Gielgud

A Theatrical Life

Gielgud as Hamlet, 1934

GIELGUD

A Theatrical Life

JONATHAN CROALL

METHUEN

Published by Methuen 2000

1 3 5 7 9 10 8 6 4 2

First published in Great Britain in 2000
by Methuen Publishing Limited,
215 Vauxhall Bridge Road, London SW1V 1EJ

Copyright © Jonathan Croall, 2000

Jonathan Croall has asserted his rights under the Copyright, Designs
and Patents Act, 1988, to be identified as the author of this work

Methuen Publishing Limited Reg. No. 3543167

A CIP catalogue record for this book
is available from the British Library

ISBN 0 413 74560 0

Typeset in Garamond by MATS, Southend-on-Sea, Essex

Printed and bound in Great Britain by
Creative Print and Design (Wales), Ebbw Vale

Contents

Contents

Introduction

THE theatre was John Gielgud's life. Nothing else really mattered. It was his occupation, his hobby, his obsession, his joy. If he was not working, he was not happy. At the age of ninety-six he was still at it. He never stopped.

One of the main problems facing any biographer is the sheer extent of his work. In the theatre, over a period of sixty-seven years, he played more than 130 roles in over 200 productions. For the cinema, starting in the silent era, he made over seventy films; on television he appeared in over sixty plays. He also played countless parts on the radio, his first in 1929, and one of his last, King Lear, on his ninetieth birthday.

For many people he was the greatest actor of the twentieth century. I was both excited and intimidated by the idea of investigating his life. But what surprised me was to discover how many roles he played in addition to that of actor. He was a director of flair and imagination, with over eighty productions to his name, both in England and America. He designed the sets for some of his productions. He was a pioneering actor-manager, and a great discoverer and nurturer of talent in others: numerous actors, playwrights and designers owed their start in the theatre to him. He was also a talented writer, an elegant stylist and witty story-teller who produced several entertaining volumes of memoirs and books on the theatre.

In trying to unravel and make sense of this extraordinary career, I have of course worked through the usual primary sources: reviews, letters, diaries, and other contemporary documents. But I have also been able to gather many personal testimonies from friends and colleagues who knew or worked with him. Once Gielgud, after a little persuasion, had agreed to my writing this biography, I was able to talk in depth with over a hundred actors, directors, writers, designers, friends and members of his family, and to correspond with many others.

What soon became clear was the enormous love and admiration people had for him, not just as an actor but as a man. This made my task of pinning down his personality more difficult than it might otherwise have been. As Dirk Bogarde succinctly put it to me early on: 'Everybody adored him, so the book might make rather flat reading.' Happily most people were willing and able to go beyond the adoration, and generously and openly share their thoughts about Gielgud's faults and foibles, as well as his many strengths and virtues.

Their recollections – eloquent, vivid, humorous and perceptive – are a crucial part of the book. I have though treated them with extreme caution. Memories are fallible even in relation to the recent past, and some of the people I talked to were casting their minds back fifty years or more. In particular I have been wary of theatrical anecdotes, which seem to develop a life of their own, changing their plot and sometimes even their characters in the re-telling. I have been told many different versions of the famous gaffes attributed to Gielgud – some of which he was not above embroidering himself.

I have also had to be wary of his own recollections. He was a modest man, and consistently downplayed or under-rated his achievement as an actor or director. This was not false modesty, but a result of the high standards he set himself. Yet if he was his own severest critic, he was not always the fairest to himself. Often he contradicted a judgement made years previously, describing as a failure a performance or production that from contemporary evidence – including his own letters – had clearly not been one.

An allied difficulty was the accuracy of his recollections. A witty and roguish raconteur of theatrical stories, he had an astonishing memory not just for names, dates and productions, but also for detail: the style of shoe worn by an ageing actress, the pillar used for the set of a wartime production, the colour of a supporting actor's wig in a long-forgotten Sheridan revival. Yet even he slipped up on occasion, making mistakes over dates, the sequence of events, and sometimes even the names of actors or directors.

He was himself a critical reader of theatrical biographies and memoirs, and hated the effusiveness that characterised some of the worst examples of the genre. What he valued was accuracy, truth and fairness. I have tried to follow these principles in putting together the story of his rich theatrical life. I had hoped he would be able to read it. In agreeing to my writing it he said: 'I shall very probably not be here when it comes out.' I never quite believed him, but sadly he was right. I would have liked to know what he made of it.

Prologue

IT was a tiny part, with just a single line. But it was a beginning, and it was Shakespeare.

Of course he is only a walk-on. He has hardly been noticed in rehearsals. But now his big moment has arrived. Nervously he stands in the wings of the Old Vic Theatre, clutching the scroll of paper tightly. His heart beats fast, his knees knock together. He tries to put out of his mind his teacher's wounding comment. He is a Herald with the English army at Agincourt, and they have to walk properly, not 'like a cat with rickets'.

Here, at last, comes his cue . . . And so, on 7 November 1921, on the first night of *Henry V*, seventeen-year-old John Gielgud walks on to the stage, hands a scroll to the actor playing the king, and speaks his first line in the English professional theatre: 'Here is the number of the slaughter'd French.'

Another time, another London theatre. Sixty-seven years have passed. The shy, elderly actor has followed his usual routine, arriving early at the Apollo, taking a nap in his dressing-room, spending time on the stage to ease himself into the part.

It seems like any other performance. But he has told the other actors this is to be the last night. And they have understood.

It has been a strain, certainly, playing in *The Best of Friends* these last three months. But what could one expect after ten years away from the theatre? Rehearsals had been difficult, especially when the lines failed to come. Or when the director said he couldn't be heard from the gallery. How frustrating that was, for him of all people. But he had come through. All he had needed was an audience.

The run had been a good one, but now it is time to stop. He always relishes those final words, knowing the audience do too. 'The Angel of

Death seems quite to have forgotten me.' Then, after just the slightest pause. 'On the other hand, I might pop off tomorrow. Who knows?'

The play ends, the applause begins, the actors take their call. Eventually the others leave him alone on stage. The audience is on its feet, cheering and applauding, refusing to let him go . . . But finally, on Shakespeare's birthday, at the age of eighty-four, Sir John Gielgud makes his exit from the English theatre.

PART ONE

Early Stages

1904–1929

I

A Terry Childhood

The theatre lay all about us in our infancy.
(Val Gielgud)

JOHN Gielgud's life as an actor, director and designer began in earnest at the age of seven, when he was given a toy theatre for Christmas. Cream and gold, with pillars decorated with gilt scroll-work and red velvet curtains, it absorbed him utterly. He spent most of his spare time in his childhood playing with it: creating and building elaborate sets, making costumes, organising the lighting, devising and performing plays. Enraptured by it, he lived in a fantasy world, largely oblivious to what was going on around him. It was a state in which he was to remain for the rest of his long theatrical life.

The toy theatre was given to him by his mother Kate. As a girl she too had been in thrall to the theatre, dazzled by its glamour and excitement. A member of the illustrious Terry family, which provided the English stage with some of its finest actors, she lived and breathed the theatre. Yet she had no desire to go on the stage, though she did take part in her aunt Ellen Terry's jubilee matinée in 1906 at Drury Lane. On that occasion, when the whole theatrical profession turned out to honour the greatest actress of the age, she was one of twenty-two members of the Terry family to appear in an extract from *Much Ado About Nothing*, with Ellen Terry playing Beatrice.

Kate's mother, also called Kate, was the eldest of the nine surviving children of Benjamin Terry and Sarah Ballard, who earned a precarious living in the circuit companies in the early part of the Victorian era. Such strolling players were legally 'rogues and vagabonds', travelling in open wagons and often playing in inns and barns. Benjamin was the handsome son of an innkeeper, Sarah the good-looking daughter of a

Scottish minister, with a deep, attractive voice. All their children were born 'on the road', and started as child actors before achieving fame.

Kate Terry, Gielgud's grandmother, joined her parents' troupe in 1850, at the age of three. At eight, as a member of Charles Kean's company, she was congratulated by Dickens on her performance as Prince Arthur in *King John*. At fourteen she played Cordelia in *King Lear*, and became a star overnight, the first to make the Terry name famous. Later she played other Shakespearean heroines, but also many modern roles. By twenty-three, with her fine voice, expressive face and great capacity for pathos, she had played a hundred parts and was the leading actress of the day. Then, to general amazement, she abandoned her career to marry a wealthy businessman and raise a family.

Arthur Lewis, a director of the haberdashery firm Lewis & Allenby, was a tall, attractive and sensitive man, and passionately interested in the arts. He was an enthusiastic painter, and often exhibited at the Royal Academy. He was also a music-lover, and before his marriage held 'evenings' in his London flat, when his friends came to smoke, eat oysters and sing part-songs. He founded the United Arts Club (now the Arts Club in Dover Street), where painters, musicians, writers and journalists could meet and talk; among the founder members were Dickens, Whistler and Thomas Hughes.

By the time of his marriage to Kate Terry he was living in Moray Lodge, a large two-storeyed house next to Holland Park in Kensington, with a billiard room, stables and a terraced garden. Here friends and guests such as the painters Millais, Watts and Leighton, and the illustrators John Tenniel and George Du Maurier, came for croquet, conversation and concerts. Lewis Carroll, who photographed the family, was a frequent visitor; Henry Irving was among the guests at their lavish parties. Oscar Wilde appeared at one, dressed in a black velvet suit with a yellow silk bow-tie and a lily in his buttonhole.

Despite these artistic surroundings young Kate Terry, born in 1868, had an ordered upbringing. With her sisters Janet, Lucy and Mabel she was schooled by governesses and private teachers in obedience, good manners and posture, as well as mathematics, French and dancing. It was a pious, improving regime, typical of the Victorian middle classes. It was also a happy one: there were picnics, outings in the dogcart, lawn tennis in the garden, and long summer holidays in a Highland cottage near Inverness. Kate was a conventional, amenable girl, 'almost too good to be true' in her grandmother Sarah's view. She never rebelled – as her sister Janet soon did – against their mother's strong, sometimes stifling presence, but played the dutiful daughter to perfection. Intelligent, perceptive, but shy and withdrawn, she poured her emotions into the theatre.

At home her mother, though retired from the stage, would act out stories for the children from Dickens, Trollope, Mark Twain and Shakespeare. At eight Kate saw her first play, from a box in the Haymarket Theatre. Her father was a friend of both Gilbert and Sullivan; after sitting entranced through *HMS Pinafore, Patience* and *Iolanthe,* Kate was taken backstage to meet the actors. At eleven she had her first taste of Shakespeare, seeing Henry Irving play Shylock, and her passion for theatre-going became intense. Later she dined at the same table as Sarah Bernhardt, Ada Rehan, Bram Stoker and other theatrical notables, listening avidly to the endless talk and gossip.

At eighteen Kate 'came out' formally as a débutante. A photograph taken on the day shows a slim, poised, upright girl, elegantly dressed without flamboyance, agreeable rather than pretty, a hint of mockery playing about her mouth and eyes. Essentially shy, and rather lacking in humour, she preferred to lose herself in a book rather than go to house parties and fancy dress balls. She had a good memory, and was acutely observant of the life going on around her. Greatly interested in art, history and literature, she had a particular passion for novels and poetry, and spoke and wrote German and French fluently. Though she had no stage ambitions, she occasionally took part with her sisters in family theatricals.

She worshipped her gentle, charming father, 'so tall and upright with such sweet eyes', as she described him. This intense relationship may have made others more difficult, for as a young woman she had no romantic attachments, or even suitors. When she was nineteen she met Frank Gielgud at a dinner party. Six years her senior, he had seen her sitting aloof in a box at the Lyceum, while he had had to battle just to get a hard seat in the pit. Now they talked eagerly of the theatre, and later he played the piano in a way that excited her. But he was married, and they were not to meet again for five years.

Frank Gielgud was the eldest son of Adam and Aniela Gielgud. The family, which has been traced back to the sixteenth century, came originally from Lithuania, before it was absorbed into Poland. For three hundred years the Gielguds lived in the village of Gielgaudskis in a fort beside the River Niemen. After the abortive insurrection against Russia in 1831 the family fell into disfavour, and Adam's father John Gielgud, a cavalry officer, fled with his wife to England. They settled in Chelsea, where Adam became first a schoolmaster, and later a clerk in the War Office and a correspondent on foreign affairs for several continental newspapers. A quiet, reclusive, hard-working man, he nevertheless had a merry sense of humour, an eye for the ridiculous, and an interest in the theatre.

Frank Gielgud's mother Aniela came from a theatrical background: her mother, Aniela Aspergerowa, was an actress of great distinction, especially in Shakespeare; her father, Wojciech, was also a leading Polish actor. A staunch Catholic, she was educated in a convent on the Île de France in Paris, and spoke French and English fluently. She was a woman of grace, intelligence and taste, with a passion for the social whirl of concerts, theatres and parties in Victorian London. Though she and Adam were not wealthy, there was enough money to satisfy her desire to move in artistic circles.

Frank, born in 1860, was the eldest of four children. Tall and dark, with long artistic hands, he learned the organ as a boy, and became a fine musician, able to play by ear without difficulty and improvise skilfully on the piano. Though he wanted to pursue a musical career, he suppressed his artistic inclinations in favour of a life in business. After a brief spell working for the Bank of England he became a stockbroker in the City, employed by L. Messel & Co., a firm founded by the grandfather of the designer Oliver Messel. In his twenties he married Evelyn Welford, the daughter of an American publisher, but their apparently happy marriage was cut short when she died during the Russian flu epidemic in the winter of 1890.

Two years later, still lonely and miserable, he met Kate Terry again at a house party in Devon. She listened sympathetically while he talked for hours about his dead wife. Later she remembered: 'There was such loneliness in the voice, such craving for sympathy and understanding, that the barriers of acquaintanceship went down, and friendship made way for easy confidence.' When he proposed a few months later, there was no question of romance. She was drawn to him by his obvious need for companionship and pity for his suffering. It was to be a marriage based on respect and compatibility rather than love.

They were married on 18 July 1892, and moved into Frank's small, red-brick house in Earl's Court Square. Reluctantly, Kate gave up her social life to become a dedicated wife and mother. She gave birth to two sons, Lewis in 1894, and Val in 1900. After a holiday in Pontresina she became pregnant again, and the couple moved to a larger house in the Old Brompton Road in South Kensington. Here at 7 Gledhow

Gardens, on 14 April 1904, delivered by a family friend, Dr Henry Huxley, Arthur John Gielgud made his entrance into the world.

His parents had disagreed over his name. Kate had chosen Arthur in memory of her father, and also because of Tennyson's poem 'Idylls of the King', then in fashion. She had wanted to add James, but Frank favoured John, his grandfather's name. According to Val, nothing would induce John or his brothers to use either name. Throughout his childhood, much to his mother's distress, everyone called him Jack.

Frank Gielgud had hoped for a daughter, and three years later he had his wish, when Kate gave birth to their last child, Eleanor. The house in which the four children grew up was a tall, narrow building, with four storeys and a basement. Spacious and comfortable, it overlooked a square with a large garden. There were all the trimmings of middle-class comfort: five maids and a cook to help run the house, and a succession of nannies and governesses for the children. A large drawing-room with gold wallpaper, housing Frank Gielgud's Bechstein grand, was reserved for parties and special occasions. 'The house was very draughty, and there was never enough hot water for the baths, but I loved every inch of it,' Gielgud recalled.

For the Edwardian middle class into which he was born the age was one of prosperity and stability. The Boer War had ended; a popular monarch was on the throne; the first motor cars were just appearing; nannies and servants were plentiful and inexpensive. London, its streets full of gaslights, hansom cabs and fogs, was still comparatively small; walking was easy and popular, life relatively leisurely and unhurried.

The Gielguds lived within easy reach of the West End theatres, then dominated by actor-managers such as George Alexander at the St James's, Herbert Beerbohm Tree at His Majesty's, and Gerald du Maurier at Wyndham's. Other stars were Marie Tempest, Irene Vanbrugh, Lilian Braithwaite, Henry Ainley, Lewis Waller and Frank Benson. The year 1904 marked the first production of Barrie's *Peter Pan* and Shaw's *Candida*, the West End début of Sybil Thorndike, Harley Granville Barker's first season as manager of the Court, the teaming of Sarah Bernhardt and Mrs Patrick Campbell in Maeterlinck's *Pelléas et Mélisande*, and the founding of the country's first drama school, the Academy of Dramatic Arts.

Blond and blue-eyed, Jack was a demanding baby, absorbing much of his mother's time. A delicate child, he suffered from sunstroke, and at six had an acute attack of appendicitis that almost killed him: too ill to be moved to hospital, he was operated on at home. Such incidents made his mother fuss and spoil him: she gave him special food, and often took over from the nanny, allowing him the luxury of a hip-bath in front of the nursery fire when he was unwell. According to Eleanor he exploited this devotion: 'He was the weakling of the family, but he was very naughty, because he used to exaggerate his illness,' she remembered. Val recalled his saying more than once: 'Mother wouldn't like me to do that, I might get sunstroke.'

The picture that emerges is of a spoilt, over-protected child. Early family photographs show a serious-looking boy with delicate features, more self-conscious and uncertain of the camera than Lewis or Val. Eleanor remembered: 'He was conceited, but it was partly his manner, he was much shyer than I realised.' But already there was a histrionic streak: Eleanor recalled a family funeral when he suddenly started screaming, fell to his knees, and 'made a real exhibition of himself'.

Despite his poor health he was generally a happy child, secure in his mother's love, and obedient to her wishes. Caring and conscientious, Kate Gielgud was devoted to all her children, but to none more than her youngest son. She was the dominant influence of his childhood, and the powerful bond created between them in his early years lasted until her death. It was she who introduced him to books, to the stories of Beatrix Potter and E. Nesbit, to Kipling's *Jungle Books* and *Just So Stories*. As he grew older she read novels aloud to him; he especially loved Dickens, whose sentimental death scenes had mother and son choking back the tears.

Kate Gielgud was strict about manners and propriety, and exercised a calm, stabilising influence on the family, holding in check the volatile Slav elements that often surfaced: 'We all talked too much, and, when we did not feel like talking, we would sulk or be aggressively silent,' her son recalled. 'My father and brothers were particularly prone to these alarming moods. But always there was my mother, sewing, writing, going about the house, watching and listening, and saying very little.' Her sense of duty and her capacity for sacrifice were immense, and she asked for little in return: Val later called her 'the most consistently self-denying' person he had met.

The children's relationship with their father was less warm and affectionate. Frank Gielgud had a moody temperament and could seem forbidding, as Eleanor remembered: 'We had a very happy childhood, but very strict. We were all very frightened of Father. He never used force, but he could be very sarcastic: if you did something wrong, you knew it.' Val recollected that he 'had something withdrawn and consequently formidable about him'. To young Jack he was a distant and sometimes terrifying figure, 'very alarming when he was angry, and very charming at other times'.

Yet he was essentially a decent man, with an earthy sense of humour. He had a certain Slav panache – when speaking he used his hands a great deal – but also a puritan streak: he hated extravagance, frowned on expensive theatre seats and restaurants, and always travelled by bus. He brought a spartan element to the children's upbringing: hard beds, tepid bath water, simple food, and fires allowed only in the drawing-room and the nursery. Val remembered 'the rice-pudding, the regime of punctuality for meals, and the abhorrence of debt'; Eleanor recalled 'practising the piano in a stone-cold drawing-room'.

There was though a more romantic and artistic side to their father. Val's main recollection was of him 'sitting at his piano, playing quite exquisitely by ear, and incredibly unconscious of the beauty of his hands'. He also had a fine voice, and shared his wife's passionate interest in the theatre. Kate was completely unmusical, but she had considerable literary talent, and wrote stylish, perceptive and informed accounts of the plays she saw for an invalid friend unable to get to the theatre.

The children inherited many of their parents' artistic qualities. Lewis was to show ability as a playwright and a translator of Latin verse, while Val had some success as a novelist and playwright. Eleanor was the most musical: at her music school in South Kensington she played a duet with the pianist Solomon, then a young boy, and there was talk of a musical career. But Jack too had a good musical ear and, watching his father play on the upright piano in the nursery, he soon learned to improvise. He took music lessons for a while, but soon gave them up. His quick facility annoyed Eleanor: 'He never learnt a note, he played completely by ear, and it drove me mad,' she remembered. 'After I had finished practising, the dear little boy would come down and sit at the piano and just reel everything off – though not always in the right key. I could have murdered him.'

With Lewis away at boarding-school, she and Val were drawn into Jack's theatricals, staged in the large, unfurnished playroom on the servants' floor at the top of the house. But while to them the toy theatre was an exciting game, for Jack, Val recalled, it became an '*idée fixe*'. Although he loved the dressing-up box kept by their mother – one early photograph shows him resplendent in Polish national costume – it was not acting but the visual element of the theatre – the colour, scenery and costumes – that first absorbed him. The toy theatre was his obsession. He stole Val's lead toy soldiers, transforming them into civilians by covering them in gold paint, and clothing them with ruffs and farthingales that he made out of wax. He borrowed furniture from Eleanor's doll's-house for drawing-room scenes, and plundered the house for materials to create exotic sets for caves and palaces. Once he even stole seed and sand from the canary's cage to create an Arabian desert.

Soon he and Val were improvising short plays. Reflecting the taste of the time, they devised mystery plays, costume dramas, and society 'love triangles', with a bias towards the exotic or melodramatic. More Val's work than Jack's, they had titles such as *Lady Fawcett's Ruby*, *Kill That Spy* and *Plots in the Harem*. Some poked fun at their Terry relations, and were guiltily performed in secret; others were played to parents and servants. Eleanor was, she recalled, 'either in the box office, or being Lady Jones, the theatre's sponsor and backer.' Their mother summed up the division of labour: 'John directed, Val produced the book of words, and Eleanor applauded!'

The boys later wrote detailed reviews of their plays in the style of the critic Clement Scott, after finding a book of his in their parents' library. Their sights were already set on West End management: the plays were performed, as their notebooks show, in the 'New Mars Theatre, in Trafalgar Square, W.1. Erected between April 1912 and March 1913 . . . Under the joint management of V.H. and A.J. Gielgud.'

As director Jack preferred stories requiring thunderstorms and firework displays, or magic effects using sparklers and magnesium flares. For lighting he used miniature torches. Alongside this love of spectacle he developed a passion for painting backcloths and pastel designs, propping up his home-made cardboard scenery on his mantelpiece, and often getting up in the middle of the night when a new idea came to him.

At seven he went to the real theatre for the first time, to see *Peter Pan*, the story of 'The Boy Who Wouldn't Grow Up', still starring the original Peter, Pauline Chase. He was introduced to the London theatre by his widowed grandmother Kate Terry, whom he remembered as a gay but slightly formidable old woman, and who soon made him aware of his family's privileged position in it. At matinées at the Haymarket she demanded and was given the Royal Box, to which the management sent tea in the interval. Sitting there with the former queen of the West End, Jack felt proud and important, especially when the actors gave them a special bow as they took their calls. 'Grandmother was a wonderful audience,' he recalled. 'She laughed and cried wholeheartedly, and I naturally did the same.'

From the start he was captivated by the theatre: the glow of the footlights, the first notes of the orchestra, the red plush curtain rising to reveal the elaborate, naturalistic sets. Kate Terry took him to see other members of the family perform. He enjoyed watching his great-aunt Marion, whom he found gracious and kind offstage. Genteel, reserved and fastidious, with an aristocratic bearing, known as 'the perfect lady' of the family, she was one of the most skilled *comédiennes* of the day, much admired for her poise, dignity and precise throwaway technique. Notably effective in Barrie and Wilde, she had earlier specialised in 'good woman' parts. But in 1892 she had caused a stir, and delighted Oscar Wilde, with her successful playing of the adventuress Mrs Erlynne in the original production of *Lady Windermere's Fan*.

Jack also admired his great-uncle Fred Terry, who had the grand manner in life as well as on the stage. A large, imposing man with red curly hair, he was renowned for his dedication to the theatre, but also for his love of gambling at cards and on the horses. A disciple of Irving, Tree and Alexander, in whose companies he had worked, he was a versatile actor, at home both in Shakespeare – he was a notable Benedick – and in melodrama. An actor-manager for many years, with his wife Julia Neilson he staged endless revivals of melodramas such as *Sweet Nell of Old Drury* and *The Scarlet Pimpernel*. He had no artistic sense, but great commercial judgement. Warm and jolly, generous with advice to younger actors, he was given to wild rages and coarse language. He also had strong prejudices, especially against modern playwrights, and what he saw as 'loose' behaviour on stage. He thought Wilde's dialogue 'unnatural', and hated homosexuals.

The idol of Jack's boyhood was his great-aunt Ellen Terry, the greatest actress of her age. For nearly a quarter of a century she was Irving's leading lady at the Lyceum, a partnership that became the focal point of the English theatre in the late Victorian years. A brilliant, joyous actress, she was unparalleled in playing pathos or high comedy. She was admired for her 'natural', spontaneous style of acting, for the vitality and freshness of her Shakespearean heroines, particularly Beatrice, Olivia and Portia.

Her success made her the darling of the aesthetes and a friend of the Pre-Raphaelites; Wilde once wrote a sonnet to her. She was loved by the great actor Johnston Forbes-Robertson, and also by Shaw, with whom she had a famous correspondence. A sweet-natured, intelligent woman with a great generosity of spirit, she was adored by the public, her mystical, medieval beauty appealing to both sexes. Virginia Woolf wrote after her death: 'While other actors are remembered because they were Hamlet, Phèdre or Cleopatra, Ellen Terry is remembered because she was Ellen Terry.'

But she was also wild, impulsive and reckless, and her private life scandalised her more respectable relatives, as well as many in the theatre and society at large. She had three husbands, the first of whom, the Pre-Raphaelite painter G.F. Watts, she married at sixteen. Her second and third husbands were both actors. She was almost certainly Irving's lover for many years; and she had two illegitimate children, Edith and Edward, from a long liaison with the architect Edward Godwin. Edith Craig grew up to become a designer, a director, and an early exponent of feminist theatre. Edward Gordon Craig became one of the most influential figures in twentieth-century theatre, both as a designer and a theoretician. In his childhood Gielgud rarely saw his famous second cousin, who had left England in 1904, the year of his birth. But the name already had an aura for him.

The Terry family were famous for certain characteristics, of which the 'Terry charm' was perhaps the most obvious. They had large appetites, gracious manners, fine voices and beautiful diction, but also a flamboyant temperament, great stamina and an enormous capacity for hard work. They were inclined to snobbery, but were capable of great kindness and sweetness. In middle age they tended to lose their memories, and had difficulty remembering their lines. Members of the Terry generations that followed Ellen, Marion and Fred had many of these qualities in different combinations, and many were passed down to their great-nephew.

Jack's early theatre visits with Kate Terry became doubly exciting when he was taken backstage to meet his Terry relatives. Fred Terry was a particular hero: once he went round to the stage door after a performance of *The Scarlet Pimpernel,* and his great-uncle emerged in his white silk and lace costume 'like some dandified deity from Olympus'. At eight his grandmother took him on stage after a performance of *Drake* to meet his cousin Phyllis Neilson-Terry, the daughter of Fred and Julia, who was playing Queen Elizabeth. As she towered over him in her regal robes he gazed around in wonder at the stagehands dismantling the set.

His first taste of Shakespeare, at the age of seven, was another family occasion. Now manager of the New, Fred Terry was staging special matinées there of *As You Like It*, with Phyllis as Rosalind, and his son Dennis playing Silvius. 'John adored it all!' his mother recorded. The following year he saw it again, with Frank Benson and Dorothy Green, at the little Coronet in Notting Hill Gate. He saw Fred Terry play Benedick in *As You Like It*, and at ten he was taken to Granville Barker's ground-breaking production of *A Midsummer Night's Dream* at the Savoy, with Dennis Neilson-Terry as Oberon. He remembered little of the plot, but was entranced by the gold-faced fairies, the gauze curtains, and the flowers around Titania's bower.

Fred and Marion came regularly to lunch at Gledhow Gardens, Fred invariably pressing golden sovereigns into the children's hands. At Christmas the whole family descended, each making a distinctive entrance. For Jack the most thrilling figure was Ellen Terry: he adored everything about her, her striking beauty, her deep husky voice, her gaiety and charm. She arrived covered in scarves and shawls, bowed and mysterious 'like a godmother in a fairy tale'. Now in her sixties, with short grey hair, she was for him 'the most thrilling and lovable' of his relations. 'Do you read your Shakespeare?' she asked him once. To his delight she later sent him her copy of Craig's celebrated book *On the Art of the Theatre*, covered in her notes and comments.

This intense involvement with the theatre, both imaginary and real, had a powerful effect. Caught up in a fantasy life, Jack had little contact with other children outside the family circle. Although the Gielgud children later enjoyed cycling during holidays in the country, none of them had any interest or ability in sports or games. Self-conscious about this shortcoming, and hating to be shown up, they preferred their own games, which were easier to excel in.

For Jack the only really worthwhile game was that of make-believe. It was inevitable then that, when the time came for school, his first real contact with life beyond the proscenium arch was neither easy nor happy.

2

Gielgud Minor

Clever but slapdash and ill-regulated.
(School report, 1919)

JACK'S education was similar to that of other boys of his class and background. When he was three his mother hired a Froebel governess to help him move on from 'making chalk-marks on the nursery walls and strange sounds on the piano'. At four he attended a local kindergarten, but only briefly. Invited to join in and play, he sat crying on the floor, wailing: 'I don't want to play, I've come to school to do lessons like my brothers!' His mother quickly moved him to a 'big school' in nearby Queen's Gate. This was more of a success: 'Learning with companions delighted but never distracted him,' she remembered. A poem he wrote at six survives: 'Up in Mamma's balloon I went/And right to the moon/Far in the sky, ever so high I went/And had tea with the moon.'

In January 1912, following in his brothers' footsteps, he was sent as a boarder to Hillside, a small preparatory school for boys situated on the edge of the countryside, near Farncombe in Surrey. The Gielguds had heard of the school through their friends the Huxleys, and Lewis had become a close friend there of Aldous and his cousin Gervas. A quick learner and brilliant scholar, he had been head boy, won a scholarship to Eton, and was about to go up to Oxford. Val, a voracious reader but less studious than Lewis, was in his turn head boy when Jack, now known as Gielgud Minor, arrived at the school.

Hillside had all the features of a typical prep school of the day: strict uniform, poor food, ramshackle buildings, eccentric masters, and an emphasis on classics and games. In his memoirs Gervas Huxley recalled its 'strange, rough and often brutal world' where 'a lot of bullying went

14

on'. While Aldous was popular, Lewis Gielgud, something of a dandy and hopeless at games, had 'had a poor time and needed a lot of protection'. The description of Bulstrode School in Aldous Huxley's novel *Eyeless in Gaza* is, according to Gervas, 'straight Hillside'. It was a world of 'new bugs', 'swots' and 'peter' (masturbation), where the boys called the kitchen staff 'servants', and affected to scorn work: 'That work was idiotic, and that those who worked were contemptible, had been axiomatic amongst them,' the narrator observes. Corporal punishment was the norm, even for minor offences. One pupil was the playwright Ronald Mackenzie, a shy boy with long curly hair who was considered a 'wet'. When he read out his stories by torchlight to the other boys in his dormitory, he was twice thrashed for this 'misdemeanour'.

According to Kate Gielgud, Jack went off to Hillside 'as happy as a sandboy'. Yet leaving home at such a tender age must have been a wrench. Certainly the school was at first a rude shock to the delicate and 'artistic' little boy, who had to endure an initiation rite in which, to his alarm, he was made to swing hand over hand on the dormitory beams, while the other boys flicked wet towels and hurled sponges at him. He was a fearful boy, and was victimised at first. He recalled being jumped out on in dark passages full of 'enormous and appalling shadows'; of being 'imprisoned by my enemies' in the library window seat, 'bent double and half suffocated, while my captors sat on the seat drumming with their boots on the cupboard doors which barred my escape'. It was a stark contrast to the gentility of South Kensington.

Gradually, however, Gielgud Minor found things to enjoy in his new life: the long Sunday walks over muddy fields, the weekly delight of baskets of fruit bought with his pocket money, the whispering of smutty jokes, the smuggling of plum cakes and figs into the dormitory for feasts after lights-out. At games, however, he was 'always a funk'. Despite lessons in the Charterhouse School baths nearby, he never learnt to swim. Somehow he made the football second team, but was described as 'an opportunist merely'. He was also chosen for the cricket second eleven, but was happier as scorer for the first, since this gave him time off lessons for away matches, the chance to eat enormous teas, and to show off his small, neat handwriting.

Academically both he and Val lived under the shadow of Lewis. 'His cleverness was continually being flung in my teeth as a reproach and an incentive,' Val recalled. Neither of them had Lewis's aptitude for learning – though Anne Messel, sister of the designer Oliver Messel, remembers that the three youngest Gielgud children 'were quoted to us as being brilliant'. As a pupil Jack did well in some subjects, but failed miserably in others. Mathematics, which he dreaded, was a closed book to him, Latin and Greek no more than a half-open one. His best subjects were divinity and English, but his musical ability was also apparent: at Sunday services his shrill treble soared above the other voices during the hymns. His histrionic tendencies were also emerging: 'I stood with my head thrown back, hoping to be seen as well as heard,' he recalled.

Unusually for a prep school, Hillside staged regular theatrical productions. 'We were encouraged to think of Shakespeare in terms of theatre instead of professional footnotes,' Val remembered. Up to now Jack had not thought about acting, but the school plays began to awaken his interest, as well as satisfy a tendency to show off. His first role was the Mock Turtle in *Alice's Adventures in Wonderland*, during which he produced the required heavy sobbing and tears, and gave an increasingly shrill rendering of the Beautiful Soup song. Then came what he recalled as a 'bland' Humpty-Dumpty in *Alice Through the Looking Glass*.

The following year he made his début in Shakespeare. Lewis, in whom his mother had seen 'a natural gift for elocution', had taken leading roles in the productions, culminating in a much-praised Shylock. Jack, hidden behind a large and implausible black beard, now gave an impassioned performance in the same part in scenes from *The Merchant of Venice*: his performance, he remembered, 'lacked artistic restraint'. But it was not just acting that interested him: as stage manager and self-taught scenic designer he also contributed ideas for the set.

In his last year, aged twelve, he played Mark Antony in scenes from *Julius Caesar*, acting with such conviction that he reduced at least one parent to tears. A photograph suggests a burgeoning awareness of his stage presence. In it he stands strikingly upright, a hand gracefully holding his toga as he gazes steadily out across an imagined Forum, while around him his fellow-senators look merely awkward, or wave wooden daggers half-heartedly. In character, aware of the camera but not showing it, he is the only one performing for it.

A surviving letter to his parents, illustrated with a sketch of himself as Shylock, reveals a fastidious, conceited and mannered boy, with a precocious relish for adult language and a strong interest in writing:

Mice seem to abound in this place. One was hunting for crumbs all through litany. You might send this epistle on to Val, as I can't be fagged to write all this to him again. The Doddie Magazine ought to be coming out soon. Val has not contributed this time. I have written a detective story skit with a moral in verse. Quite original. Que penses-tu?

He was now reading extensively, enjoying especially G.A. Henty's historical yarns and Harrison Ainsworth's swashbuckling tales. At school every morning after breakfast he would dash to the library, which became a favourite retreat. Here he would gaze enthralled at the pictures of the theatrical stars in the *Daily Sketch*, and read voraciously the notices of productions in the West End.

The life of the Gielgud family, like everyone else's, changed dramatically in August 1914 with the start of the First World War. A general mobilisation was announced in a climate of patriotic fervour, and their German nurse was ordered to return to her own country. Val, a pupil at Rugby, found his unpopularity increasing because of his foreign-sounding family name. Lewis, now at Oxford, was one of the first to enlist in the army. Frank Gielgud enrolled as a special constable and, as the bombs began to fall on a blacked-out London, patrolled the Chelsea Embankment. Kate Gielgud helped in the canteen of the munitions factory at Woolwich Arsenal, and sorted clothes for the Belgian and Polish refugees arriving in London.

For young Jack wartime London was visually merely an extension of theatre. His mother recalled the family's returning from a performance of *Peter Pan*: 'John was thrilled with his first view of the searchlights which started to criss-cross the sky as we came home. All through the holidays he watched them, going early to bed to gaze at the black square of his window across which those magic streaks flashed and faded and flashed again from every angle.'

At Hillside the headmaster and many teachers enlisted, to be replaced by others of doubtful ability, and casualty lists became a feature of morning assembly. The war impinged directly on school life, since Surrey was in the firing-line of German bombing raids. But to Jack this was all a terribly big adventure, as is apparent from 'The Zeppelin Raid on Guildford', a piece of patriotic doggerel he wrote in spring 1916, which began: 'One fine evening (so 'twas said)/While we boys were all in bed/Zeppelins passed over-head/Out to show us 'Kultur'./Back to Germany went they/(They

17

don't like the light of day)/Leaving bombs about this way/'Specially at Guildford.'

In London theatre audiences, including men on leave, found diversion in light and frivolous shows such as the musical *Chu Chin Chow*, the farce *A Little Bit of Fluff*, and the melodrama *Romance*. The accent was on pleasure, prompting one general to complain about 'exhibitions of scantily dressed girls and songs of doubtful character'. Theatres adjusted to the situation by staging six matinées a week, and only two evening performances. They suffered the occasional hit from Zeppelins: when two fell next to the Strand Theatre, causing panic and damage during a performance of *The Scarlet Pimpernel*, Fred Terry calmly stepped forward and asked the orchestra to strike up 'God Save the King'.

Sitting happily with his parents in the dress circle, Jack saw many of these wartime shows. Each night before they went back to school he, Val and Eleanor were taken to a show of their choice. Lewis, home on leave and in love with the actress Mary O'Farrell, took him to see her in *Peg o' My Heart*, with A.E. Matthews. He admired stars such as Madge Titheradge and Lilian Braithwaite, and went to his first revue, *Vanity Fair*. But it was still the visual aspect of theatre that delighted him most. With *Chu Chin Chow*, which he was to see a dozen times, he was moved less by the acting and music than by the scenery and costumes, the real goats, sheep and camels, the mysterious caves and gorgeous palaces.

Yet Shakespeare also began to appeal to him. He saw his first *Hamlet*, Irving's son H.B. Irving. In 1916 he was at the lavish Shakespeare Tercentenary at Drury Lane, where he and Val sat spellbound through *Julius Caesar*, with Gerald du Maurier, Henry Ainley, and the veteran Shakespearean actor-manager Frank Benson. They listened to speeches by Madge Kendal and Squire Bancroft, leading actors of the Victorian era, and cheered wildly with everyone else when Benson was knighted by King George during the interval. In the Shakespeare pageant that followed the Terry family featured prominently, with Ellen and Marion portraying Portia and Nerissa, Julia Neilson as Beatrice and Fred as Don Pedro, and Ellen representing the figure of Shakespearean Comedy in the final tableau. Such grand occasions, weaving together his family's history with that of the London theatre, made a deep and abiding impression.

His own acting opportunities were not limited to Hillside. Eleanor was now a pupil at the Mathilde Verne Pianoforte School in

Kensington, and Jack was roped in to play a sailor in *HMS Pinafore* in a Christmas performance for wounded soldiers. While staying with friends in Beaconsfield he, Val and Eleanor performed a short, improvised play in the house of the writer G.K. Chesterton, who roared with laughter at their effort. Aged twelve, Jack was allegedly a great hit as a 'sinister adventuress', wearing a big hat, sham pearls and a pink evening dress, and smoking a cigarette through a long black holder.

In his final year at Hillside he was made head boy. The appointment suggests he was gaining confidence, and finding it easier to get on with other boys. Much against his wishes, he now sat the scholarship exam for Eton, where Lewis had been an outstanding pupil. Not having worked much, he duly failed, chalking up a mere 4 per cent in the mathematics paper. He failed also to get a scholarship to Rugby – a result that pleased him: Val's descriptions of the school, with its ethos of athleticism and puritanism, made it an uninviting prospect. In the end he worked diligently enough to secure a place at Westminster, where he started as a pupil in September 1917.

Situated next to the famous abbey, Westminster was one of the top half-dozen public schools, and almost as exclusive as Eton. Many Members of Parliament sent their sons there to help them take their allotted place in the ruling class. The tone was strongly ecclesiastical, the boys having to attend early morning prayers in the abbey. Jewish boys were segregated for the prayers, and also at meals, where they ate specially cooked food, a policy that fomented much anti-semitism. The boys wore a uniform of a silk top hat, high stiff collar and tailcoat, played at soldiers in the Officers' Training Corps, and enjoyed imitating the 'Mr Chips' teachers who had been brought in to replace the regular staff during the war.

As a weekly boarder Jack found it hard to settle, for Zeppelin raids were a regular occurrence, and he spent many nights sheltering in the abbey vaults until the all-clear sounded. Suffering from claustrophobia, he was distressed by these disruptions, and ill-prepared for school the next morning. He was also homesick, and wrote frequently to his mother, exaggerating the horror of the raids in the hope she would let him become a day boy. He offered to make his own bed and clean his own boots if he could sleep at home; he begged to be allowed to do his homework in their library, away from the 'distractions of other chaps'.

By November he was writing home twice a day, consumed with self-pity and seeming close to a breakdown. 'All I feel inclined to do is either cry or shriek and it's so awful trying to fight against it,' he complained. In another petulant letter he piled on the agony: 'I still feel vilely rotten. Woke up this morning with a deadly fear of waking up, getting up, the day, the house, the work, the play, the meals and the going-to-bed-again. I shiver and shake and think and worry. It is too beastly. One can't enjoy a moment.'

After two terms his parents duly gave in, and he became a day boy. Much more at ease now, he gained a non-resident scholarship at the start of his second year. Although he had been top of his form at the end of his first term, he now drifted into idleness. Later he confessed: 'I tried to avoid learning anything that did not come easily to me.' At fifteen there were already signs of a restless temperament: the headmaster noted that he 'doesn't concentrate and doesn't much like classics'. In a later report he wrote: 'Must pass School Certificate, French and Maths bad.'

His saving grace was his interest in art, especially drawing, which obsessed him. Although his teacher found his still-life work incompetent, inaccurate and careless, his drawings of the cloisters or the banners and structures of the abbey were, to his mother's eyes, a different matter: 'Overhasty but eager and painstaking, appreciative of values, of contrasted light and shade, he would bring home tiny thumbnail sketches,' she remembered. The abbey helped him develop an eye for perspective and architectural detail; but it also became a refuge, a place he cloaked with mystery.

Though his parents had no strong religious views – his father was a lapsed Catholic – he had been confirmed in the Church of England, and at sixteen went through a brief religious phase. This was more a matter of sensual experience than of conviction or faith: his intense feelings were provoked by the theatrical and pictorial elements of religion, not its substance. Although he disliked prayers and sermons, he went often to Brompton Oratory in Kensington, where the attractions were the incense and the ceremony. The religious instruction at Westminster was a disappointment: 'I expected that at confirmation a great light would shine on me. It didn't, and I was greatly disillusioned.'

He endured two Officer Training Corps summer camps, sleeping on a straw palliasse, getting up at six, and taking part in drills, parades, route marches and night operations. His letters home, though critical of the stew provided ('boiling water, chunks of raw meat and potatoes with spotted fever'), reveal a delight in being able for once to forgo his normal manners: 'You should see me eating jam and sardines (together) with the same knife,' he wrote gleefully.

In November 1918 the 'war to end war' ended. On Armistice Day Jack and other Westminster pupils joined the crowds outside Buckingham Palace, waving their top hats and cheering the king and queen. Later he attended the burial of the Unknown Soldier, a memorably theatrical occasion for which, alongside other members of the Officer Training Corps, he lined the path from the street to the door of Westminster Abbey.

The war had divided his family, forcing his Polish cousin Tommie and his brother Lewis to fight on opposite sides. Tommie was killed in a battle with the Russians, while Lewis received a severe thigh wound at Loos that left him with a slight but permanent limp. Remarkably his mother, finding him close to death when she visited him in hospital in France, spent three months there. Her presence, it was clear, helped to save his life.

At Westminster Jack sat through lessons in a half-dream: all his thoughts were on the theatre. As a child he had stood outside a ticket agency near his home, learning the playbills by heart. Now, travelling to school on the underground, he tried to catch a glimpse at Sloane Square of the posters for productions at the Court. Restless if confined to routine, he often walked, or alighted at different stations to look at other posters. At fifteen, with his own latchkey, he became an enthusiastic walker, venturing as far as Kew Gardens or Hampton Court. But his Mecca was the West End. There he would wander the streets, scrutinising the photographs and playbills outside the theatres, and deciding how best to spend the shillings and half-crowns carefully saved up from his allowance. His absorption was total: even when he and Val went roller-skating in Holland Park, his interest was in the model stages, with scenes from the current plays, that were grouped in dark booths along the promenade.

Most of his friends at school were Jewish, and he hated the anti-semitism that was rife there. His two best friends, and most frequent companions on trips to the theatre, were the lean and bespectacled Angus MacPhail, later a leading screenwriter and film editor, and Arnold Haskell, who became a distinguished ballet critic. In his memoirs Haskell recalled: 'We used to cut afternoon classes and also an occasional game with impunity, because we did it with such frequency, to queue up for every type of theatrical entertainment, from *The Bing Boys* to the Russian Ballet.' They would wait for hours for a seat in the pit or gallery. Although Jack loathed his school uniform, he willingly endured the sniggers in exchange for two or three hours of enchantment.

Like Haskell, he became an *aficionado* of the ballet. He had seen Pavlova dance, but it was the glamour, spectacle and originality of Diaghilev's Ballets Russes, which played for three seasons in London after the war, that captivated him most. During one summer he went ten times, twice in one day to *Petroushka*. He was overwhelmed by the passionate dancing of Lopokova and Tchernicheva, the choreography of Massine, the music of Stravinsky. But he was also fascinated by the brilliant décor of Bakst and Derain. His first visit, in 1919 at the Alhambra, seems to have been particularly significant: 'Standing in the promenade beside my father, and walking about with him in the intervals among the cigar smoke and clinking glasses all around me, I felt I had really grown up at last.'

His relationship with his father was now easier. At twelve Jack had been given a gramophone, and bought his first record, of Kreisler and Effram Zimbalist performing the Bach concerto for two violins. He listened to it endlessly, overwhelmed by the beautiful playing. It was the beginning of a lifelong love of music. His father took him to see Beecham conducting Wagner, and to many concerts at the Queen's Hall or Albert Hall. He heard and saw some of the greatest artists of the day – Chaliapin, Pachmann, Rachmaninov, Fritz Kreisler – enjoying their platform presence and showmanship as much as their music.

His father also shared his principal passion: 'He never tried to crush my mania for the theatre, which he loved himself within more modest bounds,' he recalled. He listened fascinated to his father's stories of legendary figures such as Sarah Bernhardt, Ada Rehan, and the fine Polish Shakespearean actress Modjeska. He was taken to see Bernhardt in *Le Drapeau*, one of her last performances, and was awestruck by the elderly, one-legged actress's fine voice and her youthfulness. His father talked also of Madge Kendal, and of Irving, whom he greatly admired. 'I was haunted all through my childhood by the shade of Henry Irving,' Gielgud recalled.

His parents encouraged him to take the theatre seriously, to discuss the play before and after. From the age of thirteen he began to record his opinions of the shows he saw. Penned in a tiny, neat italic handwriting on the programme, these juvenile theatre criticisms were written the same night or the following day. At first he simply noted the date, his position in the theatre, and who was with him. At fourteen he began to add generalised comments: Gerald du Maurier's production of *Pamela* was 'A terrible show', Basil Dean's musical fantasy *Fifinella* was 'rather charming', *The Garden of Allah* 'rubbish, well put on'.

Once at Westminster he began to notice individual performances, including those of his Terry relatives. He saw his great-aunt Marion play Mrs Higgins in the revival of *Pygmalion*, with Mrs Patrick Campbell as Eliza ('Mrs Campbell too old, but still good'). He also caught her in Tolstoy's *Reparation* at the St James, with Henry Ainley, and noted afterwards: 'Marion charming. Ainley fine. Bad play – empty house.' Of the comedy *The Parish Watchmen*, which starred his aunt Mabel Terry-Lewis, he wrote with a growing independence of mind: 'Oh! What rot! and how the family revel in it.'

At a performance of *Romeo and Juliet*, in which Ellen Terry played the Nurse, he gave an early glimpse of the tactlessness for which he would later become famous. Before the play started Kate and Marion Terry entered the auditorium separately, each to a great round of applause. Bursting with pride, Jack said innocently to his great-aunt, 'Grandmother had a wonderful reception, didn't she?' Marion Terry replied, 'Did she, darling? I expect they thought it was me.' He learnt a lesson in theatrical etiquette that evening. Remarking in a loud voice during the interval 'Isn't Aunt Nell wonderful?' he was hushed by his relatives, and told he must never discuss actors aloud at a first night.

Ellen Terry was now seventy. At twelve Jack had watched her play the trial scene from *The Merchant of Venice* on Brighton pier; later he had seen her, with a young Edith Evans, in scenes from *The Merry Wives of Windsor*. 'She seemed to bring a breath of fresh air with her the moment she stepped on to the stage,' he recalled. He had also been present when she read Beatrice at a private performance of *Much Ado About Nothing* by the Shakespeare Reading Society: 'Read it! she threw away the book after the first few lines and acted it gaily, vividly, just like a young woman,' he remembered. *Romeo and Juliet* was her last engagement in a London run: half-blind, with her memory going, she kept forgetting her lines. This mattered little to Jack: 'Nell wonderful' he noted in his programme. Years later he could recall the performance in minute detail.

His parents looked upon theatre as a treat, to be indulged in only in moderation, for fear it would become an obsession. But with Jack it was already that, and he indulged in every kind of theatre: Shakespeare, farce, ballet, straight plays, Gilbert and Sullivan, thrillers, musicals, comedies, revue and pantomime. He knew all the actors' names, and waited at the stage door to see them. He adored the variety at the Coliseum, with Vesta Tilley, Albert Chevalier and Marie Lloyd: his schoolboy sense of humour, which he never quite lost, was tickled by one turn entitled, 'Pattman and his Gigantic Organ'. A favourite show was Nigel Playfair's hugely popular production of *The Beggar's Opera*, which he saw ten times at the Lyric, Hammersmith. By his eighth visit he had become a connoisseur: 'As charming as ever, the three new songs and scenes are excellent,' he wrote. He knew all the songs by heart, having bought the records and practised singing them at home, and loved Lovat Fraser's pretty, whimsical designs.

From an early age he had been easily moved to tears in the theatre, a characteristic Terry trait. By now he was positively enjoying the experience. After going alone to see Robert Loraine in Barrie's sentimental play *Mary Rose* he noted: 'Wonderful! Wept buckets.' He wrote his first-ever fan letter to an actress after seeing Haidée Wright in a revival of *Milestones*, telling her he had cried his eyes out – but was peeved to receive a reply addressed to 'Miss J. Gielgud'.

His writing took other forms. Inspired by *Chu Chin Chow*, as well as Hans Anderson's fairy-tale, he wrote a play entitled *The Nightingale*, with the humorous sub-title 'A Set of China in Five Pieces'. The dialogue in the fragment that survives is sentimental and innocently romantic, as are the precise indications for the set for the opening scene: 'Behind the wood is the lake, deep, deep blue. It is late evening and twilight is falling. Through the tree-trunks on the right may be seen the glitter and twinkle of the thousand glow-worm lights of the Emperor's palace . . .'

His ambition was now focused on being a stage designer. He spent his evenings at home creating brilliantly coloured dress designs and detailed sketches of stage sets, working at lightning speed in chalk, charcoal and poster paint. He built miniature sets with plasticene and bricks, and rigged up lighting for them with pocket torches. Fred Terry came to inspect his models, and commented: 'Much too expensive for touring; too many rostrums, my boy.'

He turned out numerous drawings, many of them extraordinarily detailed. As a birthday present for his mother he wrote out Tennyson's poem 'The Lady of Shalott' in the form of an elaborate missal, setting each verse in a frame that included tiny figures and landscapes. On the first page he wrote in gold lettering, 'To Mother July 5th, 1920. From

Jack'. His drawings were influenced by those in his fairy-tale books by Arthur Rackham and Kay Neilsen. Another influence was Edmond Dulac, with whom to his delight he once shared a box at the theatre. He was also excited by Aubrey Beardsley's work, and bought several volumes of his drawings, revelling secretly in their impropriety as well as their fine lines and precise detail. One of his many costume designs, conceived in black and red ink, shows the influence of Beardsley's intricate style.

Thrilled by the family connection, he talked a lot about Edward Gordon Craig. His cousin's revolutionary ideas about stage design, his championing of the visual and pictorial in the theatre and his revolt against realism, had already exercised a huge influence on European drama, though his genius was only just beginning to be recognised in England. Jack was interested in his designs, but at this age preferred the more conventional, heavily pictorial designs exemplified by *Chu Chin Chow*. Though he read the copy of *On the Art of the Theatre* given to him by Ellen Terry, the abstract philosophising of that provocative, uncompromising and egotistical work must have been hard going for a sixteen-year-old. Only later would he understand Craig's ideas fully, and relate them to his own work in the theatre.

Yet it was Craig who fuelled his dream of being a stage designer. 'I wanted to follow in his footsteps and create ideal physical settings for an ideal theatre,' he recalled. Exploiting another family connection, he showed Fred Terry some of his drawings, and talked to him of his ambition. To his dismay he discovered he would need to study architecture and technical drawing, which would entail an ability in maths he obviously lacked. It was this realisation that caused him to think seriously for the first time about becoming an actor.

Although there were no theatrical productions at Westminster, he had some chance there to show off his talent. Arnold Haskell recalled his 'wonderful effort' in 'Orations', the end-of-term verse-speaking competition: 'There seemed little doubt that he would find his way to the stage.' He won the competition with Othello's speech to the Senate, 'Most potent, grave and reverend signors'; on another occasion he had a success with John of Gaunt's 'This sceptered isle' speech from *Richard II*. Shakespeare was already becoming a particular passion.

There were also acting opportunities in the holidays. Amateur theatricals were much in vogue in middle-class families, and a popular pastime amongst friends of the Gielguds. Thanks to Virginia Isham, a drama student friend, he was cast as Orlando in an outdoor production in Sussex of *As You Like It*, performed in Rye, St Leonards-on-Sea and Battle Abbey. At the first performance, striding on to the lawn that represented the Forest of Arden, he drew his sword, declared, 'Forbear, and eat no more!' tripped over a log, and fell flat on his face.

The writer Naomi Mitchison, then Naomi Haldane and aged twenty-three, was a close friend of Lewis. After the war he had resumed his studies at Oxford, and soon after coming down had persuaded Val to produce Naomi Haldane's historical drama *Barley, Honey and Wine*, and John to play the role of a young Greek officer. When one actor proved inadequate the eminent scientist Julian Huxley, who also took part, told the young playwright 'we are getting Jack Gielgud, who at least can act, to take it.' No independent account survives of the one performance at the Margaret Morris Theatre in Chelsea, which Val remembered as 'very amateur'. But Huxley's comment suggests Jack was beginning to show some signs of ability.

He also got a chance to act with one of the theatrical Terrys while staying with Mabel Terry-Lewis in Dorset. To his delight his aunt, who had temporarily retired from the stage, asked him to play the juvenile to her leading lady in several performances of *The Bathroom Door*, a one-act play by Gertrude Jennings. Staged in village halls for the benefit of the local Women's Institute, it was a risqué piece for the time, with all the characters in dressing-gowns, pyjamas and nightgowns. Beguiled by his aunt's charm, Jack was more determined than ever to carry on the family tradition.

On 7 July 1921, after yet another visit to *The Beggar's Opera*, he noted in his programme: 'The evening of my leaving Westminster.' His parents had persuaded him to specialise in history and English literature so he could try for a scholarship to Oxford, where Lewis had again excelled, and Val had just completed his studies. But Jack had other ideas. He told them three years at university would be a waste of his time and their money, and that he wanted to be an actor. His parents were not at all enthusiastic: according to Val, despite their great love of the theatre 'they looked distinctly sideways at the stage as a means of livelihood'. Frank Gielgud argued that with his talent for drawing his son should train as an architect. To placate his father Jack promised that, if he had not succeeded as an actor by the age of twenty-five, he would accede to his wishes. In the meantime he would try to get into a drama school. Reluctantly, his parents gave in.

It took courage for him to stand up to his forbidding father, who badly wanted him to follow his older brothers to Oxford. In doing so he showed a single-mindedness and determination that were to stand him in good stead in his early years in the theatre. As Val remembered: 'When the question of his going to university came up his decision was quietly but firmly negative. He said that he wanted to go on the stage, and that he was going on the stage. Accordingly he went.'

3

Atkins, RADA and Playfair

He needs physical culture and rougher and
firmer movements, and a tightening up of all
his limbs.

(Drama school report, 1923)

IT was a vain, foppish seventeen-year-old who set about getting into
drama school. Excessively dress-conscious, he favoured light-grey
flannels and silk socks, a soft felt hat with a broad brim (in imitation
of Craig) and occasionally the ultimate affectation, an eye-glass (in
imitation of Lewis). He let his hair grow long, and washed it often,
believing this made him appear romantic. A photograph shows an
interesting rather than handsome face, with a delicate, chiselled
mouth, prominent nose, fine cheekbones, and a large forehead. The
impression is of an intense, serious and insecure young man.

For an aspiring actor his looks were in his favour, but in other
respects he had considerable handicaps. He walked with slightly bent
knees, and was not at all athletic; his movement was generally poor.
Although his light, high voice had a pleasing musicality, his diction
could seem affected, and he had a tendency to gabble. But his greatest
problems were his shyness and acute self-consciousness. Apparently
born with a theatrical silver spoon in his mouth, he had to struggle
hard for many years to overcome such handicaps.

Training for the theatre was in its infancy in the early 1920s, and
there were few drama schools. In 1896 Ben Greet had founded an
Academy of Acting near the Strand. The two main ones now were the
Royal Academy of Dramatic Art, founded in 1904 by Beerbohm Tree,
and the Central School of Speech Training and Dramatic Art, started
two years later by the eminent speech therapist and voice coach Elsie

Fogerty. There was a handful of smaller schools, mostly in London, and usually run by actors: May Whitty ran the Etlinger School, Constance Benson had her own school, while for children there was the Italia Conti.

Jack's first contact with a school had been in his last months at Westminster. At her school in Whitehead's Grove, Chelsea, Rosina Filippi sometimes called in outsiders – known as 'guinea pigs', because the pay was a guinea – for her productions. In January 1921, when a student fell ill, Jack took over as Mercutio in three scenes from *Romeo and Juliet*, performed at the Old Court Studio in Chelsea.

Rosina Filippi had worked with Tree and Mrs Patrick Campbell, and still appeared occasionally in the West End. The half-sister of the great Italian actress Eleonora Duse, she had been the first person to stage Shakespeare at the Old Vic. A jolly, energetic and gypsy-like woman, once reputedly the best teacher in London, she emphasised good speech, and the importance of full vowels and sharp consonants: 'No one can teach you to act, but you can learn to speak,' she told her students. Jack liked her humour in rehearsals, but was disconcerted in the performance when she accompanied him on the piano throughout the famous Queen Mab speech. She thought him promising, and offered him lessons and a run of small parts in her next productions. That Easter he played two parts in *Belinda*, an adaptation of a novel by Rhoda Broughton.

This opinion of his potential from an experienced teacher was encouraging. He now asserted his new-won independence by dropping the name Jack in favour of the more serious-sounding John, and applied for a scholarship to the small drama school set up by Constance Benson the previous year. Though inclined to be raucous and strident, she had been a leading lady in her husband's company for many years. Having played all the main female roles in Shakespeare she had an extensive knowledge of the plays. Her school in Kensington was housed in Pembroke Hall (now demolished), a small, ramshackle drill-hall in Pembroke Gardens, near Kate Terry's house. Drab and poky, it consisted of a tiny stage and auditorium, with a glass conservatory leading out into a yard, and a minute office.

Gielgud went there for his scholarship audition trembling with nerves. For Constance Benson and the actress Helen Haye he recited the poem 'Bredon Hill' from A.E. Housman's *A Shropshire Lad*. Some years earlier Henry Ainley's rendering at a charity matinée had moved him to tears; after the audition he feared it had influenced him too much. 'I thought I had shouted the roof off,' he recalled. As he was often to do later, he had under-rated his performance, for Helen Haye had given him full marks and he was offered a scholarship for one year's free tuition. 'The chief note she makes of your performance is "natural and unstrained",' Constance Benson wrote to him. Gielgud was overjoyed: he could now follow his chosen path.

He started at the school in September 1921, full of hope and confidence. But his experience there was not especially happy. Hating physical exercise he tried to shirk the fencing and dancing lessons. His self-consciousness made him miserable in the deportment classes, and he thought the elocution classes a waste of time. What he did like was the rehearsing of scenes from plays. He was one of only four young men among the thirty students, an advantage when it came to casting. In *Twelfth Night* he played Sir Toby Belch in an almost entirely female cast; in *Hamlet* he played the title-role while young women played Claudius, Horatio, Laertes and the Ghost. At the public performance, he recalled, his vanity took over: 'I was so delighted with the long black cloak I had to wear that I spent most of the first scene draping it over my arm and looking over my shoulder to see if it were trailing on the floor to my satisfaction.'

He now discovered that the Terry tendency to produce tears, diagnosed in his mother as 'poor lachrymal glands', could be a useful weapon in his technical armoury. But he was uncomfortable whenever he had to rehearse a love-scene. He recalled the horror of 'clinging self-consciously to a girl as shy as oneself in front of a classroom full of sniggering students'. The experience may have been the beginning of his awareness of his homosexuality.

While he was at school Ellen Terry had urged him to read Shakespeare; surprisingly, he had still not done so. But he had a good memory and found the verse easy to learn. He enjoyed the way his voice soared in the purple passages, and realised he could make himself cry at the sound of his own cadences. He liked the feeling of being part of a tradition, and learning bits of 'business' used by the Benson company – some of which had probably been handed down from actors who had worked with Tree and Irving. He played Benedick in *Much Ado About Nothing*, but found the character difficult to understand. Aristocratic parts, such as Sir Peter Teazle in *The School for Scandal* and Lord Stevenage in Gertrude Jennings's *The Young Person in Pink*, suited his upright bearing and patrician manner. A notice of one public performance suggests he was developing a talent for comedy. After his playing of a reverend in the farce *Lady Huntsworth's Experiment* a reviewer noted: 'The worthy parson, unctuously played by quite a beginner, drew much laughter from a critical audience.'

Constance Benson, whom he remembered as 'a deft and amusing person and a splendid teacher', was known for her sharp tongue, and she criticised Gielgud for being mannered, effeminate and conceited. Later he acknowledged the justice of her criticisms, suggesting that his initial style of playing was 'something I found in my property basket, inherited from my actor relations. In a way it was a drawback. I was so mannered as a youngster, and tended to show off to such an extent, that I frequently aggravated people.'

Early in his first term he suffered a devastating blow to his pride. In the middle of a rehearsal Constance Benson said to him with a laugh: 'Good heavens, you walk exactly like a cat with rickets!' This wounding, insensitive remark depressed him greatly. It also punctured his vanity, as his teacher probably intended it to. He was so upset he started to imagine he could only play parts that involved sitting down or lying in bed. He looked for consolation in books about Irving, a notoriously poor mover, who used to drag a leg when walking on the stage. This self-consciousness and anxiety about his movement affected him for many years.

At the Benson school he took part in two outside productions, in aid of charity. The first, *I'll Leave It to You*, an early comedy by the relatively unknown Noël Coward, was mounted by the Toc H Dramatic League, and a producer with the glorious name of Maude Fortescue-Flannery. Gielgud played Bobbie, a 'slim, bright-looking youth', a fey and narcissistic part Coward had written for himself. One wonders how this slight, epigrammatic piece, presented in a church hall in Barnet, went down later when Gielgud and the company performed it on a training ship for 'Working Boys of Good Character'.

The other production marked his first attempt at a part with which he was later to become famously identified: John Worthing in Oscar Wilde's *The Importance of Being Earnest*. The presence in the cast of his sister Eleanor as Merriman and his friend Pat Caithe as Lady Bracknell, in addition to his own role as producer, suggests the venture was his own initiative. So does the fact that the profits (£30 4s 7d) were earmarked for the Old Vic Fund, for he had recently begun what was to be a lifelong association with this famous theatre.

Situated south of the Thames in the Waterloo Road, the Royal Victoria Hall had been founded in 1880 by Emma Cons, a tireless social reformer, who laid on coffee and buns and wholesome music-hall acts to lure the working classes of Lambeth away from the pubs and prostitutes. In 1912 her niece Lilian Baylis took over as manager, aiming to provide entertainments 'suited for the recreation and instruction of the poorer classes', at prices 'as will make them available to artisans and labourers'. But it was not until the 1914/15 season that Shakespeare became the regular entertainment. By 1921, with his plays out of fashion except in the provinces, the Old Vic was the only theatre in London putting on quality productions.

It was a tradition at the Vic to recruit drama students as unpaid extras for crowd scenes. After seeing *Macbeth* there in October Gielgud wrote in his programme: 'On this evening I gained a job to walk on at the Vic in *Henry V* and *Wat Tyler*.' Possibly helped by a recommendation from a Terry relative, he was taken on without an audition. This was a significant moment for him: he was now a part, however small, of a centre of Shakespearean excellence, and able to observe at close quarters leading actors such as Ernest Milton, Russell Thorndike, Rupert Harvey, Hay Petrie and Andrew Leigh. He was also exposed for the first time to a radical tradition of staging Shakespeare, begun by William Poel and Harley Granville Barker, which was being carried on at the Old Vic by the producer Robert Atkins.

Since the war the producer, not yet called director, had taken over the stage management functions of the actor-managers, most of whom had now died or retired. Stanislavsky in Moscow, Jacques Copeau in France and Max Reinhardt in Germany had all become established as producers, but in England Barker was the pioneer. Identifying the need for someone to coordinate all the elements of a production in the service of the author and the text, he had virtually invented a new craft in the theatre.

As a young actor he had come under the influence of William Poel, the founder of the Elizabethan Stage Society. Revered as a genius and reviled as a crank, Poel freed Shakespeare from the over-upholstered trappings in which his plays had been smothered during the nineteenth century. His simple, uncluttered productions, which he toured to halls and courtyards, were a major influence on those of the twentieth century. At a time when the plays were being savagely cut and slowed down for the greater glory of the actor-manager – 'You can't see the Shakespeare wood for the Beerbohm Trees' Shaw once complained – he daringly advocated using the full text in its proper order, avoiding the interpolations and rearrangements then widespread. In place of the proscenium arch he had a wide platform stage projecting into the audience, approximating as closely as possible to the Elizabethan one. Aiming to replicate the way the plays had been performed in Shakespeare's time, he used Elizabethan costume, and a minimum of scenery and scene changes. He also aimed to get rid of the slow, deliberate method of verse-speaking in favour of one that was quicker, more flexible, and more intelligent in its choice of emphasis: 'We English seem to have lost the art of speaking swiftly,' he said.

Under Poel's influence, Barker's pre-war productions at the Savoy revolutionised the staging of Shakespeare. He abandoned the naturalistic scenery and elaborate stage effects created by Irving and Tree, and insisted on playing the texts uncut. As a producer he believed in teamwork more than individual brilliance, lavishing care on smaller parts that the actor-managers had generally ignored. Atkins followed in this tradition. He too believed passionately in presenting Shakespeare without clutter or cuts. His productions had force, clarity and speed, if not great subtlety. Now in the second of his five years at the Old Vic, during which he was to stage all thirty-seven Shakespeare plays, his work had already received great acclaim, marking a turning-point for the theatre. The critics now saw it as the most important in London: it had, according to Herbert Farjeon, 'emerged for the first time out of the rut of the commonplace'.

If Gielgud's introduction to the professional theatre came at an opportune moment, Atkins' powerful personality came as a shock. 'I was terrified of him,' he recalled. A former actor, Atkins had worked with Tree, Martin-Harvey, Forbes-Robertson and Benson. He was an erudite and industrious man with a round, rich voice and a passing resemblance to Mussolini. He was also, according to the critic Richard Findlater, 'a pagan – heavy-drinking, hard-swearing and womanising'. Actors called him a martinet, or Napoleonic, or less polite names.

Nervously over-dressed in a brown serge suit, Gielgud remembered vividly his first rehearsal in the shabby saloon bar at the back of the dress circle: 'All around me actors were sitting, crouching, muttering their lines to themselves, hearing one another from tattered little green books, slipping in and out for drinks or evening papers.' His restless nature made concentration hard; during the long rehearsals he shifted from foot to foot. 'I rushed about trying to make the business of carrying a spear look really important,' he remembered. Atkins told him to take his hands out of his pockets.

In *Henry V*, staged by Atkins 'after the Elizabethan manner', he was given the part of the English Herald. It was his first speaking role on the professional stage, though it went uncredited in the programme. Conditions at the Vic were primitive: with the other extras he had to dress in one of the top boxes, peeping through a covering curtain to check if his cue was imminent; one night the curtain fell down, revealing to an astonished gallery a clutch of half-naked soldiers preparing for Agincourt. Despite having only one line, Gielgud managed to create a bad impression with it, and was relegated to a non-speaking part in Halcott Glover's *Wat Tyler*. Though cast down, he put on a brave face in his programme note: 'Walked on in this production, part of a very good crowd. A clever play. Milton very fine in it. Most interesting to take part in.'

Delighted to be in a real theatre working on Shakespeare, he walked on in five more plays during the Easter holidays. Four were by Shakespeare: *The Comedy of Errors, Hamlet, As You Like It* and *King Lear*; in the latter he played one of Cornwall's attendants, and held Gloucester's chair while his eyes were gouged out. The fifth was *Peer Gynt*, the first public performance of the play in Britain. Atkins's ambitious and much-praised staging of Ibsen's picaresque poetic masterpiece, in which Russell Thorndike gave the performance of his career, increased the glamour of the Old Vic and brought it new audiences. Amongst the trolls and peasants the programme listed a 'Mr Giulgud'.

Mixing with such established actors, some of whom seemed to him straight out of Dickens, was not easy. 'I was terrified of them because they were real old "laddies", rushing off to the bar every five minutes and using awful language,' he recalled. As a novice actor he had a long way to go: 'I have been told that I was simply dreadful,' he wrote soon afterwards. At the time he was quite unaware of the poor impression he was making: some of the actors thought him so bad they considered advising him to give up the theatre altogether. He was not asked to stay on.

Despite this failure, he had enjoyed his first taste of the Old Vic: 'I could already sense the responsive enthusiasm of the audiences, and the cosy atmosphere of the shabby old theatre,' he remembered. Seeing how actors developed their parts had been good experience. He admired Ernest Milton, and thought his Shylock the best he had seen. But the actor who impressed him most was Russell Thorndike, Sybil's brother, who managed the staggering feat of playing Hamlet, Peer Gynt, Lear, and Sganarelle in Molière's *L'Amour Médecin* in the space of five weeks. Gielgud loved the great wit and energy of his acting, and took every opportunity to learn from him. One Sunday, defying a ban on anyone watching a dress rehearsal from the auditorium, he crept under a dust-sheet, and sat entranced for several hours watching the final run-through of *Peer Gynt*. 'Russell Thorndike remarkable, fine and clever,' he noted in his programme.

This contact with some of the best Shakespearean actors of the day increased his desire to succeed. His zest and enthusiasm were limitless: in addition to the Benson school, the Old Vic and his charity performances, he went to the theatre twice a week, returning three or four times to some productions. By now he was looking not simply to be moved or entertained, but to improve his technique by observing the leaders of his profession in action. He was much taken with the nonchalant, apparently effortless style then in vogue. He was fascinated in particular by Gerald du Maurier's lazy charm, throwaway technique and staccato accents. But he also admired Charles Hawtrey's well-concealed craftsmanship, and his ability to make dialogue seem spontaneous.

His reviews of the time conjure up a lively, well-informed young critic, with an intelligence tinged with arrogance, and an inclination to show off, if only to himself. But they also reveal signs of a discerning and critical mind, one that was becoming more confident about judging plays as well as actors. He thought Barrie's *Quality Street* 'full of charm and sentiment, without being thickly sentimental Barrie'. Disliking Shaw from an early age, he was bored by *Heartbreak House*, calling it 'dull and ill-constructed'. His comments reveal a delight in language for its own sake, as when he described the comedy opera *David Garrick* as 'a tedious and quite pointless conglomeration of meretricious operatic twaddle'. His tone could be superior, even didactic: Frances Peterson's Olivia in *Twelfth Night* was 'far too coquettish; less obvious intelligence and more obvious feeling would, I think, improve her performance'. But sometimes he was unsure of his opinion: after Milne's *The Truth About Blayds* he wrote: 'How strange that everyone thinks this play is so clever – I must see it again and re-judge it. Perhaps I was in a bad temper.'

In the summer of 1922, still only eighteen, he left the Benson school. Having failed to shine, and fared badly at the Old Vic, he faced an uncertain future. He was auditioned by Gladys Cooper as understudy for Ivor Novello in *Enter Kikki* at the Playhouse, but was rejected. Once again the Terry connection helped get him a break. His mother's opposition to his becoming an actor had never been as strong as his father's, though her claim to have given him 'my whole-hearted backing' does not square with other accounts, including Gielgud's. But once the decision was made she became his most fervent supporter. Now she recommended him to her cousin Phyllis Neilson-Terry, who engaged him for a provincial tour of J.B. Fagan's play *The Wheel.* For £4 a week he was to play a small part, understudy four others, and be assistant stage manager.

His cousin had hired him without seeing him act, though she may have consulted Kate Terry, who had been to a public performance at the Benson school. His grandmother now wrote to Gielgud warmly: 'Dear old Jack, I am delighted to hear of your intended real start in a profession you love, and wish you every success.' She then passed on advice given to her by Benjamin and Sarah Terry: 'You must not anticipate a bed of roses, for on the stage as in every other profession there are "rubs and arrows" to contend with. Be kind and affable to all your co-mates, but if possible be intimate with none of them.' Gielgud took this latter maxim to heart, repeating it often in later years.

The Wheel marked Phyllis Neilson-Terry's first step into management. Aged thirty, tall, beautiful and aloof, she had achieved early success in Shakespeare, notably as Desdemona, Viola and Juliet. Her laziness once prompted her father Fred Terry to compare her with her brother Dennis: 'I have a daughter who can act, but won't, and a son who can't act, but will.' The London production had been a hit, with a strong cast that included Randle Ayrton and Edith Evans. Gielgud had seen it in the spring, and observed: 'A rather bad play, stagily effective; most admirably acted. Phyllis gave a really beautiful performance.' He could hardly have imagined that he would soon be a member of her company.

The fourteen-week tour of the Midlands and the north proved an eye-opener. Gielgud had rarely been outside London, and had had no real contact with anyone outside his class. Now he came face to face with the reality of the touring actor's life: the long train journeys, the hard beds in dreary, uncomfortable 'digs', the poor meals, the endless hours to kill during the day.

Lodging in back-to-back houses with second-rate music-hall artists, where the coal was kept in the bath, the porridge burnt at breakfast, and the landlady kept her hat on indoors, he felt very ill at ease. 'What a snob they must have thought me!' he reflected later. He hated the factory chimneys and unfamiliar accents in Leeds, Bradford and

Sheffield; he was also dreadfully homesick. A tuck-box lovingly prepared by his mother as if he were still at school – tinned tongue, sardines and pots of jam – only highlighted the shabbiness of his circumstances. 'No wonder Irving died here, poor man,' he wrote from Bradford, where the people, he decided, were 'dull and heavy like the sheep whose wool they mangle'. Unused to an uncomfortable bed, he wrote home asking to be sent a pillow.

Socially he was out of his depth. During one of the traditional day-time pub-crawls with the other actors he disgraced himself by mixing beer and spirits in rapid succession, turning green, and fainting on the spot. Professionally, however, he was picking up a good deal. His parents had given him a proper make-up box, and his fellow-actors showed him how to apply grease-paint. He arranged the rehearsal call sheets, prepared the stage before curtain-up, held the prompt book, helped to work the special effects, supervised the get-out on Saturday night, and the get-in to the next theatre on the Monday. It was hard work physically, the first he had ever done. But the experience during the tour gave him a useful insight into the complexities of staging a production.

The Wheel was a typical melodrama of the time. Set in India, it concerns a passionate love-affair between an army captain and a married woman trying to escape from an unsatisfactory marriage. Though it has powerful emotional moments, the dialogue teeters on the edge of cliché. Ion Swinley – whom Gielgud was understudying – and Hesketh Pearson had the two principal male roles, with Phyllis Neilson-Terry herself playing the female lead, and her husband Cecil King producing. As the army officer Lieutenant Manners, Gielgud was on stage for less than five minutes. Of his two lines, the first – 'How d'ye do? Awfully jolly to find you all right' – was the more lively. He took some comfort, however, in his costume and make-up, boasting in a letter home: 'I am assured I look quite the experienced militarist in my moustache.' He also enjoyed the understudy rehearsals, in which he tried to copy Ion Swinley.

But the novelty of the tour soon wore off: 'I am bored to death with this play,' he wrote from Birmingham. His big moment came in Aberdeen, when he had to play a slightly bigger part for one performance. With only a morning to rehearse, he emerged with credit: his cousin reported that he 'did *very well indeed*', adding that 'the funniest thing of all is to see the family gestures coming out again'. Gielgud wrote to his parents: 'Everyone seems to have been not too badly impressed. I only wish we were not too far off for you to come and see me, but of course it is out of the question . . . anyway it has been quite a fairly thrilling experience.'

To his surprise, Phyllis Neilson-Terry promised he could play the part at a matinée in Oxford, where his parents could come to see him. But this second attempt at the part, due perhaps to their presence, was an anti-climax. 'My performance was dreadful,' he remembered. 'Nothing I had done before seemed to be right a second time; half-way through the play I knew that I had failed.' He was deeply ashamed when he went out to tea with Phyllis and his parents afterwards.

As the tour ended he faced a dilemma. Keen to find more work immediately, he had bought a suit, hat and overcoat to wear at interviews. 'I'm perfectly certain one creates twice the impression on managers if one's well dressed, and it's well worth the extra two or three pounds between Bond Street and Selfridge,' he wrote to his parents. But he was also aware of his need to improve if he hoped to make any progress as an actor. After the Oxford débâcle one of the actors in the company, Alexander Sarner, told him that he had an instinct for the stage, but needed to learn more control and improve his technique. He advised him to go back to drama school for at least another year, perhaps to the Royal Academy of Dramatic Art (RADA), where he himself had been a student.

During the tour he had had to turn down an offer to act in *Twelfth Night,* in a production Virginia Isham was organising with an amateur group from Oxford. 'I am quite desolated to refuse, it's really very sickening,' he wrote to her. 'I am vastly flattered, and long to play Feste of all parts on earth.' In November he wrote to her again: 'What of your plans for the future – are you really going to the RADA? I've nothing settled still . . . but I shall undoubtedly go to the Academy, for a term at any rate, if I can get a job in town, however small. It would be such fun, if we were there together – do go.'

The job he was hoping for was again courtesy of the family: Phyllis Neilson-Terry was casting her next play, *A Roof and Four Walls* by Temple Thurston. But all she offered him was a commission to design two sets. With his mother's help he made the models, and his designs were accepted. He was not, however, very happy with the end-result: 'My scenes quite successful,' he wrote in his programme, 'though I disliked certain things in the furnishings, which I think they have just spoiled.' Not long before he would have been thrilled to have such a commission, but now his ambitions lay elsewhere. With no acting work in sight he applied for a place at RADA for January 1923. Subsequently he won a scholarship, enabling him once again to avoid being dependent on his parents for the fees.

Situated in Gower Street in central London, the Royal Academy of Dramatic Art – it had acquired its royal charter and title in 1920 – was a more prestigious school than Constance Benson's and, with 146 students, much larger. Once again Gielgud found a surplus of females, in a ratio of three to one in his class. This was quite normal: at the Central School the following year, when Peggy Ashcroft enrolled, there were ninety female students, but only five male. Many young women with little or no talent went to drama school merely to be 'finished', or to fill in time before marriage and motherhood. RADA had a distinctly upper-class feel: Flora Robson, a student four years previously, recalled being 'surrounded by society girls'. Two friends of Gielgud's there were 'Honourables'.

Robert Harris was the star student of the time, while Beatrix Lehmann, Veronica Turleigh and Mervyn Johns were also at the school. Gielgud's classmates included George Howe, Benita Hume, Carleton Hobbs and Reginald Gardiner. As at the Benson school, there were classes in elocution, fencing, dancing and 'gesture', but most of the time was spent in working on scenes from plays. Again Gielgud had a good mixture of parts, playing seventeen in his year there. In addition to two Hamlets, they included Joseph Surface and Sir Peter Teazle in *The School for Scandal*, two roles in *The Admirable Crichton*, Sergius in Shaw's *Arms and the Man*, and Jason in *Medea*.

There were several lively and formidable personalities on the staff. Elsie Chester was a former actress whose career had ended tragically when she had a leg amputated after a car accident. A fierce and excitable woman with a beautiful voice, she would throw her crutch at any student who annoyed her. Rosina Filippi was there, as was Helen Haye, feared for her tart and cutting remarks, and Gertrude Burnett, a strict disciplinarian who took a part away from any student who forgot to bring a pencil. The flamboyant, red-haired Alice Gachet, who was soon to draw out the talent of Charles Laughton, was a sensitive and intelligent teacher who breathed fun and vitality into every class.

There were also visiting celebrities. Gielgud had his first sight of Shaw, who lectured about Shakespeare's use of the stage. Sybil Thorndike, then at the peak of her career, gave lessons in Greek tragedy, and rehearsed Gielgud's class in scenes from Euripides' *Medea*. The students, she thought, were 'like a lot of governesses' – except one:

'I said, "You're all terrible, no fire, no guts, you've none of you got anything in you, except that boy over there, the tall one, what's your name?" And he said, "It's John Gielgud," and I said, "Well, you're the only one." The rest of them had no voices.' She gave him some personal advice: 'Do everything at rehearsal,' she said. 'Let yourself go, make a fool of yourself, go to any lengths, and then learn how to control yourself in performance, and do much less.' It was to be a long time before he was able to follow her advice, but her visit made a great impact: 'She exuded vitality, enthusiasm and generosity, and we were all spellbound,' he remembered.

The teacher who encouraged and helped him most was Claude Rains. A handsome, dynamic and successful character actor, he had started as Beerbohm Tree's call-boy and prompter, and had reputedly lost his Cockney accent by walking round Trafalgar Square at night, practising his aitches. At RADA he was an enthusiastic and popular teacher, especially with the female students, one of whom, Beatrix Thompson, he later married. Gielgud was captivated by his Dubedat in Shaw's *The Doctor's Dilemma*. 'It was just the romantic boyish figure I hoped to be,' he recalled. With his piercing dark eyes and beautiful voice, Rains exerted a powerful but damaging influence over him. Finding he had a talent for impersonation, Gielgud compensated for his lack of technique by mimicking Rains, and became extremely mannered. 'I strained every fibre in my efforts to appear violent or emotional, and only succeeded in forcing my voice and striking strange attitudes with my body,' he remembered. In these early years he continued to be extremely susceptible to such influences.

His most intensive work with Rains was on Tolstoy's melodrama *Reparation*, for the final public performance. He was excited to have the role of Fedya, which he had recently seen played by Henry Ainley, another powerful role model, and which gave him ample scope for pulling out all the emotional stops. Helped perhaps by his Slav genes, he had a modest success. Yet in general he was finding it hard to allow his personality to invade the characters he played. Rehearsals were more difficult than performances, because there was no costume to hide behind. Still acutely self-conscious, he found it embarrassing to work 'with rows of girls sitting on chairs staring at me'.

He gained further experience in Shakespeare playing Hotspur in *Henry IV Part I*, and also Hamlet, surrounded again by a largely female cast. He was now a stern critic of professional Shakespearean productions, and increasingly confident of his opinions. Of Atkins's production of *Henry IV Part II* at the Old Vic he wrote: 'The play bored me very much, except for one or two scenes, and I am ashamed to confess to preferring Fagan's cut version.' He was appalled by Lewis Casson's production of *Cymbeline*: 'A pitiable exhibition with no apparent redeeming feature,' he wrote. 'We left after the first part – completely overwhelmed by the total lack of anything visible, audible or sensible.'

He had previously seen four Hamlets: H.B. Irving, Rupert Harvey, Henry Baynton ('an almost meritless performance') and Russell Thorndike ('exceedingly clever, particularly in the ironic passages'). Ernest Milton at the Old Vic was the fifth, but he was not impressed: 'I suppose a really satisfactory Hamlet is impossible. This performance was full of cleverness and ingenuity, but Milton was alternately too slow and too incoherent and too melancholy and too stagey.'

He was not happy with his own voice, which he described that Easter to Virginia Isham as 'rather sketchy, to say the least'; nor was he satisfied with his work at his first public performance at RADA, in *The School for Scandal*: 'I fear I was terribly bad,' he told her. If this was true, he must have improved later, for while still at the academy he was cast in two West End productions. Once again the family gave him a hand. His parents knew the Playfair family well, often joining in the Christmas theatricals at their house. Kate Gielgud now persuaded Nigel Playfair, a leading producer and actor-manager, to see her son in the pre-Easter public show at RADA. His class was staging Barrie's *The Admirable Crichton*, in which he was playing the 'silly ass' Woolley in the first half, and the title-role in the second. Playfair detected some promise, and offered him a part in May in *The Insect Play*, by the Czech dramatists the Brothers Čapek.

It was a wonderful break for a nineteen-year-old still struggling to learn the fundamentals of acting. Playfair was an experienced producer, with a gift for communicating his enjoyment of a play to his actors. Portly, genial and short-sighted, a pipe forever in his mouth, he treated the theatre as a hobby – Noël Coward recalled that he produced 'with more elfishness than authority' – yet still managed to retain integrity in his work. In 1918 he had found a derelict Victorian theatre in an old market in Hammersmith and, with the help of wealthy friends, including the novelist Arnold Bennett, had converted it into a small, attractive theatre.

Despite its position outside the West End, the Lyric quickly became one of the most popular, fashionable and interesting theatres of the day. Playfair staged a series of stylish, high-class classical revivals, including the celebrated production of *The Beggar's Opera* that Gielgud had so loved. As a contemporary jingle put it: 'No greater name than Nigel Playfair / Occurs in Thespian lore or myth / 'Twas he who first revealed to Mayfair / The whereabouts of Hammersmith.'

Playfair had a genius for spotting talent: at the Lyric he employed Herbert Marshall, Leslie Banks, and Hermione and Angela Baddeley when they were all virtually unknown. He was soon to provide Edith Evans with two of her greatest triumphs, in Congreve's *The Way of the World* and Farquhar's *The Beaux' Stratagem*, and help Peggy Ashcroft to get started. In 1923 he had taken over the Regent, a former music-hall in King's Cross, on the fringes of the West End. It was here that Gielgud made his London début.

The Insect Play is a sharp satire on contemporary morals, in which the vices and foibles of humanity are shown through the corrupt and immoral behaviour of butterflies, beetles, flies, ants and snails. In staging the English première Playfair was hoping to build on the success of Karel Čapek's satire *RUR*, which he had adapted for Basil Dean's production earlier that year. The new play's cast included Andrew Leigh as a cricket, Angela Baddeley as a beetle, a young Elsa Lanchester as a larva, and Gielgud's mentor Claude Rains in three different roles. The costumes and scenery were by the designer Doris Zinkeisen, whom Playfair had just discovered; the music was by Frederick Austin, famous for his work on *The Beggar's Opera*.

Gielgud was thrilled to be cast as Felix, the poet-butterfly. 'It's an enormous piece of luck for me getting the engagement,' he confessed to Virginia Isham, 'I have a very good part in the first act, and a small one in the third. You must come and see it: I think it's a brilliant play.' During rehearsals he was nervous, and terribly grateful if one of the older actors favoured him with a nod or a smile. But he was also excited at playing a part that had not been played before in England. Nora Nicholson, cast as an ant, remembered him as 'a slim young man, rather awkward and gangling, full of promise'. At one point Playfair, an easygoing and approachable producer, asked him for his opinion on a minor point, but he was too shy to give it. Later he became more confident, and at the dress rehearsal tentatively offered a suggestion, which Playfair accepted.

But it was not a happy début. Dressed in white flannels, with a green laurel wreath fixed on to a blond wig, and a pair of wings stuck on his shoulders, he felt he created a ludicrous effect. His lack of physical coordination led him to make a mess of a game of shuttlecock and battledore. He thought his acting indifferent, his inexperience glaring. 'I'm surprised the audience didn't throw things at me,' he recalled. James Agate, the new *Sunday Times* critic, nearly did. 'The butterflies had the gestures, and their voices the timbre, of tea-shop waitresses "mashing" their beaux,' he wrote. 'If, on scanning the programme during the first interval, I had to re-encounter these first-act names, I must have fled the theatre.'

It was a tough assignment for an inexperienced actor. Yet Gielgud may have exaggerated his ineptitude: though the *Morning Post* thought his performance 'rather on the light side', the *Weekly Dispatch* asserted that 'he had all the wistful grace that has come to be associated with the word "pierrot"'. Another inexperienced butterfly was Noelle Sonning, who later metamorphosed into the children's writer Noel Streatfeild. Gielgud remembered her as 'extremely pretty in a leggy way', and confessed that 'we were *both* very unhappy in our parts'. But his own unhappiness may have partially stemmed from a love-scene they had together, which involved a certain amount of sexual ambiguity ('What a pity you're not a girl. I know – you shall be Iris, and I'll be your Felix') and a good deal of suggestive byplay on soft cushions.

A letter he wrote to Kate Terry suggests he was not alone in having problems: 'It is all so fantastic and unlike anything else, that even the old stagers in the cast seem to find the same difficulty in dealing with it,' he told her. Although some critics, including Agate and Farjeon, admired the play's originality, and the eccentric Elsa Lanchester received rave notices, the production was not a success. Disappointed by the failure, Playfair made his feelings clear on the last night of the six-week run, when he sat in his box with his back to the stage throughout the butterfly scenes.

Depressed by this apparent rejection, Gielgud was surprised to be given another chance in Playfair's next production, John Drinkwater's American Civil War play *Robert E. Lee*. In this he was cast as an aide to General Lee, played by Felix Aylmer. Opening in June at the Regent, the play was a critical success, but the public was less keen, and the company often played to half-empty houses during the three-month run. In his minor part Gielgud, dressed in Confederate uniform, once more failed to distinguish himself, underlining his clumsiness by tripping over his sabre, and generally moving in a slovenly way.

However, Playfair had shown faith in his ability by asking him to understudy Claude Rains, who had the key part of a poet/philosopher.

Gielgud went on for him for three performances. As in *The Wheel*, he got through the first on sheer nerves, but then lost confidence. He did, however, show some ability in the more emotional scenes, finding for the first time that he could move an audience. One person who saw him perform, the actor Denys Blakelock, recalled being impressed by 'a strange emanation of emotional power'. Although technically he was still inadequate, his modest success suggests he was beginning to absorb some of what he was learning at RADA.

He was now starting to enjoy a social life. Playfair invited the company to dances at Thurloe Lodge, his Kensington house, where Gielgud was enthralled to see the Lovat Fraser drawings from *The Beggar's Opera* that decorated the rooms. Here he met Playfair's stage manager and protégé James Whale, soon to become a friend. A tall, red-headed young man with side-whiskers and a fawn-like charm, he later achieved fame in Hollywood as the director of the Frankenstein films. Despite being homosexual, he was then engaged to the slinky, exotic Doris Zinkeisen; Gielgud remembered them as 'a striking pair' at Playfair's dances.

Despite his shyness, he was relishing mixing in a wider circle. He spent part of that Easter holiday in Oxford with a group of Cambridge undergraduates, 'rather amusing in the rival camp', he told Virginia Isham. 'Such a hectic week, meeting numberless new and delightful people, but rather confusing to my foolish intellect, and I was in a state of vague wuzziness – not due to drink, as you might suppose! I wonder if you'll be going up there for Eights Weeks. I hope I may be – what fun if we met there.'

He still spent much of his spare time at the theatre, often standing alone in the pit. He was becoming interested in new plays, though there were few good ones around. Post-war audiences wanted their entertainment light, and the scene was dominated by revues, musicals, farces and thrillers. Comedy was immensely popular: the public relished the cynicism of Maugham, the sentimentality of Barrie and Milne, the wit of Frederick Lonsdale. There were revivals of Pinero and Wilde, glimpses of Ibsen and Shaw. But new and challenging work was thin on the ground.

Gielgud enjoyed Barrie's plays, but was less keen on Milne's: 'a storm in a teacup plot, as usual' he wrote of *Success*. He thought Shaw's *The Doctor's Dilemma* 'dull and wordy', but admired Maugham's work, though not indiscriminately: 'a very clever play, without the consummate brilliance of *The Circle*,' he observed after seeing the controversial but successful *Our Betters*. But he was excited by the new drama coming from Europe and America. O'Neill's *Anna Christie*, getting its first production in the West End, he thought 'a very fine play, sordid but intensely dramatic'; while Karel Čapek's science-fiction fantasy *RUR* was 'intensely interesting . . . quite the most wonderful and original play I have seen for some time'.

Every actor in London was at the New Oxford to see Eleonora Duse in *I Spettri*, an Italian translation of Ibsen's *Ghosts*. Gielgud was electrified by her technique, and wrote an impressively balanced and mature review: 'Her reserve, her dignity and her forcefulness in repose, and the wealth of her gesture with her most exquisite hands – these struck one as the palpable and exterior assets of her genius . . . She seemed to be somewhat selfish in her playing of the big scene of the second act, where her groans distracted, and drew one's attention to her from the boy, and I thought her over-acting part of the scene. But her first and third acts were magnificent.' In sad contrast, he sat alone in the gallery for a charity matinée at the Palladium, suffering agonies as Ellen Terry fumbled for her words on stage. 'Ellen very pathetic and gaga,' he wrote.

He left RADA just before Christmas, with no real distinction. His report, written by Rosina Filippi, underlined how much he needed to improve his physical dexterity and movement if he was to succeed. 'He needs physical culture and rougher and firmer movements, and a tightening up of all his limbs,' she wrote. But she also observed that 'he has inherited talent, an easy mentality and a sure sense of the stage'. As yet he had shown little evidence of an individual style, finding it easier to imitate other actors. He had a tendency to laziness: at both his drama schools he had worked at the things he enjoyed, but shirked others. He had also shown a certain arrogance in his attitude to some elements of the courses, especially elocution and voice production, which he believed he could deal with quite easily on his own.

During his RADA year the question of his name had come up. The actor and producer Donald Calthrop, after admiring his performance as Hotspur, had suggested he change it, arguing that no one would spell or pronounce it properly. For a moment Gielgud was tempted to use the Terry name, but a determination to make his own way made him keep his own. 'It looks so odd I think people may remember it,' he told Calthrop. His instinct was right, though until he became known he had to endure some odd spellings, including Gillcud, Cielgud and Grilgood; during the tour of *The Wheel* a critic noted that 'the small part of the messenger was adequately portrayed by Joan Gillseed'.

Many actors then emerging from drama school went first into the provinces, where there were some sixty companies touring. Every West End success was copied by the number one, two and three companies, in which the actors would imitate the voices, gestures and mannerisms of the big stars. But Gielgud had already set his sights on the West End, and didn't have to wait long to achieve his goal. For once the family were not involved: out of the blue he was offered the part of Charley in Brandon Thomas's evergreen farce *Charley's Aunt*, to be staged for six weeks as the Christmas show at the Comedy.

Finding this 'feed' part dreary and unrewarding, he decided to liven it up at rehearsal by wearing horn-rimmed spectacles and giving it the 'silly ass' treatment. He had reckoned without Amy Brandon-Thomas, the author's daughter and producer, who exercised iron control over the staging of her father's comedy, insisting every costume and move should be exactly as they had always been. Gielgud soon got bored with running up and down stairs twice daily, struggling to keep a straight face while one of the veteran actors tried to make him giggle. The critic of *The Times* failed even to mention his name. It was a disillusioning start to his West End career.

However, his fortunes soon changed. After Christmas he was invited to join a newly established company in Oxford. His four short seasons there were to give him his first taste of 'weekly rep', then the life-blood of the English theatre.

4

Oxford Apprenticeship

A very interesting performance from Mr
Gielgerd.

(*Isis* review of *Love for Love*, 1924)

OXFORD was a city to which Gielgud was already greatly
attached, a place he invested with glamour touched by
nostalgia. At fifteen he had visited Lewis while he was an undergraduate there, and remembered feeding the deer through the window
of his rooms in Magdalen. There had also been a moonlit picnic on the
Cherwell with Aldous Huxley and Naomi Mitchison, in a punt lit by
Chinese lanterns. His romantic feeling for the town had later been
reinforced by his enjoyment of Max Beerbohm's *Zuleika Dobson* and
Compton Mackenzie's *Sinister Street*. Having not long ago spurned the
idea of Oxford in favour of the theatre, he now enjoyed something akin
to the life of an undergraduate during the next eighteen months.

The idea of repertory was still relatively new in Britain, having been
pioneered by Barker during his celebrated 1904–7 seasons at the Court.
Reacting against the lack of intellectually challenging work for actors,
the 'continual demand for nothing but smartness and prettiness' that
dominated the West End, he and J.E. Vedrenne had presented a
startling variety of new plays, few of which would have been staged in
the commercial theatre. Works by, among others, Ibsen, Euripides,
Galsworthy, Maeterlinck, Hauptmann and Shaw were put on for a few
matinées, and if successful entered the evening repertoire, where they
alternated with other plays. The productions were not dominated by a
star: as the actress Lillah McCarthy said: 'When we went elsewhere the
part was everything; at the Court the whole was greater than the part.'

Inspired by Barker's work, the first regional repertory theatre was

47

opened in 1908 in Manchester, by Annie Horniman at the Gaiety, and Liverpool and Glasgow soon followed suit. In 1913 the first purpose-built one was opened to house the new Birmingham Repertory Company. It was under the direction of Barry Jackson, a stage-struck millionaire who was appalled at the lack of intelligent theatre in the city. The programmes of these theatres varied, from the cautious early ones of the Liverpool Repertory Theatre (which became the Playhouse in 1916), to the poetic drama, European plays and striking Shakespeare productions at the Birmingham Rep.

Founded in 1923, the Oxford Playhouse, together with the Cambridge Festival Theatre established three years later, was part of the second wave of repertory theatres. Of the two, the Festival was more avant-garde: its productions included a flamenco-style *Romeo and Juliet* and a *Twelfth Night* on roller skates. The Playhouse, which provided permanent theatre during the university terms, had more highbrow aims, as is clear from the appeal for support for its launch by leading theatrical figures, including Barrie, Shaw, Pinero, Playfair, Henry Arthur Jones, Masefield, A.A. Milne, and Gilbert Murray.

'It appears to us only right that Oxford should encourage the efforts which are being made sporadically by individuals to raise the standard of the acted drama in England – the only great country in the world where neither Government nor Municipality will move a finger to support the most democratic of the arts.' The aim was 'to present plays suited to the stage rather than to the study, and provide scope for the art of acting': citizens and undergraduates were urged to 'assist in raising the theatre to the position which it has occupied in the great cultural epochs of the past'. Or as Shaw put it more succinctly, on a visit to the Playhouse during its first season, 'If Oxford is not highbrow, what on earth *is* Oxford?'

The man behind this bold theatrical venture was a large, genial and sensitive Irishman, J.B. Fagan. Widely read and immensely cultured, Fagan was a theatrical polymath, combining the roles of actor, playwright, manager and producer. He had acted with Benson and Tree, and had written several plays. A devotee of Barker, he too had managed the Court, where in 1918 he had staged the first production of Shaw's *Heartbreak House.* He had also mounted innovative productions of Shakespeare, which Gielgud had seen there when he was at Westminster.

Fagan, who had been impressed by Gielgud's performance in *Robert E. Lee* when he had come on for Claude Rains, was exactly the kind of producer the nervy, self-conscious young actor needed to help him gain confidence. Fagan's daughter Gemma, who joined the Oxford Players later, remembers: 'My father was a gentle and humorous man, and very patient. I never saw him lose his temper, which was extraordinary for an Irishman. He was a very good director: he would come on stage and show you how to do things, but if actors had their own ideas, he would discuss these with them.' Fagan was known for his ability to fire the imaginations of his cast. Tyrone Guthrie, whom he directed in a production by the Oxford University Dramatic Society (OUDS), recalled how good he was with young actors, being neither pompous nor condescending. 'There was never any doubt that he was in complete control, but there was no fussy over-ordering about or attempt to impress us with masterful airs.'

Fagan liked to keep up with theatrical trends abroad: he was the first to bring Georg Kaiser's expressionist drama to Britain, and the first to stage a Sean O'Casey play (*Juno and the Paycock*) in the West End. In Oxford he wanted to expose 'Town and Gown' to the best in European theatre. In his first season he had provided an ambitious repertoire featuring among others Shaw, Wilde, Goldoni, de Musset, Ibsen and Sheridan. Audiences were often small, but responsive: among the keen regulars on first nights at the Playhouse were the actress Lillah McCarthy, now retired from the stage, the society hostess Ottoline Morrell, and the scientist J.B.S. Haldane.

The main audience comprised undergraduates, among them the future historians A.J.P. Taylor and A.L. Rowse ('What excitement it gave one for half a crown!'), Evelyn Waugh, and the actor Robert Speaight. For Emlyn Williams, an aspiring playwright and penniless student, the Playhouse offered a vital education, a 'three-year Fagan course in Drama, three shillings a time', during which he attended 'one draughty première after another', staged by a company which 'had no money to spend, but offered a standard kept consisently high by a lovable unbusiness-like man of the theatre'. Usefully for Gielgud, the standard was high enough to attract a few national critics.

Fagan launched his second season in January 1924 with a company almost entirely made up of young, unknown actors. He had an exceptional eye for talent. The company included Flora Robson, just out of drama school; the elfin Richard Goolden, fresh from success with the OUDS; Molly MacArthur, later a leading designer; and Peter Creswell, who was to become a BBC radio drama producer. He also hired three young men who were to make their names as directors:

Glen Byam Shaw, Reginald Denham and Tyrone Guthrie. Occasionally Fagan would use guest actors, such as Raymond Massey and
Dorothy Green.

Fagan had taken over the Red Barn, an ugly late Victorian red-brick
building in north Oxford, formerly a big-game museum (now the
Oxford Language Centre). The ramshackle theatre was no more than
a hall, with an unraked apron stage and no balcony, and tiny and ill-
equipped dressing-rooms. 'The whole place was falling to pieces it was
so rotten,' Gemma Fagan recalls. According to Val Gielgud, it was 'a
building devoid of cheer, foyer or bar', with seats, 'surely the most
uncomfortable in any theatre in the world', that creaked at the slightest
move. Often the vibrations from passing traffic drowned the actors'
words. There was no front curtain, and scenery was generally a simple
white drape with, if necessary, a table and chairs brought on by a
stagehand. Fagan grandly called this the 'presentational method'; in
practice it was simply all he could afford. Despite its drawbacks, the
theatre had a distinctive atmosphere, captured by a reviewer in *Isis*
magazine: 'There seems to be a personal friendliness, one might almost
call it intimacy, between the opposite sides of the footlights, without
which neither "théâtre intime" nor repertory theatre can exist.'

It was a tough setting for a theatrical apprenticeship, but Gielgud,
now earning what seemed to him a wonderful salary of £8 a week,
plunged into the work eagerly. The company presented a new play
every Monday, gave seven performances a week, rehearsed for six hours
during the day, and spent Sundays and Mondays helping to build and
paint the scenery. It was an exhausting schedule, though different from
normal weekly rep, since the actors had the vacations in which to
recover. But productions were often unready by the first night, and the
actors far from word-perfect. With no space for a prompter to be
concealed, the company used an old rep device, and placed lines they
had difficulty with on the back of the furniture.

Fagan's productions were often raw and unpolished, but they had
vitality and gusto. Gielgud was given a stimulating range of parts, some
minor, others substantial. In the space of six weeks he played Johnson
in Shaw's *Captain Brassbound's Conversion*, Valentine in Congreve's
Love for Love, Brian Strange in A.A. Milne's light comedy *Mr Pim
Passes By* (not long before banned by the university authorities), and
Young Marlowe in Goldsmith's *She Stoops to Conquer*. He was also
Prinzevalle in Maeterlinck's *Monna Vanna*, which was being given its
first public performance in England, having previously been banned

by the Lord Chamberlain for nearly twenty years because of its 'immorality of plot'.

Gielgud's poor movement continued to be a problem. Reginald Denham, who produced four plays in his first season, recalled 'an awkward stance that prevented his performances reaching perfection'. Yet his notices, though brief, were positive. In *Captain Brassbound's Conversion*, according to *The Times*, he 'showed both imagination and restraint in the small part of Johnson'. In *Monna Vanna*, Robert Speaight in *Cherwell* noticed that he performed 'with a strange unearthly passion'. Harold Acton wrote of the production in the same magazine: 'It is a delectable surprise for an Oxford audience to realise that Mr John Gielgud as Prinzevalle, handicapped by the beard and bandages of an artificial maturity, is as sensible to Glamour as he is worthy of the Comic Muse.' At the end of the season the female undergraduates' magazine *Fritillary* concluded: 'Mr Gielgud shows promise of that versatility which no repertory actor can afford to be without.'

His finest achievement came in *Love for Love*. Congreve's vigorous and lusty satire about love, sex and money was the hit of the season. The bawdy language and explicit sexual situations shocked many regulars, but drew so many delighted undergraduates and dons to the Playhouse that extra performances had to be put on. Wearing a striking long curly wig, Gielgud played Valentine, the intelligent young wit who feigns madness in order to win over Angelica, the woman he loves. His performance prompted some undergraduate actors to imitate his distinctive voice. They were not to be the last.

His notices were no more than reasonable. The *Cherwell* critic thought 'he looked the part admirably and spoke his lines with decision . . . our only criticism might be that he must not point at the audience'. The *Isis* reviewer noted 'an interesting performance by Mr Gielgerd', calling it 'a fine essay, but not sufficiently even or sustained', and ending sternly: 'He may become a fine actor – he has it in him – if he works and does not fall victim to easy success.' It was a perceptive comment.

But Norman Marshall, an undergraduate who later became a leading producer and theatre manager, thought his performance enchanting, remembering his 'gaiety and impudence and high spirits, fresh, ringing tones, a youthful self-confident dash and swagger'. And Emlyn Williams, observing him from a creaking chair, recalled: 'When he got going, all nose and passion and dragging calves and unbridled oboe of a voice – no peering at the back of furniture for this beginner – the creaking stopped. It was all a little large for the hall, but the tall haughty creature held the stage all right.'

Molly MacArthur, who handled the costumes, was also playing a small part. The clothes she had created for herself were more beautiful clothes than those for Flora Robson, playing the heroine. The actress recalls Gielgud sticking up for her: 'John took my part. He said, "I don't understand why, when Flora is supposed to be the rich daughter, she has the poorest clothes of all to wear." He very kindly showed me how to make the best of what I'd been given by adding frills and so forth.' It was the sort of kindness Gielgud was to show many times to his fellow-actors.

At the end of the season he was due to play the Lieutenant in Shaw's *The Man of Destiny*. But then bad luck intervened: 'Young Jack Gielgud's got the mumps,' Guthrie wrote home, as he fumigated the dressing-rooms. The invalid, his face hugely swollen, was whisked home in a hired car by his mother. But this proved a blessing in disguise, for Gielgud had unwittingly passed the mumps on to Gyles Isham, a handsome young baronet ('Quite charming' Gielgud told his sister Virginia) with whom he had lunched in Magdalen, in rooms once occupied by Oscar Wilde. Isham had just had an enormous success in the first-ever university production of *Hamlet*, produced by Fagan for the OUDS. His performance prompted one London critic to compare him with Irving. He was now planning to play Romeo during the vacation with a cast of London and Oxford amateurs. When he succumbed to the mumps he suggested that Gielgud stand in for him until he recovered.

Thrilled at such an opportunity ('I love the play,' he had written after seeing a recent production), Gielgud rehearsed with the cast and producer Eric Bush, hoping he might actually go on. To his intense disappointment Isham returned a week before the performance. But he had made a good impression, and was asked to stay on and play Paris. However, the production failed: the London press, it was reported in Oxford, 'attacked it with sledgehammers'.

During rehearsals he and his father sat in the dress circle of the New on the first night of Shaw's *Saint Joan*. Produced jointly by the author and Lewis Casson, it swept aside Gielgud's dislike of Shaw's work. 'A wonderful play,' he wrote afterwards. 'All the witty remarks and philosophical byways do not hinder in any way the drama of the situation or the clearness of the exposition.' Like everyone else he was captivated by Sybil Thorndike, for whom Shaw had written the title-role. 'Sybil Thorndike gave a magnificent performance, imaginatively conceived, and simply carried out, almost altogether without mannerism, and full of charm and sincerity,' he noted. Later, accompanied by Flora Robson, he saw it again and, at the famous moment when Joan's prayers for a change of wind are answered, they burst into tears simultaneously.

On the first night, as the actors took a dozen curtain calls at the end of four hours, Gielgud noticed their exhaustion: 'I realised, perhaps for the first time, something of the agonies and triumphs of theatrical achievement,' he recalled. He was soon to get a taste of the agony himself. At the beginning of April he received an odd, intriguing letter:

Dear Mr Gielgud
    If you would like to play the finest lead among the plays by the late William Shakespeare, will you please call upon Mr Peacock and Mr Ayliff at the Regent Theatre on Friday at 2.30pm. Here is an opportunity to become a London Star in a night. Please confirm.
    Yours very truly, Akerman May

May was an old actor working for Barry Jackson, whose high-quality Birmingham Rep productions often transferred to the West End. Jackson was shortly to provoke controversy with startling modern-dress productions of *Macbeth*, *The Taming of the Shrew* and *Hamlet*. But now, for his first production as a manager in London, he was staging *Romeo and Juliet* in conventional costume at the Regent, a barn of a theatre in King's Cross. Jackson liked to make his own stars rather than use existing ones, and was looking for a young actor to play Romeo opposite Gwen Ffrangcon-Davies. Gielgud, word-perfect in the part after standing in for Isham, was determined to get it.

The auditions, the first he had faced, were intimidating. There was no Juliet on stage with him, so he had to deliver his speeches to Jackson and the producer sitting out front, while her lines were intoned from the wings by the stage manager. The producer was a South African, H.K. Ayliff, who had recently produced Shaw's marathon *Back to Methuselah* for Jackson. Tall, grim and autocratic – Gielgud was reminded of a Franciscan Friar – he was a terrifying prospect for an inexperienced actor. Although he was a meticulous producer, he was notoriously brusque with and unsympathetic towards actors, and frequently lost his temper with them. Paul Scofield, who worked with him later, recalled: 'He spoke little, but any dissatisfaction was alarmingly signalled by his left foot, which swung ominously from his crossed knees, like a pendulum.'

Ten days after receiving the invitation to audition, Gielgud received another letter:

Dear Mr Gielgud,
I am feeling quite excited (as an old actor) to hear this morning that it is most likely we have fixed you to play in *Romeo* in London.
Best hopes and congratulations, Akerman May

To win such a part on the eve of his twentieth birthday was a fine achievement, and it excited him wildly, especially as he was already a fervent admirer of Gwen Ffrangcon-Davies, the leading lady at Birmingham Rep, who had recently become a national name after appearing in the hugely successful opera *The Immortal Hour*. Gielgud had seen it twice the year before, and after the second visit wrote: 'I still rave over Miss Ffrangcon-Davies.' But she in her turn had seen him in *The Insect Play*, and thought him disastrously bad. Having already played Juliet at Birmingham, she was aghast at the thought of him as her Romeo. When she told him this at their first meeting, it gave him a shock. But soon she warmed to his personality and his voice. 'One day during rehearsals I listened offstage as he did the Friar Laurence scene,' she recalled. 'I thought, Oh yes, this is all right, he's going to be quite good.'

Feeling extremely vulnerable, Gielgud was never to forget her kindness and encouragement. She told him not to be frightened of their passionate embraces, and he felt less embarrassed. Since they were both word-perfect, he felt he couldn't postpone the moment he always dreaded, when he had to let himself go. But he soon encountered other difficulties. He felt very uncomfortable in his ill-fitting doublet, unbecoming thick black wig parted in the middle, and orange make-up – a combination which, he recalled, made him look like 'a mixture of Rameses of Egypt and a Victorian matron'. He was also nervous and clumsy in the fights, and thrown off balance by the violent swords-manship of Mercutio, played by Scott Sunderland.

For such a romantic role these were enormous handicaps. Shortly before the opening night, with his costume only half ready, he had a crisis of confidence. Jackson had invited selected friends to watch the dress rehearsal, but when Ayliff realised the play wasn't ready, he cleared the theatre, and held the rehearsal with the safety curtain down, sitting in front of it and taking notes just a few feet from the actors. Intimidated by this experience, on the first night Gielgud had acute stage fright as he waited for his first entrance: 'What if I slipped out into the street and disappeared?' he thought, and imagined the scene. 'Everything would be in turmoil – the audience, the company – the evening would be a complete disaster, while I would be far away, completely uninvolved.'

The notices for his first major Shakespearean part were not as universally poor as he later implied. The veteran critic A.B. Walkley called him 'an exceptionally well-graced actor', and noted 'a beautiful voice, which he knows how to use'. Ashley Dukes wrote acutely: 'Here is an actor of possibilities – one who can be moulded, without being lifeless clay in the producer's hands. He seemed to me to be feeling his own way through the part with a sensitive perception.' But many did find fault with his performance, judging him too introspective, over-hysterical or effeminate. The most devastating notice came from Ivor Brown, who described him as 'niminy-piminy' and 'scant of virility', and ended cruelly: 'Mr Gielgud's body from his hips down never meant anything throughout the evening. He has the most meaningless legs imaginable . . . perhaps six months of melodrama at, say, the Bordesley Palace, Birmingham would make an actor of him. Anyhow, Mr Ayliff never will.'

The criticism of effeminacy was one that would always worry Gielgud who, as the actor Maurice Denham later put it, 'was so beautiful when he was younger he could have played a woman just as well'. One actor who saw his Romeo was Robert Farquharson, an eccentric and famously bitchy man said to be Wilde's inspiration for Dorian Grey. Coming to Gielgud's dressing-room he told him: 'You have taught me something about the part of Romeo I never knew before.' Gielgud boasted of this compliment, only to be told by a friend that Farquharson had meant it was the first time he had realised that 'Romeo could be played as Juliet'. He took a long time to get over this comment.

Ellen Terry came one night, and, being partially deaf, said after-wards: 'I now know what John looked like as Romeo.' Gwen Ffrangcon-Davies later generously called his first attempt at the part 'absolutely marvellous'. But Gielgud, who had much fancied himself in the role, felt he had failed. 'I just enjoyed indulging in my own emotions, and imagined that that was acting,' he recalled. He realised he had been rash to think he was ready to tackle a major Shakespearean role in London. Yet though his conceit was punctured and his vanity bruised, this setback made him more determined than ever to succeed.

Despite the critical hostility, *Romeo and Juliet* ran for two months, thanks mainly to loyal fans of Gwen Ffrangcon-Davies making return visits. But the critical mauling upset Gielgud, and at one matinée he blacked out during the balcony scene. Though he got through the performance, he went down with pneumonia, and was out of the play for a fortnight. The break was immensely frustrating: the chance to 'become a London Star' was vanishing fast. From the Chatsworth Hotel in Eastbourne, where he had been sent to recuperate, he wrote restlessly to a fan. His final comment, though apparently flippant, suggests a characteristic that was soon to become more apparent: a willingness to listen to criticism, even from the humblest of sources, and try to learn from it.

> Going back to the play on Monday night. You can imagine how I raged at getting ill, and they had an awful job, as neither of my two brilliant understudies either knew the part, or were competent to play it, so they've had two hectic weeks, one with Ion Swinley and the other with Ernest Milton – rather hard work for poor Juliet, rehearsing and adapting herself like that! They've all been so kind, and written me such letters and sent telephone messages that I felt quite grand – like an expiring Cabinet Minister – but I'm simply longing to get back again, and hope you'll come soon and see it. Please come round afterwards for a minute, when you do, and tell me the worst!

He and Gwen Ffrangcon-Davies now began what was to be a lifelong friendship. They went to the theatre together, were painted and sketched by Laura Knight, and were invited to smart parties that seemed to Gielgud like something out of the fashionable novels by his brother's friend Aldous Huxley. At one party they were asked by the wealthy hostess to play the balcony scene in her garden, but the occasion proved less than romantic. 'I looked round desperately to invoke the moon, but realised at last it was shining on the wrong side of the house,' Gielgud recalled.

His performance was briefly immortalised when the balcony scene was filmed as 'a presentation novelty' in a series of 'Living Paintings'. With no sound, he and Gwen Ffrangcon-Davies can do little more than make meaningful yearning gestures at each other. They were also persuaded to play the scene for a fortnight in the vastness of the Coliseum – it was then normal practice for actors to appear in variety programmes in extracts from the classics. One week they shared a bill with the comedian Will Hay, a xylophonist, a group of gymnasts and a mezzo-soprano; for the other they were preceded by a man of twenty stone who played the saxophone, and followed by the Houston Sisters, one of whom sent up Gielgud's performance ('A thousand times goodnight', etc.) in her broad Scots accent. This attempt to introduce Shakespeare to a more popular audience was greeted by only mild applause, and Gielgud was pathetically grateful when a stagehand told him towards the end of the fortnight that they had improved. His only compensation for this humiliation was a large salary.

He now returned to Oxford, where the reputation of the Playhouse was growing fast. Fagan observed: 'We are overwhelmed with applications from would-be actors and actresses all over the kingdom. Everybody seems to want to join the Oxford Players, but our numbers are limited, we have room only for a few very promising beginners.' Given his failure at the Regent, Gielgud was lucky to be invited back for the autumn season.

Having spent his first season in digs, he had now rented a two-room flat in the High Street. 'I was very proud of it, as it satisfied all my instincts for tidiness and space,' he recalled. He would wander round reciting his lines, shouting them above the music he loved to play on the gramophone. On Sunday evenings after dress rehearsals he held rowdy parties. Several of his Westminster contemporaries were now undergraduates, so there were meals with friends in their college rooms. After the Playhouse performances ended he and Richard Goolden would march down St Giles in archetypal student fashion, singing at the tops of their voices in the vain hope of being mistaken for members of the university.

The Oxford undergraduate world was then almost exclusively male. Female students, having only just gained the right to get a degree, counted for little. Post-war solemnity had been replaced by an exuberant, anarchic hedonism. For many the university was not primarily a place for study: dandyism was rampant, with students divided more obviously than usual between the 'heavies' and the 'aesthetes'. This was the Brideshead generation, with Evelyn Waugh,

John Betjeman, Oliver Messel, Graham Greene and Claud Cockburn all in residence. Prominent among the aesthetes were Brian Howard – Waugh's model for Anthony Blanche in *Brideshead Revisited* – and Harold Acton, their self-styled leader, who walked along the 'High' sporting the famous Oxford bags he had invented, and recited his poems through a megaphone from the balcony of his rooms.

Robert Speaight recalled that 'there was a good deal of flamboyant, and in many cases transient, homosexuality'. If Gielgud was now aware of his own, then Oxford was a place in which he could feel more at ease with it than elsewhere. He got to know Acton, delighting in his elegant deportment and meticulous pronunciation, and made the acquaintance of Robert Byron, an effervescent Old Etonian given to uttering unnerving wild shrieks, and described by Howard as 'looking like some possessed Hungarian prince'. He also befriended Nigel Millet, an effete young man who favoured mauve make-up, and designed costumes for the OUDS. With Tamara Talbot Rice, an undergraduate friend of Waugh's, they spent free afternoons punting on the river or walking. Once they hired a car and spent the day in Bath, returning at reckless speed for fear that Gielgud would be late for the theatre. It was a carefree, footloose life, and one that he took to with relish.

He and other members of the Oxford Players were made honorary members of the OUDS, and frequently ate and drank in its clubrooms. Emlyn Williams watched him hold court there, and recalled his fluent, unselfconscious talk, 'the poise and the swift unequivocal judgement' about the theatre, 'with every comment irradiated by a passionate interest in people and things which made his conversation quite free from self-display'. He also recalled Gielgud's sillier side: 'Just as you sat increasingly in awe of the imperious turn of the head, the pundit would toss into the air some appetising morsel of trivial West End gossip, embellished with some atrociously risqué pun . . . and then a shrill cackle, utterly at variance with the other personality.'

The foppish, charming, good-mannered aspects of his personality can be glimpsed in a gently mocking article written by Kathleen Moseley, a fellow-member of the Oxford Players:

Our beautiful young man may drift in, the ends of his grey silk scarf ('Positively my only prop') floating some yards behind him. Should this happen you must be careful not to look as if you had any acquaintance with the domestic arts, or he will undulate towards you with a buttonless coat and a disarming smile, and speaking the familiar words: It would be so kind of you . . .

The Playhouse company had undergone some interesting changes since the spring. Fagan had not re-engaged Tyrone Guthrie ('a crushing liability'), while Flora Robson, cruelly, had been told she was not attractive enough for the undergraduates' taste. He had taken on Virginia Isham, Alan Napier and Veronica Turleigh, and as assistant producer in place of Reginald Denham appointed James Whale, who had skills in lighting and design. The programme was bolder than before, and included the type of play rarely seen in a repertory theatre.

This enabled Gielgud to tackle a wider range of parts. He was Eugene Marchbanks in Shaw's *Candida*; Naisi in Synge's unfinished *Deirdre of the Sorrows*; Zurita in *His Widow's Husband* by the Nobel-Prize-winning Spanish dramatist Jacinto Benavente; Erhart Borkman in Ibsen's dark family drama *John Gabriel Borkman*; and Antonio and Augusto respectively in *The Cradle Song* and *Madame Pepita* by Gregorio Martínez Sierra. He was also in plays by Arthur Eckersley and the novelist Gilbert Cannan.

His reviews during this season were mostly positive, especially those by Harold Acton, now the regular critic of *Cherwell*. After seeing *His Widow's Husband* he wrote: 'We loved Mr Gielgud's caricature of the type of arty poet that flourishes in large numbers in baby Bohemian cafés all over the world and has even, it is said, penetrated to the Oxford Aesthetic Tea Party.' He was also impressed by his performance in *Deidre of the Sorrows*, though in the love scene with Veronica Turleigh 'there were occasions when his rougher voice jarred a little', and his Irish accent failed to convince.

His voice still seemed affected to many. But one student was in no doubt about his talent, though it was another fifty years before he would record his opinion of his performance in *Candida*. In his memoirs the critic Harold Hobson recollected: 'What struck me in Gielgud was the electric, febrile energy of the lithe, active, slim young man . . . I felt myself instantly in the presence of a great actor.' Was this hindsight? It was certainly not a general view at the time.

During the Christmas break Gielgud appeared briefly in a production at Charterhouse of *French Leave*, a farce by Reginald Berkeley. Back at Oxford for the spring-term season, he was in a concert performance of Arthur Eckersley's *A Collection Will Be Made*, and played Algernon Peppercorn in *Smith*, a minor piece by Somerset

Maugham. In this he failed to impress John Fernald, the future principal of RADA, who wrote in *Cherwell* that 'the character of Algy, at best an exaggerated and silly stagey type, received no help from the actor who spoke the lines'. But the third production of the term provided him with a very different opportunity.

Today Chekhov's last play *The Cherry Orchard* is widely recognised as one of the masterpieces of world theatre, but in the mid-1920s its reputation was low. It had first been produced by Stanislavsky at the Moscow Art Theatre in 1904. Its English première was in 1911, when it was put on by the Stage Society at Shaw's suggestion. The performance was a fiasco. The members were mainly interested in the work of Ibsen and Shaw, in theatre as a forum for airing ideas and moral problems. Chekhov's subtle, delicate, non-judgemental play seemed flimsy, aimless and incomprehensible, and most people walked out. The critics were equally bewildered, finding it gloomy and formless.

However by 1924 there was a growing admiration for his work: the plays had been translated, and his short stories had recently started a Chekhov 'craze' in Bloomsbury literary circles. Fagan was at its forefront: his enthusaism prompted the *Stage* to complain of 'the excessive adulation poured forth at the shrine of Anton Chekhov by Mr Fagan and other boosters of the so-called Drama of Ideas'. But as yet no production had caught the true spirit of *The Cherry Orchard*.

At the first reading of the new translation by George Calderon, the Oxford actors were mystified by the strange, unfamiliar work, so alien in its mood, style and structure. Fagan allowed more time for rehearsals than usual, and talked at length about the play. Though it was quite different from anything Gielgud had done previously, he seemed to understand his character straight away. During rehearsals he had a moment of revelation. Cast as the idealistic student Trofimov, he put on a black wig, a small beard and steel-rimmed glasses – and found himself looking in the mirror at a caricature version of his brother Val. Later he described the impact on him of his disguise: 'It acted as a kind of protection from my usual self-consciousness, and I felt easy and confident when my turn came to make my appearance on the stage. For once I need not worry whether I was moving gracefully or looking handsome; I had not to declaim or die or express violent emotion in fine language. Instead I must try to create a character utterly different from myself, and behave as I imagined the creature would behave whose odd appearance I saw in my looking-glass.'

For the first time he felt able to look in the mirror and know how his character would speak and move and behave. This new-found under-standing gave him an invaluable new tool as an actor. More relaxed, less self-conscious of both his graces and defects, he worried less about the audience, and concentrated more on the other characters. But though he was more sure of his own role, he remained uncertain about Fagan's production, feeling it to be clumsy and tentative. Just before the opening he wrote to his mother: 'I fancy Oxford's verdict – if favourable – is likely to be "the best farce since Flubb!"'

His prediction was spectacularly wide of the mark. The local critics called the production a triumph. It was reviewed by the national papers, the *Morning Post* praising the company's 'sure grasp of the Chekhov method of portraiture which makes each character extraordinarily alive and interesting, yet allows none to dominate the stage'. One Oxford critic pointed admiringly to 'the nervous fire of Mr Gielgud's Trofimov'. The production set Oxford alight, and on the last night more than a hundred people were turned away.

Norman Marshall, who fully expected to be bored, recalled the atmosphere at the momentous first night in January 1925: 'It was one of the most exciting evenings of my life. This play had a reality such as I had never imagined to be possible in the theatre. For the first time I was seeing ordinary men and women on the stage . . . After the long diminuendo which brings the play so movingly to its end, the audience sat for a few moments in complete silence. When the applause came it started quietly, but soon it had swelled into a roar of cheering which, in the words of the critic of one of the undergraduate papers, "would not have disgraced a football match".'

Gielgud recalled of *The Cherry Orchard*: 'Although none of us understood the play there was an extraordinary sincerity about the performance, and a feeling of discovery.' It is said the Celt and the Slav share a natural melancholy: if true, it would help to explain Fagan's rare understanding of the play, and his ability to handle its changing moods. His Slav background might also have been a factor in Gielgud's instant empathy with Chekhov's melancholy, tragi-comic drama.

Nigel Playfair, impressed by the power of Fagan's production, obtained his agreement to transfer it to the Lyric, Hammersmith at the end of the Oxford season. A year after his huge disappointment with Romeo, Gielgud was set to return to the London stage. But between the Oxford and London productions of *The Cherry Orchard* he became involved in a new play that was to shake the foundations of the British theatre.

5

Coward, Chekhov and Komisarjevsky

I'm so glad you think I'm getting rid of a few of
the bad tricks.

          (Letter to Gabrielle Enthoven, 1925)

THE London theatre to which Gielgud returned offered little that
was new or significant to serious theatregoers. The West End in
the mid-1920s was dominated by musical comedies, Aldwych
farces, thrillers, melodramas and revues. The cynicism of Maugham, the
wit of Lonsdale, the sentimental whimsy of A.A. Milne and the
journalistic plays of Clemence Dane offered a little more substance.
Galsworthy and Shaw had written most of their best work. There was the
occasional classical revival – Sheridan and Congreve, Ibsen and Synge –
and the very occasional interesting import – O'Neill and Strindberg –
but in general froth and mediocrity ruled on Shaftesbury Avenue.

Acting was changing, rhetoric and grand gesture giving way to a more
'naturalistic', conversational style. The most admired actor was Gerald
du Maurier, whose relaxed, restrained work in lightweight roles (Raffles,
Bulldog Drummond) contrasted with the bombast and declamation of
Tree and Irving (whose scripts had been marked with the word
'Applause' at appropriate moments). Matinée idols such as Godfrey
Tearle, Henry Ainley and Owen Nares were much in vogue; Tallulah
Bankhead and Gladys Cooper, representing sex and beauty respectively,
were the toast of the town, along with the brilliant Marie Tempest. The
glamorous stars were Gertrude Lawrence, Jack Buchanan, Yvonne
Arnaud, Jack Hulbert and Cicely Courtneidge, Fred and Adele Astaire.
Sybil Thorndike alternated between *Saint Joan* and Grand Guignol,

while Edith Evans showed her brilliance in revivals of Congreve, Farquhar and Goldsmith before going to the Old Vic.

The actor-managers' day was over, and producers were beginning to take their place. But Barker had withdrawn from the theatre, and there was no innovator to match the work of Stanislavsky, Max Reinhardt or Jacques Copeau. Craig, who organised an International Exhibition of Theatre Art in London in 1922, was recognised as a pioneering designer – Stanislavsky said 'he is half a century ahead of us all' – but was now living permanently in Italy. The most successful producer in the West End was Basil Dean, celebrated for his technically brilliant, lavish, naturalistic productions, most notably *Hassan*, which had a full orchestra for the score by Delius.

The picture was different in the suburbs, where pioneers such as Playfair, Norman Macdermott, Theodore Komisarjevsky and Peter Godfrey staged an exciting mix of classical and modern plays from the European and American repertoires. Their tiny theatres included a former cinema (Barnes), a back-street attic in Covent Garden (the Gate), a former drill-hall in Hampstead (the Everyman), and a furniture store in Hammersmith (the Lyric). Enthusiastic audiences packed into these newly converted theatres to see modern works by Pirandello, Cocteau, O'Neill, Joyce, Kaiser and O'Casey; plays by Gogol, Molière, Dostoyevsky, Calderón and Turgenev; and innovative productions of Elizabethan and Restoration classics.

In November 1924 the Everyman mounted a new play by a young writer that helped Gielgud take a small but significant step up the theatrical ladder. Noël Coward, still only twenty-four, was already beginning to make his mark as an original writer and performer. Beginning as a child actor, he had charmed his way into the theatre by a shrewd mixture of talent, wit, industry, conceit, and a ruthless determination to succeed. An inveterate social climber in flight from his lower-middle-class origins, he was already firmly ensconced in 'café society' where, as a homosexual, he was able to indulge his taste for guardsmen and other young men. *The Vortex*, which had been turned down by several West End managements, provoked a furore similar to that caused thirty years later by John Osborne's *Look Back in Anger*.

The play, which starred Coward and Lilian Braithwaite, centres on the intense relationship between a young man who has become a drug-addict, and his man-hunting mother, who is having an affair with a man half her age. There had been plays about drugs before, but not in a setting of society life – where in reality they were widely used. But it was not so much Coward's airing of the taboo topic of drugs as his picture of the moneyed classes at play that provoked the Lord Chamberlain to recommend that the play be banned, on the grounds that it was 'calculated to promote public disorder'. Howevere, after Coward threatened to serialise it in the press so the public could decide for themselves on its moral stance, *The Vortex* was granted a licence shortly before its opening.

The play now seems a slight, tiresome melodrama, with the endless cocktails and laughter of the first two acts only just redeemed by an over-heated confrontation between mother and son in the third. It has none of the panache, effervescent wit and dramatic dexterity of Coward's *Private Lives* or *Hay Fever*. There have been claims that Nicky's drug-taking is a metaphor for his homosexuality, then a taboo subject both on and off the stage. Yet apart from references to Nicky's 'wrong' upbringing, there is little evidence for this in the text. Yet Coward's indictment of the hypocrisy of the older generation, and Nicky's retort to his mother, 'We've all got a right to our opinions', struck a powerful chord with the younger generation. *The Vortex* was a sensation and an instant hit, and made Coward the unofficial spokesman for the 'Bright Young Things' of the new generation.

Labelled 'Our Most Daring Playwright', Coward did his best to sustain a public image of brittle, world-weary decadence that only partly reflected his real persona. Gielgud was at first unimpressed by him. In the summer of 1923, after attending the first night of *London Calling!*, a revue co-authored by Coward, who starred in it with Maisie Gay and Gertrude Lawrence, he had noted: 'Coward will be better when he's less nervous – but he's a little ineffectual and amateurish at present.' After seeing *The Vortex* he still failed to rate him as an actor, observing that he 'lacked charm and personality, and played the piano too loudly, though he acted sincerely and forcefully as far as he could'. But he thought the play 'very brilliant . . . witty, effective and original . . . an amazing achievement'.

The Vortex transferred to the West End, where it played for 224 performances in three different theatres. In February 1925, on the recommendation of the producer Allen Wade, Gielgud was invited to audition as Coward's understudy. Coward needed an actor who could handle Nicky's attempts to play jazz, classical and dance music on the piano. Gielgud, with his ability to play by ear, won the part more for his musical than his acting ability. Once he did so, Fagan generously released him from the Oxford Players.

Gielgud had seen Coward at a Kensington cocktail party not long before, and found him 'rather bumptious and pushy' – which indeed he was – and 'dreadfully precocious and rather too keen to show off on the piano'. There was a touch of jealousy in his reaction, the envy of a garrulous but shy young man of the other's social ease and panache, of his ability to take centre stage. But when they eventually met in Coward's dressing-room at the Royalty, Gielgud's hostility evaporated in the face of Coward's charm.

Understudying him was both a thrilling and a terrifying experience. Coward was inclined to be late – his first entrance was forty minutes into the play – and Gielgud would stand anxiously at the stage door, looking down the street grease-paint in hand, ready to rush off and make up if need be. He was desperately anxious to shine if needed, and prepared to work intensively. Every night he went in front for the final act, to study how Coward and Lilian Braithwaite handled the climactic scene between mother and son, the way they used inflections and gradations in their voices in what Herbert Farjeon called 'a vehicle for histrionic pyrotechnics'.

When he rehearsed he found it hard technically to reproduce the same effect as Coward. Like any understudy, he had to decide how close to stick to the original. His own rather clipped vowels and staccato manner were not unlike Coward's, and he found it almost impossible not to give a poor imitation. This led him into mannered habits, and it was to be a while before he was able to shake off Coward's influence.

Being an understudy made him long to see his name up in lights. 'I'm going to be a star,' he announced at a party. In March the moment he both dreaded and yearned for arrived. Coward decided to attend the dress rehearsal and opening night in Manchester of his new revue, *On with the Dance*, and conducted two rehearsals with a very nervous understudy. Overdoing the hysteria during the central scene with Lilian Braithwaite, Gielgud cut his hand on a bottle. His nerves were not helped when, shortly before curtain-up, he was told that a few people were demanding their money back after discovering Coward was 'indisposed'. This incident made him tremble so violently he was scarcely able to put on his make-up.

Despite his tortured feelings, his nerve held. Afterwards George Arliss, who had famously played opposite Mrs Patrick Campbell, came backstage to congratulate him, while the revue artist Violet Loraine wrote to Coward praising his performance. Coward, sensing a 'rich talent', offered him the part for the last three weeks of the run (while he himself went on holiday prior to taking the play to Broadway), and recalled later that he 'played it beautifully'. Only once did Gielgud lose his nerve: when a cat appeared on stage one night during the key scene between mother and son, he became hysterical and threw it into the audience.

Perhaps because of his intense attachment to his mother, Gielgud was always able to relate well to older women, who in turn developed a maternal fondness for him, and treated him with great kindness. Lilian Braithwaite was an early example of this tendency. Tall, dark and fifty, she had played in everything from farce to Shakespeare, but had recently been stuck in genteel comedies. With her playing of the nymphomaniac mother in *The Vortex* she broke new ground. Gielgud watched fascinated as she made her first entrance, 'bracing herself with deep breaths, like an athlete preparing for a race'. Renowned publicly for her scorching wit, she was admired in the profession for her warmheartedness and generosity. She helped Gielgud greatly during rehearsals, and gave up her holiday before the Broadway run so he could have his spell in the role. It was the first time he had worked with a leading actress, and he was impressed by her dedication, discipline and helpfulness – qualities that others were soon to admire in him.

The play's run was near its end, and no critic came to see him. Yet this may have been no bad thing, for it had not been an easy role to master: 'It was a highly strung, nervous, hysterical part which depended a lot upon emotion,' he recalled. 'I found it tiring to play because I did not know how to save myself.' With his nervous energy and reliance on instinct, he still had a lot to learn about control and pace.

With *The Vortex* he found himself in the middle of an acrimonious debate about the 'new drama', which the popular press denounced as decadent, depraved and – even worse – effeminate. One critic wrote: 'It is not the kind of drama you would wish intelligent foreigners or servants to witness.' Gerald du Maurier, who despised homosexuality, was revolted by its subject-matter, and denounced the new generation of playwrights: 'The public are asking for filth ... the younger generation are knocking at the door of the dustbin,' he declared. 'If life is worse than the stage, should the stage hold the mirror up to such distorted nature?' Coward cheerfully responded by attacking the 'fake and nauseating sentimentality' of the 'second-rate drama' du Maurier and others had been serving up, announcing his intention to write as honestly as possible on any subject he liked.

During these months in Oxford and London Gielgud continued to haunt the West End. He saw plays by Maugham, Barrie, Milne, Galsworthy, Bax, Lonsdale, and Shaw. He went to revivals of Shakespeare, Sheridan and Congreve; watched Diaghilev's celebrated Ballets Russes four times; spent three successive nights at the Royal Opera House in Covent Garden where Bruno Walter conducted Wagner's Ring Cycle; and found time to catch musical comedies such as *No No Nanette* and *Kismet*, and revues staged by Charlot and Cochrane. His reactions could be impulsive: after seeing Gwen Ffrangcon-Davies in *Back to Methuselah* he noted, 'Gwen as the Old Eve was really amazing – I had no idea she could do anything so perfectly', then rushed home to write her a wildly enthusiastic five-page letter.

Though he had firm opinions and was quick to make judgements, he was also capable of being swayed by others. After seeing *Ned Kean of Old Drury* with Angus MacPhail, now his most regular theatre-going companion, he wrote: 'My real opinion is hopelessly unbalanced by Angus' cynical comments – but it was pretty good tosh . . . I feel I should have wept without Angus, but he was quite right in his criticism, I suppose.' A tendency to self-deprecation was already apparent.

In May Fagan's production of *The Cherry Orchard* came to London. Opinion was still divided over Chekhov. When the production opened at the Lyric, Hammersmith, with Gielgud back as Trofimov, the audience received it warmly – though when he spoke his line 'All these clever people are very stupid', a woman shouted out, 'That's very true.' However, the critical reaction was violent, both for and against. Basil Macdonald Hastings called it the worst play in London, but Herbert Farjeon, a Chekhov enthusiast, called it 'immeasurably the best play in London . . . by a poet with a vision of the universe' and 'an oasis just now in a desert of jazz'.

No critic was so fervent in promoting it as James Agate, who was to play a crucial part in Gielgud's career. Coarse and witty, a voracious homosexual, he was a man about town who, in his own words, 'looked like a farmer, dressed like a bookmaker, ate like a Parisian and drank like a Hollander'. For the last two years he had been writing a sparkling column in the *Sunday Times*, and was fast establishing himself as London's most brilliant, erudite and stimulating critic. In his youth he had seen Irving and Forbes-Robertson, Ellen Terry and Madge Kendal, but also Bernhardt, Réjane, Lucien Guitry and other great

French stars. Often wayward and capricious, loving to provoke argument, he was fascinated by the art of acting, and was more interested in reviewing the performance than the play. Yet he had a wide knowledge and profound love of Shakespeare's plays. He was one of the first English critics to recognise Chekhov's importance, calling *The Cherry Orchard* 'an imperishable masterpiece, which will remain as long as men have eyes to see, ears to hear, and the will to comprehend beauty'.

Playfair shrewdly advertised the play in the press and on posters with the opinions of Hastings ('this fatuous drivel') and E.A. Baughan ('this masterpiece') placed side by side. Interest quickened but, according to Playfair, it was a letter from Lady Cunard to the *Daily Express* urging the merits of the play that ensured the production's success. Audiences doubled and doubled again, and the play eventually transferred to the Royalty in the West End for a respectable run. Norman Marshall, who saw productions in many countries over the next twenty years, thought it the best of them all, and the closest in spirit to Stanislavsky's original.

Gielgud received his share of praise. The *Stage* thought him 'notably fine', while Desmond MacCarthy wrote that 'Mr Gielgud's Trofimov and Mr Alan Napier's Gaev were the parts played best'. Most encouraging of all, Agate judged his shabby student to be 'perfection itself'. Gielgud felt he had taken a great leap forward: 'It was the first time I ever went on stage and felt that perhaps I could really act,' he remembered. He now understood how it was possible to project a personality on stage quite different from his own.

Since his Trofimov bore some resemblance to his brother, it seemed apt that Val Gielgud should be hired as his understudy during the play's West End run. After leaving Oxford without taking his degree, Val had been a commercial traveller, a sub-editor, a private tutor, and secretary to a member of Parliament. Mildly envious of his brother's achievements, he had started to write novels, mostly of a Ruritanian nature. His work in *The Cherry Orchard* led Fagan to take him on for two seasons at the Oxford Playhouse. Gemma Fagan, who acted with him in *Dear Brutus*, remembers him as 'a bit wooden, not a patch on his brother'. Of one production a reviewer wrote: 'Mr Gielgud's physical attributes inevitably remind us of his brother John. He is, however, a far finer and more subtle actor.' Val was unable to resist sending the review to his mother, who told him not to believe what he read in the papers.

In August Gielgud returned to Oxford to play the Stranger in

Ibsen's *The Lady from the Sea*, and the title-role in Pirandello's one-act *The Man with a Flower in his Mouth*, which formed part of a triple-bill with Shaw's *Overruled* and Strindberg's *The Stronger*. The *Oxford Chronicle* reviewer noted that 'he played his Pirandello with an exquisite sensibility and the most clutching appeal.' It was an upbeat end to his four short seasons in Oxford. Fagan had given him a useful training in the practical side of theatre, tested his abilities in a valuable range of parts, and made him familiar with the work of some of the most stimulating European playwrights.

The production of *The Cherry Orchard* established Chekhov's reputation in England, and awakened the interest of a wider public. Suddenly there was what one paper called a 'Chekhov boom', and Gielgud was soon in the middle of it, taking part in a season of ground-breaking productions of Russian plays staged at the small, 250-seat converted cinema in Barnes. Inspired by Fagan's production, the northern impresario and former actor Philip Ridgeway, the youngest theatre manager in London, decided to mount a season there that included *Three Sisters, Ivanov, Uncle Vanya* and *The Cherry Orchard*, as well as Gogol's *The Government Inspector* and Andreyev's *Katerina*.

The opening production in October was *The Seagull*. Its initial failure in Russia had prompted Chekhov to vow he would never write for the theatre again. It had been the first of his plays to be performed in English, in 1909 at the Glasgow Repertory Theatre. Like *The Cherry Orchard*, it had puzzled critics and audiences alike. The new production included Randolph McLeod as Trigorin, Miriam Lewes as Arkadina, James Whale as Medvedenko, and in the role of Nina a newcomer, Valerie Taylor. Gielgud was cast as the failed young writer Konstantin, a part originally played by the celebrated Russian director Meyerhold.

He was excited by this opportunity to play a romantically gloomy role in a fetching black blouse and Russian boots. The producer was A.E. Filmer, a former actor, and a producer at the Birmingham Rep under Barry Jackson. Known for his scholarly and fastidious approach to a play, and an interest in its psychological dimensions, he proved of little help to Gielgud, who needed firm guidance. Some of his friends had begun to criticise his mannerisms, while he himself was aware of his continuing tendency to show off any new technical skill he discovered. During the run he wrote to Gabrielle Enthoven, an actress and playwright friend of Coward:

I'm so glad you think I'm getting rid of a few of the bad tricks. It's a very difficult part, and the producer wasn't much use as a helper, so I've had to go tentatively about my own improvements and developments since the first night. I hope it's getting better by degrees, but it's so irritating to realise suddenly after one's been playing for some time, some perfectly obvious thing one's been missing all along.

He received some good notices. *Punch* declared his part to be 'very intelligently handled', while Agate felt he 'played the ineffective son with great sensitiveness and beautifully controlled emotion'. Prophetically, the critic of *Eve* magazine observed that he 'should of course be playing Hamlet, and was, in fact, doing so in this piece without knowing it'. Gielgud later decried his playing of Konstantin as 'somewhat highly strung', but it was obviously much else besides.

Valerie Taylor's sensitive portrayal of Nina made her name overnight. But her performance was significant in another respect. Gielgud had his own ideas about the final scene between Konstantin and Nina that leads to his suicide, and spent time working on the scene with Valerie Taylor. Enjoying the experience, it came to him that, if his acting career failed, he could perhaps consider producing as an alternative.

Although *The Seagull* was supposed to be staged in Barnes, the huge and unexpected success of the previous production there – *Tess of the D'Urbevilles*, starring Gwen Ffrangcon-Davies – meant it had to be moved to the Little in the West End. In the audience one night was a man who was soon to exercise a powerful influence on Gielgud's career. Theodore Komisarjevsky was a Russian of many talents, with direct links to Chekhov and the pre-revolutionary theatre. His father had founded, with Stanislavsky, an organisation that eventually became the Moscow Art Theatre. His half-sister Vera, thought by some to be the equal of Duse and Bernhardt, had played Nina in the disastrous first production of *The Seagull*; Chekhov later considered her one of his best interpreters. She started a theatre in St Petersburg, appointing first Meyerhold and then Komisarjevsky as her artistic director. There, and later as director of Moscow's State and Imperial theatres, he was a prolific and much-admired producer of plays and opera. The son of a well-known tenor and a princess, with a cosmopolitan background, he left Russia after the revolution and in 1919, as the critic W.A. Darlington wrote, 'arrived like a lamplighter' in England.

He soon made his mark, and by the time Ridgeway hired him for the Barnes season he was already a seasoned producer of Chekhov. In 1921 he had staged *Uncle Vanya* at the Court for Fagan, and shortly before the Barnes season he had created the first London production of *Ivanov* for the Stage Society, with Robert Farquharson in the title-role. This was the first Chekhov play Gielgud had seen from the other side of the footlights, and he was much impressed by Komisarjevsky's handling of an ensemble: 'Very fine production,' he noted in his programme. 'A fine play and all the comedy so admirably brought out.' Two months later, in February 1926, he was working with Komisarjevsky.

The brilliant Russian producer had considered Filmer's production of *The Seagull* quite ridiculous, completely un-Russian, and funny for all the wrong reasons. But he thought Gielgud sufficiently promising to cast him as Baron Tusenbach in the first English production of *Three Sisters*. The company included Mary Sheridan, Beatrix Thomson and Margaret Swallow as the sisters yearning to get to Moscow, and Ion Swinley, who excelled in Russian plays, as Vershinin. In the tiny Barnes theatre Gielgud and his fellow-actors had just one dressing-room between them, and a minute stage on which to perform twice daily. Budgets were minimal, so costumes had to be made rather than hired, and sets built in the theatre. The salaries (£10 a week) were handed out every Friday by a pimply eighteen-year-old business manager. Some of the actors disliked this cold, aloof youngster, who seemed much older than his age, but Gielgud enjoyed gossiping and giggling with him. This was his first contact with Hugh Beaumont, universally known as 'Binkie', who was later to become a close friend and play a pivotal part in his career.

Komisarjevsky was contemptuous of the conventional productions staged by timid West End managements. He believed in a theatre in which all the elements were fused together, and none dominated. With his brilliant, almost childlike imagination, he was a designer of quality, creating beautiful, romantic sets more concerned with mood than detail. A sensitive musician, he treated a play like a fugue, and was famous for orchestrating silences as much as dialogue: 'Pause' was his most frequent interjection. Bald, foxy-faced, with slanting Mongolian eyes and a sly, humorous expression, he had an irreverent and perverse sense of humour, and could be very caustic. He despised actors who put fame and money before a dedication to their craft. Often he just ignored those he disliked, or cut their lines. 'He was prone to Russian moods when things were not going well, when he would maintain a grim silence,' Gielgud recalled.

The first days of rehearsal were spent sitting round a table in Komisarjevsky's flat in Bloomsbury endlessly re-reading the play, which was unfamiliar to the actors. One of his central ideas was to dispel the gloominess in English productions of Chekhov. Komisarjevsky stressed that the plays were comedies as much as tragedies, and that Russian audiences found them very funny.

For *Three Sisters* he emphasised the play's romantic quality. He set it twenty years earlier than usual, with the sisters in bustles and chignons, and produced some startlingly beautiful scenic effects. But he also made cuts and changes to the text, some of which affected Gielgud's interpretation of his character. Chekhov makes it clear that the dreamy, ineffectual Baron is a decent but essentially plain man, and not attractive to Irina. Komisarjevsky cut all reference to his lack of looks, and dressed Gielgud in a smart uniform and sideburns. This was done, he explained, to make the character more acceptable to English audiences, whom he believed wouldn't know the play and realise what had been changed. Gielgud was torn between the pleasure of playing the part as a handsome juvenile, and dismay at Komisarjevsky's lack of fidelity to Chekov's text. Much in awe of him, he kept his doubts to himself.

He was fascinated by Komisarjevsky's authority: some actors thought him Svengali-like, but Gielgud, while recognising his destructive tendencies, saw him as 'a real artist, a wise and brilliant teacher and often an inspired producer'. Actors, he said, loved working for him. 'He lets them find their own way, watches, keeps silent, then places the phrasing of a scene in a series of pauses, the timing of which he rehearses minutely. Very occasionally he will make some short but intensely illuminating comment, which is immensely significant and easy to remember.' Other actors remembered his laconic style of comment: Fabia Drake recalled playing Portia in the casket scene in *The Merchant of Venice*, and being simply told by Komisarjevsky, 'This scene – not sentimental – physical.'

Komisarjevsky's father had been Stanislavsky's teacher, and he himself had published a book on *The Creative Actor and the Stanislavsky Theory* in 1916 – although Stanislavsky thought it a misleading account of his ideas, and wrote 'Lies' in the margin. But like Stanislavsky, Komisarjevsky looked to actors to find an inner reality in creating a character. This idea was relatively new to English actors: Stanislavsky's

My Life in Art had only been published in translation in 1924. But it was an approach to which Gielgud responded keenly.

The critics went into ecstasies about *Three Sisters*, which was translated by Constance Garnett. 'If I were given the chance to see again one production of all the thousands that lie behind me, this would be my choice,' W.A. Darlington remembered. 'It created an atmosphere in which were blended humour and pathos, a divine knowledge of man's futility and despair, and a divine sympathy with his struggles.' Gielgud was praised by *The Times* for 'a portrait at once light and subtle'. But Desmond MacCarthy, who knew the play, criticised the reading of Tusenbach, observing that 'an ugly man had been transformed into a neurotic Adonis who might well have fascinated Irina'.

Komisarjevsky's next Russian production at Barnes was *Katerina*, a minor melodramatic piece by Leonid Andreyev, a playwright who was as popular as Gorky and Chekhov in pre-revolutionary Russia. Also in the company were Ernest Milton and the highly promising Jean Forbes-Robertson. Gielgud played a hysterically jealous husband – 'a kind of Slavonic Othello' – of a tormented and promiscuous wife. 'I was amazed that Komisarjevsky should dream of entrusting this strong character part to me,' he said later. It was his first attempt at a middle-aged role: 'I found I could vividly imagine that man's character. He became a part of me and I of him.' It was an intense part, and he took to it with aplomb.

On the first night of *Katerina* the set was unfinished, the stage manager collapsed with exhaustion, the curtain went up forty minutes late, and Komisarjevsky was forced to improvise the sets for each act during the intervals, while also acting as prompter. The pianist went through her entire Chopin repertoire during the lengthy intervals; one critic felt he was 'attending a pianoforte recital with dramatic intervals' rather than a play. Despite the fiasco, the notices were good. *The Times* thought Gielgud's playing had 'the terrible colour of unendurable and inescapable suffering', while Agate noticed another quality: 'Mr Gielgud is becoming one of our most admirable actors; there is mind behind everything he does.' Under Komisarjevsky's skilful tutelage he was learning some valuable lessons.

The two seasons at Barnes succeeded triumphantly. The tiny theatre became a fashionable attraction: the smart set, who normally confined their theatre-going to the West End, streamed across the river in their Daimlers and Rolls-Royces to see talented actors such as Gwen

Ffrangcon-Davies, Claude Rains, Martita Hunt, Robert Farquharson, and the young Charles Laughton, and Komisarjevsky's simple but beautiful productions. They were to have an enormous influence on the art of producing in England. Six years later Guthrie recalled the 'wonderful sensibility' of the Chekhov seasons, and prophesied: 'Here, if anywhere, lies the future of naturalism in the theatre.'

Now twenty-one, Gielgud could afford to be pleased with his progress. Komisarjevsky's notion of building a character from within had helped him to be less tense on stage. As he relaxed more and gained confidence, so he began to be taken more seriously by the critics. Naomi Royde-Smith even described him as 'unequalled as an English interpreter of Russian drama'. If this was an exaggeration, his work in the productions by Fagan, Filmer and Komisarjevsky had brought a new depth to his acting. It also marked the beginning of his lifelong love-affair with the plays of Chekhov.

6

Man about Town

He's got arrogance, and he isn't afraid to use
and show it.
                              (Leslie Faber on Gielgud, 1926)

AFTER making great strides with Fagan and Komisarjevsky,
Gielgud's progress was fitful over the next three years. It was a
time of struggle and frustration, of minor successes in
interesting 'little' productions, and predictable failures in West End
trash. He was torn between his desire to earn a big salary and see his
name in lights in Shaftesbury Avenue, and his interest in the classics.
In the meantime he began to enjoy a lively social life, which varied
from glittering parties given by top society hostesses to the more raffish
delights of London's theatrical circles.

Many of the actors and aristocrats he met were involved in the little
stage societies that flourished during the 1920s. An early version of
fringe theatre, they included the Phoenix Society, the Stage Society,
the Three Hundred Club, the Fellowship of Players and the Play
Actors. They staged single performances on Sunday nights, sometimes
adding a second on Monday afternoons. Some existed to mount
foreign or forgotten plays, others to provide opportunities for rising
young actors, or interesting new writers unable to get their plays staged
commercially. Most were founded in response to the conservatism of
West End theatre managers and audiences.

The societies also staged plays in protest against the often absurd
restrictions imposed by the Lord Chamberlain, who granted licences
for all new plays, and whose authority was to bedevil the theatre for a
further forty years. Under the 1843 Theatres Act he was empowered to
trim or ban a play 'whenever he shall be of the opinion that it is fitting

for the Preservation of Good Manners, Decorum, or of the Public Peace'. Barker, Shaw and other playwrights had agitated in vain against the stupidity and injustice of this censorship. Among the many plays refused a licence in the mid-1920s was Eugene O'Neill's *Desire Under the Elms*, which the Lord Chamberlain described as 'just the sort of American play that should be kept off the English stage'.

The stage societies were a vital lifeline for new writers and aspiring young actors such as Gielgud. Donald Wolfit, Laurence Olivier and Ralph Richardson all benefited from their existence. The societies also gave established West End stars the chance to play in something more demanding than the 'obstinate successes' in which they were often stuck for months on end. There was little money involved: actors were paid just a guinea, and usually had to rehearse for at least three weeks.

The oldest, best-known and most important of the societies was the Incorporated Stage Society. Founded in 1899 by a group of amateur enthusiasts, it had a distinguished record, having staged the first production of works by Shaw, Maugham, Barker and, in the teeth of fierce opposition, Ibsen and Chekhov. Since the war it had specialised in new plays otherwise unlikely to be seen in England, notably the expressionist drama already popular in Europe and America. Its programme had included plays by leading foreign writers such as Hauptmann, Gorky, Tolstoy, Kaiser, Wedekind and Pirandello. Its most famous production was to be R.C. Sherriff's anti-war play *Journey's End*, staged in 1928 after it had been rejected by every West End management.

One of Gielgud's first appearances on the Sunday night scene was in *L'École des Cocottes*, a French comedy by Paul Armont and Michel Gerbidon, adapted by H.M. Harwood. It concerned a woman being schooled to become a mistress who climbs her way to fortune over a series of discarded lovers. Banned by the Lord Chamberlain, who thought it improper, it was staged by the Play Actors, a society which specialised in putting on translations of well-known foreign plays. Gielgud was cast as a young gigolo in a company that included Leslie Faber, Minnie Rayner and Athole Stewart. The star was Gladys Cooper, now at the height of her fame. Then appearing in Lonsdale's hugely successful *The Last of Mrs Cheyney*, but bored with playing the same role eight times a week, she agreed to take part in the play's Sunday-night performance at the Prince's.

Terrified of an actress notorious for being the last to learn her lines, Gielgud was thrown by her inability to give him the same cue more than once during rehearsals. He was also, despite her attempts to put him at ease, embarrassed at having to indulge in 'a lot of boyish horseplay' with her. On the night he was paralysed with nerves and, in his own view, acted indifferently. The part was clearly unsuitable: Agate thought him 'too noble for the type of Paris gigolo who keeps a mistress on three hundred francs a month'.

Some of the scenery for the play had been devised by the eccentric aristocrat Edward Bootle-Abraham, the third Earl of Lathom, who now became Gielgud's friend. Ned Lathom's parties in his Mayfair flat enabled aspiring young actors to mingle easily with the stars of the stage. Wealthy, extravagant and frivolous, he was a friend of the outrageous Tallulah Bankhead, with whom he created a 'camp' language, in which everything was 'very bijou'. He was a great enthusiast for the theatre, financing several plays, and supporting struggling writers; he bought some of Coward's early songs when he was poor. He was also a talented playwright, with a flair for caustic, witty dialogue. When his play *Wet Paint* – which some critics considered finer than *The Vortex* – was refused a licence, he set up his own society, the Venturers, to stage it himself. He did the same for two more of his plays, but both were refused a licence. He dissipated his fortune on these and other theatrical projects, contracted tuberculosis, and died virtually penniless at the age of thirty-four.

Gielgud regularly attended his 'luncheon' parties. At one he met the formidable Marie Tempest, and became covered in confusion when he clumsily dug a button-hook into her instep while gallantly trying to mend her shoe-strap under the tablecloth. He was enraptured by Lathom's flat, 'a dream of decadent luxury', and overwhelmed by its elegance: 'the Romney portraits, the library filled with lovely hand-bound books, the thick carpets, the burning sandalwood which scented the rooms'. Although Lathom laughed at what he considered to be Gielgud's highbrow tendencies, his enthusiasm for Chekhov and Shakespeare, Gielgud thought him delightful.

Lathom's plays ran foul of the censor because they invariably had a 'kept gentleman' in the story – as he did in real life. In theatrical circles homosexuality was commonplace, and attitudes were generally more tolerant than in other spheres. Some managers, however, were hostile: du Maurier announced he would throw out anyone in his company he found to be homosexual. ('Are you a bugger?' he once asked Charles Laughton. 'N-no, Sir Gerald, are you?' the young actor replied.) Since homosexual acts were illegal, and punishable by severe prison sentences, even theatre people had to be extremely discreet and constantly on their guard: careers could be ruined, not least by blackmail. Agate likened 'the peculiar tragedy of the homosexual' to that of the tightrope-walker, 'preserving his balance by prodigies of skill and poise and knowing that the rope may snap at any moment'. Some within the theatre even feigned a heterosexual lifestyle: Somerset Maugham, whose homosexuality was known to his close friends and family, used marriage as a cover for living with a man.

In these circumstances homosexuality was inevitably a taboo topic on the stage. Coward's 1926 play *Semi-Monde*, with its homosexual and lesbian characters, remained unperformed for fifty years. A performance of J.R. Ackerley's *The Prisoners of War*, staged in 1925 at the Royal Court by the Three Hundred Club, was the first play of the century to deal explicitly with homosexual desire, and for a while 'the new homosexual play' was the talk of the town. But West End audiences were not ready for a work euphemistically described as 'morbid', and its transfer to the Playhouse was a failure.

Gielgud knew Ackerley, whom he had met through Cambridge friends, and attended the performance. He occasionally visited him in his spartan riverside flat in Hammersmith, where he noticed in particular 'a statue of a Greek youth, a large bunch of bananas on the dining table, and a rather anonymous young disciple ironing shirts in the kitchen'. He also had two friends in Ackerley's play: James Whale and Robert Harris, an actor with a beautiful baritone voice, who received some of his best notices as the young officer with whom the hero falls in love. Harris was one of his theatre-going companions; others were the actors Richard Goolden, Bruce Belfrage, George Howe and Godfrey Winn.

Together with Ackerley and Harris, and the dancer Robert Helpmann, Gielgud was now part of a larger circle that racketed around town, going to cinemas, theatres and concerts, frequenting Soho pubs and bars, and eating in their favourite restaurants. He enjoyed the occasional exotic meal: bear steaks at Sovrani's in Jermyn Street, oysters and grouse at the Naval and Military Club. He was also a regular at the vast but cheap Lyons Corner House restaurant off Leicester Square, known as the Lily Pond, where actors caught up on the latest gossip and casting news.

Godfrey Winn, later a journalist, remembered 'one frequent visitor with the air of an eagle, despite the fact that his grey-flannel trousers were poorly pressed and his hair was already receding, making him appear older than his years'. The designer Cecil Beaton, whom Gielgud had come across in Cambridge rehearsing in drag for an undergraduate revue, was more waspish: Gielgud's manner repelled him, he said, after meeting him at a smart society party: 'It's so very stagey and unfresh, so suave, such a well-graduated voice.' A jealous man, he and Gielgud were to fall out in years to come.

Gielgud went to theatrical parties, getting to know Charles Laughton, whom he found 'an amiable mixture of boyish gaiety, moodiness and charm', and mingling with music-hall stars as well as actors at the Marylebone flat of the actress Naomi ('Mickey') Jacob, a colourful figure with her short black hair, mannish suits and cigars, who later became a popular writer. A friend of Val Gielgud, she was acting with him in Edgar Wallace's thriller *The Ringer*, in which Val walked on as a policeman.

The star of *The Ringer* was Leslie Faber. Gielgud admitted later that he was 'not very close to my relations, and this made me find substitutes for them elsewhere'. This seems to be a discreet reference to his distant relationship with his father, for whom Leslie Faber became a substitute. While his friendship with Ned Lathom satisfied the more frivolous side of his nature, the bond he formed with the older actor tapped into his more serious, ambitious side.

Of Danish descent, tall and strikingly handsome with a fine profile, Faber was Gladys Cooper's leading man at the Playhouse. An exceptionally versatile actor, he excelled at playing villains and seducers; Val Gielgud later rated him the finest actor he ever saw. But Faber never quite fulfilled his potential. Elsie Fogerty, from whom he had voice lessons, observed: 'He was born too soon: he belonged to a theatre that is still to come, and rarely, if ever, had a part for his brilliant intellect to work on.' Gielgud was already an ardent admirer, having seen him in a string of melodramas. He thought his drunken husband in St John Ervine's *Jane Clegg* opposite Sybil Thorndike one of the finest pieces of character acting he had seen.

Faber was shy, haughty and often bitter, but also capable of great generosity. During the difficult rehearsals with Gladys Cooper for *L'École des Cocottes* he had been kind to Gielgud. Now, lonely and unhappy after his second marriage had broken down, he befriended him, and soon became his mentor. Gielgud, despite his conceited streak, was often in doubt about his acting ability, and Faber was the first established star to notice him and give him encouragement. 'His belief in my possibilities carried me through a very difficult time,' he recalled. He felt flattered and honoured by Faber's friendship and grew extremely fond of him, perhaps in part because he found in him a mixture of qualities very like his own: vanity, confidence and self-dissatisfaction.

Faber also befriended the actress Fabia Drake: he called her and Gielgud 'my theatrical godchildren', and they became 'a triumvirate'. She remembered him as 'a man of immense charm and talent' who 'gave us his knowledge and artistic wisdom in abundant measure'. She believed he was one of the first to recognise Gielgud as a potential star, a judgement reinforced by Naomi Jacob, to whom Faber remarked: 'That young man will go a very long way. He's got arrogance. And he isn't afraid to use and show it.' Faber warned Gielgud that it took fifteen years to make a true actor; Gielgud took the precept to heart, and often voiced it in later years.

His friendship with Faber stimulated further his love of music: the pair sat up late into the night listening to Bach and Wagner. Faber also increased his interest in theatrical history, spinning tales about Wyndham, Hawtrey, du Maurier and others with whom he had worked, and playing him records of the celebrated German actor Alexander Moissi's speeches, including Hamlet's 'To be or not to be' soliloquy. He took him to the Garrick, the actors' club, where Gielgud met legendary figures such as Allan Aynesworth, the original Algernon in Wilde's *The Importance of Being Earnest*. Already fascinated by glimpsing in Piccadilly star actors of his parents' time such as Forbes-Robertson and Squire Bancroft, he listened in awe to the elderly actors in the Garrick reminiscing about Irving and his contemporaries. There he also met and befriended the ballerina Tamara Karsavina.

The 'triumvirate' socialised a great deal. Gielgud was a keen dancer, though he never took any lessons, and enjoyed dancing in the little clubs around the West End: 'I used to look at myself in the glass all the time,' he remembered. 'I thought I was awfully good.' So too did Fabia Drake, who found him 'a witty, joyful companion'. She claimed to have fallen in love with him, and at least one fellow-actress was under the impression she hoped to marry him. This unlikely scenario seems to have been based on 'one swallowed kiss in a taxi-cab'. She later admitted she was simply 'in love with love', which was just as well.

Not long after meeting Faber, Gielgud appeared in Eugene O'Neill's *The Great God Brown* for the Stage Society. O'Neill's plays were just getting known in London and even becoming fashionable. Starring Hugh Williams, Moyna MacGill, Annie Esmond and Mary

Clare, it was produced for two performances at the Strand by one of the pioneering figures in the world of the little theatres. Peter Godfrey, a former clown, conjuror and actor, was in charge of the Gate, which he and his wife Molly Venness founded in 1925 after despairing of the stale West End successes he had been producing in provincial repertory theatres. An enthusiast for the new expressionist drama, he had made the Gate the most exciting theatre in London, staging work by Kaiser, Toller, Capek, Gorky, Cocteau and Elmer Rice.

In *The Great God Brown* the actors, in order to show different aspects of their characters, had at certain moments to don masks (made by Gielgud's childhood friend Oliver Messel, who began his career as a designer in this way). Gielgud found the convention pretentious but, despite being hampered by a severe attack of laryngitis, managed to make a mark as the young, hypersensitive artist. *The Times* observed his 'deeply serious intensity', while *Punch* noted that he 'put fire and depth into Dion Anthony'. It was another 'tense young man' part, which entailed playing a character not appreciably different from his own. Also in the company was the director Peter Cotes, then a boy actor at the Italia Conti School. Cotes remembered how Gielgud seemed ill at ease at rehearsals: 'He was very remote, he detached himself, he was rather awkward with the other actors.'

He also appeared in two productions by the Phoenix Society. An offshoot of the Stage Society, it had been set up just after the war to mount the works of the Elizabethan, Jacobean and Restoration playwrights who had fallen out of favour. Most of the literary and dramatic critics, who championed Ibsen and Shaw, argued that their plays were dull, unstageable and, in some cases, obscene. William Archer criticised Elizabethan theatre as 'brutal, shallow and maladroit', while Max Beerbohm suggested productions of Ben Jonson and Congreve would be 'a mere rattling of dry bones'. The Phoenix Society productions engendered great enthusiasm for the work of these and other half-forgotten writers. They also created a stir in smart society: the performances often drew a more distinguished audience – Desmond MacCarthy called it 'the snob rush' – than weekday West End first nights. The long-term effect was profound: of the twenty-five plays staged by the society during its six-year life, many have remained in the repertoire.

Gielgud became involved with the society through the respected designer Norman Wilkinson, a committee member. He had taken to lunching in Soho, where 'the spaghetti was cheap and delicious and I drank Asti Spumante and felt very much a man of the world'. In the Gourmets restaurant he regularly shared a table with a theatrical group that included Wilkinson. Best known for his Shakespearean sets recreating the Elizabethan period, Wilkinson had done the décor for Barker's famous production of *A Midsummer Night's Dream* which Gielgud remembered from his childhood. He invited the young actor to his beautiful house in Chiswick Mall where Gielgud, with his love of the ornate, gazed awestruck at the beautiful rooms hung with chandeliers, and at the walls decorated with drawings of costume and scene designs.

Wilkinson offered him the leading part of Castilio in Thomas Otway's tragedy *The Orphan*. A programme note for the production at the Aldwych described the play as a magnificent vehicle for rhetorical acting. The *Daily Telegraph* admired Gielgud's 'flawless sincerity', and Desmond MacCarthy suggested 'Mr Gielgud with his charming voice and pleasing vivacity is sure to make his mark quickly.' But some critics felt he had missed his opportunity. Farjeon wrote: 'It was surprising to hear him deliver such a line as "Who can hear this and bear an equal mind?" in the lowest emotionless terms.'

The producer was Allen Wade, who staged many Phoenix productions. He was sufficiently impressed with Gielgud to cast him in Marlowe's *Doctor Faustus*, which the society put on at the New Oxford. Gielgud played the Good Angel and, according to Agate, gave 'an admirable performance'. The production gave him a chance to mix with a distinguished cast that included Hay Petrie, John Longdon and H.R. Hignett. He also worked for the first time with the eccentric and blatantly homosexual Ernest Thesiger, who allegedly modelled his appearance on Queen Mary, and who once silenced a party by inquiring in his piping voice, 'Anyone fancy a spot of buggery?' In *Doctor Faustus*, according to one critic, he was a 'rather ladylike Mephistophiles'.

One of the founders of the Phoenix Society was the American society hostess Emerald Cunard, a great patron of the opera and ballet, and the lover of Thomas Beecham. Many musicians and dancers came to her gatherings in Grosvenor Square. Amusing, intelligent and forthright, she called homosexuals 'popinjays'; Gielgud thought she resembled 'a brilliant canary', and enjoyed the challenging remarks she flung at her guests. Her rival hostess Sibyl Colefax liked especially to encourage young talent – Coward and Ivor Novello were two of her protégés – and filled her Chelsea house with artists, writers and theatre people. Here, in the scented panelled rooms filled with flowers and all the latest books, Gielgud met Gertrude Lawrence, Ruth Draper, Edith Sitwell and, briefly, Shaw.

He also attended one of the fashionable tea-dances held in York Terrace by Lady Wyndham, owner of the New Theatre and a backer of plays, who danced with all the young men with a Pekinese under her arm. It delighted and dazzled him to find himself mixing with actors and actresses whom he had previously only seen from a theatre pit or gallery, and he began to develop a love of repartee and sparkling conversation.

Another society was the RADA Players, set up by former students to provide acting opportunities for themselves. Gielgud appeared in three of its Sunday productions. His voice, though admired by some critics, seemed as much a handicap as an asset, and he was criticised for sounding affected. St John Ervine, reviewing the RADA Players' production of Allan Monkhouse's *Sons and Fathers*, was blunt: 'If he will consent to rid himself of certain irritating mannerisms and affectations he will become a most accomplished actor. He is at a point where he may make or mar his career . . . Dramatists are likely to become more and more reluctant to employ in their plays actors who persistently speak in a particular and uncommonly ugly and emasculated manner.'

Such attacks of course made him acutely self-conscious about his voice. He later claimed he tried to speak exceptionally well in order to distract attention from his poor movement. But he was also worried about charges of effeminacy. When he appeared for the Three Hundred Club in *Confession* by W.F. Casey, one critic complained he was not 'aggressively uxorious'. This kind of criticism worried him very much. So when Basil Dean offered him the plum role of an effeminate young man in Frederick Lonsdale's risqué play about prostitution and lesbianism, *Spring Cleaning*, he deliberately talked himself out of it by asking for twice his normal salary.

Like other, more established actors, Gielgud found himself invited to appear in the occasional charity matinée. In one of these he played Armand Duval in Michael Orme's adaptation of Dumas' *The Lady of the Camellias*. Agate wrote approvingly: 'Mr Gielgud's over-intense quality stood him in excellent stead, and he was as good an Armand as I can remember.' Among the actors with non-speaking parts was Donald Wolfit, with whom Gielgud was soon to cross swords.

Out of family loyalty he appeared in the *Old English Nativity Play*, staged at Daly's by the Pioneer Players, founded in 1911 by his cousin Edith Craig. Her aim was to put on plays of ideas – political, social and, especially, feminist – that were banned from public performance. The most celebrated had been Shaw's *Mrs Warren's Profession*, which dealt with prostitution. In Shaw's view the Pioneer Players, 'by singleness of artistic direction, and unflagging activity, did more for the theatrical vanguard than any of the other coterie theatres'.

Edith Craig was practical, energetic and industrious, with no little skill as a producer. Always in her mother's shadow, she was handicapped by a slight lisp: both factors probably contributed to her behaviour as a producer, which gained her a reputation as a dragon. Like many of the Terrys, she was a perfectionist, and was often stubborn, dictatorial and controlling. She once threatened to fine actors each time they forgot their lines. Gielgud remembered 'a picturesque figure whether in her country smock or rather striking bohemian clothes, delivering her views with brisk authority'. Now in her sixties, she had for years been producing plays in churches and pageants in parks and gardens, both in London and the provinces.

The nativity play, which she also produced, had Fay Compton as Mary, Viola Tree as Third Angel, Raymond Massey as Third Soldier, and Gielgud as Second Shepherd. It also featured a group of children – including A.A. Milne's son Christopher Robin – as angels and cherubs, and rapidly degenerated into the worst kind of bungled school production. Edith Craig and her lesbian friends Christopher St John and Clare (Tony) Atwood, disguised as monks, barked out orders amongst the mayhem, while Esmé Percy, as Herod's son, did his best to restrain a huge wolfhound on a leash. When Gielgud and his fellow-shepherds, guided by the star in the east, went to exit through the doors at the back of the auditorium, they found themselves locked in, and were forced to creep sheepishly back westwards round the edge of the stage, where the next scene was already being played.

He fared little better when he was offered a rare part in a normal West End production. *Gloriana* was a chronicle play about Queen Elizabeth by Gwen John, in which he was cast as Sir John Harington. The title-role was played by Nancy Price, whom he remembered as 'a strikingly effective battleaxe'. His opinion may have been coloured by her treatment of him in his one scene, when she placed him by the footlights with his back to the audience and his face obscured, while she expired on a pile of cushions. The play closed after a week at the Little.

Despite the shortage of good roles, he was getting to know the methods of different producers. They included Henzie Raeburn, who had worked with Komisarjevsky; Milton Rosmer, a leading actor-manager who later briefly ran the theatre at Stratford; and Lewis Casson, Sybil Thorndike's husband. He worked with Casson in *The High Constable's Wife*, an adaptation of a Balzac novel by Cecil Lewis, the first director of the BBC. Later he became fond of Casson; at the time his rigorous insistence on phrasing and diction terrified him.

During this period he had few opportunities to broaden his experience in Shakespeare. In the five years following his failure in *Romeo and Juliet* he played in just four productions, in each case for only one or two performances. Once again the stage societies came to his rescue.

7

The Search for Stardom

Never shall I forget the bitter disappointment I
had to suffer.
(Gielgud on *The Constant Nymph*, 1926)

IN the 1920s Shakespeare's plays were rarely seen in the West End.
There were exceptions, such as Lewis Casson's productions of
Henry VIII and *Macbeth*, staged in the lavish tradition of Tree. The
Old Vic, with the help of Edith Evans, continued to mount full
seasons, and the actress Lena Ashwell was doggedly touring
productions round schools and town halls. But for a young actor such
as Gielgud the opportunities were severely limited.

The society that did most to keep the Shakespearean flame alight
was the Fellowship of Players. Founded by the actress Margaret
Scudamore and others, it aimed to stage the entire Shakespeare canon,
partly so the more rarely performed plays could be seen. Gielgud
played Valentine in its Sunday-night production of *The Two
Gentleman of Verona* at the Aldwych, with Ion Swinley, John Laurie,
Florence Saunders and Beatrix Thompson. The producer was Robert
Atkins, which would have brought back memories of the 1921 season at
the Old Vic. The novice walk-on had made progress since then: the
Daily Telegraph noted 'a sound piece of work' and the *Star* called him
'a romantic Valentine'.

He had his first taste of *Hamlet* in a notorious modern-dress production, produced by H.K. Ayliff for Barry Jackson, with Colin Keith-
Johnston as Hamlet. Shakespeare in modern dress was a new concept
to London, but was actually a reversion to what had been normal
practice in the eighteenth century, when the plays were presented in
the costume of the time. Jackson's aim was to bring Shakespeare

'nearer to the man in the street', who is 'too often bored or bewildered' by conventional productions.

At the Kingsway Hamlet sported plus fours and smoked a cigarette, Ophelia was dressed in short skirt and stockings, Polonius was in spats, and the First Gravedigger wore a bowler hat. In one scene the Prince of Denmark wore a soft shirt and collar with a dinner-jacket, prompting the *Men's Wear Organiser* to thunder: 'Hamlet's evening kit was a sheer disgrace.' The production created a furore in the press, although several critics though it a valid experiment. But when Gielgud saw it he disapproved strongly, calling it, in his shortest review, 'Unspeakable'. However, this didn't stop him agreeing to play Rosencrantz in two performances of the production staged at the Court.

He also played for the first time in *The Tempest*, replacing Eric Portman as Ferdinand in two special matinées at the Savoy, with Rosaline Courtneidge as Miranda. The annual visit to London of Henry Baynton, a handsome but vain actor-manager of the old school, was a shameless exercise in self-promotion. Baynton turned Caliban into the principal character, cut the tempest, and between the scenes entertained the audience with monsterish antics, including swallowing live fish, to gain extra rounds of applause.

The result was mocked by the critics, one of whom suggested the play should be re-named *Caliban, or Come and See the Monster Fed*. Gielgud was asked to strip to the waist for one scene but, worried about the acne spots on his back, refused to do so. Somehow he managed to rise above it all. The *Daily Telegraph* called him 'a nice-looking, clear-speaking Ferdinand', while other critics thought him suitably romantic. Agate attacked producer Robert Courtneidge for the obvious lack of teamwork: 'Mr Gielgud looked exactly as if he might have been taking the air in the streets of Florence in the fifteenth century, whereas Miss Rosaline Courtneidge ... might quite well have spent the morning shopping in Kensington High Street.'

After Baynton, Gielgud had a close-up view of another large ego, but a better actor, when he played Cassio in two performances of *Othello*, produced by Filmer for the Lyceum Stage Society, with Ion Swinley as Iago and Elissa Landi playing Desdemona. Othello was Robert Loraine, a powerful, bravura actor who had been an acclaimed Cyrano de Bergerac, and a notable success in Shaw's plays. During *Othello* he behaved outrageously, ignoring Filmer at rehearsals, cutting a major speech because Forbes-Robertson had done so, throwing a tantrum over his wig and costume at the dress rehearsal, and insisting that the company clear the stage after one curtain call so he could take subsequent ones alone. Gielgud was delighted when Ion Swinley refused to do so, and Loraine was forced to share the applause with his Iago.

One actor Gielgud admired greatly was Henry Ainley. Owner of the most beautiful voice in the English theatre, he was a fine if erratic Shakespearean actor. When Gielgud heard he was to play Benedick in *Much Ado About Nothing*, opposite another of his idols, Madge Titheradge, he boldly went to the stage door of the theatre where Ainley was currently acting, and asked to be considered for Claudio. Unfortunately the part had already been cast, and soon after Ainley became ill and left the stage for three years.

Gielgud seemed on the verge of a breakthrough to stardom in spring 1926 when he was cast as the juvenile lead in Miles Malleson's *The Fanatics*. The play was a passionate plea for revolution, and an attack on the older generation that had led people into the horrors of the First World War. The starry company included Nicholas Hannen, Athene Seyler and Ursula Jeans. But as the opening night approached so too did the threat of a General Strike, which became a reality in May. Worried that the play's subject-matter might be considered inflammatory, Malleson argued successfully for a postponement. When the play was staged after the strike was over, Gielgud was unavailable.

His real chance came that autumn. *The Constant Nymph*, a romantic novel by Margaret Kennedy on the theme of 'free love', was to sell more copies than any other novel in the 1920s. It had been jointly adapted for the stage by the author and the producer Basil Dean. The leading male character was Lewis Dodd, a talented, temperamental and unconventional young composer, who escapes from his bourgeois marriage by running away to Belgium with a fourteen-year-old girl, the 'constant nymph' of the story. When another young actor, Christopher Scaife, turned down the male lead, Dean offered it to Gielgud. It was a long and difficult part that required him to sing as well as play the piano: once again his musical ability had been crucial. Gielgud could hardly believe his luck at such an opportunity: 'I was up in the clouds,' he remembered. 'Already I was thinking of myself as the actor of the age.'

Basil Dean, once an actor, was now the foremost producer of the day. He had started as a repertory actor, had become the first director of the Liverpool Repertory Theatre and in London had established his own company, ReanDean, based at the St Martin's. As a producer he was a pioneer, putting on new plays by Coward, Maugham, Galsworthy, Masefield, Lonsdale and Clemence Dane. A great admirer of the spectacular, technically brilliant work of Max Reinhardt in Germany, his glittering productions, of which *Hassan* was the supreme example, were slick, meticulous and imaginative, with brilliantly realistic sets, state-of-the-art lighting, and efficient teamwork.

But Dean, known as 'Bastard Basil', was also the most hated man in the English theatre. Tall, massive and bespectacled, he was a sadistic bully. He created a regime of fear in rehearsals, reducing actors to tears with his sarcasm and withering abuse. 'We were all scared to death of him,' Harold French recalled; one actor allegedly fainted on stage after a verbal lashing. Yet Dean often drew excellent performances from those he bullied, and because his productions were usually successful, there were always actors willing to put up with his tyranny in exchange for extended periods of work.

Once Dean had confirmed the part was his, Gielgud took a fortnight's holiday, and booked a celebratory lunch with Fabia Drake at the Ivy restaurant, London's most famous theatrical haunt. But although Margaret Kennedy wanted him to play Lewis Dodd, Dean was not sure if he was experienced enough, and had been secretly negotiating with both Ivor Novello and Coward, in the hope that one or other would take the part. Coward, initially doubtful, suddenly changed his mind and accepted. When he spotted Gielgud lunching in the Ivy, he broke the news to him. Gielgud showed extraordinary control, saying nothing of Dean's offer to him, and politely telling Coward he thought he would be very good in the part. Shattered, he saw Dean that afternoon, and was told the management had changed its mind, that Gielgud might be known in Oxford, but that in London he was 'a mere nobody'.

Gielgud was desolate. 'Never shall I forget the bitter disappointment I had to suffer,' he told a journalist not long after. 'All my pride had been taken from me, all my hopes had been dashed to the ground. I was right back where I had started – a mere understudy.' To add insult to injury Dean offered him half the original £20 salary to understudy Coward for a month, and then the full amount when he took over, with a further rise to £25 if the play was a success. Though morally and legally in a strong position, Gielgud realised the dangers of quarrelling with Dean and Coward. Swallowing his pride he accepted the offer, though he persuaded Dean to raise the understudy salary to £15.

His reaction to Dean's treachery revealed his dislike of confrontation, the difficulty he had in asserting himself, and the uncertainty he felt about his acting ability. Later he denied bearing any ill-will towards Coward, whom he claimed was kind and sympathetic throughout the episode. Yet though he later called Coward 'my enchanting friend', there was always a wariness in his attitude to him, and he never became part of Coward's inner circle. His ambivalent feelings probably date from this incident.

Depressed and discontented, Gielgud sat in on rehearsals for *The Constant Nymph*, which were predictably stormy. Coward was one of the few able and willing to stand up to Dean: as a child actor he had threatened to go 'straight home to my mother' if Dean didn't stop bullying him. The two men clashed continually: 'Basil tore himself and us to shreds over the production,' Coward remembered. But he himself was no model of flexibility and cooperation, and he argued incessantly with everyone. He threatened to walk out unless Dean stopped terrorising the actors playing smaller parts. After one row Coward told Gielgud he was giving up the part. 'My heart leapt as I thought my chance was coming after all,' he recalled. Dean asked him if he knew the lines, and he spent all night studying them. But the next day rehearsals continued as if nothing had happened.

With a company that included Edna Best, Cathleen Nesbitt, Mary Clare, Elissa Landi and Marie Ney, the play opened at the New in September. The fashionable first-night audience included Maugham, Bennett, Galsworthy, H.G. Wells and Hugh Walpole. Gielgud was too cast down to watch, and went off to see another show nearby. There were sixteen curtain calls, and the critics, who had expected the novel not to translate well to the stage, were loud in their approval.

During the third week Coward stunned the audience and his fellow-actors by crying throughout one performance. Afterwards he collapsed and, suffering from nervous exhaustion, was ordered to bed for a week. Gielgud went on for the matinée the following day, and played the part for the rest of the run. In theory this was stardom, but his response to his new status was understandably muted: 'I could not relish the distinction as I had dreamed I would; the gilt had been taken off the gingerbread,' he remembered.

The part, which he played nine times a week, was immensely demanding, with six costume changes and hardly a moment offstage. Initially he struggled with it, intensely aware, as he had been with *The Vortex*, of the shadow of Coward's voice and interpretation. His acting became increasingly self-conscious, and when Dean came to see the show after three months abroad he described his performance, perhaps not unreasonably, as no more than that of an understudy. He called an intensive rehearsal for the next day and, Gielgud recalled, 'reduced me to pulp'.

Amazingly, Coward's photograph remained outside the theatre throughout the run. Gielgud was rightly offended, but evidently refrained from making the kind of protest that would have been justified. He was also upset about the lack of star billing and publicity for his taking over of the part, both of which he had been promised. To make matters worse, relations backstage were poor. The actors resented Coward's departure: three of them refused to speak to Gielgud offstage, and Edna Best made her dislike clear. They looked on Gielgud as an intruder from the highbrow world of Chekhov and the stage societies. But perhaps he was partly to blame: his sense of humour, he later admitted, 'was strictly limited by youthful self-importance and a terror of being ridiculed'.

The rows and unhappiness continued for months, until he developed a skin rash on his face, and had to leave the cast for ten days. Dean's harsh methods were abhorrent to him: 'He would not allow people to think for themselves or develop their characters freely, and his meticulous method of giving them every inflection and tone, before they had experimented themselves, made them feel helpless and inefficient,' he recalled. It was a cry from the heart.

Despite the backbiting and humiliation, Gielgud knuckled down to nearly a year's run. This gave him a chance to experiment with his timing and vocal technique, to try to control his mannerisms, and to learn to work effectively with others night after night. He accepted the validity of some of Dean's criticisms: that he projected too much, that he forced the emotion without using his mind sufficiently, that he tended to show the audience how hard he was working. He admired the cool approach of Edna Best, who would sit absorbed in a novel waiting for her entrance, mark the page with a sigh when it was time to go on, play a big emotional scene, then calmly resume her reading.

His willingness to learn and determination to improve were apparent to others. A month after he took over from Coward the artist Graham Robertson, a close friend of Ellen Terry who had known him since his childhood, wrote to a friend: 'How do you like John Gielgud? The boy has worked very hard and conscientiously and I'm so glad that he is getting on.' That he was beginning to do so was signalled by his first appearance in *Who's Who in the Theatre*, in which he listed his recreations as 'music and stage design'. But as an inexperienced replacement for an established star he received little attention from the critics for his playing of Lewis Dodd.

'I felt that I was beginning to know how to act, but I got no particular credit for it,' he recalled. The part of the self-seeking musician was probably more suited to Coward. Sybil Thorndike, who saw both actors play it, pointed up the contrast: 'Noël's Lewis Dodd was beautiful. It was perfection . . . John gave a lovely performance, but there was not the streak of cruelty that was in Noël . . . you felt that slight jab that Noël always had.' But Ivor Brown, reviewing a revival a few years later, recalled that Gielgud was 'harsh and livid' and 'showed genius'.

During the summer of his year at RADA, when his parents were away, he had borrowed a flat from his fellow-student George Howe, and enjoyed the taste of freedom. Now, turning twenty-three, with a lively social life and a salary of £25 a week, he became restive living in Kensington, and decided to get a flat of his own. 'I persuaded my parents to let me leave home,' he recalled. Whatever his parents felt, they put up no real resistance.

One of the many actors Gielgud had met at Ned Lathom's was Frank Vosper, who had a small fourth-floor flat above a saddlery shop at 7 St Martin's Lane, almost opposite the New. Gielgud now took over the lease from him. There was no proper kitchen, and the bathroom was down a steep and narrow flight of stairs, but otherwise he found the place charming. On the ceiling of one of the bedrooms an artist friend of Vosper had painted a series of nude figures. This Gielgud thought very modern and original: it certainly struck a different note from the respectable décor of Gledhow Gardens. He was to stay in the heart of the West End for eight years.

He shared the flat with two other theatre people: Bert Lister, a witty and volatile man who was later Coward's dresser and stage manager, and John Perry, a mediocre actor then working for the florist Constance Spry. Of upper-class Anglo-Irish stock and hailing from Tipperary, he was a friend of the writer Molly Keane. Tall and gaunt, with thinning fair hair, he loved hunting, and gambling in casinos and at the races. Emlyn Williams remembered 'a mocking manner which contrived to hide a kind heart'. His easy, laid-back charm made him attractive to both men and women: Gielgud thought him handsome and witty, and they became lovers.

When *The Constant Nymph* finally ended Basil Dean offered him a four-month provincial tour in the part – though only after another actor proved unsuitable. Perhaps hoping to break free after ten months, Gielgud demanded a doubling of his salary to £35 a week and second-star billing, and was amazed when Dean accepted his terms without argument. The tour, which opened in Manchester and included Scotland, was very different from his experience with *The Wheel* four years before. The novice actor had blossomed into a cultured leading man, who sported large grey trilby hats and pearl-grey Oxford bags. In place of the dreaded pub-crawls he was able to enjoy his free time, going for long walks, seeing the local sights, and visiting museums and art galleries.

Shortly after the tour ended, in January 1928, he made his first trip to America. Leslie Faber was playing the lead in Alfred Neumann's *The Patriot*, a German costume drama about the conspiracy against Paul I of Russia. It was being produced in New York by the leading impresario Gilbert Miller, well known for bringing top British talent to Broadway. In rehearsal the actor playing the small part of the young Tsarevitch Alexander had proved inadequate, and Faber had recommended Gielgud as a replacement. The cast included two other English actors, Lyn Harding and Madge Titheradge. It looked set to be a big adventure.

Fortunately Gielgud had to make an instant decision. He hated uprooting himself, and imagined all the disasters that might befall him in a strange place. He tempted fate by asking for a good salary and a six-week guarantee, but both of them were granted. Luckily there was little time to brood: hired at very short notice, he had to sail within forty-eight hours, and learn his part during the two-week journey across the Atlantic on the *SS Berlin*. Lonely and homesick, he was greeted on his arrival by a short paragraph in the *World*, which described him as 'one of London's prominent young actors', who had 'stepped into the limelight considerably' by taking over from Coward.

For an avid theatregoer such as Gielgud there were riches in plenty to be sampled. With a record 264 productions in seventy theatres during the 1927/8 season, Broadway was booming. The shows were overwhelmingly American, with gaiety and romance the predominant spirit. But there were also straight modern plays, some of them by English writers, featuring many of America's most distinguished actors. Katherine Cornell starred in Maugham's *The Letter*; Otis Skinner was Falstaff in *The Merry Wives of Windsor*; Alfred Lunt acted in Shaw's *The Doctor's Dilemma*, and subsequently Eugene O'Neill's

Marco Millions; his English-born wife Lynn Fontanne was in O'Neill's new play *Strange Interlude*. Hecht and MacArthur's biting masterpiece *The Front Page* was a substantial hit, while at the other end of the spectrum Mae West's *The Pleasure Man* was closed by the police because of its overt sexual references. There were also distinguished musicals on offer: *Show Boat* opened, Fred and Adele Astaire were partnered in *Funny Face,* and Paul Robeson sang in the memorable first production of *Porgy and Bess.*

Gielgud's introduction to the American theatre was alarmingly abrupt. On arrival he was driven straight to the Majestic, where the first of two dress rehearsals was in progress. He was struck by the contrast with London: 'The theatre was in a state of pandemonium,' he recalled. 'The stage was covered with scenery and strewn with debris, and Faber was walking up and down, in costume, calling angrily for his dresser.' Overwhelmed by the scale and intensity of it all, unsure how to make his presence known, he crept timidly to the dressing-room in search of someone to hear his lines.

He was understandably anxious at his lack of preparation, and when Miller criticised his voice, his pace and, worst of all, his movement, he felt his confidence slipping. He was at least happy with his costume, a situation that always boosted his spirits. He thought his wig, uniform and cloak magnificent, and felt that despite just two rehearsals he might yet cut a dash on his Broadway début. He was especially keen to make an impression on Madge Titheradge, a diminutive actress of sensational emotional power whom Gielgud had admired in several London shows. To be on the same side of the footlights as this leading figure of the Edwardian theatre appealed to his star-struck and romantic sensibility.

The critic Burns Mantle noted that New York audiences generally disliked historical drama, and a headline in the *Sun* described *The Patriot* as 'A Play Produced in the All Too Grand Manner'. Gielgud claimed later that the notices 'ranged from expressions of mild approval to complete boredom'. But this was not the case. Most of them were good, some were ecstatic, and few found much fault with the acting. Despite his small part, Gielgud was mentioned favourably by several critics. Alexander Woollcott, whose views could make or break a show, wrote in the *World* that he 'gave a good account of himself as the squirmingly reluctant Alexander'. Only *Billboard* magazine dissented, observing that he was at times 'rather too stiff or too emotional'.

The audience seemed to have enjoyed the play, though Gielgud noticed less enthusiasm than was usual at a London première. After the traditional first-night party he and Faber sat in a restaurant in the early hours, drinking coffee and confidently composing self-congratulatory telegrams to send to London. But the next morning the picture looked different. Many people had walked out during the show, the notices were not good enough to sustain a run, and the play was taken off after only eleven performances.

After the final performance he and Leslie Faber stayed on for a few days to explore New York. He went to the theatre as much as possible, admiring Judith Anderson's beauty in *Behold the Bridegroom*, being charmed by Helen Hayes' brilliance in *Coquette*, and standing enraptured in the new Ziegfeld Theater to watch *Show Boat*. This first taste of New York filled him 'with wonder and delight'. He spent several nights in Harlem, saw Cab Calloway at the Cotton Club, and enjoyed celebrity-spotting in the dining-room at the Algonquin Hotel. He went to parties with Yvonne Arnaud, and 'speakeasies' with Emlyn Williams. This was the prohibition era, a time of illicit drinking, and Gielgud enjoyed the thrill of descending to mysterious basement cellars, being scrutinised through gratings, giving the password before being allowed in, and wondering if he would be poisoned by drinking the bath-tub gin. The emotional highlight was a romantic taxi-ride with Madge Titheradge, whom he found romantically enchanting: 'She kissed her hand as she waved goodbye, and wished me well in the career that I was just beginning,' he remembered.

He was encouraged to find that his playing had sparked some interest within the American theatre. Constance Collier suggested him for a revival of Maugham's *Our Betters* with Ina Claire; there was talk of a part in a play by Maurice Browne and Robert Nichols; and the Theatre Guild and other managements offered him the promise of work later in the season. He loved the excitement of New York, and the temptation to remain and try his luck was considerable. But the Miller management had failed to honour his six-week guarantee, and with no money and no immediate prospect of work, he returned with considerable reluctance to London. Yet had he remained in America, he might never have taken the step which was to alter fundamentally the direction of his career.

8

Mrs Pat and Lilian Baylis

I believe he may go quite far.
(Harley Granville Barker on
Gielgud rehearsing *Fortunato*, 1928)

ON his return from America early in 1928, Gielgud was given the chance to act with the most brilliant and most wayward actress in the English theatre.

Mrs Patrick Campbell was, in Shaw's view, 'a perilously bewitching woman'. An Italianate beauty totally without formal training, she mesmerised critics and audiences with the electric power of her personality, her superb figure, and her wonderful contralto voice. Rebecca West said 'she was as beautiful among women as Venice is among cities'. But she was also awesomely temperamental, and made many enemies. Highly intelligent, devastatingly witty and super-sensitive, she could be cruel, rude and domineering. Easily bored, she often lost interest in the middle of a performance. Her unprofessional behaviour onstage was the despair of actors and managers, and stories abounded: during a dramatic scene in Fagan's *Bella Donna* she flicked chocolates against the backcloth; in a light comedy by Ivor Novello she suddenly inserted a speech from Sophocles' *Electra*.

Some people, including Sarah Bernhardt, thought her a genius. She was wooed by Shaw, though more by letter than in the flesh ('One day he will eat beefsteak, and then God help us poor women,' she remarked): he wrote Eliza Doolittle for her, and she continued to play the part until she was nearly fifty. She had her greatest success in the title-roles in Ibsen's *Hedda Gabler*, Pinero's *The Second Mrs Tanqueray* and Hermann Sudermann's *Magda*. The toast of the theatre on both sides of the Atlantic, she was praised for replacing the old-style rhetoric with a natural intelligence and grace. In 1902 *Life* had called her 'the best actress appearing today on the English-speaking stage'.

Gielgud had already met her socially at a luncheon party given by Lord Lathom at the Metropole Hotel in Brighton. By now she had lost her looks, become stout, and was compelled by financial necessity to tour the provinces in her most famous roles. Now sixty-three, she was to play Mrs Alving in Ibsen's *Ghosts*, with Gielgud as her son Oswald, in a production for the Ibsen Centenary Festival. It was a glorious opportunity at a low moment in his career, and one that the Terry connection may have helped him to secure: though Mrs Campbell was often jealous of other actresses, she had always loved and admired Ellen, and spoke warmly of her to Gielgud when they met.

Once again the family had given him an entrée; but Mrs Campbell, who had a weakness for good-looking young men, seemed to take a special fancy to Gielgud. She told him he had acted beautifully in *Katerina* at Barnes, and showed an interest in his career, which flattered him a great deal. He was as fascinated by her offstage as he had been in the theatre, where her performances as Hedda Gabler and Paula Tanqueray had deeply affected him.

The festival's organiser, J.T. Grein, was a friend of Kate Gielgud. A playwright, critic, and ardent advocate of avant-garde European drama, Grein had started the Independent Theatre of London in 1891, a forerunner of the Stage Society, and with similar non-commercial aims. His opening production, the first performance in England of *Ghosts*, had provoked one of the most violent critical receptions in theatrical history, turning Ibsen overnight into a household name, and Grein into the most abused man in London. It must have given him immense satisfaction to revive the play for the festival.

Translated by William Archer and produced by Peter Godfrey, with Frederick Lloyd, Margot Sieveking and Fewlass Llewellyn in the company, *Ghosts* was to be given a Sunday-night performance at the Arts, and seven matinées at Wyndham's. Before rehearsals began Mrs Campbell wrote to Shaw: 'You have bashed me and beheaded me so often, do do it once more if you think I should ruin the play – I could get out of it.' But she duly turned up for rehearsals, clutching the Pekinese dog that accompanied her everywhere.

It soon became clear that, though she had never played Mrs Alving, she knew the play inside out, and was very willing to give Gielgud the benefit of her experience. 'She helped me enormously with the emotional effects of my difficult part,' he remembered. She had done much the same with du Maurier; Gielgud believed she would have made a fine producer. But some of her advice was distinctly eccentric, as when she told him: 'You must speak in a Channel-steamer voice. Empty your voice of meaning and speak as if you were going to be sick. Pinero once told me this, and I have never forgotten it.'

At first Mrs Pat – as he was now invited to call her – seemed unable to learn her lines: 'My dear, it's all like a very long confinement,' she groaned to Gielgud during rehearsal. But at the dress rehearsal she amazed him by being word-perfect and in full control. She also lived up to her reputation for unprofessional behaviour, insulting other actors behind her hand, and bemoaning in a stage whisper the poor attendance and the absence of her titled friends. Taking a dislike to Fewlass Llewellyn, playing Pastor Mandes, she distracted the audience by hanging a set of curtains during his main scene. On one of Gielgud's crucial lines she suddenly said, with her back to the audience: 'Oh I'm so hungry!' On another occasion, after he had failed to cover up a mistake, she pouted at him, 'You're such an amateur!' And when he got carried away and shed real tears, she scolded him: 'You silly boy. Now you've got a dirty face.'

His most alarming moment came in the last act, which ends with Mrs Alving holding a box of pills, and Oswald calling out 'The sun . . . the sun!' Mrs Pat decided that she, rather than Ibsen, should have the last word, as Gielgud recalled: 'With a wild cry she flung the pillbox into the footlights and threw herself across my knees with her entire weight. "Oswald! Oswald!" she moaned. The armchair cracked ominously as she lay prone across my lap, and I clutched the arms in desperation for fear they might disintegrate.' Despite such incidents, Gielgud kept his equanimity. Most of the time Mrs Pat was gracious and charming to him, and at the fall of the curtain after the first performance even thanked him for having helped her through it.

Agate compared her physical splendour to the Lord Mayor's coach. But in the first two acts 'the coach seemed empty, or at least one did not feel that Mrs Alving was in it'; only in the third act, he felt, did the great actress emerge. Alan Dent, who accompanied him, believed there was a simple explanation for this: 'She became aware half-way through this performance that the very young actor playing her son was stealing most of the audience's attention. He was tense and haunted where, up to the last act, she was merely apathetic.' Gielgud certainly received good notices: Agate thought him 'extremely fine', while *The Times* praised an 'elaborate and beautifully restrained study'.

Gielgud's friendship with Mrs Pat ripened during the rehearsals for *Ghosts*. Despite the differences in age and temperament, they had many tastes in common, including a love of food, theatrical gossip, and beautiful objects. 'I think she is almost the best company in the world, particularly if one is alone with her,' he wrote a decade later. They lunched at L'Escargot in Soho, where she taught him to eat snails. He visited her flat in Chelsea, where the Morris wallpaper reminded him she had been the idol of the Pre-Raphaelites, and been sketched by Beardsley in her slimmer days. He enjoyed her devastating and defiant humour and capacity for self-criticism: 'I look like a burst paper bag,' she once told him. Somehow he never feared her. She in turn took a fancy to the shy, garrulous and adoring young actor, with his lack of malice, his sensitivity, and his exquisite manners. Both were flattered by the attention the other gave to them, though as Gielgud's star waxed and Mrs Campbell's waned his feelings were increasingly tinged with pity as her life and career went into decline. He was to grow enormously fond of her, and remain a good friend until her death.

Meanwhile another theatrical legend was fast fading from the scene. Her memory clouding over and her strength diminishing by the day, Ellen Terry had retired to her country cottage at Smallhythe in Kent. Just before playing in *Ghosts* Gielgud, along with Mabel Terry-Lewis and other relatives and friends, had taken part in a radio tribute on her eighty-first birthday. In it they had presented scenes from Shakespeare especially associated with her, and Gielgud had played Oberon, Bassanio and Horatio. On 21 July 1928, with Edith and Edward Gordon Craig by her bedside, she died after a stroke. As the funeral cortège travelled the sixty-mile journey to London, people lined the way and threw bouquets of flowers. At her memorial service in St Paul's Church, Covent Garden, everyone wore light suits or summer dresses rather than mourning, and the atmosphere was one of celebration rather than the 'funeral gloom' she so disliked.

Attending the service with Fabia Drake, Gielgud remembered the Christmas parties of his childhood, the 'godmother in a fairy-tale' who had told him 'Read your Shakespeare'. In her recitals he had glimpsed her famous ability to catch the essence of Shakespeare's heroines, and had marvelled at it. Although he had talked to her only half a dozen times, his feelings ran deep: he loved her mixture of bohemian and great lady, her very modern desire to understand new people and new trends. In a fond and lengthy appreciation a few years later he wrote: 'She was swift and gay, and yet old and wise; an inspiration to her own generation, and an ideal of beauty and perfection to us who remember her with such great honour and affection.'

He had only once been alone with her. Earlier that summer while driving in Kent he stopped at Smallhythe on impulse, and plucked up courage to knock at her door. While waiting for her to appear he took in every detail: the flowers, the simple furniture, the poster of Irving on the wall. When his great-aunt came slowly down the staircase, red coral combs in her white hair, he was touched to see that she carried the handbag he remembered from his childhood: 'She asked me who I was and I told her. She seemed to remember for a while, and asked if I was acting now and whether my parents were well. I had on a bright-blue shirt, and she said how gay it was and that bright colours always cheered her up. She asked me to stay to lunch, but I pretended I had to go on somewhere else. She seemed suddenly to grow inattentive, and I knew I must not tire her any longer.' A few weeks later she was dead.

Beyond his intense love of Ellen Terry lay a strong awareness of the family tradition, of the baton being passed down the generations. Yet there seemed less chance than ever of his being able to pick it up. Despite his good notices for *Ghosts*, he was offered nothing of merit in the West End during the rest of the year. The three plays in which he appeared were worse than mediocre, offering poor parts that did nothing for his stalled career.

The first was the farce *Holding Out the Apple*, in which he teamed up with Hermione Baddeley. The play depended for its laughs on a woman trying to conceal the fact that she had had her teeth knocked out during a game of hockey. After a pre-London tour this immortal piece ran for six weeks at the Globe, mainly to nurses and others with free tickets. Hermione Baddeley remembered that 'the first-night audience got the pip and the playwright lost all her money'. Gielgud, playing a doctor, thought it 'an appalling concoction'. The critics noted his discomfort: J.G. Bergel concluded: 'John Gielgud is a very good actor; but not in farce . . . he was hopelessly lost, and no wonder.'

In *The Skull*, an American 'comedy mystery thriller' at the Shaftesbury with Alison Leggatt, he played a villain disguised as a detective. This pot-pourri of ghosts, skulls, chain-rattlings, screams and revolver shots was, for Hubert Griffith, the 'ultimate rock-bottom of imbecility and ugliness'. His third disaster was *Out of the Sea*, a poetic melodrama by the American humorist and poet Don Marquis. Cast as an American poet, Gielgud had to sit gloomily playing Wagner on the piano before committing suicide along with the heroine.

J.T. Grein noticed 'his fervour and his lovely voice'. The play, reviled by the critics, lasted exactly a week at the Strand.

Gielgud was restive. 'It was no fun earning a big salary in a bad part,' he remembered. Now classed as a leading man, his name in big letters at the top of the bill, he feared being typecast as a lightweight, West End actor. It depressed him to feel his name was simply being drawn out of a hat. 'The haphazard mixture of parts which had come my way made me feel I was chosen at random, and that no manager or producer cared whether or not he engaged me,' he recalled. Once again his escape route lay through the stage societies and little theatres. Here, recognised as an actor of promise, he found better work, with good directors and actors of substance.

Two of these productions were at the recently founded Arts Theatre Club, which was to prove one of the most adventurous of the little theatres. In *Prejudice* by Mercedes de Acosta, a melodrama produced by Leslie Banks for just three performances, Gielgud played Jacob Slovak, a Polish Jew. Four of the national critics commended his performance highly, but his hopes of a West End transfer were unrealised. It was in this play that he appeared for the first time with Ralph Richardson, an idiosyncratic but promising young actor who had been making his mark at the Birmingham Rep, and also treading the Sunday circuit. The two of them took little notice of each other.

The other Arts production was a revival for just seven performances of Filmer's production of *The Seagull*. Struggling to improve his playing of Konstantin, Gielgud asked in vain for the producer to be more critical, and to allow him to play differently a scene with which he had never been happy. 'What a pity you always want to gild the lily,' Filmer replied. Yet if Gielgud was not satisfied with his performance, Herbert Farjeon certainly was, describing it as 'as good as ever'.

He had yet another Slav role in *Red Rust* by V.M. Kirchov and A.V. Ouspensky, the first post-revolutionary drama from Russia to reach London. Again his performance was praised, W.A. Darlington noting his 'fine altruistic fervour' as the idealistic student Fedor. But after the short run at the Little Gielgud admitted to Gabrielle Enthoven: 'Yes, it was a very poor wraith of a part, and I'm not sorry to see the back of it. But it was fun in a way (though rather a fake too) trying to make an effect with no lines or situations to help one.'

He had more hopes of *Hunter's Moon*, a romantic melodrama staged by the Sunday Play Society for a single performance at the Prince of Wales. Set in the time of the French Revolution, it had been banned by the Lord Chamberlain because of its 'connubial frankness'. Gielgud, playing a neurotic and cowardly émigré fighting with the Austrians against the revolutionaries, starred alongside two of his mentors, Leslie Faber – who also produced – and Phyllis Neilson-Terry.

Just before the Sunday-night performance Gielgud wrote to Gabrielle Enthoven: 'The production is brilliant I think – an old-fashioned romantic play done (I hope) with brilliance and humour and imagination. I think it should be taken, with any reasonable luck.' But again his judgement was too optimistic: the play failed to interest any West End manager. Once more he received several good reviews, but with no immediate benefit to his career.

Barry Jackson was staging Tennyson's *Harold* at the Court. Though it was a poor play, the part of the doomed romantic Saxon king was a plum one: the actor had three thousand lines and was on stage virtually throughout. Jackson advertised for an experienced romantic leading man, but Gielgud's hopes of winning the role were dashed by the boldness of another young actor working with the Birmingham Rep. During the dress rehearsal of *Back to Methuselah*, to the astonishment of the watching Jackson and Shaw, he suddenly burst into a three-minute speech from *Harold*. This reckless action did the trick, and obtained the part for the twenty-one-year-old Laurence Olivier.

It was during this frustrating period that Gielgud first worked with Harley Granville Barker, an experience that was to have a profound effect on his work and his ideas about theatre. After the war Barker had been persuaded by his second wife, the American writer Helen Huntington, to withdraw from the theatre and concentrate on his writing. Shaw described this as 'a public scandal'; others found it hard to forgive what they called a desertion. But the result was the celebrated five-volume *Prefaces to Shakespeare* which, with their brilliant mixture of scholarship and practical theatrical knowledge, was to become the Bible for generations of actors and producers.

Barker and his wife had translated several plays by the Spanish writers Martínez Sierra and the brothers Serafín and Joaquín Álvarez Quintero, whose gentle, subtle work enjoyed a brief vogue in England as a result. Two of the Quintero plays, the farce *Fortunato* and the two-act comedy *The Lady from Alfaqueque*, were presented by Amner Hall in a double-bill at the Court. The producer and designer was James Whale, who invited Gielgud to join a company that included Anthony Ireland, O.B. Clarence, Virginia Isham, Miriam Lewes and John Fernald.

As translator Barker turned up for some rehearsals, and occasionally took over from Whale, giving what was effectively a master-class in producing. His technique was a collaborative one: 'If a producer only knows how to give orders, he has missed his vocation; he had better be a drill sergeant,' he once wrote. Gielgud found his method a revelation: 'He rehearsed us for about two hours, changed nearly every move and arrangement of the stage, acted, criticised, advised, in an easy flow of practical efficiency, never stopping for a moment,' he recalled. 'We all sat spellbound, trying to drink in his words of wisdom and at the same time to remember all the hints he was giving us.'

Barker, who favoured a naturalistic style of acting, rehearsed Gielgud's best scene in *Fortunato* once only. 'He just got up on the stage and did the part for me in the most simple way without really acting it, but showing me just where I was wrong, the timing and everything,' Gielgud recalled. 'Let me write it down, let me write it down,' Gielgud pleaded, but Barker replied, 'No, no, no, I have to go to lunch,' and swept out of the theatre, never to return. Gielgud was dazzled by his brilliance: Barker seemed to him infallible.

But not all the actors were so impressed. Margaret Webster, playing a small part in *The Lady from Alfaqueque*, disliked his tendency to concentrate obsessively on tiny sections of the play, leaving huge swathes untouched. During rehearsals she wrote to her mother: 'Everyone is playing their parts as about six different people – all very convinced that what Barker says must be good and right, but thoroughly upset as to quite what they are meant to be doing, and all holding their heads and calling on the Almighty. To me there is an awfully disjointed feeling, as if none of the characters have quite come alive.'

Barker's magnetism was considerable. Much of his influence on actors was due to his charm, his bubbly sense of humour, and the sheer force of his personality. Lewis Casson described him as 'eager and tireless, blazing with an inner fire that yet remained always under the steely, flexible control of a keen, calculating brain'. His charisma put many actors in awe of him: the poet and dramatist John Masefield told him: 'People have come to regard you as a kind of god.'

Gielgud certainly fell under his spell. Intellectually he admired Barker for his brilliant observations on the characters, his encouragement of actors to explore their inner life rather than give an impersonation. He was impressed by his patience and persistence, his passion for detail, his demand for speed and clarity. But there was also an emotional need, that was to appear to a greater or lesser extent with all the producers with whom he worked. Restless, impetuous, often uncertain of his abilities and ideas, Gielgud needed both a firm anchor and a guide, someone who could both inspire him, push him to the limit, but control his excesses. Only three producers would truly fulfil this role for him during his career: Komisarjevsky had been the first; Barker was the next; the third would not appear for another twenty years.

Although the first-night audience at the Court rose to the company's performance of *Fortunato*, and the critics praised its charm and simplicity, the double-bill proved of little interest to the public. Gielgud came out of it reasonably well. In *The Lady from Alfaqueque* he played the part of a poet-imposter, drawing the comment from Agate that 'for once John Gielgud was right in his Byronic suggestions'. In *Fortunato*, with spectacles on nose, he was a young architect turned amateur beggar, and was complimented on 'admirable work' by *The Times*.

More importantly, Gielgud's talent had registered with his idol, as Barker revealed soon after when he referred to the production in a letter to a fellow-producer: 'I saw something of Gielgud at rehearsals once, and he struck me as having the real thing in him. A trifle too much finesse perhaps. A little apt to let his sword-blade turn just before he made the stroke . . . he was in fact not quite crude enough for his youth. But . . . I believe he may go quite far.' Barker had noticed Gielgud's tendency towards fastidiousness and showy effects at the expense of raw power, but had recognised a true theatrical sensibility. Had Gielgud known of this assessment, it would have given him some badly needed encouragement.

His hopes rose again with a revival of *Berkeley Square*, a play of disillusion and romantic passion across the centuries freely based on Henry James's unfinished novel *The Sense of the Past*. It was already running at the Lyric with Leslie Howard and Jean Forbes-Robertson in the leading roles. The plan was for Gielgud to understudy Howard, and take over for a few matinées while the actor watched from the front in order to prepare for a transfer to Broadway. 'It will be a tough job, as it's such a huge part – imaginatively and practically,' Gielgud confided to Gabrielle Enthoven. 'The play isn't produced at all this time, it's even scrappier than it was before, and parts of it drag appallingly – but I love it all the same.' But this rare opportunity to tackle a part of substance in the West End was cruelly snatched away from him when the impresario Gilbert Miller came to rehearsals and announced he was not right for the part. Instead he had to endure the frustration of understudying Howard for a few weeks.

He made two further brief appearances on the little theatre and stage society circuit. *Red Sunday*, which had four performances at the Arts, offered him a potentially interesting role as Trotsky. A play about Russia before and after the revolution by the critic Hubert Griffith, it was directed by Komisarjevsky, who impressed Gielgud all over again with his consummate ability to handle actors and orchestrate a scene. For yet another Slav part Gielgud donned shabby clothes and his Trofimov wig and spectacles, and was widely praised for a sensitive and clever portrait of Trotsky. Several West End managers made offers for the play, but the Lord Chamberlain refused to license it, on the grounds that characters such as the Tsar, Lenin and Trotsky should not be depicted on stage.

Gielgud's other appearance was in *Douaumont*, a play by Eberhard Wolfgang Moeller about a German soldier, whose return from the front in the Great War is compared to the return of Ulysses. Directed by Peter Godfrey, presented by the Stage Society at the Prince of Wales, and starring Esmé Percy and Martita Hunt, it was, according to Farjeon, 'a thoroughly hollow play'. Gielgud, as the Prologue, took no part in the story itself, but, clothed in evening dress and a cloak, recited excerpts from Homer between the scenes. *The Times*, commending the beauty and rhythm of his language, noted that he 'used his brief opportunities with so much discernment that his appearances before the curtain were more moving than the play'.

Gielgud was 'getting the notices', but virtually no money. In the spring of 1929 he wrote in frustration to Gabrielle Enthoven: 'I'm a bit sick of rehearsing all this time, and making no money – cursed invention!!' One alternative source of income was the burgeoning film industry, now about to move out of the silent era. However, many actors looked down on the new medium. Gielgud shared this attitude, but he was also an avid filmgoer, which was rare for a stage actor. He went to the cinema three or four times a week, mostly to foreign films, many of them at the old Shaftesbury Pavilion. He saw the D.W. Griffiths silent classics starring Lillian Gish, the Chaplin and Keaton films, *The Cabinet of Dr Caligari* and the early Erich von Stroheim pictures, and admired in particular stars such as Emil Jannings and Conrad Veidt.

Five years earlier, in 1924, he had appeared in *Who is the Man?*, an adaptation of *Daniel*, the play in which Sarah Bernhardt had made her farewell London appearance. Isabel Elsom starred, and Gielgud played a sculptor addicted to morphine. By his own account he flung himself around in a melodramatic manner, making anguished expressions and feeling acutely embarrassed, while a piano and violin duo played popular melodies off-camera to inspire in him the required emotions. Yet perhaps he was not as terrible as he thought; one critic wrote: 'Mr John Gielgud gets over the neurotically pitiful Daniel with much artistry.'

Now, in 1929, he risked another bout with the cameras. *The Clue of the New Pin*, an Edgar Wallace thriller directed by Arthur Maude, also starred Benita Hume and Donald Calthrop. Gielgud played the maniac villain, disguised in a long black cloak, a black wig, spectacles and false teeth. Seeing himself on screen in these films was a chastening experience: he was horrified by his 'vulturine grimaces', the 'violent and affected mannerisms' of his walk and gestures. He also found it exhausting having to repeat an emotional scene time and time again. These early, negative experiences on the set were to colour his outlook on film work for many years.

At this difficult time in his career he at least had the backing of the Terry family. A moment of special encouragement came after the performance of *Hunter's Moon*, when Fred Terry came round to his dressing-room and announced: 'My dear boy, you are one of the family now.' Gielgud's pride at being given the Terry seal of approval knew no bounds.

As if on cue, he almost immediately achieved the breakthrough he had longed for. *The Lady with a Lamp* was a play by Reginald Berkeley having a successful run at the Garrick. Gielgud had joined the company for the last month, replacing Leslie Banks, to play the part of the man in love with Florence Nightingale. In the title-role was an actress whom he already admired hugely, and who was soon to work with him in some of his finest productions. Edith Evans was recognised as the finest exponent of English comedy. Plucked from a hat shop in 1912 by William Poel to play Cressida in an Elizabethan Stage Society production, she had toured with Ellen Terry, then spent several years playing older character parts in modern plays. Turning her back on the West End to play the Serpent and the She-Ancient in Shaw's *Back to Methuselah*, she finally achieved stardom under Playfair at the Lyric, Hammersmith, with Millamant in *The Way of the World*. After seeing it Gielgud had written: 'Edith Evans gave a marvellous performance, really at last worthy of her critics' everlasting praise.'

A plain woman with a distinctive musical voice and perfect pitch, she had wonderful timing and control, and an extraordinary capacity to make herself attractive, even beautiful, by totally inhabiting her character. Offstage she was imperious and aloof, being wary of strangers and of the superficial compliments endemic in the theatre. Other actors found her difficult to get to know: Sybil Thorndike observed that when you approached her it was as if there was a placard round her neck saying 'Keep Off the Grass'. Gielgud, fascinated but in awe, kept a respectful distance.

His big moment in the play was the scene in which, brought in on a stretcher, he had to die in Florence Nightingale's arms. He was under strict instructions from Edith Evans, who was co-producer, not to present such a romantically clean appearance, and duly covered himself in dirt from head to foot. A letter he wrote to Gabrielle Enthoven a week into the run makes clear his unhappiness with the scene, despite its obvious impact on the audience: 'You're right about the death scene – timing or something, and I'm afraid of being theatrical to excess. Besides I hear them crying in front, and get very embarrassed!! Pure chichi, of course – I'll get it right in time, I hope.'

One evening the actor Harcourt Williams came to see the show. Having just been appointed by Lilian Baylis as the new producer for the Shakespeare Company at the Old Vic, he was putting together a group of actors for his first season. He had seen Gielgud in *The Insect Play* and *Robert E. Lee*, but not been impressed: 'At that time he had a queer body carriage from the heels backwards,' he remembered. Later he heard of his work at Barnes under Komisarjevsky, and was struck by his performance in *Ghosts*. Watching him in *The Lady with a Lamp*, he realised how much he had developed. 'Artistically he had grown out of all knowledge, and the fact that he had so grown appealed to me,' he recalled. Over lunch at the Arts he offered Gielgud the position of leading man in his Old Vic company.

This was a thrilling and totally unexpected opportunity for a young actor just turned twenty-five. Yet Gielgud was in two minds whether to accept, and asked for time to consider. As he cast his net far and wide for advice, most of his friends urged him to turn it down. They argued that it would be foolish to give up the prestige of working in the West End, which anyway paid much better. While the suggested salary at the Old Vic was £10 a week for nine months' unstinting repertory work, Gielgud was getting four or five times that for West End appearances.

These were reasonable arguments, and yet the Old Vic offer was immensely attractive. While he had gained valuable experience in countless Sunday-night and club theatre productions, Gielgud's career in the West End since *The Constant Nymph* had been essentially a failure. 'I found that managers thought of me chiefly as a type for neurotic, rather hysterical young men,' he recalled. Stars such as Gladys Cooper and Gerald du Maurier thought he took himself too seriously, that his acting was too intellectual. Yet it was this element in his make-up that drew him to Chekhov and Shakespeare. 'Walking on' at the Old Vic eight years before had increased his love of Shakespeare, and a visit to Stratford had made him long to be in the company there. The words of Ellen Terry remained permanently in his mind. But his experience of the plays was still sadly limited.

There was a further consideration. He realised that the Old Vic would be a good place to learn about other aspects of theatre. Watching Komisarjevsky and Barker at work he saw that, apart from their talent and technical skills, a driving passion for the theatre lay behind their work. Recognising a similar passion in himself, he began to harbour secret desires to follow in their footsteps. Appearing on stage eight times a week was no longer a rewarding enough activity: 'If I could use my own enthusiasm, or find someone to teach me how to use it constructively, I might perhaps in time learn how to handle plays, and actors too, and experiment in putting some of my own ideas to a practical test.'

Still undecided, he boldly interrupted Edith Evans's sacred post-matinée sleep to seek her opinion. Five years previously she had played Helena in Basil Dean's production of *A Midsummer Night's Dream*. Greatly dissatisfied with her performance, she decided she must 'find out how to play Shakespeare', and that the Old Vic was the place to do it. 'Everyone, or nearly everyone, thought I was mad,' she recalled. 'But I knew where I ought to be, and I went there.' She was the first star West End actress to join the Old Vic, and her season was a triumph. When Gielgud turned up in her dressing-room she talked to him at length about her experience there, and advised him to accept the offer if he was serious about Shakespeare. Her advice proved decisive: the next day he went to meet the legendary Lilian Baylis.

The Old Vic's eccentric manager was a remarkable woman. Short and dumpy, dowdily dressed, she was variously likened to a social worker, a seaside landlady and a parish visitor. With her thick glasses, podgy face, slight squint and drooping mouth – probably the result of Bell's palsy – and a rasping voice that mixed the tones of south London and her native South Africa, she seemed an unlikely theatre manager. Yet for over thirty years she had selflessly devoted her life to the Old Vic, turning it into the country's true 'home of Shakespeare'.

She never read a play, and knew little about the technique of acting. Her secret lay in her deep, naive religious faith, and her unswerving belief that she was an instrument of God, who had given her the Vic as her life's work. Theatre, she believed, had great power to do good or evil, and in her championing of the Old Vic she proved an irresistible force. She was bossy, brusque and tactless, and often crushing in her criticisms: 'Well, dear, you've had your chance and missed it,' she told one actor. But she was also immensely shrewd and practical, and loyal to her producers. Unmarried and childless, she had a strong maternal streak: actors in her companies were 'my boys and girls', the Old Vic audience 'my people', for whom only the best was good enough – and that meant Shakespeare.

She lost no opportunity of promoting the Old Vic, declaring regularly: 'All this talk about a National Theatre – we *are* a National Theatre!' But she was notoriously penny-pinching, and famous for paying actors badly. If they asked for a rise, she would set her two terriers loose on their ankles, or consult God, who invariably sided with the management ('Sorry, dear, but God says No'). Gielgud arrived in her office in his best suit, trying to look arrogant and starry. But his attempt to fool this astute businesswoman backfired. Although the Terry connection impressed her – she spoke appreciatively of Ellen Terry's interest in the Vic – she informed Gielgud brusquely: 'We'd love to have you, dear, but we can't afford stars here.' Sensing his keenness to tackle some good Shakespearean parts, she tempted him with Romeo and Richard II, which excited him, and Antonio in *The Merchant of Venice*, which didn't. Other parts, she explained, would be decided later; no doubt he'd like to play Hamlet, 'but Gyles Isham is coming to us too, so of course we shall have to see'. By the end Gielgud was begging her to let him join the company.

Gielgud had made friends with Martita Hunt during *Holding Out the Apple*, and he made it a condition of his coming that she was engaged as his leading lady. But Lilian Baylis offered her ten shillings less than had been originally agreed with Williams, to the latter's despair. Gielgud himself held out for fifty shillings more than she initially offered him. Eventually Williams got her to agree, and brought the final contract to Gielgud's dressing-room at the Garrick for his signature. Even then he hesitated, as Williams remembered: 'We both paced up and down the room – short paces, for theatre dressing-rooms built in 1880 were not very spacious – and at last John said, "Give me a pen.""

One of the few people to have urged him to go to the Old Vic was Leslie Faber. Soon after taking his advice Gielgud read in the paper that his friend had left the cast of the play he was in because of illness. When he called at his flat, he was told that Faber had died that morning. Gielgud was stunned by the loss, which had come, he told a friend, 'just when I was most relying on him to guide my faltering footsteps on the ladder'. A decade later he confessed: 'There is no friend that I have more often missed, no actor whose loss I have more often regretted, than Leslie Faber.' His death made him determined to prove himself worthy of Faber's belief in his ability, by succeeding at the Old Vic.

Just before the season began Gielgud went secretly to the theatre, eager to see his name on the posters outside. Instead he saw only Shakespeare's. 'Was it for this I had forsaken a good salary in the West End, a comfortable dressing-room for myself, new suits, late rising, and suppers at the Savoy?' he mused as he walked back across Waterloo Bridge.

PART TWO

Lord of the West End

1929–1937

9

The Old Vic

Isn't it lovely, the dear boy is blossoming!
(Lilian Baylis, 1930)

ON 27 August 1929, sporting a red carnation in his buttonhole, Gielgud arrived at the Old Vic for the first rehearsal of *Romeo and Juliet*, the opening production of the theatre's sixteenth season of Shakespeare. Conditions were hardly less austere than when he had walked on eight years before. Lilian Baylis ran her theatre like a village hall. There was virtually no publicity, since she refused to 'waste money' on advertising the programme and performance times. The design budget was precisely £20 per production. The scenery was cheap and tatty, the costumes, endlessly recycled from past productions, worn and faded. The theatre smelt variously of size, sawdust and stale tea, or of the sausages and kippers Lilian Baylis cooked in her office and the stage box. The dressing-rooms were tiny and primitive: Gielgud's was next to the lavatory, and about the same size.

Having sacrificed his chance of going to Oxford, Gielgud gained a different but arguably more valuable education at the Old Vic. He could not have found a more suitable tutor for his course in Shakespeare than Harcourt Williams. A sweet, gentle and trusting man, a conscientious objector during the Great War, he was known universally as Billie, and as a vegetarian lived on Bemax and bread and cheese. At rehearsals he wore old flannel trousers, an open-necked shirt and sandals, and rushed up and down pulling at his untidy hair – one actor likened him to 'a harassed bee-keeper'. But behind the eccentric façade was a fanatical enthusiast for the theatre. As an actor he had been in Benson's company, worked with Barker, and been coached by Ellen Terry, who thought him a brilliant actor. As a producer he preferred, unlike Dean or Atkins, to coax actors rather than bully them. His inclusive method, ahead of its time, suited Gielgud perfectly, and a mutual respect helped to create a wonderfully fruitful working relationship.

Williams was an imaginative producer, with a great feel for Shakespeare's poetry, and a desire to introduce a more psychological interpretation of character. He was also a man with a mission: to get rid of the mannered 'Shakespearean voice', to break down the deliberate verse-speaking which made productions over-long and tedious to watch. There was to be no more traditional 'business' based on what Garrick, Kean, Irving or Tree had done; he would only use ideas that were his or the actors' invention. Scene-changes, which often held up the action, should be swift and simple. Above all, the text would be inviolate. Gielgud, with his quick, impatient temperament, embraced these ideas, and became Williams's staunchest ally in his reforming crusade.

Williams was directly inspired in his 'battle against the slow-coaches' by the ideas of Poel and Barker, both of whom he knew personally. He discussed his first two productions with Barker, who was to give him invaluable advice and moral encouragement throughout the season. Gielgud, already a disciple, was now exposed through Williams to Barker's innovative ideas on staging Shakespeare.

Williams had also absorbed Craig's ideas on non-naturalistic design, and discussed them with him. As rehearsals began Craig wrote to him: 'I hear that you are now at the Old Vic as producer, and that Jack Gielgud is with you. I hope you will have a good time and put through some of the things you've wanted to do . . . and don't be unhappy because you can't get them all through.' Craig underlined his belief in Williams in a letter to Gielgud, advising his cousin: 'Stick absolutely loyal to Harcourt Williams, then great things are possible.' It was to prove good advice.

The first rehearsal for *Romeo and Juliet*, with the Old Vic 'students' perched round the room clutching their Shakespeare volumes, took Gielgud back in time. 'It was rather like the classes at the academy all over again,' he remembered. 'Lilian Baylis arrived, and made her usual motherly opening-of-term speech, while we all stood round sheepishly summing each other up.' Williams had put his faith in a young company with little experience of Shakespeare. Even Martita Hunt, who had trained with Sarah Bernhardt and shone in Chekhov and Ibsen, had virtually none. Gyles Isham had been a sensational Hamlet for the OUDS, but Richard Ainley and Adele Dixon were relatively untried. Only Brember Wills, Margaret Webster and Donald Wolfit – who had already toured Shakespeare round the provinces for two seasons – had any significant experience of the repertoire.

Williams quickly made his intentions clear: 'Ladies and gentlemen, please – all of you – right through this play I want pace – pace – pace.' He had the proofs of Barker's Preface to the play, and encouraged the actors to read it. Gielgud was excited by his ideas, and discussed them avidly over lunch with Martita Hunt. On their way back they looked into the auditorium, and in his mind's eye Gielgud recalled the fine productions he had seen there. He slipped into the ramshackle wardrobe room, and gazed at the well-worn robes and doublets, the crowns and armour. Among the costumes he saw the black velvet robe with ermine sleeves which Ernest Milton had worn as Richard II, and which he himself would soon be wearing. Up front it had looked magnificent, but close to it was shabby and moth-eaten. Despite this disappointment, the idea of the continuity of theatrical tradition stirred his romantic imagination. 'I went back to the rehearsal bursting with a great desire to prove myself worthy of the noble inheritance I had come to the Old Vic to claim,' he recalled.

Deciding to take literally the Chorus's description of 'two hours' traffic of our stage', Williams brought a stop-watch to rehearsals. This intimidated some of the more established actors, who resisted the idea. Even the younger actors struggled with his notions of verse-speaking: 'They had no vowel sense,' he recalled, 'the words are clipped out of all recognition and, what is worse, have no carrying power.' But Gielgud and his leading lady proved the exceptions. After the dress rehearsal Williams's wife Jean Sterling Mackinlay, also a producer, wrote to him: 'You will be criticised of course for excessive speed, but how worth while, when one gets the whole spirit and vitality of the play. And as you say the pendulum will settle in its swing when everyone is used to it. All cannot have Martita's skill in this respect, and Gielgud's.'

Her predictions proved correct. The critics made sardonic comments about 'steeple-chasing exercises' and a 'world speed record'. But Gielgud, and Adele Dixon as Juliet, were generally exempted from such criticism. Gielgud was seen as a fresh, handsome young Romeo, who spoke the verse with feeling and delicacy, and a good sense of its rhythm. But the *Punch* critic noted a familiar problem: 'Mr John Gielgud was not, I think, quite the ardent lovesick stripling of our imagination. He was adequate in elocution (occasionally a little noisy), spirited in movement, but there was no quality of rapture in his wooing.'

Although he had progressed since his ill-fated 1924 Romeo, Gielgud thought this second attempt 'rather a failure', finding it required more technique than he yet possessed. Harcourt Williams too was disappointed, describing it later as his least interesting performance at the Vic: 'He certainly gave little hint of the power to come, albeit it was a thoughtful, well-graced performance, and he spoke beautifully,' he recalled. He felt Gielgud had failed to come to grips with the final scenes, 'to bring off the distracted joy jolted by disaster into full manhood; the ecstasy, too, of the last moments transcending death escaped him'.

The audience, however, were enthusiastic. Unlike theatres in the West End, which relied on 'the carriage trade', the Old Vic had a regular, young, serious and well-informed audience, who were attracted by the combination of informality – casual dress was the norm – low prices, and a serious classical programme. The writer Hugh de Selincourt noted the atmosphere in the interval of a performance of *Romeo and Juliet*: 'Full of keen young'uns, bright-eyed with enthusiasm. The feel of the whole place was RIGHT.' Those in the gallery were especially vocal in their criticism, fierce in their loyalties, and possessive of their favourites. Unlike the smart, well-heeled West End audiences, they cared little for reputations or critical opinion, and were notoriously hard to please. New faces were not welcome until they had proved their worth, and Gielgud had yet to do that.

Some of the regulars were not happy about the radical change in style. Williams received several poisonous anonymous letters, and was verbally abused at the stage door by his more fanatical critics. Hurt and disheartened, he was 'consumed with a desire to fling up the whole thing'. But the criticism drew the company together. 'We ranged ourselves behind Harcourt Williams with increasing devotion,' Gielgud recalled. 'We did our best to cheer him up, and hide the poorer notices from him.'

Williams pressed on with his reforms in *The Merchant of Venice*, in which Gielgud played Antonio. Barker saw half the production, and noted: 'Antonio good, if a little timid.' Williams himself thought Gielgud brought sympathy and distinction to the part. 'He made a young and picturesque Antonio,' he remembered. 'He was far less solemn than most Antonios, and never dreary.' *The Times*, however, thought him miscast, as he did himself. Most critics disliked the production: there were references to its 'breakneck speed' and 'a general tendency to gabble'.

When Williams received more anonymous letters he offered his resignation. It was refused. Lilian Baylis had read no Shakespeare, and was thought never to have sat through a performance in the Old Vic. Yet she had an instinct about her producers, and a feel for what would go in her theatre. She also had a hatred of the critics, whose judgement of her actors she believed too hasty: 'Why should we give the bounders free seats and then let them earn their wretched livings by saying scurrilous things about us?' she said. Now she scolded Williams for his cowardice. How, she argued, could a man who had stood up for his pacifist principles in wartime give up in the face of a few adverse reviews and abusive letters? Moved and heartened by her support, Williams returned to his task with renewed energy and greater authority.

'Harcourt Williams was our great strength and rallying point,' Gielgud recalled. 'He ruled us by affection and by the trust he had in us, a trust almost childlike in its naivety.' Unusually for the time, Williams gave his actors a lot of freedom in rehearsal, and encouraged their ideas. He now began to have lunchtime discussions about the plays with Gielgud and Martita Hunt, inviting them to make suggestions. 'We'd chatter away and give him countless ideas,' Gielgud recalled. It was these sessions that fuelled his now intense longing to produce.

As a *de facto* assistant producer he grasped the chance with relish. He roughed out ideas for sets, and suggested John Masefield's Shakespeare plot summaries be printed in the programme. His ideas found favour with Williams who, according to Margaret Webster, was 'much influenced by his two leading actors'. Gielgud also began to be in demand as a speaker: 'I have for my sins to lecture at a girls' school in Chichester on Sunday,' he told Gabrielle Enthoven. 'Might I borrow your big Shakespeare again? It gives me such moral support.'

The Old Vic traditionally staged an occasional non-Shakespearean production, usually a well-tried Sheridan or Goldsmith play. Williams, however, chose Molière's trenchant satire on hypochondria and the medical profession, *Le Malade Imaginaire*. This gave Gielgud his first chance since *Love for Love* at the Oxford Playhouse to play in classic high comedy. With Brember Wills in the title-role, he played the minor part of Cléante, suitor to the *malade*'s daughter, played by Adele Dixon. Williams thought the two of them played and sang the delightful music lesson scene 'with just the right touch of burlesque', and the critics thought Gielgud debonair and decorative. His performance gave glimpses of his developing comedic skills, as well as further evidence of his pleasing tenor voice.

The fourth production of the season was *Richard II*, for which Williams decided to moderate the pace slightly. The role of the young, headstrong and self-absorbed king luxuriating in his downfall had always attracted Gielgud. The fact that Leslie Faber had also played it gave the role an extra resonance. Previously he had been impressed mainly by the play's pictorial qualities; now he became excited by the beauty of the poetry, the exquisite melancholy of the later speeches. He also identified readily with Richard: 'I seemed to be immediately in sympathy with that strange mixture of weakness and beauty,' he recalled. 'He was a shallow, spoiled young man, vain of his looks, with lovely things to say. I fancied myself no end in the part, but even that seemed to help my acting of it.'

He was supported by Gyles Isham as Bolingbroke and Brember Wills as John of Gaunt. On the first night the Old Vic audience rose to their feet, shouting and stamping their delight at 'their' new young actor's moving interpretation, and his fine speaking of the verse. Eric Phillips, playing Bushy, recalled the occasion: 'The infinite variations of his beautifully modulated voice hypnotised both audience and actors. It was an instinctive creation, drawing breath from inconsistency, conceived by the actor not in parts but as a whole. The turn of his head, the curve of his body, the movements of his hands each told a story of their own, and were beautiful to watch.'

The playwright Christopher Fry, then twenty-one, remembers the delicate balance he achieved in the speech in Pomfret Castle. 'The precision with which he was creating it without losing the inner music was remarkable. It had a most extraordinary effect on me, and I can hear it to this day.' Writing in the *Old Vic Magazine*, Harcourt Williams observed that 'his playing of the Coronation scene will live in my mind as one of the great things I have witnessed in the theatre'. Of all the Richards he had seen, 'none have touched his poetic imagery and emotional power'.

The critics showered Gielgud with praise: his Richard was masterly, exquisite, beautifully controlled. 'This young actor is profiting visibly from his repertorial experience, and grows steadily in power,' Horace Horsnell wrote. Only Agate, who thought the part the most subtle in all Shakespeare, had reservations: Gielgud, he felt, had been unable to bring out the artist side of Richard's dual nature. But he admitted that 'the other half of the character, the weakly, understandable half, was beautifully presented, with a command of noble pose and gesture, a gracious melancholy mien, and a lovely handling of the language to which one would not refuse the highest admiration'. It was Gielgud's most important review to date.

Public demand forced the Old Vic to revive the production shortly after Christmas. Its success boosted Gielgud's confidence: 'I had a tremendous kick from playing the part, and felt I'd found something I could do well,' he recalled. He now settled in to the Old Vic's demanding routine. Each play had just three weeks' rehearsal, and was performed only thirteen times, sometimes alternating with another production. Rehearsing one play during the day, performing another in the evening, attending dress rehearsals at the weekend: all this put a heavy strain on the actors. Yet Gielgud, his spare frame bursting with energy, revealed a stamina that was to prove one of his great assets over the years. He thrived on the work, and the speed with which the productions were staged. 'They were whipped on very quickly, and the results were very exciting, though often unfinished,' he remembered. 'It was a marvellous training-ground.'

For the next production, *A Midsummer Night's Dream*, Harcourt Williams again broke with tradition, inspired by Barker's controversial and mould-breaking 1914 production at the Savoy. He went a step further than Barker, dressing the lovers in Jacobean costume, making Bottom and the 'rude mechanicals' English yokels of the Warwickshire countryside, and replacing the Mendelssohn music with English folk music and dances collected by Cecil Sharp. Once again there was opposition, including anonymous letters. Even Lilian Baylis was heard to say: 'I suppose I'm old-fashioned, but I do like my fairies to be gauzy.' Williams referred to 'a battle royal' with the company, who for once thought he was going too far. Gielgud, however, supported him steadfastly. In an article in the *Old Vic Magazine* he spelt out his support for experiment and fresh ideas, revealing his passionate concern to keep Shakespeare fresh and alive:

If we are content to resign Shakespeare to our bookshelves and only play him traditionally, the interest in him will die out among audiences more and more. We cannot hope that among all the experiments there will be more than an occasional success, but that is so with all experiments. And we must remember that the isolated success among these experiments will probably establish the tradition which the next generation of actors will have to break ... Judge fairly of our creations apart from the pre-conceived ideas you have of the characters, either in your imaginations or from pictures, or from other productions you have seen. You go to any other kind of play with open minds, so why not to Shakespeare too?

Gielgud was now a spokesman for change and a key prop to Harcourt Williams, who began to rely on him for support and ideas. He even allowed him to take other actors aside and rehearse them separately. 'John's influence in the company was always electric,' he recalled. 'He sparked with ideas and would beget ideas in other people which would spark back again, and even our disagreement was constructive.'

In the *Dream* Gielgud was a dark-faced Oberon, while Puck was played by a guest actor. Small and sprite-like, Leslie French was a trained dancer and boy chorister. He and Gielgud became good friends, developing on stage what Williams described as 'a perfect camaraderie of acting: the one gay, elegant gossamer, the other witty, buoyant, quicksilver in motion, but always of the same spirit sphere as his master'. French ascribed the success of their partnership to a mutual sympathy and love of mischief: 'John was a lovely man, and we clicked absolutely. It was a marvellous rapport, we each seemed to know what the other one wanted, and be able to give it. He had a tremendous sense of fun. Sometimes it was difficult to get through a scene without laughing. I used to improvise a little, and he liked that, he liked a giggle.'

The first night of the *Dream* roused the Old Vic audience to a pitch of excitement unequalled since Atkins's landmark production of *Peer Gynt*, in which Gielgud had played a troll. The quicksilver production played to packed houses, and was much admired by the critics who, Williams recalled, 'came over to our side wholeheartedly'. Ivor Brown wrote approvingly: 'No endless trippings of fairies in muslin, no flights on wires, no droves of rabbits and small deer, but just the play as it might have happened "on the night of production". What a blessed change is here.'

Gielgud felt his verse-speaking was improving. 'It gave me a wonderful sense of power to feel that I was beginning to control the lovely language, which at rehearsals moved me so much that tears would spring to my eyes.' However, according to French 'his Oberon was all voice'. This criticism, which was to become a familiar one, was also made by some of the critics: Farjeon thought him 'a musical if rather meaningless Oberon'. But the production exploited the humour in the play, and Gielgud's performance, according to *The Times*, was not one of mere vocal beauty: 'Mr Gielgud's Oberon knows exceptionally well how to be a monarch and a poet, with a discreet tongue in his cheek and a twinkle in his eye.'

The company were helped with the dances and movement in the *Dream* by a young woman Lilian Baylis had taken on to develop ballet alongside the Old Vic's opera and Shakespeare. Ninette de Valois, who had recently worked with Diaghilev, was soon to launch the pioneering Vic-Wells ballet company. 'I used to give deportment lessons or something dotty to Miss Baylis' boys, as we called them,' she remembers. 'It was the fashion to have a choreographer help a pro-ducer, and I used to do all the entrances and exits with them.' She remembers Gielgud's personality and impact: 'He was the one that people spoke about with a lot of awe, as if he was going to do something. He was talented, good looking, and very nice.'

The company's pacey, uncluttered style was now becoming accepted even by the diehards in the audience. *Julius Caesar*, the first production of 1930, was praised by the critics for injecting freshness and psychological insight into a play that was often treated as little more than a series of famous speeches. Williams felt Gielgud's Antony fulfilled his aim of bringing out the politician as much as the soldier, and getting away from the pretty juvenile idol which had become the norm. The *Morning Post* called his performance 'capital'.

Gielgud was very popular with his fellow-actors: 'His keenness, his modesty, his infinite capacity for work, spread their influence through the company,' Williams wrote at this time. The same could not be said of Donald Wolfit, a jealous man who resented Gielgud's rise, and complained constantly about the parts he had been given. Wolfit's resentments were excessive, and he rarely concealed them. Leslie French recalled the contrast with Gielgud: 'John was a very gentle person, very caring, with a lovely sense of humour. Donald was a joke, a terrible actor with no sense of humour, who believed he was the greatest in the world. Once John and I took a call together in front of the curtain; Donald collapsed in tears because he wasn't called.'

The characters and backgrounds of the two rising young stars were strikingly different. A selfish, tactless and overbearing man whose marriage was failing, Wolfit stood aloof from the other actors at the Vic. Two years older than Gielgud, a scholarship boy from a working-class provincial background, he had been struggling for nine years with only limited success to establish himself as a classical actor. 'He felt people were spoilt if they didn't make their own way,' his daughter Margaret says. 'He thought those with a theatrical background had an unfair advantage.' Gielgud, with his public-school education, com-fortable middle-class background and valuable theatrical family links, seemed to him to have had it easy. Sensitive, generous with praise for others, and fast becoming an excellent team member, he had now, with only minimal previous experience of Shakespeare's plays, suddenly become the star player. A man as prone to jealousy and self-pity as Wolfit was could find ample cause for resentment.

Physically the two could hardly be more different: Gielgud slim, elegant, endowed with a graceful beauty; Wolfit coarse-featured, saturnine and beetle-browed. Their styles of acting reflected their con-trasting appearances and temperaments: Gielgud's poetic, lyrical and romantic, Wolfit's marked by raw power, virtuosity and the grand manner. Gielgud seemed modern, Wolfit a leftover from the era of Tree and Irving. Although Gielgud admired Wolfit's power, he found his acting tasteless, and over-reliant on old actor-manager trickery. The two had nothing in common but ambition, and a passionate love of the theatre. Before long they were to clash again.

Gielgud believed he was not good as Antony, and his next part, that of the rather characterless Orlando in *As You Like It*, held no special interest for him. He did, however, enjoy himself in *Androcles and the Lion*, which Williams presented in a double-bill with *The Dark Lady of the Sonnets*. These were the first Shaw plays to be staged at the Vic, and both were uproarious successes. Shaw himself came to a matinée and received a great ovation from a crowded house. Gielgud enjoyed himself playing the Emperor, 'with a red wig, a lecherous red mouth, and a large emerald, through which I peered lasciviously'. The critics also enjoyed his performance: S. R. Littlewood suggested there was little to choose between his and Leon Quartermaine's in the original Barker production in 1913. It was a useful moment of light relief before the two formidable challenges now awaiting him.

With his slender build, melodious voice and highly strung sensi-bility, Gielgud would have been few producers' choice for Macbeth, a character then invariably played as a brawny Scot, and a part that few actors have triumphed in. He was as surprised as anyone when

Harcourt Williams, who had played Macbeth at the Birmingham Rep, now offered it to him. To be entrusted with a major tragic Shakespearean role that seemed to most people well beyond his range was a clear sign of Williams' belief in his potential.

As with Richard, he had held an image of Macbeth in his mind since childhood. For guidance he turned to Irving. Though he was too young to have seen Irving act, he sometimes felt he had done so. He had read all the books about him, including Ellen Terry's memoirs, and all the notices of his productions. Now he looked at the drawings of him as Macbeth in the Lyceum souvenir programmes his mother had given him. He was keen to bring out Macbeth's visionary quality as well as his weaknesses, but knew he would have difficulty suggesting his warrior side. Hoping to match Ellen Terry's description of Irving as a 'gaunt, famished wolf', he made up for the last act with bloodshot eyes and whitened hair. He even imitated Irving by carrying his sword on his shoulder in the early scenes.

At the dress rehearsal Lilian Baylis purred with pleasure to Eric Phillips, 'Isn't it lovely, the dear boy is blossoming!' Gielgud rose supremely well to the challenge of the most physically demanding of the great Shakespearean parts. He found the role exhausting, but with only three weeks' rehearsal had little time to be overwhelmed. His approach was essentially intuitive: 'I acted it for the main development and broad lines of the character, without worrying about the technical, intellectual and psychological difficulties,' he recalled. 'I played it from scene to scene as it seemed to come to me as we rehearsed.'

The first-night audience gave him a thunderous reception. The critics observed that his performance would have been astonishing in a player twice his age. For the first time he was compared to great Shakespearean actors of the past: one critic suggested there had not been a Macbeth since Irving 'to whom one could honestly give precedence either in speech, passion or imaginative power'. Ivor Brown, perhaps recalling his wounding review of Gielgud's 1924 Romeo, observed that his acting had filled out: 'It has ripened into a rich masculinity. His delivery of verse is clear, strong and various; in the vocal flow and rhetoric of acting he is the Henry Ainley of the rising generation.'

Even Agate was won over: 'In the old phrase, the actor carried us away,' he wrote. 'Vocally he was superb.' During the interval he had paid Gielgud a surprise visit. He congratulated him on doing the murder scene better than anyone he had seen, explaining that he was telling him this now as he was sure he would be unable to handle the rest of the play. Understandably self-conscious for the rest of the performance, Gielgud was astonished to read Agate's appreciative notice that Sunday, in which he admitted that 'for the first time in my experience Macbeth retained his hold upon the play till the end'.

Macbeth broke records at the Old Vic box-office. For the first time Gielgud had shown himself capable of creating a character whose nature was markedly different from his own, of playing strength as well as weakness, savagery as well as neurosis. Williams, his decision vindicated, felt he gave Macbeth weight and authority, and played the part exquisitely: 'John is never a copyist . . . yet he often makes one think of Irving.'

Gielgud was always pleased and proud when one of his Terry relatives approved of his work. His great-aunt Marion Terry, now eighty-seven, had already seen him in the *Dream*, and now came to *Macbeth*. After the performance, still in his make-up, he had gone to her box to receive her congratulations, and been moved to find an old woman with white hair and a bowed back. 'It was sad to see the great Terry relatives disabled by time at last, in spite of their powerful vitality,' he recalled.

If Harcourt Williams had helped him to make rapid progress, so too had his leading lady. The Argentinian-born Martita Hunt, three years his senior, had shown her versatility in playing Juliet's Nurse, Rosalind, Portia, Helena in the *Dream*, and now Lady Macbeth. She was a cultured, intelligent woman and a perceptive critic, and Gielgud often sought her opinion of his work. Tall, slim and elegant, with a bony, sculptured face, she was soon to gain a reputation for being 'difficult'. But as with Mrs Pat, Gielgud warmed to her offbeat, high-spirited personality, and the two became inseparable. It was a relaxed friendship: Leslie French recalled Gielgud saying: 'Martita dear, if you gather any more poise you'll fall over backwards.'

By now there could be no doubt, even in Lilian Baylis's mind, that Gielgud rather than Gyles Isham should play *Hamlet*. As with other Shakespearean parts, he had no difficulty in memorising the lines: 'I had learnt them in the womb,' he said. Yet in assuming this most challenging of stage roles, in a play that has had more written about it than any other, he was more conscious than ever of the weight of theatrical history on his shoulders.

By now he had seen a dozen Hamlets, two of them at the Vic. He had also attended a lecture given by Forbes-Roberston, during which the actor widely considered the supreme Hamlet of the previous century had spoken one of the great soliloquies. But the Hamlet he had admired most was John Barrymore's, whose interpretation had been the culmination of his stage career. Gielgud saw the production at the Haymarket in 1925 and wrote in his programme: 'Barrymore is romantic in appearance and naturally gifted with grace, looks, and a capacity to wear period clothes, which makes his brilliantly intellectual performance classical without being unduly severe, and he has tenderness, remoteness, and neurosis all placed with great delicacy and used with immense effectiveness and admirable judgement.'

In preparing his Hamlet he once again read the memoirs of Ellen Terry, Irving's Ophelia, to see how he had played a part which he had studied for fifteen years. Irving was an inspirational guide: with certain scenes, such as when Horatio tells Hamlet of his father's Ghost, Gielgud followed his reactions precisely. He was determined not to 'whitewash' or sentimentalise Hamlet, not to ignore his less pleasant aspects as others had. But he also feared giving a hotch-potch of all the performances he had seen. 'How could I seem great enough, simple enough to say those hackneyed, wonderful lines as if I was thinking of them for the first time?' he wondered.

Rehearsals alarmed him for another reason. Although Martita Hunt had told him, 'Don't be afraid to be yourself,' he found it hard to banish that fear. Macbeth had been a character part, in which he could submerge his personality behind the make-up. With Hamlet, a role in which an actor cannot *but* be himself, fear and vulnerability were holding him back, paralysing his imagination and making it impossible for him to live the part. 'All through rehearsals I was dismayed by my utter inability to forget myself while I was acting,' he recalled. 'How could I put into the part my own personal feelings – many of which fitted the feelings of Hamlet – and yet lift them to a high classical style worthy of the character?'

To add to his difficulties, Williams was keen to stage two versions: the usual heavily cut version, and 'Hamlet in its Entirety' (or 'Hamlet in its Eternity' as some weary actor called it). Rehearsing the two versions simultaneously placed terrifying demands on the company. Gielgud was also rehearsing Pirandello's one-act play *The Man with a Flower in His Mouth* and, less than a week before the *Hamlet* opening, taking part in the annual Shakespeare Birthday Festival, in which he appeared in Maurice Baring's *The Rehearsal*, and played Oberon, Antonio and Richard II in scenes from the plays. Coming at the end of a strenuous season when, as Harcourt Williams recalled, 'our nerves were strained to breaking-point', his burden was excessive.

For the first night in April the company presented the uncut version, which lasted four and a half hours, with only one interval. Around him Gielgud had Martita Hunt as Gertrude, Donald Wolfit as Claudius, and Adele Dixon as Ophelia. More than other Shakespeare plays, *Hamlet* requires a close rapport between the main character and the audience, most notably in *Hamlet*'s great soliloquies. This Gielgud achieved in electrifying fashion. Confronted with a sympathetic audience he lost his self-consciousness, and allowed his personality to come through. 'I thought, Well, unless I am myself, with all my own faults and my hates of myself, they won't be interested. I threw myself into the part like a man learning to swim, and I found that the text would hold me up if I sought the truth in it.'

A packed and excited house applauded tumultuously. The critics were dazzled: with this young, imperious and passionate *Hamlet*, Gielgud seemed suddenly to be on the threshold of greatness. Hamlet was normally tackled by leading actors later in their careers when their reputations were established: Barrymore was forty-three when he came to the part, Irving thirty-seven, Forbes-Robertson forty-four, while Benson was still playing it at seventy-two. Gielgud, little more than six months into his Shakespearean apprenticeship, was just twenty-six. For many this enhanced the tragedy of the early scenes: 'I have never seen a Hamlet so utterly thrown down by the discovery of his father's murder,' wrote E.A. Baughan. For Harcourt Williams Gielgud's youthful interpretation 'broke the heart'.

Equally crucial was the intelligence Gielgud brought to the part. J.T. Grein, who had seen Irving's Hamlet and Forbes-Robertson's, noted 'the profound study that he bestowed, not merely on the soliloquies, but on almost every line of the text, some of which shone in a new light in the illumination of his reading'. Agate picked out the same quality: 'This Hamlet is noble in conception. It has been thought out in the study, and is lived upon the stage, with the result that you feel that these things are happening to Hamlet for the first time, and that he is, here and now, creating the words which shall express the new-felt emotions.'

The acclaim within the profession was equally ecstatic. Lilian Baylis remarked during the first night: 'It's like a crowning, isn't it – after all the struggles.' In the early hours after the performance Sybil Thorndike wrote to Gielgud: 'I never hoped to see Hamlet played as in one's dreams . . . tonight it was Hamlet Complete. When you spoke your final word I said to myself what I said when I read the first chapter of *Moby Dick*, "This is too good to be true" . . . I've had an evening of being swept right off my feet into another life – far more real than the life I live in, and moved, moved beyond words.'

Marion Terry was also greatly impressed, as she wrote to her brother Fred. 'I was in the *uncomfortable* stalls for Hamlet, for just *five* hours, and didn't *want* to move . . . It's very young, very thoughtful (without dragging it for long pauses and mouthing), graceful without effort, and every word distinct, and of course he looks charming.' When she saw Gielgud afterwards to tell him how proud she was, he replied that 'he was proud of knowing he had some of the Terry blood in him, and hoped to go on doing better'. A few months later his great-aunt was dead: of the Terrys of her generation, only Fred remained.

Hamlet was a sensational success. The five performances of the complete version were sold out, with people standing throughout, and many others turned away. The production marked a significant moment in the fortunes of the Old Vic, both artistically and financially. For Harcourt Williams it vindicated the policy to which he had pinned his faith: 'It put a definite nail in the coffin of slapdash, unreasoned methods, which, however ornate and splendid, are no longer easily tolerated by press and public.' The production began to attract a wider public to the Vic: West End theatregoers crossed the river in droves. Such was the acclaim for this new, fresh young Hamlet that arrangements were immediately made to transfer the production, in its cut version, to the Queen's.

After years in which Shakespeare had rarely been sighted in the West End, for a brief moment at the start of the decade he became the most-performed playwright there. Within the space of a month audiences had the chance to see no fewer than three Hamlets – those of Gielgud, Henry Ainley and the leading German actor Alexander Moissi – and the Othello of Paul Robeson. The man behind most of these productions was the American actor and producer Maurice Browne, who had made money from staging the hugely successful *Journey's End*, produced by James Whale. Now Browne wanted to prove that there was a public for Shakespeare in the West End. He persuaded the Old Vic company to stay on at their meagre salaries, but to take a share of the profits; in return he kept seat prices low, to attract as wide an audience as possible.

His gamble was not a great success, for none of the Hamlets did very good business. At the Queen's the cheaper seats were full every night, but the stalls and dress circle were not. Gielgud was very disappointed. 'What was the use of being praised, extravagantly perhaps, by the critics if one was to fail with the public?' he mused. Yet this was hardly a 'failure'. At the first night there were twenty curtain calls, and his fan mail was his biggest yet. Many who wrote told him he was the best Hamlet they had ever seen. Gielgud was touched when his former teacher at RADA, Alice Gachet, told him: 'I have seen many Hamlets and you alone have absolutely satisfied every craving and longing in this part.' Fred Terry wrote: 'I thought him the best Hamlet I've seen in forty years. Henry Irving still holds my imagination, but John easily comes next. Young virile bearing – yet he never "tortured" Shakespeare.'

Gielgud's parents were in the audience that night, and wrote separately to him afterwards. The contrast between their two letters says a lot about their very different relationships with their son. The one from 'your critical old father' contained a brief congratulatory sentence, but went on to criticise him for losing control in the more violent speeches. Frank Gielgud also suggested a way in which he could improve one speech ('I would like you to touch your breast when referring to the aching heart within'), and ended by exhorting him to 'husband your strength with plenty of rest and proper food'. He added: 'Your mother was quietly resting when I left this morning, and her joy at your success was very moving.'

Two days later Kate Gielgud also wrote. Where her husband was formal, precise and critical, she was overflowing with emotion and approval. Her letter offers striking evidence not just of her critical perceptiveness and literary skill, but of her adoration of her son, and her profound belief in his talent:

I love your enthusiasm for the fine things in your art, your exquisite sense of rhythm and proportion, your grasp of character, your 'readings' and that great gift of translating them to the audience . . . You can dominate but I have never seen you step out of the canvas to distort the picture – only to fill it – You do not demand the centre of the stage in and out of season – but you can hold your audience spellbound by a whisper, and their eyes with a gesture. When I see *Hamlet* again I'll probably find scenes and speeches to praise individually – now it is the wholeness of your conception, the dignity, the variety in its constancy, the beauty and breadth and simplicity of the delivery of your lines – the power and restraint of it all – that fills my heart with wonder and admiration. Hamlet is many men in one – so too is John Gielgud – you understand – and you make us understand – and give us joy and delight past expression – and to no one more than your devoted mother.

Of the three Hamlets in the West End, Gielgud came off best in the critics' eyes. Ainley, now fifty and only recently back in the theatre after illness, was praised for his magnificent stage presence and the beauty of his elocution, but was thought too stagey. Moissi was deemed good in the soliloquies, but lacking in emotional strength, and too obviously reliant on technique. Gielgud, on the other hand, was praised for making Shakespeare's poetry seem natural, and for presenting a Hamlet of remarkable breadth and completeness.

Of all the glowing reviews, it was Agate's that did most to establish Gielgud as the definitive Hamlet of the age. Re-visiting the production, he wrote:

His performance is subtle, brilliant, vigorous, imaginative, tender, and full of the right kind of humour. It has elegance of body and elevation of mind, it is conceived in the key of poetry, and executed with beautiful diction. I have no hesitation whatsoever in saying that it is the high water-mark of English Shakespearean acting of our time.

From a man who idolised Irving this was praise of the highest order.

The last night of *Hamlet* at the Old Vic marked the end of the season. In the traditional curtain speech given by the leading actor, Gielgud expressed the hope that his performance would improve. The modesty was genuine: he was to be consistently dissatisfied with his own performances. The season had been a strain, as he told Gabrielle Enthoven: '*Macbeth* was awful the day you came. I was too tired to concentrate, and to jerk back for just two performances after all the *Hamlet* business was rather too much for me.' Yet Williams recalled how as Macbeth Gielgud was skilfully refining his technique: 'His resourceful ingenuity in harbouring his voice and strength to stand the physical strain of such a part was remarkable.'

During the season Gielgud had enjoyed the rehearsals, the challenge of doing a new play every three weeks, the vigorous lunchtime discussions in the pub or the station buffet at Waterloo. It had been a happy time. He loved to walk slowly home after rehearsals, mumbling his lines as he crossed Hungerford Bridge in the late afternoon sun. Friends would drop into his flat, where he had a baby grand piano, a small gramophone, a few books, and an Irish cook to do his meals. After first nights, accompanied by Martita Hunt and Leslie French, he would turn up at the smart Savoy Grill, eager not to be forgotten by the theatrical establishment.

In May he reflected on what he had gained from the experience: 'Playing in Shakespeare gives one breadth, sense of character, and ability to handle big situations in a simple, broad and effective way,' he explained. 'Such work is fascinating, and gives one the opportunity to exercise all the sides of one's equipment as an actor. I enjoyed very much playing Oberon one night and Macbeth the next. Luckily I have a wonderful memory and can make a quick study of any part.' He spoke also about verse-speaking: 'One has to practise continually, and possess a good sense of rhythm. Actors must have good ears, and Shakespeare is a wonderful trainer of ears.'

The annual report gave him full marks for versatility beyond his years and, to no one's surprise, he was invited to return the following season. Gielgud had got on well with Lilian Baylis, but he was amazed when she agreed 'without a murmur' to increase his salary to £20 a week. Once again he was uncertain if he had done the right thing. 'Alas, I must go back to the Vic,' he told Gabrielle Enthoven:

> They more or less blackmailed me into it over the contract for the Queen's, and so I trusted to the fates and gave in. I hope it will not prove to be a bad mistake – and I shall *not* expect my good friends to waste their time a second year by pestering them to come down to the performances. But the company is to be much better, I think, and we are doing fine work – so bother the West End. I shall anyhow be able to resist the ever-present danger of playing bad parts in dreadful plays because I'm hard up.

Around this time Beverley Nichols met him in a tea-shop. When Gielgud told him he was returning to the Vic 'because I don't think I act well enough yet', Nichols said he was mad not to return to the West End. 'He turned up the collar of his mackintosh, held his chin very high and said, rather sharply: "You wait and see. I may make a corner in Shakespeare one day."'

10

Matinée Idol

He was a kind of brilliant butterfly.
(Ralph Richardson, on Gielgud in 1930)

DURING the summer Gielgud eagerly accepted an invitation
from Nigel Playfair to appear at the Lyric, Hammersmith in
Wilde's 'trivial comedy for serious people', *The Importance of
Being Earnest*. He fancied himself in comedy, but had been given little
chance to show his mettle since *Love for Love* at the Oxford Playhouse.
He also welcomed the prospect of a break from his heavy
Shakespearean roles. The part of John Worthing was one which over
the years would bring him almost as much acclaim as Hamlet. The two
roles catered for contrasting sides of his personality, the romantic and
soulful on the one hand, the witty and superficial on the other.

Playfair, with characteristic panache and originality, mounted a
black-and-white-and-silver production in the style of Aubrey
Beardsley. Gielgud acted elegantly, speedily and with wonderfully
exaggerated solemnity, revealing a feel for the period, a command of
the artificiality of Wilde's language, and an ability to play comedy with
speed and precision. Darlington commended the way he slightly
exaggerated 'that admirable seriousness of his' to make 'point after
comic point'. Only Agate demurred: 'Mr Gielgud is totally unfitted for
the part, not because he is a tragic actor, but because he is a serious
one,' he wrote. Agate was never to change this view, which was soon a
minority one, of Gielgud's inability to play comedy.

The role suited Gielgud's innate stylishness and his haughty
demeanour, and the production was a roaring success, with a cast that
included Anthony Ireland as Algernon, Jean Cadell as Miss Prism and
– to Gielgud's delight – his aunt Mabel Terry-Lewis as Lady Bracknell.

She had returned to the West End during the 1920s after a long absence, to play a series of aristocratic roles. Gielgud admired her gracefulness and instinctive qualities, but her memory was now shaky, and she needed frequent prompting. She also, to his embarrassment, lacked a sense of humour, and failed to understand why the audience laughed at her lines. Despite this, her dry wit and precise delivery of Lady Bracknell's sallies were much acclaimed, and provoked a performance of equal precision from her nephew. *The Times* critic thought they were brilliant together, that they alone caught the rhythm of the play. Gielgud matched the standard set by Mabel Terry-Lewis: 'His phrasing is quick; he maintains the tension of the dialogue; he discovers the music of this astonishing artificiality.'

He also got the giggles, a habit that had already got him into trouble. In *Charley's Aunt* a veteran actor had made him giggle and then reported him to Amy Brandon-Thomas, who had lectured him severely. Now, during a poorly attended matinée at the Lyric, he succumbed again, after noticing some elderly women asleep in the stalls, 'hanging down over the edges of their seats like discarded marionettes in a Punch-and-Judy show'. He and Anthony Ireland, playing Algernon, became hysterical during the muffin scene, provoking the audience to laugh at them rather than at Wilde's witticisms. 'I was so ashamed I hardly knew how to finish the performance,' Gielgud recalled. The incident nearly got the two of them the sack. As with many actors, giggling was a form of nervous release. Yet though he considered it 'a disgraceful habit', it was one he never fully learned to control.

Gielgud's name and face began to appear regularly in newspapers and magazines. His Hamlet had turned him into a matinée idol, propelling him into the ranks of stars such as Lewis Waller, Owen Nares and Ivor Novello, men whose personalities provoked fluttering hearts and ardent worship amongst theatregoers, and deferential articles in the popular press. He acquired a 'following', and received shoals of letters, photos to be signed, flowers, books and other presents; one admirer sent him an old map of Elsinore. His adoring fans, mostly young and female, would wait patiently at the Old Vic stage door to catch a glimpse of their idol. Early in the new season, in September 1930, a reporter caught him emerging after a matinée of *Henry IV Part I*, nattily dressed in trilby hat and dark suit, and surrounded by a bevy of young women in cloche hats:

Out comes Mr Gielgud. Inside he was the fiery, youthful, impetuous Hotspur, a man of easy and gallant bearing, guaranteed to sweep the most cynical and sophisticated modern girl right off her feet. Outside, however, he is just shy John – at least he was until he got used to being a matinée idol. John can now say 'Hello, girls!' without a qualm. He carefully signs all there is to sign, warmly shakes every hand that is placed before him, and laughs himself away with a 'Good-bye, girls!' To which all the girls reply in ecstasy, 'Good-bye! . . . John.'

Despite his shyness, Gielgud enjoyed the attention, and his fans' enthusiasm for Shakespeare: 'I know them, they are the galleryites and the pittites, the kind of people whose support of Shakespeare makes you glad to be alive. These girls of the new generation – and the young fellows too – are a fine lot. They know their Shakespeare. I do not in the least object to their waiting until I come out. They are always so nice about it.' He was aware, though, of the need to retain some mystery. 'Some of my correspondents want to make my acquaintance personally, but I have to draw a line there.'

One adoring young fan was the translator and agent Kitty Black, then studying *Richard II* for her school certificate. 'After five minutes I realised I had fallen passionately in love with The Voice,' she remembers. 'All the other teenagers were just as mad about him, he exuded sex appeal. We used to cluster sobbing at the stage door to collect his autograph.' The director Joan Littlewood, also at school, was much affected by his Hamlet: 'It had me on the edge of my seat all afternoon,' she recalled. 'Then I rushed home to read the play, and learned "Oh what a rogue and peasant slave am I!" by heart.' Another worshipper at the shrine was the designer Tanya Moisiewitch, step-daughter of John Drinkwater. Aged sixteen, and painting scenery at the Vic, she watched dress rehearsals, and would make sketches of Gielgud. 'He obviously knew I was soppy about him, but he didn't rebuff me,' she recalled.

Gielgud was also in demand in the press. Editors sought his views on the theatre and on Shakespeare, commissioning articles and interviews that enabled him to spell out his developing ideas. His season at the Vic had convinced him of the value of teamwork and the great advantages of the repertory system: 'When you have worked with the same people for some time, you get to know instinctively what the other man will do, and are able to cover up each other's faults and help each other in countless ways,' he explained during the run of *Hamlet*. 'That is the secret of the success of the many important repertory companies abroad. I should like so much to collect six good actors for a season of plays on similar lines.' Even now he was beginning to set his sights on a company of his own.

During the summer Gielgud helped Williams to select the actors for the next season: 'I consulted John a good deal when considering the new cast, not only because I knew it was in his power to "influence" personalities that could work with him, but also because his advice was good,' Williams recalled. One decision was straightforward. Wolfit had made clear his dislike of Gielgud's Hamlet, and had unjustly accused him of influencing Williams to cut down his part for the West End, grumbling throughout the run at the Queen's. By now he was very unpopular, and to his great disappointment he was not retained. Others not re-engaged included Adele Dixon, Gyles Isham and Brember Wills. In came Leslie French as a permanent member and, among others, Gielgud's friend from RADA days, George Howe.

Finding a new leading lady to replace Martita Hunt proved problematic. Gielgud's first two candidates – Fabia Drake and Peggy Ashcroft – were unavailable. But the eventual choice was much to his liking. 'They've engaged Dorothy Green for the Vic, which I am very pleased about,' he told Gabrielle Enthoven. A versatile, unselfish and often under-rated actress, she had played most of the major Shakespearean roles with Benson's company, and worked with Fagan, Playfair and Komisarjevsky. She had been Rosalind when Gielgud, aged eight, had seen the play for the second time. He had also seen her play all the major parts at Stratford in 1925, when her Cleopatra had been acclaimed as the finest of her generation.

He was less certain about another new recruit. Ralph Richardson, two years his senior, with his precise, distinctive voice and oddball face, was showing a flair for playing 'ordinary' characters, and had begun to play minor Shakespearean roles, most recently Roderigo in the Robeson *Othello*. Williams liked his vitality, his humour, and his 'dash of impertinence', but Gielgud doubted his suitability. However, Williams knew Gielgud would not stay for a further season, and saw Richardson as his successor.

At first there was mutual wariness between the two young actors. 'We were inclined to circle round each other like suspicious dogs', Gielgud remembered. Richardson thought him affected and conceited, too much the dandy: 'I found his clothes extravagant, I found his conversation flippant,' he recalled. 'He was the New Young Man of his time, and I didn't like him.' He summed up the essential difference between them: 'He was a kind of brilliant butterfly, while I was a very gloomy sort of boy.' On the first day of rehearsals he told Gielgud that he had almost rejected the Old Vic offer because of his presence in the company. Gielgud, who found this bluntness endearing, roared with laughter.

Their stage partnership began with *Henry IV Part II*, which Gielgud had suggested; he now had a voice in the selection of plays. But rather than the noble Prince Hal, he opted to play the fiery and impetuous Hotspur. It seemed a risky choice, not least vocally, for a character supposedly 'thick of speech'. On the first night Gielgud's following was out in force: there was standing room only, and several women fainted at the back of the stalls. The critics loved his swashbuckling performance. 'He plunged into the part of Hotspur with enormous energy and gusto,' observed A.E. Wilson. 'He played with strength and variety, and filled the lines of splendid rhetoric with fire and impetuosity.'

Gielgud displayed a dash and vigour that had rarely been seen before, and suggested his Terry blood had been of great help: 'For one thing, I know, it has made me play for melodrama. Sometimes, when I have been doubtful about a scene or a character, I have just let go and gone for it, realising that acting is worthwhile for its own sake. I was not pleased with myself as Hotspur, but the audiences seemed to like it, and I feel I must thank the Terry part of me for that.' But he could also thank a growing confidence in his own ability, and his increasingly fruitful partnership with Richardson.

Williams thought them 'an astoundingly happy pair' as Hal and Hotspur, Gielgud proving 'vivid and debonair' and Richardson 'real and witty'. When it came to the sword-fight 'the encounter had a thrilling quality . . . all gallant and full of young life'. The combatants, however, saw it very differently. Neither was brave physically, and both were apprehensive about the fight, which was under-rehearsed. Gielgud's anxiety increased when Richardson called out audibly during the fight: 'Left . . . right . . . now you hit me, cocky . . . now I hit you.'

It was the next production, *The Tempest*, which marked the real beginning of their friendship. Richardson was struggling with the role of Caliban, and Gielgud offered to run through a scene with him after rehearsals. He accepted grudgingly, but when Gielgud made some shrewd suggestions about ways of illuminating Caliban's character, he changed his attitude. 'The scales fell from my eyes,' he recalled. 'I thought, "This chap I don't like is a very great craftsman, he's a wonderful fellow, he knows an awful lot about his job."' Richardson had discovered the man of the theatre behind the flippant dandy. It was the start of one of the most rewarding relationships of Gielgud's life.

Gielgud saw in Richardson something of the temperament and integrity of his old friend Leslie Faber. Yet apart from a shared passion for Shakespeare it was an unlikely friendship, a clear case of the attraction of opposites. Richardson was fascinated by machinery, and delighted in fast cars and motor-bikes; Gielgud was the the least mechanical of men. Richardson took an interest in politics; Gielgud ignored them. Richardson cared little for theatrical gossip, while Gielgud found it endlessly fascinating. Richardson was by his own admission 'rather a cross man' and occasionally flew into rages; Gielgud was often impatient, but almost never lost his temper. Richardson was shrewd, cautious, often mysterious; Gielgud was impetuous, mercurial and often tactless. Richardson was heterosexual, and married to the actress Kit Hewitt; Gielgud was homosexual, and married to the theatre.

With *The Tempest* Williams again broke new ground. He gave it an oriental décor, and made Caliban a Mongolian monster. Both he and Gielgud were keen to avoid the traditional concept of Prospero as a venerable bearded magician. Clean-shaven, in turban, flowing robes and sandals, he looked more like an Eastern potentate.

Leslie French was the first male actor to play Ariel since the nineteenth century. He and Gielgud now wove another spell. Williams thought they 'acted together in a way that may be taken as an example of interplay between actors'. Their continuing rapport was due in part to French's refusal to be fazed by Gielgud's glowing reputation: 'The company was quite in awe of him, but I never was, I just got on tremendously well with him,' he remembered.

Gielgud rose to the challenge of playing an older character. 'Prospero, who is usually made into a dull old boy by most actors, in John's sensitive hands became a being of great beauty,' Williams recalled. The critics too were taken with the freshness and maturity of his interpretation. S. R. Littlewood declared Gielgud 'in some respects the finest – certainly the most poignantly human and dramatic – Prospero within memory'. Gielgud loved playing the part: the sublime poetry and complex character were to make it his favourite Shakespearean role.

His interpretation won another accolade from Fred Terry, who wrote to Kate Gielgud: 'John gives a fine performance – his movements were those of a man of 50, tired & worn – this is in itself (to me) a great accomplishment – I know the difficulties and tho' I watched for it I NEVER saw him "break". His voice, and delivery, are beautiful.' But the appearance of Leslie French in little more than a loincloth and a golden helmet shocked him profoundly, as it did others of his generation: 'My dear, nakedness in man or woman on the stage is abhorrent to me. It is NEVER NECESSARY . . . Nakedness is reducing an artist to the level of the slave market! And a foul slave market it is!'

Lilian Baylis also had a puritanical side. Notorious for asking actors if they were 'pure', she constantly checked up that her 'boys and girls' were not 'mating in the wings'. Ninette de Valois remembers: 'She didn't really appreciate the ballet, all she watched out for were the dirty movements, and we were always having to take things out.' But according to Leslie French, when watching the dancers she used to remark, 'All the boys have such pretty bottoms.'

He remembered that *The Tempest* was not to her liking: 'At the end of the dress rehearsal she came round, and said: "All I can say is, thank God for Leslie's legs!"' But it was Ariel's skimpy costume that gave the production its lasting memorial. 'I don't think people remember whether I was good or bad,' he said, 'they only remember that I had nothing on.' The sculptor Eric Gill invited him to pose naked for a statue of Prospero and Ariel, which now perches above the entrance to the BBC headquarters in Portland Place.

While playing Prospero Gielgud had one moment of disillusion. Gordon Craig came to a performance, but left after the opening scene. Shortly afterwards, to Gielgud's excitement, Craig invited him to lunch at the Café Royal, but then patronised him: 'I felt we ought to get to know each other, as you seem to be quite popular here in London,' he announced. He laid into Lilian Baylis, the Old Vic, and everything it stood for, and also, on the basis of a single scene, into Gielgud's performance. 'My vanity was piqued,' Gielgud recalled. 'He criticised me unmercifully, and I was hurt.' Although he was never quite sure if Craig was pulling his leg, this first meeting with his boyhood hero was a severe disappointment.

Gielgud now tackled a lighter, non-Shakespearean role in George Colman's once popular eighteenth-century play *The Jealous Wife*, a mediocre work which, as one critic put it, has nine fairly good parts and no very good one. Only Gielgud and Dorothy Green – who both 'scintillated', according to Williams – rose above the material. Ivor Brown, noting that 'the omnicompetence of John Gielgud' helped to ensure the success of their scenes, picked out the 'exquisite levity' he achieved as the mincing French coxcomb Lord Trinkett. His skill in artificial comedy was developing fast.

Armed with Barker's Preface, Williams next risked *Antony and Cleopatra*, a play many people thought as difficult to stage as *King Lear*, and one which had not been seen in London for twenty years. Few great actors have enhanced their reputation by playing Antony, and the reckless, lusty Roman was not a part for which Gielgud was obviously suited, physically or temperamentally. Williams acknowledged this, but felt that 'like all his performances, it was vibrant, colourful and romantic'. John Allen, who joined the Old Vic company two years later, felt Gielgud was convincingly virile: 'I was eighteen and highly impressionable, but I remember to this day how he and Dorothy Green made their opening lines heavily erotic.'

Gielgud himself was unhappy in the role. He read Barker's Preface and thought it brilliant, but there were whole speeches he didn't understand, and not enough time to discuss them properly: 'I wore a Drake beard and padded doublet and shouted myself hoarse and seemed to get some sort of result, but was very miscast all the same,' he recalled. Although the critics tended to agree, they also found much to praise. The *Manchester Guardian* noted that 'he has hard work to be the animal that is Antony, but he fully discovers just that subtle sensual quality, that Renaissance refinement on barbarism, which makes Antony the most exciting of all Shakespeare's Romans'. Even Agate felt Gielgud and Dorothy Green, while 'miscast for the amatory hurly-burly', acted superbly in the closing scenes, where 'there is no further question of the body. All is spirit, and to this these fine artists rendered justice.'

The production did record business, and ran for an extra week. The Old Vic audience was wildly enthusiastic: on the first night Gielgud was unable to begin his curtain speech for a full five minutes because of the applause. Barker came, saw and approved, making some technical suggestions which Williams took on board. Williams remarked: 'John Gielgud is a growing thing, and that's what makes our association so devilish exciting. Our minds run so well together in harness, with just that spice of difference, thank Heaven! that occasionally strikes vital sparks, and keeps us from getting humdrum.'

By now Gielgud, Richardson and George Howe had become an informal sub-committee, plying Williams with advice and suggestions. Their discussions began to create in Gielgud an intense longing to produce. On *Antony and Cleopatra* he worked briefly as co-producer: Williams had two minor parts, and sought his help when he was on stage. 'John threw a critical and guiding eye over my scene, and saved me from giving a reproduction of some memorised performance,' he recalled. 'He sat in front and made me toe the line.' Theirs was now a close and harmonious partnership, as Lilian Baylis observed to Williams: 'She told me how much she liked to see us working in that way, taking and giving criticism. But then we always did.'

Gielgud's potency in Shakespeare was formally recognised when Herbert Farjeon, a Shakespearean scholar as well as a perceptive critic, chose him as his actor of 1930:

To call him the cat's whiskers would ill befit his work. But perhaps I may call him the Swan's feathers. His Hamlet was a masterpiece. His Hotspur, his Richard II, his Antony scaled the peaks. In bitterness and desolation he was superb. If he sticks to Shakespeare he will be recognised as our leading actor.

The first production of the new year was a significant moment in English theatrical and musical history. For many years Lilian Baylis's aim had been to bring enlightenment – in the form of Shakespeare, opera and ballet – to the 'ordinary people' of north as well as south London. After years of battling, fund-raising and praying, she at last fulfilled her dream. On a foggy and frosty night in January 1931 the Sadler's Wells Theatre in Islington, where Mrs Siddons, Samuel Phelps and Edmund Kean had all acted, but which had been closed since 1915, re-opened with *Twelfth Night*, with Gielgud as Malvolio, Richardson as Sir Toby, and Dorothy Green as Viola.

It was an evening of great ceremony, attended by a very un-Vic-like celebrity audience: Gielgud remembered that 'the four front rows were like all the gossip columns come to life'. Before the play there were speeches by stage dignitaries, including Forbes-Robertson in one of his last public appearances. During the hour-long ceremony Gielgud became impatient: 'I was feeling that the play was the thing, and itched to speak my line, "Have you no wit, manners, nor honesty, but to gabble like tinkers at this time of night?"' After the play Lilian Baylis, who had an honorary MA from Oxford, made a speech dressed in her full academic regalia, clutching for no obvious reason a basket of fruit. Carried away by her oratory, she sent the fruit flying, Gielgud burst out laughing, and the audience followed suit. The awful solemnity hanging over the new 'people's theatre' was broken.

Twelfth Night was one of Gielgud's favourite plays, but the production was one of the least effective of the season. This was due in large measure to the poor conditions at the Wells. 'How we all detested Sadler's Wells when it was opened first!' Gielgud recalled. 'It looked like a denuded wedding-cake, and the acoustics were dreadful.' The other disadvantage was that, with two theatres available, the company now played eight times a week rather than nine times a fortnight, a much more exhausting schedule.

Gielgud thought the production poor: 'Hope you weren't too bored by the play,' he wrote to Gabrielle Enthoven. But his Malvolio was much liked by the critics. Alan Parsons thought it 'a performance of rare merit and shining intelligence', observing that he 'resolutely refuses to clown: his Malvolio was more than any "a kind of a Puritan", and one felt that he was indeed "sick of self-love"'. The clarity of his speaking was very apparent: Farjeon noticed that, despite the acoustics, he alone could be heard wherever he stood.

Gielgud was now starting to think more seriously about the actor's craft. In an eloquent article entitled 'Yes – Actors Do Work' he made clear his opposition to the star system and his growing belief in the virtues of a balanced ensemble:

> If we have no Irving today, it is because the public taste has changed. It no longer demands a melodramatic vehicle for a star actor, but expects a well-balanced cast headed by actors who can create within the limits of their parts, and can be trusted not to throw the play out of proportion, nor yet under-act selfishly to gain their effects. And so we have artists such as Cedric Hardwicke, Gwen Ffrangcon-Davies, Edith Evans, Diana Wynyard, and men like Dean and Komisarjevsky. To see these men and women at rehearsal is to watch a six-week miracle of concentration, a slow, painstaking building up, an infinite patience that will surely bear comparison with the physical efforts of the most acrobatic chorus.

He and Richardson, whose Sir Toby in *Twelfth Night* was hailed as masterly, were becoming an increasingly compelling team. This was confirmed in the revival of *Richard II*, in which Richardson was Bolingbroke. Though such a straight, blustering part might not seem tailored to his talents, in Williams' view 'he lifted the whole play to Gielgud's level'. Meanwhile Gielgud's Richard seemed to have lost none of its magic: 'I came out of Sadler's Wells having cried so much that I dared scarcely face the light,' Naomi Jacob wrote to him. Farjeon thought Gielgud spoke Richard's 'For God's sake let us sit upon the ground' speech 'more poignantly than I have ever heard it spoken'. He ended: 'Must he too one day leave the Old Vic for the West End, and dwindle into a lounge suit?'

The Vic's next offering, Shaw's delightful anti-militaristic *Arms and the Man*, gave Gielgud a chance to see the famous playwright live, and at his scintillating best. Shaw, now seventy-four, still loved to be involved in rehearsals, and entertained the company with a spirited reading of the text. Roaring with laughter at one point, he said: 'You must forgive me, I haven't read this play for a long time, and you know it's really very funny.' Gielgud thought his rendering highly amusing: 'He read with marvellous pace and skill. He seemed to enjoy himself thoroughly, as he illustrated bits of business, and emphasised the correct inflexions for his lines. We were so amused that we forgot to be alarmed.'

Gielgud was Sergius, the pompous and hypocritical upholder of chivalric ideals, while Richardson's idiosyncratic personality fitted the anti-romantic 'chocolate cream soldier' Captain Bluntschli. Shaw came to the dress rehearsal, sat muttering and groaning in the circle, gave the actors 'a leathering' and detailed notes at the end of the first act – which, Gielgud remembered, 'reduced everyone to a state of disquiet' – then vanished. Despite his adverse comments, the production was well received. *The Times* critic felt the moustachioed Gielgud had captured well Sergius's mixture of 'the heroic, the craven, the unscrupulous, the honourable, and the purely comic'.

Gielgud now returned to Shakespeare with *Much Ado About Nothing*, which had fallen out of fashion in recent years. For Gielgud it had potent family connections. As Beatrice opposite Irving's Benedick at the Lyceum, Ellen Terry had captivated audiences with her gay, swift and witty performance. Shakespeare, it was said, must have written the part with her in mind. Gielgud had been present at the first night of a production with Henry Ainley and Madge Titheradge, after which Ainley had stepped forward and, bowing to a figure half hidden in the stage box, declared: 'We have had the honour of playing before the greatest Beatrice of all time.' Gielgud had also seen Fred Terry's fine interpretation of Benedick: though only a child, he remembered 'his lovely voice and his tenderness'.

Benedick was later to become one of his most treasured roles. Fearing he could not be able to find the bluff, soldierly aspects of his character, he played on his courtly qualities. Some critics felt he achieved both: Darlington was astonished at his versatility: 'Nobody who had seen him only in Hamlet would have recognised him in the hearty young soldier and wit who wooed Beatrice last night,' he wrote. 'His Benedick is the personification of virility and spontaneous gaiety.' Agate paid him a supreme compliment, suggesting a special matinée for actors so they could learn from Gielgud 'how to speak English prose with beauty, point, and audibility'.

No Benedick can succeed without a Beatrice to match him in their battle of wits. Dorothy Green was the first in a line of actresses to partner Gielgud with consummate skill. 'There is nothing in the part that Dorothy Green could not twist around her little finger,' Williams remembered. 'She and Gielgud were now playing superbly together.' The critics agreed, noting how well they caught the spirited essence of the play, and the delight each took in the other's performance.

Gielgud had originally worn his Benedick costume for the Old Vic's annual fancy-dress ball. It had been made for him by three shy, genteel but ambitious young women. Elizabeth Montgomery and the sisters Margaret and Sophie Harris were art students and enthusiastic regulars in the cheap seats at the Vic. Collectively they used the name 'Motley', and were soon to form a partnership with Gielgud that would be of immense importance to all their careers. Margaret Harris recalled their first contact:

'We used to go many times to the Vic, and send him drawings of himself as Richard, Macbeth and other characters, painted on lampshade paper, most of them by Elizabeth. He loved them. He would pay ten shillings for each, but sometimes he'd say he would have three if he could pay 7s 6d and wait until pay day on Friday.'

Gielgud was particularly delighted by Elizabeth Montgomery's sketch of him as Richard, and postcards from it sold like hot cakes. His popularity with the younger generation was greater than ever, as the London correspondent of the *New York Evening Post* reported: 'There is a young actor in this town who has taken the place the way John Barrymore took New York, when he was known as "Jack" and was knocking the flappers out of their seats. His pictures sell like mad among the earnest young students who flock to his performances.'

By now Gielgud had decided to move on from the Old Vic. For his final part Williams invited him to choose between *King Lear* and a revival of *Hamlet*. It was a measure of his delight in taking risks that, despite Agate privately warning him not to, he opted for Lear. Any anxiety he had about playing the eighty-year-old king at the age of twenty-seven he kept private. 'Lear shrieks out to be acted, and if I may say so in all modesty, I am not terrified by the part,' he stated during rehearsals. 'Vocally I do not find it as trying as Macbeth, in which the last act is a terrific strain.' He dismissed the view that the play was unactable, arguing that it could only be really appreciated on the stage. 'Certain scenes appear to be very complicated, but they become much clearer when you begin to act them . . . Whenever I play these great tragic characters I know that Shakespeare must have been an actor.'

He knew the play well, not least through having walked on in Atkins's 1921 production. He had also seen Komisarjevsky's magnificent 1927 OUDS version, which had helped to shift opinion about the play's suitability for the stage. 'It moved me so much that after crying nearly all the time I came out of the theatre exulting in the beauty of the play,' he remembered. For Williams's production two guest actors were brought in – Robert Speaight for Edmund and Eric Portman for Edgar – while George Howe played Gloucester, Dorothy Green was Goneril, Leslie French was the Fool, and Richardson played Kent.

Gielgud felt more at ease with the part than he had with Hamlet, where 'so much of oneself and one's own emotions get mixed up with the character'; with Lear 'one seems to be able to lose oneself, and while on stage to be the part. Lear is like a god, whereas there is something of all of us in Hamlet.' But the role obviously presented huge problems. Rather than play Lear as 'a doddering old man with a long beard', he decided to emphasise his physical strength and vigour, which remain even after he loses his mind.

Gielgud later claimed his Lear had been only partially successful. 'I was wholly inadequate in the storm scenes, having neither the voice nor the physique for them,' he recalled. 'Lear has to *be* the storm, but I could do no more than shout against the thundersheet.' Leslie French, much admired as the Fool, remembered differently: 'It was astonishing, because he was far too young, and yet he gave a tremendous performance.' The poet and playwright Gordon Bottomley was also impressed, writing to Gielgud: 'I cannot believe that you or anyone else can ever be (or can ever have been) more convincingly Lear than you were last night. It was a piece of the greatest kind of art that will go on living in everyone who heard it. Homage.'

The critics admired Gielgud for tackling the part so young, but several thought he lacked the necessary weight and power, most notably in the storm-scene. *The Times* critic summed up the adverse views: 'It is a mountain of a part, and at the end of the evening the peak remains unconquered.' But others felt that, while he lacked physical power, he overcame this by means of his art. Ivor Brown wrote: 'He sweeps to a fullness of voice and a declamatory power which he has hardly touched before.' Agate suggested he would conquer the part later: 'In the manifest intelligence displayed throughout, and in the speaking of the verse, it is fine; time only can do the rest.'

A few days later, shortly before he left the Vic, Gielgud wrote to Agate to thank him for his support during the two seasons:

Dear James,

Your notice of *Lear* was extremely instructive and much better than I deserved, especially after your sage counsel not to attempt the part. But it seemed to me a more exciting wind-up than the revival of *Hamlet*, which would otherwise have been the order of the day. My great fear with this was that it would be either funny or quite negligible, neither of which I hope is entirely the case. Certainly you and Ivor Brown have taken me most seriously, and I am greatly pleased and flattered that it should be so. You have indeed been a tower of strength these two seasons in doing me good turns (and the theatre too) and I shall always remember your really fine championing both of *Hamlet* and *The Cherry Orchard* with much gratitude . . . I must anyhow tender you my thanks for your interest and advice in Waterloo Road. I imagine that to have to see the same actor more than three times in a year is a trial to any critic – perhaps it's just as well you're a Shakespeare fan apart from – or shall I say despite – all efforts at performance.

Sincerely, Yours etc, John Gielgud

The graciousness and modesty that characterise this letter were among the qualities that made Gielgud a favourite within the Old Vic 'family' he was now leaving. 'With every reason for adopting the aloofness of a star, John Gielgud has sensed the spirit of the Vic truly enough to be as approachable as the humblest member of the company,' the *Old Vic Magazine* commented: 'One of the many things we shall remember about him is that, with a rehearsal in the morning and a very exacting role in the evening – it was Richard II – and a thoroughly reasonable excuse for staying away, he yet came to help feed five hundred poor children at one of the Jabberwock parties at the Old Vic – and that is a very exhausting afternoon's work even for the most confirmed child-lover.'

Gielgud performed other duties, such as giving away the prizes at the annual fancy-dress dance. The theatrical photographer Angus McBean recalls winning first prize for his costume: 'I heard that extraordinary, idiosyncratic and quite beautiful voice saying: "What an extraordinary costume – but, dear boy, I'm deeply embarrassed to have to give you this." It was a set of records of him orating Shakespeare's most famous soliloquies: heavy, twelve-inch, single-sided 78s.'

The family spirit at the Vic also affected Gielgud's mother. Relatives and friends were allowed to attend weekend dress rehearsals, and Kate Gielgud was always present 'to look out for possible flaws'. She offered criticisms and, equally importantly, large supplies of food to the impoverished actors. Harcourt Williams remembered her graciousness and lively interest: 'Her advice was ever helpful and sound – as were the juicy pear and delicate sandwiches which she would slip into my hand in moments of exhaustion.'

Her constant presence in the theatre was yet another mark of her devotion to Gielgud, and the intense closeness of their relationship. While he was at the Vic she wrote to him: 'I can't tell you what joy it gives me to have you give up your spare time and forsake your many friends, to come along here and let me share your interests, to weigh the pros and cons of the future, to be ever my dear sympathetic loving son as well as the brilliant artist.' Now sixty-two, she had gained a new lease of life from Gielgud's achievement, as Graham Robertson explained to a friend: 'His last year of great success has greatly rejuvenated his mother, who had been ailing for some time, and is now herself of about thirty years ago again.'

In a world of large egos and all-pervasive vanity, Gielgud's tendency towards self-deprecation had also won him friends. Later that year he wrote to Harcourt Williams after returning to the Vic to see his production of *King John*. Apologising for 'my domineering carping ways in the past', he added: 'It was such a joy to be there and see a lovely bit of work of yours untrammelled by my own egotistical view of it.' But this was not how Williams viewed his behaviour: 'He had opportunities in full for throwing his weight around as a leading man. He never took one. Of his many ideas at rehearsal and elsewhere he never put forward a suggestion that glorified his own part. It was always for the play as a whole.' To him Gielgud was 'a dear comrade who always held his position in the company with absolute fairness and consideration for his fellow-artists'.

During his two years at the Old Vic Gielgud had developed at an extraordinary pace. Despite his age and obvious physical limitations, he had tackled some of the toughest Shakespearean roles. His Hamlet and Richard II, the parts on which he drew deepest from his own personality and feelings, had established him as a player of intelligence, imagination and intense poetic sensibility. His bold attempts at Lear, Antony, Prospero, Macbeth and Malvolio had revealed a hitherto unseen and unsuspected strength and versatility. His sensitive and beautiful verse-speaking was a revelation, dispatching overnight the ponderous declamatory style of his predecessors. Overall the Vic had been a superb training-ground for his later attempts at the major Shakespearean roles.

He had quickly won over the Old Vic audience, as was noted in the annual report: 'In the two years here he has again and again sent the audience home the richer for a beautiful thought or a new insight into a particular character ... Never has any actor been more rapturously received, even in this theatre, which has great traditions regarding applause.' He had been lucky in his leading ladies: both Martita Hunt and Dorothy Green had given performances of the highest quality. He had found a wonderful foil in Ralph Richardson, whose talents were to merge with his much later – though never again in Shakespeare. Richardson had come to admire him as an actor: 'He was so brilliant, he shone, he was so handsome, and his voice was so splendid,' he recalled.

Gielgud was now hailed as the finest Shakespearean actor of his generation. It was an astonishing rise, and one for which he owed much to his innovative, talented and humane producer. Williams had enabled him to unleash his imagination on a wide range of challenging and contrasting roles. He had also provided a stimulating apprentice-ship as a producer: his revolutionary ideas would later influence Gielgud's own productions. But the benefits had been two-way: Williams would have found it almost impossible to carry out his reforms without Gielgud's enthusiastic, determined and loyal support.

On his departure from the Vic Lilian Baylis wrote a prophetic letter to Kate Gielgud:

You know how proud we were in the first instance to have a Terry with us – we are prouder than ever to feel that he is going out to conquer new fields with something added to his art, and himself, by the work he has done here. I know that he will miss the joy of playing a series of such parts, just as we will miss seeing him in them, but I look forward with keen pleasure to the day when he will have his own theatre, and when we may hope to see him again in parts of huge size.

Harcourt Williams's enormous gratitude was reflected in his farewell present, a glove given to him by Ellen Terry, which Irving had worn as Benedick. He too was in no doubt about Gielgud's potential to achieve great things. In a farewell letter he wrote:

Your enthusiasm and 'theatre etiquette' have been a shining example and of untold service to me. I know from these foundations that stand beneath your power as an actor that you will grow and expand until you shatter that theatre falsely termed commercial . . . and create one – either of brain or brick, I don't care which – that we shall be proud of.

His hopes were to be realised quicker than he could have thought possible. Gielgud's sights were now fixed on the West End, but he had no intention of 'dwindling into a lounge suit'.

II

Young Producer

His energetic, fresh and dancing imagination
was evident from the first rehearsal.
(Peggy Ashcroft on *Romeo and Juliet*, 1932)

BACK in the West End Gielgud set about fulfilling certain aims.
Sick of the intense, neurotic roles he had been playing there
before, he was determined to expand his range and establish
himself as a serious actor. The politician Harold Nicolson noted in his
diary: 'Talk to Gielgud, who is a fine young man. He does not want to
specialise in juvenile parts since they imply rigidity. He has a high view
of his calling. I think he may well be the finest actor we have had since
Irving.'

He was also determined to achieve what he now called his 'real
ambition', to become a producer. The attraction the job had for him is
clear from a piece he wrote while at the Vic, in which he underlined its
importance:

What a task, then, for the producer! To take down the book from
the shelf, dust it carefully, read it carefully, consider it, and
interpret it clearly and fully in his mind. Now he must cast it,
arrange the scenery, costumes, cuts, music, exits, entrances,
groupings – and then come to rehearsal and put all these things
into practice, as well as observe how an actor fits his scheme here,
and falls short of it there . . . The task is really one of herculean
labour, and the actor must ever be aware, when he answers the
applause at the curtain night by night, how much he owes to the
man on whom the whole responsibility really rests.

First, however, he opted for some light relief, agreeing to appear in the stage version of J.B. Priestley's *The Good Companions*. This jolly, picaresque novel had been a huge popular success two years before. The story of the Dinky Doos, a third-rate, end-of-the-pier touring company, and their adventures on the road had met a need for gaiety and humour in a time of economic depression and unemployment. Priestley had adapted it for the stage with the actor and dramatist Edward Knoblock; Gielgud was to play Inigo Jollifant, a disillusioned schoolteacher who joins the company to write its songs. Some surprise was expressed that he should accept such a light, unchallenging part – though one commentator labelled it 'a comeback after Shakespeare'. Writing to Agate before the opening, Gielgud appeared slightly shamefaced about it: 'I trust you will soon be taking a summer holiday, otherwise I shall send you myself a whole parcel of bricks to hurl at my head in *The Good Companions*, a very strange pot-pourri of English life!'

The demanding schedule he faced before the opening revealed his astonishing energy and appetite for work. The first night was just three days after he left the Old Vic. Rehearsals began while he was playing Benedick and rehearsing for Lear. There was then a pre-London tour, where an understudy took over his role – though he managed to play it for two nights when there was no performance at the Vic. In the space of seven days he played his last performance as Lear, tackled Hotspur again for a children's matinée, played Benedick at the emotional last night of the Vic season, went up to Leeds to re-join *The Good Companions* for one performance, and was in its London opening.

The cast included Edward Chapman as the lovable Yorkshireman Jess Oakroyd, and Adele Dixon as the troupe's star Susia Dean. With sixteen scenes, forty speaking parts, two real cars, and vivid sets by Laurence Irving, the spirited production by Julian Wylie was an immediate success at His Majesty's, transferred to the Lyric, and ran for nearly a year. Gielgud's light, breezy part required him to smoke a pipe, fall in love with Adele Dixon, play the piano, and sing.

On the first night the Old Vic 'gallery girls', the solid core of his following, turned out in force, and gave him a tremendous reception on his entrance. Agate observed that 'some part of the applause might be taken as a tribute to all those kings over the water whose sceptres the young tragedian had just laid down'. His bravura performance was liked by the critics for its zest, sparkle and romantic feeling. For once he had no trouble with the love-scenes: Farjeon noted that 'he has little to do beyond emphasising the charm of youth and making amiable love, in both of which he is entirely successful'. Gifts from his many admirers – including horseshoes, lucky black cats and miniature pianos – came flooding in.

Gielgud soon tired of this conventional juvenile role. But he liked having money again: 'Suppers at the Savoy were no longer a luxury, and sometimes I enjoyed hearing people say "That's John Gielgud" as I passed,' he remembered. But *The Good Companions* also gave him a taste of the more raffish side of theatre life. Julian Wylie was a cultivated, cigar-smoking impresario, best known for putting on pantomime. From boyhood Gielgud had loved the romance of panto- mime, and he now sat enthralled amongst the pictures of pantomime and music-hall favourites in Wylie's Charing Cross Road offices. Some of the show's company had been in revue and pantomime, and one veteran actor was continually upstaging him and ruining his lines. Gielgud sought the help of Fred Terry, who advised him to retaliate by walking in front of the actor while he was speaking, forcing him to come downstage. Gielgud did as he was told, and it worked.

It was the show's co-writer who prompted Gielgud's most celebrated gaffe. Edward Knoblock, an American-born writer with such hits as *Kismet* to his name, was notoriously dull and garrulous. While he and Gielgud were dining together at the Ivy a man passed their table, and Gielgud remarked: 'Thank God he didn't stop, he's a bigger bore than Eddie Knoblock.' He was to drop many similar bricks, the best known being at a dinner party when he called someone's performance 'as dreadful as poor, dear Athene on a very bad night'. In the silence that followed he suddenly realised Athene Seyler was among the guests. 'Oh not you Athene,' he said hastily. 'Another Athene.'

Such incidents suggest crass insensitivity or supreme malice, or both. Yet in Gielgud it was a combination of a patrician vagueness, a mer- curial mind, and a fatal inability to censor his thoughts before they turned into words. Even most of his victims were convinced that such gaffes were unintentional, and committed without malice – though Gielgud certainly loved to re-tell, and sometimes embroider, the more appalling ones.

Many people within the theatre now began to see him as the great white hope of his generation. The critic Hubert Griffith set him apart from others on the London scene: 'Sometimes it seems that of actors under thirty we have only an array of stiff boys with magazine-cover profiles doomed to walk into lounge halls carrying tennis racquets to make love to hard-faced stage girls of the contemporary convention – that we have only these, and John Gielgud.' Citing his Lear, he marvelled at his versatility: 'That he could slip from it to the piano-playing schoolmaster in *The Good Companions* is in itself an assurance that he is sustaining the burden of mantle- and torch-bearing that we have laid upon him.'

Gielgud was now searching for interesting new plays. His name prompted many writers, new and established, to send him their latest work. One play immediately took his fancy, though at first merely for personal reasons. *The Discontents* was set in Poland, and was written by Ronald Mackenzie, who reminded him in an accompanying letter that they had been at prep school together. Gielgud's initial reaction to a script was invariably impulsive: he relied on his intuition to sense its potential, and if it excited him he would be casting it mentally within minutes. Immediately enthusiastic about *The Discontents*, he invited its author to lunch to discuss a possible production.

Mackenzie was a young, introverted and impoverished Scot, who had led a nomadic life working in the mines and as a logger in Poland and Canada. He had become assistant stage manager at Wyndham's, a job he hated. Scornful of the Edgar Wallace thrillers that played there, and of the West End commercial theatre in general, he sat in the prompt corner writing his own plays, and reading Chekhov and Tolstoy. Gielgud found him bitter and cynical about the world: 'I attempted to meet the somewhat aggressive air which he affected with a little facile charm,' he recalled. 'This he probably found thoroughly patronising and obnoxious. An uncompromising vegetarian, he glowered darkly at me over his carrots.' Mutual shyness was to prevent the two men from getting to know each other at all well.

Gielgud had recently signed a contract to appear in three plays under the joint management of Bronson Albery and Howard Wyndham. During the 1930s Albery was to play a central role in his career. A leading West End manager and the son of Lady Wyndham – who had recommended Gielgud to him as an interesting young actor – he was a courteous, self-effacing but astute man of the theatre, with a great interest in new plays and a shrewd sense of the public's taste. He controlled the Criterion, the New and Wyndham's, and was a director of the Arts, the leading small theatre for experimental and new writing. He was just what Gielgud needed: a good businessman who had vision and taste.

Gielgud thought Mackenzie a talented writer, but was aware that his play, with its overtones of Chekhov and Turgenev, might not be a commercial proposition: five managements had already turned it down. Fortunately Albery liked it, and offered him the chance to stage it at the Arts for four performances, under its revised title, *Musical Chairs*. Gielgud's judgement and faith in the young writer were gloriously vindicated when the curtain rose in November on what Agate called 'the best first play written by any English playwright during the last forty years'.

Musical Chairs dealt with the tensions created by the arrival of a young American woman into a family living in the Polish oil-fields. Albery, as Harcourt Williams had done, recognised Gielgud's passionate interest in all aspects of theatre, and involved him in choosing cast and producer. While taking the leading male role himself, Gielgud suggested Frank Vosper for the father. The rest of the company were rising young actors: Roger Livesey, Jessica Tandy, Finlay Currie, Margaret Webster and the American Carol Goodner.

Gielgud also recommended his favourite producer to Albery. Komisarjevsky was scornful about theatre managers – 'Albery is just a tradesman!' he told Gielgud – but he was immediately in sympathy with Mackenzie's play. He still handled actors sensitively, as Margaret Webster recalled: 'He guided us, but he never pushed; he allowed the subtle relationships between the characters to develop gradually, with a hint there and a comment there, until we had absorbed the play into our blood, into our skins.' Rehearsing the part of the consumptive, sensitive but cynical young pianist Joseph Schindler, Gielgud warmed once again to Komisarjevsky's methods, which gave actors plenty of room to be creative. At the first rehearsal he led Gielgud to the middle of the stage and said: 'There is your piano, and there on it is the photograph of that girl who was killed. Build your performance around those two things.'

Seven months later, when Gielgud was free of Inigo Jollifant, the play was produced commercially at the Criterion. Before the opening Gielgud was gloomy about the prospects for Mackenzie's sombre, neo-Chekhovian work. Komisarjevsky had become involved in another play, and had only come to a few rehearsals: 'I had to take over: it was chaos,' Gielgud recalled. But after three nights he wrote: 'We are all very nervous of the play, but I believe all is well, especially as the critics have done us proud.'

They had come out in a rash of superlatives, Ivor Brown stating that its fierce emotions 'make the average West End piece seem as substantial as a puff of cigarette smoke'. Desmond MacCarthy called Gielgud's performance 'a wonderfully convincing mixture of nervous exasperation and real emotion'. After the opening Gielgud gave a supper party at the Savoy. The celebration was merited: *Musical Chairs* had at last brought him a good part in a new, classy West End play.

His acting was maturing. Komisarjevsky, with his acute musical sensitivity, had coaxed him out of his habit of playing on all four cylinders, and taught him how to vary his emotional pitch. He also gave him confidence in an area in which he still felt exposed. 'I had never before tackled such violent love scenes in a modern play, and the smallness of the Criterion, as well as one or two dangerous lines, had made me nervous,' he recalled. During a rehearsal for one tense love-scene some offstage hammering caused an uncharacteristic loss of temper, and he shouted at the stagehands. 'But Carol Goodner's perfect timing and clear-cut technique gave me just the confidence I needed.' Komisarjevsky also helped him, by demanding 'an inner understanding of character which I was able to carry a stage further than I had ever done before'. He no longer fought shy of using his own personality. Given his difficulties with Hamlet, this was a real breakthrough.

There were, however, moments of panic, brought on by his habit of observing individuals in the audience. Required to play Bach and Chopin on the piano, he became self-conscious one night when he noticed the famous pianist Arthur Rubinstein in the stalls. Another night the presence of Noël Coward had the same effect: he continually checked Coward's responses to his lines. Coward failed to return after the interval, leaving Gielgud hurt and offended. Later Coward wrote to him: 'I thought you were over-acting badly and using voice tones and elaborate emotional effects, and as I seriously think you are a grand actor it upset me very much.' Gielgud claimed this cured him of the habit; but the cure was only temporary.

Fred Terry and Julia Neilson also came to see his performance. Gielgud, thrilled as ever by a visit from an illustrious Terry, sent a large bouquet of carnations to their box. Afterwards they came backstage, and Fred complimented him warmly on his playing. Gielgud's memory of his visit is tinged with affection and nostalgia: 'He stood, that evening, framed in the iron pass-door leading from the stage, leaning on his stick, looking like a benevolent Henry the Eighth. Julia was by his side, looking radiantly beautiful, with the flowers we had sent her held loosely in a dark mass against her light dress. There they stood as if they were taking some magnificent call at the end of a play in which they had made a great success.' It was the last time he saw his uncle, who died the following year, the last Terry of his generation.

Musical Chairs ran for three hundred performances and nine months. After a while Gielgud was beset by the problem facing any conscientious actor involved in a long run: how to keep his performance fresh. He felt he was wasting time repeating a part he felt he had perfected. Some nights he fought against losing his concentration by reciting passages of Shakespeare in his dressing-room. He became nervy and lost weight, prompting a woman who came to the play to ask Ralph Richardson: 'Is your friend Mr Gielgud really as thin as that?' Eventually he took a fortnight off in the south of France. On his way back to London he picked up a paper, and was devastated to read that Mackenzie, also in France on holiday, had been killed in a car accident. His promising discovery was just twenty-nine.

Gielgud now had a burning desire to produce. The spark that had been set off by his toy theatre, and ignited in Barnes and at the Old Vic, now became a flame. Acting was no longer a sufficient outlet for his restless temperament and intense fascination with every aspect of theatre. Having worked with and observed at close quarters most of the leading producers – Atkins, Fagan, Playfair, Dean, Komisarjevsky, Harcourt Williams and, briefly, Barker – he was ready to tackle the job himself.

His first opportunity had come shortly before *Musical Chairs* had opened at the Criterion, when he was asked to produce *Romeo and Juliet* for the undergraduate group, the Oxford University Dramatic Society (OUDS). This proved an historic event, as well as a first sketch for Gielgud's later production. It brought together a group of exceptional talents on whose lives the production was to have an immediate effect. Many of their subsequent careers were to interweave closely with Gielgud's over three decades, and in different ways have a major impact on the development of the English theatre.

Technically his first production was only semi-professional. It was an OUDS tradition to invite well-known names in the theatre to help with student productions. In recent years Gyles Isham had produced *Twelfth Night*, and Basil Dean had helped with a production of *Hassan*. Gielgud was now invited to take his turn by the OUDS president, the portly, bespectacled twenty-one-year-old George Devine. An admirer of the Komisarjevsky productions in Barnes, Devine and the OUDS committee came to his dressing-room during the run of *The Good*

Companions. Gielgud was repelled by his 'rather ungainly and gross' appearance, finding him 'very greasy, spotty and unattractive'. But he also detected humour and intelligence in the burly undergraduate. And Devine's offer, though it was unpaid, was too good to turn down.

Casting was negotiated with the OUDS committee. While Gielgud approved of the young poet Christopher Hassall as Romeo, William Devlin as Tybalt, and Hugh Hunt as Friar Laurence, he was not convinced that Devine, an erratic actor, could manage Mercutio. Devine, however, exercised his right as president to choose his part. The female leads were a more complicated matter. Women undergraduates had not been allowed to take part in OUDS productions until 1927, and the tradition was still to recruit professional actresses, who were not paid but, in Devine's words, were 'put up and loved'. However, Gielgud was entirely happy with the committee's choice for Juliet.

Peggy Ashcroft, a promising young actress admired for her freshness and sincerity on stage, had come to prominence three years earlier playing opposite Matheson Lang in *Jew Süss*, and had confirmed her promise in the Robeson *Othello*. Gielgud had been deeply impressed by her Desdemona, her first Shakespearean role: 'When Peggy came on in the Senate scene it was as if all the lights in the theatre had suddenly gone up,' he recalled. 'Everything she did on stage seemed right and natural.' Dispirited after playing a series of unchallenging parts, she eagerly accepted Juliet, a role she had long dreamed of playing. Two weeks before the opening Gielgud carried off another coup, persuading Edith Evans to take on the Nurse, a part she had played to great acclaim at the Old Vic. He also overcame Devine's objections to using unknown designers from outside Oxford, and persuaded him to use the Motleys for the costumes.

He was now poised to put into practice what he had learned from Harcourt Williams: the need for speed, continuity of action, and a strong design. Despite his inexperience, and a fear of 'not being very good with the boys', he quickly established a good rapport with the actors. 'I got on extraordinarily well with the whole cast, and it was wildly exciting for me to see some of my long-cherished ideas of production actually being carried out on the stage,' he recalled. 'Working with amateurs gave me confidence, and I seemed for the first time to gain real authority.' Ever-conscious of his own handicap, he showed Christopher Hassall how to walk straight. The undergraduates not only liked him, but were impressed by his abilities, especially his efforts to improve their verse-speaking. To William Devlin he seemed like a benign headmaster: 'He really taught us, rather than produced us, which was the right method for intelligent undergraduates with flexible voices.'

Peggy Ashcroft was also impressed. 'His energetic, fresh and dancing imagination was evident from the first rehearsal,' she recalled. 'His conception of the essential youthfulness of the play, which fitted his undergraduate cast, was something that inspired us all – amateur and professional; it had a marvellous zest and speed.' Edith Evans was friendly and encouraging to the company, though stern with any latecomers to rehearsal. Gielgud was still in awe of her, and offered his ideas timidly.

One aspiring student actor among the extras was Terence Rattigan, playing one of the revellers who discover Juliet's death. The future playwright was fascinated to observe Gielgud, the first star he had seen in action. But despite patient coaching – Gielgud recalled giving him 'endless demonstrations of disapproval' – he was unable to get his one line right, and kept provoking an inappropriate laugh. This traumatic episode persuaded him to concentrate on writing rather than acting; later he was to make use of the experience of working with Gielgud in two of his plays.

As the lights went down and the music started to play for the dress rehearsal at the New in Oxford, Gielgud experienced a deep thrill. 'A wonderful play was about to be performed, and it was for me alone. I felt like Ludwig of Bavaria.' But on the opening night he was shaking with nerves, much more than he did when acting: this time he felt utterly helpless. When the curtain stuck for two minutes towards the end he 'nearly died with anxiety and mortification'. However, his work delighted the critics, who thought it the best OUDS production in years. The writer David Cecil later described it as 'easily the best performance of the play I have ever seen: straightforward in inter-pretation but fresh with youthful lyrical rapture, so that it seemed at once wholly in tune with Shakespeare's intention, and yet as if it had been written yesterday'. There was praise for the fresh and youthful passion of Peggy Ashcroft's Juliet, and the humour and integrity of Edith Evans's Nurse. Devine got the best notices of all the undergraduates; even Gielgud had to admit that his Mercutio was 'suddenly remarkably good'.

The production marked down Gielgud as a bold, imaginative and dedicated producer, clearly well equipped to tackle a West End play.

Charles Morgan, a former OUDS president, rhapsodised over his achievement: 'Here is an artist, honoured by his task and devoted to it, whose imagination is fired by *Romeo and Juliet*, and who is so far skilled in the theatre that he can give to the acted play the unity, the pulse, the excitement of his inward imagining of it.' It was a brilliant début for a twenty-seven-year-old.

At Albery's invitation he brought the play to the New for two Sunday-night performances, in aid of what he called 'my school', the Old Vic and Sadler's Wells. But the production had other, more significant returns. For the Motleys it was the beginning of an enormously fruitful and creative collaboration with Gielgud that was soon to bring them to the forefront of stage design. It launched George Devine on a career that would eventually, through his founding of the English Stage Company at the Royal Court, have far-reaching consequences for the English theatre. It re-awakened Edith Evans's interest in the classics, prompting her to return again to the Old Vic. It persuaded Komisarjevsky to offer Peggy Ashcroft a role in his next play, and Harcourt Williams to bring her to the Old Vic. It was the springboard for a theatrical partnership between Ashcroft and Gielgud that was to delight and enchant audiences for the next thirty years.

Gielgud's second career now developed rapidly. He read a play by Rodney Ackland, then twenty-four and virtually unknown. A former actor, Ackland had been inspired to write by Komisarjevsky's 1925 production of Chekhov's *Three Sisters* at Barnes. His first three plays made little impact; a critic described one as 'nearly as boring as Chekhov'. But it was precisely the Chekhovian moods and subtleties of his new play, which had already had a try-out at the Embassy, that appealed to Gielgud. *Strange Orchestra* dealt with a set of bohemian characters living out their tragi-comic lives in a seedy Chelsea boarding-house. Unlike so many West End plays, it reflected real life. Still not entirely secure with his own ideas, Gielgud decided to produce it 'in the style of' Komisarjevsky.

For the cast he recruited Robert Harris, Leslie French, Hugh Williams and (after failing to get Celia Johnson) the mysterious Jean Forbes-Robertson who, alongside Peggy Ashcroft and Jessica Tandy, was seen as a young actress of immense promise. It was a talented company, but in the early rehearsals Gielgud had his hands full dealing with his leading lady. Despite his difficulties with Mrs Patrick Campbell in *Ghosts*, he had persuaded her to play the part of the bohemian landlady. He faced rehearsals with trepidation, all too aware that 'she was liable to treat a producer as dust beneath her chariot wheels'. Mrs Pat behaved true to form, turning up late every morning, claiming not to understand the play ('Who are all these characters? Where do they live? Does Gladys Cooper know them?'), insulting one of the actors, and worrying ceaselessly about her Pekinese dog, now in quarantine. She frequently argued with Gielgud, and also quarrelled with the sensitive Ackland, provoking him to storm out of rehearsals.

Also in the company was Mary Casson, who had been playing Wendy in *Peter Pan* for the previous six years. Then eighteen, she remembers Gielgud's reaction to Mrs Pat: 'She was very strange and eccentric, and John found it very difficult to cope. After a few days he was getting very uneasy.' That unease was as much to do with Mrs Pat's continual threats to leave as with the difficulties she created, for he was convinced he had a success on his hands. But after two weeks she carried out her threat to leave and spend more time with her dog. 'I was in despair,' Gielgud remembered. 'She had rehearsed the part magnificently.' Fortunately he was able to engage in her place Laura Cowie, once Forbes-Robertson's leading lady.

He now decided he enjoyed producing even more than acting. His quicksilver mind brimming with ideas, Gielgud was constantly changing his mind – over an entrance, a move, a piece of stage 'business'. Some actors found his restless, impetuous method stimulating and inspiring; others became anxious, frustrated and sometimes despairing. Even in these early days, he admitted, he was 'prissy and meticulous'. With *Strange Orchestra*, Leslie French remembered, 'he changed everything from day to day, which made rehearsals very difficult'. But Mary Casson found his search for perfection refreshing: 'It wasn't so much changing his mind as evolving the production as he went along, as new ideas came to him,' she recalled. 'I found it quite helpful, and enjoyed rehearsals enormously.'

The critics recognised in Ackland a dramatist of great promise: Agate thought his play 'as much superior to the ordinary stuff of the theatre as tattered silk is to unbleached calico', while Ivor Brown commended 'its abundant freshness and force'. They also applauded Gielgud for the masterly way he conducted this strange, disparate orchestra of players. 'Great plays inspire great acting,' Alan Parsons wrote. 'This is what I call great production.' The public were less certain about the play, which had only a modest three-month run. But the production greatly enhanced Gielgud's reputation as a producer.

His next aim was to produce a Shakespeare play in the West End.

For a moment *The Winter's Tale* seemed a possibility, under the management of C.B. Cochran, who was normally associated with revue and musicals: 'I have read *The Winter's Tale* twice since I saw you, and I think I would like very much to have a shot at it,' he wrote to Cochran. His mind already racing, he poured out a flurry of casting suggestions, which included Charles Laughton or Cedric Hardwicke for Leontes, Leon Quartermaine as Polixenes, and Ernest Thesiger as the Chorus: 'I believe men who speak verse so well as these and yet are good modern actors would be the types to get,' he wrote. As usual he had already visualised a design, to consist of 'Renaissance classical dresses and decorations, a great terrace and Veronese colouring in rich dark and tawny materials for the court scenes, then the pastoral could be light and delicate in contrast'.

But the production failed to materialise, and his first chance to produce Shakespeare professionally came, aptly enough, at the Old Vic, with *The Merchant of Venice*. Harcourt Williams was desperate to break the tradition of drab sets and costumes imposed by Lilian Baylis's strict housekeeping, and Gielgud now made him a generous and ingenious offer: he would forgo his producer's fee on condition the production was properly designed. The budget was £90 instead of the usual £20. Marius Goring, then at the Vic, remembered that Lilian Baylis 'nearly had a fit' when first told of the idea.

Gielgud gathered together a strong company. Peggy Ashcroft, now leading lady at the Vic, was to play Portia, Malcolm Keen was Shylock, and Roger Livesey, Marius Goring, George Devine and Harcourt Williams were also cast. In the *Old Vic Magazine* Gielgud made clear his intention to look afresh at the play, and ignore the fashionable view that it was uneven, fantastic and boring: 'In thinking of *The Merchant* and reading it continually, I have never found it had any of the faults commonly attributed to it, although I think any performance is fraught with pitfalls and difficulties,' he wrote. He pleaded for tolerance from the Old Vic regulars: 'If at first it all seems a little strange and unlike what you have been used to expect, please believe that we wish, not to be clever or highbrow, but to try to give a fresh, lively, imaginative performance of one of the loveliest dramatic fairy tales in the English language.'

Gielgud designed the set himself, although it was executed by the Motleys. Tanya Moisiewitch remembers it as 'very simple, but very telling and beautiful'. Gielgud decided, daringly for the time, that the costumes should be conceived individually in relation to each character. He based some of them on memories from his youth of the

Russian ballet. But Margaret Harris was not sure the experiment succeeded: 'He tried to use the costumes without any period: they were quite fun, but not really very good, they came out awfully camp,' she recalled. They were certainly inexpensive, thanks to the resourcefulness of the Motleys: Shylock's was made of dish-rags, while others were made out of mosquito-netting or bath-towelling.

A painting by Roger Furse shows Gielgud rehearsing Peggy Ashcroft in the trial scene. Slim, angular and besuited, head held high and one hand in his pocket, he stands with knees slightly bent, pointing imperiously at the actors. He seems at ease, but in fact he was under pressure: there were only ten days of rehearsals, half of which he missed through his acting commitments; on these occasions Williams took over. In the circumstances the result was remarkable: the production was the success of a lacklustre Old Vic season. Anthony Quayle, then at the start of his career, remembered it as 'the one production that stood out shining like a jewel . . . Behind everything there was a brain.' The Old Vic audience, unused to such relative sumptuousness, applauded rapturously.

The Merchant of Venice was a mould-breaking production. Ivor Brown wrote that it 'confirms the overthrow of the Bensonian tradition', and called it 'a young man's play made young again'. Guthrie, now provoking controversy with his bold productions at the Cambridge Festival Theatre, wrote to Gielgud, praising 'a Shakespeare comedy which was not heavily and boringly trying to be funny, but was instead elegant and witty, light as a feather, and so gaily sophisticated that beside it Maugham and Coward seemed like two Nonconformist pastors from the Midlands'.

Farjeon wrote that 'the words of the play are more intelligently spoken than usual'. Gielgud, now dubbed the finest speaker of Shakespearean verse, was keen to help raise standards by passing his ideas and technique on to others. Quayle, playing the Prince of Morocco, was the first of many to benefit from his tuition: 'I got off the ground, and that I did so was entirely due to John,' he recalled. 'There could not have been a better teacher to bring me face to face with the lifelong vocal problems of our trade – breathing, resonance, diction, phrasing.'

In just over a year Gielgud had established himself as a producer of the highest quality. He had also revealed a flair for spotting exciting new playwrights, a talent which was now to give him one of his most memorable roles.

12

Richard of Bordeaux

You are a very strange and very beautiful actor.
(Lynn Fontanne, 1933)

NOT long before his production of *Romeo and Juliet* Gielgud and John Perry had temporarily taken a house in Oxfordshire. A substantial gabled building with a large garden and a thatched summer house, Woodhill was set in Harpsden Woodland, on a hilltop above Henley-on-Thames. It was in a secluded spot, screened by rows of fir trees. Here 'the Two Johns', as they were known, were able to relax and socialise with their theatrical friends.

Perry was a great gambler, and the regular and very lively house parties often turned into all-night poker schools. Among the many guests were two young actors, Robert Flemying and the beautiful Peter Glenville, and Terence Rattigan, still a student at Oxford but now a close friend of Perry. Rattigan was overawed by the starry company, but especially by Gielgud: 'He was the greatest figure alive, and I never dared talk to him,' he recalled. Desperately guilty about his homosexuality, Rattigan enjoyed Woodhill because he could relax, and drop the pretence he had to keep up elsewhere.

The climate for homosexuals was still an oppressive one. In 1889 Shaw had protested against a law 'by which two adult men can be sentenced to twenty years' penal servitude for a private act, freely consented to and desired by both, which concerns themselves alone'. Forty years on nothing had changed: such acts were still illegal, and every year more than three hundred people were convicted for 'gross indecency'. Nancy Astor's son had recently been imprisoned for several months as a result of 'homosexual offences'. Blackmail was an ever-present threat: Beverley Nichols, also homosexual, threatened to give the police details of Agate's private life after a row over his review of a play by Nichols.

Many actors felt the need to maintain in public a pretence of being heterosexual. Gielgud was no exception. Asked while at the Vic what he felt about being besieged at the stage door by young female admirers, he replied: 'I don't mind – who would, with English schoolgirls, fresh and lovely as they are.' Later, during the run of the Priestley play, he was invited to write about 'Girls Who Make Good Companions'. The article was a conventional cover for his homosexuality, but also a wistful description of a relationship he seemed half to desire.

Actresses, he explained, had provided him with so much sympathy and understanding that 'I have never felt the need, or even the desire, to look for them elsewhere'. His ideal companion would need enough sympathy and intelligence 'to know instinctively just when to leave me alone'. This, he suggested, was always 'a great gift', for 'a supreme necessity of good companionship is occasional and even frequent solitude'. Good temper and a sense of humour were also vital, 'much more so than actual beauty, which I, for one, would never insist upon, or even specially desire'. He also wanted his 'good companion for life' to be a good reader, able to talk intelligently about pictures and music, but be a good housekeeper and cook – and 'on these latter and practical points I should personally be very firm'. He concluded that she 'must not give all her attention to pets, at least when I am about', but that 'I should rejoice in all the loving companionship and care she devoted to children'.

As a matinée idol, Gielgud was not conventionally good-looking in the manner of Owen Nares or Ivor Novello. Spotting him in the Ivy, a friend of Agate's remarked: 'It's a rum sort of head: the profile's Roman Emperor, but the rest is still at Eton.' One writer described him as 'slight in build, occasionally effeminate in manner, at times suggestive of ill-health'. Despite his vigorous massaging of his temples every day, his hair was thinning rapidly. He still moved awkwardly, as Alec Guinness remembered: 'He walked, or possibly tripped, with slightly bent knees . . . His arm movements were inclined to be jerky and his large, bony hands a little stiff.'

Yet his garrulous charm, his obvious intelligence, and in particular his mellifluous voice disarmed journalists, many of whom wrote gushing, deferential but not always accurate pieces about the new West End idol. After a three-hour lunch, during which he talked virtually

non-stop, one woman journalist was qu
is delightful, the nicest I've ever heard,'
unless he has something really interest
fearfully ambitious – yet not an egoist, wl
Unlike most people on the stage, he's shy. F
patronise night clubs. Neither do his friends

Gielgud confessed that 'my work is my
interests outside it'. His appetite for reading
childhood, and he was now devouring theatr
books about the plays and players of the past. H
for the short stories of Chekhov, Maugham and
still browsed through his favourite novels by Di
Reading in bed last thing at night provided rare mo
'The theatre is a merciless taskmaster, affording me
he admitted. 'That calm finale spent with a small an
book has a soothing effect on the nerves.'

There were many calls on his time. He was in deman
the Critics' Circle invited him, along with Irene Vanb
Bliss and A.P. Herbert, to their annual dinner, where rece
been Shaw and Barrie. The main topic for discussion was
actors' trade union formed in 1929, with Godfrey Tearle, Be
and May Whitty among its moving spirits. Gielgud had
added to its council, along with Cedric Hardwicke, Gerald du
and Gertrude Lawrence. Though he was not especially act
election underlined his growing status within the profession.

In his continuing search for good new plays he was facing an
battle. The West End fare of the early 1930s was essentially cosy
undemanding. Most of the forty theatres staged revivals, light dome
comedies, thrillers, musicals and revues. Popular 'serious' playwrigh
were few; they included Coward, Priestley, James Bridie and John va
Druten. Shaw's heyday was past, Maugham's career was on the wane.
The prevailing atmosphere was genteel: an orchestra played before
curtain-up and during the interval; the public, especially those in the
expensive seats, still wore evening dress. This was the climate in which,
with thoughts of building a company, Gielgud was looking not for a
star 'vehicle', but for plays that would provide substantial parts for
several actors.

One that came to him for possible revival was *Advertising April*, a
farce by Herbert Farjeon and his fellow-critic Horace Horsnell which
caricatured the lives of two glamorous film stars. He had seen Lewis

riginal production in his youth, with Sybil Thorndike
around in silk pyjamas and Frank Cellier burlesquing her
and had thought it 'prodigiously amusing and entirely
' and 'a deliciously absurd entertainment'. But in replying to
n his new role as producer he had to be more hard-headed:

frankly I don't see an ordinary audience with a Pit and a
ry being able to cope with it. For my own part, the types in
so painfully like the real thing that I fear their prototypes in
udience would be either really insulted, or 'not amused'! . . .
s, from my point of view, I think I am too 'straight' a per-
ality to play the part. I see more the conventional actor type,
h as Ainley or Ernest Milton, either of whom would, in their
veral ways, be immensely interesting and amusing . . . I feel
ther churlish in refusing the play for myself, and I am greatly
attered that you should have offered it to me first.

But one play that arrived interested him greatly. Gordon Daviot was
e pseudonym of Elizabeth Mackintosh, a grocer's daughter from
verness and a former games teacher, who had been writing plays
nce childhood (and who later wrote successful thrillers as 'Josephine
ey'). After seeing Gielgud in *Richard II* at the Old Vic, she had been
inspired to write a version of Richard's story using modern idiomatic
language, charting the king's progress from young, impetuous idealist
to bitter, disillusioned cynic. She called her play *Richard of Bordeaux*.

Gielgud read it through several times, and realised that the part of
Richard was 'a gift from heaven': while Shakespeare's king had no
humour, Daviot's had. Though he saw weaknesses in the play, he liked
its charm and originality, its mixture of romantic melodrama and
modern comedy, the fact that, like Shaw's *Caesar and Cleopatra*, it
showed kings and nobles talking like ordinary human beings. But he
was doubtful about its chances in the West End. Once again Albery
offered him the Arts, for two Sunday performances. Unable to engage
Komisarjevsky as producer, and hesitant about producing on his own
while playing such an exacting part, Gielgud persuaded Harcourt
Williams to co-produce. Around him he gathered the kind of quality
company that was soon to be his trademark: he cast Gwen Ffrangcon-
Davies as his wife Anne, and hired Robert Harris, Roger Livesey,
Anthony Ireland, Anthony Quayle and Margaret Webster. He also
engaged the Motleys as designers.

The try-out performances in the summer of 1932, staged not at the Arts but at the more spacious New, received a muted welcome. Horace Horsnell, one of the few critics to attend, wrote of 'many well-dressed scenes and clear-cut characters', but felt the play 'hardly develops or fully redeems its admirable opening promise'. Gielgud, easily influenced by the critical comments of friends, and still worried about weaknesses in the play, suggested detailed changes to the author, then forgot all about her. Several months later he received a revised version, and found to his surprise that Daviot had added, subtracted and rewritten scenes exactly as he had suggested. His enthusiasm was re-kindled. Although Albery was opposed to the idea of stars acting as their own producers, Gielgud decided to produce it himself because 'I knew more about this particular play than anyone else except the author'. It was the first of many productions in which he took on both roles, an arrangement that was to create many problems.

About half the original cast, including Gwen Ffrangcon-Davies, was available for the commercial run. Among the newcomers were Francis Lister and Richard Ainley. At the very last minute Donald Wolfit was brought in as Mowbray ('A poor part, but I hope to make it effective,' he wrote in his diary). Working with older actors such as Ben Webster and Frederick Lloyd, who had acted under Benson and Tree, Gielgud faced a severe test of his authority. Anthony Quayle remembers 'how courteous he was to the older and very distinguished members of his cast – and well he may have been: though God-like to me in his eminence, he was only twenty-eight.' To Gielgud's relief, the old guard responded to his suggestions: 'They obeyed me without question and had beautiful manners,' he remembered.

But two of the younger actors were less pliable. Wolfit, Gielgud recalled, 'took the part with a very ill-grace and sulked all the time and we became really quite strong enemies'. But it was Henry Mollison who caused the most trouble, by refusing to play Bolingbroke the way Gielgud wanted him to. In frustration Gielgud wrote to Albery asking him to sack Mollison, but the actor returned to rehearsals the next day provocatively waving Gielgud's letter to his manager. Most producers would have forced a showdown in the face of this rebellion. Gielgud, disliking confrontation and rarely capable of letting out anger, allowed Mollison to remain. According to Emlyn Williams, his behaviour greatly distressed Gielgud. While discussing some other matter he would suddenly say: 'What d'you think he muttered last night in front of the whole company?'

Gielgud was never a dogmatic producer, and was willing – sometimes too willing – to listen to the opinions of others. He had devised two tableaux in the style of Beerbohm Tree, one planned as a 'magnificent stage effect', with Richard burning down Sheen Palace. Just before the dress rehearsal, under pressure from the company, he reluctantly accepted that such ideas were outmoded, and dropped them. But he was also capable of taking decisions without due consultation. Margaret Harris recalled one such incident: 'We came into the theatre and saw that the fleur-de-lis on the end of the pediments in the set had been sawn off. We were asking the carpenter what had happened when a voice came from offstage: "I'm sorry, girls, but they couldn't see me from the gallery." It looked absolutely terrible, but it was too near opening night to re-build it.'

His mother was among those attending the dress rehearsal, as Tanya Moisiewitch recalls: 'She was in the front row and I remember her saying, "Pineapples only came in with Queen Anne" – so out went the decorative dish of fruit.' Overall the rehearsal was a disaster and, with the strain of his double responsibility taking its toll, Gielgud had almost lost his voice by the opening night in February 1933. But his performance provoked what Darlington described as 'a glorious full-throated roar such as the West End seldom hears in these sophisticated days'. Yet though some critics thought *Richard of Bordeaux* the best historical play since *Saint Joan*, others saw it as merely competent. It was Gielgud's production that won the plaudits. He was praised for transforming an interesting work into a gloriously moving one, skilfully knitting together the design, costume, lighting, music and acting. Agate wrote of a production 'flowing like music', while the *Manchester Guardian* marvelled at Gielgud's 'extraordinary ability to mould young actors while building up a beautiful performance of his own'.

Gielgud himself believed he had matured considerably as an actor. He felt he had more inner power to draw on, had reduced his tricks and mannerisms, and was learning how to relax. Most importantly, he had learned to be less wary of exploiting aspects of his own personality to interpret a character. Even so, the ecstatic response to his playing of Richard must have surprised him. *The Times* argued that 'he is acquiring the authority and presence that are the marks of a great actor', while Desmond MacCarthy wrote: 'In my opinion he is now the first of English actors. The range of his emotional scope, and the intelligence with which he conceives his parts, put him right at the top of his profession.'

Gielgud was in raptures for days: 'I felt so happy and exhilarated that I went for a long walk on the Downs in a heavy snowstorm,' he recalled. Richard was the perfect part for him to exploit his lyricism, humour and acute sensibility. But it was the romantic tenderness and nobility of his playing that reinforced his matinée-idol status. 'Dressed in cream or cloth of gold, the sculptured cheekbones and proud poise of the head nobly accentuated beneath the red-gold flame of hair, Gielgud was a royal figure with the hereditary Terry radiance,' the critic Audrey Williamson rhapsodised.

Once again he was impressed by the skilful, unselfish work of Gwen Ffrangcon-Davies, who received excellent notices as Anne; Agate thought there was no better actress in England. Gielgud found her wonderfully responsive to his playing, and admired the way she 'selected and economised her emotional effects from day to day, watching carefully how the other actors developed their performances, so that hers might grow with them in the most helpful possible way'. Their partnership was a close and harmonious one: 'I needn't tell you how happy it makes me to be with John again,' the actress wrote after the opening.

Wolfit noted in his diary. 'First night of *Richard of B* a big success. Everybody predicts a run, including Albery. Should get seven weeks out of it at least.' His prediction proved wildly pessimistic. The play was a sensational success, running for 472 performances and fourteen months at the New. From the window of his flat Gielgud gazed in delight at the queues coiling round the theatre. The play's pacifist theme appealed to a public beginning to look warily at the rise of fascism in Europe. It even received royal approval: King George and Queen Mary attended a gala performance at which, nervously uncertain whether he should wear his crown in their presence, Gielgud was presented to them in the interval.

The elegant but simple costumes and settings that Motley created for *Richard of Bordeaux*, based on the mille-fleurs tapestries in the Victoria and Albert Museum, marked the real beginning of a collaboration that was to prove crucial to Gielgud's success in the coming years, and launch the trio on their highly successful careers. Elizabeth Montgomery was the artist of the group; Margaret Harris – usually known as Percy – was the craftswoman, specialising in set design; while Sophie was the expert in making costumes. 'Liz was very neurotic, Sophie a bit frail, and Percy the more solid,' a friend remembers. They had now moved into a derelict third-floor studio in

Garrick Yard, a former workshop of Thomas Chippendale situated off St Martin's Lane and virtually opposite the New.

The production also brought about a visual revolution in the West End. In place of the usual expensive, elaborate costumes, the Motleys created simple but beautiful sets and costumes, made from inexpensive materials often picked up in the sales. For *Richard of Bordeaux* they used among other items dish-cloths, mosquito-netting and unbleached calico. Under Gielgud's influence they treated the costumes as an integral part of stage character. 'We got rid of all the fustiness, and tried to get the essence of the period without fussy detail,' Margaret Harris said. 'The play was the thing that had to be interpreted, and that was John's influence. He wanted us in our designs to encourage the audience to use their imagination, to suggest rather than fill the stage.' Gielgud found them ideal collaborators and constantly praised their taste and ingenuity: 'They are scientists as well as artists,' he explained. 'They try in the first place really to interpret what the producer wants. They come and ask me what I want to do with the floor-space, and have long conferences discussing "lines of sight". They think of the pretty costumes last.'

The three young women had taken their collective name from Jacques' remark in *As You Like It*, 'Motley's the only wear'. Gielgud tried to get them to drop it. 'John hated it, he thought it so arty,' Margaret Harris recalled. They had at first been thrown into paroxysms of shyness by Gielgud's tendency to hurl remarks over his shoulder, and to speak so fast he was barely intelligible. But now they were more assertive. 'He said he would ask Mary MacArthur to do the sets for *Richard*, but we said we wanted to do them. He said, You don't know how, and we said, We'll find out. It was very brave of him, but he was like that, if he thought something was right he would go for it.' The partnership soon blossomed. 'He used to come to our studio after a show, and work half the night on the model for the next play. It was very difficult to tell which were his ideas and which were ours. It was all great fun but terribly hard work.'

Gielgud was now a major star earning £100 a week, with a greater following than that of any other young stage actor. He had, the *Daily Express* reported, 'definitely established himself as the supreme idol of the pit and gallery, where most of the intelligent playgoers sit'. According to *Truth*, people felt 'the thrill of hero-worship in the air as soon as he takes the stage'. At Golders Green, on the last night of an eight-week tour of the play – described by one journalist as 'a sort of

Royal procession round the country' – the police had to hold back the crowds surging round the stage door waiting for their idol to emerge.

Gielgud was pleased by this massive adulation, but it also embarrassed him, and eventually bored him. Flattery made him feel awkward, as the actor Peter Copley remembers: 'I was seventeen and wanted to be an actor, and a mutual friend took me to his flat. In my well-mannered public-school way I said, "It's a tremendous honour to meet you." And he replied, "Don't be such a bloody little fool!" I was terribly embarrassed. But I realised he was shy.'

Many of his adoring followers saw him play Richard thirty or forty times. Alec Guinness, who sat in the gallery more than a dozen times, remembered: 'He came on to the stage with simplicity and a certain sort of beauty, and that beautiful diction, and of course that fabulous voice, which was like a silver trumpet muffled in silk.' Laurence Alma-Tadema, a friend of the family, wrote to Gielgud's mother: 'John gave me a certitude of greatness that so moved me I could hardly sleep last night . . . at times he reached, without the help of words, depths and heights of creative understanding which only the greatest ever reach.' Alfred Lunt and Lynn Fontanne, now at the top of the profession in America, came to a matinée in Streatham. Later the actress wrote to him: 'You are a very strange and very beautiful actor.' Gielgud was dizzy with delight: 'My head whirled round like a piano stool,' he confessed.

Now the toast of the West End, he was photographed, painted, caricatured and interviewed, and deluged with white harts (Richard's emblem) designed in flowers, embroidered on handkerchiefs and stamped on cigarette boxes. On the hundredth performance he was presented with a silk bedspread embroidered with Richard's coat-of-arms. Bordeaux dolls appeared on the market, and women clamoured to have the Motleys create medieval dresses for them. One fervent female admirer sent Gielgud fruit, flowers and expensively bound books several times a week; another commissioned a bust from Epstein to put in her sitting-room.

Girls and young women were especially smitten. The actress Judy Campbell, then sixteen, remembers: 'I saw it four times and went weak at the knees. I would wait outside the stage door just to get a glimpse of him.' Some young fans followed him in the street; others knocked unannounced at his flat; he answered telephone-calls from giggling schoolgirls phoning for a dare. Diana Wynyard, playing nearby at Wyndham's, observed: 'Every evening as I leave the theatre I find hundreds of autograph-hunters. Unfortunately they've all got their backs turned to me. They are waiting for Mr Gielgud!'

During the run Gielgud was forever making 'little additions and improvements' to the production. Despite this, and the regular cast changes which required fresh rehearsals, he began to be bored with Richard. Though he was learning to control his emotions better, he felt he was becoming exaggerated and insincere, and self-conscious in the moments for which he had been especially praised. To revive his flagging interest he considered combining *Richard of Bordeaux* with *Richard II*, presenting the latter at matinées. 'Oh my God, you do like work, don't you?' came the horrified response from Francis Lister. Gielgud dropped the idea. Eventually fatigue took over: members of the company told him he was emotionally exhausted, that he was becoming mannered. After six months he was given a fortnight's holiday from the production.

Gielgud was rarely happy away from the theatre, and after a few days touring the West Country he became restless. He took a suite in a Brighton hotel, and littered it with scripts. Unable to stay away any longer, he returned to London and, with Emlyn Williams, sneaked unseen into a box at the New to watch Glen Byam Shaw, his understudy. Williams recalled: 'At the end of one emotional scene between the king and his wife, I stole a look behind me: John was not just moved, he was weeping. I was in the company of a child playing with double mirrors.'

Playing one particular hysterical scene eight times a week strained his vocal cords, and he turned to Elsie Fogerty for advice. The founder and director of the Central School of Speech and Drama had helped many leading actors, notably Sybil Thorndike and Lewis Casson. After seeing *Richard of Bordeaux* she prescribed some simple exercises for Gielgud, and tried to get him to relax: 'Imagine your head is a two-pound pot of marmalade,' she told him. 'Now slacken every muscle, every limb, by slow degrees.' He found that 'her calmness and practical advice were immediately reassuring'. The problem went away, and never returned.

During the run Gielgud reinforced his growing reputation for tactlessness. Many of his gaffes were committed during the traditional curtain speeches. At the first night of *Romeo and Juliet*, holding Edith Evans and Peggy Ashcroft by the hand, he had declared, 'I hope never to have two such leading ladies again.' After the opening of *The Merchant of Venice* at the Vic he had thanked his co-producer Harcourt

Williams, 'who has done all the donkey work'. After a year of *Richard of Bordeaux*, he told an audience filled with regulars: 'I know that many of you have been to see us thirty or forty times.' He then paused, looked along the line of the cast until his eyes rested on Jack Hawkins, who had replaced Francis Lister. Then he added: 'In spite of changes in the cast.'

Touring *Richard of Bordeaux* after fourteen months at the New proved taxing. After a week in Glasgow he and Gwen Ffrangcon-Davies took to the hills. That evening he wrote from Ballachulish: 'The country here is grand, and the theatre merely, for once, an excuse for making a little filthy lucre!' The week had not been a fruitful one: 'Glasgow was foul to begin with, but the houses and weather are improving, and we are becoming gradually more cheerful. But when even Leslie Henson is disappointed at his business, what hope has poor Richard?' Complaining about the long run, he added: 'One must make hay, and money, while the sun shines.'

It was principally money that had persuaded him to suppress his dislike of filming and appear in two of the new talking films. 'I am in the throes of my first "talkie" – profitable, but I fear unattractive otherwise – and plunge into oriental cafés at Elstree,' he told Gabrielle Enthoven. *Insult*, shown in July 1932, was a convoluted and undistinguished Foreign Legion drama. Also starring Hugh Williams and Elizabeth Allen, it was directed by Harry Lachman, an American with a reputation as a photographer and painter, and a tendency to scream at actors. Gielgud, playing the son of a major, admired his scenic compositions but not his temper. It was the first of many occasions when he was compelled to ride a horse for the screen, and he did so gingerly, relieved that a double could do the mounting and dismounting in longshot.

Film Weekly called the film 'an insult to one of his ability'. He was on surer ground in his second film, *The Good Companions*, in which, though reluctant to do so, he repeated the role of Inigo Jollifant. Shown in February 1933, and directed by Victor Saville, this phenomenally popular film launched Jessie Matthews as a musical star. Yet her acting now appears forced and insincere in contrast to the easy charm Gielgud brings to his role. He gives a carefree, physically relaxed performance, leaping on to tables and chasing his co-star round the piano. He plays several songs with dexterity, sings in a light, melodious voice, and delivers his lines swiftly, with more than a hint of clipped Coward. He even copes well feeding quick-fire lines to the comedian Max Miller.

Only in two brief kisses does he seem hesitant and awkward. Jessie Matthews was aware he found these scenes an ordeal, and felt sorry for him. She found him a pleasure to work with: 'He was one of the nicest and easiest of leading men, no tantrums, no side, always cooperative and gentle and helpful,' she remembered. But Gielgud was not comfortable. With the long hours, the early rising, and having to play Richard in the evening, he found filming exhausting. Still a novice in front of the camera, he was disconcerted to find that in some scenes which he had played carefully only the back of his head was visible. The critic Caroline Lejeune wrote of the film: 'It suggests a long screen career for John Gielgud.' But in the next twenty years he was to make only two films.

In March 1934 Beverley Nichols wrote in his diary: 'John Gielgud to lunch. Very gay and charming. Told me he had just bought a country house for £1000.' The success of *Richard of Bordeaux* enabled Gielgud to fulfil a long-standing dream of owning a house in the country. His search took him as far from London as Warwickshire: 'We shall all be flying in a year or two, and it will only be a few minutes from London to anywhere,' he remarked cheerfully. Finally he and John Perry bought an old farmhouse in north Essex called Foulslough – a name he refused to change, despite its gloomy connotations. Set in four acres of land just outside the beautiful village of Finchingfield, with a long, narrow garden and stunning views across the cornfields, the handsome, isolated house provided him with tranquillity at the weekends. A visiting journalist found him relaxed, 'looking almost as romantic in blue shirt, grey shorts and sandals as in his *Richard of Bordeaux* splendours', and claiming to be loath to return to London.

It was a new, unexpected role, that of a country gentleman enjoying walks in the fields with his two Schnautzer dogs. But Gielgud soon became attached to the house. Its long, low-ceilinged sitting-room had space for his growing book collection and his grand piano; the two guest-rooms made it easy to have friends to stay. He added a new wing, and had a tennis-court and swimming-pool built, and a thatched barn in the garden converted into quarters for his cook-housekeeper and valet-butler-chauffeur. Yet the theatre was never far away.

As at Woodhill, there were frequent weekend house parties for theatrical friends. Geoffrey Toone was a regular guest: 'It was a lovely house, and John was absolutely charming, naughty and splendidly mischievous, but never malicious,' he remembers. 'He loved gossip and silliness, which is very different from foolishness.' The East Anglian theatre colony soon grew: the playwright Dodie Smith had just bought a cottage in Finchingfield, and both Gwen Ffrangcon-Davies and Diana Wynyard were to move into villages nearby.

Success also enabled him to improve his London home: he took over an upstairs attic, and turned it into a spare room and a studio. He was enjoying his celebrity status, as Emlyn Williams found when he visited the flat during the run of *Richard of Bordeaux*. 'I must remember to order three hundred more postcards,' Gielgud said. 'After the show I sit signing them in my costume as people come round. Yes, I know it's vulgar, but I can't resist it: I'm a star!'

13

Hamlet

Until then the London scene was a desert.
(Glen Byam Shaw)

DURING the fourteen months in which he appeared in *Richard of Bordeaux*, Gielgud produced two other plays. So began a pattern that was to continue for forty years, the parallel pursuit of two demanding careers. His appetite for work was voracious, his energy boundless. Often he would be simultaneously rehearsing a company as a producer, acting in another eight times a week, and planning the designs for a third. 'He was a terrifically hard worker, and he never stopped,' Margaret Harris remembered.

Sheppey was his first production of a play by an established living author. Somerset Maugham's witty and cynical plays had been fashionable in the West End for more than a quarter of a century. Recently he had been producing more serious work, but had become disenchanted with the theatre. The year before he had told the critic and playwright St John Ervine that 'in a very little while I propose to make my final experiment in that direction'. That experiment was *Sheppey*, a re-working of an earlier short story, which Albery asked Gielgud to produce. It was the story of a hairdresser who wins a large sum on the horses, but decides after 'seeing the light' to give it to a thief and to a prostitute rather than to his family.

Gielgud admired Maugham's plays, and was excited at the idea of reading a new script by him. But he found *Sheppey* a curious mixture of styles – part Pinero, part Shaw, part tragic fantasy – that made it difficult to produce. He also had problems with its author, who came over from France for the later rehearsals.

Diffident, self-contained and hampered by a lifelong stutter,

Maugham had no real enthusiasm for the theatre, and was never comfortable discussing his work with a producer. He was, however, prepared to consider changes; but Gielgud was too in awe of him and inexperienced to suggest anything radical. 'Do you want this scene played for comedy or pathos?' he asked deferentially. He found Maugham correct, polite, but unwilling to offer any opinion. 'He seemed dispassionate, quite untouched by the expectant atmosphere in the theatre,' he recalled. When he invited the playwright to a matinée to get his approval for minor cuts, Maugham remained virtually silent.

Gielgud blamed their failure to communicate on 'my actor's egotism' and 'my violent enthusiasms and youthful impetuosity'; but Maugham's austere and withdrawn manner intimidated many other people. Yet he clearly approved of Gielgud's work: at a dinner at Claridge's after the opening he drew him into the cloakroom, muttered a few polite words, and gave him a copy of the published script of *Sheppey*. Gielgud was surprised and flattered to find it was dedicated to him.

Starring Ralph Richardson, Laura Cowie, Angela Baddeley and Eric Portman, the play puzzled and divided the critics, though Ivor Brown thought Gielgud had 'extracted the uttermost' from a flawed and confused play. He certainly extracted a fine, unsentimental performance from Richardson as the bluff, saintly hairdresser: *The Times* thought his portrait 'masterly', while Desmond MacCarthy called him 'a perfect interpreter of a dramatist's subtler intentions'. But the play, which ran for only eighty-three performances, was Maugham's last: for the rest of his life he concentrated on novels and essays.

Gielgud's friendship with Richardson had survived a chance encounter during a recent holiday in the West Country. He had been staying at remote inns, eating enormous cream teas, taking long walks, and absorbing the picturesque scenery. Suddenly Richardson appeared over the horizon in his drophead Lagonda touring car, and whisked him away in it at ninety miles an hour. The trip was transformed, as Gielgud remembered: 'We visited tin mines, salt mines, pottery works, and listened attentively for several minutes while a workman at one of the slag heaps explained the technical details of his occupation to us.' This was all beyond Gielgud's grasp, and Richardson's interest bewildered him.

After Maugham, Emlyn Williams must have seemed like a tonic. Now a successful dramatist and actor, the Welshman was funny, cheerfully malicious, but industrious. His play *Spring, 1600*, about life in Shakespeare's acting company, centred on a young woman who dresses as a boy, comes to London, and falls in love with the actor Richard Burbage. Gielgud liked it, but was unable to persuade Albery to present it: 'Bronnie soit qui mal y pense!' he quipped to Williams. The two of them, together with a mutual journalist friend, Richard Clowes, decided to finance the production themselves. Almost by accident, Gielgud drifted into a third career as a theatrical manager.

Williams had known Gielgud only from a distance, and thought him affable but haughty. Now, in their discussions about the play, he saw the enthusiast, a 'melodious machine-gun' scattering verbal grapeshot punctuated by shrieks of laughter. 'I loved your play, how d'you feel about the last act? But there's so much to the rest. Peggy for the girl d'you think, or Jessica or Celia? What about Edna? She was beastly to me in *The Nymph*, but she has quality. Then there's Angela, she wouldn't play it Baddeley, but Edna might be Best.'

Later they worked together cutting and re-shaping the text, in sessions that Williams likened to 'a vigorous game of tennis'. He was impressed by Gielgud's close study of the script, and thrilled by the torrent of imaginative suggestions that came pouring out. Discussing the part of a whore that Isabel Jeans might consider if it was extended ('Let's call the play *Whores for Tennis!*'), he rattled on: 'Perhaps a scene in her palatial lodgings, with a couple of dabs of paint the Motleys would make them look like gorgeous Tiepolo draperies, a rostrum on wheels perhaps, Burbage drunk on her bed, panic in his theatre . . .'

Gielgud toyed with the idea of casting Richardson as Burbage, but decided against it: 'His is fundamentally a clown's face,' he told Williams. 'I'm afraid I told him so, and I do hope it's not the end of a long friendship.' A much more fanciful idea was to offer the female lead to the internationally famous Austrian actress Elisabeth Bergner. Then Europe's greatest stage star, she had played classical roles in Max Reinhardt's company, and had just fled to London to escape Hitler's Germany. Her accent alone would have prevented her from playing a young English country girl. But Gielgud, who had admired her films and photographs, thought it 'an exciting idea'.

He insisted on sending her a script, and even met her for lunch. Another guest at the table enjoyed watching the two of them 'talking together about the theatre with tremendous enthusiasm, yet without any affectation or pretentiousness'. So began yet another lifelong friendship with a distinguished, temperamental older actress. Unhappily for Gielgud, Bergner chose to play in Margaret Kennedy's

Escape Me Never, so he offered the part to Edna Best. 'I rather enjoy the thought of employing somebody who's been rude to me,' he told Williams. She came to the first rehearsal, then returned to America. Gielgud remarked: 'It's Bart of course, I did hear he's been a bit footloose in Hollywood' – an unfortunate way to describe her husband Herbert Marshall, who had an artificial leg.

The part was turned down by Celia Johnson, and finally given to Joyce Bland, who joined Isabel Jeans, Ian Hunter, Frank Pettingell and Margaret Webster in the company. Rehearsals featured Gielgud's usual search for perfection, as a watching journalist testified: 'One little scene – a matter of only a few lines – was gone over again and again. By the time the producer was satisfied, I think the actors themselves were half-hypnotised into believing they *were* the characters they had to play.' But Gielgud's painstaking approach was not welcomed by all the cast: Margaret Webster remembers being frustrated by his 'unending stream of new notions and suggestions and changes and improvements'.

Williams sat through rehearsals watching the play 'lurch and grow under the feverish, merciless care of its director; nobody could have guessed that he was playing an arduous part eight times a week'. At the first run-through, forgetting Williams was behind him, Gielgud announced through a megaphone: 'Sorry everybody, but you're all being too slow, we must get it tearing along here. Emlyn agrees with me that from now on this last act is thin.' Williams said, with remarkable equanimity: 'John, I agree with you that it's thin, but *please*, not through a megaphone.'

Gielgud's heavy workload caused him to make a serious error. Preoccupied with *Richard of Bordeaux*, he forgot to check the running time, and was horrified when Frank Vosper pointed out that the dress rehearsal had lasted three and a half hours. His decision not to make further cuts proved costly. Although his beautiful production prompted *Queen* magazine to dub him 'the greatest producer on the English stage', others commented on the play's inordinate length: J.G. Bergel suggested it was 'half an hour too long and fifteen miles an hour too slow'. Williams, too nervous to watch from the front, did so from a distance up in the 'flies'. At one stage he was forced to relieve himself in a wash-basin. 'You must be the first playwright who's pee'd over his own play,' Gielgud observed.

Devastated by the reviews, Williams made substantial cuts, thereby losing forty-five minutes. Before the second night Gielgud assembled the actors on stage. Williams recalled the scene: 'John rapped out, "I'm told you were all so good last night. Please remember the critics are in tonight too, those dreaded weeklies, so please give the same splendid show." He was not a Terry for nothing. The actors left, mouthing the cuts like sour wine, but mollified.' It was too late to save the play which, hampered by an all-enveloping fog, closed after less than three weeks at the Shaftesbury. 'Oh dear, I am sad for you,' Gielgud told Williams. 'We don't seem to have quite got away with it, all that work and love and then it just evaporates.'

As usual he took much of the blame himself, this time appropriately: 'My suggested additions overweighted the production,' he remembered. 'The slender plot sank deeper and deeper into a morass of atmosphere and detail.' He had also been extravagant with his production budget, engaging madrigal singers, a large orchestra, and a crowd of walk-ons, at a cost of £4000. 'It was rather a disaster,' Margaret Harris remembered. 'We spent too much money, including a fortune on creating an Elizabethan theatre. We even hired a monkey, which kept biting people.' It was a poor start to his career as a manager, and highlighted the damage that could be done if his love of decoration went unchecked, as well as the danger of committing himself to too much work.

His commitments included several charity matinées, to which leading actors were then expected to give some time. There were also annual events such as the Shakespeare Birthday Festival, and the Shakespeare summer event at Smallhythe Place. Ellen Terry's last home was being run as a museum by Edith Craig, who mounted a memorial performance of scenes from Shakespeare on or around the July anniversary of her mother's death. They were enacted in the tiny 100-seat barn in the garden, which she had converted into a theatre. Many leading actors performed there, and Gielgud was a faithful participant in its early years. Between 1930 and 1933 he played Hamlet, Benedick, Macbeth and (for the only time) Orsino; in 1934 he read a selection from the *Sonnets*. His nostalgic feeling for the occasion, and the Terry associations it evoked for him, are perfectly captured in a letter he later wrote to Edith Craig:

Every year the atmosphere of the memorial performance seems to grow fresher, and more touchingly unique in its simplicity and charm. The gathering of friends in that beautiful place looking over the marsh, the hospitable greeting, and then the unforgettable silence and warm responsiveness of the audiences crammed into the little barn: the rushes, and the red fire buckets, dressing in the cottage, and speaking magic words on that little intimate stage, with the dress baskets labelled 'Sir Henry Irving' just behind the wing, and Tony Atwood's beautifully executed properties and scenery to work with – all this makes up an occasion that I have delighted in every year, and which is quite unforgettable. I think in its strange mixture of professional and amateur, of gaiety and sadness – the ease of a country garden party and the solemnity of a tribute to a great artist, whose work was done in cities – it is amazingly fitting and right, and I believe Nell would have loved it as much as you and I do. It expresses much of her character through you, in the same way as her cottage still does, and her lovely garden, and her spirit which surely moves about the place wherever one goes.

There was also a family connection in his radio work. Val Gielgud had been head of radio drama at the BBC since 1928, having been offered the post after just six months as an assistant on the *Radio Times*. His appointment was a surprise: he had no radio experience and minimal technical knowledge, though he had produced plays for the BBC's amateur dramatic company. What he did possess, he suggested, was 'a wide if fairly undiscriminating knowledge of plays and players', and a burning desire to produce professionally. His presence at the BBC was to prove invaluable to Gielgud – and to others: in 1931 the *Old Vic and Sadler's Wells Magazine* noted approvingly that 'Mr Val Gielgud, with the weight of the BBC behind him, has been a constant sympathiser with the work'.

These were pioneering days in the BBC's primitive studios at Savoy Hill. In the early 1920s theatre managers had boycotted 'outside broadcasts' of plays from their theatres, fearing it would adversely affect the box-office. Ten years on radio drama was still a poor relation of the stage, and only one play a week was broadcast. The work was not taken seriously by actors: Val Gielgud recalled the typical view 'that there was nothing in broadcasting but script-reading and the equivalent of cigarette money'. A pioneering producer, he raised a storm when he suggested Shakespeare could be interpreted better on the radio than on the stage.

The first radio drama, scenes from *Julius Caesar*, had been broadcast in 1923; the first play specially written for radio came two years later. Once his brother joined the BBC Gielgud soon became involved. He made his début in 1929 in Pirandello's *The Man with a Flower in his Mouth*, and while at the Old Vic took part in scenes from *Richard II* and in an adaptation of *The Tempest*. Having also broadcast scenes from *Hamlet*, with Margaretta Scott, Martita Hunt, Jack Hawkins and Robert Donat, he and some of the company gave a repeat performance at Harrow School, where the smaller parts were read by the boys. Michael Denison, then a pupil, recalled 'a golden-haired young man, who was deeply impressive'.

In 1932 Val Gielgud produced him in *Othello*, in which he achieved his burning ambition to work with Henry Ainley, playing Iago to his hero's Moor, with Peggy Ashcroft as Desdemona. By now Shakespeare broadcasts were allotted two whole hours, and were being broadcast virtually uncut. But actors still found it hard to adjust. When Ainley played Othello he would step back during his main speeches as if he were addressing a large theatre audience, and had to be continually led back to the microphone.

Good voices like Ainley's were a minimum requirement for radio drama, though tone, pitch and volume all had to be modified. The critics had just started to review radio drama, but concentrated on its limitations. Reviewing Gielgud's 1932 Hamlet, Darlington compared 'the tremendous effect in the theatre of John Gielgud's magnificent acting as the finest Hamlet of our time' with 'the faint emotions I felt yesterday as I heard his voice borne over the ether'. Val Gielgud clearly had an uphill task.

After the success of *Richard of Bordeaux* Gielgud was sent dozens of similar costume plays. 'People seem to think I want to go on playing young romantic and neurotic parts and nothing else,' he complained. At the same time he made clear his refusal to avoid the conventional career path of an acknowledged leading West End actor. 'I do not always want to play star parts, I am as keen as ever on acting for its own sake,' he said. 'I would rather play a solid, well-conceived character in a good play than a star role in a poor one.'

He was now desperate to find a good, modern role: 'If my public don't see me soon in a pair of trousers they'll think I haven't got any,' he remarked. He found a pair at last in Ronald Mackenzie's second play *The Maitlands*, a tragi-comic tale of family life in an English seaside town, which Mackenzie had completed just before his death. Gielgud had been a little hurt not to have been shown the script by Mackenzie, or by Komisarjevsky, with whom the playwright had discussed it while writing it. But both of them had felt he was not

1. Felix the Butterfly in *The Insect Play*:
'I'm surprised the audience didn't throw things at me.'

2. Kate Terry Gielgud:
a devoted and conscientious mother.

3. Frank Gielgud:
a distant, moody and artistic father.

4. Unwillingly to school? Arthur John, also known as 'Jack'.

5. 'Masquerade', a drawing at 18 by the budding designer.

6. At 21, the year he understudied Noël Coward in *The Vortex*.

7. Early family influences: Ellen Terry and Edward Gordon Craig, at the Lyceum, 1891.

8. Making up as Romeo, 1924, as sketched by Laura Knight.

9. With Lilian Baylis (below) and Dorothy Green, the Old Vic, 1931.

10. As John Worthing in Wilde's masterpiece, 1930.
11. As Richard of Bordeaux, 1933.

ROMEO AND JULIET, 1935
12. Rehearsing Olivier, Peggy Ashcroft (left) and Edith Evans.
13. The rivalry begins: Olivier as Romeo, Gielgud as Mercutio, Edith Evans as the Nurse.

FOUR AT THE QUEEN'S, 1937/38
14. As Joseph Surface in *The School for Scandal*.
15. As Richard in *Richard II*.
16. As Shylock in *The Merchant of Venice*.
17. As Vershinin in *Three Sisters*.

18. Mother and son at the Haymarket, 1948.
'I can only be thankful that I lived to see John so wholly master of his art.'

suitable for either of the principal male parts. Their judgement was probably right, for when Komisarjevsky did send him the script, his instinct was to accept neither. John Maitland, the actor-brother of the family, seemed initially the more suitable, but Komisarjevsky persuaded him to go against type and play Roger Maitland, an impoverished, unhappily married schoolteacher.

The production starred Jack Hawkins, Catherine Lacey, May Whitty, Frederick Lloyd, and the promising young Stephen Haggard. It provoked extraordinary scenes on its first night at Wyndham's. Queues for the pit and gallery, mainly of young women, had been building up all day. As the curtain rose to reveal Gielgud in a shabby sports jacket, flannel trousers and a pencil moustache, a delirious yell broke out, followed by boos, catcalls and cheers, and a vigorous argument between members of the audience. 'Meanwhile I stood on the stage, paralysed with nervousness, waiting to speak the opening lines of the play,' Gielgud recalled. At the end there was booing amongst the tumultuous applause, and when Gielgud responded to calls for a speech, a cry of 'Rubbish!' came from the gallery. Although he managed to quieten the house with an emotional tribute to the dead author, the headlines the next morning were 'WILD SCENES AT WYNDHAM'S' and 'AUDIENCE IN ARGUMENT'. Their idol's sudden dwindling into ordinary clothes in a non-star part had been too much for some of his followers.

Agate thought the booing was by people who preferred escapism to the 'truth to life' which Mackenzie showed them. Other critics also praised the piece, which they believed showed Mackenzie was not merely a one-play wonder. Gielgud's notices were positive, though more muted than most recent ones. But he was uncomfortable as the down-at-heel schoolteacher, especially when he had to play drunk. His innate fastidiousness made him dislike such behaviour, real or imaginary. 'The more I see it, the more I detest drunkenness on the stage,' he had written at eighteen, after seeing a production of Galsworthy's *Windows*. He was never a convincing drunk, and despite endless rehearsals made a terrible hash of the scene in *The Maitlands*. He was also, for the first time, dissatisfied with the work of Komisarjevsky, who had somewhat Russianised the English seaside town atmosphere. While praising him in public, he privately felt he had failed to exploit 'a brilliantly effective piece of theatre, full of bitter wit and observation'. After a transfer to the Criterion, the play ran for a modest four months.

During the run Gielgud was saddened by the comparatively early death at sixty of Nigel Playfair. In an eloquent letter of condolence to his widow, he wrote warmly of their theatrical relationship:

I always felt at ease with him and able to talk to him naturally and freely as I could with hardly any of the older generation in the theatre. He and Leslie Faber were the only two men of that age I knew at all and could consider my friends, and I regret very much that they should be taken so soon, for I should always have valued so greatly their friendship and advice.

Recalling Playfair's 'lovable personality', he added:

His simplicity and approachableness were always so remarkable when one remembered all the very grand things he had achieved, and that amusing attitude of his that the whole thing was just a hobby – when his own red-hot enthusiasm had turned it into a real artistic, and even a commercial, success – was always a most endearing and attractive quality to me.

One evening Gielgud was visited in his dressing-room at Wyndham's by a strange, thin young man, dressed in shabby grey-flannel trousers and a skimpy sports jacket. Alec Guinness, aged twenty, had recently won a prize at a public performance at Fay Compton's drama school, at which Gielgud had been one of the judges – he later remembered 'being greatly struck by the evident talent of a skinny boy with a sad pierrot face and big ears'. Some months before that Guinness, who already hero-worshipped Gielgud, had found out his telephone number and boldly rung him for advice. Gielgud responded kindly to this total stranger, and advised him to take voice lessons from Martita Hunt, which Guinness had done. Now desperate for work – he was understudying for £1 a week – living on apples, milk and jam sandwiches, he was emboldened to approach Gielgud in person.

What followed highlighted not just Gielgud's keen eye for talent, but also his generosity towards other actors. 'He was friendly and kind,' Guinness remembered. 'He painted his eyebrows for a moment or two in silence and then became immensely practical.' He suggested auditions Guinness could attend, and insisted he report back to him every evening. But Guinness had no luck, and after an audition at the

Old Vic – at which after two lines the producer Henry Cass yelled at him 'You're no actor: get off the fucking stage!' – he returned in despair to Gielgud's dressing-room. 'All I had left was the proverbial half-crown,' he recalled. 'On the side of his make-up table was a neat pile of one-pound notes. "The next time I do a play I'll give you a part," he promised, "but you are far too thin. Here's twenty pounds – for God's sake go and eat properly."' Guinness, proud but afraid of getting into debt, politely refused the money. But Gielgud would not forget him.

For some time now people had been asking why, after his Old Vic triumph, he did not return to Shakespeare. He had certainly not lost interest in the plays. Some months before in a letter to *The Times* he had defended Guthrie's controversial production of *Measure for Measure* at the Old Vic. He called it 'a most beautiful and satisfying production . . . entirely original, and modern in conception, and yet executed with a sureness and power worthy of the best and oldest traditions of our stage'. Now, prompted again by Barker's work, the subject was on his mind: 'There is so much room for enterprise in Shakespearean production, but opportunities are continually neglected.'

Although it was only four years since he had played Hamlet at the Old Vic and the Queen's, the idea of mounting his own production had been preoccupying him for nearly a year. He had been mentally casting it, and arguing endlessly with the Motleys about costumes and sets. It was fortunate he had done so, for when Albery suddenly suggested he stage it at the New in November with a cast of his choice, he had little time to gather a company, and only four weeks in which to rehearse.

He and Albery were taking a risk in staging *Hamlet* in the West End. In London Shakespeare was mostly confined to the Old Vic, although productions in the Open-Air Theatre in Regent's Park, begun two years before by Robert Atkins, were proving popular. At Stratford the new theatre had only recently opened, and standards there were erratic, although Komisarjevsky had recently staged iconoclastic productions of *The Merchant of Venice* and *Macbeth*. Shakespeare was occasionally staged in the West End, but his plays were not considered commercially viable. Fresh in Gielgud's mind was the time when Ainley's, Moissi's and his own Hamlet at the Queen's had all failed at the box-office. Ernest Milton's more recent staging of *Othello* and Godfrey Tearle's of *Julius Caesar* had suffered the same fate. The New was cautiously booked for just six weeks.

Gielgud had set himself a formidable task. It was the first time he had combined the roles of producer and leading actor in a Shakespeare play, and he was doing so with one of the most complex and physically demanding parts in the classical repertoire. In addition, during the early days of rehearsals he was still playing in *The Maitlands* in the evenings. Graham Robertson recorded: 'He told me that he was playing badly, as he was rehearsing *Hamlet* every day and could think of nothing else.'

His cast was a strong one, a shrewd blend of experience (Laura Cowie as Gertrude, Frank Vosper as Claudius, George Howe as Polonius) and youth (Jessica Tandy as Ophelia, Jack Hawkins as Horatio, Glen Byam Shaw as Laertes). Frank Vosper was now a close friend. A talented playwright as well as a fine actor, he had a distinguished record in the classics: he had already played Claudius in the 'Plus Fours' *Hamlet*, and Romeo and other leading parts at the Old Vic. He had also scored a success in Mordaunt Shairp's controversial *The Green Bay Tree*, a play which had dared to hint at the existence of homosexuality. Vosper, homosexual himself, was sleek and lantern-jawed, full of warmth, wit and vitality. A fellow-actor described him as 'a great big orange pussy cat'; Mackenzie had based the character of the actor in *The Maitlands* on his personality.

As with Richardson, his friendship with Vosper was an attraction of opposites. Restrained in his behaviour and intellectual in his tastes, Gielgud was drawn to Vosper's playful, bohemian personality. 'He loved ragging me about my highbrow activities,' he recalled. 'Some people thought him affected and rude, but I loved his sublime disregard for other people's disapproval.' Vosper's tragic death three years later – he fell overboard from an Atlantic liner – shocked him greatly. 'I miss him continually,' he wrote not long after.

During rehearsals for *Hamlet* Gielgud's impatience and tactlessness were much in evidence. 'He sat in the dress circle with his feet on the rail, and shouted at the actors and changed everything every minute,' Margaret Harris remembered. Faced with his patrician manner and formidable reputation, the younger actors were 'absolutely terrified of him'. The young ones included George Devine, the Player King: 'Oh, why is your voice so harsh?' Gielgud asked. 'It really is quite ugly. Do *do* something about it.' There was also Sam Beazley, who eventually gave up acting for many years as a result of Gielgud's treatment of him.

Frith Banbury was another victim: 'I think John took against me, something about my personality irritated him,' he recalls. 'He never stopped picking at anything I did. One speech went on rather; he interrupted me with, "Banbury, don't be prim," and gave the rest of it to Jack Hawkins. It was awful. Then at the dress rehearsal I missed my entrance, and had to climb down the stage revolve like some bloody gazelle. John stopped the rehearsal and said: "Banbury, I can forgive you for being late, but what I cannot forgive is you standing like that when you do arrive." I felt very, very small.'

But the actor who suffered most was Alec Guinness. Gielgud had kept his promise to find him work, and cast him as Osric and the Third Player. 'It was torture, because he was very, very impatient and would say totally the wrong thing,' Guinness remembers. 'It took me a long time to throw off the self-consciousness he instilled in me.' The shy young actor was overwhelmed by 'a rapid stream of commentary, together with wildly contradictory instructions from the stalls', such as: 'Come on from the left. No! No! The *other* left! Oh, someone make him understand! Why are you so stiff? Why don't you make me laugh?' All this, without pause for breath, was interspersed with remarks to his designers: 'Motleys! Motleys! Would it be pretty to have it painted gold? Perhaps not. Oh don't fidget, Frith Banbury. Alec Guinness, you are gabbling. Banbury, your spear is crooked. Now turn upstage. No, not you. You! Turn the other way. Oh, why can't you all *act*? Get someone to teach you to act!'

Guinness's script, filthy grey from all the changes to his moves, was also 'smudged with tears'. After a week Gielgud said: 'What's happened to you? I thought you were rather good. You're terrible. Oh, go away! I don't want to see you again.' Shattered, Guinness asked him a little later if he was fired: 'No! Yes! No, of course not. But go away. Come back in a week. Get someone to teach you how to act.' When he re-joined the production, Gielgud showered him with praise for his work – although Guinness was sure he was doing nothing different. But at Christmas Gielgud gave him an edition of Ellen Terry's letters, inscribing it 'To Alec, who grows apace', and adding Hamlet's advice, 'The readiness is all'.

Gielgud could disarm actors with his humour and self-mockery. But even the Motleys couldn't always cope with his ever-changing demands. Sam Beazley, one of the Players, recalls him saying: 'Oh, the Motleys are in tears again.' Banbury, later a leading director, suggests his behaviour came from an inability to put himself in the shoes of another actor: 'Because acting came easier to him than to most, he didn't realise how difficult it was for us. He wouldn't wait for you to get it right: before it came out of your mouth, he would correct you. This was surprising, because he was quite humble about his own work.' Guinness, who called him 'a living monument of impatience', believes it was part of his quest for the highest standards: 'He was a strict disciplinarian, intolerant of any slovenliness of speech and exasperated by youthful tentativeness.'

Having seen twenty productions of *Hamlet*, Gielgud wanted to get away from 'the hackneyed Gothic style of decoration, in which the King and Queen look like playing-cards, and Hamlet like an overgrown Peter Pan'. He had been impressed by Fagan's 1924 OUDS production, for which the characters were dressed in the style of Dürer, 'suggesting admirably the atmosphere of luxury and intrigue, of sensuality and crime and supernatural happenings'. This was the basis for the costumes: the Motleys ingeniously suggested magnificence while essentially using little more than canvas and paint spray. The set, unusually for the time, was a permanent one, heavily influenced by Craig, who had designed Stanislavsky's famous 1910 production of *Hamlet*.

Gielgud was so busy concentrating on working with the other actors that he neglected his own part. Often he would skip some of the longer speeches in rehearsal, 'for fear of wasting the company's time', and rehearse them himself at home. There was another problem. 'I am apt to be swayed in my views about certain details, both by outside criticism and my own judgement,' he told Graham Robertson. Margaret Harris recalled: 'Martita Hunt came to the dress rehearsal and said John looked awful, he must have a new costume. He believed in Martita, so we had to make a new one overnight. It was a nightmare. It still wasn't quite ready just before the performance, and his dresser used to run over every ten minutes to ask where it was. So he went on never having worn it before. But he seemed to take it very calmly.'

Gielgud's status had changed significantly since his 1930 Hamlet. The critic M. Willson Disher observed that 'besides inspiring hero-worship in schoolgirls who have never set eyes on him, he excites more true playgoing zeal than you will find anywhere else in London.' Interest in his new Hamlet was huge: the production attracted record advance bookings for a non-musical play, and the number of applications for seats for the first night in November was the most the New had ever received.

Hamlet ran for four and a half months and 155 performances, the longest run since Irving had staged it in 1874. For the last two performances hundreds were turned away. The production then toured for five weeks, and was acclaimed all over again. Yet for a performance which was to become legendary, and which provoked a torrent of cheers and a dozen curtain calls on the first night, Gielgud's reviews were very mixed. Several critics referred to his inaudibility in certain speeches; others found his performance 'subdued', 'too curbed in its emotional display', and even 'cold'; one referred to a dangerous tendency to 'speak the speech too trippingly'. Agate wrote: 'This Hamlet abounds in loveliness, but one feels that this actor's treasury could yield more.'

The explanation lay in Gielgud's exhaustion, brought on by the burden of producing himself in a role of immense complexity. 'I never saw an actor look so utterly tired out as he did,' one critic wrote of his curtain speech. 'He looked as though he might collapse at any moment.' Val Gielgud, emerging from the theatre, realised 'he was dead to the world'. This was an under-rehearsed Hamlet: Gielgud missed out key lines in the closet scene, and improvised at other moments. He had started to think seriously about the part only a few hours before the opening, after a long talk with a friend (almost certainly Martita Hunt) who attended the dress rehearsal. 'I told this friend how I thought Hamlet should be played and, after advice, I found myself playing my own version,' he explained after the opening. 'I shall be playing Hamlet better in a week. I shall have shaped the part and put everything into working order.' It was an astonishingly casual approach to such a formidable role.

Yet his performance also won great praise. Darlington called it 'the finest Hamlet of our time', while Grein praised his 'relentless insight and psycho-analytical profoundness'. J.C. Trewin was thrilled by his voice, which 'had the range of a violin, a Stradivarius controlled by a master'. Ashley Dukes wondered at his ability to make Hamlet's thoughts seem new-minted, as if they had just occurred to him. But some critics missed the youthful exuberance of his first Hamlet. Ivor Brown, recalling how it 'had fired the general imagination, and moved the gods to approving thunders', found his new interpretation too cold and rational; others thought it too intellectual. But Agate, who had felt he lacked pathos before, felt Agate's had now been 'remedied to a very remarkable degree'. This allayed one of Gielgud's anxieties, for, as he told Graham Robertson, he felt Agate's earlier criticism had been right.

Gielgud welcomed the diversity of opinion, and the continuing challenge of the part. 'People do seem to find it stimulating and controversial, and that is very important,' he observed a month into the run. 'I suppose one cannot hope ever to play the part entirely to one's own satisfaction, or anyone else's either, which gives one impossible ideals to strive for, and is very exciting.' His production was widely acclaimed: 'If I see a better performance of the play than this before I die, it will be a miracle,' Charles Morgan declared. But Farjeon made what was to become a familiar criticism: 'You cannot do justice to your own Hamlet if you are thinking half the time about the right way to play Ophelia and Polonius and the gravediggers, with scenery, lighting, effects, and the other multitudinous harassing details that must crowd a producer's mind,' he wrote.

For the younger actors Gielgud provided an object lesson in acting. Guinness, who was to play Hamlet four years later, and who watched Gielgud 'at least a hundred times from the wings', remembers in particular 'the courtliness and the charm, mixed with the mordant wit'. Sam Beazley was awestruck by his performance: 'He had great magnetism and power. I used to watch him in the great soliloquies, with this bright light on him: there was this electric, quivering silence between him and the audience, it was really magical. He didn't vary his delivery, and yet it always seemed spontaneous, fresh and vital. It was a great experience, and all the company were aware of that.'

Trewin later called it 'the key Shakespearean revival of its period'. Gielgud had proved that Shakespeare could be made profitable in the West End: the production costs of £1500 were paid off in the first two weeks, and the play took £33,000, an enormous sum for the time. Hundreds of people who had queued for hours for the last two performances were turned away. Gielgud was attracting devotion and hero-worship from theatregoers of different ages, on a scale which had not been seen since Irving's days at the Lyceum. His success was due in part to the new audiences he attracted to *Hamlet*. 'Gielgud wants it to be a "show" for the common man who may or may not have seen it before,' *Era* reported. A fellow-actor observed: 'He is playing nightly to houses half of which have never read *Hamlet* and the other half never even heard of it.' *Vogue* noted that *Hamlet* had become 'almost as much the thing as any Cochran revue. Its fame has spread even to the dormitories of Eton and Harrow and Dartington and Bedales; so that many parents, wondering whether to take young home-for-the-holiday-makers to *Peter Pan* or *What Happened to George*, have been surprised to learn, almost before the trunk was on the taxi, that Shakespeare is not only for all time, but for Christmas too.'

Gielgud had also set new standards of design and production for serious plays. Glen Byam Shaw, later a producer himself, recalled the production's seminal influence: 'Nobody could believe his *Hamlet* could run five months in a West End theatre. Until then the London scene was a desert. There was no production as we understand it now at all. There were some good classical actors, but their costumes and scenery were unbelievably tatty and awful. The change really started after John's productions of *Bordeaux* and *Hamlet*. Directly after that, when other talented young actors saw that you could have that sort of success from doing interesting plays instead of light comedies, they all followed suit. The standard went right up.'

At the age of thirty, Gielgud was already at the top of his profession. 'For the second time within a year a delicate-looking young man whose fair hair is thinning rapidly on top overshadows everybody else in the London theatre,' the critic Stephen Watts wrote, adding prophetically of his Hamlet: 'His performance will be one of the monuments to our time in the history of the theatre.'

14

Saint-Denis and *The Seagull*

Chekhov is not in the Terry blood.
                    (Shaw on Gielgud, 1936)

FROM his newly eminent position in the profession Gielgud now joined the long-standing debate about establishing a national theatre. Begun in the nineteenth century, it had been fuelled by Barker and William Archer's 1907 book *The National Theatre: A Scheme and Estimates*. In it they advocated a purpose-built theatre, a permanent repertory of plays, and a company of actors on three-year contracts. As a result a committee was set up to raise the money, a site was bought in Bloomsbury, and Shaw, Barrie, Galsworthy and others gave their support. Although the First World War put a halt to further progress, the pressure to move ahead intensified in 1930 when Barker updated his book, advocating the building of two theatres under one roof on a site on the south bank of the Thames.

One of the main obstacles to progress had been the rivalry between the supporters and governors of the two theatres seen as most likely to form the basis of any national theatre: the Shakespeare Memorial Company at Stratford, and the Old Vic. Stratford had had a poor record artistically with its Shakespeare summer festivals, but had been doing well financially since the opening of its new theatre. The Old Vic, on the other hand, was producing much exciting and innovative work, particularly under Guthrie, but was still hampered by a chronic lack of money. But in Lilian Baylis's eyes, 'When I think of all the work that has been done by our three companies . . . I know we are the National Theatre.'

In the spring of 1935 Gielgud argued that a 'Shakespeare theatre' was needed more than a national theatre: 'Good new plays of the classic order are very hard to come by – and the producer at the National Theatre may find himself torn between tripe and Shakespeare!' He questioned the wisdom of building a new theatre in central London, advocating instead the amalgamation of the Old Vic, Sadler's Wells and Stratford, with the Old Vic being the principal base. 'It does not seem to me very worthy that there should be in existence three imperfect Shakespeare theatres which could so easily be turned by money, goodwill, and fine organisation into one really worthy of England and able to influence the country by producing the plays continually, finely, and alternately in the big cities.'

Meanwhile he ventured into management for a second time, with Rodney Ackland's adaptation of Hugh Walpole's novel *The Old Ladies*. Walpole, already famed for his Herries novels, was rated alongside writers such as Arnold Bennett and John Galsworthy. The novel, set in a boarding-house in an English cathedral town, told the story of three lonely, impoverished old women, driven by conflicting desires, ambitions and greed. It was one of Gielgud's favourite books: he had approached its author not long before about collaborating on a stage version, but Walpole had been busy completing the Herries sequence. Gielgud greatly liked Ackland's adaptation, but was unable to persuade Albery or any other manager that this macabre, downbeat story with a small, all-female, elderly cast – Edith Evans, Jean Cadell and Mary Jerrold – would attract West End audiences. Once again he took a risk, persuading Richard Clowes to co-present the play with him. Clowes, a known wit, remarked: 'I'm just a bird in a Gielgud cage.'

Rehearsals began while Gielgud was still playing Hamlet. A journalist captured him in action: 'Suddenly, from the darkness of the dress circle, a voice rang out, authoritative, rich, clear and incisive, and a most vibrant, *living* quality.' Rehearsing with Edith Evans required all these qualities, especially since she was playing her first part since her husband's death from a brain tumour only weeks before. During rehearsals Gielgud confided anxiously to a friend: 'Edith will I hope be easier to manage when we get a theatre – at least her assertion of personality is a sign of returning vitality, which is something to be thankful for – and she will give a wonderful performance, which is another.' But her way of asserting her personality could be irritating. Her relationship with Walpole, who was homosexual, was not warm: when he asked her if she liked the novel, she replied innocently: 'Oh, is it from a book?' During one rehearsal at which he and Ackland were both present, she called out: 'Oh Mr Author . . .' When both men stood up, she asked provokingly: 'Oh, shall I call *you* the author and *you* the authoress?'

But Gielgud's prediction proved correct. Her playing of the terrifying harridan Agatha Payne was, according to *The Times*, 'a slow nightmare of macabre genius'. Under Gielgud's guidance she sublimated her grief and gave a powerful, chilling and bravura performance. But the work of Mary Jerrold and, especially, Jean Cadell was also widely admired, and Gielgud was given due credit for the high-quality acting. Darlington said he was 'a producer with more than a touch of genius', while *The Times* thought 'the performances, orchestrated by Mr Gielgud, collectively flawless'. In his diary Agate included Gielgud alongside Komisarjevsky, Guthrie, Dean, Atkins and Casson in his list of the ten best producers of straight plays.

Yet while it enhanced his reputation as a producer, *The Old Ladies* did nothing for Gielgud as a manager. Despite enthusiastic notices, it closed after playing for less than two months, first at the New and then the St Martin's. Gielgud blamed his inability to find a small theatre for Ackland's intimate piece and, less convincingly, the public's preoccupation with King George V's 1935 jubilee celebrations. Yet the risk he took in backing Ackland's clever adaptation underlined his determination to produce works of quality in the West End, rather than merely to strive for commercial success.

However, raising West End standards required good producers. Opening an Easter school organised by the British Drama League, Gielgud bemoaned their shortage: 'There are only four or five of whom any of us would say, "I should like to be produced by him." All the others are only actors who produce plays themselves because there are so few good producers.' He identified three on his quality list as Komisarjevsky, Guthrie and Basil Dean, but felt it would be 'invidious' to name more – presumably because one would be John Gielgud.

After *Hamlet* Gielgud needed a different acting challenge. 'Never have we had a young actor of established popularity less content than he to rest on his laurels,' one critic noted. Most of the new plays sent to him he considered 'poor stuff'. He was interested enough in one about the life of Sir Thomas More by John Palmer to buy the rights, but nothing more came of it. He finally found what he wanted in *Noah*, a modern version of the story of the Flood by the French playwright André Obey.

Noah was a simple, charming and humorous play – 'a nursery tale for adult minds' one critic called it – in which Noah spoke directly to God, and actors impersonated the animals in the ark. Albery had brought the original version to London in 1931, and again the following two years. Performed by the Compagnie des Quinze, a group of actors, acrobats, mimes and musicians, *Noé* had caused a sensation. English audiences, unused to a non-naturalistic way of playing and brilliant ensemble work, were mesmerised. The play had also had a great impact on the profession: 'It was like a delightful ballet, only it had fifty times more content than any ballet ever had,' Guthrie wrote. Gielgud too had been impressed, admiring the teamwork of the troupe, 'who are making people realise the power and potentialities of simplicity'. Hearing that Pierre Fresnay, the creator of the title-part in Paris, had succeeded with it in New York, he got Albery's enthusiastic support for a London production of an English version, with himself as Noah.

As producer Gielgud brought in Michel Saint-Denis, who had staged the original production, and also taken over as Noah during the London run. Like Komisarjevsky, Saint-Denis was to have a significant impact on his work as both actor and producer – as he was also to have on that of Guthrie, Devine, Olivier, Ashcroft, Byam Shaw, the Motleys and others. Soon he was to found the London Theatre Studio (LTS), a school famous for its innovative ways of training actors. Now, based in London and hoping to start his own company, he was still a newcomer to the English theatre.

His antecedents connected Gielgud to a radical European theatrical tradition that embraced both Craig and Stanislavsky. Saint-Denis was the nephew of Jacques Copeau, founder in 1913 of the Théâtre du Vieux-Colombier – a small, shabby theatre on the Left Bank in Paris – and a great influence on European and American theatre. An admirer of Stanislavsky's work, Copeau was dissatisfied with the rigidly traditional productions of the classics at the Comédie Française, and with the shallowness and poor standards of acting and production in contemporary plays. 'Let's have no more stars!' he proclaimed. 'Yesterday's queen is today's servant; everyone must be trained, educated and disciplined in a single-minded manner and completely united under the producer.' He was influenced by Craig's ideas on design, and presented plays with only minimal sets. He took his own company, Les Copiaus, to the French countryside, where for years he trained them to represent stories dramatically through mime, rhythm, noise and music. Going back to the roots of popular theatre, the company performed 'diversions' for peasant audiences using their ensemble style of theatre.

In 1929 the troupe disbanded, but immediately re-formed as the Compagnie des Quinze. Saint-Denis, who had been stage manager and assistant producer, and one of their best actors, took over as producer. In February 1935 he came to England, hoping to form a similar troupe. Two of the London cast of *Noah*, Marius Goring and George Devine, were already enthusiasts: Devine told him he was looking forward to 'a show by your company which may, by the Grace of God or Bronson Albery, bring some light to the messy dirge of our theatrical life'. He became a disciple of Saint-Denis, whose ideas were to influence his later work at the Royal Court. Gielgud, always alive to new ideas, admired his work enormously, but from more of a distance.

Fastidious, pipe-smoking, with the face of a peasant, Saint-Denis was a painstaking and disciplined producer. The American director Harold Clurman, one of the founders of the Group Theater, later called him 'the most cultivated, innately refined, spiritually pure person' he had met in the theatre. But though like Gielgud he was a perfectionist, he was less human and flexible, and immensely intimidating. Yvonne Mitchell, who trained at the LTS, recalled: 'He had enormous strength, physical, moral and mental. His only weakness seemed to be that he could not admit weakness in others.'

Chattie Salaman, another student there, got to know him well. 'He was a great man, the first person to talk of theatre as an art-form, which was a shock at the time,' she remembers. 'But actors found him difficult, because he always had this vision, and would push and push people to try to get there, without making allowances for who they were. He was horrible to most people.' Gielgud was no exception, as Margaret Harris recalled: 'Poor John, I don't think he enjoyed *Noah* very much, Michel gave him rather a hard time.' After the production Gielgud described Saint-Denis as 'extremely patient, quite inexhaustible, demanding that one shall concentrate and labour unceasingly, as he does himself'. But after his death he was more forthright, calling him 'something of a martinet with a very orderly French mind'.

He certainly felt constrained by Saint-Denis's rehearsal method. Working from the Quinze prompt book, the Frenchman repeated exactly his previous production. He came with detailed notes about movements, business and characterisation, leaving the actors no room for invention. Alec Guinness, playing a Wolf, remembered being 'driven mad by Michel's meticulous little moves'. Saint-Denis insisted that Gielgud reproduce Pierre Fresnay's performance to the last detail, making him feel like 'a good cook trying to cook a dinner that's been ordered but which he has not quite created himself'.

There were other difficulties. Saint-Denis's poor English made communication difficult. He was used to a rehearsal time of more than four weeks, and was not good at working at speed. To complicate matters further, the translation was too American, and featured remarks such as 'Hey, you floozies!' Gielgud found it hard to translate the colloquial original into appropriate English. He also struggled with the physical demands of the part, which required him to balance precariously on a ladder, climb through trap-doors, crouch doubled up on the ground, and play the handyman. 'I suffered agonies trying to learn how to hammer the nails in the boat I was supposed to be making, of giving the impression of a man who worked with his hands,' he recalled.

As well as Goring, Devine (predictably cast as the Bear), and Guinness and Merula Salaman (who were later to marry), the cast included Colin Keith-Johnston, Marjorie Fielding, Harry Andrews and Jessica Tandy. The Motleys created a series of delightful masks for the actors playing the animals. The play opened in a heatwave, putting enormous physical demands on Gielgud, who wore a padded jacket underneath heavy peasant clothes, and was soaked through; during one rehearsal he actually fainted onstage. It took an hour and a half every night to turn himself into the 600-year-old Noah, with his wig, long white whiskers and beard, eyebrows, blacked-out teeth, and make-up.

'HIS ADMIRERS DID NOT KNOW HIM' ran a headline the next morning – though this hadn't stopped two hundred of them, mostly women, from besieging the stage door after the performance. But for the first time since he became a star, Gielgud's first-night entrance was met with silence. The audience were stunned to see their idol and acclaimed Hamlet reborn as what Ivor Brown called 'a prodigious mixture of Lear, Job, Tolstoy, and the Old Man of the Sea'. Sean O'Casey writing in *Time and Tide* called it 'a tour de force of mimicry' and 'grand acting'. But Agate, writing apparently with inside know-ledge, wrote that 'Mr Gielgud for the first time has created nothing, but allowed himself to be clay in the hands of the producer'.

Audiences were unsure how to respond to the play's mixture of pathos and comedy, and to the stylised technique taught by Saint-Denis. Many of Gielgud's fans, unhappy to find their idol hidden behind his costume, stayed away. But *Noah* still ran for a respectable three months at the New during a blisteringly hot summer. It was welcomed as an antidote to the prevailing realism, and Gielgud's performance was much liked. Graham Robertson noted: 'His Noah is a colossal figure distinctly over life-size and on the heroic scale, an illusion which no amount of make-up or padding could produce without the Something Else that he supplies. And he's such a slip of a boy – when he sheds Noah's character and his garments in his dressing-room there seems to be nothing left.' He was also impressed by Gielgud's dedication, the way in which he 'goes on working and striving towards some goal which he has set up for himself, never resting on his oars and allowing his head to swell gently'.

Working with Saint-Denis was difficult but rewarding. Gielgud had been terrified the Frenchman's approach would destroy his fragile self-confidence and belief in his own talent. Saint-Denis, he admitted, made him feel lazy, ignorant, self-satisfied and 'very humble'. Yet these emotions merely spurred him on to work harder. Always eager to explore new ideas, he relished the chance to learn how to use mime and the stylised technique of the French troupe, both quite alien to English actors. He was grateful to the steely-minded Saint-Denis for another reason. Noah was a character part in every sense of the word, and Gielgud had never concealed his own personality so successfully. His admiration for Saint-Denis was so great that when the Frenchman said at the final performance, 'At last you are beginning to find the way to play the first act,' Gielgud was encouraged rather than cast down.

Like others, Saint-Denis found Gielgud reserved: 'He is not distant, but he keeps his distance,' he observed. 'He is not a person you get to know easily.' But he also perceived and admired Gielgud's inner toughness, and his capacity for hard work: 'The impression he gives from the stage is an impression of frailty, of subtlety, of delicacy. Yes; but see him in the garden of his country house in Essex, in shorts, standing solidly on two strong legs . . . There I realised that behind this apparent frailty was real physical strength and resistance . . . Without such strength one cannot play Hamlet eight times a week.'

Gielgud's parents were devoted attenders of all his first nights, his mother regal and upright, his father wearing a top hat. But Kate Gielgud's involvement in his career often went beyond this. Margaret Harris remembered an incident during *Noah*: 'She came over to the studio and asked if we could think of some other way of giving him Noah's shape without all the padding; perhaps a cane superstructure? She was very protective.' Gielgud seemed unembarrassed by her interventions: a friend who arrived in his dressing-room minutes after the opening performance found his mother solicitously waving a large feather fan over her son's head. But Frank Gielgud also put in the occasional appearance, sometimes dropping in to the Motley studio and playing Chopin elegantly on the piano. 'He was a very gentle character, and very kind,' Margaret Harris recalled.

Gielgud's status in the theatre was highlighted when he took part just before *Noah* in a matinée at Drury Lane to celebrate Marie Tempest's fifty years on the stage. The highlight was a masque written by John Drinkwater and produced by Guthrie. Gielgud led on a starry company representing theatre past and present: Irene and Violet Vanbrugh, John Martin-Harvey, Edith Evans, Lilian Braithwaite, George Robey, Lewis Casson and many more. In his diary Agate wrote that of the 250 actors who took part the one he admired most was Gielgud. 'I wonder whether John is a *great* actor? His grace and poise are remarkable, and his voice would melt the entire Inland Revenue.'

As a national celebrity Gielgud's views were being sought on many topics. In a lengthy article in a popular paper on his 'Programme for Living', he confessed that 'even at the risk of losing friends and becoming a bore' he felt an increasing need 'to put the theatre first and everything else afterwards'. He also stressed the enormous pleasure he derived from his life. 'I never cease to be grateful for the enthusiasm with which I was born, which makes the routine of my profession a delight instead of a penance,' he wrote. 'It is not difficult to work hard at a thing when it is one's business, one's hobby and one's chief pleasure and interest all combined.' This indeed was one of the keys to his unflagging absorption in the theatre; away from it, one writer noticed, 'he is a little abstracted and pale and spent'.

His 'ordinariness' offstage was sometimes remarked on: 'You would not see the sort of physique that blinds sensible women to the shortcomings of the tea served at matinées,' one critic wrote. 'His proud, pale face is pleasingly erratic. His clothes are comfortable rather than elegant. His hands have the tapering grace of the pianist – which he is. Yet that normal-looking man of thirty is one of the really great actors.' Another writer noticed his shyness: 'He gives the impression of wanting to be polite and not offend, but not quite knowing how to to set about it!' He was invariably obliging to journalists, who wrote warmly of his modesty, enthusiasm and charm.

His flippant side emerged in a questionnaire-style feature published in a theatre programme, in a series entitled 'The Truth, the Whole Truth':

Favourite book? – Ellen Terry's memoirs
Preference if not actor? – A gentleman of leisure
Favourite dish? – Scrambled eggs
Pet aversion? – Lapdogs
Happiest moment? – When I went on the stage
Favourite actor/actress? – Conrad Veidt/Gwen Ffrangcon-Davies
Most frightful experience? – Every first night
Ideal holiday? – Sleep and motoring
Peculiar weakness? – My bed

His social life was still intensely active. He went to genial lunch parties at Emlyn Williams's house in Chelsea, where Coward, Rodney Ackland and the dancer Robert Helpmann ('I'm Outback and I'm Outrageous!') were frequent guests. At other parties he played the piano; at one he and Beverley Nichols jointly entertained the guests with 'a programme of melodious memories' from the 1920s revues of his youth. In his West End flat he held cocktail and dinner parties: Alan Dent remembered one with Coward as a guest which was 'at once august and frivolous', and another where Mrs Pat arrived booming, 'Who is there here who still *loves* me?'

Sometimes Gielgud even let journalists into his flat, to report on the décor and furnishings. They tended to do so in gushing style. 'Here we are back again in the sitting-room,' wrote one. 'Don't you admire the beige-brown upholstery? Mr Gielgud is very proud of the fact that this is – hessian. *There's* a hint for you, if you want to re-upholster *your* sitting-room.' The writer added coyly: 'A soft beige is the general colour scheme of his bedroom. Isn't the bedspread a surprising note in a man's room – a glorious soft rose-pink silk!'

Nine months after *Noah* Gielgud affirmed his belief in the value of an ensemble by assembling a cast of extraordinary quality for *The Seagull.* Chekhov was now accepted as a great dramatist, one whose poetic naturalism and truthful delineation of character revealed a subtle portrayer of human unhappiness. His plays had reached the Old Vic, where Laughton had appeared in Guthrie's production of *The Cherry Orchard.* Farjeon exclaimed in delight: 'Chekhov popular! Can there be some hope for humanity after all?'

Gielgud engaged Komisarjevsky to produce what was the first full-length production of *The Seagull* in the West End. Chekhov had described it as a comedy with 'much talk of literature, little action, and five bushels of love', and it proved the ideal play for the top-quality ensemble Gielgud gathered together, with Edith Evans as Arkadina and Peggy Ashcroft cast as Nina. Gielgud could still have played the more romantic part of Konstantin, but gave this to Stephen Haggard, opting instead for the vain, weak and selfish writer Trigorin, the part played by Stanislavsky in the Moscow Art production. He assembled a classy supporting company, which included George Devine, Leon Quartermaine, Martita Hunt, Clare Harris, Frederick Lloyd and, in a non-speaking part, Alec Guinness. It was, as one critic put it, 'a Cabinet of all the Talents'.

Komisarjevsky came armed with his own translation and costumes, and with ambitious if costly ideas about the set design. But he also brought along some provocative opinions. At the first reading he astonished the company and upset Gielgud by delivering a harangue on what he saw as the dreadful state of the English theatre, peopled by wretched actors completely lacking in style. This tirade was doubtless provoked in part by the presence of Peggy Ashcroft, now his wife. Later she admitted it was admiration rather than love that persuaded her to marry Komisarjevsky: 'I was got by his genius,' she said. Although they had been married only a year, the notoriously unfaithful Russian – known backstage as 'Come-and-seduce-me' – had recently left her for another woman.

The critic Hubert Griffith, who sat in on rehearsals, described Komisarjevsky's method: 'He is the quietest of producers. I have never heard him give an actor an intonation, or say how a line should be spoken. He will discuss what the character is thinking or feeling, and leave it to the actor to work out.' But he could also be destructive. Edith Evans, infuriated by his initial remarks, eventually worked well with him. But once, when she failed to follow his direction exactly, he said to another actor: 'How can such a stupid woman be such a great actress?' He also remarked that, 'John Gielgud and Edith Evans are so successful now they only want to play themselves.'

Fortunately for their working partnership Gielgud only heard of this comment later. It was, however, well wide of the mark. Since teaming up with Albery he had been at pains to avoid being typecast. Often he had followed a romantic role with a strikingly different one, sometimes to the consternation of his public. *The Seagull* was a classic example. As ever, he wanted the chance 'to make experiments in character work, and to contribute in a supporting part without spoiling the balance of a fine team'.

However, as with Tusenbach in *Three Sisters* at Barnes, he failed to see eye to eye with Komisarjevsky over his character. No doubt aware of Gielgud's West End following, Komisarjevsky wanted him to play Trigorin as a fashionable gigolo, and gave him a pencil-slim moustache and elegant evening dress to help him achieve this. Gielgud, unhappy about the interpretation, nevertheless fell in with it, as he was so often to do with producers he admired. Afterwards Komisarjevsky told him that Stanislavsky and other Russian actors who had played Trigorin had all been dressed elegantly. But Gielgud's view was closer to Chekhov's own. In Moscow, where Stanislavsky had played the part 'in the most elegant of costumes and a handsome make-up', Chekhov had said that he should instead have worn check trousers and shoes with holes in them.

Gielgud's decision to play Trigorin surprised some critics, though others applauded his courage in taking on such an unsympathetic part. Most found his performance thoroughly satisfying and proof of his versatility, though the *Morning Post* critic, stuck in the age of Irving, noted sadly: 'His Trigorin does not give him anything like a full actor-manager's chance.' Some critics thought he made the character too charming, allowing the matinée-idol Gielgud to overshadow Trigorin's callousness. Others complained of a lack of passion in the love scenes, while Agate ambiguously labelled his performance 'an exquisite exhibition of sensitive Gielgudry'.

The production, set in the Edwardian period, was ecstatically received. More naturalistic and less melancholy than many English versions of Chekhov, it was lauded for its beautiful settings: Gielgud thought it 'masterly in conception and finely carried out'. There was praise too for the ensemble acting: Farjeon thought it 'as flawless as it is tender'. In his traditional first-night curtain speech Gielgud, loyally putting aside his reservations about the interpretation of Trigorin, called it an 'inspired' production, adding that Komisarjevsky had made the company love the play as much as the producer did himself. It became a much-talked-about production, as Gielgud acknowledged to a friend during its first week: 'It is exciting that everybody likes and dislikes different performances and points of production. We are playing to wonderful business.'

The Seagull increased Gielgud's admiration for the artistry and dedication of Edith Evans. Though she had done so successfully in *The*

Old Ladies, she generally disliked playing unsympathetic parts. Once, playing a kleptomaniac, she explained: 'No, no, she just likes pretty things, she doesn't steal.' When Gielgud handed her *The Seagull* and suggested she play Arkadina, he added: 'Of course she's rather a bitch.' Having read the play she disagreed with his analysis. Gielgud recalled: 'I knew then she was going to find the sympathetic side of the character and play it as all unattractive parts must be played.' She received glowing notices for her Arkadina. 'Her performance was full of the most subtle touches of comedy, alternating with passages of romantic nostalgia,' Gielgud remembered.

His own notices, and the attention to detail he brought to Trigorin, were a reminder of his ability to empathise with Chekhov's lonely, yearning, sometimes absurd characters. He also enjoyed the contrast with Shakespeare, the chance to play, as Stanislavsky put it, 'with the fourth wall down', almost as if there were no audience present. 'Playing in Chekhov isn't like playing in any other way,' he pointed out. 'One gets so quickly away from the ordinary stage conventions that playing in Chekhov to me is like playing a part in a novel.'

After seeing *The Seagull* Marie Tempest wrote to him: 'You are a grand artist, my dear, and with your taste *and* sanity, will go very far.' But Shaw, who may have known nothing of Gielgud's Slav ancestors, took a different view of his performance. Now eighty, and disenchanted with the theatrical scene, he wrote to Edith Evans in typically perverse fashion: 'I went to *The Seagull*, and disliked it extremely. You kicked it round the stage; and Gg (Gielgud) killed it dead every time he walked on. Chekhov is not in the Terry blood.' After declaring 'Komisar has lost his old Russian touch', he ended: 'Gg's nullity was stupendous, considering that the man *can* act when the stuff suits him.' But Shaw, as so often, was in a minority of one.

Many critics commented on the fine playing of the lesser roles. 'Throughout we have the rare and exhilarating spectacle of seven or eight first-rate players playing perfectly into each other's hands for a purely Chekhovian end,' Agate wrote. Such comments reinforced Gielgud's determination to create a more or less permanent company to present the classics. It was a notion both Komisarjevsky and Peggy Ashcroft believed in fervently, as did Saint-Denis. His experience with *The Seagull* led Gielgud to consider the idea more seriously.

He had already reinforced this conviction by lending his support to the London Theatre Studio, which Saint-Denis had just opened in conjunction with George Devine and Marius Goring, in Diaghilev's former studio in Soho (it moved after a few weeks to Islington). Saint-Denis' intention was that the students should form the nucleus of a permanent company after three years. After Albery and Guthrie had put money into the scheme, Gielgud, Laughton and Olivier followed suit. Gielgud also joined its committee, and there were plans for him to 'instruct pupils in the speaking of verse'.

A theatrical circle was now forming around him in the West End. Its base was the Motleys' studio, which became an unofficial social club, and the scene of intense discussions about theatre. 'The *joie de vivre* was marvellous,' Gielgud remembered. At the core of the group was George Devine ('very bohemian, like an artist from the Quartier Latin with his pipe and corduroys'), who was now the Motleys' business manager, and was soon to marry Sophie Harris. Also in what Agate called the 'Gielgud coterie' were Glen Byam Shaw and Angela Baddeley, Peggy Ashcroft, Jack Hawkins and Jessica Tandy. Regular visitors to the studio included Edith Evans, Gwen Ffrangcon-Davies, Robert Donat, Michael Redgrave, Rachel Kempson and Alec Guinness. Another habitué was Anthony Quayle, who remembered it being full of 'friends who enjoyed each other's company, shared each other's aims, and were to a greater or lesser extent under John Gielgud's patronage. At its centre was John himself, lord of the London stage.'

Yet this lord was already being rudely challenged by an ambitious, thrusting young actor, who would soon become his greatest rival, and remain so for more than half a century.

15

Enter Larry

I was the whipping boy, he was the adored god.
(Laurence Olivier on *Romeo and Juliet*, 1935)

OLIVIER'S career was in the doldrums. He had made his mark in the Stage Society production of *Journey's End*. He had also supported Coward and Gertie Lawrence in *Private Lives* in London and New York. Despite being fired from playing opposite Garbo in *Queen Christina*, he had gained some success in Hollywood, where he hoped to become the new Ronald Colman, and where he was taught gymnastic tricks by the arch-swashbuckler Douglas Fairbanks. But he had done little of merit recently in the theatre. 'I'm washed up, I'll never make it,' he protested despairingly to Emlyn Williams.

Like other young actors he had been influenced by Gielgud; he thought his first Hamlet 'wonderful'. The actor Roland Culver recalled accompanying him to an Old Vic production in 1929, unspecified, but probably *Richard II*: 'He was transfixed by Johnny's performance – by the grace of it, by the insight that flowed from its understated eloquence.' Until then Olivier's acting had been aggressively masculine; he had deliberately suppressed his more feminine impulses. 'Then he saw Gielgud letting his own femininity flow free, and he was thoroughly impressed by the way it enhanced Johnny's performance, giving it complexity, surprise and a mysterious depth.'

It was then, Culver noted, that Olivier first started talking about becoming a classical actor. But by 1934, when he came to work with Gielgud for the first time, his ambition had still not been realised. Jack Hawkins, who was Horatio to Gielgud's Hamlet that year, recalled Olivier telling him 'he'd like to give old Hamlet a try, to see if he couldn't do it better than Gielgud. It was a bizarre idea, really, since one didn't think of Larry in Shakespearean terms – he just didn't have the voice.' At the time Olivier was giving an athletic performance in *Theatre Royal,* a thinly disguised satire on the Barrymores. Hamlet was for the future, but Gielgud was about to set him on the road as a classical actor.

He was planning to produce Gordon Daviot's next play *Queen of Scots.* While touring *Richard of Bordeaux* he and Gwen Ffrangcon-Davies, for whom the play had been specially written, visited all the castles and palaces in Edinburgh connected with Mary. From Manchester Gielgud wrote to his mother of 'a hectic week of telephones and telegrams, trying to arrange about Mary with Bronnie'. He had hired the famous poster designer E. McKnight Kauffer to do the sets, but was dissatisfied with the results: 'I have remodelled all Kauffer's sets, which were all quite useless,' he told her.

He was, however, pleased with his 'first-class working cast', which included George Howe, Mercia Swinburne, Glen Byam Shaw, Frederick Lloyd, Margaret Webster, William Devlin and, from the Old Vic, the young James Mason. Gielgud handled this rich array of talent and temperament with dexterity: Margaret Webster later described it as 'the gayest, friendliest and most harmonious company I have ever been in'. But he made one mistake, casting Ralph Richardson as the passionate, arrogant philanderer Bothwell. In rehearsals Richardson predictably struggled with this flashy, romantic role, feeling shy in the love-scenes with Gwen Ffrangcon-Davies. Eventually he asked to be released, and suggested Olivier as his replacement.

Gielgud knew Olivier only casually, but had seen him in several productions, and admired and envied his bold physicality. Despite there being only eight days before the opening, Olivier jumped at the chance to play the dashing, brawling, philandering Bothwell, in doublet, high boots and red goatee beard. So great was his excitement about his first costume role that he took his cloak home to wear at the weekend. Gielgud rehearsed with him for fourteen hours a day.

The critics thought his performance 'virile' and 'excellent through-out', but also 'rather exaggerated', 'unconvincing' in the love-scenes, and 'more Hollywood than Holyrood'. Agate felt he was too light in the voice, 'which has the tennis club, will-you-serve-first-partner-or-shall-I? ring about it'. Olivier's athleticism was already in evidence; one night he broke his ankle jumping over a balcony. 'One thought of oneself as a sort of Tarzan,' he recalled. Gielgud, who thought of himself as anything but, nevertheless recognised Olivier's talent. The part helped to revive Olivier's flagging stage career.

The production was greeted with the kind of critical comment Gielgud's work now regularly attracted: 'a joy to the eye at every point', 'masterly in every detail', and so on. But he himself had found the play uneven, and thought his production the same. It enjoyed nothing like the success of *Richard of Bordeaux*, and an August heatwave helped to kill it off after only a couple of months at the New.

It was the elderly actor-manager John Martin-Harvey who was responsible for bringing Gielgud and Olivier together again. After finishing with *Hamlet* Gielgud conceived the idea of adapting Dickens's novel *A Tale of Two Cities* for the stage. His collaborator, suggested by John Perry, was Terence Rattigan. Though he had written half a dozen plays Rattigan, still only twenty-four, had yet to achieve any real success; to make a living he was working as a scriptwriter for Warner Brothers. He recalled the manner in which Gielgud offered him the job: 'I can't find anyone to do this *Tale of Two Cities*,' he said. 'I'm sure you're not doing anything. Would you like to do it?' Then came the instant second thoughts: 'I wonder if it's all right to have someone without any experience?'

The two of them worked on the script at Foulslough, Gielgud planning the structure and scenario, Rattigan writing the dialogue. They worked fast: the third act was completed in just over a week, and Albery agreed to stage the play at the New, with Gielgud doubling as Sydney Carton and the Marquis de St Evrémonde. Martita Hunt, Fay Compton, Mary Clare and Leon Quartermaine were hired, and the Motleys designed a set. For Rattigan, weighed down by rejection slips, it seemed like the break he was hoping for.

Two weeks before rehearsals were due to start Gielgud received a 'violent letter' from John Martin-Harvey. Now seventy-two, the actor-manager had worked under Irving at the Lyceum, and had been considered by some to be his natural successor. Although he had been acclaimed in many classical roles, including Hamlet and Oedipus, the part for which he was best known was Sydney Carton, in the adaptation of Dickens' novel entitled *The Only Way*. He had first played this romantic role at the Lyceum in 1899, and had toured it since all over the world. Poised for yet another 'farewell performance', he resented the idea of any competition, and wrote to Gielgud: 'For you to usurp the part of Sydney Carton would be like proposing to stage *The Bells* while Irving was still alive.'

Gielgud thought this ridiculous, and was very upset. He showed the letter to Albery, and the two of them met Martin-Harvey at the

Garrick. He also rang Agate and a few other critics who, to his astonishment, told him that to continue would be disrespectful, and 'taking bread out of an old man's mouth'. Gielgud, foolishly he later thought, deferred to the old actor, and the production was abandoned. The Motleys were in despair; but it was also a cruel blow for Rattigan, made worse by the way Gielgud told him about the alternative. 'It's a pity about Martin-Harvey, isn't it?' he said. 'But it's lucky, the design works for *Romeo and Juliet*, so we can do that instead.' This was all news to Rattigan: 'I went away and cried quietly,' he remembered. 'John was delighted with himself. He never said he was sorry at all. He hadn't seen it from my point of view. It was just, what's good for the theatre, is good.'

For both men the disappointment proved a blessing in disguise. Gielgud, perhaps from remorse, persuaded Albery to send Rattigan a cheque for £50 for the work he had done. Albery invited him to submit another play, which Rattigan immediately did. Albery took up an option, but after nine months it lapsed. Then Gielgud came across it in Albery's office. 'To everyone's amazement, and my own joy,' Rattigan recalled, 'he liked it enough to tell Albery that, whenever he did it, he himself would be glad to direct it. This was the spur that was needed.' In fact Gielgud was not available to direct *French without Tears* when it was staged by Albery in 1936, but the play was an overnight sensation and made Rattigan's name.

An alternative to *A Tale of Two Cities* now had to be found quickly, otherwise Albery would have to abandon the lease of the New. This threat, together with the availability of Peggy Ashcroft and Edith Evans, and his realisation that the set the Motleys had designed for Dickens could be adapted for Shakespeare, led Gielgud hastily to suggest *Romeo and Juliet* as a replacement. Ever since his OUDS production Gielgud had longed to stage the play professionally, and improve on what he considered his inadequate earlier attempts at Romeo. Apart from the 1924 production in which he had first played the part, there had been no significant revival in London since the 1919 one at the Court, starring Basil Sydney and Doris Keane as the young lovers. Gielgud stressed the need for every generation to re-discover Shakespeare for itself: 'I believe one must try to create the pace and general spirit of a Shakespeare play anew at rehearsal, and treat it as if it were a modern work which has never been produced before,' he said.

At the New he succeeded gloriously, with a production that became a landmark in British theatre. It transformed Peggy Ashcroft from a promising young actress into a West End star and classical player of the first order. It confirmed Gielgud's belief in the value of working with an ensemble of top-class actors. It reinforced what his *Hamlet* had already shown, that Shakespeare could be profitable in the West End. But it was also celebrated for bringing Gielgud and Olivier together on stage for the first time, to alternate the parts of Romeo and Mercutio.

In retrospect this seems like a brilliant scheme designed to set the town alight. There were precedents: Phelps and Macready had alternated Iago and Othello nearly a hundred years earlier, as had Irving and Edwin Booth at the Lyceum later. But this was not what Gielgud originally planned. He knew from experience that Romeo was a difficult part for him, and was worried that a good Mercutio would eclipse him – as Quartermaine had done to Basil Sydney. He therefore thought it safest to play Mercutio, whose early death would also allow him more time to concentrate in rehearsals on his work as producer.

He then decided to alternate the two parts with Robert Donat, another half-Polish actor, a friend, and a fine and sensitive classical player. But Donat, who had just turned down an offer from Hollywood to play Romeo opposite Norma Shearer's Juliet, was planning his own production. He agreed to withdraw, but declined to play in Gielgud's production. Gielgud then approached Olivier – and was astonished to discover that he too was working on a production, in which he would play Romeo opposite his wife Jill Esmond. Olivier privately boasted that both he and Donat would be more suited to the part than Gielgud. But seeing where the greater opportunity lay, and that Gielgud already had a theatre, he dropped his plans, and accepted Gielgud's offer with alacrity.

There is an alternative, more plausible account of the casting. This has Gielgud offering Donat only Romeo, which he turned down because of other commitments. When no suitable alternative could be found, Gielgud in desperation considered playing Romeo himself. Hearing of his problem Donat suggested Olivier for the part; but Gielgud had already decided he would be too showy and boisterous. Donat thought otherwise, and brought Gielgud and Olivier together for lunch at the Ivy. Afterwards Gielgud, though still believing Olivier too coarse for Romeo, offered him the role – but only on condition he also learn Mercutio, so that if the critical reaction was negative the two of them could switch roles. Olivier was offended by this, but Gielgud insisted on it as an insurance against commercial failure.

Either way, the notion of the production being planned as a clash between the uncrowned king of the West End stage and the young pretender to his throne is a fanciful one, based mainly on hindsight and later accounts. Although Olivier had achieved some success under Gielgud's direction in *Queen of Scots*, he had little Shakespearean experience, and none at all in a major role. He had also been consistently criticised in recent stage appearances for his poor use of his voice: Agate accused him of confusing realism with unintelligibility.

Because of the late decision to stage the play Gielgud had only three weeks in which to rehearse the cast. Once again there was a shrewd mixture of youth (Ashcroft, Byam Shaw, Devine, Guinness and Harry Andrews) and experience (Edith Evans, Frederick Lloyd, H.R. Hignett). But Gielgud soon clashed with his chosen Romeo. Olivier had shaved off his film-star moustache but, self-conscious about his low, weak forehead, decided – as he would frequently do later – to wear a false nose. Gielgud remembered that he was 'tempted to remonstrate' about this bizarre notion for playing Romeo. According to Olivier he actually did so: 'I remember him being upset about this and begging me to take the thing off. I was obdurate.' Olivier claimed that when Gielgud asked Albery to back him up, he himself said to Albery: 'Perhaps you would like to have it taken from me by force? But then, how would you force me on to the stage?' His blackmail worked: the nose remained in place.

Rehearsals revealed the clash of two theatrical cultures. While Gielgud wanted to preserve the beauty and rhythm of the verse, Olivier preferred to stress the reckless, passionate, impulsive youth of sixteen. Harry Andrews observed: 'I don't think the interpretation pleased Gielgud greatly, but there was no quarrel.' Others in the company say there *were* arguments, focusing on Olivier's refusal to play the part in the way Gielgud thought appropriate. Significantly, Gielgud was most annoyed by the ardent way in which Olivier played the love-scenes, and asked him to tone them down.

One cast member recalled that 'Larry was out to dominate the play by the sheer force of his presence, to ride roughshod over the rest of us as we went about things in our rather restrained Gielgudian fashion'. There were certainly fundamental differences over the verse-speaking, though Gielgud later refused to blame Olivier for them: 'I daresay I was somewhat smug after a few recent successes, and perhaps was inclined to patronise him from my position of authority,' he observed. 'I bullied him a great deal about his verse-speaking, which, he admitted himself, he wasn't happy about.'

But Olivier admitted no such thing. By his own account he was 'carrying a torch, I was trying to sell realism in Shakespeare'. He rebelled against what he saw as Gielgud's over-lyrical, musical approach, believing that 'Shakespeare was now being handled in a certain way, and that because of the extremely strong influence that a man of Johnny's power and gifts would have on the company, all the company would be going that way'. His playing was not to the liking of one Gielgud protégé: 'We all admired John greatly, but we were not so keen on Larry,' Guinness recalls. 'He seemed a bit cheap and vulgar, striving after effects and making nonsense of the verse.'

A week before the opening Gielgud was emphasising the musicality of the lovers' roles: 'I want to set Romeo and Juliet in contrast to the other characters – poetry in contrast to prose,' he explained to the critic Stephen Williams. 'I want to set them almost on an operatic plane, so that they shall *sing* those marvellous duets while the other characters speak their lines.' This was precisely the effect Olivier claimed he was trying to avoid. Yet if he was hostile to the notion then, he was not showing it publicly. Coming off the stage after rehearsing the nuptial scene he was very much the humble pupil, remarking to Williams: 'In other plays you have to draw on your own knowledge; in Shakespeare you are learning all the time.'

Romeo and Juliet opened in October, and was acclaimed by public and critics alike. Gielgud's production was commended for its speed, clarity and vigour, for its beauty, grace and ingenuity. Barker told him it was 'the best bit of Shakespeare I've seen for years'. Peggy Ashcroft's performance was praised for its naturalness, for her ability to balance the child and the woman in Juliet; Darlington called her 'the finest as well as the sweetest Juliet of our time'. Edith Evans, playing the Nurse for the fourth time, triumphed again, although some thought her performance almost too powerful for the balance of the production. The all-round quality of the acting was marked; even George Devine as Capulet's servant attracted good notices. There was also praise for the Motleys' innovative permanent set, which enabled the action to flow more freely than usual: with only one curtain drop and the briefest of black-outs, the action was not constantly held up by applause, as normally happened. Gielgud was breaking with tradition.

But the spotlight fell inevitably on the performances of the two principal actors. Gielgud (who also played the Chorus) had found Mercutio a difficult part; his early death seemed to give little time to develop his character: 'You have to strike twelve in every scene,' he explained. But several critics thought he did so brilliantly, giving a light, easy performance full of impudent raillery, in which his swift rendering of the famous Queen Mab speech stood out. Farjeon found him 'speaking beautifully (but not too beautifully) and lighting up like the flash of sunlight on the blade of a rapier'. Gielgud himself enjoyed the gaiety of Mercutio, a part he had long been fascinated by.

Olivier later exaggerated the critical reaction to his Romeo, referring to a 'sledgehammer of opprobrium' which 'struck its blow from every critic to a man'. In fact the critics liked many elements of his performance: he looked suitably Italianate and every inch a lover, and his acting was thought virile, fiery and full of animal magnetism. Agate called him 'the most moving Romeo I have seen', and Guthrie wrote to him praising his 'speed and intelligence and muscularity'. But for Olivier such comments were outweighed by the scorn poured on his handling of the verse. Stephen Williams observed that 'his blank verse is the blankest I ever heard'; another critic declared 'Mr Olivier plays Romeo as if he were riding a motor-bike'; and Agate concluded: 'One wanted over and over again to stop the performance and tell the actor that he couldn't, just couldn't, rush this or that passage.'

Gielgud had clearly failed to douse Olivier's 'torch of realism', his determination to play the part his own way. But Olivier, who had 'always seen myself as the one and only Romeo', was shattered by the criticisms. Before the second performance he told Albery he was prepared to give up the part. Albery refused to let him, and Peggy Ashcroft, who admired his performance, also encouraged him to continue. Shortly afterwards Olivier disingenuously asked John Laurie, who had been at the Old Vic: 'What is this thing called blank verse?' When Laurie explained about the five beats in a line he said: 'Is that all?' Ironically, once he recovered from the opening night, during which he had shown obvious nerves, he developed considerably in the role. St John Ervine, who came to a later performance, described him as the best Romeo he had ever seen.

Shortly before the change-over of parts after six weeks, Olivier was indisposed for one performance, allowing Gielgud an invaluable try-out as Romeo. 'Better than a week of rehearsals,' he told a reporter. But he was worried about what he saw as Olivier's loudness and extravagant tricks as Mercutio. After the dress rehearsal he told Byam Shaw of his 'serious premonitions' about the critics' likely response to Olivier's performance, and his worries about he might handle it. There was also a real problem: in their scenes together they kept trying to speak on each other's cues. 'If I was not very careful I used to say the Queen Mab speech with my lips, while I stood as Romeo, watching Larry as Mercutio,' Gielgud recalled.

When they changed roles the critics turned out in strength, ready to compare the rival performances of the two parts. Most preferred Gielgud's more traditional, poetic Romeo, full of tenderness and musicality. Darlington's view was representative: 'Mr Gielgud's Romeo is more romantic than was Mr Olivier's, has a much greater sense of the beauty of the language, and substitutes a thoughtfulness that suits the part for an impetuosity that did not.' On the other hand, they felt Olivier was more at home with the dashing swagger and sardonic wit needed for Mercutio – though even here *The Times* noted that 'he turns on the poetry in the way that athletic young fellows turn on the morning bath'. Gielgud unconsciously revealed his opinion of Olivier's Mercutio during a matinée. Olivier came offstage muttering, 'It's a terrible lot out there – I can't get a smile out of the bastards.' Gielgud at once replied: 'Of course not, there are no cheap parts in front.'

Gielgud's Romeo was seen as less convincing than Olivier's in one important respect. Agate asked: 'Is this Romeo ever really in love with anybody except himself?' and suggested that he 'never warms up to Juliet until she is cold'. In a broadcast Agate summed up: 'If Romeo were just a lovesick gumph, occasionally falling into a deeper trance in which he speaks unaccountable poetry, then Olivier is your Romeo. But if it is a question of playing Shakespeare's analytical and critical lover, then Gielgud's the man.'

Members of the company took a different view. Peggy Ashcroft observed: 'I thought John's extraordinary, darting imagination made him the better Mercutio, but Larry was the definitive Romeo, a real, vigorous, impulsive youth.' Sam Beazley, aged nineteen and playing Paris, agrees: 'Larry was very handsome and sexy, you really felt he wanted to get up the balcony and get at Juliet, which you didn't entirely feel with John.' Alec Guinness recalls their different qualities: 'As Mercutio John was absolutely glorious, funny, witty and mercurial, whereas Larry was a bit coarse-grained and heavy-footed. But with Romeo John didn't quite get it, you didn't believe in his passion, whereas Larry was very romantic and tragic, and looked wonderful.'

Gielgud resolved never to play Romeo again. He justified his view with critical remarks about the placing of Romeo's big scenes, arguing that he was really only a feed for the other characters. But his decision must have been influenced by the critics' comments on his failure, compared with Olivier, to play the young lover with conviction.

Geoffrey Toone, playing Tybalt, remembers vividly their contrasting approaches to the fight scene: 'Larry used to get so over-excited, so physical. On two occasions he hurled his sword into the audience, and someone handed it back. I wasn't brilliant at the fighting, but John was even worse. He came round the wrong way with his sword once, and practically cut my thumb off. I was supposed to be dead, and I lay on the ground with huge drops of blood dropping into my gauntlet. I was off for more than two weeks.'

Much of the intense debate about the respective merits of the two actors came later: according to Geoffrey Toone, 'it wasn't the talk of the company, any kind of rivalry'. The seed of it was certainly sown by their partnership in *Romeo and Juliet*. But the rivalry, both now and later, was more in Olivier's mind than in Gielgud's. On this question, their later recollections of the production are revealing.

Olivier's were peevish, self-aggrandising, tinged with jealousy, and sometimes unfair. He suggested, against the general opinion of the time, that Gielgud's voice 'dominated his performances'. He referred to his 'acolytes' leading him by the nose, and suggested that he too readily 'believed his publicity'. He over-dramatised his role as the upstart outsider vying with the Establishment represented by Gielgud, complaining that 'everybody was in his favour, while I was on another planet', that 'I was the whipping boy, he was the adored god'. He continued: 'I know that my Romeo, to say the least, was controversial, but it was also ultimately a success.' This was quite at odds not just with the majority of critical opinion, but with his own feelings at the time. He also observed of Gielgud, quite incorrectly: 'He harks back every now and then to how terrible he thought I was as Romeo.' Not once did he mention the huge debt he owed Gielgud for launching him on his career as a classical actor.

Gielgud, on the other hand, was gracious and generous about Olivier's bold performance, and played down his own. Three years after the production he wrote: 'Larry had a great advantage over me in his commanding vitality, striking looks, brilliant humour and passionate directness. As Romeo his love scenes were intensely real and tender, and his tragic grief profoundly touching.' Later he admitted to feeling jealous of Olivier's 'tremendous energy', his 'wonderful plastique, which is absolutely unselfconscious, like a lithe panther. I had been draping myself around the stage for weeks, thinking myself very romantic as Romeo, and I was rather baffled and dismayed that I couldn't achieve the same effect at all.' He was also generous about Olivier's verse-speaking: 'He was much more natural than I in his speech, too natural I thought at the time, but now I think he was right and I was wrong and that it was time to say the lines the modern way.' Olivier on the other hand was still savagely indignant fifty years later at the thought of the critics' disapproval: 'Me? Not speak Shakespeare's verse?' he said. 'What they meant is that I didn't *sing* it.'

Gielgud's production marked the longest-ever run of *Romeo and Juliet*. Its 186 performances in six months at the New were followed by a five-week provincial tour (without Olivier), during which the company played to large and appreciative audiences. 'Am I going to do more Shakespeare with Gielgud? Sure to!' Albery announced gleefully. With around £43,000 taken at the box office, Shakespeare had again proved a paying proposition in the West End. Albery took the production off when it was still a success, leaving open the possibility of a further revival. But Gielgud and Olivier were never again to appear on a stage together.

During the run of *Romeo and Juliet* Gielgud had given up his West End flat. Increasingly his privacy had been invaded by fans camping on his doorstep at all hours, hoping for a word or an autograph. He moved to Avenue Close in St John's Wood near Regent's Park, to the top floor in one of a cluster of new blocks of flats, well set back from the road and surrounded by trees and sedate Victorian villas. With his collection of books and 'hundreds and hundreds of gramophone records', he now had both peace and privacy within reasonable distance of the West End. A visiting journalist observed his fondness for order: 'On the desk, as everywhere else in the flat, everything must always be in its exactly right place – Gielgud has a positive horror of untidiness.' He also had the use of a garden in which to exercise his Schnautzer dog, Tanis – although sometimes he would walk it around the streets without a lead, when it would wander into the road and bring traffic to a halt.

While playing Mercutio Gielgud was seduced into producing *Richard II* for the OUDS. Even he with his boundless energy realised he would be unable to work unaided while acting every night at the New. After failing to persuade Devine to help, he appointed as co-producer Glen Byam Shaw, now a regular member of his unofficial West End company. A sensitive, gentlemanly man, he had never much enjoyed acting; this was his first attempt at producing. After the war he became a leading director of plays and opera, notably at the Old Vic, Stratford and Sadler's Wells. Gielgud had set him on his way.

Michael Denison, then a student at Magdalen College, remembered Byam Shaw being 'as stimulating, as firm and as courteous to his undergraduate cast as to any professional company'. Gielgud he found more impetuous, but also stimulating. 'It was a sea-change in my life,' he remembered. 'At the beginning of the rehearsals I had no intention of being a professional actor; by the end I had no intention of being anything else. It was John's sheer presence that did it, and the energy and passion that he and Glen brought to the theatre.' When Denison later wrote to Gielgud about a possible stage career, Gielgud was silkily discouraging: 'There are already many more actors than there are positions available in any one season, and perhaps your abilities would point to success in some other profession?' he wrote.

Continuing the OUDS tradition of hiring professional actresses, Gielgud persuaded the American Florence Kahn to play the Duchess of Gloucester, a small role with a single scene. It was a striking, unconventional choice, made partly from his sentimental attachment to older actresses, but also in an attempt to lure to Oxford her husband, the critic and writer Max Beerbohm, half-brother of Beerbohm Tree. Renowned for her playing of Ibsen's heroines, Florence Kahn had recently returned to the stage after a long absence, scoring a huge success at the Old Vic as Åse in *Peer Gynt*. But in rehearsals for *Richard II* her style seemed mannered and old-fashioned to the undergraduates. Beerbohm's biographer David Cecil wrote: 'In particular they were amused by her habit of accompanying every phrase with an illustrative gesture. If she spoke of her heart, she pointed her finger at her left breast; at the mention of a spear, she flourished an imaginary weapon in the air. This practice tended to slow down the pace.'

Gielgud tolerated what he saw as the 'old-fashioned declamatory passion' of this formidable-looking actress, as well as her continual efforts at the first rehearsal to upstage a shy and diminutive under-graduate, Joseph Adamson. 'This traditional actor-manager behaviour completely destroyed the confidence of poor John of Gaunt,' he recalled. He also had to put up with her habit at the end of each of her speeches of asking her husband, who attended rehearsals, how she had done. But Gielgud enjoyed escorting the celebrated writer to rehearsals: 'It was fascinating to watch Beerbohm descending the staircase at the Randolph Hotel, dressed in a white suit with a flower in his buttonhole and straw boater in his hand, looking exactly of the period, jaunty and debonair.'

The only other female role, Richard's Queen, was played by a twenty-two-year-old actress desperately keen to break into the classical theatre. Nine months before, Vivien Leigh had caused a sensation with her second West End appearance, playing a prostitute in the costume drama *The Mask of Virtue*. Public and critics were both overwhelmed by her beauty and obvious intelligence, though doubts were expressed about her speaking – Agate thought it 'displeasing to the fastidious ear'.

Having already marked out Olivier as her future husband, and being determined to meet him, she had come to see *Romeo and Juliet* several times. Their first lunch date together was at the Ivy – with Gielgud, who agreed with Olivier's suggestion that she should audition for the OUDS production. There are conflicting memories as to whether Olivier was present when she auditioned at the New for Gielgud and Byam Shaw. Since he was not involved in *Richard II*, it seems unlikely that he was there. It was certainly Gielgud who saw Vivien Leigh's potential, as Byam Shaw remembered: 'She was very nervous at the reading and I must admit that I was not very impressed, but John said she would be very good, would look divine, and that all the young men at Oxford would fall in love with her.'

Two of Gielgud's predictions proved correct. Vivien Leigh's impact on Oxford was akin to that of Max Beerbohm's heroine Zuleika Dobson ('A hundred eyes were fixed on her, and half as many hearts lost to her'). Michael Denison remembered that 'she was at the absolute height of her beauty, and so the whole of Oxford was spinning'. The critics too were captivated by her appearance, writing of her 'appealing charm' and 'an enchantingly pretty figure', and describing her performance as 'incredibly lovely'. The only significant judgement on her acting came from the critic of *The Times*, who warned that 'she has yet to make herself at ease with Shakespearean verse' – a criticism that was to dog her career. Gielgud remarked politely that, though the part was not interesting, 'she managed to endow it with every possible grace of speech and movement, and wore her medieval costumes with consummate charm'.

Richard II ran for its allotted week in February 1936 at the New in Oxford. The décor and costumes were again by Motley, the music was by Herbert Menges, and the stage manager was Robertson Davies, who became an actor and playwright before making his name as a novelist. But the person who gained most from the production was the undergraduate David King-Wood, who subsequently became a professional actor. His playing of Richard was praised for its maturity, subtlety, and fluent and sensitive verse-speaking. Darlington recognised Gielgud's contribution: 'So strong is the Gielgud influence on his playing of this particular part that I find it almost impossible to judge him separately.'

As if his life wasn't already full enough, Gielgud returned to a film studio during *Romeo and Juliet*. Actors were coming under increasing pressure to appear in films during the 1930s: by the middle of the decade over 60 per cent of the profession was working regularly in the studios. But film companies were still unsure about what the public wanted. In 1935 London Film Productions sent out a nationwide questionnaire, asking people for suggestions for new films, and suitable actors to appear in them. According to one report, 'An unexpectedly large number of them replied by demanding that John Gielgud should be made into a film star, so that the provinces could see more of him'.

Gielgud received plenty of offers around this time, but turned most of them down. Films were then seen as a threat to the stage, and he was, he said, 'first and foremost a stage actor'. Like others, he looked down on cinema as the poor man's theatre, and film as an inferior medium. He also disliked the fragmented nature of filming compared with the reassuring routine of the theatre. Wary of exposing his personality, he still felt acutely self-conscious in front of the camera. His impatience made him hate the idea of 'doing something which does not reach an audience until six months have passed'. All this helped him resist the money, which was six or seven times as much as he could get in the theatre.

Some of the film parts with which he was linked were pure fantasy. In newspaper discussions about a proposed film of the story of King Arthur, the public voted him a leading contender for the title-role, alongside Ronald Colman and Alfred Lunt – although some understandably feared he might be 'too gentle to be seen galloping round on a charger'. And *Vogue* magazine must have been teasing its readers when it intimated that in a forthcoming film of the life of Nijinsky, Charles Laughton would play Diaghilev and Gielgud would portray Nijinsky.

Among parts for which he was seriously considered, two eventually went to Conrad Veidt. The first was the title-role in *Jew Süss*, the second that of the Stranger in the adaptation of Jerome K. Jerome's play *The Passing of the Third Floor Back*, a part made famous on the stage by Forbes-Robertson. There was also a possibility he would appear with Elisabeth Bergner in *Saint Joan*, but that project fell through. In principle he was opposed to the filming of stage plays; but he was prepared to make an exception of *Richard of Bordeaux*. He was even willing to see the story adapted to suit a more popular taste: 'The film people seem to think that there's not sufficient love-interest in it,' he explained. 'But this, of course, could be built up if it were really necessary.'

He turned down an offer to play opposite Norma Shearer in George Cukor's version of *Romeo and Juliet* ('Boy Meets Girl – 1436' as the posters put it). When he saw the finished result, with Leslie Howard playing Romeo, he walked out in disgust after ten minutes. He was also unable to sit through Max Reinhardt's inventive but bizarre film of *A Midsummer Night's Dream* ('Three centuries in the making!'). Appalled, he wrote to Peggy Ashcroft of 'the cuts and the squandering of idiotic money and the whole damn thing', adding that 'it's really like having an operation to see anything you really love, like this superb play, butchered in such an unspeakable way'.

He also rejected Alexander Korda's suggestion that he put his Hamlet on film. 'When I dined with him at the Savoy Grill I tossed my head and said I didn't think that Shakespeare was any good on the screen,' he recalled. Though actors he admired, notably Forbes-Robertson (Hamlet) and Godfrey Tearle (Romeo), had appeared in Shakespeare on film, few had been successful. 'I didn't feel I could risk my stage reputation by appearing in what might have been very unsatisfactory film versions of the same plays,' he said during the run of *Noah*. Hollywood's efforts at filming Shakespeare were, he felt, 'too grandiose'; and to film Shakespeare was as bad as re-writing the Bible.

He was not alone among the leading actors of his generation in being wary of the medium. Though Edith Evans had appeared in two silent films, she was not to return to the screen until *Queen of Spades* in 1948. Peggy Ashcroft, who also disliked working in the studios, managed a brief but moving appearance in Hitchcock's *The Thirty-Nine Steps*, but made only sporadic appearances in films in the next thirty years. In 1937 Olivier, with significant experience under his belt, including a disastrous Orlando opposite Elisabeth Bergner's Rosalind in *As You Like It*, called film 'this anaemic little medium which could not stand great acting'. Richardson, however, took a more positive attitude, accepting a contract from Korda in 1935, and notching up several excellent performances in the following years, notably in *South*

Riding and *The Four Feathers*. 'You sell to the cinema what you've learnt in the theatre,' he remarked.

During 1935 Gielgud refused more Hollywood offers than any other British actor. It was Hitchcock who enticed him back to the studios, to play the title-role in his thriller *Secret Agent*, based on Maugham's *Ashenden* stories. After spending so long in costume on stage, Gielgud welcomed the idea of a modern part, and of being directed by Hitchcock, 'whose work I admire enormously, and who will, I know, make as good a job of me as a film actor as it's possible to make'. The money was becoming harder to resist: 'It's a great temptation to make a heap quickly and put something by,' he confessed.

Having failed to hire Donat, Hitchcock had tempted Gielgud by describing Ashenden as a kind of Hamlet in modern dress, an agent reluctant to kill. In fact the role was a light, inconsequential one, which to his chagrin became less prominent as filming progressed. His performance was overshadowed by the relaxed playing of Madeleine Carroll as his wife, and the scene-stealing antics of Peter Lorre as his sidekick. He was unsettled by Lorre's habit of improvising on camera, though publicly he claimed to admire it: 'You know, improvisation – the sort of thing the old Commedia dell'Arte did – is something the stage has got to learn all over again from the cinema,' he said during a break from shooting. 'We theatre people today are so desperately self-conscious.'

Hitchcock himself remarked that Gielgud 'was rather on the nervous side at first, but he gained confidence every day'. Gielgud confessed during filming that Hitchcock 'has often made me feel like a jelly and I have been nearly sick with nervousness', but added: 'I have realised the tremendous help he has given me with his quick mind, his humour, his ability to sense what is needed of each character.' Screen work, he realised, 'teaches you to have all your wits about you, to know what to a split-hair is over-acting and what is under-acting'. Hitchcock was evidently ruthless in his efforts to get him to adapt his technique: 'His stage experience is no use to him here,' he observed. 'I've had to make him rub out everything and start blank. I've had to rely purely on his intelligence.'

He called Gielgud's final performance 'remarkable'. The critics disagreed, describing it as bloodless, stilted and even inept, and accusing him of merely walking through the part. What *was* remarkable was his stamina and sheer appetite for work. He had originally planned to complete the film while playing Mercutio ('I haven't too much to do in the play,' he explained). But shooting took longer than planned, and for several weeks he was filming in Shepherd's Bush during the day and playing Romeo in the evenings, sometimes returning to the studio again after midnight. Yet the long hours of waiting on the set made him keener than ever to act before an audience. 'Seldom have I more sincerely enjoyed speaking the words of Shakespeare,' he said.

While working on *Secret Agent* he gave himself an ultimatum: 'If I do not satisfy myself in this very interesting part, I shall not act for the films again.' Aside from one wartime effort, he was not to make another for nearly twenty years.

16

A Prince on Broadway

Well-Known British Thesp Makes Good.
(*Variety* headline for *Hamlet*, 1936)

GIELGUD'S second taste of Broadway was very different from his first, eight years before. For some time now the American producer Guthrie McClintic had been trying to persuade him to play Hamlet in America, but his West End commitments had prevented his doing so. He had also refused the offer for fear of competing with Leslie Howard, who intended to play the role in New York. But when Howard announced he had abandoned his plans Gielgud decided in autumn 1936 to pick up the gauntlet.

McClintic, who had seen his Hamlet, told him he could provide 'a much better production' than his own. This rather nettled Gielgud, but he then decided it would make sense in New York to work with another producer, leaving him free to concentrate on his own per-formance. The company was an enticingly strong one, a mixture of American and English actors: Judith Anderson as Gertrude, Malcolm Keen as Claudius, Arthur Byron as Polonius, Harry Andrews as Horatio, and as Ophelia the one-time star of the silent films, Lillian Gish.

Though not producing, Gielgud was still involved in the early production discussions. In his London flat there were noisy late-night sessions into the early hours with McClintic and his designer Jo Mielziner, where they pored over the design sketches. They continued in the Riviera sunshine, in an old farmhouse which Gielgud rented near Grasse. Totally absorbed by his career, he had not taken a proper holiday for five years. Now he spent three weeks in France with friends, eating, lying in the sun, reading, dancing and gambling. But misgivings about the forthcoming American trip made it hard for him to relax.

He became depressed about the idea of uprooting himself from his usual surroundings, joining a new company, facing strange audiences. He was convinced his Hamlet would be a failure: 'I wished with all my heart that I had never agreed to go,' he remembered. Despite his love of new challenges in the theatre, offstage he had a basic fear of the unknown and the unfamiliar. At the end of August he boarded the liner *Normandie* alone, feeling 'very important but extremely lonely', trying to appear jaunty, but 'secretly a prey to fears'.

Word of his triumph had crossed the Atlantic, and whetted New York's appetite for his arrival. Since the war there had been a dearth of good Hamlets on Broadway, and none of any note from England. Raymond Massey, a Canadian, had played it in 1931, but in a version drastically cut by the producer Norman Bel-Geddes, who preferred scenery and action to philosophy; Leon Quartermaine, as Horatio, was heard to whisper at the opening, 'Forgive us, Master Will, for what we are about to perpetrate.' But one performance was still fresh in the memory. In 1922 John Barrymore had played a vibrant, moody and passionate Hamlet that had been ranked alongside Edwin Booth's, previously considered the greatest American interpretation.

Once in New York Gielgud's despair soon gave way to excitement. For the first week he stayed in McClintic's old house on the East River. Small and slight, with a little black moustache, McClintic loved to talk about the theatre as much as Gielgud did. Although he was homosexual he was married to Katherine Cornell, the acknowledged First Lady of the American stage. Gielgud enjoyed telling how he had spent the first night in her bed – adding that she was in Europe at the time. He met Judith Anderson, who came to McClintic's house, her hair dyed and waved in readiness for playing Gertrude. 'Why not wear a wig?' Gielgud suggested tactlessly. 'It looks better, and it's so much less trouble.'

He had already met his Ophelia in London. Lillian Gish had made her début in the theatre at the age of six, and played many child roles, once acting with Bernhardt. One of the first stars of the silent films, she had returned to the stage in 1930, playing in Chekhov and O'Casey, and as Marguerite Gautier in *The Lady of the Camellias*. Gielgud had expressed doubts to McClintic about her age; she was now forty-three, though her prettiness and vulnerability made her seem younger. Three days later she had visited Gielgud in his dressing-room at the New, decked out in a little-girl outfit with a white-straw hat and velvet ribbons. 'Am I too old to play Ophelia?' she asked. Recalling from his youth the posters on the underground advertising her films, Gielgud was beguiled, and decided she was ageless.

Before rehearsals began he was dismayed to find he was expected to give separate interviews to the main New York critics, and a press conference ('rather like a criminal at a line-up before the police'). He confessed that 'to feel one is representing the English theatre as Hamlet is a terrifying ordeal'. But his appearance and manner made a good impression, though some reporters could be unnervingly blunt. One described him in *Time* magazine as 'a sensitive and intelligent Englishman with a nose the size of a hockey puck'; another said he could play Cyrano without benefit of putty.

One writer noticed how different he was from the old school of Shakespearean actors: 'He strikes no poses. He can go for days without quoting Shakespeare. He is a pleasant-appearing young man of medium height. He has blue eyes, and his light-brown hair is slicked back over his rather high forehead.' He concluded: 'John Gielgud is well-tailored, polite and very British. He may not spout Shakespeare, but he talks pretty incessantly.' Another wrote: 'Tall he is, yes, and inclined to spareness. He is not to be called handsome, but his features are strong and pronounced – large in fact – and his face is mobile and animated.' He then perceptively summarised Gielgud's character: 'A half-hour's conversation with him left one with an impression of abundant nervous energy, a rather finely drawn emotional capacity, and a keen and discriminating mind.'

As to Hamlet, he confessed to being sorry that he lacked the demonic quality he knew Irving had brought to the part. He admitted the role was not his favourite, because there was no way you could hide your own personality, as you could with Prospero or Macbeth. He dismissed the idea that Hamlet was 'a neurotic', and when asked what he thought of the Freudian notion of Hamlet being in love with his mother, replied with uncharacteristic brevity and fierceness: 'Rubbish!'

Rehearsals began in the Martin Beck Theater during a heatwave. Gielgud, casually dressed in a sleeveless shirt, blue linen trousers and sandals, was excessively nervous. The schedule, from one o'clock to six without a break, was different from the one he was used to in London. The only familiar faces were Malcolm Keen and Harry Andrews. At the first reading McClintic, a sensitive, restless, volatile man blazing with enthusiasm, tried to cover his nerves with a stream of jokes. Judith

Anderson and Lillian Gish, almost invisible under hats with enormous brims, murmured their lines softly.

Uncertain whether to behave as 'the Great Star' or 'Modest Stranger from England', Gielgud opted to go all out. Knowing the part by heart, he began at a high emotional pitch, giving what was in effect an instant performance. One startled journalist described the impact of his first scene: 'Heavens, is he speaking lines or disclosing his despairing soul! His speech is most beautiful; like sculpture – not a syllable slurred or scarred.' He added: 'For the first time I know how much this boy loved his father. He *is* good. How good, I wonder. As good as Irving?' Gielgud recalled: 'I gave my all at those rehearsals, so anxious was I to impress the company.'

McClintic, once an actor himself, was an innovative and distinguished producer. His mother had raised him on tales of Edwin Booth's Hamlet, and when he ran away at sixteen to go on the stage he dreamed of playing the part. Since then he had seen seven Hamlets, including Forbes-Robertson's in 1913, a performance which had made him want to direct the play. Many of his best productions, including his 1934 *Romeo and Juliet*, had featured his wife. A painstaking producer, with a scholarly interest in past Shakespearean productions, he liked to immerse himself in the literature. Having re-read *Hamlet*, he was determined to bring to the stage 'the thrill, the whirl, the unrelenting doomsday feeling of inevitable tragedy marching to catastrophe that I got when I sat in the library and read the play'.

American audiences were used to a cut version, which tended to show Hamlet in a more heroic light, the 'sweet Prince' rather than the cruel young man who banters coarsely with Ophelia, and is sardonically direct with his mother. But McClintic went for a virtual 'Hamlet in its Entirety': he cut no scenes, merely lines or parts of lines. 'I retained every quotation, the lousy ones as well as the eternal ones,' he explained. 'I snipped out things I considered could be missed in our race with a three hours' curtain time.' It must have been skilfully done: the complete *Hamlet* at the Old Vic had taken four and a half hours.

McClintic was a volatile producer, talkative, nervous, and famous for his explosive rages: the critic Alexander Woollcott wrote an article on his style of directing entitled 'The Terror of the Tantrum'. The situation with *Hamlet* was potentially tricky: Gielgud knew the play intimately, and had his own ideas about how to play the part. Sometimes he disagreed with McClintic: he rebelled, for instance, against his idea of having Hamlet stand during his final speech rather than die in Horatio's arms – but then decided it was an excellent departure from tradition. But fundamentally he had confidence in McClintic: he was in tune with his aim of presenting a less noble Hamlet – the basis of his own production at the New – and with his desire for a swift, fast-moving production.

Complimented by the company, and feeling at the top of his form, Gielgud began to enjoy rehearsals. Katherine Cornell, unseen in the stalls, came to watch him. Woollcott also dropped in, and praised his playing of the closet scene. The only setback came during the fight with Laertes, for which the actors were using real swords. Wounded in the arm by John Emery, Gielgud had to be taken to a local surgery, and given gas and ether and eight stitches.

The pre-Broadway opening was in Canada. The company gave five performances in the Royal Alexandra, a large, shabby theatre in Toronto. Because of delays with the set there had to be two dress rehearsals. As he began his first soliloquy, Gielgud was horrified to see himself reflected in the mirrors at the back of the pit, and hastily had them covered up with felt. Then, true to form, with six days left before the New York opening, he demanded a complete rearrangement of the final scene, and several other major alterations.

The opening in September was described as 'the greatest first night in Toronto for many years'. The critics felt McClintic's production made the play clearer and more intelligible than before. Gielgud's Hamlet was admired for its speed, clarity and modernity. The critic Augustus Bridle drew an evocative picture of his performance: 'He speaks most of his lines at tremendous tempo; moves with cat-like speed; looks intense, luminous, gay, sombre, tragic, melancholy; dresses slouchily, with a sort of Byronic elegance; glows with jungle-like ferocity, or coos like a dove. So variegated a Hamlet we have not seen here.' A reporter visiting his dressing-room found Gielgud in a brown silk dressing-gown, 'receiving the congratulations of a gallery of men', and clearly exultant. 'The actor was talking in quick, excited sentences, and it was obvious that the impetuous Hamlet had not yet subsided into the usual British reserve.' In *Variety* a headline announced 'WELL-KNOWN BRITISH THESP MAKES GOOD'.

There were two further sell-out performances in Rochester in New York State, in a huge theatre holding three thousand people, with a mighty Wurlitzer organ standing in the orchestra pit between actors and audience. But then Gielgud caught a heavy cold. On the night train back to New York he lay exhausted but sleepless, trying to distract himself by reading *Gone with the Wind*. He felt acutely claustrophobic in his solitary compartment. Once in New York, desperately worried that he would lose his voice, he retired to bed and missed the dress rehearsal. The following day, which marked the opening, he had revived. 'This morning he came at twelve o'clock and took me to lunch,' his ardent fan Gwendolyn Jefferson reported. 'John has got thinner but he is very gay.' In the afternoon, trying to forget the ordeal that lay ahead, he went to the cinema.

Once in the Empire, and opening scores of telegrams from well-wishers, he became less agitated. This was the first big night of the season; one observer described it as 'the most orchidaceous evening Broadway has seen since the first nights of the great Ziegfeld'. The lobby was 'navel-deep in mink', the celebrities out in force: Noël Coward, Moss Hart, Beatrice Lillie, Fredric March, Burgess Meredith, Walter Huston and many others were there. Lillian Gish came to Gielgud's dressing-room and put a garland of white carnations round his neck for luck. It was the most nerve-wracking moment of his career so far, and one he recalled vividly not long after:

> I made up slowly and put on my costume. It was curtain time. The first scene came to an end, and I walked blindly to my place in the darkness. The light rose on the second scene. There was a roar of applause from the audience, a warm, reassuring burst of welcome that brought a big lump into my throat. I gulped it down, took a deep breath, and steadied myself to begin to speak. The cue came at last, and I heard my voice, far away in the distance, beginning the familiar words: 'A little more than kin, and less than kind.'

After the applause at the end of the scene he remembered little, except the palpable sympathy emanating from the audience. In the middle of the first act he thought, 'This is like the Old Vic all over again.' At the finish the audience cheered for fifteen minutes, and there were sixteen curtain calls. 'The reception moved and touched me so much I could hardly speak,' he recalled. Coward was the first into his dressing-room. 'He leaped about with joy and told me the audience were still standing up in their seats and cheering.' Outside the stage door the police had to force their way through crowds of autograph hunters to escort him to his car. Lillian Gish cabled his parents: 'Your darling son has just had his greatest triumph.' Next morning he awoke to headlines proclaiming 'GIELGUD'S TRIUMPH', 'BROADWAY GOES DELIRIOUS', and 'BARRYMORE RIVAL, SAYS NEW YORK'. 'This morning I am feeling grand,' he told a reporter. 'It was terrific to hear the cheers and see the hard-boiled audience applauding Shakespeare as though it had been the slickest revue.'

The critics were deeply impressed. The influential Burns Mantle called his performance 'masterful to the point of being inspired'. John Mason Brown enthused: 'Such a voice, such diction, and such a gift for maintaining the melody of Shakespeare's verse even while keeping it edged from speech to speech with dramatic significance.' Robert Benchley wrote of 'a Hamlet that you will remember – intelligent, sensitive, and at times inspired to the point of lifting your orchestra chair a few inches off the floor'.

When it came to the inevitable comparisons with Barrymore, Gielgud was generally judged to have come second. Richard Watts Jr missed 'the demoniacal humour and thrilling theatrical eloquence that Mr Barrymore brought to the role', John Anderson 'the bite and ferocity, the malevolent humour and sheer mischief' of the American. Brooks Atkinson wrote that for intellectual beauty his Hamlet ranked with the best, but he concluded: 'There is a coarser ferocity to Shakespeare's tragedy . . . and that is wanting in Mr Gielgud's art.'

Yet Gilbert W. Gabriel wrote: 'His Hamlet has quite all the intellectuality of Forbes-Robertson's, and all the sardonic force and feeling that were Barrymore's.' In a radio broadcast, Woollcott also bracketed Gielgud with his illustrious predecessors, speaking of 'a great play so beautifully done' that he wanted 'to ring the church bells and arrange with the mayor for dancing in the streets'. Only the unpredictable George Jean Nathan dissented. He suggested Gielgud was a bogus intellectual with mental equipment fifty times greater than that needed for the role, and that he looked as if he had tuberculosis. 'The delicate mannerisms and fastidious graces of the actor give the exhibit the air of a drawing-room version of the play,' he wrote, adding caustically: 'I can't wait to see Ivor Novello's Macbeth.'

According to Lillian Gish, Nathan wrote this vituperative review because he was in love with her, and was resentful of her obvious and intense fondness for Gielgud. 'Honey, he knew I loved you,' she told Gielgud later. The feeling was mutual: Gielgud was greatly taken with his co-star, to such an extent that he later claimed she was the only woman he thought of marrying. This seems more of a testimony to the actress's romantic allure than to Gielgud's belief in such a scenario.

After his battle with Hamlets past, he unexpectedly had to face one in the present. English stars were much in evidence during this season. Maurice Evans and Jeanne de Casalis were playing in R.C. Sherriff's *St Helena*, Noël Coward and Gertrude Lawrence were appearing in *Tonight at 8.30*. There was also Peggy Ashcroft, who had accepted a part in Maxwell Anderson's *High Tor* after seeking Gielgud's advice ('Play a mixture of *The Tempest* and *The Flying Dutchman*. Strongly advise', he had cabled her enigmatically). Now, a month after he had opened in *Hamlet*, another English actor appeared. Popular, experienced, handsome – he was forty-three but looked younger – Leslie Howard, whose following in America was as large as Gielgud's in London, had decided after all to play the prince on Broadway.

The news upset Gielgud, who admired Howard and had no desire to compete with him. But he also had a lingering feeling of inferiority towards the older actor, going back to when he understudied him in *Berkeley Square*. However, he put a brave face on it, as the *New Yorker* reported: 'He regrets that he will be competing with Leslie Howard this winter, but isn't sore; thinks, on the whole, that maybe the rival Hamlets will stimulate public interest.'

His instinct was right. Howard's *Hamlet* was produced by the young and talented John Houseman, with Gertrude Elliott, Forbes-Robertson's wife, cast as the Queen. Sensationally, just before the dress rehearsal in Boston, the distinguished American actress was replaced. Despite this setback, Howard attracted excellent notices in Boston and Philadelphia. But the opening at the Imperial in New York was a disaster. Where Gielgud's adrenalin had flowed, Howard was paralysed with nerves, and had to be given a massage in his dressing-room. His performance was uncharacteristically hesitant and unsure, and the critics attacked him cruelly and viciously.

John Mason Brown called the production '*Hamlet* with the Hamlet left out', and others were withering in their scorn. In despair Howard announced there would be no second night, but was then prevailed upon to change his mind. The next night he gave an infinitely better performance, got a huge reception – but spoilt the effect by coming down to the footlights at the end and asking, 'It wasn't so bad, was it?'

Howard took his *Hamlet* off after just a month, although he then toured it successfully round the country. There had been rumours that he and Gielgud had been to a matinée of each other's production, wearing dark glasses. Neither visit actually took place, though the idea caused Gielgud a moment of anxiety: 'The audience might be watching Leslie more than me,' he reflected. In fact the two actors were on friendly terms and exchanged good-luck telegrams. But the supposed rivalry was kept going by the press, which dubbed it 'The Battle of the Hamlets'.

That autumn and winter *Hamlet* became the centre of attention on Broadway, and many who had never seen the play went to both productions. The *Stage* reported: 'Half the theatrical gossip recently has been of Hamlet; the revues burlesque Hamlet; and the wireless blares Hamlet.' Even the taxi drivers joined in: 'Which of the Hamlets from England are *you?*' they would ask Gielgud when he directed them to the Empire, then fire questions at him until they reached the stage door.

Gielgud had been pessimistic about the chances of his production, cabling his parents that the run would be six weeks at the most. But Howard's relative failure boosted attendance at the Empire and, Gielgud admitted, his own self-confidence. Many New Yorkers had been waiting for the critical verdict, and his *Hamlet* now became a commercial as well as an artistic success: people were standing every night and scores were being turned away. The production moved to the larger St James's, and on 7 January 1937 Gielgud broke the Broadway record for the longest run in the part. This had been held by John Kellerd, with 102 performances in 1912; but the totals that really mattered were Edwin Booth's 100 and Barrymore's 101. Gielgud passed them both, finishing with 132, followed by a further 30 on a three-week tour of Boston, Washington and Philadelphia.

A vivid first-hand impression of his last performance on Broadway survives. Peggy Ashcroft, playing at the Martin Beck, was able to catch the final scenes. 'I could sense, from the audience's tenseness and their faces, as much as from the wonderfully relaxed and intimate way John was playing, what a performance it had been,' she wrote. 'I have seen John's Hamlet so many times now but I have never been more moved, and I have never heard him say "The rest is silence" as he did then: it was one of those special moments in the theatre that one never forgets.'

Some months later Rosamond Gilder, editor of *Theater Arts* magazine, published her book *John Gielgud's Hamlet*. Having seen his performance seventeen times she compiled a scene-by-scene record, using the prompt book to describe every gesture, movement, thought and emotion. A paean of praise to Gielgud, 'the prototype of all lost and lonely souls', it was one of the closest examinations ever made of an actor's interpretation of a part. She offered many shrewd judgements about his virtues: his ability to listen, his skilful use of gesture and facial expression, the precision of his movement, the energy of his attack. She found his voice 'an instrument delicately attuned to his intention and responsive to his will', and concluded:

> He combines the power to convey subtle movements of the spirit, delicate shades of thought, the inner workings of mind and heart, with a knowledge of theatrical technique and an ability . . . to tear off a 'passionate speech' with the best of them as occasion requires. He can fence with words as lightly and humorously as he can bludgeon with them. He has, above all, an ever-renewed freshness of attack. In his hands Hamlet seems born again every night.

It was one of the most brilliant notices he was ever to receive.

For his 'towering performance' as Hamlet, 'the greatest Prince of Denmark of this generation', Gielgud gained the *Stage* newspaper's prestigious annual acting award. A dinner was held for him at the Players Club, organised by two eminent men of the American theatre, Walter Hampden (a former Hamlet) and Otis Skinner (a former Shylock). Telegrams were sent by Forbes-Robertson and, most gratifyingly for Gielgud, by John Barrymore, who said of his Hamlet: 'It's not only stimulating but thrilling that you have made him so supremely your own. Congratulations on your brilliant success.' Gielgud remembered it as one of the most wonderful events of his life.

His colleagues were also unstinting in their praise. McClintic called his performance 'a sensitive synthesis of cerebral and emotional intensity, flawless technique, and rare vocal beauty'. Judith Anderson, making her début in Shakespeare – she was soon to be a memorable Lady Macbeth – put it more plainly: 'There's never been anything like him. You can't call it anything else but an inspiration to work with him. He's perfectly magnificent.'

There was also approval from a more unexpected quarter. Kate Gielgud received a letter from a family friend, Bertha Hunt, who reported the comments of a leading physician, Dr Davenport West: 'He himself is a great Shakespearean student, and had no adequate words for Jack's performance, but also said: "We have discussed it in medical meetings and all the psychiatrists agree that every reaction he has in the character of Hamlet to the situation is exactly what it should be medically and mentally."'

Gielgud at first lived modestly on the fourth floor of a brownstone apartment building in the East Fifties, but later moved to a penthouse apartment on Fifth Avenue, with a fine view across the city to the Hudson River. When the lights came on and the church bells began to ring, his romantic feelings were stirred by the spectacle, and by sounds that reminded him of Oxford: 'An extraordinary fairyland atmosphere suddenly descended on the city, in striking contrast to the brittle, hectic restlessness of its daytime aspect,' he recalled. 'I felt strangely removed from life. The noises of the streets were hushed, and I was alone with the twinkling lights and the sound of the wind and the bells.'

As he plunged deep into the city's social life, there seemed no limit to his stamina. 'John is in love with New York City!' Gwendolyn Jefferson told his mother. 'He has won all hearts by his charm.' Gielgud was rarely in bed before three in the morning. The speakeasies from his last visit were now restaurants, but he managed to visit many night clubs. He went to parties at the Lunts' house – where he saw Alfred's toy theatre – at Helen Hayes's, and others. He got to know Katherine Cornell, 'one of the most gentle, kind and unassuming women I have ever met'. He lunched with Gladys Cooper, played party games with Noël Coward and Beatrice Lillie, met Stravinsky, and was entertained by the critic and novelist Carl Van Vechten and his wife in their Chinese pyjamas and kimonos. With Lillian Gish and Ruth Gordon he was invited to dinner by Alexander Woollcott ('Mr Woollcott collects personalities as other people collect postage stamps or old china'), where he enjoyed a lively discussion about Barrymore's Hamlet with his witty, acid-tongued host. Also there was the playwright Thornton Wilder, whom Gielgud described as 'a funny, nervous little man like a dentist turned professor'.

Lillian Gish took him to the White House to meet Roosevelt. Gielgud described the President as 'charming, urbane and gracious, rather like Godfrey Tearle in manner', while Eleanor Roosevelt seemed 'pleasant and unassuming'. He also spent an unlikely afternoon there discussing Shakespeare with J. Edgar Hoover, the future head of the Federal Bureau of Investigation, whose 'erudition made me feel woefully ignorant'.

One memorable evening he took part in the Beaux Arts Ball, the main event of the New York winter season, held at the Astor Hotel. He and Gertrude Lawrence were persuaded to represent Night and Day in a 'Pageant of the Hours', he in plumed helmet and cloak on a black horse, she in a white net costume and diamonds on a white one. Somehow Gielgud managed to mount his steed, overhearing Gertrude Lawrence mutter as she did the same, 'If this is a buck jumper there'll be no matinée tomorrow.' They entered alongside Gloria Vanderbilt, borne on a litter as the Goddess of the Sun, then sat on enormous thrones as King and Queen of the revels, gazing at the back of Gipsy Rose Lee as she performed an elegant striptease for the company. Both having matinées the following day, they made their excuses and left early. Gielgud's account of this truly kitsch event shows him torn between embarrassment, amusement, pride, and a sneaking delight at the awfulness of the occasion.

His inexhaustible energy enabled him to drink deeply of the New York theatre scene. His taste was as catholic as ever. He saw Helen Hayes in *Victoria Regina* and the Lunts in Robert E. Sherwood's anti-war comedy *Idiot's Delight*; three plays by Maxwell Anderson, including Peggy Ashcroft in *High Tor*; Rodgers and Hart's pioneering show *On Your Toes*, with the celebrated ballet 'Slaughter on Tenth Avenue' choreographed by Balanchine. He also caught Sidney Kingsley's *Dead End*, with its cast of child actors, and George Kaufman and Moss Hart's *You Can't Take It With You*, which won the Pulitzer Prize that year. Looking at it all with a producer's eye, he observed how much more variety there was on Broadway than in the West End. He was impressed by the standards of production and the leading players, though he felt the supporting casts were often weak. He noticed approvingly that the daily critics often wrote longer articles developing their first notices.

Since *Ghosts* he had continued his friendship with Mrs Patrick Campbell, who had meanwhile alienated yet more people by her erratic behaviour and refusal to be helped with her fading career ('She is like a sinking ship firing on her rescuers,' Woollcott observed). Not long before, searching for a play for her to appear in, Gielgud had found what he thought a suitable one, about an ex-opera star and her daughter living in an Italian mountain village. But Mrs Pat, now over seventy and extremely fat, astonished him by saying: 'I suppose you want me to play the daughter.'

In New York, hearing she was living alone with her Pekinese, he visited her in a very ordinary hotel room. Soon after she wrote to Shaw: 'John Gielgud found me there and brought me flowers with tears in his eyes – the Terrys weep easily. He took me for a drive in the park – gave me his arm and I walked slowly – and Moonbeam ran about. He asked me to come and see his Hamlet and criticise.' Gielgud wrote to his mother: 'She looks well but is very sad . . . She stays in bed a great deal here – is writing another bad book – no maid or companion but the eternal pekineses – but she is as grand and majestic as ever.'

One night at the theatre he received a note from her: 'I am in front – give me the beauty I long for.' Afterwards she told him not to distract the audience by walking about during one of his soliloquies. As so often with someone he admired, Gielgud took her advice. After seeing the play again she wrote to him: 'It was wonderful last night. With "To be or not to be" you performed a miracle – I felt I had never heard it before.' Later she waxed lyrical in the *Stage*: 'If the great ones are watching from Olympus they must recognise in John Gielgud their son, and smile with love and satisfaction that they are so well remembered,' she wrote. When she read the piece out loud at a small lunch party he gave during the run, Gielgud was moved to yet more tears.

One night, after seeing Charles Laughton in the film *Rembrandt,* they listened in the Plaza Hotel to Edward VIII making his abdication speech. Mrs Pat burst into tears, insisted they send the ex-king a telegram, and dragged Gielgud to the nearest post office, where she announced: 'This is the greatest thing since Antony gave up his kingdom for Cleopatra.' Only with difficulty did he persuade her to send a telegram instead to Laughton, saying how much they had enjoyed the film. Another time, when Gielgud invited her to a party that he gave with his two female co-stars, she said to Judith Anderson à propos Gertrude: 'Why did you sit on the bed? Only housemaids sit on the bed.' Later, when the party became rowdy, she boomed: 'Why must people always scream like the French Revolution?' Despite such incidents, Gielgud remained a faithful friend.

Mrs Pat arranged for Gielgud to meet Edward Sheldon, an encounter he later described as 'among the most remarkable and inspiring of my life'. Sheldon had been a brilliant man of the theatre in his youth, a successful playwright, and a friend and encourager of John Barrymore. In 1917 he had been struck by arthritis, which gradually immobilised him, leaving him blind and paralysed and confined to his apartment in New York. Despite this cruel affliction he remained steadfastly charming and philosophical, and was much visited by theatre people; Katherine Cornell, Ruth Draper, Lillian Gish and Mrs Patrick Campbell were among his intimate friends; Helen Hayes always had dinner with him before her first nights. He would listen to their ideas, and advise and inspire them; in return they performed for him in his home.

Gielgud found him stretched out on a great bed, smartly dressed, but with his head tipped back and his eyes covered in a black mask. He had not left his room for fourteen years, but never referred to his illness, nor allowed anyone else to do so. Within minutes Gielgud had forgotten about his condition: he and Sheldon were talking 'as if we had known each other all our lives'. He was impressed by Sheldon's wisdom, and his skill in drawing him out. 'He at once put me at my ease and made me wish to appear at my best before him,' he recalled. 'He was amazingly well informed, especially about the theatre, and seemed to know everything that was going on. He spoke of my Hamlet as if he had seen it.' Later he did so: Gielgud returned to his apartment to act out certain scenes. 'I never played to a more sensitive or appreciative audience.' Only out on the busy New York street again did he experience 'a momentary feeling of desolation'. His liking for Sheldon was mutual: the American kept regularly in touch, even during the war. When he died in 1946 – now deaf and mute as well as blind – Gielgud penned an affectionate and moving tribute for *The Times*.

Before his arrival in America there had been serious talk of his playing in *Richard II*, which had not been done on Broadway for nearly sixty years. With *Hamlet* coming to an end he revived the idea with McClintic, who apparently replied, 'Oh, a pansy king, that will never do in America. No, no, you must go on the road and play Hamlet for another six weeks.' Hearing the news Maurice Evans, who had played the part at the Old Vic, but now worked in America, asked Gielgud if he would mind *his* staging a production. When Gielgud returned to New York after touring *Hamlet* he was considerably put out to discover that Evans had scored a sensational success as 'the pansy king', a part that led him to become America's most admired Shakespearean actor.

McClintic wanted to extend the *Hamlet* tour to all the main cities, but Gielgud was committed to a new play in London. He had also, he confessed, 'had his fill of Shakespeare for the time being'. Towards the end of the run he was ticking off his performances 'like a schoolboy at the end of term'. So the tour was confined to Boston, Philadelphia and Washington, where he did an additional thirty performances. In Boston, where an extra matinée was put on in aid of a flood relief fund, he was stretched to the absolute limit, with four performances in thirty-six hours.

His third Hamlet had greatly enhanced his reputation, gaining him enormous respect and admiration in America. 'It is hard for elderly Americans to give up their memories of Edwin Booth,' Bertha Hunt wrote to Gielgud's mother, 'but I've not heard one who hasn't said Jack was the greatest.' Later Gielgud described it as his most thrilling Hamlet, because of his desire to win over a totally new audience. It had also deepened his understanding of the role, as is clear from an extended essay on 'The Hamlet Tradition' he wrote soon afterwards for inclusion in Rosamond Gilder's book. His aim was 'to describe some of the problems and questions that have occurred to me during fifteen years of reading, seeing and thinking about the play'. It revealed an astonishingly detailed knowledge of the many different productions and interpretations of *Hamlet*.

Just before returning to England, he announced that he was too old to play Romeo again, and would not attempt Hamlet after reaching thirty-five. With Romeo he kept his word; with Hamlet, as with so much else, he was soon to change his mind.

PART THREE

Shakespeare in Peace and War

1937–1948

17

Actor-Manager

One of the rarest blazes of theatrical light of the
century.

> (Harold Hobson on Gielgud's
> 1937/38 season at the Queen's)

AFTER his triumphant success as Hamlet, Gielgud had been besieged by offers from Hollywood film companies. 'I'm a free agent, and I don't intend to accept them,' he said defiantly after the opening. Stepping off the *Queen Mary* on his return to England in February 1937, he said: 'I love the stage and all that goes with it, and I think my best work as an actor has been done on it. I think a stage-acting life lasts about ten years, and I intend to make the most of it.'

He now took up a play Emlyn Williams had written for him, *He Was Born Gay*, the story of the last Dauphin who would have become King Louis XVII of France had he survived. The title was taken from his mother Marie Antoinette's comment, '*Il est né gai*'. The role of the half-mad princeling appealed to Gielgud: 'It's a part I'd like to play: it's costume, it's poetic, it's romantic,' he enthused. With his contract to Albery at an end, he decided to go into management again, with Williams as co-producer. The cast included Harry Andrews, Gwen Ffrangcon-Davies, Glen Byam Shaw, Carol Goodner and Williams himself, with sets and costumes by Motley.

During rehearsals he began to have doubts about the play: 'The theatrical quality of it is strong and it is charmingly written – but I fear the worst if the critics should take it into their heads to find fault with the logic and the construction,' he wrote to his mother. 'However, if we can make them believe in such frankly romantic melodrama it will be one up to us.' On the pre-London tour he embarked on his favourite activity: making changes. 'The notices here were marvellous, and we have changed a great deal for the better this week,' he wrote from Manchester. In Edinburgh, Guthrie McClintic 'had some most constructive points for me in the last act, which are all improvements'. In Birmingham the play seemed 'to have strong popular appeal – my poisoning act seems to go very big, though it's rather Grand Guignol!' Provincial audiences were enthusiastic, the critics mostly favourable. From Oxford he wrote: 'We are certainly having magnificent receptions here, and I am beginning to feel very happy about the play.'

While staying in Stratford during the Birmingham week he had a brief encounter with a bygone age, lunching with the elderly American actress Mary Anderson, a famous beauty and a celebrated Rosalind fifty years before. 'She is old now and no longer strong, but even so extraordinarily gracious and dominating in the most charming way,' he told his mother. 'She talked much of Nell and Forbes-Robertson.' He also at Stratford had a welcome near-miss: 'Mr Wolfit wished to be photographed with me – Hamlets past and present – for the local press, but I was not to be drawn, and was in my bath!'

In May, the day before the London opening, Williams wrote with a hint of foreboding to Kate Gielgud: 'Whatever is the fate of the play, I shall consider the experience more than worthwhile for having meant my working again with John.' Its fate proved unhappy, and London audiences more demanding, for it closed after just twelve performances at the Queen's. The critics savaged it for its confusing mixture of comedy, tragedy and farce, its unbelievable situations, and its over-literary language. The *New Statesman* wondered why Gielgud had wasted himself on a play so 'grotesquely ham', reflecting: 'He has won the devotion of a vast public, and certainly need not appear in a play which he perceives to be trash.'

His own performance also came under fire. Stephen Williams thought he was 'so obviously Acting that everything he spoke became unreal', while *The Times*, during his big speech, prayed 'that no one will laugh out loud before it is over'. The problem was obvious: with author and star actor co-producing, the production had no observer able to give an independent opinion, and to curb Gielgud's histrionics. Margaret Harris of Motley remembered: 'It was not a good play, and it pandered to all John's tricks.' One critic thought he had been blinded by the apparent 'fatness' of his part. This was a factor, but another was his friendship with and loyalty to Williams. It was, nevertheless, a serious misjudgement.

The failure made him consider his next step very carefully. McClintic had promised to send him a new play by Pearl S. Buck, hoping he might do it in London and New York. He had offers to broadcast Oberon's speeches on the radio, and to do scenes from either *Hamlet* or *Richard of Bordeaux* for the fledgeling BBC television service. All of these he turned down – as he did the chance to return briefly to America (and earn £500) for a Shakespearean broadcast with Helen Hayes. He also declined an offer from Elisabeth Bergner to produce her in *The Boy David*, Barrie's last play, which he had written especially for her. Gielgud didn't care for this further re-working of Barrie's 'lost boy' theme, and this time his judgement was surer: when the play was eventually produced by Komisarjevksy, it was lambasted by the critics.

There was renewed pressure to return to films. The editor of a film magazine wrote him an open letter, suggesting the studios had 'failed to take full advantage of your gifts', that he 'must not ignore the fact that many thousands are genuinely anxious to see you on screen'. In fact he had just come to an agreement with Jack Buchanan's new film company to film *Richard of Bordeaux* in colour, the one film project that tempted him. Miles Malleson wrote a skeleton scenario, but after various delays the threat of war led to it being shelved. Gielgud's only compensation was the £2000 Buchanan paid him not to make the film himself.

With the coronation of George VI imminent, the critic and theatre manager Sydney Carroll suggested the celebrations would be incomplete 'without John Gielgud in some play or other of Shakespeare', and that Albery should organise some gala performances. Gielgud replied promptly:

> I do not like 'scratch' revivals of Shakespeare. Every time I have played in one of his plays I have worked afresh, with a different approach and a new cast and production . . . I am very gratified to feel that these classic plays have gained me some popularity, but I cannot help wishing to break new ground, to play in other kinds of plays, and to create a new character by a modern author . . . I do not wish to play another great Shakespearean part without considerable thought and adequate preparation, and I do not care to take the more obvious course and stage revivals of past successes which might lack the spirit and enthusiasm of the originals.

Gielgud was critical of the 'frequently prim and unimaginative atmosphere of the West End stage'. At the same time he was cool about a national theatre, which was now beginning to look more of a reality: 'The public are not interested in practical schemes, managements, or committees,' he argued. 'They demand sensational theatrical fare attractively served up by expert and popular personalities.'

He now decided to realise his long-standing dream to go into management with a season of classical plays. He wanted to prove that short runs, with a permanent company, were not only possible economically but desirable artistically. 'The strain of playing in long runs is not only intense, but death to the art of an actor,' he said. 'The most stimulating thing about repertory is the keenness with which everyone is possessed. Rehearsing for the next play while appearing in the present one prevents any danger of staleness.'

Sparked off by his experience at the Old Vic and his admiration for the Compagnie des Quinze, the idea had been simmering in his mind for some time. In his essay on *Hamlet* he had written of the desperate need for more preparation and rehearsal time, enabling a different relationship to develop between actors and producer, in which the latter would 'not merely impose his personality and order them about like sheep', but 'study with them, work with them, discuss with them'. Everyone, he felt, would gain from this two-way contact: 'This, I am sure, is one of the secrets of companies like that of the Moscow Art Theatre and some of the famous Continental repertory companies.' He wanted to bring the English theatre into line with the innovators in Europe. In this he was again following Barker, who had argued that a permanent company, 'used to each other's methods, and working in harmony, may be trusted to give a far sounder performance of any play than the most brilliant scratch company that can be got together'.

Gielgud now formed his own company to undertake a nine-month season of four plays at the Queen's under his management. He and John Perry put in £5000 each to finance it. The plays – *Richard II, The School for Scandal, Three Sisters* and *The Merchant of Venice* – were to be put on for a minimum of eight weeks and a maximum of ten. He offered the actors contracts for the entire thirty-two-week season, and put the leading ones on a percentage. Instead of the usual three weeks, at least seven would be allowed for rehearsals, a rare luxury. 'More time and hard work at rehearsals are of greater use than masses of money spent on scenery and costumes,' he argued.

His company was bursting with actual and potential talent. He had no difficulty in choosing Peggy Ashcroft, now an established star, as his leading lady. 'Her enchanting lightness and spontaneity were a continual joy and inspiration to me,' he had said of her Juliet. A backbone of experience was provided by Frederick Lloyd, Leon Quartermaine, Harcourt Williams and George Howe, all of whom he knew well and had worked with often. Among the younger, less proven actors were Glen Byam Shaw, Michael Redgrave, George Devine, Harry Andrews, Dennis Price, Anthony Quayle – and Alec Guinness, now 'a freer, less inhibited man and much more sure of myself'. Gielgud engaged as guest stars four leading actresses whose work he knew intimately: Carol Goodner, Gwen Ffrangcon-Davies, Dorothy Green and Angela Baddeley. To complete the 'family' he had the Motleys as designers, and Herbert Menges as musical adviser.

The announcement of his plans created huge excitement. It was the first time for a long while that an actor-manager had risked a classical repertoire in the West End. 'Mr Gielgud's programme already looks like a counterblast to the "National Theatre",' one writer suggested. 'Indeed if a Gielgud Art Theatre is a result of this tentative programme, anxiety about the future of the British drama will become superfluous.' But privately Gielgud was agonising over the wisdom of the venture.

In his essay on *Hamlet* he had written: 'If only Mr Granville Barker would answer the prayers of us who love the theatre, and instead of writing his brilliant treatises from far away, would come and work with us at the practical task of presenting Shakespeare in London and New York as he alone knows how it should be presented!' He now sought an opinion from Barker, who was in London briefly. His reply reflected Gielgud's dilemma over priorities, but also revealed Barker's confidence in him:

I am only afraid that my counsel – such as it would be – might increase rather than lessen your distraction. For distracted – if I guess right – you must be, between two aims: the one, which is really forced on you, a personal career, the other, the establishing of a theatre, without which your career will not be, I think you rightly feel, all that you proudly wish it to be . . . The question is, have times changed? Can you yet hope to establish a theatre? If not the blessed 'National Theatre' (but names mean nothing), then such a one as Stanislavsky's or Reinhardt's of thirty years back? For that you'll gladly sacrifice as much of your personal career as need be – this I see; but naturally you don't want to make

the sacrifice in vain. Is a compromise practical? I don't know . . .
It is no longer for me a practicable question, therefore I can still
say *theatre or nothing* and not suffer. For you a devilishly practical
one; so, who am I to counsel you? . . . You have given us some fine
things and you'll give us more, I don't doubt – by whichever path
you go.

Gielgud's bold venture was a revolutionary one for England. No one
had tried anything similar since the Barker–Vedrenne management in
1904. Henry Ainley, Godfrey Tearle, Owen Nares, Phyllis Neilson-
Terry and Sybil Thorndike had all ventured into management, but not
with a permanent repertory company. Yet though he was now an actor-
manager, Gielgud's aims were very different from those of Irving,
Alexander, Tree and Martin-Harvey. They had surrounded themselves
with lesser lights in order to shine more brilliantly themselves, and
chosen plays mainly as vehicles for their own talents. Following Barker
Gielgud, a company man by temperament as well as by conviction,
believed passionately in the virtues of an ensemble, and was prepared
to submerge himself from time to time in smaller roles. While this was
all part of his search for fresh experiences, he also looked back with
fondness on his repertory years at the Old Vic and at Oxford – 'my
happiest times as an actor', he now admitted.

There were teething problems over the choice of plays for the
Queen's season. Olivier was now at the Old Vic, where he and
Guthrie planned to include *Richard II* and *Macbeth* in the forthcoming season. Since Gielgud also planned to do both, a trade-off was
agreed: he would steer clear of *Macbeth* and Olivier would avoid
Richard II. He looked at several options for the modern classic,
though one playwright was immediately excluded: 'I do not care for
Ibsen,' he confessed. 'To me there is something dead about his work,
although I appreciate his wonderful craftsmanship.' He considered
Shaw's *The Doctor's Dilemma*, but feared the medical dialogue might
be dated. Maxwell Anderson suggested his *The Masque of Kings*, but
Gielgud was uncertain about a verse play. He also thought about
doing Barrie's *Dear Brutus*, but rejected it because du Maurier's
performance was still too vivid in his mind. *Our Betters*, which he
thought a comic masterpiece, was another contender, but the
company's particular talents didn't seem to fit Maugham's characters.
Some people thought his final selection too conservative, to which
Gielgud replied that 'the public is apt to stay away from wild

experiments'. With a substantial sum invested, he needed to be pragmatic as well as adventurous.

The season opened in September with *Richard II*. Again he had a great popular success with his playing of the weak, neurotic king. 'Critics enthuse, dowagers are melted, highbrows seek in vain for foot-faults,' wrote the novelist Elizabeth Bowen. Most critics who had seen his acclaimed Old Vic performance thought this one even better: his acting was simpler yet more mature, and he had shed most of his mannerisms. Agate's comment was particularly welcome:

> His present performance lays greater stress on the artist without losing any of the kingliness. His reading has gained in depth, subtlety, insight, power. The last act is not only the peak of his achievement to date; it is probably the best piece of Shakespearean acting on the English stage today.

But Gielgud was not just concerned with his own notices: a great deal rested, both artistically and financially, on the response to his new ensemble. In *The Times* Charles Morgan underlined the season's importance to the theatre in general, suggesting that 'its failure would give disastrous opportunity to those who cry that the living theatre is a sick man that can't save himself'. But the reviews were very favourable: the critics remarked on the balance and beauty of Gielgud's production, and the high all-round quality of the verse-speaking. Peter Fleming wrote: 'It might almost be a Russian company, so compact and smooth is the texture of a large cast.' The fullest praise came from Ivor Brown: 'The chief note of his first venture is the teamwork and the giving of distinction to routine elements or seemingly inconsiderable parts by shrewd casting and rich performance. Mr John Gielgud is not only a fine actor himself, but a source of fine acting in others.'

The most detailed critique, and the one Gielgud would have valued most, came to him privately. Seeking Barker's advice, he had asked him if he had written a Preface for the play. 'I've done no Preface to it, nor am like to do,' Barker replied. However, he met and talked with Gielgud, and after seeing the production wrote to him at length about its virtues and faults – effectively a mini-Preface to the play. Overall he thought Gielgud's production first-rate, and the lists scene 'as good a piece of Shakespearean staging as I can remember'. But he was critical of what was usually reckoned one of Gielgud's strengths, the verse-speaking.

'I am preaching; forgive me – everything the actor does must be done *within the frame* of the verse,' he wrote:

> The *pace* you may vary all you like. Clarity there must be, of course. But here, it is really the breaking of the rhythm that destroys it . . . You must not turn W.S.'s quavers into crochets or semi-breves – or semi-quavers for that matter . . . The thing got more and more hung up as it went on, and you began to play more and more astride the verse instead of in it.

He also noticed the pervasive influence of Gielgud's voice: 'I think each character ought to have his own speech. I thought during the first half of the play they were imitating each other; then I found they were imitating you.'

In reply Gielgud defended his interpretation of Richard. But he also took to heart Barker's concern about the slow pace: at the next performance, he told Barker, he shortened the playing by eight minutes without making any cuts – 'simply by speeding up: and how it improved the performance!' Barker, impressed by Gielgud's receptiveness, replied:

> Bless you – for you are really a most satisfactory person to write to, and it pleases me no end that you should have been able to turn all that talk to some practical use . . . I know how comparatively easy it is to criticise and how hard to do the thing right. I appreciate that difficulty, of avoiding reciting, in giving life to a conventional form, of getting sense and music combined.

In his letter and talks with Barker, Gielgud had tried hard to persuade him to return to the theatre, perhaps to produce him in a play. For the moment he failed, but at the end of his critical review of *Richard II* Barker underlined his confidence in Gielgud's abilities, and offered to help him in the future:

> As to me – oh no. I have to put it all into books now, and as quick as I can before my time is up. I doubt if I'd *be* any good as a producer any longer – other reasons apart, I doubt if I've energy and patience left. But an argument with me – just the two of us – might clear your mind sometime, and mine. And, you see, you have *got* it in you.

No endorsement of his talent could have given Gielgud greater satisfaction.

Barker's point about actors imitating Gielgud was a valid one. Some of the younger members in the company were heavily influenced by his voice, technique and stage presence. The two most severely affected were Guinness and Redgrave. Guinness later admitted to indulging in 'pale, ersatz Gielgudry', describing his own *Richard II* as 'a partly plagiarised, third-rate imitation'. Like many actors he was particularly affected by Gielgud's Hamlet: when he came to play the part in Guthrie's modern-dress production at the Vic he was, by his own modest account, 'merely a pale shadow of Gielgud with some fustian, Freudian trimmings'.

Redgrave, only four years younger than Gielgud, had joined the profession comparatively recently. Tall, handsome, intellectual and conceited, after shining as an actor at Cambridge he had become a teacher at Cranleigh School in Surrey, where he had played several Shakespearean leads in the productions. He admitted later that his Hamlet there owed so much to what he had seen at the Old Vic in 1930 that 'I must have seemed like Gielgud's understudy'. He had avoided seeing his 1934 Hamlet, 'knowing that if I were to play the part myself I should want to clear my imagination of his presence'.

At the start of rehearsals for *Richard II* he had been overawed by Gielgud: 'John, even at the first reading, was as near perfect as I could wish or imagine,' he recalled, adding that he could see 'no way of improving on the dazzling virtuosity of phrasing and breathing'. Fifteen years later at Stratford, when he played Richard as overtly homosexual, and reviewers found traces of Gielgud in his performance, he said: 'If you have seen a performance which you consider definitive you cannot help being influenced by it – and why not?'

Gielgud helped him to paint a lucid portrait of the ruthless, thick-skinned Bolingbroke, which provided an admirable foil for his Richard. His approach to Redgrave and the other actors was glimpsed by a journalist sitting in on a rehearsal, who noted one point he continually made: 'It is not enough to speak your lines, however much feeling you put into them,' he told the actors. 'First of all you must let the audience see the sense of the lines come into your own head: they must be given the illusion that you yourself, not Shakespeare, thought of the lines. Trick yourself into thinking so, too.' This illusion of fresh thought was already and would remain one of the hallmarks of his own work in Shakespeare.

The second play of the season was Sheridan's *The School for Scandal.* During its run Peggy Ashcroft's divorce from Komisarjevsky was finalised, and the popular press now resurrected an extraordinary rumour which had surfaced some weeks before, that she and Gielgud planned to marry. 'I could not be more surprised if Oxford won the boat race!' Lilian Baylis declared, as the two actors issued 'a categorical denial'. Gielgud would have been alarmed at his private life being aired in the press, however ridiculous the story. But he dealt with it skilfully. On the day the Queen's season began a reporter had suggested that nothing would give theatregoers greater pleasure than such a 'Romeo and Juliet contract'. Gielgud replied suavely: 'Nothing would give me more pleasure also; the rumours have been so persistent. But the lady has to be consulted.' Peggy Ashcroft also played it straight: 'Romance for me even with Mr John Gielgud at the moment must be strictly confined to the stage,' she said. 'The suggestion that we are engaged or likely to be engaged has a basis only in imagination.' Later Gielgud recalled: 'Peggy had the good taste never to refer to the episode.'

The School for Scandal was a perennial favourite of repertory companies and amateur groups, and Gielgud felt the cobwebs around it needed sweeping away. Having decided to produce only two plays himself in the season, he engaged Tyrone Guthrie for Sheridan's comic masterpiece. Guthrie had come a long way since their Oxford Playhouse days together. A tall, gangling Ulster Scot, with short hair and clipped moustache, his military image was dented by his quirky voice, and also his unconventional dress: in a company where suits, bow-ties and suede shoes were the norm, he favoured sandals and an old grey cardigan. His manner was confident and straightforward, sometimes brutally so: 'Tony Guthrie was about as ambiguous as a sword thrust through the ribs,' Anthony Quayle remembered.

Now seen as the *enfant terrible* of the theatre, praised for his daring, fresh and irreverent productions, notably of Shakespeare, he was also criticised for being an exhibitionist, too fond of elaborate business and startling visual stunts. A great visionary and risk-taker, he worked at a furious pace, dashing back and forth between the stage and stalls. For Guinness, who was to work with him often, and become a friend, 'there was a spontaneity in all he did, a sort of whirlwind of activity and invention'. Guthrie liked to create an atmosphere of play: the results were never boring, always stimulating, and often brilliant. But by his own admission he had an exaggerated regard for originality, and his wanton showmanship sometimes resulted in spectacular failures.

He was also a sworn foe of all that was fashionable and metropolitan. He now announced that he had never seen *The School for Scandal*, and was approaching it with a completely fresh mind. Yet it was, according to Guinness, the least satisfactory production he ever did. Given the circumstances this was not surprising. Guthrie was not only preoccupied with his heavy workload at the Vic, where Olivier was about to open with *Macbeth*; he was also involved in a rare excursion into acting, in a film with Charles Laughton, *The Vessel of Wrath*. As a result his involvement with the Sheridan play was less than it should have been, and at rehearsal Gielgud often stood in for him. Ominously, late in the day the opening was postponed for a week, to give the company time for extra rehearsals.

Artistic differences also arose. 'John and Tony never really got on, and I don't know why,' Guinness says. Tanya Moisiewitch, who later worked with Guthrie, recalls: 'Tony's admiration for John was enormous, but perhaps his method didn't suit: they were both notorious for changing their minds.' Alastair Bannerman, a junior member of the Queen's company, remembers that the two men 'crossed swords' once or twice during rehearsals: 'Tony wanted John to go faster all the time, and John was quite determined to go his own pace.'

Such resistance on Gielgud's part was uncharacteristic. He had a great affection for Guthrie, based partly on family links: Guthrie's mother had been his mother's bridesmaid, and the two women were friends. He liked Guthrie's warmth, humour and enthusiasm, and appreciated the generous letters he wrote to him about his performances. He recognised 'a terrific pioneer' and 'an exciting pageant-master of the theatre', and enjoyed his 'boy scout way of rallying people's morale, which was terribly amusing'. Ultimately, though, he felt Guthrie lacked integrity: 'Tony's was a wayward talent, for all its brilliance,' he said.

Once again Gielgud avoided the obvious role, that of Charles Surface, and chose to play his smooth-tongued brother, the urbane hypocrite Joseph Surface. Playing a relatively small part – the character has only three scenes and is on stage for around forty minutes – was another sign of his willingness to take on less sympathetic, even secondary roles, for the sake of the company. Guthrie supported this surprise move: 'We thought it might be rather good for Gielgud fans to see him in something where he is not suffering,' he said caustically. But once rehearsals began tensions started to appear.

Guthrie was notorious for ignoring the leading actors in favour of those playing minor roles, to whom he liked to give amusing, often grotesque pieces of byplay. Guinness pinpointed the problem at the Queen's: 'Some of the older actors wished everything to be "lovely", fluttering lace handkerchiefs and with a lot of fan-work; they resented Tony's harsher attitudes, and the result was an uncomfortable compromise.' Guthrie was more interested in working with young people, and 'was not hugely respectful of the elderly ladies in the cast'.

The play was a personal triumph for Gielgud, whose Joseph Surface, clothed in silver brocade and lace ruffles, oozed silken hypocrisy and subtle villainy. Farjeon enjoyed 'the exquisite clarity and icy humour with which he creates the outline of a calculating scamp'. Fabia Drake wrote: 'It is only very rarely that one sees such great distinction in a performance, and it was allied with a wit and a force that I am afraid rather left the majority of the company like Peter in the New Testament, "following, afar off".' Barker told Gielgud he was 'the best Joseph Surface I remember or am likely to encounter. Forbes-R was good, but even then, elderly, and the more inexcusable. I liked your dandyism, and shallowness.'

His Joseph Surface was the start of a new line: Peggy Ashcroft later described it as 'one of the most dazzling comedy performances I can remember', while Olivier went one step further, calling it 'the best light comedy performance I've ever seen, or ever shall see'. While Gielgud would never be able to tackle a totally evil character, he was now quite at home, at least in comedy, when playing the hypocrite, the plausible villian or the scheming prig.

The production, however, divided the critics. Those who liked experiment and innovation thought Guthrie's attempt to find 'the itch beneath the powder' fresh, imaginative and gloriously iconoclastic. Those who preferred a more conventional treatment took umbrage at his heretical ideas, which included a row of fake footlights, sketchily painted backcloths, and a scene in which the actors bounced up and down on a huge sofa. The critic of *The Times* wrote: 'If the emphasis is to be neither on the dialogue nor the character nor Sheridan but on pattern-making and elegant diversions, then all is well. If not, not.' Agate was almost apoplectic: 'Mauling is too rough a word, fantastication too smooth, and treatment too colourless for the way in which this revival has been mishandled.'

Gielgud's dislike of confrontation was partly to blame for this relative failure. Guthrie attended only half a dozen rehearsals, and was generally cavalier in his approach to working on the play. 'He seemed rather slapdash and eccentric,' Gielgud remembered. Yet he was unable to assert himself sufficiently to discuss Guthrie's ideas with him. 'In the end I just shut my eyes to the production and tried to play my own part as well as I could,' he confessed. It was not the best of recipes for creating high-quality ensemble work.

However, there were mitigating circumstances on the first night. Earlier in the day the theatre world had been stunned by the news that Lilian Baylis had died from a sudden heart attack. Gielgud and his company, geared up to play an evening of high comedy, were deeply shocked and upset. In his review J.G. Bergel felt it was unfair to judge the actors since 'the death of Miss Baylis lay heavily upon them, individually and collectively'. Gielgud was deeply affected, and had to take his opening line from the prompter, the first time this had ever happened.

The strength of his emotion was understandable, for Lilian Baylis had been a crucial figure in his career. Since he had left the Old Vic, he had looked upon her as a personal friend. In her turn she had taken a fond, almost maternal interest in his progress: 'I know we all feel most proprietary about his great success!' she wrote to Gielgud's mother after his Broadway triumph. 'He really seems to belong to us, and all at the Vic feel this.' At her memorial service in St Martin's-in-the-Fields Gielgud read one of the lessons, and shortly afterwards wrote an eloquent tribute to her, revealing some of the human qualities he held most dear: 'As her servant in the theatre she loved so well, I reverence her clear trust in those who worked for her, and her own selfless example of perseverance. As her friend I mourn her delightful unique humanity, and the real goodness of her character, which a strong sense of humour made to shine more brightly. She inspired me with awe, with admiration, and with affection – and I salute her passing with deepest personal regret.'

If the equilibrium of his company had been upset by Guthrie's intervention and Lilian Baylis's death, the third production of the season, *Three Sisters*, directed by Michel Saint-Denis, did more than put it back on an even keel. Gielgud had longed to stage Chekhov's play ever since Komisarjevsky had directed him in it at Barnes, but after *Noah* he was wary of working again with the autocratic Frenchman. Yet now the Saint-Denis meticulousness came as a relief after Guthrie's slapdash approach.

Since coming to London Saint-Denis had been very taken with Gielgud's work as a producer. 'I have never seen a single production of

Gielgud's without feeling stimulated by the quality and justice of his inventions,' he observed. Still hoping to form a troupe along the lines of the Compagnie des Quinze, he saw an opportunity to work with the nearest the English theatre had to a permanent company. 'A play of this kind needs teamwork and meticulous rehearsal,' he remarked before starting rehearsals. This was the first Chekhov play he had produced, 'my first experience of realism' as he put it later, and he had help with it from a retired Russian actress living in Paris. He was already an enthusiast for the work of Stanislavsky. In 1922, after seeing the Moscow Art Theatre production of *The Cherry Orchard* in Paris, with Chekhov's widow Olga Knipper playing Madame Ranevsky, he had talked about it with Stanislavsky into the early hours.

It was via Komisarjevsky and Saint-Denis that Stanislavsky's ideas filtered through to the English theatre, influencing many actors, notably Redgrave and Ashcroft. Gielgud had just read Stanislavsky's 'working textbook' *An Actor Prepares*, and reviewed it enthusiastically for *Theatre Arts Monthly*: 'I was entrapped by it, I could not put it down,' he wrote. He was fascinated by Stanislavsky's ideas about the actor's inner preparation for a part, about the relaxation and control of the body, about the audience and the 'fourth wall'. Significantly, he felt the book was of less value to actors than to producers and students: what Stanislavsky wrote was what actors knew but had been unable to express, what they realised without being conscious of it. But he doubted whether his methods would penetrate the English theatre: 'In Russia and on the continent the theatre is taken seriously as an art. In Anglo-Saxon countries it is, if you generalise, a business. Alas, the modern commercial theatre is bound to be a bitter disappointment to those trained in Stanislavsky's theories. But it is our theatre which is wrong, and not the training.'

In casting *Three Sisters* he and Saint-Denis had different ideas. Though there was no obvious part for him, Gielgud had opted for Andrey, the weak brother; but Saint-Denis, who had the final say, wanted him to play the soldier/philosopher Vershinin, a part in which Stanislavsky had given one of his greatest performances. Gielgud then suggested Redgrave for Andrey, but Saint-Denis cast him as Baron Tusenbach, and George Devine as Andrey. In all this, Saint-Denis wanted to avoid typecasting: 'An actor must be able to transform,' he argued. 'Casting to type slowly kills acting ability.' Such a notion fitted in with Gielgud's determination to test himself in the broadest possible range of parts.

With eight weeks to work in, the company was able to spend almost a week reading the play before beginning to rehearse, and then to dig much deeper into their characters than was normally possible. Gwen Ffrangcon-Davies had never had so long to rehearse: 'I thought I would be stale, but on the contrary, it changes one's whole attitude to one's work,' she told Saint-Denis. Gielgud, initially anxious about surrendering control, gradually relaxed and enjoyed himself. 'We were able to take it very slowly, and we didn't find a moment of it boring or too hard work,' he recalled.

Saint-Denis saw acting as the point of balance between technique and inspiration. He once described it as being like a hand holding a bird: 'If you clench your fist you will kill it. If you loosen your hand too much it will fly away.' With *Three Sisters* he stressed the importance of atmosphere, suggesting the mood was sometimes more important than the text. He found that 'Gielgud likes character-acting, and that he has a fine sense of characterisation which would develop if he felt free to develop it'. Such a freedom was always to be crucial for Gielgud's ability to create such a character.

Opening in January 1938, *Three Sisters* was acclaimed as a masterpiece, and the outstanding theatrical event of recent years. Words such as 'perfection', 'flawless' and 'unsurpassed' littered the review columns, as the critics eulogised Saint-Denis' magical evocation of Chekhov's provincial world. Agate exclaimed, 'Dear God, the very furniture seems to breathe!' The production prompted leading articles in several newspapers: A.E. Wilson noted that it 'had stirred the emotions of playgoers more deeply, and has caused more admiration and excited discussion, than any play since *Journey's End*'.

The critics praised the company's ensemble work, and Saint-Denis' ability to make the smallest part count for something. Ivor Brown observed: 'It is all real acting and no egotistical nonsense'; Darlington described it as 'more like an orchestration than a production'. *Three Sisters* was seen as a glorious justification of Gielgud's decision to create a company in which the actors, who had now been together for five months, were able to harness their talents to the group effort. Several critics thought this production alone made the season worthwhile; Agate suggested that Gielgud's decision to include it 'ranks with his finest performances as an actor'.

Morale among the company was high: 'Wasn't it a wonderful night and isn't it heaven to think it's going to be a success!' Gwen Ffrangcon-Davies wrote after the opening. 'We all adore it so much that to have success as well seems almost more than one deserves!' Alec Guinness remembered that 'it was like going to some delightful and sad party: we couldn't wait to get back to the place every night'. Cochran, the king of revue, wrote to Gielgud: 'Not many times in my life have I seen anything as good, anywhere.'

Ironically, Gielgud's own performance was liked the least. The critics felt he caught Vershinin's vanity and shallowness, but failed to suggest his loneliness. Rachel Kempson, Redgrave's wife and an ardent admirer, felt 'he was too self-conscious and couldn't quite believe in himself in the part'. Initially he had thought Vershinin a simple, even dull role. But in rehearsal he admitted there was more to Chekhov's garrulous colonel than he had thought. Soon he was describing it as one of the most difficult tasks he had yet set himself. Later he reflected: 'Michel Saint-Denis told me all about the character, but I managed to put very little of myself in it.' Agate, who thought him miscast, saw things differently. 'The trouble, of course, was the necessity for subduing the Gielgud graces to this play. Well, they just won't be subdued. If you subdue them there is nothing left but compromise, since if there are two things which the Terry blood for ever forbids, they are the warped and the sombre.' Gielgud was to prove him wrong on this score in several later parts.

Gielgud's mother and his brother Val were in the first-night audience for *Three Sisters*. Although the beard and eyeglass Gielgud wore as Vershinin were supposedly modelled on how Stanislavsky looked in the part, there was also a startling resemblance to Val, the 'possessor of the best-known beard in the BBC'. One journalist claimed that on his entrance several first-nighters turned to make sure Val was still in his place, and that Gielgud 'only needed to don one of Mr Val Gielgud's flowing evening cloaks to be received in Portland Place with the repect due to the BBC's director of drama'.

Among all the luminous performances, Gielgud especially admired Redgrave's gangling Baron Tusenbach, which he reckoned infinitely finer and truer to Chekhov than his own playing of the part at Barnes. So he was particularly upset when Redgrave asked to be released from playing Bassanio in *The Merchant of Venice*, the final play of the season. He had been offered a five-year film contract worth five times his salary, starting with the lead in Hitchcock's *The Lady Vanishes*. Gielgud was not pleased, telling Redgrave it would look as if he was leaving after having played his best parts – as indeed he was. He also feared his departure might start to break up the company. Yet though he could have insisted that Redgrave stay, he preferred not to retain an unhappy actor. The dispute led to 'an acrid correspondence', and soured relations between them in subsequent years, though Gielgud continued to admire Redgrave as an actor.

The Merchant of Venice was a new departure for Gielgud: for the first time he was producing himself in a leading Shakespearean role without having played the part before. To make his task easier, he asked Glen Byam Shaw to act as co-producer; he also used Alastair Bannerman, who resembled him physically and vocally, to speak Shylock's lines while he observed from out front. Once again he was worried about ghosts from the past: 'The trouble with all these big Shakespearean parts is tradition,' he said. 'Once Irving and Ellen Terry had played them they should have been put away in cold storage for a hundred years! . . . I'm always being asked: Are you going to do this, or that, as Irving did? . . . Tradition is very hard to get away from, just as it's hard for me to put out of my mind recollections of Moscovitch and Ernest Milton in the part.' He had seen Milton at seventeen, and thought him 'the best Shylock I've seen – including Moscovitch'.

Although he liked to look at every Shakespeare play afresh, Gielgud was not a wildly unorthodox producer, as he now made clear in what seems like a thinly veiled reference to Guthrie. 'We have got into the habit of playing altogether too many tricks with Shakespeare,' he said. 'We are doing this play without any of the pretty business. Mark you, the revolt from tradition was wholesome, because it made us think for ourselves more; but it has gone ridiculously far. In *The Merchant* we are keeping our eye on the ball, just as Michel Saint-Denis did in *Three Sisters*. It is to be a straightforward production in a semi-permanent setting.'

Again he consulted Barker, who wrote to him of Shylock as a 'sordid little outsider, passionate, resentful, writhing under his wrongs – which are real – and the contempt of the Venetians'. In rehearsal he tried to develop Shylock as a man rather than a monster, but found this no easy task, and often needed reassurance. Once, standing in the wings with Merula Salaman, playing a lady-in-waiting, he suddenly said: 'I don't know how to play a Jew. You're one: how do you do it?' He even asked his father if he had any Jewish blood, and was disappointed to hear that he hadn't.

The play opened in April, with Peggy Ashcroft as Portia, Leon Quartermaine as Antonio, and Richard Ainley replacing Redgrave as Bassanio. The morning after the opening Gielgud wrote to a friend: 'I was a bit dashed by some of the notices. But I don't falter from my feeling that the reading is a legitimate one, though I hope I may execute it better as time goes on.' His was a modern, unsentimental interpretation, faithful to Shakespeare's text and clearly influenced by Barker. He avoided the roaring, demonic figure of the old actor-managers, who made Shylock the towering storm-centre of the play. In refusing to play the Great Actor, and so unbalance the production, he again gave the other actors more scope to shine.

But his realistic interpretation disappointed those critics who preferred a more heroic, passionate Shylock. Agate in particular found fault. Having seen Irving's forty years before, he wanted a Shylock who was 'malignant and terrible, ready to shatter the inconsiderable world about him'; Gielgud's Jew was by contrast 'merely a wet blanket at a party'. Charles Morgan, on the other hand, thought it a refreshing performance: 'The fireworks of the part are sacrificed to Mr Gielgud's conception of the truth of it, and so clearly does he establish the truth that a new Shylock emerges from his playing.'

Gielgud later claimed he received very bad notices, and failed in the part 'because I find it practically impossible to be disliked onstage'. Once again he was re-writing history to his own disadvantage. Shortly after the play opened he wrote to his father: 'Thank God it seems to be a real success – in spite of Agate. The press was really fine, and I do value Morgan's praise.' Agate was in a minority; most critics thought him a very fine Shylock. Desmond MacCarthy's view was typical of many: 'Never have his remarkable gifts been shown to greater advantage,' he wrote. 'When he is on the stage you can feel the whole house motionless under the painful weight of his realism.' Olivier later rated Shylock one of his finest creations.

Immediately after the opening Gielgud wrote to a friend: 'It seemed a very smooth evening as far as the production was concerned, and I do think the company acted beautifully.' The ensemble work was widely praised, as it had been throughout the season: he had created the company spirit so vital for achieving and sustaining good teamwork. 'His companies were always happy ones,' Guinness recalled. Temperamentally Gielgud was not a natural leader, but his fellow-actors warmed to his enthusiasm and optimism, and were galvanised by his sheer presence. 'It was splendid to see that the press realise what John's season means to the real theatre,' Dorothy Green wrote after the first night of *Richard II*. 'How we all love him and wish him the greatest possible success!'

Why did Gielgud inspire such devotion? Few people knew him better than the Motley trio, who had now designed fifteen of his productions. Margaret Harris remembered: 'He was wonderful to work with because he was so volatile, so exciting, and always very enthusiastic about everything he was doing. He had this extraordinary mind, which never stopped working. But he also had a wonderful generosity towards other actors, which is such a big quality, and so unusual in the theatre. He was much loved for that, and for his amazing kindness.'

As a producer he continued to annoy as well as stimulate. Although Peggy Ashcroft liked the abundance of his ideas, and the scope for argument that he gave the actors, she found his changes of mind 'provoking'. Others suffered from moments of thoughtlessness. At the final rehearsal for *Richard II*, in which Guinness played the Groom, Gielgud told him unhelpfully: 'You're not nearly as good in the part as Leslie French was when I did it before.' Harry Andrews was another victim. Reminiscing with the company about his Hamlet in America, Gielgud remarked: 'I had a rather poor Horatio. Oh, it was you, Harry. Well, you've improved so much since then.'

His season at the Queen's gave a great boost to several careers. George Devine grew in stature with two fine comic performances in *Three Sisters* and *The Merchant of Venice*. As Tusenbach, and also as Bolingbroke in *Richard II*, Redgrave demonstrated a new ability as a character actor of power and intelligence. Of Peggy Ashcroft's playing, Anthony Quayle observed: 'John helped her to achieve status. She was the spring-queen of the time.' She enhanced her reputation with a poignant Irina in *Three Sisters* and, building on her earlier performance for Gielgud at the Vic, a fresh, lyrical and humorous Portia. Later she described the season as 'by far the most formative part of my acting experience'.

Gielgud also drew from Guinness an unexpectedly fine romantic rendering of Lorenzo in *The Merchant of Venice*, of which Ivor Brown wrote: 'He lifts the final scene to an unspectacular, meditative, star-struck beauty that takes the breath away.' After seeing this performance, Guthrie asked Guinness to play Hamlet and other parts at the Old Vic. Not long afterwards Gielgud met him in Piccadilly and said: 'I can't think why you want to play good parts. Why don't you stick to the little people you do so well?'

The season was a success in other respects. By making a small profit, Gielgud had proved that a repertoire of classics was viable in the West

End. The *Tatler* noted that 'he can keep a London theatre packed with appreciative humanity for months and months on end with classic plays that have hitherto been looked upon as inevitable failures'. He had shown the value of keeping a first-class company together for an extended period. As a producer he had been praised for *Richard II* and *The Merchant of Venice*, despite playing the lead in both. As an actor he had further demonstrated his versatility.

In the long term the season, described later by Harold Hobson as 'one of the rarest blazes of theatrical light of the century', was enormously influential. The supreme quality of the ensemble acting showed that, if conditions were right, the English theatre could produce work to rank alongside that of the Moscow Art Theatre, the Comédie Française and Max Reinhardt's company in Germany. Gielgud had shown the way to actors such as Redgrave, who later formed his own company; to Quayle and Byam Shaw, who were to spearhead the revival of Stratford in the 1950s; and ultimately to those such as Olivier, Peter Hall and Trevor Nunn who were to form the Royal Shakespeare Company and the companies at the National Theatre.

18

Binkie, *Earnest* and Elsinore

He will either be the Henry Irving of his age, or
he will be nothing.
                    (St John Ervine on Gielgud, 1939)

AFTER *Three Sisters* Gielgud's admiration for Saint-Denis had
increased enormously. He claimed to have learnt more about
acting from working with him on that play and *Noah* than
from productions in which he had achieved a greater personal success.
Yet though the two of them shared many ideals about the theatre, their
paths were now to diverge completely, and not meet again for nearly
quarter of a century.

Ironically it was Gielgud, at the moment of breakthrough, who drew
back. As Peggy Ashcroft later put it succinctly: 'He gave us the
opportunity to form what was really the first ensemble, and then just
waved goodbye to it all.' Saint-Denis now assumed his mantle. In
partnership with Albery he took over the Phoenix that autumn with a
repertory programme of Chekhov, Ibsen, Shakespeare, Molière and
Bulgakov, and a company largely drawn from Gielgud's group. 'If he
should fail in establishing a permanent company in London it will be
a lasting slur upon the taste and appreciation of everyone who loves the
very best that the theatre stands for,' Gielgud declared.

By this time he had temporarily abandoned his dream. Saint-Denis,
who found him 'tired and worried' at the end of the Queen's season,
pinpointed the dilemma he faced between furthering his career and
advancing the cause of theatre more generally: 'His interest in the
plays, his preoccupation with giving good opportunities to his actors,
had taken the place of the star actor's policy,' he suggested. 'Added to
this conflict was his responsibility as a manager, having to bear the

weight of a company for nine months, and he was feeling that weight.'

Gielgud's enthusiasm for the repertory set-up had at first been boundless. He had contemplated adding several weeks to the season, and changing the play every day. He had thought about touring, and even considered taking three of the productions to America with the same or a similar company. He had wondered about adding modern plays 'of slightly less obvious popular appeal' to the repertoire. But as the weeks went by his zest faded. 'One cannot go on doing classics continually, and so far I have not found any suitable new plays,' he said. Finally he reluctantly disbanded the company.

The year 1938 marked the centenary of Henry Irving's birth. To Gielgud he was still a kind of theatrical god: among his possessions was the cigar-case Irving used to take with him on tour. It was fitting then that he should play a significant part in the centenary matinée at the Lyceum in May, in which he closed the first half by leading on to the stage the surviving members of Irving's company. Yet this was the precise moment when he abandoned the role of actor-manager in which Irving had shone so brilliantly.

The man behind his unexpected change of direction was Hugh Beaumont, known throughout the theatre world as 'Binkie'. Beaumont was to be the most important figure in Gielgud's professional life over the next two decades. Only thirty, he was effectively running the management company H.M. Tennent. Before long he was to become the most powerful man in the West End – and the most feared. Already he was proving a shrewd businessman wih a nose for what the public wanted. Having privately invested £1000 in Gielgud's season, and helped him to lease the theatre on favourable terms, he had made a profit on his investment.

Neat and suave, always immaculately dressed, Beaumont could be charming, devious and manipulative, sometimes all in the same moment. Guthrie observed that 'the iron fist was wrapped in fifteen pastel-shaded gloves'. Rattigan, a close friend, described him as 'bland, smiling, courteous and ingenuous-seeming'. The smile rarely left his face, but behind it was a capricious, cruel and ruthless man, as many in the theatre were to discover. 'Binkie would put the dagger in anyone who crossed him,' the director Peter Cotes said.

Dark, feminine-looking and homosexual, Beaumont now became John Perry's lover. Ironically, it was Gielgud who introduced them. During the Queen's season he had come to Beaumont's office with Perry to suggest he produce his friend's play *Spring Meeting*. Accounts differ as to whether Beaumont agreed to do it because he liked it, or because he saw it as a way of getting Gielgud on to Tennent's books. Either way, Perry stopped living with Gielgud and moved into Beaumont's flat in Piccadilly. According to one actor-friend of Perry, his relationship with Gielgud was very close, but non-sexual. Kitty Black, who was later to work for Tennent's and knew all three men, says: 'I don't think John was bitter, but it must have been a shattering experience.' Gielgud later admitted he had been hurt. But the theatre was more important to him than any relationship: he set aside his wounded feelings, and remained friends with both men.

Perry's co-author on *Spring Meeting* was his childhood friend and the future novelist Molly Keane, then writing under the pseudonym of M.J. Farrell, and soon to become a good friend of Gielgud. The play, set in a crumbling mansion in Tipperary based on Perry's house, centred on an eccentric, impoverished Irish family obsessed with betting on the horses. The company included Zena Dare, Joyce Carey, Roger Livesey, Nicholas Phipps and Margaret Rutherford. Gielgud's production of this fresh, whimsical play was much liked by the critics – 'Mr Gielgud gets more than a breath of the blarney-stone across the footlights,' Agate wrote – and it ran for nearly a year at the Ambassador's.

It made a star of Margaret Rutherford, whose career until then had been in routine comic character parts. Her outstanding performance as the semi-crazy spinster aunt established her as an actress who could suggest the pathos behind an outwardly comic character. Gielgud also rehearsed a second company, including Robert Flemying, Jean Cadell and A.E. Matthews, to tour the play in the provinces and take it to New York. It was headed by Gladys Cooper, to whom he wrote deferentially: 'I can hardly believe I am that same man whom you guided so kindly through the mazes of *L'École des Cocottes* – and now I am producing you in a play, and you look exactly the same as you did then. It must be very nice to feel you make time stand still for everyone who looks at you.'

While championing Perry, Gielgud was also defending Rattigan. His friend's *French without Tears* had been running successfully in the West End for more than a year, despite a running attack on it by Agate, who thought it childish nonsense without wit, plot or character. When he put it at the bottom of a list of plays running in the West End, Gielgud was moved to write to the *Sunday Times*, protesting at the critic's continual sneering at a play which he himself considered 'delightful and original both in conception and execution'. He ended: 'It seems to me most discouraging to a promising young author that he should be baited so ignominiously in your columns on the occasion of his first success, especially at this time when the theatre is so greatly in need of young writers.'

The letter is interesting less for Gielgud's opinion of the play, which was shared by most critics, than for his vigorous defence of young writers. It is also notable for his support for popular, lightweight theatre: his taste was always to be catholic. It was a courageous gesture to risk antagonising the most powerful of the critics, as Rattigan acknowledged shortly afterwards. 'I wonder if anyone not actually in the theatre can understand the moral courage involved in the writing of that letter,' he asked. 'Agate's goodwill must, I know, have meant just as much to Gielgud as it did to all of us.'

Gielgud disliked writing to the newspapers, believing critics always had the last word. His vigorous defence of Rattigan reflected his ambivalent attitude to Agate, whose witty, learned and influential notices had been crucial in shaping his career. He became enraged when Agate took advantage of their offstage friendship: 'He was always giving me advice and pontificating, and I wished I'd never been introduced to him,' he recalled. 'He was also very rude and behaved badly at first nights. He was a strange man: a great, great talent when he praised, and rather spiteful when he didn't.

Binkie Beaumont now effectively became Gielgud's manager. In July Beaumont was approached by Olivier, who was looking for financial backing for a bold and ambitious project he had conceived. After *Romeo and Juliet* with Gielgud he had set his sights firmly on becoming a classical actor. Inspired by Gielgud's example, he accepted an offer from Guthrie to go to the Old Vic. In preparing to play Hamlet there he was, according to Guthrie, 'afraid he would suffer dreadfully in comparison with Gielgud'. His energetic, passionate prince was admired but not universally liked, and there were again criticisms of his verse-speaking. But by the end of his second season, after a magnificent Coriolanus, he was being acclaimed as a potentially great Shakespearean actor.

He now planned to stage the four great Shakespearean tragedies in repertory, with Vivien Leigh as his leading lady. But Beaumont would back him only if he agreed to alternate roles with Gielgud: Othello and Iago, Lear and Gloucester, Hamlet and Laertes, Macbeth and Macduff. He also wanted Gielgud to have a share in the directing during the proposed season. Unsurprisingly the negotiations collapsed, apparently through Olivier's refusal to be directed by Gielgud.

On his return from France Gielgud began rehearsals for a new play, *Dear Octopus* by Dodie Smith. She had written several plays during the 1930s, and in 1937 had been described as 'the most successful woman playwright in the history of the theatre'. Yet most of her work has not survived: only *Dear Octopus*, a regular choice for repertory and amateur companies, is now revived. The play centres on a family reunion held to mark a couple's golden wedding anniversary, and the tensions and conflicts that emerge during a weekend get-together of three generations. Marie Tempest and Leon Quartermaine were cast as the couple, with Gielgud playing their son.

It was a dull, conventional and undemanding part in a superficial and genteel play, and it was a measure of Gielgud's temporary loss of crusading energy that he took it. But he may also have been motivated, as earlier with Emlyn Williams, by loyalty to the author. While writing the play Dodie Smith had been to *Three Sisters*, and when she went backstage Gielgud had complained of the shortage of new plays. She then decided she wanted him in hers, and wrote a key speech with him in mind. 'John was my most admired living actor, and while writing the Grand Toast to the family I had often thought how beautifully he would speak it. But the rest of the part was nothing like good enough for him, and how Binkie persuaded him to accept it I don't know.' The answer lay in his mental and physical exhaustion after the Queen's season, in his constant desire for change, and the large salary that Beaumont used as bait.

There was also Marie Tempest, now seventy-five and playing what was to be her last role. A hard-working actress of elegance and wit, with exquisite diction and timing, she was also a martinet, a bully and a supreme egotist. She insisted actors wore dinner-jackets to rehearsals, and refused to watch any in which she was not involved. She never listened properly to the dialogue, but simply waited for her cues. She upstaged rival actresses with an array of tricks, and if she forgot her lines blamed other actors. Her lack of interest in the script of *Dear Octopus* led her to think the play's title referred to her own character, rather than to the Family, 'that dear octopus from whose tentacles we are never quite able to escape, nor, in our inmost hearts, do we wish to do so'.

Gielgud managed to penetrate her intimidating mask, and they became good friends. During the provincial tour they went for drives together; in London he was invited to her dressing-room during his waits offstage, to be served with French bread and coffee by her dresser. It was all very Edwardian, and very much to his taste. His admiration for the short, plump but stylish actress was fuelled by a shared passion for clothes: 'She was always perfectly soignée, with beautiful shoes and crisp little hats,' he recalled. In his fondness for eccentric elderly actresses he perhaps glimpsed nostalgically the shadows of his Terry relations in his youth, and was prepared to forgive their many faults and foibles. They in return, apart from enjoying the company of a star actor, warmed to his old-fashioned courtesy, kindness and humour, and his obvious and unceasing dedication to the theatre.

Gielgud had proposed himself as producer for *Dear Octopus*, but Beaumont feared his mercurial methods would be disastrous with Marie Tempest. Murray Macdonald, Beaumont's first choice, thought all three principal actors were miscast: 'None of them can be other than they are, and it will be a waste of time to try and force them into an unnatural mould,' he said, declining the job. Yet if Marie Tempest always played herself, Gielgud's versatility was proven. But so too was his indecisiveness. Beaumont finally hired Glen Byam Shaw, an inventive producer whose gentle manner concealed a strong will. Knowing Gielgud well, he stressed the importance not just of planning the actors' moves, but of being sure of the reasons for them. Dodie Smith recalled Gielgud saying, 'You and Glen have been very clever over these moves. I can't find anything to change.'

The first night at the Queen's in September was overshadowed by events on a larger stage. Fears of war had become acute with Hitler's invasion of Czechoslovakia, and during the first act the audience sat grave and unresponsive. According to theatrical legend, the critic Charles Morgan arrived in the interval from *The Times* office, and revealed that Chamberlain was to fly to Germany the next day to meet Hitler. The news spread, the audience relaxed and started to laugh, and the play was received rapturously. At a party at Beaumont's after the signing of the Munich agreement Gielgud, like most people, was relieved at the apparent easing of the crisis, after Chamberlain had waved his famous piece of paper promising 'peace for our time'. Never abreast of current affairs in any detail, he was puzzled when Coward arrived 'white with fury' to denounce Chamberlain's action.

During rehearsals Dodie Smith admired Gielgud's integrity, and the gentle assistance he had given Glen Byam Shaw in rehearsing Valerie Taylor, who was struggling with her part as Gielgud's sister. But on the first night she was hurt by a rare moment of unkindness on his part. Against convention, it had been agreed that she would eventually join the company onstage to receive the applause after the performance. Marie Tempest, who disapproved, refused her outstretched hand, and when she offered her other one to Gielgud, he did the same. 'He later said that, if he took my hand, it would make Marie's rudeness seem even more pronounced,' she recalled. Having to offend either his leading lady or his author, Gielgud chose the safer option.

The critics recognised in the comfortable, sentimental and virtually plotless *Dear Octopus* – one called it 'a great big sofa of a play' – the recipe for West End success with a public keen to forget the gathering storm in Europe. But many felt Gielgud was wasting his talent on such a flat and unprofitable part. The *Sunday Referee* compared its challenge to Paderewski playing 'The Lambeth Walk'; Alan Dent congratulated him on choosing 'this splendid way of taking a nice long holiday'. Talk of his 'betraying the higher theatre' and 'bartering his soul for gold' provoked him to defend his decision: 'One part of the public likes me in modern light plays – another thinks I'm wasting my time in that way,' he explained. 'I want to please both of these sharply divided sections – after all, they are both entitled to consideration – and I gain rest from change and freshness as they gain satisfaction.' It was a valid, undogmatic stance, and one that he would maintain throughout his career.

Although contracts for actors were then normally for the run of a play, Gielgud left *Dear Octopus* after ten months in June 1939. He was soon channelling his energies in another direction. The year before, with the help of Richard Clowes, he had written some auto-biographical articles for *Woman's Journal,* and these he now expanded into a book. One of his principal aims was to record the details of his childhood and the theatrical Terrys while they were still clear in his mind.

In *Early Stages,* published by Macmillan, he also wrote in detail of his career, from the day he walked on at the Old Vic up to his Hamlet in America. He conjured up people and places in a graceful, vigorous and easy style, shot through with wit and humour. In her review the novelist G.B. Stern wrote that, in describing his illustrious family, 'John Gielgud betrays an ironic gift of discrimination; a flair for selecting what incident, what fragments of dialogue, what entrances and exits would reveal them from the most telling angle.'

But the book also revealed his skill as a raconteur, his extraordinary memory for detail, and his modesty. Theatrical memoirs of the time tended to be self-applauding and gushing, and dominated by success and gossip. Gielgud's was startlingly different, not least in drawing attention to his failures and deficiencies as much as his successes and positive attributes. St John Ervine, often critical of his work as a producer, was deeply impressed by 'the true modesty of mind, the frank acknowledgement of defects as well as the equally frank acceptance of worth', while Ivor Brown called the book 'a feat of self-effacement'.

Gielgud offered his own critique of it in an epilogue: 'I have three besetting sins, both on and off the stage – impetuosity, self-consciousness, and a lack of interest in anything not immediately concerned with myself or the theatre. All three of these qualities are abundantly evident to me in reading over this book.' It was an accurate self-appraisal, but none of the qualities marred the book; indeed his obsession with the theatre was one of its assets. Also remarkable was his generosity towards his fellow-actors – even Donald Wolfit escaped censure – and his touching portraits of Ellen Terry, Leslie Faber and Harcourt Williams. There was nothing hostile or indiscreet: by temperament and upbringing he was averse to pulling others apart in public.

Early Stages was published in May 1939 shortly after his thirty-fifth birthday, giving the critics a chance to assess his position in the theatre. Agate put him at its forefront, 'since of all practising English actors he has aimed higher over a longer period than any of his confreres'. The reviewer in *The Times* observed that 'there are few actors who can look back on a career dedicated so wholeheartedly to the best things in the theatre'. But St John Ervine was more critical, noting that 'Mr Gielgud cannot make convincing love, and he lacks dash', and suggesting his future depended on whether he could meet 'his supreme need for an increase in flesh and blood as well as mind and spirit'. He concluded provocatively: 'He will either be the Henry Irving of his age, or he will be nothing.'

While playing in *Dear Octopus*, Gielgud had found a project to fill the daytime hours. Ever since appearing in Playfair's production of *The Importance of Being Earnest* in 1930, he had wanted to produce Wilde's classic comedy. Early in 1939 a request for help from the Hospital for Women in Soho prompted him, with Tennent's support, to stage eight special matinées at the Globe, the proceeds to be divided between the hospital and five theatrical charities.

It proved a landmark production. The company included Joyce Carey and Angela Baddeley as Gwendolen and Cecily, Ronald Ward as Algernon, Margaret Rutherford as Miss Prism and, most famously, Edith Evans as Lady Bracknell. Gielgud decided, with the Motleys, to set the production in the early Edwardian period, mainly so he could indulge his taste for lavish sets, and allow Lady Bracknell to wear imposing hats. It was a period that had a special meaning and resonance for him, through his parents' lives and his own childhood memories of pre-war London. He even based the outdoor set for the second act on his grandmother Kate Terry's Regency house in Kensington.

The philosophy of *The Importance of Being Earnest*, Wilde declared, is 'that we should treat all trivial things very seriously, and all the serious things of life with sincere and studied triviality'. Determined to get the style right, Gielgud talked to members of the original company, who had performed the play under the actor-manager George Alexander, the original John Worthing. From Irene Vanbrugh he learned that Wilde had wanted the actors to play the piece as naturally as possible. This became his intention too: to ensure they played it lightly but with deadly seriousness, to heighten the comedy and avoid turning it into caricature.

The production gave Edith Evans the most celebrated role of her career, and one with which, to her chagrin, she was ever after identified. She modelled her performance in part on the titled women to whom she had been forced to defer as a young milliner. Gielgud had first discussed the role with her at Foulslough. 'We took the play out of the bookcase and read the handbag scene together,' he recalled. 'At the end we all laughed and thought it was so marvellous, and she shut the book and said: "I know that kind of woman, she rings the bell and asks you to put another lump of coal on." There was a kind of resentment which made it a comment on the whole quality of those kind of *nouveau riche* people.'

His production was visually beautiful, the furnishings heavy and ornate as he intended. The costumes were widely admired, though the budget had to allow for an idiosyncrasy of Edith Evans: 'She insisted on having all the right underclothes right down to the skin,' Margaret Harris recalled. 'Fortunately we could buy them for sixpence in the Caledonian Market. We also got her a beautiful cloth suit for ten shillings, and other amazing things like that.' The trouble was worth it: the production was a triumph for what Agate called her portrait of 'dragonhood'.

One reason for its success was the more equal relationship she now had with Gielgud. Disliking the frivolous aspects of theatre that he adored, she nevertheless warmed to him in his more serious moments. 'I like him so much on his own,' she told Gwen Ffrangcon-Davies not long after *Earnest*. She did though have one difficulty with him: 'I respected John, but he used to say my part for me on the stage. I found that very odd.'

Gielgud admired her as 'a model of behaviour and professionalism' – though this presumably excluded their joint inclination to giggle during the famous handbag scene. He also admired her dedication to her work, her refusal to be malicious, and her subtle skills as an actress. 'She taught me to give up my own impatient inclination to drive actors about the stage in order to give a scene excitement long before the dialogue demanded it,' he recalled. But her grand manner amused him. One of the Wilde matinées was attended by Queen Mary, who sent for the company after the first act: 'The Queen, half a head shorter than Edith Evans, looked almost like her on a small scale,' he remembered. 'When Edith curtseyed, one felt she should really have curtseyed back.'

After the first matinée Allan Aynesworth, the original Algernon, said approvingly: 'They've caught the gaiety and exactly the right atmosphere, it's all delightful.' The production was greeted with joy by the critics, and Guthrie later called it 'the high-water mark in the production of artificial comedy in our epoch'. Gielgud's John Worthing was greatly relished: Darlington felt he 'combined a very exact feeling for Wilde's language with a capacity for imitation grief which he might have learnt from the Mock Turtle himself'.

Richard Clowes once quipped that the nearest Gielgud ever got to politics was the plot of *Julius Caesar*. Yet he now made a rare foray into political theatre, and a brief return to management. 'I gamble there as other men do on the Stock Exchange,' he remarked with bravado. *Scandal in Assyria*, which he staged at the Globe for two performances in April and May for the London International Theatre Club, was a re-telling of the biblical story of Esther as a modern satire on totalitarian racial theory. Attacking anti-semitism, the author, 'a Continental dramatist who writes under the pen-name of Axel Kjellström', preferred to conceal his identity.

The piece was a thinly veiled parody of conditions in Nazi Germany, but an uneasy mixture of tragedy, comedy and farce. Critics noted that Gielgud as producer was more at home with the jokes than the history or politics. In a cast that included Jack Hawkins, Ernest Thesiger,

George Howe and Francis L. Sullivan, he was felt to have drawn the best performance from one of his boyhood idols, Ernest Milton, who, according to *The Times*, provided 'the only portrait that is genuinely and consistently moving'.

His brief political phase continued with *Rhondda Roundabout*, a story of the struggles of a Welsh mining community by the novelist and playwright Jack Jones. Believing he was on to a winner, Gielgud put up most of the money himself: 'It seems to me like a play by O'Casey, but without O'Casey's terrific pessimism,' he announced. The producer, Glen Byam Shaw, toured south Wales and recruited amateur actors to complement the professionals, who included Hugh Griffith, Mervyn Johns, George Devine and Raymond Huntley. The critics decided that what the play lacked in craft it made up for in warmth and sincerity. Agate declared 'it was too good for the West End theatre; in other words it was provocative and interesting'.

But at a time of deepening international crisis the public was not attracted to a play dealing with unemployment and communism, and it was only saved from immediate closure by a public appeal for support from Gielgud, Sybil Thorndike, Clemence Dane, Emlyn Williams, and others. 'I have never known an appeal meet with such an immediate response,' Gielgud said, as the pit and gallery filled up. But the play still closed after six weeks, leaving him out of pocket.

During its run he unwittingly provoked controversy in the press. While giving away the prizes at a London school, he suggested children should not be taken to see Shakespeare until they were at least sixteen, since his plays required 'a trained ear and a matured intelligence'. His remarks, made off the cuff, were prompted by memories of special matinées at the Old Vic, where children had 'rustled their programmes like autumn leaves, fidgeted, and were bored stiff'. It seems he had forgotten his own enjoyment of *A Midsummer Night's Dream* and *As You Like It* at roughly half that age. But the debate, prompting many letters and a leader in the *Daily Telegraph*, allowed him to express his dislike of recent productions of the *Dream*, 'disfigured by female Oberons, cascades of Mendelssohn, flying ballets, and tedious horseplay in the comic scenes'.

As war became increasingly likely, he became conscious of a world outside the theatre, and tried to respond to it. He read through scores of new plays to find something appropriate. To the many demands that he return to Shakespeare, he replied: 'Why on earth should one try to cut oneself off from the modern theatre with its risks and adventures?'

Yet however worthy his aims with *Scandal in Assyria* and *Rhondda Roundabout*, such plays were ultimately not congenial to him. Finally he surrendered to public pressure and, despite having reached thirty-five, the age at which he had promised to abandon the part for ever, decided to make a fourth attempt at Hamlet. After his exhausting run in America, the thought of repeating the role had at first repelled him. But few of his decisions were ever final, and events now conspired to make him change his mind.

The first was Olivier's Hamlet at the Old Vic. According to legend, Gielgud told him on the opening night, 'Larry, it's one of the finest performances I have ever seen, but it's still *my* part.' Despite his well-known tactlessness, this grandiose remark seems out of character, and was probably never made. It is not included in any of the main Olivier biographies, perhaps because on the opening night in January 1937 Gielgud was still playing Hamlet in America. But he did later admit that when he read Olivier's better notices, he burst into tears.

The following year he had been 'stirred and provoked' by another Guthrie production, this time with Guinness as Hamlet: 'I was deeply touched by Alec's performance, which I thought grew in distinction and quality all the time,' he told Guthrie. He offered his opinion on the virtues and faults of the production in a way that suggest renewed interest in the play. And it was around this time that he read Barker's Preface, which had appeared since he had played the part on Broadway. It was this, he now admitted, that had cured him of his 'revulsion' for the play. 'Barker really set me thinking again about Hamlet,' he said. 'It's a wonderful piece of work – full of ideas and understanding.'

The clinching factor was an invitation from the Danish government to stage *Hamlet* in the very place where Shakespeare had set the play, Kronborg Castle at Elsinore. Olivier had played there two years before in Guthrie's production. Gielgud tried again to get Barker to produce him, but Barker declined: 'The Preface is an intellectual discussion more valuable than my presence,' he told Gielgud. 'I have written why I think certain things ought to be done; it is for you to find how they should be carried out.' It was almost a rebuke.

With only eight performances scheduled in Denmark, Gielgud was uncertain whether he could recruit a good enough cast. It was Edith Craig who suggested he should stage *Hamlet* for a week in London beforehand, in a theatre with powerful associations for them both. Despite widespread protests and several rescue attempts, the Lyceum was due to be demolished that summer to make way for a block of flats and shops. Sixty years before Irving had begun his reign as actor-manager there with Hamlet, with Ellen Terry later playing an acclaimed Ophelia. It seemed fitting that his apparent successor and her great-nephew should close it with the same play, in a part which he had already made his own.

But Gielgud was worried about the short rehearsal time. 'I wish to heaven I had more than three weeks,' he said. 'I should like to have ten days with the cast, just sitting round a table and speaking the verse. Nothing else. We are in danger of losing the purely vocal magic of Shakespeare in our concern with the psychological problems.' This last comment was not so much an attack on Stanislavsky as on the current vogue for Freudian interpretations of Shakespeare – including Olivier's Hamlet – for which he had little time. 'If Hamlet had an Oedipus complex Shakespeare, I feel, would have said so right out,' he suggested.

During rehearsals he heard that Barker was to be in London; hoping for guidance, he invited him to a run-through. Barker agreed to come on condition that 'there won't be any press or publicity – my name is not to be used in any way'. The next day Gielgud was summoned to the Ritz, where for three hours he sat at the feet of his master, frantically scribbling while Barker gave him some 'marvellous notes'. Most of them suggested simplifying his characterisation of Hamlet, and cutting much of the business. Some of Barker's observations – 'The King is a cat, you see, and he ought to be a dog' – were decidedly cryptic; but Gielgud was inspired by what Barker had told him. Desperate to put it into practice, he persuaded the company to rehearse the following day – despite it being a Sunday – so he could try them out. Barker's influence was as powerful as ever.

He had recruited a high-class company, with Laura Cowie and George Howe repeating their Gertrude and Polonius from 1934 and, in a bold innovation, Jack Hawkins playing both Claudius and the Ghost. Harry Andrews was Laertes, Glen Byam Shaw played Horatio, and Marius Goring the Player King. Ophelia was Fay Compton, who had played the part with Barrymore. There were further historical links: her aunt Isabel Bateman had been another of Irving's Ophelias, and her grandfather H.L. Bateman had been manager of the Lyceum. For Gielgud the associations could hardly have been more thrilling.

The weight of history hung heavy over the performances. Gielgud's sword, which his mother had given him, was the one used by Edmund Kean in *Richard III*. The foyer and corridor walls were lined with portraits of Irving and Ellen Terry and programmes of Irving productions, lent by Gabrielle Enthoven. 'I love your frames and pictures in the theatre,' Gielgud told her before the opening. 'They will do so much to make it look more attractive, and the only difficulty will be to get the audience in from looking at them in time to look at the play!'

Barker, leaving for France, sent his good wishes to 'the best Hamlet going today'. Nearly three thousand people packed into the theatre for each of the six performances, the last night being attended by Queen Mary and members of the Bateman and Terry families. The demand for seats that night was so great that hundreds of people had to be turned away, including four hundred trying to get into the gallery. In his curtain speech Gielgud, visibly moved, paid tribute to those involved in the Lyceum's long history. 'This historic occasion is tinged with sadness, but like all things of the theatre that pass, it will become a memory,' he said. He ended on a suitably rousing note: 'Long live the memory of the Lyceum! Long live the memory of Henry Irving! Long live the memory of Ellen Terry!' Afterwards people besieged the stage door, among them actors and actresses who had come from other theatres still wearing their make-up, to get a last glimpse of a theatre which many had thought to be as permanent as the Bank of England.

Despite these distractions, the looming shadow of Irving, and the burden of playing the part six times in four days, Gielgud came up with another fine Hamlet. In the inevitable comparisons with his 1930 and 1934 versions, most critics felt he had grown in authority and depth of feeling, producing a more bitter, more venomous Hamlet while retaining the sensitivity. Agate thought it an immense advance, which had 'shed nothing of its nobility and poetry', a performance 'of great intelligence, abounding interest, increasing vigour'. But Darlington felt his new strength failed to compensate for the loss of his 'boyish, romantic quality'.

While it had not been easy to fit a production designed essentially for a castle courtyard into a conventional proscenium theatre, Gielgud and the Motleys had devised a set of great simplicity, with an apron stage and a small inner stage. The results were liked: *The Times* critic noted the production's 'excellent precision and lucidity', while S.R. Littlewood wrote: 'The whole thing is a good deal nearer to Shakespeare than it is to Irving. It is human, alive, bright and "close-up", with no needless gloom of atmosphere, and yet exquisitely poignant.' Several critics thought Fay Compton one of the finest

Ophelias they had seen, commending her for her restraint and simplicity. Gielgud, declared the *Bystander,* was 'almost a National Theatre in himself'.

Elsinore was a very different experience. The festival, dreamed up by a Danish journalist, had been inaugurated in 1937 by the Guthrie/Olivier Old Vic production. Gielgud, travelling for the first time by plane, made a preliminary visit in the spring. 'The stone castle is disappointing,' he wrote in his diary. 'Hamlet's grave is said to be a fake. It is even supposed to contain a cat. But everybody is very agreeable.' When he returned for the real thing, he was treated like an ambassador, which effectively he was: the company's visit was intended to promote good relations between Britain and Denmark at a critical moment internationally. His arrival at his hotel was marked by a small cannon being fired in his honour; he was invited to unveil a bas-relief statue of Shakespeare in the walls of Kronborg Castle; and a prologue written specially for the play in both English and Danish ended, 'But is our Hamlet lost for evermore? / John Gielgud, bring him back to Elsinore!'

Kronborg Castle, with its thick grey walls, its spires and gables and green-coppered roofs, stands on a promontory jutting out into the narrow sound that separates Denmark from Sweden. In its spacious cobblestoned courtyard the audience for *Hamlet,* equipped with fur coats, mufflers and rugs, sat for nearly four hours on hard wooden benches. They came from all over Europe, and even America, where seats could be booked along with a berth on a special liner. Many people came for the experience as much as for the production, for the chance to walk beforehand on the battlements where Shakespeare had set his opening scene, and where Hamlet first sees his father's ghost.

The production was beset with problems. The weather was atrocious: in a postcard to Kitty Black, Gielgud described the performance as 'extracts from the Lyceum production with wind and rain accompaniments'. It rained nearly every day, causing one performance to be cancelled, another to be abandoned during the graveyard scene, and a third to be interrupted for several minutes. The small apron stage – one critic likened it to a marionette theatre – was dwarfed by the castle walls. The wind blew the actors' cloaks into their faces, and the large colourful banners designed by the Motleys flapped noisily in the wind, losing their effect because of having to be strapped down. Worst of all the ghost scenes at the start of the play, performed in broad daylight, lacked any real atmosphere.

Unused to playing in the open air, Gielgud felt acutely vulnerable in the early scenes: 'I hate being able to see the audiences so clearly,' he wrote. 'We feel defenceless, with our painted faces, until halfway through the evening, when the artificial lights are turned on.' One night he was disturbed by two of his fans: 'Two admiring ladies from England, conspicuous in brightly coloured headscarves, keep moving their seats so as to sit right in front of me. This makes me very self-conscious, and I change my moves to thwart them.'

None of these problems affected the Danish critics, whose notices were fulsome. Three of the leading Copenhagen papers headed their reviews 'WORLD'S BEST HAMLET'. The *Nationaltidende* thought Gielgud virile: 'The big, prominent nose, the broad Slav cheekbones, speak of maturity and strength, of masculine force.' The critic of *Politiken* wrote: 'Never has English sounded more beautiful from the human mouth.'

The visiting English critics were more divided. Ivor Lambe thought Gielgud held the cosmopolitan audience, despite the fact that most people in it could not understand the words. 'They forgot the hardness of the seats, the wind and the rain. His voice, echoing sometimes from the roof, rose over the sirens of ships in the Sound and the noise of the sparrows.' But W.E. Williams, who had seen the Lyceum production, thought him less effective: 'Gielgud is a parlour Hamlet, not a platform Hamlet,' he wrote. 'Something of the delicacy of his production dissolved in the wide spaces of Kronborg courtyard, and sometimes the light and shade of his beautiful voice failed to carry the distance.'

One of his 'admiring ladies', Margaret Drew, wrote effusively: 'The glory of last night is still filling me – I rejoiced so much that the Danish people realised and acclaimed to the full his greatness . . . He is a star and sun and moon and sometimes all the Universe. He is so *lit* from within.' Another of his fans passed translations of the Danish notices to him while the company was having dinner. Without checking them Gielgud started to read them aloud, and found himself saying: 'Miss Compton has neither the youth nor the looks for Ophelia, but she obviously comes of good theatrical stock.'

Elsinore was a unique occasion, but not an especially enjoyable one for Gielgud, who was never at ease in the role of goodwill ambassador. 'We earn some critical praise for our performance, but I do not find myself deriving much pleasure from the experience,' he wrote. He disliked in particular the formal occasions. But there was one compensation. At one performance a young Danish poet noticed a dark-eyed woman in a hat 'whose lips could form every speech in *Hamlet* as perfectly as the prompter'. This was the Danish writer Karen Blixen, who wrote *Out of Africa* under the pseudonym Isak Dinesen. Gielgud was introduced to her at one of the 'tedious lunches' he had to attend. Twenty years his senior and a great enthusiast for Shakespeare, she was to him 'mysterious and fascinating'. They became good friends, and were to meet often. Once again he was bewitched by an elegant older woman with a passion for the theatre and feather hats.

The company was inevitably conscious of the growing threat of war. Torpedo boats flying the swastika were anchored in Elsinore harbour, and one night, to the actors' displeasure, a group of German sailors occupied the whole front row. The tension came out in practical jokes and childish pranks, with Marius Goring the ringleader. Live chickens appeared in people's beds, and cannons in the corridors. Once Gielgud returned to his room to find four of the company, including Fay Compton, tucked up in his bed. After a last-night party even he caught the mood, as Margaret Harris remembered: 'We all assembled on the beach, and started to throw people into the sea. Nobody quite dared to do that to John. Finally he said, "Isn't anyone going to throw me in?" So we did.'

One day all the swastikas disappeared from the hotel dining-room. With several Nazis among the guests, the manager feared an international incident, and appealed to Gielgud. Reluctantly assuming the role of an authority figure, he asked the culprit to own up, whereupon Marius Goring confessed to having stuffed the flags down the toilet. Some replacements were found, but they too disappeared, presumably in similar fashion. 'I think we all feel some kind of premonition of violent change,' Gielgud wrote in his diary. 'There is a curious end-of-term melancholy as we pack up and say good-bye.'

Back in London all the signs pointed to war: the sandbags around Broadcasting House, the trenches being dug in the parks, the gas masks and uniforms in the streets, the children being evacuated to the country. Anticipating air raids, Gielgud moved his most precious books and pictures from London to Foulslough, and made plans to move his parents to Ireland. Yet even now, just three weeks before the outbreak of war, he was looking eagerly to the future and bursting with ideas.

He talked of parts he'd like to play: Lord Foppington in Vanbrugh's *The Relapse*, Arnold Champion-Cheney in Maugham's *The Circle*.

More unexpectedly, he expressed a desire to play Iago to Godfrey Tearle's Othello – but then changed his mind in mid-thought, adding that 'perhaps someone like Laughton or Emlyn Williams ought to take the part?' He underlined his need for variety: 'I want continually to ring the changes on Shakespeare, modern comedy, the classics, modern drama, with New York visits, and production periods when I am neither seen nor heard, to keep the public's interest from being satiated.' But he had cooled on the idea of commissioning plays: 'I don't want a part that has been made to measure according to a dramatist's idea of me, or a play that has been built round a part.' He still talked of a permanent company, with Saint-Denis, Komisarjevsky and Norman Marshall as producers. He even mused on the possibility of taking *Hamlet* to America.

One role he coveted and had come near to playing was that of Lord Harry Monchensey, the modern Orestes in T.S. Eliot's new verse drama *The Family Reunion*. Gielgud was intrigued by this complex play, but found it hard to understand. It was announced he would play the part and produce the play in a series of matinées at the Globe. He had assembled a cast that included Sybil Thorndike, May Whitty and Martita Hunt, but then Eliot asked to meet him at the Reform Club, for oysters and a talk. Gielgud felt intimidated by his austere personality ('He was just like a civil servant, with striped trousers'), and rattled nervously on about practicalities such as the set and the positioning of the French windows. Eliot became increasingly silent. Shortly afterwards Gielgud heard – though not from Eliot – that he had decided against his doing the play, on the grounds that he was not religious enough to understand the motivation of the characters. This seems an unlikely reason since Michael Redgrave, who also had no faith, was given the part shortly afterwards. Gielgud may have been nearer the truth in thinking that Eliot feared he was going to turn it into a fashionable Shaftesbury Avenue comedy.

Another possibility was *A Tale of Two Cities*. He and Rattigan toyed with the idea of working again on their ill-fated adaptation and staging it in a large theatre such as Drury Lane. Gielgud envisaged an elaborate production: huge crowd scenes, real coach and horses, music in the style of that used in the Fred Terry melodramas. But when Tennent's suggested inviting an American composer to write a musical version, he was horrified. The ill-starred adaptation was finally done on the radio in 1953, with Eric Portman as Sydney Carton.

The build-up to war was now intensifying. According to a story related by Beverley Nichols, Gielgud was so preoccupied with the theatre he scarcely noticed what was going on. Nichols found him in a state of gloom one morning, surrounded by newspapers full of news of troop movements and diplomatic manoeuvres. When he asked Gielgud what had happened, Gielgud replied: 'The worst: Gladys has got the most appalling notices. And so has the play. I don't know what the world is coming to.' While there may be an element of truth in the story – Gielgud always turned first to the theatre notices – he was certainly not oblivious to the ever-worsening situation in Europe.

He was worried especially about its effect on his parents. His father had been ill and was recovering from an operation, his mother, now seventy-one, was greatly apprehensive. When they resisted his attempts to get them to stay with John Perry's family in Ireland, he suggested they move out to Foulslough. But then he discovered a large airfield was being constructed near Finchingfield and, seeing searchlights combing the sky, realised East Anglia would be a vulnerable area. In the end he persuaded his parents that if war were to be declared they should remain in Somerset, where they were then staying.

Although war now looked almost inevitable, Binkie Beaumont was not to be deflected by a mere dictator from planning his autumn season. 'This silly war just isn't going to happen,' he announced in July. 'As far as the management and I are concerned, it's business as usual.' One planned production was an adaptation of Daphne du Maurier's novel *Rebecca,* published the year before. Gielgud, up to date as always with the new novels, persuaded Beaumont of its excellence, and together they convinced the author she could adapt her hugely successful novel for the stage. Gielgud was engaged to produce, and play the brooding hero Maxim de Winter. The production went into rehearsal on 29 August, with Jill Furse as the second Mrs de Winter, and Margaret Rutherford an unlikely choice for the evil housekeeper Mrs Danvers.

In the meantime Tennent's had revived Gielgud's production of *The Importance of Being Earnest* for a planned six-week run at the Globe. The cast had been strengthened since the special matinées: Jack Hawkins was now Algernon, and Gwen Ffrangcon-Davies and Peggy Ashcroft played Gwendolen and Cecily. In addition, making his only appearance under Gielgud's direction, John Perry took over as Lane the butler. Opening on 16 August, the production played to capacity houses. But West End attendances fell dramatically during the following week. When Hitler invaded Poland on Friday 1 September,

Gielgud and other Tennent stars – Marie Tempest, Rex Harrison, Diana Wynyard, Anton Walbrook – assembled in Beaumont's office, to be told that all Saturday-night performances of the firm's productions would be cancelled. Most of them were close to tears; Walbrook, a Jewish refugee from Germany, shed real ones.

That night Gielgud dined with Ralph Richardson and Alan Dent. On the Sunday he joined Saint-Denis and his cast rehearsing *The Cherry Orchard* in the Queen's, to sit on the stage and listen on a tiny radio to Chamberlain's announcement that Britain was at war with Germany. Some of his closest associates were there: Peggy Ashcroft, Edith Evans, Richardson, Beaumont and Albery. Afterwards there was a farewell lunch for Saint-Denis, who was returning to France. The actor Basil Langton recalled: 'Gielgud joined us but left the table early; as he crossed the floor he turned to Saint-Denis and said, "Bonne chance!" I thought this a very chic thing to say to a soldier; like a line from a well-made play. It was the end; it was the break-up of the family.'

19

Barker and *King Lear*

He was the master, the Toscanini, the absolute genius.

(Gielgud on working with
Barker, 1940)

AT the start of the 1930s Gielgud made a list of the things he wanted to do in the theatre. When war broke out he found he had done them all; now he had to do several of them again. Though he never saw active service, for the next six years he did his bit for the war effort in the only way he knew how, by working in the theatre. Living precariously from production to production, working ferociously hard, he provided a mix of classical drama and lighter fare which helped to maintain morale during the dark, dangerous and often dreary war years.

As soon as war was declared the theatres were closed down until further notice. Like other actors, Gielgud faced an uncertain future. *Rebecca*, along with *The Cherry Orchard* and other productions in rehearsal, was shelved. Edith Evans wailed self-pityingly: 'What am I to *do*? I am an actress. I can't act with bombs falling!' But no bombs fell, and the 'phoney war' began. Within days the government, realising people needed entertainment more than ever, announced that theatres in designated 'safe areas' could be re-opened. Much of the credit for this was due to Beaumont, who led a deputation to Downing Street from the Theatre Managers' Association, and made personal calls to Anthony Eden and Clementine Churchill. After further pressure from the profession, the government agreed to make work in the theatre and cinema a 'reserved occupation', enabling actors to carry on while there was a 'reasonable demand' for their services. To prevent those actors who did so being branded shirkers, some theatres printed a programme note stating: 'All the actors in this production are either unfit for military service or awaiting call-up.'

Gradually the leading actors disappeared into the armed forces. Richardson enlisted in the Fleet Air Arm, where he was belatedly joined by Olivier, who was heavily criticised for remaining in America during the first year of the war. Alec Guinness entered the navy, Anthony Quayle and Jack Hawkins the army, George Devine the artillery. Gielgud, having initially signed up for reserve service, volunteered in October for active service, before his age-group was called up, but was told he was not needed for at least six months. For someone of such a fastidious nature and physical awkwardness, unused to mixing with the 95 per cent of the population who never went to a theatre, the news may have been not unwelcome.

Ten days after Chamberlain's announcement he had already resumed work with his production of *The Importance of Being Earnest*, which re-opened the Golders Green Hippodrome, playing there for a week. It was the first large theatre to re-open in London, and the occasion had great symbolic importance. Queues formed from an early hour, and the actors arrived wearing gas masks. Outside the theatre Gielgud was cheerful: 'It has been a gloomy time for everybody since the theatres closed, and we are all delighted to be back,' he said. He promised that 'the theatre will go on somehow throughout the war'.

As his first wartime task he took *Earnest* on tour, delighting audiences in Blackpool, Brighton, Cardiff, Bristol, Streatham, Oxford, Birmingham, Manchester, Newcastle, Glasgow, Edinburgh and Liverpool. A huge success, the production returned to London and ran until the end of February 1940; in 1942 it was to sell out the Phoenix for a further two months. In those early days, amidst the blackout and the sandbags, it met the needs of the hour. After the Golders Green opening Alan Dent observed: 'Everybody seemed to forget about Europe during these three hours of witty nonsense.'

Edith Evans's Lady Bracknell was relished more than ever: her famous cry, 'A handbag?', soon to enter theatrical legend, was compared by one critic to an air-raid siren. Gielgud's John Worthing, full of witty mock gravity, was showered with yet more praise, as was the production. The critic of *The Times*, who felt it 'would surely gain the applause of Congreve and the gratitude of Wilde', decided that 'if the past theatrical decade had to be represented by a single production this is the one that many good judges would choose'. Gielgud's reputation as a producer was never higher.

After one performance Lord Alfred Douglas, Wilde's lover and the cause of his downfall, came round to his dressing-room. For Gielgud the meeting was a great disappointment. Although he continually questioned 'Bosie' about the original production of *Earnest*, Douglas only wanted to talk about his relationship with Wilde, and how he had influenced his writing of the play. His visit frustrated Gielgud, but also saddened him, for Douglas had lost all his good looks.

As the phoney war continued he made a more personal contribution to keeping up morale. Mindful of his Polish roots, he lectured in several cities on 'Shakespeare – in Peace and War', the proceeds going to the Polish Relief Fund and the Red Cross. Devised for him by Ivor Brown, his 'lecture' consisted mainly of reading passages from the plays. But he also encouraged people to turn to Shakespeare as a relief from the war, to learn from a writer who had covered so many of its aspects. He introduced a lighter touch, with quotations made relevant to air-raid wardens, reserve policemen, the blackout, and aerial warfare. He gave his services free, and was warmly received: in Bristol he was said to have 'performed a service to many who have already suffered mental wounds, and who by his lecture will be encouraged to seek solace in the pages of Shakespeare'.

While touring he was invited by Rudolf Bing, manager of the Glyndebourne Opera House, to produce *The Beggar's Opera*, with the composer Frederick Austin conducting. It was a welcome but difficult assignment. The famous Playfair production at the Lyric, Hammer-smith, for which Austin had re-arranged the music, had been one of the highlights of his youth, and twenty years later the details were still imprinted on his memory. Before the production was announced, he sought support for the revival from Playfair's widow May:

I do hope you won't be very much hurt by this. You know how enormously I admired Nigel and his work – above all the *Beggar* at the Lyric – but I believe that he would have been the first to say of it now, Let's do it again in quite a different way . . . The thing is a masterpiece in itself, and should be revived afresh at intervals, just like other classics, with fresh interpretations – don't you agree? . . . A poor copy is the most lifeless work imaginable. This new production may fail altogether – it is bound to be received with suspicion and comparison – but I should like to feel – and Austin feels as I do – that we had your goodwill in undertaking it.

May Playfair duly obliged. Gielgud was so anxious not to imitate Playfair and Lovat Fraser, so desperate 'to avoid limping in their footsteps', that he and the Motleys set the opera in the Regency period rather than in 1720. He had come to see Playfair's production as over-stylised, feeling some of the 'squalid satire' had been lost. He wanted to stick closer to Gay's original, and provide a more naturalistic, dramatic version, with the songs – some of which had not been used at Hammersmith – arising more easily out of the action. 'They will not be sung with a bow to the audience,' he explained during rehearsals. 'I am hoping very much that the audience will not demand encores all the time.'

The production had Audrey Mildmay as Polly Peachum, Michael Redgrave in his first singing role as Macheath, and support from leading singers in the Glyndebourne company. After a seven-week tour it re-opened the Haymarket, one of the few London theatres to have remained closed since the war began. Gielgud later described as 'a dangerous attempt at originality' his decision to shift the action forward: 'It changed the colour of the play and gave it a Dickensian atmosphere.' But he had support for the idea, notably from Ivor Brown, who argued that his 'experiment in bringing the opera closer to the London earth is successful as well as exciting'. Others baulked at the innovation: the *Bystander* noted that 'the orthodox rightly complain that there is too little Gay and too much Gielgud'; Lionel Hale suggested it was 'preferable to limp in anyone's footsteps rather than fall flat on one's face in one's own'.

Redgrave, a rare example of an actor who could sing, made a charmingly roguish Macheath, but some music critics felt his voice was not up to the role. Gielgud concurred, as he wrote to May Playfair: 'Redgrave has enormous charm, but of course lacks experience as a singer, and his performance certainly lacks humour and breadth.' There was tension between them, a residue of their dispute over Redgrave's departure from the Queen's company. But Gielgud's methods as a producer were also a factor: 'John had muddled me in rehearsal, giving me one direction one day and countermanding it the next,' Redgrave recalled. Yet Gielgud could be reasonably satisfied with his first opera production: according to *Theatre World* it did more than any other show in London to make people forget 'the unpleasant realities of the world outside the Haymarket'.

Having regretfully sold Foulslough at the start of the war, Gielgud was living permanently in his St John's Wood flat. He now received his call-up papers, to general consternation at Tennent's. Beaumont acted swiftly, cutting through red tape and obtaining exemption for him until the end of the war. Gielgud later claimed he was unaware of this intervention, and kept on wondering why he hadn't been called up. This seems surprising, for in February he pledged himself publicly to play nothing but Shakespeare and the classics for the duration, promising to take productions anywhere in the world where troops needed to be entertained.

In fact plans were already in motion: the British Council had approached him about heading a 'mobile touring company' to go to the Mediterranean and the Balkans. It would perform his Lyceum *Hamlet,* and also *The Importance of Being Earnest,* with Sybil Thorndike replacing Edith Evans. But in January, as the proposed tour ran into planning difficulties, he had written to a friend: 'I can't think it will happen now as the war seems to be spreading. I have no plans really, but something is sure to turn up. Hope you are keeping well in these dreary times.'

In fact something had already turned up. At the start of the war Barker had written to Gielgud from Paris: 'If this war goes on for long, something should be done to save the theatre from falling into the pitiable state (from the point of view of the drama itself) into which it fell during the last. And I think you are chief among those who can do this.' He proposed a scheme for plays to be performed by a company on a non-profit-making basis. In reply Gielgud suggested Barker should be the producer for such a company, but his mentor was not to be tempted. Gielgud then asked him if he would produce him in his latest assignment at the Old Vic. There, at the invitation of Guthrie, he and Lewis Casson were to head a company which would re-open the theatre with a three-month season of classics.

The theatre had been closed since the outbreak of war, and damaged by fire, and the announcement of the season was widely welcomed. 'Mr Gielgud, Shakespeare, the Old Vic and its audience are four major powers that have been too long parted,' declared the *Sunday Times.* 'Their projected alliance will come as near to making theatre history as these hard times allow.' Gielgud had never forgotten his debt to his theatrical training-ground, and decided to resume where he had left off in 1931, with *King Lear.* What the press and public didn't know was that he had persuaded Barker to work on the production, though only on certain conditions: that his involvement was kept secret, and that Casson, already cast as Kent, would co-produce but be named as sole producer. Casson called this 'humbug' but, revering Barker as much as Gielgud did, thought it a fair price to pay to get him back into a theatre.

Gielgud and Guthrie assembled a distinguished company, none of whom was paid more than £12 a week. Cathleen Nesbitt and Fay Compton were Goneril and Regan, Jessica Tandy was Ophelia, Jack Hawkins played Edmund, Robert Harris was Edgar, Nicholas Hannen played Gloucester, and Stephen Haggard was the Fool. Barker came over from France for a weekend, and Gielgud read his part to him in the manager's office of the Queen's, weeping during the more emotional scenes. When he finished Barker told him he had read only two lines correctly, adding: 'Of course you are an ash and this part demands an oak, but we'll see what can be done.' Where most actors would have been devastated by this reaction Gielgud, overwhelmed by Barker's presence, was merely hungry to learn more.

When Barker returned temporarily to France Gielgud, Casson and Guthrie laid the foundations of the production, using Barker's 1927 Preface as a guide. Its author then appeared, and scrapped nearly everything they had done. 'He was like a god coming back,' Gielgud remembered. 'You felt if you could satisfy him the puzzle was solved for ever.' For ten days the company worked intensively with Barker, sometimes from 10.30 to midnight. 'His knowledge of the stage, of the tricks, of the ways and vanities of the actors, is enormous,' Gielgud said. 'If you think you are going to see the old-time ranting Lear next week, you are mistaken. I shall rant hardly at all in this production.' He later called these days with Barker one of the great experiences of his career. In his excitement, and against Barker's wishes, he invited actor friends to slip into rehearsals, to witness 'something absolutely extraordinary'.

He admired Barker's meticulous methods, perhaps because they were so different from his own: 'From the moment he stepped through the stage door at the Old Vic, he inspired and dominated everyone like a master-craftsman, and everyone in the theatre recognised this,' he recalled. 'He began to work with the actors, not using any notes, but sitting on the stage with his back to the footlights, a copy of the play in his hand . . . quiet-voiced, seldom moving, coldly humorous, shrewdly observant, infinitely patient and persevering . . . He neither coaxed nor flattered, but at the same time, though he was intensely autocratic and severe, he was never personal or rude. The actors had immediate respect for his authority. They did not become paralysed or apathetic, as can so often happen when a strong director is not excessively sensitive.'

He was not alone in worshipping Barker. John McCallum, playing a servant, recalls that 'the rest of the cast ate out of his hand'. Guthrie dropped into rehearsals, and found Casson 'playing the raw apprentice, hanging on Barker's every word'. Stephen Haggard wrote to his father of 'nine ecstatic days' of rehearsals: 'Oh my! how exhilarating he is to work for. He has taken the whole dead thing and made it sit up and look at you . . . He's an object of reverent admiration for the whole cast (and that's a feat in itself).' But he could also instil fear. Alan MacNaughtan, just out of RADA and playing the King of France, recalls: 'He was an absolute martinet, and for Gielgud and the others their god. They were just like children, they were all petrified of him.' He himself rebelled when Barker made him go over one line endlessly. 'Something snapped, and I said, "But I did exactly as you said." Lewis Casson muttered anxiously, "Don't answer back! Don't answer back!" He and everyone watched Barker to see what terrible thunderbolt was going to fall. Barker looked at me in amazement, then grinned, and said, "All right, do it just once more."'

Gielgud was absorbing everything he could from 'the finest audience and the severest critic I ever had to please'. His confidence in him was absolute: 'When Barker told me anything was good, I never wanted to change it again,' he admitted. 'He was the master, the Toscanini, the absolute genius.' Barker tried to get him to be less declamatory, to find the witty and sly side of Lear. 'Get your scaffolding right, and leave your big moments to chance,' he told him. Praise from him was rare, and often implied rather than stated. Once he said to Gielgud: 'You did some fine things today in that scene: I hope you know what they were!' – then produced a page of 'shattering, critical notes'. But Gielgud relished being pushed to the limits: 'To me he was like a masseur who forces you to discover and use muscles you never knew you possessed.'

To the actors' dismay Barker left before the dress rehearsal: news of his presence had got out – perhaps through the friends Gielgud had invited to rehearsals – and there was growing anxiety in Paris about the German advance. But before the opening he wrote Gielgud an encouraging note: 'Lear is in your grasp. Forget all the things I have bothered you about. Let your own now well-disciplined instincts carry you along, and up, simply allowing the checks and changes to prevent your being carried *away*. And I prophesy – happily – great things for you.'

Two days before the opening a journalist wrote: 'A slim, slightly untidy young man in a pullover mingles with Londoners daily, usually unrecognised. He is our leading actor, John Gielgud, 36 tomorrow, and the busiest young man in London.' The label was an apt one. The previous week, while rehearsing Lear, he had been compelled to play Macheath for four performances of *The Beggar's Opera* when both Redgrave and his understudy fell ill. It was the first time he had sung onstage since *The Good Companions* nearly a decade before, and with seven solos, three duets, two trios and two ensembles to learn at a day's notice, it was a much greater challenge. But he acquitted himself well, and received a great ovation: 'He carried it all off with an air, and every word that was sung could be heard,' the *Daily Telegraph* noted. His curtain speech was humorously self-effacing: 'I remember Mr C.B. Cochran once had the temerity to put on the stage a singing duck. I'm afraid you must have felt this performance was rather like that.'

A letter he wrote to his father just before the opening of *King Lear* underlines the pressures he faced during these threatening days. It also reveals his understanding of the value of playing Lear at such a momentous time, not just for the public benefit but for his own self-respect:

I am in the usual chaotic despair before a first night. Barker has tried us hard – and still demands further ideals – but his work is fine – I have learnt much this week – and everyone has struggled bravely and uncomplainingly, though I am very disgusted with the Vic people who have foundered badly with all the stage organisation – wringing their hands and making excuses – the war, etc – instead of putting their backs into it and getting things in order to give us the light and confidence we need. But such is the birth agony of the theatre – was in the beginning, is now, and ever shall be, I suppose. Nothing but such a master as Barker and a mighty work like *Lear* could have kept one so concentrated these ten days with such a holocaust going on around us. One must be grateful for such work at a time like this – I'm glad I didn't do *Rebecca* – I think a West End commercial success of that kind wouldn't have been much pleasure to one's self-respect at such a moment – though these birthpangs are painful and disagreeable, and to some extent unnecessary, which is a pity.

King Lear opened as the phoney war ended. Hitler had invaded Norway only days before, and in the Old Vic auditorium the atmosphere was tense and expectant. Celebrities were greeted with rounds of applause by what one critic called 'a hysterical house'. Another wrote: 'People crowded every seat, stood all down the aisles, hardly dared breathe, certainly dared not cough.' Gielgud's parents were present for what *The Times* called 'the first genuine theatrical occasion of the war'.

The production got a mixed reception, some finding it slow and uncertain. Barker didn't see Gielgud's performance, but admitted to him shortly afterwards: 'Lear really is difficult, next door to impossible.' Yet despite all the pressures Gielgud attained new heights in the part. What had previously been a mere essay was, according to Alan Dent, a major performance, capturing both the terror and the pity of the play. But Agate, who seemed to have heard of Barker's comment, thought there was too much ash and not enough oak in it. In his diary he wrote: 'John, with his tenor voice, is a *light* tragedian. Hamlet and Richard II, yes. Lear and Richard III, no.' Yet he found his performance one of 'great beauty, imagination, sensitiveness, under-standing, executive virtuosity, and control'. Others praised the way he conveyed Lear's progress from worldly to spiritual authority, and the rare pathos and stillness of his final scenes with Jessica Tandy's Cordelia. Only in the storm scene was he again thought to have fallen short.

There was praise too from colleagues. Guthrie told Gielgud's mother: 'I think his performance is *very* fine – a really memorable achievement and a contribution to the sort of theatre that is worth fighting and tussling to preserve.' Edith Evans wrote admiringly: 'There is so much you do that is *new* in your work that I wanted to rejoice with you at your growth . . . You had eliminated to an amazing extent all your Johnisms.' Even Gielgud himself thought he had improved, telling a friend that 'within my own scope of personality I do feel, with Barker's wonderful guidance, that now I have some of the range and gradual ebb and flow of the character'. Given his penchant for rigorous self-criticism, this was high praise indeed.

Despite the war the run had its frivolous moments. As in all Gielgud's companies, his voice came in for a lot of imitation. One night onstage Laurence Payne was unable to suppress a giggle after one particular burst of the Gielgud tremolo. Afterwards, Alan MacNaughtan recalls, 'Gielgud asked him why he had laughed, then insisted he do the tremolo himself. "Oh my God, did I really do it like that?" he said. "Well, you mustn't laugh." At the next performance he went outrageously over the top, but Laurence didn't utter a sound. When he came off Gielgud said, "Good boy." The next night he did it again, but began to giggle himself.'

Servicemen helped to pack out the Old Vic during the run. 'Army officers, even more numerous than their men, were craning necks over side seats in the gallery,' Ashley Dukes wrote. 'People were not going to see *The Country Wife* or *Abraham Lincoln*; they were coming to see *Lear*.' Many experienced a kind of catharsis in the king's anguished journey: they told Gielgud they had been uplifted 'like after hearing Beethoven', that his performance had given them the courage to face the imminent threat of bombing and invasion. At first Gielgud found it hard to grasp how such a cruel, violent and bleak play could appeal at such a time. But after three weeks he observed: 'It is wonderful that people are so ready to come, and seem to be so still and moved – even with all the troubles in the world. I think the superb poetry is a sort of comfort and release.'

Despite his exhaustion, the morning after the opening he read the lesson at a memorial service for Mrs Patrick Campbell, who had died in France the previous week. Her last months had been lonely and sad, and from her death-bed she had telegraphed Gielgud, one of the few to remain loyal and keep in contact. Only a few of her theatrical friends – Violet Vanbrugh, Esmé Percy, Ernest Thesiger – came to the church in Chelsea. In an affectionate and eloquent tribute, Gielgud expressed his hope that the public would remember 'not only the deep-voiced prima donna uttering brilliant witticisms and driving authors and managers to despair', but also 'the generous, warm-hearted, creative artist, shrewdly critical, passionately fond of beauty and eager to find it wherever it might be'.

After *King Lear* the plan was to stage a classical comedy, such as Pinero's *Dandy Dick* or Boucicault's *London Assurance*. Once again Gielgud was seeking variety in a lighter part. But in the changing circumstances it was decided to stage *The Tempest*, with Gielgud playing his second Prospero. This time Barker declined to produce, saying it was not a play on which he had anything to offer. Guthrie gave the job jointly to Marius Goring, who was also playing Ariel, and George Devine. Also in the company were Alec Guinness as Ferdinand, Jessica Tandy as Miranda, and Jack Hawkins as Caliban, while the costumes and scenery were by Gielgud's childhood friend Oliver Messel.

After the exhilaration of working with Barker, he found Devine 'not very helpful'. The master–pupil relationship was clearly the wrong way round; Devine was 'too much under my control' and 'a bit embarrassed' to be producing him. He was also slow in comparison with his own quicksilver temperament. Lack of experience may have been another factor, for this was only Devine's second production, and Gielgud always needed firm direction. But Devine, a complicated mixture of assurance and self-doubt, was in awe of the man who had effectively started him in the theatre.

As a result, Prospero was Gielgud's interpretation much more than Devine's. Often considered a dull character – Agate called him 'a crushing bore' – Prospero was his favourite part: his 'strong mystic imagination' appealed to his own imagination. He decided to play him as a man of forty: 'There is no reason why he should be an ancient with long whiskers,' he said. A few critics thought him too young for the part, or not harsh and commanding enough. But Ivor Brown welcomed 'a clear arresting picture of a virile Renaissance notable', a Prospero that was 'very far from the usual mixture of Father Christmas, a colonial bishop, and the president of the Magicians' Union'. T.C Worsley, who had seen his 1930 version, wrote to him: 'I think you need have no fear that you have not grown into it in the meantime . . . now there's a dignity – a result of understanding and experience which is greater.'

The season was marked by moments of panic and potential tragedy. While playing in *King Lear* Stephen Haggard disappeared for a week; unknown to the company he had been accidentally trapped on board a destroyer, which took him to Norway and back. Just before a matinée of *The Tempest* Lewis Casson, playing Gonzalo, heard that his son John was 'missing, believed killed' in a raid over Norway (in fact he survived). Gielgud remembered: 'Every line in the Alonso scenes seemed to refer directly to the agonising situation. We dared not meet each other's eyes or his.' But he himself provided some light relief. Jessica Tandy, whose notices had been lukewarm, had decided to take her child to America, and been replaced by Peggy Ashcroft. Gielgud said in a curtain speech: 'Ladies and gentlemen, I know you will rejoice with all of us in relief at the news just received – Jessica Tandy is safely in America!'

During the run of *King Lear* he had been invited to mount a Shakespeare season at the Lyceum, now closed but still equipped for performances. Money from the Treasury and a charitable trust was available, so Gielgud wrote to Barker for advice. Barker outlined a provisional repertoire, and the parts he felt Gielgud should play. He suggested 'an Arab Othello' (with Emlyn Williams as his Iago), and told him 'you'd make a first-rate Malvolio'. But the scheme was a victim of the deteriorating international situation. So too were the plans of Devine and Goring to make the Old Vic a national theatre, using the Gielgud company as its permanent ensemble, under the direction of Guthrie. With government recognition looking likely, they planned to celebrate by taking *King Lear* and *The Tempest* to Paris. But as the lights began to go out all over Europe, Guthrie decided to close the Old Vic.

The evacuation of the retreating British army from Dunkirk was reaching a peak as *The Tempest* opened on 29 May. During the run children in their thousands were being sent into the country, and the first bomb fell on the fringes of London. Farjeon thanked the Old Vic 'for a draught of loveliness in these violent, mortal and suspicious times'. Gielgud gave a defiant curtain speech, saying the actors were 'speaking lines that have endured through several wars, and will endure after this one has been won'. Prospero's farewell seemed especially poignant, and never more so than at the final performance on 22 June, the day France surrendered. Gielgud's final lines – 'As you from crimes would pardoned be, / Let your indulgence set me free' – were the last to be spoken in the Old Vic in wartime. Soon afterwards the theatre received a direct hit. For Gielgud and countless others, it was a heartbreaking moment.

20

ENSA and *Macbeth*

Alan Dent says my knees are not suited to the
exhibition of high tragedy.
> (Gielgud on tour with *Macbeth*, 1942)

DURING the first part of the war Gielgud was involved in many
offstage activities. With Ivor Brown, Bernard Miles and others
he founded the Market Theatre Rural Entertainment Society,
to provide entertainment in rural areas for evacuees of all ages. He made
an appeal on behalf of the Institute of Psychiatry and, on the anniversary
of Hitler's invasion of Poland, another in aid of the thousands of Polish
refugees who had fled to England. In it he referred to his great-
grandfather who 'struggled for Poland's freedom and came to England
in exile in very similar circumstances to those of the present time'.

With Holland and France over-run and Britain preparing for
invasion, questions about life and death were becoming insistent, if
sometimes a trifle melodramatic. Alan ('Jock') Dent asked Agate
whether he would sacrifice his life and see his work obliterated in order
to put an end to war for ever: 'It appears that Hugh Walpole, John
Gielgud and all Jock's friends would jump at the chance of such an
honour,' Agate wrote in his diary.

Gielgud's hatred of war was certainly intense. It led him to take a
rare political step which, had it been known about, would have got him
into trouble. In March, with Shaw and Sybil Thorndike, he signed a
secret letter to the Prime Minister, Neville Chamberlain, urging him to
'give sympathetic consideration' to any proposals for peace sponsored
by the neutral countries. This aligned him with the Communist Party,
which after the Nazi–Soviet pact of August 1939 was opposed to war
with Germany. But Gielgud had no interest in politics, and was

probably persuaded to sign up by Sybil Thorndike, an ardent socialist. The letter's existence only became publicly known more than fifty years later.

With the Old Vic closed and Europe occupied, Gielgud set about fulfilling his earlier pledge. The Entertainments National Service Association (ENSA) had been established before the war by Basil Dean and a group of actors. It was already sending out singers, comedians and variety artists to entertain the troops and factory workers, on the basis that 'Entertainment is an Essential War Industry'. Artists had to devote six weeks every year to this kind of work, but since the stars could do only so much, the standard was variable: servicemen dubbed ENSA 'Every Night Something Awful', and jokes on the lines of 'Abandon hope all ye who ENSA here' became common currency.

Gielgud chaired the ENSA Advisory Drama Council and, according to Basil Dean, 'led the way for other stars of the serious drama'. Dean, though he had mellowed, was still wildly unpopular, and was not rated highly as head of ENSA. Though troop audiences showed an unexpected interest in serious drama during the war, some of his proposals for them were quite peculiar. Once, to Gielgud's dismay, he suggested he tour *Diplomacy*, a creaking nineteenth-century melodrama based on a play by Sardou, with four elaborate sets and period costumes. Gielgud thought the idea impractical and ridiculous.

In July, heading a small Tennent's company that included George Howe, Joyce Carey, the singer and mimic Ivy St Helier and the much-loved Beatrice Lillie, he set out with a more appropriate programme, comprising three short plays. He had tried in vain to get Rattigan, now in the RAF, to write one. Two of the three he finally chose were *Fumed Oak* and *Hands Across the Sea*, from Coward's *Tonight at 8.30*. The third was *Swan Song*, a one-act trifle by Chekhov, featuring an elderly actor brooding on his past successes. Gielgud re-titled it *Hard Luck Story* and adapted it to include key speeches from *Hamlet, King Lear, Romeo and Juliet* and *Richard II*. The last was John of Gaunt's 'This England' speech, which acquired extra meaning for his audiences at a moment when the Battle of Britain was taking place in the skies above 'this sceptred isle'.

The troupe toured Wales, the Midlands and East Anglia for six weeks in July and August, playing on makeshift stages in schools, camps, hospitals and aerodromes. Many who came had never before experienced live theatre. Audiences were very mixed: one in a convent school in Ross-on-Wye consisted of priests, boys aged between seven and fourteen, and an evacuated girls' school from Kent. For the troops Gielgud persuaded Beatrice Lillie to make her material more risqué, and the men loved it. The show was so successful he added Shaw's *The Dark Lady of the Sonnets* – with Martita Hunt playing Queen Elizabeth – and the Darnley murder scene from Gordon Daviot's *Queen of Scots*, and called it *Plays and Music.* He spent a further three weeks giving what one reviewer described as a 'glorified pierrot show' in Manchester, Edinburgh and Glasgow.

He also repeated his Shakespeare lecture in several places, raising substantial sums of money for the war effort. He made changes to suit the prevailing mood: out went the more pacifist passages, in came the speech before Agincourt from *Henry V*, with which he now rousingly ended the lecture. Some months later he recalled: 'I was quite amazed by the reception given to the Shakespearean speeches by the forces. All through "To be or not to be" the house was perfectly quiet, and the men were very enthusiastic about "Once more unto the breach".'

As bombs started to fall on London theatre performances began earlier, so audiences could get home before the blackout. If an air-raid siren sounded during the show, people normally stayed put, and the actors carried on. Occasionally they would break off during a raid, and entertain the audience with music-hall and wartime songs. Gielgud's ENSA company, despite the blackout, the travel restrictions and the sporadic raids, got off relatively lightly. 'All this time we never heard a gun – though we missed raids three or four times,' he wrote to a friend. But in Manchester his troupe worked overtime: 'When the sirens went just after we had finished a Saturday night, we had to stay in the theatre and try to keep the audience amused by playing the piano and singing for an hour or more.' In September the last dates of the tour, Streatham and Golders Green, had to be cancelled. The London Blitz had begun, and within days almost all the West End theatres had closed down.

Gielgud vividly captured the atmosphere in a letter to Rosamond Gilder:

> People walk to and from their work in London in long processions through the parks and back streets in this lovely autumn weather, and the shops board up and open again with amazing cheerfulness . . . The tubes are rather dreadful to see, with families queuing up to sleep there at five in the afternoon with bedding, food etc, children and old women all along the passages and platforms, but they seem fantastically gay and even

hilarious sometimes, in that real Cockney way which is so endearing . . . Mayfair looks very dramatic – we walked round the other night before the raid began, about 6.30, and it needed a painter to do it justice – the big houses with windows blown out and torn white curtains still streaming out, and trees and railings down here and there – then whole streets quite untouched, and suddenly round a corner another big lump of devastation – with rooms gaping open to the sky, yet mirrors and pictures often still hanging on the side walls quite untouched . . . Of course everything closed down a fortnight ago, and the cinemas even are closing at seven o'clock at night – one just goes home about then, dines, and settles in for the night.

His parents were now back in London, living in a flat in Kensington, weathering the Blitz like millions of others. 'People are very quiet and very brave,' his mother wrote to a friend in America. 'My husband, who, as you know, is eighty years old, goes five days a week to the City by devious ways, returns and sleeps on a couple of chairs in the basement shelter, while I write letters and knit.'

At the BBC Val Gielgud too was in a 'reserved' occupation. When war broke out he was evacuated with his radio drama department, first to Evesham in Worcestershire, and then to Manchester. But he still came frequently to London, where he had a flat in Covent Garden. He joined the Home Guard, wrote a topical play called *Bombshell*, and continued to attend first nights in his crimson-lined opera cape. His reputation as a rake – he had a penchant for slim, attractive blonde women, many drawn from the BBC repertory company – was highlighted when he was caught in bed with the wife of a Polish count, and allegedly chased across the rooftops by the husband brandishing a sword. 'He had quite a turnover of girlfriends,' the actress Olga Edwardes remembers. 'He had the Terry charm, and he was a wonderful dancer. With his beard and theatrical hat and cloak, you would have thought he rather than John was the actor.' The writer Julian Maclaren-Ross thought 'he gave the impression of a character in an Edgar Wallace who might turn out to be someone else disguised'.

The war disrupted Gielgud's living arrangements. In 1938 he had moved to 27 St Stephen's Close, a third-floor flat in a block similar to the one he had previously lived in near Regent's Park, and only a stone's throw from it. Now the flat was commandeered by the War Office to house refugees from Gibraltar, so he moved in temporarily with Perry and Beaumont, in their basement flat at 142 Piccadilly, opposite Green Park. One night, while they were preparing a 'wholesome blackout dinner', a direct hit on the house next door shattered their skylight, and glass, girders, plaster and floorboards crashed on to the kitchen table. Despite this lucky escape, Gielgud stayed in the firing line: with Beaumont and Perry he moved into a flat in 55 Park Lane, a red-brick, ten-storey block opposite Hyde Park, where he remained until the end of the war.

Several London theatres were seriously damaged or destroyed by the wartime bombing. The Queen's was an early casualty. 'That debris is one of the saddest sights in all London,' Gielgud mused to a friend as they surveyed the wrecked shell of the theatre shortly after it was hit. The Little, where he had played in *The Vortex* and *The Seagull,* was destroyed, as was the Shaftesbury. The Saville, the Palladium and Drury Lane, where ENSA was based, were all hit, but survived; the Royalty, Kingsway and the Gate were irreparably damaged; and the RADA theatre in Malet Street was reduced to rubble by a land-mine and a direct hit.

The heart of the Tennent empire also came under fire, as Gielgud reported to Rosamond Gilder: 'There were incendiary bombs on the Globe one night, and Binkie and I went dashing up Piccadilly with the barrage going on all round us, feeling very heroic and terrified, to find the fire out and the stage deep in water – a lot of glass lying about and scenery soaked and damaged, but no one hurt and no real damage.' The Motleys' studio was another casualty: the morning after, all Gielgud could find among the wreckage was his cloak from *Richard II.*

Just before the war Agate had labelled him 'quite the worst film actor I ever saw'. Despite his antipathy to filming, the crisis atmosphere persuaded him to break his resolve. During the Blitz he spent seven weeks at Teddington studios playing Disraeli in *The Prime Minister,* directed by Thorold Dickinson, with Diana Wynyard as his wife. Bombing raids were occurring daily, and as filming ended the studio was hit and the manager killed. The film was essentially propaganda, and full of obvious references to 1940: 'Peace can be purchased at too great a price', 'There's more to politics than party', and, from Gielgud, 'England is at the mercy of the most ruthless band of villains the world has ever seen.'

In his delivery of the older Disraeli's speeches in the House of Commons Gielgud's tone is almost Churchillian, although overall his performance is more reminiscent of his Shylock. There is much pursing of lips, grimacing, and other mannerisms in what now seems an embarrassing performance. Yet it was well received at the time: C.A. Lejeune called him 'a spell-binder, in whom a creative personality is combined with a high technical proficiency', while Dilys Powell thought his Disraeli 'a character wisely grasped and beautifully held'.

By Christmas, as the blitz ended, some theatres had re-opened, though initially only for matinées. Gielgud had been overwhelmed with ideas for his next production – by the public, by his friends, by Tennent's. As so often he vacillated, considering and rejecting a dozen parts, including Tamburlaine, the Jew of Malta, Mirabell in *The Way of the World*, and Oedipus. Finally he decided on Dearth, the jaded artist gone to seed in Barrie's *Dear Brutus*. Gerald du Maurier had given a fine, affecting performance in the original production at Wyndham's, during which his daughter Daphne, aged ten, had to be led from her seat in tears. Gielgud, only thirteen, had been entranced by it, and afterwards saw the play several times. He remembered du Maurier's playing as 'a masterpiece of understatement, acted with a mixture of infinite charm and regretful pathos'. Fearing comparisons, he had steered clear of the part until now.

Barrie's whimsical fantasy concerned a group of characters who, given a chance to re-live their lives, make the same mistakes as before. It had been a success during the First World War, taking the public's mind off the slaughter in France. This may have prompted Beaumont to persuade Gielgud, against his better judgement, to set aside his commitment to the classics and stage a piece of bitter-sweet escapism. With only eight theatres open at the start of 1941, his return to the West End was seen as reassuring: it seemed to one critic 'as though the London theatre was approaching something like stability again with Mr Gielgud back in the fold'. Another 'cabinet of all the talents' was assembled, to include Roger Livesey, George Howe, Leon Quartermaine, Zena Dare, Margaret Rawlings, Nora Swinburne, Ursula Jeans and Muriel Pavlow.

The play opened at the Globe in January 1941. 'I kept remembering how marvellous du Maurier had been,' Gielgud said later. 'I could not touch him in the part.' This was also the view of Desmond MacCarthy, who felt that 'Gielgud's charm lacks the *crispness* of Gerald du Maurier's personality, so necessary to counteract the sentimentality'. But Graham Greene observed in the *Spectator*: 'To the notorious and unremunerative part of Dearth Mr Gielgud devoted his immense talent – nobody could make it more palatable.' Afterwards Gielgud felt he should have had someone other than himself as producer.

To enable the audience to get home before the night-time raids *Dear Brutus* played six 'morning matinées' a week, and an extra performance on Saturday afternoon. Some thought the play the perfect antidote to the war, others, such as the *Manchester Guardian* critic, suggested 'we need our tears for more real matters'. Agate railed against the waste of an all-star cast: 'Why assemble so many steamhammers to crack this fragile little nut?' he wrote. 'With such a force behind him Mr Gielgud could have flown at anything; I suspect his difficulty to have been a doubt of the wartime audience and its taste in dramatic flying. My advice to him is scrap this play and put on *Hedda Gabler*.' Edith Evans too thought he had made an error: 'It's the commercial element that brings out all his "safety-first" qualities that I don't like,' she complained to a friend. 'He could have been so much more adventurous.'

Yet the production ran for four months, and its success encouraged other London theatres to re-open. Gielgud then took the company on a fourteen-week tour. Wartime conditions made touring a hazardous and often tedious business for the many companies criss-crossing the country. Crewe, where everyone changed trains, became a great centre for meeting up with fellow-actors. It was there that Gielgud once opened a carriage door in a blacked-out train to find Wolfit sitting inside. 'Oh my God, it's the enemy!' he cried, and rushed away.

In Manchester, which had just suffered an air raid, he raised a laugh in his curtain speech by saying: 'I'm sorry to see your beautiful city laid waste.' It was, a reporter observed, the first time anyone had called Manchester beautiful since the eighteenth century. In Cheltenham he stressed the importance of touring, speaking of 'the refreshment to be derived from playing in a new town every week, the stimulus of a completely new audience'. Privately, however, he was often less enthusiastic. 'This is a vile hole,' he wrote from Llandudno. In Cheltenham he confessed: '*Brutus* hangs a bit heavily around my neck – but the end is in sight.' For three more weeks the company toured army camps in and around Aldershot and the Salisbury Plain.

There was one moment of tragedy. In Llandudno Nora Swinburne received news that her actor husband Esmond Knight had lost an eye in the action that sank the *Bismarck*. 'John was terribly upset for me, and very kind; he took Zena Dare and I away for a quiet weekend,' she recalled. Easily moved by people's distress, Gielgud was already becoming known for his many acts of kindness, large and small. Muriel Pavlow remembers one during *Dear Brutus*: 'We were in the wings together, just before one of his entrances, and he said, "What are you doing, sitting there looking as solemn as Hamlet?" And I said, it just burst out, "I really don't want to go on playing children until I'm forty!" He smiled, then made his entrance. Ten days later, at exactly the same moment in the play, he said, "There's a part you should do in the new John van Druten play, I've told Binkie to cast you," – and then went straight onstage. That part in *Old Acquaintance* started my career as a grown-up actor.'

Gielgud was becoming something of a cultural activist and spokesman for the English theatre. In October, with Russia now Britain's ally, he wrote an article for the *Anglo-Soviet Journal*, sending 'greetings and admiration to our brother and sister artists in the Theatre of the Soviet Union'. After a summary of the differences between the Russian and English theatre, he ended: 'May our theatre be united and contribute to one another in the years of freedom which we know are to come, when our great struggle is at an end, and you are rewarded for the wonderful sacrifices of your great nation, which has given such a wealth of creative art to our civilisation.' In print, if not in person, he could be positively statesmanlike.

He was often in demand for concerts and other fund-raising activities around the country. He took part in a gala matinée at the Palace in aid of the Red Cross, in which he and Edith Evans played the Millamant–Mirabell scene from *The Way of the World*; and in a concert in aid of the London Fire Service Orphans' Fund. In Manchester he was the Orator in Bliss's symphony 'Morning Heroes' and Elgar's 'Carillon', performing with 'a fine grace, dignity and subtlety' according to the *Manchester Guardian*. In Cambridge he compèred a concert featuring Hermione Gingold and Stephane Grappelli, and played a scene from *The Importance of Being Earnest* with Peggy Ashcroft. And in a concert in aid of King George's Fund for Sailors at the Albert Hall, on a bill that included Vera Lynn and George Formby, he recited poems by John Masefield.

He also became a leading advocate for the Sunday opening of theatres, for which the profession was agitating in order to obtain parity with the cinema. When the government proposed to allow it for the first time since 1781, Gielgud described it as 'the greatest step forward in the history of the theatre since Cromwell'. When the proposal was defeated in the House of Commons he was bitterly disappointed. He thought it 'an inexplicable mystery' that his company could give a Sunday performance of *Dear Brutus* for BBC Radio, but was not allowed to open the theatre in which it was being performed.

Ignoring Agate's advice to give the public a dose of Ibsen, Gielgud wrote to a friend: 'I have this nice gay farce to produce in October, which should brighten London for the winter.' The farce was *Ducks and Drakes* by M.J. Farrell. Soon after he wrote: 'The comedy is admirably cast, and I have hopes of its success, if we do not get blitzed again at the end of the month.' But this was one of his more spectacular misjudgements. Despite the presence of veterans such as Lilian Braithwaite and Ronald Squire, this leaden comedy set on a duck farm was booed by the gallery after its first night at the Apollo, and withdrawn after a short run.

He had hoped the comedy would 'cheer me up before I descend into the pit of hell'. This description of his planned *Macbeth* proved not far wide of the mark. After Lear and Hamlet, Macbeth was the other great Shakespearean role he was determined to conquer. Although his 1929 performance at the Old Vic had been greatly acclaimed, it had not been up to his own high standard. His wartime Shakespearean crusade now gave him the chance to improve on it. Against Beaumont's advice he decided to produce it himself, thus making a difficult task almost impossible.

Because of conditions in London *Macbeth* began with a twenty-one-week tour. During the war audiences in the provinces were better served than before, with London managements competing to use the theatres. In 1941 the government, believing the arts should be protected, and accepting for the first time the idea of state subsidy, had established the Council for the Encouragement of Music and the Arts (CEMA), the forerunner of the Arts Council. This reflected a growing belief that the arts should not be the prerogative of a cultured elite living in London and the big cities. Among the first beneficiaries of CEMA support were Lewis Casson and Sybil Thorndike, who took productions of Shakespeare and Greek tragedy to the mining villages of south Wales. The Old Vic, temporarily based in Lancashire, toured extensively in the north and midlands, while the Pilgrim Players took drama to village halls. Donald Wolfit – who had provided 'lunchtime Shakespeare' at the Strand – also toured with his own company. Even Coward toured three of his plays for six months, from Inverness to Bournemouth.

In preparing for *Macbeth* Gielgud had already consulted Barker, who replied from New York: 'I fear I can't be very helpful. I have a five-year-old draft for a Preface here – a solitary copy which I managed to bring away. But when I shall be able to return to it I don't know.' He never did, and Gielgud turned for advice instead to David Cecil and, in particular, John Masefield. He had long admired Masefield's ideas on Shakespeare, and was impressed by his knowledge of *Macbeth*: 'He spoke of each line with such love and tenderness and understanding that you really felt he had lived with this play all his life and it was as dear to him as a child,' he remembered. 'It was extraordinary, it was so wise.'

He drew on all kinds of sources for *Macbeth*, as he explained in *Theatre Arts Monthly*: 'When one is studying an ambitious new stage production, it becomes related to everything one sees and hears during the months of preparation, the novels one reads, films and plays, even the newspapers and the reactions to the war on the faces of people in the street.' One source of inspiration was the cinema, in particular two films then showing in London. He took ideas from Eisenstein's *Alexander Nevsky*, with its stirring music by Prokofiev, basing his make-up partly on that of the Russian actor Nikolai Cherkassov. He was also influenced by Orson Welles's *Citizen Kane*, which he thought remarkable for its lighting and composition.

He hired Michael Ayrton and John Minton to design the sets and costumes, and bombarded Ayrton with ideas, suggestions, sketches and criticisms. ('Torches! Torches! Candelabra at the banquet? Cloak with hood for Macbeth's cauldron scene?') He devised a hugely complex sound-effects score, adding and subtracting up to the last moment, until there were 140 separate cues. He commissioned William Walton to write the music, and was impressed when after attending just a single rehearsal Walton composed a piece to fit in with the rhythm of the witches' incantations.

But the war, he wrote, made it difficult to plan ahead:

The theatre has not been able to break much new ground these last two years, but it has made a valiant effort to stagger along from day to day, and amazingly it has stood up to the strain. Theatres destroyed, actors in hundreds in the forces, stagehands, electricians gone – canvas, timber, clothes rationed – even grease-paints scarce and programmes cut in half till they look like little books of labels. Large audiences, yes, but fluctuating and somewhat more incalculable than usual – all permanent residents on the move, many small towns packed, many larger ones half empty – travelling complicated, trains crowded, hotel accommodation difficult.

Casting was a major problem, even though Equity had produced a register of those unfit for military service who could be cast in emergencies. While touring *Dear Brutus* Gielgud gave Ayrton a running report, including casualties. 'It seems likely we have lost Bobby Helpmann, and we still have no Lady Macbeth,' he wrote from Nottingham. 'I shall probably have all women for the Weird Sisters – or is Ustinov still available?' A month later he was in Cheltenham: 'I think I may have Peter Glenville for Malcolm – he wears clothes extremely well – some of the others may be a bit on the young side – but we'll have to fake that somehow.' Back in London he admitted: 'Our search for men does not progress well – everyone so much in demand, if they are still free, and contemptuous of the bad parts in *Macbeth*!'

He hired Leon Quartermaine for Banquo and Milton Rosmer for Macduff, but finding a Lady Macbeth proved a nightmare. He offered the part first to Edith Evans, who felt unable to get to grips with such an evil character: 'I could *never* impersonate a woman who had such a *peculiar* notion of hospitality,' she allegedly said – though Gielgud thought her rejection was because she felt the part was incomplete. Other candidates were too young, or too inexperienced in Shakespeare. In desperation he held open auditions, but to no avail. With cancellation threatening, he finally persuaded Gwen Ffrangcon-Davies to cut short a tour in South Africa to take on the role.

Unlike many actors Gielgud was not superstitious about 'The Scottish Play'; but subsequent events must have given him pause. In Manchester Beatrix Fielden-Kaye, understudying a weird sister, died after the opening night, while another sister, Annie Esmond, suffered a heart attack. She was replaced by Ernest Thesiger, who at rehearsal pranced around the cauldron in a double-breasted grey suit and immaculate suede shoes. Soon Gielgud had further trouble to report: 'Marcus Barron has been taken ill, and Rosmer and Cadell are both out of the cast, so we are playing under great difficulties, and I am sick of rehearsing and shifting the cast around.' Barron, playing Duncan, died soon afterwards; his understudy proved inadequate, and was fired; *his* replacement, Bromley Davenport, had his part written out on a scroll, but couldn't read it without glasses; the next candidate was too young; and finally Nicholas Hannen took over.

Another problem was Michael Ayrton. Despite his relative inexperience as a theatre designer, Ayrton behaved arrogantly during rehearsals, and upset many in the company. He came into conflict with Gielgud when he asked for extra money. Gielgud sent him £25, promising him 'a private bonus from me' if the production was a success, but then underlined sternly his own financial position: 'All the money I have, I have earned with the sweat of my brow, and it all goes back into the theatre except what I keep to live on and pay away in taxes – and things like the ENSA tour and the *Macbeth* rehearsals are whole months when I earn nothing at all.'

Later a disagreement over changes to the set provoked him to rebuke Ayrton: 'At the risk of you thinking me unpleasant I must say I intend to carry out the changes whether you agree to them or not,' he wrote:

If a man as experienced and as brilliant as Walton can show such modesty and collaborate with such complete unselfishness, I feel you should do the same, and I do deplore the fact that you haven't got on better with all the people you have come into contact with in this production, which has made the atmosphere sometimes lacking in constructiveness and ease. You will find if you want to go on working in the theatre (which perhaps you don't) that a capacity for extemporising in an emergency, tolerance and patience are three of the most essential qualities.

The provocation must have been extreme, for Gielgud rarely put anyone in their place, and never so firmly and directly. As leader of the company he generally inspired loyalty and affection. 'He was wonderfully modest and thoughtful, and we'd all do anything for him,' recalls Frank Thornton, who had just worked with Wolfit, and was playing Angus. In his diary/scrapbook he wrote: 'I found JG infinitely approachable and more unGod-like than Wolfit. In fact a charming, ordinary (in the best sense) sort of man.' In one scene he was centre stage while Gielgud was down left. 'Mr Gielgud reprimanded me at rehearsal for playing the scene as a rather nervous, self-conscious young actor playing to the star. "That's how Donald Wolfit has taught you to act: I don't want it," he said.'

Although Gielgud was staging *Macbeth* because he felt 'its stern theme would match our stern times', not everyone got the message. In

Glasgow and Edinburgh matinées were disrupted by schoolchildren, who screamed with laughter through the sleep-walking scene and the soliloquies, and threw paper cups down from the dress circle. 'I was determined not to interrupt the performance, so I just kept making Macready pauses and frowning at the audience,' Gielgud recalled. At a dinner in Edinburgh he good-humouredly referred to the inter-ruptions the players had to suffer in Shakespeare's day, but also deplored children's inability to concentrate. 'I beg of you, if you have children, don't let them read a book, eat an orange, and listen to Beethoven all at once,' he pleaded.

Life on the road was exhausting and frustrating, especially as he often fitted in extra concerts for the troops on Sundays. The dress rehearsal for the opening in Manchester went on until four in the morning. From Glasgow Gielgud wrote: 'This week has been hell. Not one light right – panatropes breaking down, sparse audiences, stupid giggling schoolchildren, vile weather, etc, etc . . . It's a big strain with these awful moves, and old switchboards managed by still older gentlemen with not a thing to be depended on.' In Liverpool there was a lighter moment when the local paper described George Woodbridge, who was playing the Porter, as 'an engaging Portia', prompting Gielgud to remark that 'the quality of Mersey is not strained'. That week he complained about his heavy schedule: 'I've had to play at two and six on matinée days, murder indeed, and I should like to know what Messrs Macready, Irving and Salvini (to put myself in no more distinguished company) would have said to such an effort.' But Gwen Ffrangcon-Davies had no doubts about his ability to handle the part: 'John is wonderful, he grows in stature daily,' she wrote from Glasgow. 'He is heaven to act with.'

As usual he was very open to ideas from outsiders, and at the start of the tour Guthrie, Guinness and Ivor Brown all offered what he felt were constructive criticisms. Alan Dent gave him detailed comments, suggesting he needed to be less violent in certain scenes. ('You know, dear heart, you always tend too easily to indignation.') But one of Gielgud's main concerns was his physique: 'Will my arms look beefy enough?' he anxiously asked Ayrton before the tour began. Later he lengthened his tunic for the last act, 'as Alan Dent says my knees are not suited to the exhibition of high tragedy, and I fancy he speaks some truth'. In Blackpool he decided he needed some armour for his throat because 'my neck is too thin and scraggy'.

In June the company reached Bournemouth, Agate's home town,

and Gielgud called on the critic. As described in Agate's diary their meeting, like so many in wartime, had an unreal quality. 'He showed me an interesting collection of things written about the Macbeths of Garrick, Kean, Kemble, Macready, Booth, Rossi, Irving. I was looking through this when the sirens went. They were raiding Poole across the water, and after watching it for half an hour from the balcony we resumed our talk, and didn't break up till the All Clear about 4am.'

Macbeth finally arrived in London in July, where it ran for three months at the Piccadilly, and divided the public as much as the critics. 'Some people don't care for it, others think it is the best thing he has done,' Graham Robertson noted. Despite Gielgud's efforts at disguise, several critics felt he lacked the necessary martial air. But Guinness disagreed: 'I see the press has attacked Gielgud's Macbeth for lack of soldierly qualities,' he wrote to a friend. 'They seem to have some notion that fine fighting-men look like prize-fighters, and that Macbeth must above all suggest a great eater of beef. Actually Gielgud manages to suggest great physical activity and alertness.'

In other respects his Macbeth was considered a fine, even a magnificent achievement. Dent, who had seen it in Manchester and Edinburgh, was impressed by how much he had worked on every syllable and gesture, and judged that he had 'never played with more finesse, subtlety, poetry, fire, clearness and authority . . . It is now one of his best things.' Roger Marvell, however, wrote that Gielgud, 'whose voice is a magnificent organ, treats it like a Wurlitzer, pulling out different stops on every other word'. He himself felt that, in contrast to his instinctive rush at Macbeth in his youth, he had now become over-concerned with technique. He also worried about his appearance, observing later: 'The point about Macbeth is that he doesn't look like a man who would see ghosts. But I look as if I see ghosts all the time.' His insecurity in the role was reflected in his reaction to Alan Badel, playing Lennox, who came to his dressing-room and told him where and how he needed to improve his performance. 'He's quite right you know,' Gielgud told Gwen Ffrangcon-Davies. Badel was eighteen.

During the tour he had exchanged friendly, scholarly letters with Agate about the motivation of the Macbeths and the time-lapses between the scenes. After Agate saw the show in Bournemouth he confided to his diary: 'John will never be happy vocally with Macbeth; his voice is neither deep nor resonant enough. But what sheer acting ability can do, he does.' But after the London opening he wrote to Gielgud: 'I never admired you more . . . You are the best Macbeth I have seen, except perhaps old Mollison, who hadn't much poetry but remained a soldier.' He then dedicated his new book, *These Were Players*, to 'John Gielgud, our first player'.

After *Macbeth* ended in October Gielgud did two further months as John Worthing in the revival of his production of *The Importance of Being Earnest*. He then took up the ENSA banner again, for what was to be his only wartime trip abroad. Just before Christmas, in a company assembled by Beaumont that included Edith Evans, Beatrice Lillie, Michael Wilding, Jeanne de Casalis and the singer Elisabeth Welch, he flew in a blacked-out RAF bomber to Gibraltar, where Anthony Quayle and John Perry were on the governor's staff. Here, for four weeks, the company entertained the troops stationed on the Rock.

The revue, *Christmas Party*, consisted of musical numbers, sketches, and recitations of poems and speeches, as well as extracts from *The Importance of Being Earnest, The Way of the World, The Merry Wives of Windsor* and *The Dark Lady of the Sonnets*, and a finale written by Noël Coward. The company, which gave its services free for ENSA, performed forty-eight shows on the uneven boards of the 750-seat local theatre, with soldiers as scene shifters, and the garrison orchestra providing the music. Overall they gave three shows a day, including concerts in hospital wards, army camps, and on board ships.

All this was a new departure for Gielgud, and he found it both moving and exciting. The audiences, he wrote to his mother from Gibraltar, 'are extraordinarily well-mannered, and never fail to listen politely to the next turn, however much they have been shouting and whistling at the end of the one before'. This was a heartfelt compliment, since he sometimes had to appear immediately after the ever-popular Beatrice Lillie. His patriotic contributions included Clemence Dane's poem 'Trafalgar Day', about Nelson and the bombing of St Paul's in the blitz, which he performed in an old trilby hat and raincoat; A.E. Housman's 'Bredon Hill'; and, inevitably, 'Once more unto the breach' from *Henry V*.

He also sang with Michael Wilding and Beatrice Lillie, and recited a comic poem 'Mussolini and the Eagle'. Wilding, who shared a dressing-room with him, thought him 'as near a saint as anyone I have ever met', citing in evidence his humility about his performance of the Mussolini poem. At first, dressed in a dinner-jacket, Gielgud spoke it deadpan, to great laughter. Carried away by his reception, the next night he donned a funny uniform and adopted a silly walk – and no laughs came. When Wilding told him he was being too obvious,

Gielgud stopped straining for laughs, and next time received a standing ovation. Wilding recalled: 'He rushed back to the dressing-room and embraced me with tears in his eyes. "What a clever pusskin you are, Mike!" he cried.'

The show went down well with the troops, who had been badly starved of professional entertainment. The local critic wrote: 'Everything that goes to make true theatre was there – suppressed excitement on both sides of the curtain; true artists on the stage; an audience quick and appreciative of every change in mood.' Sometimes the mood was decidedly blue, which offended Edith Evans, who disliked this brand of humour. But Gielgud revelled in it, and resisted pressure for there to be fewer risqué jokes and more straight pieces: 'It is quite hard enough to hold them with the best and simplest kind of straight stuff for six or seven minutes, and we are much impressed to find the *Importance* scene, which is twelve minutes, does really go very well,' he reported.

Concentration was not easy for the actors, especially when they had to perform on an aircraft carrier or a battleship for an audience of more than two thousand men. Gielgud recorded one such occasion:

On the neighbouring ships we can see others focussing on us with field-glasses. Aeroplanes fly overhead, and occasionally attempt to drown us with the noise of their engines. During my Nelson recitation, the commander rushes to the telephone and abuses a neighbouring ship roundly for sending over an aeroplane at such a moment. I almost feel I have stopped the war for twenty seconds.

Gibraltar was a welcome respite from England. 'London and the war seem amazingly remote, and in that way the trip is quite a rest, in spite of the continued rushing about,' he wrote to his mother. 'It is more like a Riviera holiday, with a dash of the theatre.' He and John Perry drove to Algeciras, delighting in the picturesque villages *en route*: 'The Spanish country looks very romantic and much as I expected – richer and more full of character than Provence, with beautiful avenues of eucalyptus trees, donkeys, tidebirds, and ragged-looking soldiers stringing along with a mulecart in their midst, covered with sacks and luggage, like a war drawing by Goya.' Yet even in these surroundings Gielgud talked of little else but the theatre. One night he, Perry and Beaumont, sharing a bedroom, discussed a potential production into the early hours, until silenced by exhaustion. When he awoke, Gielgud continued: 'And do you think Dolly can be trusted with the wigs?'

On New Year's Eve the company was entertained at Government House. One night they were taken by the governor to the top of the Rock to see the barrage defence exercise. 'Masses of guns let off from every nook and cranny and shivers of tracer bullets, rockets etc flying out over the sea – an extraordinary sight,' Gielgud reported. 'The sea so smooth under the gunfire and searchlights and the masses of little racing sparks like fireflies scurrying out over the surface.' Even in war, his focus was on the visual effect of the scene.

The visit had a postscript. Gielgud flew back from neutral Portugal early in 1943. A few weeks later Leslie Howard, lecturing there for the British Council, died on the same journey from Lisbon, his plane being shot down in circumstances that remain unexplained. Soon after Gielgud was offered the film role Howard was to have played next. Horrified to find the script was based on the greatly mourned actor's private life, he flung it across the room, and rejected it roundly.

21

The Haymarket Season

Thank God for paint when golden youth is on
the wane at last!

(Gielgud to his mother, 1944)

ALTHOUGH he had little time for Shaw's plays, there were two
roles that Gielgud had always wanted to play: Captain Shotover
in *Heartbreak House,* and the doomed painter Louis Dubedat
in *The Doctor's Dilemma.* Four days after returning to England he
unexpectedly found himself playing the latter at the Haymarket, when
both Peter Glenville and his understudy fell ill.

He had to learn the part over the weekend – a challenge he relished
– then play it for a week. His performance was less astringent than
the part required, too heavily influenced by Claude Rains's romantic
interpretation he had seen while at RADA. But his appearance did
the trick for Tennent's, as the critic Barbara Brighouse wrote: 'I so
much enjoyed watching the faces of the people confronted with the
presager of doom – a slip in the programme – and seeing them slowly
realising their luck. It was a grand week and did much good to the
whole cast.'

Gielgud was delighted to be in the dressing-room at the top of the
famous theatre once used by du Maurier and Tree, in the company of
'Mac', the dresser he had recently inherited from Martin-Harvey. With
its historical associations and beautiful architecture, the Haymarket
soon became his favourite theatre. The part also enabled him to act for
the first time with Vivien Leigh, now married to Olivier. Their
friendship blossomed from this time, despite being put to the test soon
afterwards. During discussions about an ENSA concert party in which
she was due to appear, Vivien Leigh suggested she might try the potion

scene from *Romeo and Juliet*. Gielgud burst out: 'Oh no, Vivien! Only a great actress can do that sort of thing!'

For a moment it seemed they might appear together in another Shaw venture, a planned film of *Caesar and Cleopatra*. Shaw, who had written the play for Forbes-Robertson and Mrs Patrick Campbell, agreed that the Hungarian Gabriel Pascal could direct it if he could get Gielgud to play Caesar. Arriving in New York Pascal announced: 'John Gielgud is Caesar! Vivien Leigh is Cleopatra. Wonderful, no?' His boast was premature. Shaw got wind that Gielgud had turned down the part – he had taken an intense dislike to Pascal – and tried to persuade him to change his mind: 'I know of no one who could follow Forbes-Robertson in the part with any chance of getting away with it except yourself,' he wrote, adding: 'You will have to play Caesar one day, just as you have had to play Hamlet and Macbeth. You owe it to your repertory.' Gielgud was flattered, but immovable: 'I do not like filming, and should be terrified of risking giving an indifferent performance,' he told Shaw.

The war drew him into some unusually political assignments. He acted as narrator for *Unfinished Journey*, a filmed tribute about the death of the former Polish Prime Minister, General Sikorski. He also took part in a mass celebration in the Albert Hall, commemorating the twenty-fifth anniversary of the founding of the Red Army. Staged by Basil Dean and filmed for showing in Russian cinemas, it included a speech from *Alexander Nevsky* spoken by Lieutenant Laurence Olivier, contributions from Sybil Thorndike and Lieutenant-Commander Ralph Richardson, an appearance by Marius Goring as a Nazi SS officer, and Gielgud as the voice of Moscow Radio, 'summoning the eyes and ears of the world to the heroic defence of Stalingrad'.

Gielgud was now the number one star in the Tennent firmament, the most powerful management in the West End. His position enabled him to exert a huge influence on the plays selected by Beaumont. He would often accompany him on his round of unannounced visits to West End theatres. Although Beaumont had no particular knowledge of the classics, he had an instinct for what an audience liked, and Gielgud often took his advice about his own productions. 'At a dress rehearsal he knew exactly what to say,' he recalled. 'He immediately put his finger on what was wrong, advising us on cuts and all sorts of other details that were admirably constructive and not in the least discouraging.'

Despite Gielgud's commitment to the classics, there were times when he yearned for something different. On the eve of his departure to Gibraltar he had written to Herbert Farjeon: 'Did someone whisper there was a play on your shelves about an actor which might do for me? If not, I wish you could invent one – I'd so love to play something new and modern for once.' But while he was looking for a comedy, he was unsympathetic to one wartime hit: 'Oh God! the dreariness of *Arsenic and Old Lace*,' he wrote to a friend. 'Why does anyone think it funny, or is my sense of humour completely lacking?'

His choice finally fell on Congreve's *Love for Love*. The play had not been done in the West End for seventy years, although Guthrie had produced it at the Old Vic in 1934. With the war dragging on into a fourth year, and the memory still clear of his success as Valentine under Fagan at the Oxford Playhouse, he felt a revival of this bawdy, spirited play would be an attractive idea.

As designer he engaged the talented young artist, illustrator and designer Rex Whistler, who provided some strikingly naturalistic sets. Because Whistler was training in the Guards he had no time to do the costumes, so Gielgud hired Jeanetta Cochrane, an authority on the period. With so many men in the services, he had to use actors who were older than their characters: Leon Quartermaine, now seventy, was cast as a young rake, and other seasoned professionals included Leslie Banks, Yvonne Arnaud, Miles Malleson and Angela Baddeley.

Gielgud's eminence and prestige were such that he was able to persuade stars to play smaller roles in his ensemble. His casting was often imaginative, inspiring an actor to move in a new direction. This happened with Yvonne Arnaud, whom he had seen in Fagan's *And So to Bed*, but who had since become stuck in lightweight comedies demanding a French accent. Later she admitted it was a relief to have a small and worthwhile part such as that of Mrs Frail, instead of having to carry the whole weight of inferior plays on her shoulders. Gielgud delighted in the presence of such a brilliant performer.

When Leon Quartermaine declined his offer to produce *Love for Love*, Gielgud decided to do it himself. His aim was to avoid the over-stylisation he felt had marred his last two period plays, his own production of *The Beggar's Opera* and Guthrie's *The School for Scandal*. He discussed the play at length with Quartermaine, who convinced him it should be played in a more naturalistic manner, with the 'fourth wall' down. Usually, when he combined producing with acting, Gielgud would use the pre-London tour to work on the other characters, and only put his own in as a sketch, using his understudy to walk through his scenes. This made life difficult for the other actors, and often left him under-prepared. This time, already word-perfect with many of Valentine's speeches, he was ready.

Love for Love arrived at the Phoenix in April after a five-week provincial tour. It was a huge success, running for more than a year and for 471 performances, the most in the play's history: Desmond MacCarthy called it 'the best performance of a Restoration play I have seen'. Several critics highlighted the ensemble work, marvelling at Gielgud's ability to knit the disparate company together so skilfully. The production was naturalistic and vigorous, in tune with the times as well as the text. A long way from Playfair's prettifying style, the play was attacked in some papers for being improper and obscene.

Gielgud's Valentine provoked unanimous delight, especially for a scene in which he had to feign insanity. In it he managed not only to impersonate his own pretended madness as Hamlet, but also his playing of Romeo, Lear and Macbeth. His witty self-parody signalled a new versatility. 'This is a performance to startle even those who already think Mr Gielgud the best of the younger school of actors, and to convert those who do not,' Alan Dent wrote. Alfred Lunt, working in England, gave him the ultimate accolade, calling it 'about as near perfection as anything can be in the theatre'. In his diary Agate noted: 'Gielgud would fill the theatre whether he played John Worthing, Macbeth, Valentine, Box, Cox or Mrs Bouncer.'

During the run Gielgud's parents celebrated their golden wedding. Together with Lewis, Val and Eleanor he organised a special lunch to mark the anniversary. It was a nostalgic occasion, with his great-aunt Julia Neilson and his aunt Mabel Terry-Lewis among several Terry guests. Frank Gielgud, replying to a toast, said he hoped the younger generation would 'attempt to restore the graces to life'. He also suggested he and his wife could compliment themselves on producing a 'quartet of not unpresentable children'. Self-deprecation, it seems, was an inherited trait.

Lewis was now working in the War Office, Eleanor was doing a stint in the Globe box-office, while Val was still in charge of radio drama at the BBC. In May 1943 he produced Eric Linklater's patriotic play *The Great Ship*, in which Gielgud played a wounded officer in the Western Desert. According to Val, he was still finding it hard to adapt from the stage to the microphone: 'It was amusing, if a trifle disconcerting, to watch John at rehearsal, discarding first tie and then jacket, sweating and gesticulating,' he recalled. It was a very emotional part, and after the recording the actors were amused to see the two brothers both emerge in floods of tears.

Radio had become an immensely popular medium during the war, and not just because of the news: readings of classic novels such as *War and Peace* drew large audiences, and those for radio drama doubled. Gielgud was a frequent broadcaster: his work included a shortened version of *The Laughing Woman*, a play about the sculptor Henri Gaudier and the writer Sophie Brzeska, which Gordon Daviot had originally written for him and Edith Evans. He also did radio versions of *The Importance of Being Earnest* and *Richard of Bordeaux*, and of *The Pilgrim's Progress*, in which he played Christian. He even took part in the variety programme *Hi Gang!* But his most notable contributions were in Shakespeare plays.

His *King Lear*, produced by Peter Creswell and broadcast on the eve of the blitz, was promoted as 'a symphony of the wracked soul of man'. The cast were mostly middle-rank actors, but for his *Hamlet* he had a star line-up, with Celia Johnson playing Ophelia, Emlyn Williams as Claudius and Martita Hunt as Gertrude. In her review Grace Wyndham Goldie praised the 'exquisite and sensitive clarity' of the acting, suggesting Gielgud's playing had even more strength than his performance onstage. This was the first full-length Shakespeare broadcast of the war, and there was a predictable uproar when, due to a mix-up in the studio, the producer broke in just before the final act with the words, 'And there we must leave them.'

During the run of *Love for Love* Gielgud produced three plays for Tennent's, partly to ward off the boredom of a long run, partly to help Beaumont. The first, *Landslide*, he directed without payment, as a favour to Kitty Black of Tennent's, who had helped translate Julien Luchaire's play. A weak, artificial piece about a group of young mountaineers stuck in a small Alpine hotel, it was scorned by the critics: 'Was it for this that Shaw and Galsworthy bled?' asked Beverley Baxter.

Kitty Black remembers that Gielgud re-wrote the script practically every morning: 'It was absolute murder.' Dulcie Gray, one of the stars, found him an inspiring producer: 'He generated such excitement, you wanted to work your head off for him,' she recalled. But his impracticality could be vexing: 'Just before the opening he said, "You should be doing something here, dear. Why don't you crochet?" I said: "But I've never crocheted in my life." He replied: "Oh, I expect there's time to learn."'

Like other actors she was astonished at his modesty, 'which made him ask advice from anyone around'. Olga Edwardes, also in *Landslide*, recalls an example: 'At a party I told him I had a record of him speaking poetry. He said, "Do tell me what you thought of it." Quite spontaneously I said I thought it was absolutely lovely, but that some of it was quite mannered. Even as the words came out I was horrified at what I was saying. But he just said, "Do you think so? Which parts in particular?"'

His quest for perfection required great patience from his actors. Many were frustrated by his methods, but were won over by his charm and sincerity, or were too intimidated by his manner or reputation to argue. The results were often unpredictable, as with his production of *The Cradle Song* by Gregorio and Maria Martínez Sierra, the classic Spanish comedy about life in a convent, which opened at the Apollo in January 1944. Agate thought it exquisitely acted and 'the most beautiful thing produced in London' in the last year. He and other critics called Gielgud's production faultless.

But in rehearsal he confused some of the younger actors. Wendy Hiller, in only her second West End role, remembers: 'He wasn't very good, he was more nervous than we were. During the dress rehearsal he was pacing up and down deep in thought, and we started to chatter a bit, and he suddenly called out, "Be quiet everyone: I'm in a frenzy!"' Yvonne Mitchell, a West End newcomer, was initially overwhelmed by his presence: 'He so fascinated me as a person that for the first few days of rehearsal I could not listen to what he told me,' she recalled. 'I was so impressed with the beauty of his eyes.' Gielgud wanted her to speak in a higher register, a change which she felt wrong for her low-pitched voice. She complied, but received poor notices, after which Gielgud told her: 'Sorry darling, just do it as you would if I hadn't produced you.'

At rehearsal he would dart about the stage and auditorium, never still for a moment, constantly correcting and advising the actors. A reporter from *Picture Post* observed him in action during his production of Eric Linklater's *Crisis in Heaven*:

You three people have got to represent the crowd of five hundred who are behind those doors. Stylise it! Give me big movements! . . . Lloyd, I don't feel your intention to go to that chair and sit down. Stop by it only because you are still talking . . . Barry, raise the scene now. Don't put it on the floor when the maid goes.

Move the chairs to make it more intimate if you like . . . Adele, not so emphasised, darling. You'll have the clothes and everything for it, so keep the throb out of your voice.

A photograph shows him dressed in a sober suit and tie, clutching the back of a chair, his angular body bent like a bow, cigarette in mouth, head raised imperiously as he watches the rehearsal intently.

Crisis in Heaven was an allegory featuring Voltaire, Helen of Troy, Pushkin, Florence Nightingale, Abraham Lincoln and Aristophanes. A dull and didactic hotch-potch, with sets and costumes by Cecil Beaton, it came off after only a month at the Lyric. Linklater had been inspired to turn from writing novels to plays by a radio performance by Gielgud, as he explained in a letter to him: 'I've discovered (I mean you have discovered for me) an old truth – that words are meant to be spoken, that paper is a cold thing, that the human voice can not only be lovely to the ear but mighty significant to the mind.'

After *Love for Love* finished Gielgud produced *The Last of Summer*, a play about bitter family relationships in an Irish country house. It was adapted for the stage by John Perry from the novel by the best-selling Irish writer Kate O'Brien. If Yvonne Mitchell had been too compliant with Gielgud, Margaret Johnston, playing the young heroine, was the opposite. Geoffrey Toone recalls his problem: 'John got very fed up with her. Eventually he found out that her husband, the agent Al Parker, was sending her to some voice coach, who had a great theory about acting, and took her off to shout in a barn. As a result, she said yes to everything John suggested, and then didn't do it.' Gielgud's frustrations eventually came to the boil, as Guinness – who was not in the play – recalls. 'Someone questioned whether yet another change was necessary, and he fired the whole cast, including Fay Compton. Then he burst into tears, and ten minutes later everyone was brought back.'

The Last of Summer opened at the Phoenix on 7 June 1944. But now the war intervened once more. Recently there had been few serious raids on London, and the D-Day landings the previous day had sent the country into a ferment of excitement, inducing a belief that the war was as good as over. But a few days later the V2 'buzzbombs' started to rain down, and theatre attendance fell dramatically. Yet of those people who came, hardly any left when the sirens sounded. For actors it was a testing time. Hearing the engines of the pilotless planes cutting out, they had to continue performing while waiting for the explosion, while some of the audience hid under their seats. Eventually all the theatres – apart from the Windmill revue theatre – closed down. *The Last of Summer* managed just nineteen performances.

After nearly five years of almost continuous work, Gielgud was exhausted. This led him to reject what might in other circumstances have been a tempting offer. The Old Vic company had spent most of the war touring in the provinces from its base in Burnley. Guthrie and the governors now wanted to re-establish it in London, and in the spring of 1944 invited Ralph Richardson and the producer John Burrell, a protégé of Saint-Denis, to form a new company. With backing from CEMA, and the aim of restoring the damaged theatre in the Waterloo Road, there seemed a basis for the long-awaited National Theatre.

Richardson accepted the challenge on condition he was given help. 'I realised that my name alone was not enough to bring people back to the Vic,' he recalled. 'What we needed was a real crowd-puller.' He then invited Olivier and Gielgud to join him. Had the plan come off, the National Theatre would almost certainly have been established sooner than it was, and the careers of both Gielgud and Olivier taken a different turning. Richardson appealed to Gielgud's patriotism, but he declined the offer, adding: 'It would be a disaster, you would have to spend all your time as referee between Larry and me.'

It was surely a wise decision. Despite Richardson's close friendship with both actors, the scheme would surely have foundered on the rocks of their difficult relationship. According to Richardson, 'Johnny still thought Larry tended to overact and found it hard to understand his popularity', while 'Larry looked on Johnny as being too much on the cool, remote side'. Ironically, Burrell said later that Olivier only agreed to join after Gielgud had refused the offer. Had Gielgud known that Olivier would have refused had he himself accepted, his decision might have been different.

He also hesitated over an enticing offer from Beaumont, who had formed a bold plan. After the success of *Love for Love* he suggested Gielgud keep the production going by building a repertoire of plays around it, using some of the same actors for a permanent company, and taking over the Haymarket for a season in conjunction with Tennent's. But Gielgud felt he had played all the classical parts within his range, and that the triple burden of acting, producing and managing was too much for him to carry.

Beaumont, however, was a very persuasive man, who knew how to play on Gielgud's lack of certainty and resolve. Before long he had signed him up for a season comprising *Hamlet, Love for Love,* Maugham's *The Circle, A Midsummer Night's Dream* and Webster's *The Duchess of Malfi.* To lessen his burden, three outsiders – William Armstrong, Neville Coghill and George Rylands – were to come in as producers. As part of the bait Peggy Ashcroft was engaged as leading lady, to play Titania, Ophelia and the Duchess. The company also included Leslie Banks, Leon Quartermaine, Yvonne Arnaud, Miles Malleson, Angela Baddeley, Max Adrian, Isabel Dean and Rosalie Crutchley.

Rehearsals were seriously affected by the buzzbombs, and many had to be held underground at the Piccadilly. One elderly actress insisted on keeping a whistle around her neck for fear of being buried alive. Peggy Ashcroft was hurt by flying glass from a V2, sustaining a knee injury that bothered her for the rest of her life. In a letter to Gielgud's parents Beaumont announced that 'to open in London under present conditions would be ridiculous'. Instead he arranged a three-month tour of *Hamlet, Love for Love* and *The Circle.*

Although not delighted at the prospect of a tour, Gielgud found reserves of energy once it began. His letters to his mother show his passion returning as he becomes involved with the productions. From Manchester, where *Hamlet* was a sell-out, he wrote proudly: 'Three and a half hours solid playing, and nobody budged.' He thanked his mother for 'the beautiful new kerchief, which went on to the stage to give me courage', and added: 'My clothes are very successful – also the new wig! Thank God for paint when golden youth is on the wane at last!' From Leeds he wrote of Peggy Ashcroft's success as Ophelia – 'her mad scene most striking and original'. At Cambridge he found a model audience: 'Very moving and exciting playing in the tiny theatre last night – pindrop silence and attention, and wonderful appreciation from everyone one meets.'

His detachment from 'ordinary' people was reflected in some of his comments on provincial life. In Manchester he remarked on the 'vast crowds of hideous people thronging the streets and bus queues'; in Leeds the town was 'packed with horrible people, but they are quite a good audience'; in Bournemouth the theatre was full of 'typical holiday vulgarians'. To compensate for these hideous sights there was dinner with the Lunts in Manchester, and lunch with the Rothschilds in their twelfth-century oak-beamed house near Cambridge.

On tour there were problems. Bristol was 'dirty, war-worn and depressing' and crowded with evacuees, the Hippodrome there 'like the Coliseum – dirty, noisy staff, and crossing the stage is like doing the quarter mile! However it goes wonderfully, despite a few drunks in the gallery who are expecting Evelyn Laye or a Negro Band!' In Edinburgh Yvonne Arnaud contracted laryngitis, and was unhappy with one of her dresses. 'No one dares to have a row with her over it, as she will undoubtedly take finally to her bed if she is crossed,' he confided. But in Bournemouth in late August he wrote excitedly: 'We passed an enormous American convoy bound for France. The news is wonderful – I think we ought to go and play *Hamlet* in Paris at the end of September instead of going north again – or perhaps it will be able to be London.'

By October the bombs had temporarily ceased, and the Haymarket season opened with *The Circle*. It was the first West End revival of Maugham's cynical comedy of manners, and its success established it as a modern classic. In 1923 the first production had been booed in the same theatre, mainly because it ended with a wife running away with her lover. Gielgud had seen it, and particularly admired Ernest Thesiger as the prim, priggish and insipid Arnold Champion-Cheney, the self-centred politician who prefers his furniture to his young wife. This relatively small part, which he was now playing, gave him a chance to display again his exquisite comic timing in an unsympathetic role. Lionel Hale exclaimed: 'What an actor this is! He can poise a line like a foil and put it home with a most delicate turn of the wrist.' Agate, meanwhile, repeated his minority opinion that 'Mr Gielgud is not by nature a comedian'.

The director of *The Circle* was the experienced William Armstrong, a refined, gentle Scot who had worked with Mrs Patrick Campbell and Benson. Tall, thin and bronchial, he had been for many years artistic director of the Liverpool Playhouse, where he had given Michael Redgrave his first break. He was a calm, diplomatic producer with an enchanting sense of humour, who handled actors with a loose rein, and 'got the greatest pleasure' from producing Gielgud.

The season continued in true repertory style, with *Love for Love* opening the night after *The Circle*, and *Hamlet* following the next night; thereafter the play was changed two or three times a week. Congreve's comedy entranced audiences all over again. It also marked the moment when two young men who were later to have a significant impact on Gielgud's work entered his orbit: the director Peter Brook and the critic Kenneth Tynan.

Brook, a nineteen-year-old Oxford student, was already an aspiring producer. One day he sneaked into the Haymarket through a side-door, keen to see how an experienced producer worked. He glimpsed Gielgud 'in the middle of the stalls, his long legs bent over the seat in front of him, a trilby hat covering his bald head, calling his instructions to the actors'. One evening he slipped past the stage door to the dressing-rooms, to ask Gielgud, then making up, if he could briefly use the set of *Love for Love* to shoot a scene of a film he was making of Sterne's *A Sentimental Journey*. He was astonished when Gielgud granted his request, giving him his first experience of 'those lightning impulses, those generous flashes' that he was soon to know at first hand.

Tynan, seventeen and still at school in Birmingham, was already an ardent London theatregoer, and like Gielgud before him recorded his views of the productions he saw. After seeing *Dear Brutus* he had generously awarded Gielgud '96 marks out of 100', but his review of his performance in *Love for Love* was more sophisticated. Seeing him 'posturing beautifully' in front of Rex Whistler's sets, he wrote that in the mock-madness scenes 'he extended the intense raptness, the silent inner lightnings which he shares with Irving, until they reached delicious absurdity'. He suggested that Gielgud refused to compromise with an audience, and demanded they come up to his intellectual level. But in criticising his 'aloofness and rigid dignity' he was already setting down a marker for his later, more withering reviews.

Gielgud now approached his fifth Hamlet. At forty he felt he was too old for the part, but Beaumont had flattered him that he could pass for thirty onstage. By chance a fragment of his performance survives on film, in Humphrey Jennings's moving documentary *A Diary for Timothy*, where he is captured doing the 'Alas, poor Yorick' speech. The only visual record of his Hamlet, it reveals a prince well into middle age.

His producer was George Rylands, a Shakespeare scholar with a passion for the theatre. A friend of Forster, Eliot and Virginia Woolf, he was a fellow at Cambridge, where he had directed countless students in productions for the university's Marlowe Society, of which he was the moving spirit. His speciality was a close scrutiny of the text and the encouragement of clear verse-speaking. It was a risky choice, and one that Gielgud soon came to regret.

Rylands found experienced professionals very different from obedient amateurs. 'That naughty old Quartermaine resented him, and made some difficulties,' Gielgud wrote from Manchester. The actors disliked Rylands' didactic approach, and his tendency to keep his eye on the book rather than on the stage. They wanted less from him on inflection and rhythm, and more on character motivation, stage moves and 'business'. But when they turned to Gielgud for help he hesitated to give any behind Rylands' back. Yet he too was having problems with Rylands. In rehearsal he was uncertain whether to approach Hamlet afresh, or to use what he had learned from Harcourt Williams, McClintic and Barker. On this question Rylands offered him no guidance.

Despite these tensions *Hamlet*, played almost 'in its Entirety', was well received both in the provinces and London. After the opening in Manchester Beaumont wrote to Gielgud's parents: 'It was a magnificent night, a great triumph for John, and I really think far and away his best *Hamlet* production.' His performance was greatly though not universally admired. 'How heavily he has scored with his new reading!' Graham Robertson wrote. This was a more intellectual prince than before, more given to disgust than horror at the actions of Claudius and Gertrude, and showing a more profound range of emotions. The youthful spontaneity had gone, to be replaced by a new dignity and strength, and a fiery intensity that many found thrilling. But two elements that distinguished all his Hamlets remained unaltered: the poetry and the intelligence.

His Hamlet touched both young and old, and had a great influence on the next generation of actors and directors, many of whom saw it while still at school. Denis Quilley was studying the play for his Higher Certificate: 'It was the first time I had seen a text I was studying come alive,' he recalls. 'It was magical, it sprang to life before my eyes.' Peter Hall saw it in Cambridge, and still reckons it the most complete Hamlet he has seen. In Manchester Peter Barkworth was with a group from school, and had to hide his tears of delight from the other boys. In his diary he wrote: 'Gielgud was marvellous, absolutely wonderful, I've never seen acting like it, and I learnt more by simply watching him than I ever have done at a lesson.' That afternoon he decided to become a serious actor: Gielgud had become his 'idol and guiding star'.

Sybil Thorndike declared that those who saw the production 'have a memory of something hauntingly beautiful for which to be grateful all their lives'. Guthrie told Gielgud: 'You stand quite alone, in my opinion, as a speaker of verse. It was a distinguished, sophisticated, masterful, gracious and imaginative performance. The lack of youth is more than counterpoised by the authority and sophistication of maturity.' Barker, however, was less impressed. Although he felt Gielgud's Hamlet had matured well, that in the scenes with Ophelia and Gertrude 'there's no one at present who can touch you at them', he thought he lacked clarity later on: 'I was troubled now and then by the sudden outbursts of rather forced emotion,' he told him. 'We can be held – at least you, I am sure, can hold us – by quiet, or at any rate *controlled* tension.'

The most significant review came from Agate, who had seen all his previous Hamlets in England, as well as those of Irving and Forbes-Robertson, and thought this his greatest. In his diary he wrote: 'Mr G has now reached the right age; he is at the height of his powers; and the conjunction is marvellously happy.' In his review he concluded:

Mr Gielgud is now completely and authoritatively master of this tremendous part. He is, we feel, this generation's rightful tenant of this 'monstrous Gothic castle of a poem'. He has acquired an almost Irvingesque quality of pathos, and in the passages after the Play Scene an incisiveness, a raillery, a mordancy worthy of the old man. The middle act gives us ninety minutes of high excitement and assured virtuosity: Forbes-Robertson was not more bedazzling in the 'Oh what a rogue and peasant slave' soliloquy. In short, I hold that this is, and is likely to remain, the best Hamlet of our time.

Tynan too saw *Hamlet*, and coolly drew up a balance-sheet of Gielgud's qualities:

His face is best in repose: in the eyes there is noble rebuke, in the pursed lips and sunk cheeks you discern a defiant melancholy, overcast by wisdom and the traditional poet's sadness. The voice is thrilling and bears witness to great suffering; an east wind has blown through it . . . Yet with all these powers, he is not an intemperately exciting actor: too wire-drawn, too thin-spun and fugitive, essentially unanchored to earth. The voice, too, tends to fly too high, and resorts too often to a resonant alto headnote which, though it certainly expresses demoniacal possession, will not do for all the variety of demoniacal rage, terror, love and scorn.

It was a shrewd and brilliant diagnosis.

Gielgud had mixed feelings about returning to the part: 'It is a great *adventure* every time one plays it, and one is never sure of the success of its effect,' he wrote to an acquaintance. 'So much depends on one's own *personal* mood – the *reactions* of the audience and the other actors too seem to matter more than in other plays.' As his own severest critic, he felt later he had been trying too hard to imitate his younger performance, and had created nothing more than 'a pallid looking-back'. He found the part a strain, especially on matinée days, when he would say to himself: 'I could do it in a week's time, but not twice today and once tomorrow.' There was the added burden of having to fire-watch from the roof of the theatre – sometimes he slept in his dressing-room – and cope with the buzzbombs. During one performance an explosion burst open the scene-dock doors while he lay 'dead' at the end of the play. 'We felt that at any moment there might be fearful chaos in the theatre and people would be killed,' he remembered. 'But the audiences took it with amazing calm.'

His producer for *A Midsummer Night's Dream* was also from the university world. Neville Coghill was a fellow of English at Oxford and director of the wartime OUDS. He had less interest in verse-speaking than Rylands, but more in spectacle. Again there was a lack of rapport with the actors, who disagreed with his ideas, and told Gielgud so. 'It was awkward for me because I always felt the dons would think I was trying to undermine their authority,' he recalled. Forced to arbitrate, he took over much of the direction himself. A journalist glimpsed him at work: 'His figure was in silhouette – lounge suit, muffler flung loosely around his neck, felt hat on the back of his head, his long legs shuffling to and fro across the footlights like a man walking through sand. Every correction he suggested to the players brought the lines to life.'

Distracted by his extra work, Gielgud neglected his own performance. He was preoccupied with his costume, as Graham Robertson told a friend: 'John is rehearsing Oberon and is quite excited about his "lovely Leonardo Da Vinci helmet and dark green hair". How hard he works!' But Agate thought the end-result terrifying, and too reminiscent of the ghost of Hamlet's father. Other critics variously remarked on his resemblance to Julius Caesar or the Demon King. Panicking, he totally changed his conception of the part, discarding his perspex helmet and green make-up, and coming up with a more youthful Oberon, clean-shaven and sporting a flaming red wig. Audrey Williamson came a few nights later and found Oberon 'all faery charm and eloquence'.

But the critics had disliked his performance for other reasons: they thought him too worldly, aloof and self-conscious. One wrote: 'He spoke Oberon's glorious lines as if dictating letters to a typist.' Edith Evans, by contrast, scolded him for wallowing in the beauty of the speech 'I know a bank where the wild thyme blows', telling him, 'If you cry less, the audience will cry more.' The production was dull and laboured, and Gielgud decided his earlier, lighter interpretation at the Old Vic had been better, that he was now too old to play Oberon.

He had originally discussed possible sets for the *Dream* with Rex Whistler, who had subsequently withdrawn from the production because of his war service. Gielgud was deeply upset when he heard that Whistler was killed during the D-Day landings in Normandy. He wrote feelingly to his mother of Whistler's 'unaffected patriotism and sense of duty' and his 'most enchanting personality'. A tribute he wrote for *The Times* underlined his passion for design and the taste he shared with Whistler for the romantic, graceful and ornate:

His exquisite draughtmanship was evident in his love of painted detail – whether of shaded pilasters, cornices and mouldings, or in some delicate suggestion of distant woods, staircases or prim streets. Even his book illustrations, with their cupids, festooned curtains, and formal groupings, had an immediate kinship with the artificial, crisp, cardboard grandeur which appeals to the child in us all when we first visit a theatre.

The final Haymarket production was *The Duchess of Malfi*. Peggy Ashcroft had largely agreed to do Ophelia on condition she could also play the title-role in Webster's dark, bloody and neglected tragedy. Gielgud chose to play Ferdinand, her evil brother who plots her death, while Cecil Trouncer had the key role of the scheming Bosola. Rylands, already invited by Gielgud to produce, knew the play intimately, having played not only Bosola and Ferdinand, but also the Duchess, in which role he had been photographed by Cecil Beaton for *Vogue*.

Again there was trouble. Some of the actors were unsympathetic to the play, and in rehearsal rebelled once more against Rylands' academic approach. Led again by Leon Quartermaine, they argued that no one would like the play, that it was bound to fail, and that it should be abandoned. Peggy Ashcroft conveyed their sentiments to Gielgud, who passed the buck to Beaumont, who broke the news to his producer. Rylands was incensed: 'I told them they were cads, cowards and philistines and went at them with all guns blazing,' he recalled.

The mutiny was quelled, but the mutual distrust lingered on. Rylands believed the actors were failing to understand their parts, while they felt he was unable or unwilling to help them understand them. Gielgud sympathised with some of the actors' criticisms, feeling Rylands failed to give them confidence on key matters. When he asked him whether Ferdinand's relationship with the Duchess was incestuous, Rylands replied: 'Just follow the text, and it will all come out.' This was unhelpful to Gielgud, who liked clear directions on motivation, especially when trying to get to grips with an evil character.

As head of the company he tried to act as peacemaker behind the scenes while avoiding outright confrontation. Rylands wrote to him shortly afterwards: 'It was your sweetness of nature, your distinction and your enterprise – and nothing else – which made the season a success – both with the highbrows and the Great British Public. What a team you had to work with! Oh dear, oh dear! No one but you could have stuck it and held them together.' But later he said of the affair: 'I think John was a bit feeble.'

The Duchess of Malfi was well received, some critics calling it the best modern revival of the play. At the time the papers were full of photographs of the death pits at Belsen, which for many made Webster's corpse-strewn drama both less horrific and more gruesomely familiar than usual. Peggy Ashcroft's Duchess was praised – except by Agate, who called her 'Little Miss Muffet' – but Gielgud teetered on the edge of over-playing his part. Some people admired his frenzied, tortured Ferdinand: 'I was able and even forced to forget that you were John Gielgud,' Coghill told him. Others thought him braying and shrill, and the critic of *The Times* labelled him 'a petulant pervert'. It was an unsubtle part that he took little pleasure in playing: such unadulterated evil was quite foreign to him. Rylands, who thought him 'a little uncertain and patchy', told him: 'Something inside you disliked or feared the part, so it was always a struggle for you.'

The season had been a difficult one. Recruiting Rylands and Coghill had not been a success. The repertory system to which he was so firmly committed in principle proved difficult to manage in wartime, and his company's talents were limited. The renewed bombing put a severe strain on rehearsals and performances: 'It's something of a privilege to be able to act at all under these conditions,' he confessed during the raids. 'The difficulty is that life in London lately has become even more dramatic than anything you're likely to see or hear on the stage.'

On the other hand he had managed to keep a difficult, middle-aged company on an even keel, while producing a trio of fine performances himself. Agate complained that 'Mr G is too often thrown away on parts unworthy of his eminence'. Yet if his Oberon had been a failure, and Ferdinand beyond his grasp, he had scored well in the Maugham, scintillated all over again in *Love for Love*, and given what some thought his finest interpretation of Hamlet.

This was assumed to be his last Hamlet, and it attracted full houses. There was now a Shakespeare boom: his plays were reported to be enjoying a greater popularity than in any war period since the Napoleonic era. Wolfit contributed to this boom, notably with a much-praised Lear. Yet the most exciting productions of the 1944/5 season were undoubtedly at the New. This was now the home of the re-formed Old Vic company headed by Olivier and Richardson, which also included Sybil Thorndike and Margaret Leighton. Its success was phenomenal, with people queuing for hours to see *Peer Gynt*, *Richard III*, *Arms and the Man* and *Uncle Vanya*. Together, the seasons at the Haymarket and the New re-established the repertory system in the English theatre, at the very moment when some of the great European houses had been bombed into silence. 'Continental leadership has passed,' Ashley Dukes reported.

Both Olivier and Richardson were at the height of their powers, and at the New each gave what was widely considered to be their finest performance so far, Richardson with a superb, dreamy Peer Gynt, Olivier with his satanic and richly comic Richard III. Gielgud paid tribute to his work. 'It has been a great year for Laurence Olivier,' he wrote in *Theatre Arts Monthly*, praising him for his mesmerising Richard III, but also for his screen version of *Henry V*.

During the run of *Richard III* the sword of Edmund Kean, which Irving had worn on his first night in the part, was presented to Olivier onstage. On its blade was a newly engraved inscription: 'This sword, given him by his mother Kate Terry Gielgud, 1938, is given to Laurence Olivier by his friend John Gielgud in appreciation of his performance of Richard III at the New Theatre, 1944'. It was an extraordinarily generous gesture, reflecting not just Gielgud's deep sense of theatrical history, but also his genuine admiration for Olivier's power as an actor.

It also seemed to symbolise a growing belief that the leadership of the profession was passing into Olivier's hands.

22

Travelling Player

I'm very proud to be the general of this ship.
(Speech to the troops after *Hamlet*, India, 1946)

IN later years Gielgud claimed he felt guilty and upset at not being called up during the war. Yet the authorities had clearly recognised, as he himself acknowledged, that he would have made a poor soldier, and was much better employed in the theatre. As it was he had done the state no little service in his contribution to the war effort.

On VE night in May 1945 he gave a dinner party for Barker and his wife, Beaumont and Lady Cunard. He was disconcerted to see that Barker had aged, and upset to hear that he had missed the first act of his Haymarket *Hamlet* because he was still at lunch. Within a year Barker was dead, and before long Gielgud was looking on his long exile from the theatre in a positive light. 'Now that he is dead, I cannot help being glad that the writer in him triumphed over the actor-director, for his prefaces give a wonderful composite picture of his many brilliant gifts,' he said.

Shortly before the war in Europe ended Gielgud wrote a letter to the editor of *The Times* – not about post-war reconstruction or the national theatre, but a more pressing matter. 'I shall shortly be removing from 55 Park Lane to 16 Cowley Street,' he explained. 'I am wondering if you could suggest a newsagent or stationer who could supply me with *The Times*.'

His new home was a small, elegant, eighteenth-century house in Westminster, close to his old school. A tall, narrow and attractive four-storey building, with a small walled garden filled by a giant fig-tree, it was the first house he had owned in London. He had made relatively little money during the war, and was able to afford the deposit only as a result of one of his acts of kindness. Annie Esmond was an elderly actress he had admired in his youth, and grown fond of during *Macbeth*; knowing her to be poor, he had occasionally bought her lunch. When she had begged him to give her a part at the Haymarket, however small, he had taken pity on her loneliness, and obliged. She was then taken ill, and from hospital asked to see him. He found her gasping for breath, desperate and incoherent. 'I sat at her bedside for twenty minutes, while she held my hand tightly and gazed at me beseechingly,' he recalled. She died that day, and in her will left him £5000.

The new house was close to theatreland, but in a secluded street. From the top floor he had a clear view across the rooftops to Westminster Abbey, with all its potent associations with his childhood. He had room for his period furniture, precious china, snuff-boxes, and modern paintings. He filled the shelves with his vast collection of plays, volumes of criticism, and books on the history of the theatre; and the walls of the staircase with Victorian playbills and prints of famous actors and actresses. The décor he chose reflected his taste for tradition, elegance and the sumptuous: pink walls, brocade and silk damask curtains, fitted carpets of deep burgundy. Even here there were theatrical associations: a pine china-cupboard from the Queen's, a patchwork cushion of velvet and silk made from the *Richard of Bordeaux* costumes, a screen in the bedroom filled with pictures of Irving and Forbes-Robertson. 'Don't open a drawer or Ellen Terry's teeth will fall out,' John Perry joked.

Living what was then known as a bachelor existence, Gielgud was afraid of appearing precious. 'There's a danger of becoming old maidish about having your things just so when you live alone,' he told a journalist. Once he had made all the alterations he desired, he settled into a comfortable routine. In the evenings after a show he would take a cold supper, often alone, then play his mini-piano, read or play records. But he was also very sociable: helped by his valet and cook he held regular intimate supper parties for his theatrical friends.

In the post-war London theatre the mood was for fun, colour and spectacle. 'People want most of all to forget the horrors of the last six years,' Gielgud suggested. 'For the moment they want laughter more than logic.' He now met this need with a revival of *Lady Windermere's Fan*, another play with strong family associations. Marion Terry had been in George Alexander's original 1892 production, and at the end of her life was still re-enacting the play's big scene at charity matinées with

Mabel Terry-Lewis. For his production Gielgud enlisted Wilde's son Vyvyan Holland to help with the period detail. His production, with Athene Seyler, Isabel Jeans, Geoffrey Toone and Dorothy Hyson, was not particularly distinguished: the sets overwhelmed the story, and the characters' humanity was felt to be lost beneath the glitter. But it was just what the public wanted. Battered and starved of beauty during the war, emerging from the blackout into a world of austerity, coal shortages and utility clothes, they packed the Haymarket for 428 performances.

Aside from Wilde's celebrated wit, the main attraction was Cecil Beaton's sumptuous sets and costumes. This was Beaton's break-through into theatre, as he recorded exultantly in his diary after the dinner with Gielgud and Beaumont which settled his engagement: 'All at once I felt confident that a whole new vista was opened up to me,' he wrote:

> This was a play I knew I could do well. As I walked upon air with Gielgud up the Haymarket, I kept pumping him with a stream of suggestions as to how the production should look: over-charged, richly stuffed and upholstered, with a great use of *trompe l'oeil* and enfilades, in false perspectives, of Victorian stucco and heavy chandeliers ... He seemed a bit overwhelmed, and laughed nervously, but made no objections.

Although Gielgud later referred to 'scenic disputes' with the 'spiky' Beaton, they remained for the moment on reasonably good terms. When Beaton took a small part on the production's transfer to America, Gielgud told him merrily: 'Your English style will no doubt put all the other gentlemen to bed. I speak figuratively, of course.' Sharing Beaton's love of elegance and lavishness he was happy to spend freely, as Geoffrey Toone recalls: 'We had the most wonderful clothes. The men's costumes were made by a Savile Row tailor who was cutting in the days of Wilde. I remember John saying, "We'll cheer up that last scene, we'll have you riding in Rotten Row." That meant tailor-made riding breeches, and handmade boots from the most expensive shoemakers.'

The term 'producer' was now starting to fall out of fashion, to be used instead in its modern meaning. But if Gielgud was now a 'director', his mercurial methods remained unchanged. Denys Blakelock was in the company on the pre-London tour of *Lady*

Windermere's Fan: 'His inexhaustible supply of nervous energy never ceased to surprise me,' he recalled. 'Even at the dress rehearsal, on the morning of the opening night, there were innovations.' This all proved too much for Dennis Price, cast as Lord Darlington, who resigned after a week of rehearsals.

Gielgud was also to blame for another cast change. His aunt Mabel Terry-Lewis had not worked for two years, but because of his fondness for her he rashly persuaded Beaumont to cast her as the Duchess of Berwick. At seventy-two her memory was deteriorating, and in rehearsals she kept calling characters by their wrong names. She also crossed swords over her costume with Beaton – who remembered her as 'a frail, forgetful and irascible old lady' – and resisted all Gielgud's efforts to get her to remember her lines. After a month on tour he reluctantly agreed to her being replaced, as Geoffrey Toone remembers: 'There was a terrible moment when it was clear that she wouldn't do, and John had to say to Binkie that he couldn't tell her. He was desperately upset.' It was a cowardly evasion, as he later admitted, but an understandable one: to sack a member of the Terry family was almost a sacrilege.

Many actors were loath to go abroad just as the war was ending, but Gielgud felt bound to honour his ENSA commitment. Many companies went to the newly liberated areas: one of the first was the Old Vic, led by Olivier and Richardson, which re-opened the Comédie Française in Paris. But there were still troops in action or waiting to be demobilised further afield, and Gielgud had agreed to take a Tennent's company to India, Ceylon and the Far East for ENSA, with John Perry as its manager.

'I rather wanted to do *Charley's Aunt*,' he said before leaving, 'but everybody assures me it is a mistake to play down to the troops.' So, in addition to Coward's *Blithe Spirit*, he was compelled to wheel out *Hamlet* yet again. There were considerable casting problems, as many actors had yet to be released from the services. Those who were available were much in demand. Tennent's called in a shy, promising young actor, to whom Gielgud apologised for only being able to offer him Osric and Guildernstern. 'I don't think I can accept, because Barry Jackson has offered me Henry V at Stratford next season,' Paul Scofield replied.

There was also trouble over Ophelia, caused by an act of misplaced kindness on Gielgud's part which was understandably seen as nepotism. Isabel Dean had attracted praise at the Haymarket when she had gone on for Peggy Ashcroft as Ophelia, but was overlooked in favour of Gielgud's cousin Hazel Terry, a lesser actress whose personal life was in confusion, and for whom Gielgud felt pity. His second-rung company eventually included Marian Spencer, Ernest Hare, Irene Browne and George Howe. 'Good luck in India,' Barker had written, in his last letter to Gielgud. 'You'll find the Indian Shakespeare scholars very nippy.'

Packed with colour and incident, the tour opened Gielgud's eyes to many vivid, hot and unfamiliar new worlds, as well as to the extremes of wealth and poverty. In Delhi he was put up at Government House by Lord and Lady Wavell; in the humidity of Singapore he stayed at the famous Raffles Hotel. In Bangalore he met the dancer Ram Gopal, who performed for the company in his house. They visited the huge Mysore Palace, where he was particularly struck by a group of sacred elephants, which greeted their approach with massive erections. In Bombay he was surprised naked in his hotel room by a large, enthusiastic Indian woman inviting him to lunch, at which a small poet in a white suit read a long poem in his honour.

The colours of India reminded him nostalgically of productions from his youth. From Bombay he wrote home:

> There are bits of *Beau Geste*, *Chu Chin Chow*, Charing Cross Station in a fantastic jumble – the worst is the smells and beggars and ugliness and squalor, the best the wonderful touches of colour – mostly in the scarves and sashes and turbans, all washed and washed till they are the most exquisite shades of blue and yellow and crimson, and those colours stand out with unexpected and dazzling brilliance against all the rest which is cheapjack and sordid and often depressing.

His company worked under difficult, often hazardous conditions. In Bombay they rehearsed in an open-air cinema, while children played noisily around them, banging the walls, throwing pebbles, and giggling at the actors. In Saigon they performed in a private house while shooting was going on outside; in Rangoon they played in a converted chapel. They also performed *Blithe Spirit* in an isolation hospital for wounded airmen. In Singapore the windows of the theatre had been blown out, and there were no doors. The performance was constantly interrupted by street sounds, birds flying around, and music from the concert hall next door, where the pianist Solomon was playing. On his night off Gielgud went round to the hall: 'I stood at the back of the packed house to listen to an orchestra of soldiers recently released from prison camps, who were learning to recover their skills in playing instruments that they had not been able to touch for years,' he wrote. 'Behind me, in the harbour, was a line of dark battleships spread out under the night sky. It was extraordinary to hear a Beethoven symphony performed so movingly under such strange conditions.'

As usual he thrived on a challenge. In Madras the company was booked to play *Hamlet* in the large Senate House, where the stage was separated from the semi-circular auditorium by a large orchestra pit. With a monsoon cascading down, Gielgud realised the actors would not be heard, and suggested the pit be covered to make an apron stage. In six hours he re-lit and re-rehearsed the entire production. Having to speak the soliloquies close to the audience he found exhilarating; he gave there what he felt to be some of his finest performances.

Jack Hawkins was ENSA's representative in India. In November he reported to London that Gielgud was 'sweeping the Far East', adding: 'Frills, legs and variety, so necessary an antidote to battle strain, have given place to a wish for good theatre. A new taste for the theatre has been awakened in the men, and I believe it will live when they come home.' Shakespeare and Coward were immensely popular with troops accustomed to dead-beat ENSA acts, and they queued for hours to see Gielgud. Although he was not a fan of *Blithe Spirit*, which he thought over-written and little more than an extended joke, he had expected it to be the more popular play. But the greater demand was for *Hamlet*. There was no lowering of standards, as one company member, Nancy Nevinson, recalls: 'Before we left people said, "*Hamlet* for the troops, are you *mad*?" But whether it was the Haymarket or a barrack room, John was always magnificent. There was never any easing off, ever. It was swift and magnificent, and you could hear a pin drop.'

While flying from Singapore to Saigon, Gielgud and the company narrowly escaped death. Their plane was buffeted by violent weather, and nearly came down in the China Sea. While all around him were being sick, Gielgud sat quietly doing *The Times* crossword. Asked whether he had been frightened, he replied: 'I don't know really, I thought it was better to concentrate on something.' But the constant travel and endless performances sometimes took their toll. Rowland Smailes, then in the RAF, recalls *Hamlet* in Bombay: 'Gielgud had lost his voice, its tone was almost inaudible, yet every word was clear.' Often he was uncertain how troops unfamiliar with Shakespeare would react. Jack Wood, the company's stage director, remembers the response in Singapore: 'John gave a wonderful performance, but the play was received in total silence. You could feel it, they'd been in Burma for four years, and they were thinking of home. He came off at the interval, very worried. At the end I brought the curtain down, then up again to show the final tableau. They were still silent. But when I raised it again and the cast gathered, the applause was absolutely tremendous.'

The actors' affection for Gielgud was expressed in a sketch that included the flawed if heartfelt limerick: 'There once was an actor called Gielgud / Whose Hamlet we all think is still good / But when he gets back to London / We fear he may be undone / If he doesn't make up his mind.' One of its authors, Nancy Nevinson, was playing small parts and understudying. 'I was rather shy, so he was a bit of a God to me,' she recalls. Extracts from her diary give glimpses of the impression he made on a young actress:

'*London.* First day of rehearsal. Watching J rehearse *Hamlet*, it was nothing less than thrilling. He's so helpful to each person without getting fussed, and so pliable and unset.'

'*Malta.* Lucca aerodrome, sleeping in a barrack room. Poor John G was sick. He's such a sport though, very simple and sweet and friendly.'

'*Madras.* JG really is a nice fellow. Apparently he had tactlessly told Irene that I was good as Arcati, so naturally that upset her.'

The gaffe with Irene Browne was not an isolated case. In Saigon at the end of the performance he announced: 'I'd like to thank my company, particularly the ladies, who have travelled so many thousands of miles to give you all so much pleasure.' In Cawnpore, where he learnt there had been a mutiny in the camp, he remarked: 'I hope you got what you wanted.' Other moments underlined his unworldliness, as when he told an audience of troops after a performance of *Hamlet*, 'I'm very proud to be the general of this ship.'

His mischievous side was never suppressed for very long. At one performance of *Blithe Spirit*, in which he played Charles Condomine, he had an uncontrollable fit of the giggles. He was not above testing out other actors. 'His eyes danced, he tried to make you laugh with a twinkle,' Nancy Nevinson recalls. In Bombay Donald Sinden, going back to England after ENSA duty in Burma, asked him what he considered the most important elements of acting. 'He thought for a second, then replied, "I should say feeling and timing," and then he flashed me a look out of the corner of his eyes, and gurgled, "I understand it's the same in many walks of life."'

On the way home the company gave nine performances of *Hamlet* in Cairo. In the Opera House, originally built for the first production of *Aida*, Basil Dean had organised an ENSA Festival for the servicemen. But the actors played to half-full houses: riots had broken out in Egypt, and Cairo was off-limits to the troops. The last performance began farcically: Lee Fox, playing Horatio, fell into Hamlet's arms in an epileptic fit, and Gielgud shouted crossly: 'Drop the curtain, put something between his teeth, fetch the understudy.' Busy making up for Guildenstern, Julian Randall was ill-prepared: when he warned Hamlet of the approaching Ghost with, 'Look, my lord, it comes,' Gielgud replied, 'No, you fool, the other way!'

Gielgud received the usual accolades, the *Egyptian Gazette* declaring: 'Here is a Hamlet before whom even the most cynical, hard-boiled critic could only bow in awed admiration.' At a reception before the first night he announced yet again that this would be his last Hamlet – then told the Russian ambassador he would love to play the role in Moscow. But this time, nearing forty-five, having played it more than five hundred times from New York to Rangoon, he kept his word.

The tour had been exhausting. He had done eighty shows in eighteen weeks; travelled thousands of miles; given his lecture 'Shakespeare – in Peace and War' in aid of the Red Cross; and tried to play the ambassadorial role expected of him. At its end he talked of the theatre as 'a great force for peace and better understanding among the nations', and reflected on the increased popularity of theatre and radio drama with the troops: 'This war which has produced so much destruction has developed a demand for serious theatre, at least among the forces. Long hours alone have given many time to think. The radio has had a tremendous role to play and the troops eagerly listen to broadcast drama.'

The next three years were frustrating ones. Although he had some successes, he played many roles which were either not his choice, or really suited to him. As all actors do when they reach middle age, he worried about the growing number of parts he was unable to play. As a director he was more at the mercy of other people's wishes, especially Beaumont's, and his choice of play was often less than assured. Significantly, he neither acted in nor directed any Shakespeare plays, and spent much of the time in America. For the first time since he achieved stardom he seemed to be losing his direction.

His first engagement on his return to London, Rodney Ackland's adaptation of Dostoyevsky's *Crime and Punishment*, encapsulated his problems. He was not Beaumont's first choice as director: the job had been marked down for Michael Benthall, and Olivier, Redgrave and Peter Glenville were all considered before Gielgud was persuaded to take it on. The cast included Edith Evans and Peter Ustinov, with Robert Helpmann playing Raskolnikov, the penniless student who murders an old woman pawnbroker to prove his superiority over other men. But when Helpmann had to withdraw through illness Gielgud agreed to take over the role, and leave the direction to Anthony Quayle.

This was Quayle's first job as a director, and he made a success of handling a complex play containing over forty characters. As the original director Gielgud was in a position that required diplomacy, not his strongest suit. But in Quayle's view he trod the fine line between advising and interfering. Once, however, he fell from grace. While blocking Edith Evans' death scene, Quayle suggested Maria Britnieva, playing her daughter, should run offstage for a glass of water. From the stalls Gielgud cried out, 'No, no! Everybody will be watching little Maria!' To which Edith Evans replied, 'I think I'll risk that.'

As the consumptive Madame Marmeladov she had given Gielgud problems, distracting him during a key scene with a rather too emphatic cough. Maria Britnieva recalls his reluctance to confront her about this apparent piece of upstaging: 'He would wait in the wings afterwards and say, "Can't you keep her quiet, darling?" He was too cowardly and too kind to say anything himself.' Despite such incidents, he continued to admire Edith Evans' powers: 'She's got a badger's way of sniffing out things, of isolating what's best and most actable in a part,' he said.

Gielgud was really too old to play Raskolnikov. Despite his Slav ancestry he found it difficult to develop his dark, tortured, ruthless character. It was a part much better suited to Helpmann's sinister and macabre personality. But Quayle, hailed as a promising director, worked sensitively with him to improve his movement, and to bring out more forcefully Raskolnikov's terror in the final scene. From Manchester, where the play opened on tour, Gielgud wrote: 'I hope to get less mannered as I gain confidence – it was already simpler last night and I know better now what to begin to eliminate – especially some of the gulps and snorts and my standing positions.' During the run he wrote to a friend: 'I'm very pleased about the success of C and P which was an exhausting and complicated piece of work to enact.'

Playing the Chief of Police who gradually closes in on Raskolnikov, Ustinov thought Gielgud too tremulous to be convincing: 'It was awfully difficult, because I felt his guilt was apparent the moment I saw him, and my instinct was to arrest him immediately,' he recalled. But others felt he gave a sensitive performance that conveyed superbly Raskolnikov's intense suffering: Agate even thought it 'the best thing after Hamlet he has ever given us'. Ackland's skilful adaptation was much liked, and the play ran for 161 performances, first at the New and then at the Globe.

Ustinov had a good rapport with Gielgud, and remembers him as 'one of the kindest men I have come across, as well as one of the shyest'. But he also noticed the change that came over him as soon as he faced an audience, the way his ego blossomed and took over. As the curtain fell on the first act of the opening night of *Crime and Punishment* Gielgud called out, 'If there are going to have to be all these people in the wings, they *must look at me!*'

While he was playing in *Crime and Punishment*, and Olivier was playing Lear at the New, a newspaper canvassed the views of the national critics as to which of them was the greater actor. It was the first of many attempts to play up a supposed rivalry between them. But artists are not athletes, and many critics dismissed as odious and futile any attempt to create an order of merit. Ernest Betts replied: 'This is an insane question, for the two actors have nothing in common except their eminence and devotion to the theatre.'

The few who ventured an opinion deemed Olivier the more versatile actor, having more power and attack, greater control, and a wider range of expression. Gielgud, on the other hand, was agreed to have the finer voice – especially for poetry – a greater poignancy, and more subtlety. 'For those who like question, Gielgud is the better actor; for those who like forthrightness, Olivier' was Darlington's view. The subjective nature of the exercise was shown when one critic called Gielgud the romantic and Olivier the thinker, while another recorded a totally opposite view.

Tynan, not yet a paid critic, also considered the question: 'For the large, shattering effects of passion, we look to Olivier; for the smaller, more exquisite effects of temper, to Gielgud. To use an old and respectable critical terminology, it is the contrast between Nature and Art. For the best-ordered idealizations of that with which we are familiar, Gielgud carries off the palm; for the exploration of new, strange territories and planets, Olivier is our guide.' Although he refined these opinions later, he was never to change them.

Early in 1947 Gielgud left England once again. 'Safely stowed.

Staying McClintic til Sunday', he cabled his parents from New York. For his third visit to North America, the first with his own company, he had planned a thirteen-week tour of *The Importance of Being Earnest* and *Love for Love*. Asked why as a great tragic actor he had brought over two comedies, he cited the inevitable critical comparisons. Broadway had recently seen Olivier's magnificent Oedipus; Maurice Evans was playing Hamlet; Wolfit was also in New York, playing Lear. Gielgud, who had thought seriously about doing Lear, added diplomatically: 'We're all friends, as well as countrymen, and I think it would be a disservice to all to set up such an obvious target.'

In his letters to his mother he expressed his guilt at the hardships he had left behind. England was still in the grip of post-war austerity, and experiencing the coldest winter of the century. Several theatres had to close through lack of heating; in those that remained open the audience came ready with heavy sweaters and rugs. 'I simply can't bear the thought of you all in such a wretched crisis in London – the cold and discomfort must be appalling, to say nothing of the general atmosphere of depression,' Gielgud wrote from the Ritz-Carlton in Boston. 'I do really feel a pig to be away from it all and living in such luxury and ease.' To atone for his high living he sent his parents hot-water-bottles, boots, soap, and several food parcels. Meanwhile he revelled in the unaccustomed brightness and plenty of America: the brilliant neon signs, the shops full of good things, his suite on the thirteenth floor of the Plaza Hotel in New York, where he gazed across at the skyscrapers and dined on oysters, chops and ice cream.

There were several changes from the London cast of *The Importance of Being Earnest*. Edith Evans had grown weary of her celebrated part ('I still think she was a fool not to play Bracknell,' Gielgud complained), and Margaret Rutherford had taken over. Robert Flemying was Algy, Gwendolen was played by Pamela Brown, and Jean Cadell was Miss Prism. 'Margaret and Flemying are definite weaknesses in this performance, but it is remarkable how well the play re-adjusts itself,' Gielgud reported. His production received ecstatic reviews, Brooks Atkinson calling it 'a theatre masterpiece', and it picked up one of the newly established Tony awards, for best foreign import. Gielgud's Jack Worthing was considered immaculate, brilliant and dazzling. Richard Watts Jr, one of the few who had not liked his 1936 Hamlet, thought he fitted Wilde perfectly: 'It is difficult to imagine a more satisfying example of actor, role and play in complete harmony,' he wrote.

The notices for *Love for Love* were not so fervent, but still admiring, though Gielgud's own were mixed. 'We had been acting it for a long time in England, and I think I had become stale,' he recalled. Nevertheless his scene of feigned madness was voted by the *Stage* 'probably the most triumphant single comedy sequence of the past twelve months'. The production suffered from being compared with the brilliant Wilde revival, though most critics blamed Congreve for writing an erratic, over-complicated plot.

The most curious response was in Boston, where the play had never been staged. On advice from the Theater Guild, Gielgud cut certain anti-religious and anti-papal remarks. After the first night the City Fathers insisted on the removal of words such as 'whore' and 'pimp', but failed to notice the coarser jokes. The bawdy dialogue was likened by one critic to the collected works of Mae West, and allegedly 'pinked the cheeks and lifted the eyebrows' of the audience. But Boston loved the play's racy elegance, and the week was a complete sell-out.

In Baltimore Gielgud took part through a long-distance radio link in an event of great sentimental significance to him, a special broadcast marking the centenary of the birth of Ellen Terry. Excerpts from her most famous parts were read by stars such as Helen Hayes, Eva La Gallienne, Ingrid Bergman and Cornelia Otis Skinner. Gielgud brought it to a close with the lament from *Cymbeline*, once spoken by Edward Gordon Craig to his mother's Imogen: 'Fear no more the heat o' the sun / Nor the furious winter's rages . . .' It was among his favourite Shakespeare speeches, and one he was to recite later in countless memorial services.

As a director his changes of mind were still causing problems. During a matinée of *Love for Love* in Washington he asked Robert Flemying, in a stage whisper in the middle of the concluding gavotte, to move down to stage right. Afterwards Flemying caught him on his way to the dressing-rooms. 'Surely, John, I was not in the wrong place, was I?' he asked. Without pausing in his stride Gielgud replied: 'I thought it might be better there – but it isn't.'

New York as always put him in good spirits: 'Soft winds and blue skies, the city looks magnificent and sparkling, and one feels so well,' he wrote. He had lunch at the Colony and dinner at '21', went to three musicals in three days, saw Ingrid Bergman in Maxwell Anderson's *Joan of Lorraine* ('I was bored stiff and left at the interval') and went to a modern version of Gay's *The Beggar's Opera* ('a lot of vulgarity, but very intelligent and lively'). He renewed old friendships – with his beloved

Lillian Gish, with Lynn Fontanne, Guthrie McClintic and Katherine Cornell. At a party he talked at length with Greta Garbo, noticing her 'hideously cut dress' and 'lovely childlike expression'. Her film career was now over, and she told him her life was empty and aimless. 'All this with twinkling eyes and great animation, not at all the mournful tones of her imitators,' he noted. 'I couldn't make out whether her whole attitude was perhaps a terrific pose.' Garbo annoyed him by pretending not to know Cecil Beaton, with whom she was then intimate. 'But whenever I see him he's always telling me you're going to get married,' Gielgud told her.

In London, Ontario he gave a 'quiz lecture' to five hundred students, and complained of the 'rather ENSA-like hospitality – club luncheons and the like – a great many professors and elderly gushing ladies in rimless glasses'. While in Boston he gave several talks at Harvard about playing Hamlet and Lear. The playwright and director Jerome Kilty was at one of them: 'He was in his element, we sat at his feet and he made us feel we were in touch with greatness,' he recalled. Gielgud was flattered to discover his recording of *Hamlet* was still selling in the New York shops. He now recorded *The Importance of Being Earnest*, prompting John Mason Brown to write: 'If ever perfection has been caught by a disc, it is so captured on this record.'

At the beginning of 1947 Richardson was awarded a knighthood in the New Year's Honours List. This infuriated Olivier, to whom such things mattered inordinately, and who thought himself the more deserving: '*I* should have been the fucking knight!' he complained loudly. In May, after intensive lobbying by his friends in high places, and also by Richardson, his wish was granted in the King's Birthday Honours List. The main obstacle had been his divorce, then frowned on in royal circles. At thirty-nine he was the youngest actor to receive a knighthood.

Gielgud, whose claim was clearly stronger than both Olivier's and Richardson's, was passed over because of his homosexuality, which was viewed even less kindly than divorce. Coward, too, had been overlooked for what Olivier discreetly described as 'entirely the wrong reasons'. Olivier now wrote to Gielgud, claiming to be embarrassed at having been honoured before him. The press made much of the issue. Asked about Richardson's knighthood, Donald Wolfit barked: 'No comment!'

Gielgud remained in America to direct Judith Anderson in Euripides' *Medea*, in a new translation by the poet Robinson Jeffers.

Once again he helped out in a crisis: no suitable actor could be found for Jason, and Judith Anderson persuaded him to play the part. 'Apparently browbeaten, but a gentleman', as one critic put it, Gielgud had grave doubts about playing such a young, athletic, virile role, especially as he was also directing. But he had never done a Greek tragedy, and sniffed a challenge: 'If I could get a really striking make-up, wig and clothes, and play it as a character part – a sort of young Macbeth – I think the strength of the character would be very effective for me,' he decided. 'It is something a bit different from anything I've done and that always tempts me.'

A journalist watching rehearsals was impressed by his sensitive ear, his strong musical sense, and his care for the stage picture. She noted down several of his instructions to the actors:

> Pay no attention to the punctuation. That's one way writers torment actors. It's the meaning you must observe . . . You must look for the opposite colours. In a strong person like Creon, for example, find the tenderness. There's too much Goering now. Don't ever be obvious . . . This whole passage is like a song, diminuendo here, soaring there . . . So much of good acting is knowing when and how to pause. You must time to the split second . . . Simpler, make it simpler. You're doing too much.

Later she watched him acting with Judith Anderson: 'The bodies of these two obeyed their thought like well-drilled soldiers while their voices registered every nuance,' she wrote. 'Their skills were beautifully matched.'

The critics failed to share her view. *Medea* played in Philadelphia for a fortnight before opening at the National in New York in October. Under Gielgud's direction Judith Anderson gave a tempestuous, passionate performance, generally seen as the finest of her career. But she overwhelmed Gielgud as Jason, and his performance seemed colourless by contrast. Aldous Huxley met him soon after in the street, and wrote to Lewis Gielgud: 'He looked, I thought, romantically battered – perhaps as a result of playing opposite Miss Judith Anderson as Medea.'

A worse battering was to come with the US production of *Crime and Punishment*. Keen to improve his Raskolnikov, Gielgud persuaded the management to bring in Komisarjevsky to re-direct the play. Now sixty-five and running a drama school in New York, he disliked almost everything about the production – the set, the adaptation, many of the new cast. Rehearsals were chaotic: he introduced new parts to give work to students from his school that he brought in to the production, and spent too much time on their characters. Finally, as late as the first dress rehearsal, Gielgud insisted on taking over, and with Komisarjevsky present rehearsed until four in the morning.

The move appeared to have worked. 'Wonderful ovation for play excellent press especially *Times*', Gielgud cabled his parents after the opening at the National in December. Several reviewers commended his performance, as well as those of Lillian Gish and Dolly Haas as Katerina and Sonia: Brooks Atkinson thought his 'sharp, lean, tormented characterisation composed a masterpiece'. But there were criticisms of the production and its 'irrelevant Slavic pageantry', and the management took the extraordinary step of asking Gielgud to re-direct the play. Out of loyalty to Komisarjevsky, though very reluctantly, he agreed to do so. As he was about to start Komisarjevsky appeared, delivered a withering denunciation of the supporting actors' abilities, and took over once more. It made little difference: after four weeks the show was scheduled to close, and it only lasted a further month because the actors took cuts in salary.

One of Gielgud's greatest assets as an actor was his ability to support others on stage. Victor Sokoloff, playing the Chief of Police, remembered his technique: 'Each performance to me was just like a first performance. Gielgud is so flexible, so hospitable to each nuance you give him, that there was always something new to find in what you yourself did. I enjoyed the way he would take it and answer it. In our three big scenes, I felt as though we were playing tennis with the audience, the ball going to the audience and then back to the stage . . . It was such bliss to act with a man like that.'

Despite Komisarjevsky's behaviour, Gielgud said later that 'nothing could shake me in my personal affection for him or in my admiration for his diversity of talents'. It must have been painful to have witnessed the dissipation of a great talent in a man who had once so inspired him. Yet he still believed Komisarjevsky had improved his performance, and he was not alone: many of those who had seen both productions felt his Raskolnikov had strikingly mellowed and deepened.

At the end of the run Gielgud decided it was his best part since Hamlet. Disappointed by the failure, he attacked American audiences with unusual severity. He scolded them for not appreciating the kind of full-blooded, uninhibited tragedy represented by *Crime and*

Punishment, arguing that poorly acted film melodramas had made them allergic to such emotional displays. A Russian audience would be sympathetic; in America the men 'are embarrassed by a grown man beating his breast'.

In November a newspaper ran the headline 'GIELGUD DENIES HE WILL BECOME AMERICAN CITIZEN'. Friends in London, the source for the story, were wondering whether he would settle there permanently. Gielgud was angry about the rumour: although he loved the glitter and excitement of New York, his affections and loyalty lay with the English theatre. Like other actors, he had been criticised for taking companies abroad, where conditions were thought to be easier than in England. In his defence he spoke of the need 'to widen one's outlook and to bring back new and interesting ideas to one's home stage'. With little innovation in the West End, it was a valid defence.

There were other reasons for returning. One was money: he was now paying income tax in both countries. Another was his parents, about whom he was anxious: his mother had turned eighty, his father was eighty-seven. Finally there was his reputation. Articles were appearing in England speculating whether he could ever again match the brilliance of the Old Vic company headed by Olivier and Richardson.

It was clearly time to come home.

PART FOUR

Rise and Fall

1948–1968

23

Rattigan, Fry and Burton

It's always better when it's different!
(Gielgud rehearsing
The Lady's Not for Burning, 1949)

SURVEYING the post-war scene, Gielgud declared: 'The theatre flourishes, but where are the new plays?' Returning to London he found a theatrical desert. While Arthur Miller and Tennessee Williams were emerging in America, in Britain new dramatists were almost non-existent; the West End depended on established figures such as Coward, Rattigan, Priestley, Emlyn Williams and Rodney Ackland. The world had changed: managements were unsure about public taste, writers uncertain whether to explore or ignore war themes. There were few good plays of note: Priestley's *The Linden Tree* and Rattigan's *The Winslow Boy* were rare exceptions.

Since his vigorous championing of *French without Tears*, Gielgud and Rattigan had been friends. Their friendship survived Gielgud's rejection, without explanation, of the part of the lawyer in *The Winslow Boy*. Rattigan had written it for him, and had been hurt when he turned it down. Gielgud promised to 'do something else for you', and Rattigan now wrote four one-act plays, with a part in each for him. Subsequent events illustrated vividly Gielgud's notorious indecisiveness.

He liked the idea of playing four separate characters over two evenings, and when he read *The Browning Version* he was 'mad about it'. *Harlequinade* was disliked by Beaumont, who didn't even show it to him. It was therefore agreed to drop *Perdita* and stage a single double-bill, consisting of *High Summer* and *The Browning Version*, with Gielgud as the repressed schoolmaster Crocker-Harris. From America Gielgud announced: 'I'd like to bring Terry's plays to the

States, and then tour the country, which I've never done.' But he then became pre-occupied with *Crime and Punishment*. Rattigan, in New York for the Broadway opening of *The Winslow Boy*, finally pressed him for a decision during a walk in Central Park.

There are two versions of what followed. According to Gielgud he told Rattigan, 'I have to be very careful what I play now.' But Rattigan remembers him saying, 'They've seen me in so much first-rate stuff, do you really think they will like me in anything second-rate?' Either way, it was an insensitive remark, even if not intentionally malicious. Rattigan was deeply wounded; even five years later he was unable to speak of the incident. With Gielgud still failing to make up his mind, he told Beaumont he was prepared to postpone the plays until after *Crime and Punishment* had finished. Beaumont wrote to Rattigan: 'Let us pray madness will shortly lift as cannot feel *Crime* will prosper.' For several months Rattigan pleaded with Gielgud, who then decided he didn't like *High Summer* after all, and turned down both plays.

Totally frustrated, Rattigan wrote releasing him from his commitment. In his reply Gielgud attempted to justify his behaviour:

> You know my childish and impetuous nature. If I don't start into something right away in the first flush of enthusiasm it is liable to go cold on me and then I am beset by doubts and fears . . . You are forgiving and sweet and believe me I do appreciate it and rejoice that our friendship has not been knocked, for I should regret that even more than having a failure in the theatre.

The Browning Version, with Emlyn Williams as Crocker-Harris, was such a success that after the London opening Gielgud shamelessly inquired about the possibility of playing it on Broadway. Once again other plans intervened, and it was ten years before he turned again to Rattigan.

Harlequinade was a light-hearted farce about a company rehearsing *Romeo and Juliet* in a Midlands town. Beaumont had kept it from Gielgud for some while, fearing he would react badly to what was clearly a send-up not just of Alfred Lunt and Lynn Fontanne, but of Gielgud himself. The play centred on Arthur Gosport, a scatter-brained, ageing actor-producer, who changes his mind up to the last moment about the best position for a pot of flowers. As with his first play *First Episode*, Rattigan drew on the traumatic experience of being directed by Gielgud in the OUDS *Romeo and Juliet*. He also satirised his habit of linking outside events to his current production; thus the General Strike was 'the year Gladys Cooper opened in *The Sign of the Door*'. Beaumont's dislike of this trifling piece took no account of Gielgud's new delight in self-mockery, as shown in his parody of his Hamlet in *Love for Love*.

When Gielgud finally came to work again in London, it was not as an actor but as a director, and of an American rather than an English play. *The Glass Menagerie*, first performed in New York in 1945, had established Tennessee Williams as a significant new playwright. His status had been confirmed two years later by *A Streetcar Named Desire*, for which Beaumont had the London rights. Up to now he had avoided staging it, feeling its powerful exploration of insanity and brutality, and its implicit homosexuality, would be too much for traditional West End audiences. So in July 1948 *The Glass Menagerie* became the first Tennessee Williams play to be staged in England.

It was Gielgud's first attempt at directing an American play, and at first he was reluctant to do it, especially with its American cast. Once again he was the victim of circumstances. Laurette Taylor, unforgettable as the mother in New York, had died, and Helen Hayes had agreed to replace her for the London production – even though she loathed the play. She suggested Elia Kazan as director, but Beaumont offered her either Guthrie or Gielgud. Williams suggested another American, Joshua Logan, but Beaumont stood firm, and the job went to Gielgud. Once engaged he became very enthusiastic: 'Fascinating play . . . extraordinary mixture of great gentleness and sudden brutality . . . all kinds of strange half-tones that make it terribly exciting for the director.'

The play, put on at the Haymarket, marked Helen Hayes' London début. In New York Gielgud had thought her superb as Queen Victoria in *Victoria Regina*, but he found her personality 'somehow too practical' for *The Glass Menagerie*. Later he described her as 'most professional and expert and a great pleasure to direct'; but Williams, watching rehearsals in Brighton, had a different recollection: 'The great Gielgud has never been, I'd say, much of a director, but Miss Hayes should not have happened to John,' he said. At one of the last rehearsals she called author, director and company to her dressing-room, and announced grandly: 'At this point in the making of a play, I know if it will go or it won't go.' She then shook her head slowly. Williams, fearing a disaster, decamped to Paris to join his friend Gore Vidal, and missed the London opening. A week later he passed through London: 'I saw a performance and it was just as bad as I had expected.

Menagerie can't be tricked. It has to be honestly and more than competently performed and directed.'

Although the critics found his dreamy, nostalgic memory play unfamiliar and difficult to take, they applauded the acting, and poured adulation on Helen Hayes. Some, including Coward, thought Gielgud's direction too deliberate, but others praised its assurance and delicacy. Harold Hobson, who had taken over from Agate at the *Sunday Times*, felt he directed faultlessly. Gielgud later described the production as a failure, which it clearly was not. It ran for 109 performances at the Haymarket, and prompted Sybil Thorndike to write to him: 'I've no words, I was moved intolerably – never since Duse has an actress moved me quite like this.' His negative opinion of the production was a reflection of his problems with Helen Hayes, and also with Williams, who never warmed to what he saw as the closed, effete theatrical circles in which Gielgud moved.

Gielgud tasted real failure, however, with the English production of *Medea* in September. Judith Anderson refused to play the title-role again, so Beaumont engaged his newest young star, the Scots actress Eileen Herlie, with Ralph Michael to play Jason and Cathleen Nesbitt the Nurse. Although Herlie thundered and blazed with great spirit in the try-out at the Edinburgh Festival, the critics compared her unfavourably with Judith Anderson, and attacked what they saw as a pedestrian and vulgar translation. Gielgud felt the production should not be brought to London, and on the first night at the Globe in September pointedly went to another play. *Medea* closed after just sixty-one performances.

Eileen Herlie's inability to convince stemmed in part from Gielgud's vacillation, as Elspeth March, one of the chorus, remembers:

His directing was awful. We would go through everything down to the last detail, and he would say it was absolutely perfect. Then he'd come in next morning and say he'd changed his ideas. This happened every day until the dress rehearsal, when Eileen decided enough was enough, and told him she was not going to change a single thing again. So of course he had to accept that. Later he wrote to me saying what a ghastly production it was, and how he'd failed us dismally.

After lunching at the Ivy with Gielgud that summer, Harold Hobson wrote in his diary: 'Found him very conscious that much is expected of him, and therefore careful about choosing a play for his return to the London stage after two years' absence.' It was eight months since he had acted anywhere, the longest gap yet. For a moment it seemed he might return to the Old Vic, but agreement about the choice of play proved too difficult. Having spoiled his chances with Rattigan he saw nothing new that attracted him. 'Just stick a crown on his head and send him onstage' was the attitude within Tennent's. But he had grown weary of the public's desire to see him in costume plays. 'They want another *Richard of Bordeaux*. Don't we all?' he said. 'But until one presents itself, I feel it better to appear in a museum piece of quality, rather than to stage a poor romantic play from the pen of a contemporary author.'

While St John Hankin's *Return of the Prodigal* was certainly a museum piece, dating from 1905, its quality was more in doubt. It was Sybil Thorndike's enthusiasm for the play that fired Gielgud's desire to appear in it. A slight story of a charming wastrel returning to cause mayhem amongst his respectable family, its satire now seemed inoffensive, its epigrammatic wit merely watered-down Wilde. Significantly, a bitter speech in which the hero denunciates society had been cut. But Gielgud defended his choice, saying the role 'gives me a golden opportunity to test my versatility, as it calls for a different style of acting. After all, I cannot go on playing Hamlet for ever.'

The play opened at the Globe in November, directed by Peter Glenville, and with a cast that included Sybil Thorndike, Irene Browne, Rachel Kempson and David Horne. Gielgud was nervous about his return to the London stage. 'I didn't really feel at ease on the first night,' he confided to a friend soon afterwards. Most critics felt he had been prodigal with his talent, in a role which required him to do little but be roguish, and loll about in a hammock in a youthful wig and plus-fours. Stephen Williams wrote witheringly: 'Anyone who saw him this week for the first time might be excused for wondering how he gained his resounding reputation.' The actors seemed uncertain whether to burlesque the story, while the sumptuous sets by Cecil Beaton tended to swamp the comedy. Beverley Baxter called it 'the best dressed and best acted bad play in London', and it closed after sixty-nine performances. 'It got too smart, too over-dressed,' Sybil Thorndike remembered. But Beaumont remarked grandly: 'It is caviare, and something that only appeals to us and the small group who are still interested in style, convention and manners.'

By this time Tennent's were dominating the West End with their expensive, star-studded 'Fortnum & Mason' productions. In May 1945 they inhabited eight of London's thirty-six theatres; by the following May the number had doubled. This domination, which continued throughout the 1950s and after, gave Beaumont enormous power, and led to questions in Parliament. Beaumont had strong likes and dislikes, and with his disproportionate influence could, as Guthrie pointed out, make or break the career of almost any actor in London. Many actors believed he had a spy in every company. 'I think that was true,' says Judy Campbell, a friend who later quarrelled with Beaumont. 'They were people who were playing small parts, or who had fallen on hard times and were happy to understudy. So Binkie knew everything that was going on.'

Beaumont's powerful position also prompted accusations that he gave favourable treatment to homosexuals when casting his productions, that there existed 'a gay mafia'. In an apochryphal story which reflected that belief he asked one of his directors: 'What did you cast *him* for, he's normal?' To which the director replied: 'I know Binkie, but it doesn't show on stage.' The director Bryan Forbes, then a young actor, has said that 'the Hollywood casting couch was for starlets in the States and stud boys in London'. But most actors, then and now, dismissed such a notion as rubbish. 'People got jobs because they were good,' Geoffrey Toone says. 'If they happened to be friends and also gay, there was no special treatment. The idea of a casting couch was ludicrous, as was the one that Binkie made a pass at all the good-looking boys.'

The post-war climate was still a dangerous one for homosexuals. The actor Max Adrian was one of many men imprisoned at the time for 'importuning'. Agate was on the point of being sacked by the *Sunday Times* after a police raid on a male brothel, and was only saved by his status as the country's leading critic. But the threat was not just from outside the profession. Wolfit, who believed theatre everywhere to be 'controlled by an international cartel of poufferie', received a letter from St John Ervine in which the critic stated: 'I like to see manly actors on stage. You're one. The next great crusade will be to purge the theatre of its pansies; but I can't get an article on the subject into print. Editors go all a-trembling at the very idea, yet everybody is *talking* about it.'

Gielgud of course was Tennent's greatest asset, but he now badly needed to re-establish his reputation. Despite problems with *The Glass*

Menagerie and *Medea*, he was still held in esteem as a West End director. When Beaumont drew up his short-list of first-class directors it consisted of Gielgud, Anthony Quayle, Peter Glenville and Michael Benthall. It was Gielgud that he now turned to in a crisis. *The Heiress*, an adaptation by Ruth and Augustus Goetz of Henry James's story *Washington Square*, starring Richardson and Peggy Ashcroft, had been in rehearsal for three weeks. But with only a week to go before the opening in Brighton the director John Burrell had been sacked.

The public story was that he had disagreed with the authors over his interpretation of their play. In reality he simply had difficulty in moving the actors around the stage. The result was a lifeless and static production, chaotic rehearsals, and an unhappy company. The design was by Motley, and there were angry exchanges over the set between Margaret Harris and the Goetzes. Richardson had rows with James Donald, who ended up hitting him. Gillian Howell, a junior member of the company, recalls: 'There was a huge amount of drama, with people being sacked daily: we were all convinced it would be us next.'

Gielgud arrived to take over after an evening performance of *The Return of the Prodigal.* 'An appalling botch has been made of the mechanics, and they are floundering in a morass of despair, so I can only try to do my best,' he wrote to a friend. 'It's a sheer exercise in improvisation ... but I fear it can be a patched result at best.' Beaumont had assured the company that 'this time John won't have time to change his mind', but the actors, including Peggy Ashcroft, were dubious. Gielgud assured them he only wanted to help, and would not change anything. Pauline Jameson recalls the effect of his arrival: 'He told us he'd had no time to read the play, so if we'd just run through the first act, he might be able to offer a few thoughts. This we did, starting about midnight. Then he began changing entrances, furniture, positions and moves. We could have gone all night, everyone became so alive.'

Gielgud felt that 'the blocking was appalling – they were strung out from side to side like a football team', that 'it was like a railway station, they never stopped milling around'. He tried different groupings, and reduced the action so attention could be paid to the dialogue. He created more atmosphere by altering the lighting, and had the set re-painted. Concerned about the period detail, he had new furniture brought in, and different pictures hung on the wall. He also helped the actors re-interpret their lines, and coaxed Richardson, who had just been in the film, to open out his performance for the theatre.

Peggy Ashcroft felt a weight being lifted from her shoulders. 'It was wonderful the way John came to our rescue and pulled us all out of a slough of despond,' she wrote after the opening. 'He has a quality hard to describe – "radiance" I think is the nearest word to it – that no one else has, and I think it is that which makes everyone love working for him.' Richardson wrote that 'he was in great form and has done a fine job'.

The Heiress was a brilliant success, both in Brighton and at the Haymarket, where it opened in February 1949, and ran for 644 performances. Thanks in great measure to Gielgud, the two principal actors attracted excellent notices. Hobson wrote of Peggy Ashcroft's beautiful rendering of James's jilted heroine that 'all superlatives are pale and feeble things', while Beverley Baxter suggested Richardson's Victorian father 'touches greatness'. Gielgud's fertile mind, so often a trial to actors, proved ideal for such an emergency. The Goetzes told him they preferred the production to Jed Harris's one in New York. Later Gielgud described it as 'one of the great moments of my life'.

In April his father died at the age of eighty-eight. Though he had often been ill in recent years, he had gone on working well into his eighties, refusing to accept retirement, until his employers simply removed his desk from his office. Gielgud's relationship with him had remained affectionate and solicitous, but distant: when he wrote home from abroad or on tour his letters were invariably addressed to his mother.

By now his mind was full of a play which was to give him his greatest success in a new work since *Richard of Bordeaux*, and restore his reputation as a great romantic actor. He owed the break to the actor Alec Clunes, who was establishing the Arts as a theatre doing interesting new plays. He had commissioned a work from the theatre's resident dramatist Christopher Fry: the result was the verse play *The Lady's Not for Burning*.

Fry, a conscientious objector, had based his hero Thomas Mendip on the tramps he had seen wandering around in army greatcoats at the end of the First World War. A disillusioned soldier who wishes to die, Mendip falls in love with a woman accused of being a witch, who wants to live. While Gielgud was in America Clunes had scored a brilliant success in the role, under the direction of Jack Hawkins. Now he generously agreed to sell the play to Tennent's, knowing it would have a better chance of a commercial run with Gielgud in his part.

Believing poetry allowed a playwright to say twice as much as prose in half the time, Fry had first been inspired to write plays in verse after seeing Gielgud's *Richard II* at the Old Vic. 'It released my thoughts about writing and creating something,' he says. Since then there had been isolated examples of verse plays, notably Eliot's *Murder in the Cathedral* and *The Family Reunion*, and Auden and Isherwood's *The Ascent of F6*. E. Martin Browne and Ashley Dukes had recently taken over the Mercury Theatre to stage plays in verse, which included Fry's *A Phoenix Too Frequent* as well as works by Norman Nicholson, Anne Ridler and Ronald Duncan. But it was *The Lady's Not for Burning* that brought verse drama into the West End, and prompted its brief flowering during the early 1950s.

When Gielgud read the script he thought it 'one of the finest plays I have read for many a day'. He then spent six months tortured with doubts about it. In October 1948 he wrote to Fry: 'My mind is going on about *The Lady* like a squirrel in a cage, and I read it at odd moments in my dressing-room and everywhere else with increasing pleasure.' In the weeks following he bombarded him with casting ideas and developments: 'Audrey Fildes would be awfully good as Alizon . . . I wonder if Esme Percy might do Skips . . . Nigel Stock is strongly fancied for Humphrey . . . Napier still not well: I like him so much and hate to drop him, but we must be practical.'

Pamela Brown was to star with Gielgud. Many in the final cast – Harcourt Williams, Nora Nicholson, Esmé Percy, Eliot Makeham – were on the elderly side. But Gielgud also recruited two promising youngsters: Claire Bloom, eighteen and just out of convent school, and a pock-marked young Welshman with fine features and mesmerising blue-green eyes, then under contract to Tennent's. Aged twenty-three, Richard Burton had just been dropped during rehearsals from Rattigan's *Adventure Story*, and was excessively nervous at the audition. Reading for the part of the clerk, he was confused and inaudible. But Gielgud scented talent, as Fry remembers: 'Pamela and I watched from the wings while Claire and Richard did the scene. Afterwards she said to me, "The girl's all right, but I don't think the boy's going to be very good." But John realised how nervous he was, and told him to talk to me about the part, then come back the next day.'

To avoid his usual actor/director dilemma, Gielgud persuaded Esmé Percy to act as co-director, to observe his performance from the front and offer criticisms. Percy was a versatile actor, who had trained in Sarah Bernhardt's company, and played nearly all the main parts in Shaw's plays, including Higgins in *Pygmalion* opposite Mrs Patrick

Campbell's Eliza. Short and plump, with only one eye – the result of being savaged by a dog – he had been notably handsome when young. He and Gielgud shared a love of theatrical history and a delight in telling stories, and they became close friends.

Fry had specially written the part of the supposed witch for Pamela Brown, an intelligent actress whom he admired for her ability to 'walk that little tightrope between tragedy and comedy'. A courageous woman, she had been hit by arthritis at sixteen, and had to be given injections during performances to ease the pain. Gielgud became immensely fond of her, while she referred to him affectionately but ironically as the 'Young Master'. Fry recalled: 'The two of them chimed together in and out of the theatre. They each had a relish for the comicalities of life, and neither had any touch of self-importance.'

Gielgud took a while to get to grips with the meaning of his lines. Pamela Brown remembered one rehearsal when he delivered a speech in a breathtakingly brilliant manner, and then without a pause said, 'Christopher, do tell me what it's all about, I don't know what I'm saying.' He became anxious about the play, and persuaded Fry to cut and re-write in several places. 'I entirely agreed with his suggestions, so it was easy to work with him,' Fry recalls.

It was not so easy for some of the younger actors. Peter Bull, terrified of working with him in his first major West End role, felt 'he was pretty bored by frightened actors'. He remembered the effect of Gielgud's continual changes: 'Most of the company were reduced to tears at some period, and one member succumbed to jaundice and disappeared into the night.' Claire Bloom found him short-tempered and disapproving. 'Do watch Richard and *try* to be natural!' he told her. As a result she became increasingly tense.

Even experienced actors such as Nora Nicholson were left floundering: 'At one rehearsal I called out to John, "I don't know how to say this line!" From the stalls came the stentorian command: "Say it!", and in some trepidation I said it.' But his notes to actors were often apposite, as Denis Quilley recalls: 'I was understudying Burton, and he said to me one day, "It's very nice, Squilley, very Norman and rounded, but can we get it a little more Gothic and pointed?" It was a good note: it needed more delicacy.'

During the pre-London tour Fry re-wrote further at Gielgud's instigation, and the cast rehearsed incessantly, submitting to yet more changes. 'It's always better when it's different!' Gielgud announced. Fry recalled that 'the spate of his directorial inventiveness was sometimes difficult to check'. Gielgud acknowledged the problem for the actors. 'I suppose one's mind can be too fertile,' he admitted. 'It just wells up in me.'

Audiences in the provinces seemed bewildered by the play, and some theatres were half empty. But in London, where it opened at the Globe in May, it created a sensation. There were criticisms of its slight plot and of Fry's failure to develop character, and some felt the play to be too over-stuffed with imagery, too self-consciously learned. But overall it was seen as a breath of fresh air in a time of austerity, what Alec Clunes called 'a release into the light'. Comparisons were made with Jonson, Marlowe, even Shakespeare; Darlington called Fry 'a young Shaw with a poet's mind'.

Fry was revealed as a writer of brilliant fancy and robust humour who used the English language to dazzling effect, producing verse full of fire and music that could be spoken with the speed of prose. Earthy and spiritual, grave and gay, his work had none of the solemnity of earlier verse drama, and it suited Gielgud perfectly. T.C. Worsley called *The Lady's Not for Burning* 'the best acted, best produced play running in London', while Tynan decided that 'Mr Gielgud's company spoke better than any other group of players in England; and for this the credit must be his'. The striking décor by Oliver Messel added to the romance and colour of the production.

Gielgud had brought a potentially uncommercial work to the West End, and the risk paid off: the play ran for nearly nine months before transferring to Broadway. It made Fry's reputation, and restored Gielgud's confidence and enthusiasm. 'Gielgud, letting loose his vocal music with a new and ringing vigour, played Mendip with unexpected virility of approach,' Audrey Williamson wrote. 'This was a transformed Gielgud, dirt-encrusted, black with scorn, robust rather than picturesque.' Yet many who had also seen Clunes in the part felt he failed to catch the rough, soldierly side of Mendip. Fifty years on Fry agrees: 'Alec was more ironic, he caught the bitter element, while John was more lyrical and romantic. His performance worked, but it wasn't the character I had seen in my mind.'

Fry was impressed by Gielgud's persistent desire to improve, his 'never-diminishing eagerness to learn his craft, as though he were always at the beginning of his career, and still seeing the fun of it'. Even after the play opened he remained unsatisfied, sometimes changing an entire scene between a matinée and an evening performance. After two months he wrote to Fry: 'Pam and I have overhauled the love scene a little, and I think it is better. Come and have a look at us again soon, so that we don't get too ragged.' Three months later he wrote: 'I had a good afternoon a week or so ago rehearsing the first act, simplifying and freshening. I play all the beginning far more slowly and detachedly and try to get your bomb-happy tipsiness.'

Gielgud later defended his doubling of the roles of director and leading actor: 'If you're in the play yourself, you can, two or three times a week, send little notes down, or you can rehearse a little bit before the play begins, or a little bit after,' he said. More than thirty years after *The Lady's Not for Burning* he was still sending little notes down to Fry: 'What fun to do the *Lady* again. Why not in modern dress? Stuffy parlour – Mayor in rabbit fur – Hippie boys in jeans – Jennifer dressed by Lanvin – Thomas in battledress.'

The production pushed Burton into the theatrical spotlight. With his powerful brooding Welsh presence he virtually stole one scene from Gielgud and Pamela Brown, even though he had few lines, and was on his knees scrubbing the floor for most of it. Far from being put out, Gielgud was impressed by his theatrical instinct: 'The first time we went through the scene he felt immediately, without any direction, exactly where he should matter in it, and where he should obliterate himself,' he recalled. 'He just did everything right, and he seemed to have no fear.'

Burton, he felt, was 'a dream prince'. He now invited him to play a key part in the last scene of *Richard of Bordeaux*, which he had agreed to perform for a charity matinée in aid of Equity. The role still held its potency for him, as Peter Bull recalled: 'At the first reading John sat in a chair wearing a hat and reading from a script. Suddenly he threw hat and script away and played the rest of the scene word-perfect with tears rolling down his cheeks. We were moved to speechlessness and very near tears ourselves.' His performance at the Coliseum, Bull remembered, 'brought the house down. As he went offstage Gielgud turned to the other actors with glistening eyes and said, "Well, we had a jolly good blub."'

Never keen to rest, he took on another directing assignment during the run of *The Lady's Not for Burning*. A gentle farce by M.J. Farrell and John Perry, *Treasure Hunt* was set in an Irish country-house, and bursting with eccentric Irish characters. Though lacking the bite and freshness of the writers' earlier *Spring Meeting*, it ran for nearly a year at the Apollo. It was typical Tennent's fare: cosy, undemanding, with a glitzy cast that included Lewis Casson, Marie Löhr and Sybil

Thorndike, whose playing of an eccentric aunt *Theatre World* called 'the comedy performance of the year'. Gielgud wrote to Fry: 'Wonderful that *Treasure Hunt* is a big hit. It has very funny things in it, though also some very thin patches – we are lucky.'

It was the first time he had directed Sybil Thorndike, who had picked him out at RADA all those years ago. Her generosity, diligence and modesty reminded him of Ellen Terry, and he warmed to her as he never did to Edith Evans: 'Edith was the greater actress, Sybil the greater woman,' he observed. 'Sybil was a leader, a giver, not self-centred – professional to her fingertips, disciplined, punctual, kind.' He admired, perhaps even envied, her ability to get on with all kinds of people.

In rehearsal some of the less experienced actors felt the edge of Gielgud's tongue. Terence Longdon remembers him sacking one actress: 'John didn't like her, he used to say to her, "You point too much, you have such big fingers." He told me off too: "You're too like Roger Livesey," he'd say. I don't think he meant to be unkind, those sharp, spiky remarks just slipped out.' Meanwhile Tanya Moisiewitch, the play's designer, was steadily adding items to the set as Gielgud's ideas mushroomed. 'One day,' she recalls, 'when I queried how a set of Chinese armour would find its way to Ireland, he replied: "Never mind, it will be a good item to have for the treasure hunt."'

With the Fry and Goetz plays continuing, he now had three successes running simultaneously in the West End. 'I think he is rather exhausted with directing and acting,' his sister Eleanor wrote. 'I hope he may take it a bit more easily for a bit, though knowing him, I doubt it!' She was right. Keen to work with Burton again, and enchanted by Fry's *The Boy with a Cart*, he risked giving this slight, immature work its first professional production, in a double-bill with Barrie's *Shall We Join the Ladies?* at the Lyric, Hammersmith.

Written for a local amateur festival in 1938, the play concerned the early life of St Cuthman. Burton, in the title-role, gave a moving performance; Gielgud thought him 'spell-binding'. Fry remembers that he rehearsed Burton with tears running down his cheeks, working hard 'trying to get him loosened up'. Beaumont noticed that he was getting Burton to lose some of his rough edges, and allowing his natural charm to surface. As a result of his performance, Burton was offered the parts of Prince Hal and Henry V in Stratford's Festival of Britain offering of the *Henry* plays. His career then went into spectacular orbit. Gielgud remained his idol for life.

Around this time one astute critic observed: 'To renew himself as a true player of roles Mr Gielgud needs to divest himself of all he has put on, pare himself down to the bone, and start out in a different direction.' This he now did in dramatic fashion, working for the first time with a director who, like Komisarjevsky and Barker, was to have a profound influence on his continuing development as an actor.

24

Stratford and Peter Brook

I feel like a new boy at school.
(Gielgud at the start of the
Stratford season, 1950)

G IELGUD had never acted at Stratford. Ever since his success at the Old Vic the critics had been suggesting he was exactly the kind of actor needed there. But the Memorial Theatre was then more a local than a national theatre. Its productions were cheap, shoddy and old-fashioned, and between the wars many actors considered it professional suicide to play there. Change came under Barry Jackson, who began a post-war renaissance by creating a permanent company of young actors.

In 1948 Anthony Quayle and Michael Benthall took over, and introduced a policy of using West End stars. Determined to make Stratford 'the highspot of Shakespearean acting and production' – the Old Vic was now on the wane – Quayle recruited Beaumont on to the board of governors. 'Beaumont could go to an actor like Gielgud, and say, "There's nothing in London for you at the moment, so go off to Stratford like a good salmon, and swim in the sea,"' he recalled. Indebted to Gielgud for helping him as a young actor, he now offered him for the 1950 season the plum parts of Lear, Cassius, Benedick, and Angelo in *Measure for Measure*.

Despite the meagre salary of £50 a week, Gielgud agreed without hesitation. Here at last was another chance to play Shakespeare in repertory. 'The big tragedies cannot be played night after night; they are too exhausting,' he told the press. It was five years since he had played Shakespeare in England, but his drawing power was undiminished. Quayle, sensing the demand, began the season in

March, a month earlier than usual. More than 70,000 seats were sold in advance for what the critic of *The Times* labelled 'a festival that promises to be the most important in the history of Stratford'.

The company was the strongest yet assembled there. Gielgud's leading ladies were Peggy Ashcroft, Diana Wynyard, Gwen Ffrangcon-Davies and nineteen-year-old Barbara Jefford. Among the men were stalwarts such as Harry Andrews, Leon Quartermaine, Andrew Cruikshank and Quayle himself. The rising stars included Alan Badel and Maxine Audley. Gielgud was apprehensive: 'I feel like a new boy at school,' he said. 'It's awful to have reached a stage when you worry about possibly making a fool of yourself in front of other actors.'

The director of the first play of the season in March, the rarely staged *Measure for Measure*, was Peter Brook, at twenty-six already considered the most exciting young director in the English theatre. Small, dapper, he was likened to a malicious cherub; Barry Jackson called him 'the youngest earthquake I know'. He had already caused a stir at Stratford four years before with his startlingly original productions of *Love's Labour's Lost* and *Romeo and Juliet*, prompting comparisons with Komisarjevsky's revolutionary work there. Combining a genius for invention with great visual flair, he not only designed his own sets and costumes, but also created the lighting and music.

Fifty years on Brook has become a revered figure, admired for his brilliant experimental work and his uncompromising approach to theatre. But actors have often feared him, or disliked his severe, purist approach, and in 1950 he was already known as an *enfant terrible*. Yet Gielgud took to him immediately, even though they sometimes disagreed. He found Brook 'approachable and jolly', and admired his thoroughness, his cosmopolitan taste and fertile imagination. 'Peter gets on magnificently with those actors he gets on with,' he said later. Brook respected Gielgud's flexibility and openness, and his restless quest for perfection. 'The experience of working with him has been amongst my most special and my greatest joys,' he wrote later in *The Empty Space*.

Brook found a way to channel Gielgud's torrent of ideas. 'His mind worked at fantastic speed, and he had so many ideas going at once, you had to encourage him to explore in every direction possible, then help him to do the editing he wouldn't do without you,' he recalls. He wanted Gielgud to curb his histrionic tendencies and his love of emotional effects. 'I made it quite clear to him that the more romantic sort of acting no longer fitted the bill, and he was totally open and sympathetic to that.'

Gielgud always worked well with directors who were straight with him without being destructive, and he respected Brook's honesty. 'One wants to be told when one is bad and false, but one doesn't want to be put down so that one loses confidence,' he said. Deeply self-critical, he was willing to cut and discard, usually without regret. Brook later compared his adaptability to Olivier's rigidity, observing of the latter that 'once a conception had taken root in him, no power could change the direction in which the ox would pull the cart'.

To play Angelo Gielgud exploited his repressed sexuality to explosive effect, notably in the scene when Angelo first realises he wants to seduce the chaste Isabella: one observer said it seemed as if he had an orgasm when he first touched her. On the first night he experienced the same feeling of relaxation he had felt as Trofimov in *The Cherry Orchard* at Oxford, but which for some years now had eluded him. It was a sign that he had found the character.

After the opening he wrote cheerfully to a friend: 'We had a wonderful reception and I look forward to a very happy season.' In his chilling, unsparing performance, Hobson wrote, it was as if Angelo was 'looking into his soul for the first time'. Worsley suggested that he had always been haunted by Hamlet: 'Now with his Angelo he makes a break – it may be a complete break – with his past'; in his characterisation 'there are no traces of the romantic gestures, no echoes of the youthful tones'. The tone fitted Brook's production, which was less showy than his earlier ones at Stratford, imaginative rather than merely inventive – a change, Tynan suggested, that reflected Gielgud's moderating influence.

Gielgud retained his new toughness in *Julius Caesar*. He had opted to play the lean and hungry Cassius rather than the more obvious choice of the idealistic, gentler Brutus, a character often seen as a first sketch for Hamlet. When they were boys his brother Val had told him Cassius was the best part, and he had wanted to play him ever since. On the first night he gave a performance of such sustained vehemence that it electrified not only critics and audience, but also his fellow-actors. Andrew Cruikshank, playing Caesar, was listening from below the stage to his first scene with Brutus: 'Cassius' vitriolic passion I had never heard the like of before. "What's happening?" I said to Quayle. Gielgud had done nothing like this at rehearsal.'

His outpouring stemmed partly from a build-up of frustration and anxiety, for rehearsals had been fraught. The original director, Michael Langham, had never worked with a big company before, nor with an actor of Gielgud's stature. In his memoirs Quayle records that after a few days Gielgud said he could not cope with Langham, that he would have to go, and that he duly went. But Langham, now a leading director, remembers a different scenario:

> John obviously regarded me with suspicion, this callow youth, speaking when he wasn't asked to speak. I was very nervous of him, and there's nothing more frightening for a leading actor than to feel he's being directed by somebody who doesn't know how to cope with him. He didn't know how to cope with me either, but I didn't understand how nervous he was, I thought everything was my fault. After a couple of weeks Tony Quayle said he thought it would be better if *he* directed the scenes in which Gielgud appeared. My relationship with the rest of the company was excellent, so I continued with the production. But I was devastated, I felt a complete failure. Once the play was on John was extremely kind. We talked and he said, 'I'm sorry, I've been an absolute pig, but I was very nervous.'

The other problem concerned Gielgud's interpretation of Cassius, which Quayle told him was overly romantic, and more suited to Brutus. He tried to get Gielgud to find the tough, embittered soldier in Cassius, suggesting he think of 'the hard men in bowler hats coming out of the Ministry of War', disappointment on their faces because they had been passed over for promotion. Gielgud at first resisted Quayle's idea, but then complied, and surprised everyone, himself included, with the blazing intensity of his performance.

Although the production was a success with the public, Gielgud disliked the large Stratford stage, which made it difficult to be heard above the noise of the citizens and soldiers. Geoffrey Bayldon recalls his frustration: 'As a fellow-conspirator I was just behind him for one entrance. My neck was hurting because of the spirit gum used to attach my wig, and I suddenly heard myself saying, "I hate this fucking play!" The toga in front of me quivered, and I held my breath: this was a time when one didn't swear in the presence of the Almighty Ones. Gielgud looked over his shoulder, said "So do I!" – and strode on to the stage.'

The season continued with a production that was to become one of his most cherished. At Quayle's invitation he had directed *Much Ado About Nothing* at Stratford the previous year, with the elegantly beautiful Diana Wynyard and Quayle himself as Beatrice and

Benedick. It was a light, witty and assured piece of work – the critic Richard Findlater thought it among the best Shakespearean productions he had seen – and was praised for the colourful Renaissance sets and costumes designed by Mariano Andreu: 'Loveliness is the mark of all Gielgud's work,' Hobson wrote.

For the 1950 revival Gielgud took over as Benedick. The new Beatrice was Peggy Ashcroft, also making her début at Stratford, and acting with Gielgud for the first time in five years. Gielgud saw a chance to exploit the showy, romantic, Fred Terry element in his acting; but he also saw it as 'a wonderful partner part'. Yet the partnership did not click immediately, for Ashcroft saw the role differently from Diana Wynyard. Gielgud told her, 'You must come on with a lot of panache,' but she resisted, preferring to play Beatrice as natural, blunt and tactless rather than witty and sophisticated. She also refused to wear the grand dresses and headgear worn by Diana Wynyard. In both cases Gielgud wisely let her follow her instincts.

His usual last-minute changes irritated Harry Andrews, playing Don Pedro. 'I can't cope with this sort of thing at this stage,' he said angrily. Gielgud replied: 'Oh yes, of course, Harry, you are rather slow, aren't you? All right then, just do it your way.' Once again he neglected his own part in rehearsal, making Ashcroft increasingly nervous. But on the first night, she remembered, 'he *saw* Benedick. I've never experienced it before, he gave such a dazzling, brilliant performance, suddenly it was like dancing with a partner you can follow.' They had, unusually, drunk a bottle of champagne before going on and, according to Gielgud, 'never played so well in our lives'. He was twenty years too old for the part, but this was forgotten in his relaxed and witty playing, and the gaiety and harmony he and Ashcroft found as they fought the 'merry war' of words.

His Benedick established Gielgud's mastery of Shakespearean high comedy as never before. The writer Eleanor Farjeon came five times, and told him that 'Henry Irving is the second-best Benedick I have ever seen'. Of the fresh and sparkling performances which Gielgud and Ashcroft achieved, Worsley wrote: 'Over-riding everything else, they play so beautifully together, they set off each other's best points, call out in each other the highest art ... They double the value of their individual performances.' It was a partnership that gained from being based on a warm and loving professional relationship.

During the season Gielgud still had problems with his appearance. At the dress rehearsal for *Much Ado* he appeared wearing padded tights that gave him tremendous great calves ('I thought it would make me a more manly Benedick'), but reluctantly discarded them after Quayle told him he looked ridiculous. He never did find Benedick's more soldierly qualities to his own satisfaction. Years later, when Donald Sinden was rehearsing the role, he suggested to Gielgud that it was Beatrice rather than Benedick who was the witty one. Gielgud replied: 'Oh you're perfectly right. I made a great mistake there. Benedick is a very boorish fellow; you'll be much better than I was.'

Peter Brook recalls a more fundamental visual error over his costume for *Measure for Measure*: 'Inspired by Angelo's name, he came on at the dress rehearsal in a great Pre-Raphaelite head of locks, which a wigmaker friend had made secretly. "John!" I cried out in horror. "Don't you like it?" he said. "It's dreadful, outrageous, you can't possibly go on the stage like that!" I replied. He paused for a moment, looked disappointed, then pulled off the wig, and said: "Farewell my youth!" – and played for the first time with a bald head.'

Such incidents endeared him to the company, as did his unselfishness on stage, remembered by Barbara Jefford: 'I was just out of drama school, and very nervous at playing with such august people. But he was exceedingly generous, telling me at certain moments to get in the dominant upstage position because it was my bit.' She was also surprised by one aspect of his technique: 'He used to turn up stage, and swallow in a certain way, and when he turned round he'd be streaming with tears. You could hear them falling on the stage.'

Young actors tended then to be more reverential towards the stars. This, and Gielgud's detached manner, could make for awkwardness offstage. 'He was always a little apart when notes were given,' Geoffrey Bayldon remembers. 'He wanted to be easy, but found it difficult. He would come to the pub and try to be one of the boys, but it creaked a bit, he was elegantly distant and people were rather nervous of him. He was at his best sitting in the green room, talking about the Terrys, and Fred and Julia touring in open cars with their furs and caviare.'

Then and later, actors were amused by his unworldliness. John Nettleton remembers a long dress rehearsal for one Stratford production: 'Gielgud said, "We'll have a break now, and we'll all go away and have our lovely dinners." I was on £7 a week and only had about four shillings left.' Another time he asked Paul Hardwick where he was living, whether he was in a flat. Hardwick started to explain that it was just a single room, at the top of the stairs, with a gas ring – 'Oh don't go on, it's too sordid!' Gielgud interrupted. Later he asked Oliver

Cotton the same question, adding: 'Do you have someone who comes in and does for you? I do loathe making my own bed.'

During the 1950 season he joined in happily with the Shakespeare birthday celebrations: 'I am just recovering from making endless speeches and walking in processions, but it was all rather fun,' he told Christopher Fry. He also carried out other civic duties, including judging the Stratford floral queen competition. More appropriately, he gave a speech at the unveiling in the theatre of a memorial window to Frank Benson, in which he diplomatically claimed to have 'admired and loved Lady Benson for all she had taught him, and had founded all his work on her teaching'.

He ended the season with his third attempt at Lear, with Peggy Ashcroft as Cordelia, Maxine Audley and Gwen Ffrangcon-Davies as Goneril and Regan, Leon Quartermaine as Gloucester, and Harry Andrews as Edgar. 'I have very careful notes of the Granville Barker production, which Mr Quayle and I intend to follow,' he explained. With Quayle as notional co-director, the pupil remained devoted as ever to his master's ideas. Andrew Cruikshank, playing Kent, recalled him at rehearsals, consulting his copy of the play, then shouting out: 'Barker told me that I should play this scene as though there were a pain shooting through my head!' Alan Badel, however, preferred to develop his own concept of the Fool. Having recommended Badel to Quayle, Gielgud let him go his own way to avoid a confrontation. He found his arrogance intimidating: during one performance one of the actors was alarmed to find him standing in the wings on the wrong side of the stage. 'Don't worry,' he explained, 'I'm just hiding from Alan Badel.'

Fifty years later Barbara Jefford remembers Gielgud's Lear as 'the best I've ever seen, it was so deeply moving'. Peggy Ashcroft thought he brought 'a robust virility to the role'. At the dress rehearsal he had many actors in tears. After the opening he reported: 'We had a wonderful reception and absolute stillness for three and a half hours, which was a wonderful tribute.' But as usual on first nights – there were then no previews – he was nervous and exhausted. His playing seemed to some critics subdued and detached, though still intensely moving in the reconciliation scene with Cordelia. Worsley, one of the more perceptive critics, sensed he had more to offer, and returned the following night. He found a Lear transformed.

On the first night, he wrote, you admired Gielgud's performance intellectually; on the second it drew you in emotionally, so that he no longer seemed to be acting. He made the inevitable comparison with

Olivier. 'If Mr Gielgud is the great tragic actor par excellence of our generation, is it not by virtue of his ability to exhibit the particular kind of simplicity that lies at the heart of passion in highly conscious, complicated personalities?' Both Olivier and Wolfit, he suggested, 'strike harder, clearer, louder at the note of the majestic or the terrible, but they oversimplify'; Gielgud, by contrast, gives due weight to 'the ironies, the irresolutions, the subtleties' of the character.

One elderly woman who had seen Irving's Lear wrote after the first night: 'As the final curtain fell, and I wiped my tears, I would fain have had the whole begin again that I might realise and remember the more completely the glory of it all.' Kate Gielgud, at eighty-two, was still a fervent admirer of her son's work, and still attending all his first nights. 'I can only be thankful that I lived to see John so wholly master of his art and his public, great actor and great artist,' she wrote. 'To have heard his voice break in "Howl, howl, howl, howl" and die in infinite tenderness on a final "never" of utter desolation is to hold a memory unspeakably exquisite.'

The season did wonders both for Stratford and Gielgud. It considerably enhanced the theatre's reputation for staging Shakespeare, and laid the foundations for the high-quality work produced in subsequent seasons under Glen Byam Shaw and Peter Hall. It also broke all records at the box-office: the season was extended for an extra month, and towards the end people were queuing all night for unreserved seats. For Gielgud it was a milestone, and a welcome return to repertory. He had taken risks, overcome his fear of playing unsympathetic parts, exploited hitherto unseen facets of his personality, and in doing so deepened and widened his range. Peter Brook saw a new Gielgud, saying of his Angelo that 'there was more of the essential John in it than had been seen for a long time, and less of the superficial, extravagant and tricksy John'.

In the autumn *The Lady's Not for Burning* was performed in America. Gielgud had decided not to play Mendip on Broadway, but then wrote to Fry: 'I don't really think it's much good trying to get anyone to replace me if it's to be only a second-grade actor – if I may be excused for appearing conceited in saying so. Donat, Olivier and Scofield seem to be the only real attractive possibilities, and you'd not get any of them. Portman, Clunes, Clements – none of these seem very exciting to me – but perhaps you disagree?' He eventually opted to continue in the part, with a company that included Pamela Brown and Burton, but Penelope Munday in place of Claire Bloom.

In November Tennessee Williams wrote to a friend: 'There is a feeling here that his play will be a tremendous hit.' It was exactly that in Boston, especially amongst the young; but its poetic humour was received in silence at the previews at the Royale in New York. The first night was little better: soon afterwards, writing to Fry, who was now back in England, Gielgud complained about the 'fiercely antique' and 'deadly' audiences, but was still hoping for 'a few normally chuckling reactions'. New Yorkers were having problems with Fry's rich vocabulary as well as the English accents: one observer noticed that the lines getting the best response were those reprinted beforehand in the *New Yorker*.

Ultimately the play was a success, and with 151 performances ran into spring 1951. Brooks Atkinson said Fry had 'restored the art of literature to the stage'; the text of his play entered the best-sellers' list; and *Time* magazine ran an eight-page profile of him. A buoyant Gielgud, praised again for his virtuoso performance, told Fry: 'All the reporters clamour for intimate details of your life and personal behaviour, till I tell them I am getting bored describing you as a dear, and modest and ideal to work with.' He was, he confessed, still tinkering with the text: 'I made one or two little cuts in Boston, and I do hope you wouldn't mind them too badly. The first cut was tricky the first night. Richard *will* drop the last three words of his sentences so he gets too flat in his opening scene.'

When Burton had to leave to prepare for his Stratford season, he was replaced by Trader Faulkner, a raw young Australian. 'Gielgud could really lash with his tongue, and he gave me a terrible time,' he recalls. 'Once he said to me, "There's a terrible compost in your vowels: go round the block saying, 'Brown's cows go round and round the town house.'" But the more I tried to please him, the more awkward I became, which irritated him even more. Another time he said: "You have the most unfortunate crooked teeth, you really should have something done to straighten them," – so I had a brace put in. It was all very hard to take. Then one night he said, "You were every bit as good as Burton", and I just burst into tears.'

Gielgud enjoyed Burton's company as well as his looks, and went with him and others to night clubs in Harlem. He also relished the company of Esmé Percy, who held court in Greenwich Village after the show, entertaining people with impersonations of Sarah Bernhardt and a fund of theatrical stories to match his own. But he also had time for the less assured members of the company. Penelope Munday recalls:

'He was quite protective towards me, he invited me to dinner with the others, and generally kept an eye. That slightly superficial, cultured, upper-class charm was very beguiling, you couldn't help but love him for it. And he was always so full of life and energy.'

Gielgud found much to criticise in New York, as he told Fry:

The kindness and welcome are overwhelming, but there is too much money, food and drink, and too much respect for success – while endeavour and failure are just ignored, or swept away, as if there wasn't any time or place for them . . . The people here are hungrier even than ours for new beauties, only sometimes the trash theatre that is sold and fed them in such relentless streams cloys up their spirits with vulgarity.

As a contribution to the 1951 Festival of Britain he next played Leontes in *The Winter's Tale*, under the direction once more of Peter Brook. Despite the fairy-tale quality of the mysterious and disconnected story, and the obscurity of much of the verse, Gielgud liked the play's theatrical surprises, and believed it could be made convincing if staged imaginatively. Having seen the 1948 production at Stratford, he had been intrigued by the character of the insanely jealous Leontes, but doubted if he could convey convincingly an emotion he so rarely felt. His Angelo and Cassius had made him change his mind.

The company included Diana Wynyard as Hermione, Flora Robson as Paulina, George Rose as Autolycus, and Virginia McKenna as Perdita. Brook wanted to break Gielgud of his habit of watching the other actors' performance, and neglecting his own. 'He had that tremendous rapidity of improvising, so he could wing it,' he says. 'But he knew that wasn't really as good as being in the part. If he trusted a director, he could start work on his own part earlier.'

With *The Winter's Tale* he seems to have done this almost too well. Virginia McKenna was off for the first few performances, and Gielgud called Tennent's to say her understudy, Frances Hyland, was a disaster. Brook came to see her, and told Gielgud that on the contrary she was just perfect. 'Yes, she's absolutely right,' Gielgud agreed. Brook said: 'But I got a message from you that she was terrible.' Gielgud replied: 'I did say that, but I hadn't looked.'

According to Margaret Wolfit, who played an attendant, it was not a happy production. 'Peter Brook was a difficult man and he stirred up trouble, though I don't think he meant to,' she recalls. 'It was all a bit fraught.' Virginia McKenna has a similar recollection. 'I was just starting out and felt apprehensive and insecure. Peter didn't have that touch that puts young people at their ease and brings the best out of them.' Her memory of Gielgud is different. 'He was very kind and friendly, he relaxed you. He had no side, no grandeur, he just made you feel one of the team. He was wonderful with the young actors, you could ask him anything. I loved him.'

As with Angelo, Gielgud found it harder than before to learn a new Shakespearean part. But his concentration on his own role paid off with a performance of intense power. John Barber wrote: 'Dressed in hectic red, tall and tortured and rigid, he commands the bare, black stage like a fury.' Yet he made the monstrous Leontes seem human, even pitiable, and his apparently motiveless jealousy of his wife believable. In the famous reconciliation scene and the unveiling of Hermione's statue he created moments of supreme poignancy.

He was much helped by Brook's simple, straightforward production, which integrated the pastoral and court scenes much more effectively than usual. Brook talked about journeys, about Shakespeare's feeling for going on an adventure and coming home, and about reconciliation, and Gielgud found this valuable. Building on his work at Stratford, he showed that his new-found ability to 'tear open his soul' was no temporary development. His Leontes, Findlater observed, was 'lit by the incandescent fire of maturing genius'.

The production, opening in June, set a new record for the play, its 166 performances at the Phoenix beating Forbes-Robertson's 1887 production at the Lyceum. Once again Gielgud was promoting the classics in the West End by, as Worsley put it, 'turning the Number Two Shakespearean parts into Number One achievements'. He had not been seen in London for eighteen months, and his return was greeted rapturously. 'Wonderful, wonderful,' the gallery chorused on the opening night. Yet a month into the run, while being photographed for *Picture Post* as he made up for Leontes, Gielgud was in a mood of uncertainty, expressing the fear that 'London may tire of me'.

His fears were shown to be groundless when, at the start of 1952, he revived *Much Ado About Nothing* in London. It ran for a record 225 performances at the Phoenix, surpassing the 212 achieved by Ellen Terry and Irving at the Lyceum. His Benedick was hailed all over again for its abundant gaiety. Paul Scofield, playing Don Pedro and acting with Gielgud for the first time, was struck by his spontaneity in a role he had played so many times: 'John's style and wit were superlative,' he recalls. 'He would seem to have spoken a witticism before he realised what he meant by it; his understanding of what he had said was simultaneous with the moment of impact of the line.'

Chattie Salaman, in a walk-on part, recalled another aspect of his performance: 'Diana Wynyard was a bit stodgy and not very confident, but John helped her along, he nurtured her with incredible courtesy.' But there were signs that he was tiring of the play. In the middle of the dress rehearsal he called out to George Rose, a much-admired Dogberry, 'Oh George, *do* be funny!' Trader Faulkner also received another verbal lashing. Dressed in 'Botticelli green' as the messenger who begins the play, he was required to leap about from rostrum to podium: 'For God's sake stop swinging backwards and forwards like a green-baize door,' Gielgud said. 'You're not in vaudeville.'

Twenty-one and making her West End début as Hero, Dorothy Tutin had joined the cast with great expectations. 'I'd been told that John was very imaginative and inventive, and that you must be very open to his ideas,' she recalls. 'But he didn't seem to know what to do with me. I remember him saying, "This scene is a terrible bore, what can we do with Dorothy? I know, give the poor girl a fan." So I walked up and down with this fan, trying to be bright and sparky, and he said, "Oh that's so much better." That was the last note I had from him.'

Yet once the play was running Gielgud kept trying to improve it. John Moffatt, playing Verges, recalled him suddenly announcing: 'These Watch scenes are getting dreadfully common. Send all the costumes to the cleaners, and George, take that terrible nose off and wear a ring!' The next day, in their newly cleaned costumes, the actors decided to go over the top. They changed their make-up, dropped the comic voices, and played the scene younger, in the accents of a vicarage tea-party. Moffatt remembered Gielgud standing in the wings, tears of laughter running down his cheeks.

During the run he had a rare encounter with Donald Wolfit, whose daughter Margaret was understudying Beatrice. 'My father came to see me when I had to go on one night,' she recalls. 'Afterwards he went round to see Gielgud, and told him he thought I'd done quite well. Then he said rather grudgingly, "And you've had quite good notices too." This was passed on to me by Gielgud with a degree of humour.'

Despite his personal success at Stratford two years earlier, Gielgud had not been satisfied with the overall standard of verse-speaking. He was still talking about the need for a permanent company 'that would combine the best traditions of style and beautiful speaking with the vigour and thrust of the modern world', and advocating an Elizabethan stage so that a Shakespeare play 'would speak for itself'. But when he returned to Stratford in 1952 to direct Ralph Richardson and Margaret Leighton in *Macbeth* he was looking for a middle way: 'If one is too revolutionary, people are horrified; if one is too conventional, people are bored,' he said. 'The secret is to take the best of the old and the new, neither despising tradition nor being a slave to it.'

Macbeth was one of the rare productions for which he designed the set himself, in this instance with Michael Northern. He avoided the traditional attempt to reflect eleventh-century Scotland, and instead used black velvet drapes to suggest a timeless setting. 'The less realistic we can make it, the better, because it is a story of the timeless conflict between good and evil,' he announced. In an effort to avoid the usual 'melodramatic horned helmets, cloaks falsely baronial, bagpipes, tartans and the rest of it', he commissioned Samurai-style costumes based on Japanese prints he had seen in the British Museum. His bold, innovative set design owed a debt to Craig, and anticipated abstract settings later used by Devine and Brook.

John Nettelton, playing an attendant, remembers Gielgud in rehearsal: 'He was forever on the balls of his feet, dancing and watching, chain smoking his Turkish oval cigarettes, and leaping forward to change things all the time. At the dress rehearsal we came on for the final walkdown with flaming torches. Suddenly there was a shriek from the stalls: "It's too much like *White Horse Inn!*" So at the last minute the scene was completely re-set.'

In public Richardson praised Gielgud's work: 'He brings no detailed notes, he has no obsession about unalterable positions,' he said. 'He fits in with the mood of the players, his mind superbly flexible.' But Gielgud was having enormous problems with him. Richardson was not made for the great, blazing tragic roles: his elusive, poetic skills made him more suited to characters of comic pathos such as Cyrano or Falstaff, or roles such as Bottom, Caliban or Enobarbus. Before the war he had failed as Othello, and the evil, ambitious Macbeth, a man without humour, was quite beyond his range.

At odds with the part, he was a picture of misery in rehearsal. Gielgud became increasingly anxious, and told him he seemed more like a businessman than a murderer. 'You could see Ralph wasn't satisfying him,' Ian Bannen recalled. 'As time went by he got more critical and more agitated; he would get very tense when something wasn't right. I overheard him in the corridor saying to Ralph: "You're standing all wrong, you have to stand foursquare, Macbeth is a man of iron and steel." But Ralph's confidence never improved.'

His mood was also caused by the collapse of his affair with Margaret Leighton, who had fallen for Laurence Harvey, playing Malcolm. Richardson's lack of belief in himself was apparent, and he walked through the opening night in a puzzled, trance-like state, his verse-speaking betraying his anxiety. The critics had a field day. Tynan declared himself 'unmoved to the point of paralysis', and venomously attacked both actor and director: 'It was John Gielgud, never let us forget, who did this cryptic thing . . . who seems to have imagined that Ralph Richardson, with his comic, Robeyesque cheese-face, was equipped to play Macbeth . . . The production assumed, or so I took it, that the audience was either moronic or asleep.'

Richardson summed up his failure for Gielgud: 'If I can't see the dagger, cocky, can you wonder the audience can't either?' Yet Gielgud admired his performance, writing to Christopher Fry: 'I did think the critics a bit too much, especially for poor Ralph, who is so much more worth watching, even when he lacks the last jump, than some conceited and showy actors we could think of. I do hope he will recover from the blows and steadfastly build up the fine things in his performance, which are many.' Playing Leontes in London, he never saw the play in performance. 'I am desolated not to be able to see it with an audience, and give notes on pace – that is, I think, where much of the weakness lies,' he told Fry.

Even after finishing in *The Winter's Tale* he was unable to get to Stratford: the day after the last performance he flew to America, for a very different Shakespearean assignment.

25

From Hollywood to Hammersmith

> He sure knows his way around the meanings.
> (Marlon Brando, on working with Gielgud
> on *Julius Caesar*, 1952)

GIELGUD had not made a film since *The Prime Minister* in 1940. 'I detest filming: the stage is my medium,' had been a constant refrain for years. Yet having scorned Hollywood, and made clear his dislike of Shakespeare on film, he had agreed to appear in the MGM version of *Julius Caesar*. What changed his mind?

His attitude to filming had already softened during the war. He had asked Olivier if he might play the Chorus in his film of *Henry V*, but Olivier had turned him down, offering him only the small part of the King of France. The film was hugely successful, and in 1947 Olivier again directed himself in Shakespeare on the screen, this time in *Hamlet*. This may have prompted Gielgud's surprise announcement the following year that he would not appear in another film unless he directed it himself. Few actors were less cut out for the role, as he later admitted. Yet this was never a serious ambition. In 1950 Michael Denison offered him on behalf of a film company the chance to direct *The Importance of Being Earnest*. Gielgud replied: 'Oh no, I don't think so. I seem to have been doing the *Importance* all my life. In any case, I don't think it would make a film.' After a pause he added: 'It might be rather fun to do it in Chinese.' The film was successfully made by Anthony Asquith, with Edith Evans reappearing as Lady Bracknell, but Michael Redgrave preferred to Gielgud as John Worthing.

It was Joseph L. Mankiewicz who persuaded Gielgud to return to the screen. He was cast almost by accident: Mankiewicz wanted Paul Scofield for Mark Antony, came to Stratford to see him in *Much Ado About Nothing*, and after seeing Gielgud play Benedick hired him as Cassius. One of Hollywood's most literate directors, Mankiewicz was known for his intelligent and subtle handling of dialogue; two years earlier he had won two Oscars, as writer and director, for *All About Eve*. Determined to show that Hollywood and Shakespeare could mix, he planned to cut only two minor scenes, film in black and white, and focus on character rather than spectacle. After Gielgud discussed the script with him he was won over: 'I trust his judgement and ability,' he said. 'I'm assured the essential Shakespeare will remain. That's why I've agreed to go.' But another factor was the $20,000 fee, a fabulous sum compared to the £50 a week he had been getting in Stratford.

The film's producer, John Houseman, who founded the Mercury Theater with Orson Welles, was at the first reading on the MGM sound stage. 'Gielgud sailed through the part of Cassius with terrifying bravura,' he recalled. James Mason, playing Brutus, remembered his vocal skill: 'He spoke with such richness and authority and was charged with such emotion.' Gielgud in turn was envious of Mason's technique. After seeing some rushes he observed: 'I blink and fidget still in close-up and my eyes wander, as if I was looking to see if a policeman was coming to arrest me. Mason is so steady and clear in his facial acting that I get very jealous.'

Gielgud later said of his role on the set: 'I was afraid the Americans would think I was the star actor from London who had come over to teach them how to play Shakespeare, so I kept my mouth shut as much as possible.' At the time he remarked: 'No one dared change the smallest word without my approval. They seemed to imagine I was in some sort of contact with Shakespeare.' In fact he became a kind of mentor to some of the actors, including Deborah Kerr, who as a schoolgirl had been thrilled by his Romeo. 'John was so kind to me, helping me as Portia through my scenes with James Mason,' she recalls.

But his main influence was on Marlon Brando, whose casting as Mark Antony had provoked both disbelief and scorn. The brooding, beautiful young actor had scored powerfully on both stage and screen in Tennessee Williams's *A Streetcar Named Desire*, but was out to prove he could play other than just brutal parts. Apprehensive about plunging into the classics, he had been working on Antony's key speeches for a month, using Shakespeare recordings of Barrymore, Olivier and Maurice Evans as his model.

According to an actor friend, Brando was at first dismissive of Gielgud, finding it hard to imagine how 'this effete person in spats' could handle such a virile role. 'When Gielgud finally got into a breastplate, Marlon was just astonished,' he remembered. 'Gielgud was now the formidable Roman soldier, he'd grown into the part, and as soon as his character began to emerge, Marlon's admiration was boundless.' Fascinated, Brando would appear surreptitiously on the set whenever Gielgud was rehearsing a scene.

Gielgud described Brando as 'a funny, intense, egocentric boy of twenty-seven with a flat nose and bullet head, huge arms and shoulders, and yet giving the effect of a lean Greenwich Village college boy. He is very nervous indeed and mutters his lines and rehearses by himself all day long . . . I think his sincerity may bring him to an interesting performance. His English is not at all bad . . . but I think he has very little humour.'

Brando asked Gielgud deferentially if he would record two of Antony's speeches into his tape recorder, to help him with his diction. He also sought his advice about Antony's scene with the conspirators over Caesar's body. Impressed by his diligence and apparent modesty, Gielgud took him through the speech, suggesting emphases, phrasing and colour. ('He sure knows his way around the meanings,' Brando said afterwards.) When the young American followed his suggestions precisely during filming, he was impressed; but he was less taken with his rendering of the 'Friends, Romans, countrymen' speech. 'I thought he was just imitating Olivier, doing some great shouts and things,' he said. But overall he defended Brando's controversial performance. Such was his admiration for it, he invited him to play Hamlet under his direction. But Brando had no desire to return to the theatre.

Gielgud found the process of filming disconcerting: 'One minute it's like Waterloo Station in the rush-hour. Then everything stops dead. It's like acting in a graveyard.' He was missing a live audience: 'I shall never quite get used to this cold, mathematical technique of standing in a set position, saying a few lines, stopping while someone powders your face, and then starting again at the blow of a whistle.' He had other anxieties, such as whether he would appear sufficiently virile. 'I'm afraid sometimes I walk in an exaggerated fashion and I seem to play over-elaborately,' he told Mankiewicz.

Although he knew the part of Cassius intimately, he realised he had to scale down his Stratford performance. He tried to be 'a little more confidential in delivery, preserving the high style without the high volume', but also playing it faster, as he had wanted to at Stratford. It helped him that the actors, unusually for a film, had three weeks' rehearsal in an empty studio before shooting began, and that the scenes were shot nearly in sequence. It was to be some years before he was fully confident in front of the camera but, apart from having to ride a horse again, he had enjoyed much of the work.

The experience converted him to the idea of Shakespeare on film: *Julius Caesar*, he decided, was *better* on screen than on stage. Just before it was released Brando said of his performance: 'He's good in the movie – damn good.' The American critics agreed, rating his vigorous, edgy, black-toga'd Cassius the outstanding performance in a film that many ranked with Olivier's *Henry V*. Peggy Ashcroft told Gielgud he had killed the film, because he was the only one 'acting Shakespeare'.

His visit to Hollywood was, according to one writer, the social occasion of the season: 'In anticipation the Beverly Hills hostesses decanted the sherry, dressed up the poolside buffets with the best silver and damask, and dusted off the butler from central casting.' Gielgud enjoyed star-spotting: 'Kirk Douglas!' he would cry with glee. 'Why it's a fairyland!' In a letter home he described a cocktail party he and Burton attended at the house of the producer David O. Selznick. Here he met Chaplin, who told him about the early Beerbohm Tree productions he had seen from the gallery, and did an imitation of Eleonra Duse: 'He is weary and neat, with carefully waved white hair and wonderful little expressive hands, and alternates between rather pretentious philosophical generalities and sudden bursts of very natural sweetness and warmth,' Gielgud wrote. Yet though he enjoyed such occasions, he was uneasy about Hollywood life, finding it 'restless, exhausting, highly efficient, and rather frightening'. He compared it with London: 'One begins to scent the jealousies and disappointments and ambitions, much as in the theatre – only more concentrated out here – like actors crossed with Anglo-Indian civil servants who have a perpetual chip on their shoulders.'

On his return to England he announced: 'I've played all the parts I want to play. I don't want to go back.' But Beaumont tempted him into a 'Coronation Season' under his management at the Lyric, Hammersmith. It was agreed he would play Mirabell in Congreve's *The Way of the World* and Jaffeir in Otway's *Venice Preserv'd*, and direct the Congreve as well as a production of *Richard II*. A strong repertory company included Paul Scofield, Pamela Brown, Eileen Herlie, Margaret Rutherford and Eric Porter. Each play was to run six weeks, and the season would begin in December with *Richard II*, with Scofield in the title-role.

Gielgud had seriously considered playing Richard himself, but decided he was too old. At thirty Scofield was already at the forefront of the next generation of actors, with experience in a wide range of Shakespearean parts, including a Hamlet at Stratford that Tynan said had ousted both Gielgud's and Wolfit's from his mind. So how, it was asked, would Gielgud direct him in a role that had marked one of his own greatest performances?

Peter Sallis, also in the company, recalls the delicate situation: 'Richard was John's part, he knew every comma, every line, and how he wanted it spoken, and I think he limited Paul a bit.' Scofield himself remembers the pressures: 'John was sensitive to the fact that his own performance was for most theatregoers the definitive one, and he made no attempt to use his own interpretation as a model for mine. Nevertheless the music of the verse was so embedded in his whole being, that a divergence from that pattern must have been difficult for him to accept. But it was a pattern that could never be reassembled by another actor. I was probably not ready to impose my own, and perhaps never found it; but this was not John's fault.'

Although Gielgud at first held back from too much direction, two days before the Brighton opening he suddenly produced ideas based on his own interpretation of the part. He seems not to have noticed any problem, writing to a friend: 'I am very pleased with the way things are going at Brighton, and Paul Scofield gives a beautifully sensitive performance.' But Scofield was constricted rather than released by the role, giving an intelligent but remote performance that lacked the soaring, self-pitying lyricism of Gielgud's. Although Hobson and others praised his verse-speaking, most critics were disappointed. The revue artist Joyce Grenfell wrote to a friend: 'Gielgud has turned the actors into beautifully elocuting dummies. The result is disastrous. There's no life, no fire, no breath in anyone ... Perhaps actors shouldn't be producers?' As with Richardson and *Macbeth*, Gielgud was unable to direct another actor effectively in one of 'his' parts.

He was haunted by a very different ghost in the next production, *The Way of the World*, which opened in February 1953. Edith Evans's dazzling Millamant in Playfair's production had imprinted itself for ever on his mind. Now he was producing the play himself, and in Playfair's old theatre. Unable to shake off these memories, he failed to help Pamela Brown find her own line on the character. He was also dissatisfied with Mirabell, a part he would normally have relished, despite his having only two decent scenes. Peter Sallis recalls: 'When we first read the play John put the script down and said, "Mirabell isn't a very good part, is it?" That set the tone, from then on he was encumbered by it.' During rehearsals he complained: 'I'm not inside it, I don't get this part at all.' His unhappiness was such he tried, so it was rumoured, to dissuade Beaumont from bringing the play in to Hammersmith.

After the Brighton week he was clearly unhappy. 'I promise you it will be much better in London,' he helpfully told the audience during his curtain speech. But on the first night at the Lyric he was ill at ease, and uncertain of his words. The only two real successes were Margaret Rutherford, playing the man-hungry Lady Wishfort with magnificent vitality and all chins blazing, and Scofield, unexpectedly funny as the mincing fop Witwoud. 'I think I overplayed it dreadfully, but John seemed to enjoy this excess of mine,' Scofield recalls. Gielgud himself seemed subdued and indecisive, even in the wonderful 'conditions of marriage' scene with Millamant. One critic wrote: 'He gave the impression his mind was on other things.'

He was in fact profoundly saddened and depressed by the recent death of his elder brother Lewis. Apart from his spell in London during the war, Lewis had continued working in Paris for the International Red Cross. On his death at the age of fifty-eight, his close friend Aldous Huxley wrote to Naomi Mitchison: 'He was a gentle man as well as a gentleman, with all the qualities of humaneness connoted by both expressions. Lewis was not only one of the best, but one of the sanest of human beings.' Val later called his death 'the greatest personal grief and loss I have ever known'. Gielgud's relationship with Lewis had been affectionate and admiring, but not especially close, but his sadness was compounded by anxiety about the effect of his death on their mother.

Kate Gielgud, now eighty-four, was writing her memoirs. Her daughter Eleanor recalled: 'Lewis died while she was in the middle of the book, but she'd sent the first chapter to him, and he'd been very impressed, so she felt he would have wanted her to go on. That gave her something to hang on to.' Her book is a lively, intimate portrait of a life drenched in theatre, written with modesty and quiet humour by a woman with a sharp eye for detail and a phenomenal memory, two attributes she passed on to her youngest son. In a foreword written just after Lewis's death Gielgud paid a tribute to 'my remarkable mother', whom he described as 'superb in crisis, dignified in grief'. He ended: 'She is simple, natural, infinitely patient, and endlessly appreciative. She demands nothing and gives everything. What more (as Lady Bracknell says) can one desire?'

He bounded back to top form in May with *Venice Preserv'd*, the hit of the Hammersmith season. Free to concentrate on his acting, he was working again with Peter Brook, now acknowledged as the foremost director of the day. Otway's savage Restoration tragedy had not been performed publicly for eighty years, but like *Othello* it contained two strong male roles of equal stature. Gielgud, very taken with Craig's set for his 1905 Berlin production, saw it as a good melodramatic vehicle for himself and Scofield, as it had been for leading actors in the eighteenth century.

He and Brook cut, edited and even re-wrote the text in places. The critics approved: Gielgud had restored to the stage what might have been just a museum piece. In doing so, he re-discovered his confidence. The part of Jaffeir, a man torn between loyalty to his wife and his best friend, bore traces of both Brutus and Hamlet, and gave him a chance to exploit his ability to convey anguished spiritual indecision. Brook, whose clear and vigorous production was much liked, remembers: 'John adored being excessive, and usually as a director you have to check him. But for this play there was less need to discourage his natural histrionics. His poetic style was in total opposition to Paul's, and they worked very well together.'

Scofield remembers the positive effect of Gielgud's unselfish acting: 'This was the first and only time that he and I acted closely together, and his gentleness and encouragement during our scenes remains for me the perfect example of how an actor can help another simply by acting *with* him. My character was required to be dominant on stage at certain moments, and John allowed this to happen, by acting *with* me, rather than *at* me.' The production also restored Gielgud's humour. At the costume parade, watching the actresses in their long dresses, he remarked: 'I suppose I'm The Man Who Watches Trains Go By.'

The Hammersmith season surprised and pleased him: he had thought a repertory system was no longer viable. Yet the company had played to packed houses. The Lyric, he felt, was the right kind of setting for such plays: 'The season has proved what I have always felt, that Shakespeare and the classics are better acted in a small theatre.'

Just before it began, the *Sunday Times* had said of him: 'No actor of such superb talent has, in modern times, served the theatre with such undivided devotion and such absence of self-glory.' It added: 'For twenty years he has been at the summit of his profession, and at the moment his genius is at flood-tide.' This was a common view amongst critics and theatregoers – and also the Establishment: not long before Gielgud had acted as linkman for what turned out to be George VI's final Christmas Day broadcast. Now, on the day of the coronation of a new queen, his services to the theatre were recognised officially: among the Knights Bachelor featured in the Honours List of 2 June 1953 there appeared 'Gielgud, Arthur John, Actor'.

Both Olivier and Richardson had personally lobbied Churchill to enable Gielgud to join them as a theatrical knight. Coward, passed over once again, was delighted at the news, and thought the award long overdue, as did the *Stage*: 'No other living actor has inspired such devotion amongst his colleagues, displayed such integrity of purpose, and worked so faithfully and well in the service of his art,' it stated.

The Lyric company witnessed the first public reaction to his knighthood. Peter Sallis recalls the scene: 'All we underlings crowded into the wings for his entrance. When he came on the place erupted, and we erupted too, and he stood there trembling, and the tears were cascading down his face, and the audience were on their feet, and it went on and on and on.' Scofield, who later turned down a knighthood, was also watching, waiting for his cue: 'It was a huge and howling ovation such as I have never heard before or since. He waited – and waited, tears streaming down his face. At last he spoke, totally in control. When his speech ended, I came on stage, and the following scene was just as we had always played it. That impression of his emotion and his control remains indelibly in my memory.'

For Gielgud it had been a season of mixed emotions, finally vindicated by the triumphant Otway production. Yet once again he shied away from making his company a permanent one. Now approaching fifty, he had lost his former ambition. 'One must move on, find a new line, tackle different problems,' he insisted. Never a great planner, he needed the stimulus of 'unlooked-for surprises, sudden and unexpected developments'. Tynan, a passionate advocate of a national theatre, deplored the waste: 'At Hammersmith Messrs Gielgud and Brook have the nucleus of a great repertory company: in a few short weeks it will, so to speak, be broken up and re-sold. Nobody of course will complain. The English tradition of improvidence will have been upheld; and I, in the English tradition of understatement, will have to confine myself to a scream of rage.'

Tynan's provocative and iconoclastic reviews, first for the *Evening Standard* and then the *Observer*, made him the dominant and most influential critical voice of the 1950s. Gielgud, whom he viewed as part of the Establishment, was to suffer as much as anyone from his witty, shrewd but often cruel and unjust comments. 'They're wonderful – when it's not you,' he remarked. During the Hammersmith season Tynan was already warming up. He called *Richard II* 'a triumph of style over humanity', suggesting Gielgud had perpetrated 'an essay in mass ventriloquism', catering for 'an audience for whom elocution is the whole of acting, an audience which no longer exists'. And in *Venice Preserv'd* he accused him of self-pity, writing: 'The temptation sometimes proves too much for him: inhaling passionately through his nose, he administers to every line a tremendous parsonical quiver.'

Meeting Gielgud in person, Tynan admired 'the cogency, speed and charm' of his conversation. Before the Hammersmith season he had received a surprise invitation to supper at Cowley Street. 'We talked until three, I coaxed into silence by his beauty, he garrulous and fluttering as a dove,' he told Cecil Beaton. At the season's end he described Gielgud as 'a high priest in a profession mostly made up of short-sighted heretics', and pinpointed eloquently his influence within the profession: 'Gielgud is not so much *an* actor as *the* actor: his uniqueness lies in the fact that he is far greater than the sum of his parts. He is a theatrical possession, a figurehead and a touchstone: and he bears the same relationship to the everyday traffic of acting that a helmsman bears to a galley slave.'

Yet the tribute was to Gielgud's position in the profession, not to his technique as an actor. Here Tynan would always prefer Olivier, as he made clear in his first book *Persona Grata*, published that year. In it he suggested Gielgud's acting lacked heart and stomach: 'When Olivier enters, lions pounce into the ring, and the stage becomes an arena,' he wrote. 'Gielgud, on the other hand, appears; he does not "make an entrance"; and he looks like one who has an appointment with the brush of Gainsborough or Reynolds.'

Tynan also suggested Gielgud had dropped 'bricks enough to re-build the Globe Theatre'. His already legendary tactlessness led Tennessee Williams to describe him gleefully as 'that famous London Brick Factory'. In Paul Scofield's view the bricks he dropped were 'never malicious and never quite innocent', and 'a great deal more devastating than he would wish them to be': those on the receiving end, he says, were victims rather than targets, and usually quick to forgive.

The Hammersmith season added another brick to the edifice, as Peter Sallis ruefully remembers: 'When I auditioned for *Richard II* he told me in three minutes flat exactly how he was going to produce the play, what the sets would be like, the king's relationship with Bolingbroke, and with his henchmen Bushy, Bagot and Greene. At the end he said, "Do you agree?" I wasn't going to spoil it, so I said, "Yes, if I was doing *Richard II*, that's just how I'd do it." He turned to John Perry and said, "He might be Greene," then turned back to me and said, "We have two very beautiful men playing Bushy and Bagot: you might make a good contrast."'

After Hammersmith Gielgud took *Richard II* to Southern Rhodesia. When the Rhodes Centenary Festival invited him to perform it there for ten days, it was on condition he play Richard himself. While directing Scofield in the part he had been aching to do so, and against the advice of several friends he accepted at once. In Bulawayo he defended his decision: 'When one reckons that one has only, at the most, six or seven more highly active years in the theatre, one must organise life to do as many things as one feels like.' As with his other major parts, the lines were still there: 'Under a dust-cover they lie, and if I need them again, up comes the dust-cover.'

During rehearsals in London he seemed to have lost none of his power as Richard. Paul Daneman was among a group of actors present when he announced he would just 'walk through' the deposition scene: 'He thrust his hands into the pockets of his elegant double-breasted suit, clapped his trilby on the back of his head and a Turkish cigarette in his mouth and, stepping forward with that curious tip-toe shuffle of his, began: "Alack, why am I sent for to a king . . . ?" He had barely started when down came the tears and the rest of us were forgotten. We fed him cues and watched, hearts in our mouths, while he re-created the legendary performance most of us were too young to have seen. At the end, he mopped his eyes and said: "So sorry, I seem to have made rather an ass of myself."'

Unfortunately Bulawayo was not the Lyric, and the corrugated-iron theatre, built like an aircraft hangar, proved totally unsuitable. 'The theatre is unheated and seats three thousand people on a raked stone floor with no balconies,' Gielgud reported. 'The proscenium is as wide as the Festival Hall in London, and our poor little sets from Hammersmith look like children's screens, so we mask them as best we can with enormous curtains. But it still takes us five minutes, or so it seems, to cross the stage, and all the entrances and exits have to be rearranged in the shortest possible time.' In these conditions, and to his huge disappointment, he found no joy in playing Richard. 'I could only imitate the performance I saw when I was a young man,' he recalled. He was now, he realised, too old for such 'romantic juvenile parts'.

Despite his political naiveté, even he could not help noticing the existence of apartheid in Rhodesia. Hearing that a group of African actors was in the audience, in segregated seats, he made his own small protest. To the consternation of the organisers, he insisted on meeting them in his dressing-room afterwards. As one newspaper put it: 'Much to his embarrassment, all the dusky girls swept into deep curtsies when they were introduced.' But his political awareness deserted him during his speech after the last performance, when he said: 'It's been a great experience, and I want to thank all the people in this theatre, both back and front, who have worked like blacks – er, who have worked extremely hard.'

After spending a week visiting Durban and Kruger National Park with John Perry, he rented a villa in the south of France for a month. It was a rare holiday, but the theatre was never far away. He called on Rex Harrison in Portofino, and gave him a quick lesson in verse-speaking on the roof-garden of his villa. He visited Max Beerbohm and Cecil Beaton and, according to Beerbohm, 'amazed Cecil with his tunnel-vision dedication to the theatre'. Beaton enjoyed his gentle self-mockery: 'John has appeared wearing a ridiculous white linen hat, sitting bolt upright in a rowboat as formally as if he were at a board meeting,' he wrote in his diary. 'He is always the first to realise how comic a picture he presents, and in no way resents our amusement; in fact his eyes twinkle with the fun of the absurdity as, unmindful of waves or splash, he continues, in his rich, foghorn voice, to extol the work of Granville-Barker, or explain where he went wrong with Hamlet.'

With his sister Eleanor he also called on Edward Gordon Craig at his *pension* in Vence. He had not seen his famous cousin since their awkward encounter during his Old Vic days. He found Craig contented and affable, cracking jokes and singing snatches of music-hall songs. Gielgud was touched by the simplicity of his small but beautiful room, and absorbed every detail. Their relationship was now a more equable one: Craig was over eighty and slightly deaf, and Gielgud enjoyed his 'rather wicked and yet childishly attractive kind of fun and defiance'. They talked of the theatre, about which Craig was still immensely well informed, and of design. Gielgud told him that as a young man he had thought it would be inspiring to play in front of wonderful scenery, and had been disappointed when he realised that on stage you never saw it, because it was behind you. Faced with this childlike admission, Craig suggested he instal mirrors at the back of the auditorium. Afterwards he wrote: 'Johnny Gielgud has been here for a month – we had two days talking shop – quite delightful – for me.'

Craig also mentioned 'his dear sister Eleanor', calling her 'quite a heroic person'. Eleanor had married during the war, but been widowed soon afterwards. Her mother called her 'the business head of the family', who unselfishly 'put other people's interests and needs ever before her own'. Since 1946 she had acted as Gielgud's secretary and general factotum, driving him to the theatre or film studio, dealing with his correspondence, looking after his business affairs – and trying to prevent people taking advantage of his kindness. 'I went to help John for a fortnight and stayed twenty years,' she recalled. 'He was absolutely hopeless over business, which is why he was taken to the cleaners so often. His cheque book would be out before you could say Knife, it made me despair sometimes. He was also terribly impractical: I tried to teach him to drive once, and he nearly went into Hyde Park Gate. But he was generous to the point of no return; he always gave me the most expensive things like fur coats and jewellery.'

On his return to London Gielgud faced a dilemma. He had not appeared in a new play in modern dress since *Dear Octopus* in 1938. Now he had two contrasting offers. *Marching Song* was a play by actor-writer John Whiting, who had been in his companies at the Phoenix, and written the leading part with him in mind. Gielgud was sufficiently impressed to persuade Beaumont to take out an option. Whiting's previous play *Saint's Day* had been dismissed as claptrap by the critics. An unusual mixture of symbolism, realism and dream, it was a harbinger of the new drama that was soon to emerge. Gielgud had defended it vigorously in a joint letter to *The Times* with Peggy Ashcroft: 'We found it beautiful, moving and fascinating – subtly directed and finely played,' they wrote. 'Is obscurity an unforgiveable crime in a playwright?'

Had Gielgud tackled Whiting's strange play, his next few years might have been less difficult. He opted instead for *A Day by the Sea*, an unexciting, sub-Chekhovian work by N.C. Hunter. Beaumont offered him not just a leading part, but the chance to direct a starry cast that included Sybil Thorndike, Lewis Casson, Ralph Richardson and

Irene Worth, and to do so at the Haymarket. Once he would have relished testing himself on the more difficult, original work, but now he settled for the safer, more glamorous option. In doing so he identified himself more than ever with the traditional West End fare Beaumont was to serve up throughout the 1950s.

Rehearsals began for *A Day by the Sea.* Then, just a few days before its provincial opening, Gielgud suffered a traumatic experience that threatened to bring his illustrious career to a sudden and humiliating end.

26

Dark Days

The friendship and loyalty that has surrounded
me has almost made up for so much vileness.
(Letter to Raymond Mander and
Joe Mitchenson, October 1953)

THE bare facts alone suggest the tragedy. Around midnight on
the evening of 20 October 1953 Gielgud was arrested in a public
lavatory in a Chelsea mews. He had been drinking, and when
arrested said: 'I am sorry.' He was taken to the local police station, and
there charged with 'persistently importuning male persons for immoral
purposes'. He gave his name as Arthur Gielgud, and said he was a self-
employed clerk living in Cowley Street on 'approximately £1000 a
year'. He was told to report to the magistrates' court the following
morning, and released.

Like other homosexuals forced to live outside the law, he had
remained discreet about his private life. In 1953 the moral climate was
still hostile: the authorities, led by the Home Secretary, David
Maxwell-Fyfe, seemed to be engaged in a witch-hunt. This was the
period when the MP William Field had to resign his seat in Parliament
after being caught 'importuning', when prominent figures such as the
journalist Peter Wildeblood, the novelist and biographer Rupert Croft-
Cooke and, most sensationally, Lord Montagu of Beaulieu, were tried
and imprisoned for homosexual offences. The press revelled in the fate
of these 'evil men'. Meanwhile prominent figures such as Benjamin
Britten and Cecil Beaton were attracting the attention of the police.
Some homosexuals preferred suicide to having their private lives
exposed to the public gaze.

Distraught and unable to sleep after his arrest, Gielgud briefly considered this option, but decided it was too melodramatic. He dreaded telling his mother, fearing the publicity might kill her. He felt too ashamed to telephone Beaumont, whose contacts in high places might conceivably have kept the case out of court: he 'did not wish to be a nuisance', he later told a producer friend. But he also felt that having got into trouble he should face the consequences. In court the next day, wearing horn-rimmed glasses in the dock, he pleaded guilty to the offence, adding: 'I cannot imagine I was so stupid. I was tired and had a few drinks. I was not responsible for my actions.' The magistrate told him: 'I suppose on this occasion I can treat you as a bad case of drunk and disorderly, but nobody could do that again.' He fined Gielgud £10, and added: 'If this is what you do when you have taken more drink than you are able to control, you would be a wise man if you did not take that amount of drink. See your doctor the moment you leave here.'

The matter might have ended there had Gielgud's voice not been recognised by a passing reporter – or, according to another version, his face recognised by a barrister with whom he had been at school. Either way, when he returned to rehearse *A Day by the Sea* that afternoon he found his case on the front of the lunchtime edition of the *Evening Standard*. According to legend, Sybil Thorndike broke the atmosphere of shock and embarrassment pervading the rehearsal room by embracing him, and saying, 'Oh John, you have been a silly bugger!'

That night, in the Westminster house Beaumont shared with John Perry, he attended a crisis meeting with the Tennent hierarchy and their legal advisers. According to Beaumont's biographer Richard Huggett, Gielgud offered to give up his part in the play, and retire from the theatre until the scandal had died down. But Beaumont refused to let him, arguing that if he didn't face the public now he would never be able to do so. He also said it was too late to find another actor to replace him before *A Day by the Sea* opened in Liverpool in four days' time.

But another version suggests a more dramatic confrontation. It involved Val Gielgud, who told it to Monica Grey, whom he was to marry soon afterwards. When he arrived at Gielgud's house he found his brother in bed and 'gone to pieces', with a doctor in attendance. Beaumont argued that Gielgud should not open in Liverpool because of all the adverse publicity, but Val was determined he should carry on with his career. He therefore threatened that, unless his brother was allowed to continue, he would publicly expose the homosexuals within Tennent's. Beaumont gave way.

That night Lewis Casson wrote to his son: 'Our excitement about the new play has been terribly complicated by this unfortunate Gielgud business ... We were all in fits as to what would happen, but Tennent's and he decided to go on.' Casson put the incident down to Gielgud accepting too much work. 'Rather foolishly he took on the job of producing and playing a very long part. Got very strained and tired ... and there you are.' Fatigue was certainly a factor, as was the drink he had consumed at a party that night. But Gielgud had had no close long-term relationship since John Perry had left him for Beaumont, and loneliness may have also played a part.

The scandal provoked varied responses on the play's pre-London tour. At the opening in Liverpool Ralph Richardson, fearing Gielgud would be booed, re-wrote the script by joining him in his first entrance, then turning back. But to everyone's surprise he was met by cheers and a standing ovation. Alma Cohen, a student in the audience, recalls: 'It was spontaneous, we wanted to reassure him that we were there to see the play. The applause stopped him in his tracks.' In Edinburgh there was a different response. As was still the custom outside London, the audience applauded each star as they arrived on stage – except Gielgud, whose entrance was met with silence. Nora Williamson was in the gallery with other students: 'We looked at each other, but our nerve failed,' she remembers. 'We were horrified and ashamed, but Edinburgh audiences were very hidebound then.' It took great courage for Gielgud to continue in the face of such hostility.

Sybil Thorndike showed her mettle throughout the episode. On tour she ticked the company off for talking endlessly about the incident, telling them to work on the play as normal. Gielgud was sent several abusive letters, some with 'Sir' underlined. Most were intercepted by Alison Colvil, Tennent's stage manager, but a few were addressed to Lewis Casson and Sybil Thorndike, asking how they could possibly work with 'this filthy pervert'. From Liverpool Sybil Thorndike wrote consolingly to Gielgud's mother: 'It has been an anxious time but John has been splendid – and he has played beautifully. Please don't worry too much about him – he is surrounded by people who love him.' Gielgud himself wrote: 'The friendship and loyalty that has surrounded me has almost made up for so much vileness – but I wish I had not caused distress to so many dear friends.'

His mother had received the news with remarkable stoicism, merely telling Gielgud the incident wouldn't be mentioned again. Soon after she wrote to a sympathiser: 'John has nothing to his discredit save one

toast too many at a Chelsea party.' With other members of the family
she loyally attended the first night at the Haymarket, where there were
rumours of a hostile demonstration from the gallery. At his first
entrance Gielgud was paralysed with fear and unable to come on stage.
Sybil Thorndike, already on, walked across to the wings and whispered
to him, 'Come along, John darling, they won't boo me!' and brought
him on. Led by the Gielgud family in their box, the audience cheered
and applauded and gave him another standing ovation. Gielgud stood
there, the inevitable tears streaming down his cheeks. Afterwards
Beaumont, fearing the crowd at the stage door might still cause
trouble, advised him to leave by the front, but he insisted on leaving by
the normal route. Once again he was met by enthusiastic cheers rather
than hostility.

His standing in the profession, and the widespread love and
affection he inspired, was made clear by the countless letters of support
he received from his fellow-actors, some of whom knew him only
slightly. As usual he replied to every one, though in some cases with a
standard printed letter, which read: 'Thank you so very much for
thinking of me on the first night. The warmth of the audience, and
their enthusiastic reception, was touching and thrilling, as you can
imagine, and I have never been more aware of the kindness and love
that has surrounded me at this time.' He was deeply touched when
Craig wrote, enclosing a card in Ellen Terry's handwriting which she
had once sent to comfort him in a crisis of his own.

But many people were hostile. There were calls for him to be
stripped of his knighthood – though legally this was impossible – and
one member of the House of Lords even suggested he should be
horsewhipped in the streets. When the conductor Malcolm Sargent
came backstage to see Sybil Thorndike, she asked him if he would go
and see Gielgud too. Sargent replied: 'I don't think I can: you see, I mix
with royalty.' A few actors, including Edward Chapman, wanted him
expelled from Equity. Michael Denison, a council member, recalled
the critical meeting: 'I had written a speech of fire, but fortunately
didn't have to use it, because all but two members said this was
absolute nonsense, that it had no effect whatsoever on his professional
skill and integrity, and therefore should not be considered.'

The incident came as a great shock to other homosexuals in the
theatre. Rattigan remarked, only half-jokingly: 'There'll be no Sir
Terry now.' Coward, while sympathising with Gielgud's distress,
privately berated him for his carelessness, stupidity and selfishness. But

the criticisms were not confined to homosexuals. On hearing the news Edith Evans remarked magisterially: 'When I consented to become a dame, I gave up the privilege of going on the streets if I felt like it.'

The incident aroused extreme reactions in the press. A boycott of theatres where 'actors with queer habits' were playing was suggested. An extreme though not untypical reaction came from the columnist John Gordon, who argued that homosexuals should be made social lepers: 'It is utterly wrong that men who befoul and corrupt other young men should strut in the public eye, enjoying adulation and applause, however great their genius,' he wrote. Students in Manchester booed and jeered Greer Garson when, during a promotional tour for the film of *Julius Caesar*, she mentioned Gielgud's name. But at the film's British première the same month there was spontaneous applause for his opening speech as Cassius, an unprecedented break with tradition by an English cinema audience. Shortly afterwards the British Film Academy named him Best British Actor in a Hollywood Film for his performance.

Ironically, the incident prompted calls for the reform of the law to bring Britain into line with other, more tolerant countries. In the wake of Gielgud's court case the *Sunday Times* published a pamphlet reprinting their moderate leader, together with a selection from the many letters published on the subject. The movement for reform had begun, and four years later the Wolfenden Report recommended a change in the law – though it took another ten years for it to be implemented.

'This damnable business will be forgotten in a few weeks,' Dodie Smith wrote to Gielgud. She was mistaken. His application to join the Garrick Club, though proposed by Olivier and Guinness, was not accepted until 1970. More immediately, a planned trip to America had to be cancelled. Asked to play Prospero in America for the Stratford company, he had been reluctant to go, fearing adverse publicity. After the American producer Robert Whitehead persuaded him to accept, pressure was applied by the British Embassy in Washington. It was made clear that both the Foreign Office and Buckingham Palace would prefer the tour to be cancelled, on the grounds that Gielgud's presence in the USA as a representative of Britain would be an embarrassment. It was to be five years before he felt confident enough to visit America again.

There are differing views as to whether the incident was a set-up, whether Gielgud had been already warned about such behaviour, or whether he was simply careless. Whatever the facts, he showed great dignity, courage and resilience in his reaction to the affair. But there is no doubt that it took its toll emotionally. Having just received his knighthood, he felt he had disgraced the Queen and the royal family. A few months after the incident he had what amounted to a brief nervous breakdown. He also developed eye-muscle strain and double-vision, and had to wear an eye-patch for a few weeks while acting in *A Day by the Sea*. He tried to make the best of it – 'It gives me a rather dashing, piratical look, don't you think?' – but admitted that 'it's a terrible bore wearing it, and I feel I could scream at times'.

It also appeared to damage him professionally. Over the next five years he lost the impetus he had found in his brilliant season at Stratford. He acted in two new plays, neither of them a success; his three forays into Shakespeare were in parts he had played at least twice before; and his six productions were of very varying quality. Most of the time he seemed content to stay under the cosy, safe Tennent blanket.

This was the time when Rattigan mounted his notorious defence of 'Aunt Edna', arguing that the West End theatre could not afford to offend this mythical figure, whom he defined as 'a nice, respectable, middle-class, middle-aged maiden lady with time on her hands'. She would certainly have not been disturbed by *A Day by the Sea*. The play gave the starry cast a chance to display their craft, and Gielgud, as a cold, priggish civil servant, had the opportunity to wear modern clothes on a London stage for the first time for fifteen years. But it was ultimately an empty piece without story or action, providing what Tynan called 'an evening of unexampled triviality'. Its long run meant Gielgud played no new part for eighteen months.

At a time when Peter Hall was starting out as a director with a season of Lorca, Goldoni and Gide at the Arts, and Peter Brook was working on Fry's *The Dark is Light Enough* with Edith Evans, Gielgud's next directing assignment for Tennent's was yet another revival of *Charley's Aunt*. John Mills, who began his career in the farce, and now starred with Gwen Ffrangcon-Davies, remembers Gielgud's obvious boredom: 'Binkie wanted it to be beautifully dressed, very chic and well-manicured, but it wasn't really very funny. During the dress rehearsal I rushed around the stage in this heavy black frock, and ended up with my wig all over the place. I peered out into the auditorium and said: "Are you there, Johnny? How was it?" He replied: "Absolutely interminable, my dear fellow!"' Gielgud's production was too elegant for this knockabout classic, and when it opened at the Strand in February 1954, at the same time as *Alice Through the Looking Glass* and a play about Little Lord Fauntleroy, the critics bemoaned the West End's 'relapse into infantilism'.

Gielgud was always able to console himself with Chekhov. His next production, *The Cherry Orchard* at the Lyric, Hammersmith in May, was a rare beacon of light in these dark days of his career. Chekhov's star had risen since Fagan's groundbreaking production in the same theatre in 1925, and his plays were now embedded in the modern classical repertoire. The production marked Gielgud's début as a director of Chekhov. But he also branched out into another role, that of adaptor and translator. With the help of Chekhov's biographer David Magarshack, and the Russian actress Maria Britnieva, he created a more colloquial version than usual, using an existing literal translation.

The critics heaped praise on his atmospheric production. Following Chekhov, Gielgud emphasised the comedy while retaining the pathos in the plight of Madame Ranevsky and her family. He drew out a subtle creation of the peasant-turned-landowner Lopahin from Trevor Howard, who said of him: 'He radiates happiness to all those who work with him.' He also prompted strong yet delicate playing from another fine ensemble that included Gwen Ffrangcon-Davies, Pauline Jameson, Esmé Percy, Robert Eddison and David Markham. His affinity with Chekhov's work was underlined by the critic of *The Times*, who wrote of 'his extraordinarily complete stage realisation of the peculiar elasticity of Slav melancholy'.

His success, however, was tinged with sadness. During rehearsals news came from America of the death of Komisarjevsky. Gielgud's eloquent tribute in *The Times* was notably honest. He grieved for 'a great *metteur en scène*, an inspiring teacher, and a master of theatrical orchestration', whose methods were 'friendly, patient and meticulous', but who could also be 'cruel, aloof and destructive'. He regretted Komisarjevsky's disdainful attitude towards businessmen, which prevented him from managing a theatre and a company of his own in England – a company which, though he made no mention of it, Gielgud would probably have been asked to lead in the 1930s.

In the autumn he returned to Shakespeare on film. After *Julius Caesar* he had been amused to hear of a supposed offer to play Antony opposite Garbo's Cleopatra. Back in the real world Olivier gave him two short scenes as the Duke of Clarence in his film of *Richard III*.

19. Stratford, 1950: 'A fresh start in a glorious season.'

20. With Jessie Matthews in *The Good Companions*, 1933.

21. With James Mason in *Julius Caesar*, 1953.

22. With Pamela Brown and Richard Burton in *The Lady's Not for Burning*, 1949.

23. A magical partnership: Peggy Ashcroft and Gielgud as Beatrice and Benedick, *Much Ado about Nothing*, 1950.

24. 'I thought I looked rather silly.' The 'Noguchi Lear', with Claire Bloom as Cordelia.

25. 'A useful meal-ticket for my old age.' Even Tynan admired the *Ages of Man* recital.

26. With Dorothy Tutin (left) and Judi Dench in *The Cherry Orchard*, 1961.

27. Inspired by Auden, as Spooner in *No Man's Land*, 1975.

28. Old friends, new plays: with Ralph Richardson, his partner in Storey's *Home* and Pinter's *No Man's Land*.

29. As Edward Ryder in *Brideshead Revisited*, 1981.

SCREEN TRIUMPHS

30. With Ellen Burstyn in Alain Resnais' *Providence*, 1977.

31. As Prospero in Peter Greenaway's *Prospero's Books*, 1990.

32. Gielgud at the Gielgud:
'At least I shall recognise one name when I walk
down Shaftesbury Avenue.'

Olivier's terrifying pantomime villain, bordering on the camp, dominates the film, but both Gielgud and Richardson, playing the Duke of Buckingham, give subtle, intelligent performances.

Gielgud's noble, sad and ill-starred Clarence, a part he had not played on stage, was widely praised. His speech in the Tower, in which he anticipates his death by drowning, is a masterly combination of speedy and anguished verse-speaking. But the scene was poorly lit, and shot in the middle distance. Was this, as was suggested, the director's jealous hand at work? At all events, Gielgud seemed more relaxed and easy in front of the camera. He was justifiably upset when the prison scene was cut by half for American distribution – and removed altogether for continental audiences.

He and Olivier worked together again the following spring, but now the roles were reversed. Olivier, now in his late forties, had not played a major Shakespearean part since his 1946 Lear. Stung by criticisms that he was coasting, he accepted Glen Byam Shaw's invitation to lead the 1955 company, in conjunction with Vivien Leigh. During the season he scaled the heights once more, first with a dazzling Macbeth, then under the direction of Peter Brook with a powerful Titus Andronicus, a performance that persuaded Tynan that he was 'the greatest actor alive'. But these productions came later: the season opened with Gielgud's production of *Twelfth Night*, with Olivier as Malvolio and Vivien Leigh playing Viola. Twenty years after *Romeo and Juliet* the two actors clashed again, with near-disastrous results.

Directing or acting, Olivier always came to the first rehearsal with his ideas meticulously planned, and then made sure they were carried out. Malvolio was no exception: not only had he created the character in his mind, he had also worked out his walk, decided on a particular tone of voice and even a speech defect, and fixed on yet another false nose. As Olivier would have known, this was totally opposite to Gielgud's more spontaneous, instinctive approach. When Vivien Leigh asked him before they began if he'd been working on *Twelfth Night*, he said: 'No, no, I'm waiting to see what the actors give me.'

Gielgud was unhappy with Olivier's lisping, whining Puritan Malvolio, a characterisation which he likened to that of a Jewish hairdresser. Nor did he think much of his acrobatics: 'He insisted on falling backwards off a bench in the garden scene, though I begged him not to do it,' he recalled, adding carefully, 'He was inclined to be obstinate.' Angela Baddeley, playing Maria, recalled the bad atmosphere: 'The basic antagonism between Larry and Johnny came out during rehearsals. I think Larry was a bad boy about it. He was very waspish and overbearing with Johnny, and Johnny became intimidated by him and lost his authority. Almost everyone in the cast sided with Larry, laughing at his wisecracks about Johnny's direction. I felt very sorry for Johnny.'

Vivien Leigh was a further complication. Gielgud was entranced with her, and admired her attitude to her work: 'She studied and experimented continually, and always brought to rehearsal a willingness and technical flexibility, which was the result of unceasing self-criticism and devotion to her work,' he recalled. But just as Olivier was going his own way with Malvolio, so he was also, Gielgud felt, attempting to influence his wife by rehearsing her privately: 'Part of her sympathised with what I was trying to do, part of her with what Olivier clearly thought she should be doing,' he remembered. Olivier admitted only to 'the occasional practical hint'.

The situation was not improved by Gielgud's unceasing flow of ideas. Dilys Hamlett remembers: 'In the mornings he would come in and say, "I've had a lovely idea in the night," and everyone would groan.' Vivien Leigh complained that for the duel between herself and Michael Denison, playing Aguecheek, he was altering the moves for one without telling the other. Trader Faulkner, playing Sebastian, says that when Gielgud asked him to change his sword to his other hand, Olivier came over and said, 'Trader, baby, I have to admire the way you're not kicking him up the arse.'

But Keith Michell, playing Orsino, enjoyed his methods: 'At the first reading I began, "If music be the food" – and he broke in, "No, no, if *music* . . ." It took us about two hours to get through that speech, but I loved every minute of it. Here was the greatest speaker of Shakespearean verse giving me a class. I felt honoured, I just soaked it up. He said what he thought, and I found that refreshing. At least you knew where you stood. Later I was doing another speech of Orsino's, and he said, "Keith, it's like Hotspur on a day off."'

Gielgud's butterfly methods could sometimes work to an actor's advantage. Rehearsing Aguecheek's first scene, he asked Michael Denison to wave cheerily to Toby Belch and Maria. Denison tentatively suggested that his character was sad and depressed at this moment. 'Sad, sad?' Gielgud responded. 'No no, terribly gay!' Denison did what he was told. 'I sat down next to Larry, who whispered in my ear, "You're absolutely right, you know. Would you like me to do something about it?" When he and Vivien and John came back from lunch, John said enthusiastically: "Larry's had the most marvellous idea, he thinks you should be sad at the beginning of that scene." I was about to say it was my idea when I saw Larry giving me a warning look. So I said, "That's very helpful, thank you, John." And he said, "Oh don't thank me, thank Larry."'

According to Gielgud, 'Larry didn't like accepting criticism from me at all'. But some of his criticisms might have been less forthright. According to Trader Faulkner, at one rehearsal he told Olivier that his Malvolio was vulgar. 'He didn't mean to, it just came out. Everyone was watching, and it pulled the rug from under Olivier. He stopped, and said, "Johnny, you've just winged me."'

In the fourth week of rehearsal Olivier talked to Glen Byam Shaw and then, in front of the actors, asked Gielgud to leave rehearsals for the next three days, so they could work without further changes. 'I'm afraid he was a bit hurt,' Olivier recalled, 'but for the sake of avoiding a disaster I had to be firm and insist.' It was a humiliating put-down for Gielgud, who nevertheless did what he was asked. Olivier later claimed he made no changes, but simply brought a much-needed discipline to rehearsals. 'I wouldn't quite put it that way,' Gielgud observed, without elaborating.

Whatever happened in those three days, the production was a disappointment. Olivier's eccentric Malvolio, in a fuzzy, straw-coloured wig, was the focus of attention, but his style was out of keeping with the wistful romanticism of the production, and his notices were mixed. Gielgud thought Vivien Leigh enchanting, but her performance was generally dismissed as lacking variety and warmth; Tynan referred to her 'dazzling monotony'. As usual Gielgud blamed himself, his despair being encapsulated in a remark he made later to Vivien Leigh. After they had touched on Edith Evans's temporary absence from the stage, he said: 'Oh dear, I've directed this play so badly, I don't suppose any of you will ever want to work with me again,' then added after a moment, 'Except perhaps Edith, at a pinch.'

Vivien Leigh was suffering from what was later diagnosed as manic depression, and her marriage to Olivier was already falling apart. Ironically, given his difficult relationship with Olivier, Gielgud and she were by now close friends, and he was an occasional guest at the Oliviers' home. More widely read and cultured than Olivier, she shared Gielgud's delight in language and poetry, in changing fashions and theatrical tradition – and in doing the *Times* crossword. He in turn was charmed by her beauty and gaiety, and her determination to become an accomplished stage actress rather than merely a film star. Later he said of his visits to Notley: 'I loved to gossip with Vivien about who was having an affair with whom, while Larry was in his barn making plans.'

He admired her courage in the face of her developing illness. When Olivier had encouraged her to play the unstable Blanche Dubois in *A Streetcar Named Desire*, Gielgud was one of those who had thought it an unwise decision. He remembered her as 'shaking and white and quite distraught at the end of it'. According to his sister Eleanor, Olivier sometimes called on him for help: 'When Vivien was in a really difficult mood, Larry would ring and say to John, "For God's sake come down, you're the only person she will listen to," and he would go.'

While she and Olivier continued at Stratford through the summer, Gielgud and Peggy Ashcroft headed a second Memorial Theatre company, which during 1955 played *Much Ado About Nothing* and *King Lear* in eleven European cities, six British ones, the Palace in London, and finally Stratford itself. After seeing *Much Ado* in Liverpool one actor wrote: 'The entire Liverpool Playhouse company went to the matinée last Wednesday and were transported! It was a flawless performance in every way . . . a lesson to us all.' The production's continuing success led to suggestions that it should be preserved on film. But Gielgud disliked the idea of simply filming a stage performance. He also felt that having cameras on the stage would paralyse him with self-consciousness.

The production of *King Lear*, known as the 'Noguchi Lear', was one of the most controversial of his career. The inspiration for it came from George Devine, who co-directed with him. Poised to set up his own regime at the Royal Court, and disdainful of what he considered conventional productions at Stratford, Devine commissioned sets and costumes from the American/Japanese sculptor Isamu Noguchi, who had designed ballet sets for Martha Graham and Balanchine. He wanted a simple, basic design which would emphasise the 'timeless, universal and mythical quality' of Lear's story, and free it from the usual 'historical and decorative associations'.

Gielgud was not in fact the first choice for Lear, as Margaret Harris recalled: 'George first asked Michael Redgrave to do it, but Michael said, "When I do Lear I'll do *my* Lear, not Noguchi's Lear." John agreed to do it, but said, "I'll have to change my whole conception of Lear – but perhaps that's a good thing?"' He had seen Noguchi's sophisticated but simple settings for the ballet, and was enthusiastic. In his 1952 Macbeth he had been moving towards a more abstract design, less anchored in a specific time or place. Here was a chance to develop the idea further with an innovative designer.

From New York Noguchi produced some startling abstract and geometric designs, which included moving screens, airborne prisms and a large floating wall, the shapes and colours of which reflected different aspects of the story. Devine and Gielgud were thrilled. The costumes were another matter. Noguchi had never designed any before, a fact known to Devine, but not apparently to Gielgud. Instead of the usual drawings, he submitted tiny dolls dressed in miniature versions of the costumes, which were hurriedly made up.

When they were shown to the company, the actors were aghast – not just at the bizarre designs, but at their impracticality. Helen Cherry remembers the problems created by the Alice-in-Wonderland-style dresses she and Moira Lister had to wear as Goneril and Regan: 'They were like tents, and you had to put your hands on them to stop them swaying as you walked. The critics said it was a new stylised way of acting, but we were just trying to keep these awful costumes under control.' Peggy Ashcroft refused to wear her tubular structure, and defiantly exchanged it for a plain dress before the first night.

His face surrounded by dense white horsehair, Gielgud wore a crown resembling an upturned milking stool, and a cloak full of holes, which symbolically grew larger as Lear's mind disintegrated. At the dress parade Devine told him his costume was marvellously telling, that the whole play was in it. 'Oh that's a relief,' he said. 'I thought I looked rather silly.' Later he claimed he and Devine had lacked the courage to make any drastic last-minute changes, that it would have been unfair to a brilliant designer to do so. 'If I tore them off and threw them on the floor, everyone would do the same,' he said. In fact he tried to persuade Devine to abandon the costumes, and create instead simple cloaks to give a Blake-like effect to go with the settings. But Devine held firm to his conception – though Gielgud did win a compromise by getting a white quilted silk dressing-gown for his last two scenes.

Peggy Ashcroft felt that without the Noguchi costumes *King Lear* 'would have come off magnificently', but that with them 'I didn't see how anybody could act'. The costumes and the intrusively weird sets all but obliterated the play and the actors' performances. Supposedly designed, according to a rash Devine–Gielgud programme note, to allow 'the play to come to life through the words and the acting', they had precisely the opposite effect.

There was also a battle over styles of acting. Much influenced by Saint-Denis and his work at the London Theatre Studio, Devine wanted a more detached, less rhetorical approach, to match the oriental-style décor. Gielgud was in effect being asked to re-think Lear from scratch. Yet as with the wartime *Tempest*, there was still a master–pupil element in his relationship with Devine, who again failed to assert his authority. 'He didn't quite have the reins tight enough,' Moira Lister remembers. 'He had a bit to contend with in John, who wanted to go one way while he wanted to go another.' Gielgud admitted that 'we couldn't work together somehow, he'd respected me for too long'. According to Jocelyn Herbert, who later lived with Devine: 'George tried to get Gielgud to control his voice, and in rehearsals he was fine, but he got cold feet on the night, and went back to the old style.'

Gielgud had certainly re-thought the character. He now saw Lear as neither a saintly nor a romantic figure, but simply a stubborn and obstinate old man, the victim of his own tyranny. Yet, unhappy in his heavy, cramped costumes, he seemed caught between two styles. Some critics accused him of breaking up the poetry into fragments of prose, or losing it altogether by adopting a thin, dry, rasping voice. Others felt he had recaptured his old mastery, especially in the final scenes with Cordelia. Was this his Barker-inspired interpretation breaking through?

The critics went to town on the costumes, pointing to the wisdom of Lear's remark 'I do not like the fashion of your garments . . . let them be changed', and sneering at what they saw as a science-fiction land-scape inhabited by aliens. Trewin wrote sadly: 'We think of another Lear and of the Jumblies who went to sea in a sieve', while Milton Schulman thought the effect 'about as "timeless" as Oliver Messel designing a cosy for a hydrogen bomb'. Gielgud was variously compared to the Wizard of Oz and a Gruyère cheese, and in tribute to his progressively shrinking costume dubbed 'Gypsy Rose Lear' by Emlyn Williams. But there was some support for the bold, unconventional production, notably from Worsley, who observed: 'Experiment is the lifeblood of any art, and the English theatre is not so noticeably lively at the moment that we can afford to scoff when it tries to be adventurous.'

Despite the adverse critical reaction *King Lear* played to packed houses in London. Gielgud defended the production: his call for more experiment and adventure showed his continuing desire to remain open to new ideas. 'At least we can say we have done something experimental and fresh – and there hasn't been much of this in our theatre for a long time,' he said. 'Experiments such as this can have a lasting influence. They can encourage others to do better and go farther, and people can learn from our mistakes.' His words proved prophetic: when Peter Brook directed Scofield as Lear seven years later, he was inspired by the 'Noguchi Lear'.

In Europe *King Lear* was praised for its boldness, though some critics found difficulty in reconciling it with the more conventional *Much Ado*: 'Where is the director?' one asked. The tour took in Austria, Switzerland, Holland, Germany, Denmark and Norway. Moira Lister was staggered at Gielgud's professionalism. 'It's very difficult to get to the heart of each line every night, but even though we did it all over Europe for six months, he and Peggy did so in *Much Ado*. I stood watching in the wings, and their integrity and depth of concentration was quite staggering. It was always truthful, it never became mechanical.'

The company played to huge acclaim. In Vienna after every performance people surged to the front of the stalls, demanding endless curtain calls; afterwards hundreds applauded Gielgud and Peggy Ashcroft as they left by the stage door. As leader of the company he had to make the usual quasi-ambassadorial curtain speeches. After a performance of *Much Ado* at the National Theatre in Oslo one critic wrote: 'The applause was overwhelming. Finally Gielgud came forward and speaking in that intimate, wonderful manner of his, made a brief and touching speech of thanks. He said what a joy it was for him and the others to stand face to face with a Norwegian audience, who had been England's nearest and dearest allies in the darkest days of the war.' His speech-making was now much more adept.

To the company he remained an aloof figure. Moira Lister recalls his offstage persona: 'He was always kind and helpful to the young people, but he wasn't a great mixer. He was very shy, he needed someone to say, "Let's go out and do this or that." Otherwise he was apt to go off alone. When you did get close to him he was fun and sweet and just lovely. He wasn't one to embrace you, but he put you at ease at once, without the gush. Once you got on to his humorous side you could have a lot of laughs. Of course he loved puns and punning. When he saw me writing a travel article he said: "Careful, dear girl, or you'll get Reuter's cramp."'

In Berlin the company met Brecht and his wife Helene Weigel, and at Devine's instigation went to the East to see the Berliner Ensemble in Brecht's *Trumpets and Drums*, an adaptation of Farquhar's *The Recruiting Officer*, at the Theater am Schiffbauerdamm. On the way back Gielgud got on the wrong train, and was briefly separated from the rest of the company. In retrospect it seems like a symbolic action: while Devine, impressed by Brecht's 'people's theatre', chugged off to the Royal Court and became the pivotal figure for the new playwrights creating a theatrical revolution, Gielgud found himself shunted on to an artistic branch-line, in a carriage marked 'H.M. Tennent'.

The following summer the Berliner Ensemble came to London. Their productions of *Mother Courage* and *The Caucasian Chalk Circle* stamped Brecht's ideas irrevocably on the work of emerging directors, designers and actors. But Gielgud, like Richardson, was never in sympathy with Brecht's plays, nor with his theories. In 1949 an article by Brecht had appeared in an English theatre magazine. In it he argued that Stanislavsky had shot his bolt, that what was needed was 'Chinese rather than Chekhovian' acting, a style that distanced the audience from the action rather than involved them in it. Gielgud dismissed the article as 'obscure, pretentious and humourless'. Brecht's notion of the 'alienation effect' ran totally counter to his idea of theatre as a form of magic: 'The theatre only lives before an audience,' he wrote of Brecht's ideas, 'and the less that audience knows how the miracle occurs, the better.'

He also had no time for the haunting, nihilistic *Waiting for Godot*, which opened in London in 1955. Beckett's play was unlike anything ever seen in the English theatre, and was hugely controversial. It might have reached the West End earlier had it not been for Gielgud, who found it incomprehensible when he read it in 1953. When Richardson was offered the part of Estragon, Gielgud told him the play was 'a load of old rubbish', and persuaded him to turn the part down – a decision Richardson later described as one of the greatest mistakes of his life. But Gielgud was not alone in being bewildered by the play: Peter Hall admitted he had no idea what was going on before he began to direct it. When Gielgud finally saw it he thought it miserable, sordid and pessimistic: 'I had practically to be chained to my seat,' he said.

After the débâcle with Olivier over *Twelfth Night* he needed to tread warily on his next assignment. Enid Bagnold's artificial comedy *The Chalk Garden* had been written especially for Edith Evans, who had become unhappy with Gielgud's directing. 'When something is halfway there, it's like a child,' she complained. 'You can't say, "It's not a boy now, it's a girl."' Having been unwell recently, she only agreed to his directing her after Beaumont made him promise not to constantly change her moves.

The play, which also starred Peggy Ashcroft, was generally dismissed as pretentious, irritating and absurd. But it ran for 658 performances at the Haymarket, and Gielgud's work was admired for its grace and delicacy. 'What a beautiful job dear John has made of the production,' Beaumont wrote to Kate Gielgud. 'Quite lovely.' Gielgud recalled his method with the two stars: 'I just put up the tennis net and clear the court and act as referee, because they know much more about what they want to do than I do.' Mavis Walker, in a small part, remembered his restraint: 'Edith and Peggy were debating the end of the last act and who should have the final thought, and a great chill came over the rehearsal. John let them fight it out themselves.' His method paid off: according to Peggy Ashcroft, Edith Evans decided 'she never wanted to be produced by anyone but John for the rest of her life!'

While Gielgud hated *Waiting for Godot*, he was much more receptive to John Osborne's *Look Back in Anger*. Tony Richardson's production opened at the Royal Court three weeks after *The Chalk Garden*, and changed the face of British theatre. If Beckett's play ushered in the experimental work of Harold Pinter, N.F. Simpson, Ann Jellicoe and (in translation) Ionesco, Osborne's opened the door to writers such as John Arden, Edward Bond and Arnold Wesker, three very different talents united by their commitment to political change. Ironically, it was a quality that Osborne himself lacked: *Look Back in Anger* succeeded because Jimmy Porter's protest against drabness and conformity resonated with a new, idealistic but disaffected generation.

'It stinks, a travesty on England, a lot of bitter rattling on', was Olivier's first reaction. At its opening Beaumont left in disgust at the interval, while Rattigan, who only stayed on under protest, suggested afterwards that Osborne was merely saying, 'Look, Ma, I'm not Terence Rattigan.' But Gielgud's reaction to Osborne's bitter attack on middle-class complacency was more mellow and thoughtful, at least in recollection: 'I remember going and not expecting to enjoy it, and enjoying it hugely, and thinking, Oh I see now, this is a whole new lot of people. I remember coming away thinking, Now I know how a new sort of class has evolved, politically and socially and everything, and it's very well shown in this play, it's very dramatic, but I don't see there's any place in it for me.'

As it turned out, there was – but not yet. The revolution in the English theatre set in motion by Beckett and Osborne gathered pace only slowly. In the years immediately following the setting up by Devine of the English Stage Company at the Royal Court, the West End was still dominated by established playwrights such as Rattigan and Coward, and remained, in Arthur Miller's succinct phrase, 'hermetically sealed off from life'. Of the twenty-one straight plays running in London in the summer of 1959, sixteen were farces, light comedies or detective stories.

Gielgud complained of the lack of plays 'with big, romantic themes', and the abundance of light comedies. Reluctantly he went into Coward's new play *Nude with Violin*, a mediocre, whimsical and heavy-handed attack on art critics, in which he played an oily butler. He had distinct reservations about the play: 'It's very broad and a bit vulgar, but full of surefire situations and brilliant curtains, and I think it could not fail to be a success,' he wrote, 'but I should have to be rather clever at creating a character out of a "type" which does not really exist in life.' He also feared it might be difficult to avoid an imitation of Coward in a part that was so obviously a mouthpiece for his ideas. But his loyalty to Tennent's over-rode his artistic doubts.

He also made a mistake in agreeing to direct it. Coward admired him greatly as an actor, but of his directing he was less confident. This was the first time Coward had not been involved in the first production of one of his plays, and he and Gielgud spent a weekend in Paris talking it over. It was to begin its pre-London tour in Dublin, where it was agreed Coward would 'supervise' Gielgud's production after it had opened. At the first-night supper Gielgud declared: 'Mr Coward has been most considerate. He has stayed away from rehearsals in order not to interfere with any of my ideas.'

It was not to last. When Coward arrived in Dublin he thought Gielgud's production over-fussy, and decided to re-direct it. He re-wrote two scenes, made other adjustments, and took several rehearsals. Feeling Gielgud had been ignoring his own part, he tried to help him build it up. In this embarrassing situation Gielgud behaved with exemplary unselfishness, as Coward acknowledged, showing no annoyance or resentment. Coward was astonished at his humility and generosity of spirit.

They did, however, have one difference. Peter Sallis recalls the occasion: 'I was cast as an American character, which John suggested I play like Robert Eddison had played Donovan Mall in *Present*

Laughter. So I tried that, but after a few days he said I should play it like Marlon Brando. Can you imagine two more dissimilar characters? Then Noël said he didn't believe in me as an American, and I was replaced. I felt sick about it – but John was devastated. He took me to lunch in Wicklow, it was very touching. When I said goodbye he was in tears. "Oh, it's all my fault," he said. A lovely man, I absolutely adored him.'

The morning after the Dublin opening Gielgud gaily announced: 'I'm never any good in a play until I've been in it six weeks.' But Coward said he was thrilled with the wit and quiet authority of his performance. However, in London the play was met with hostility: 'Described as a comedy, it emerged as a farce, and ended as a corpse,' Philip Oakes wrote. Though the critics admired Gielgud's suave, Wildean performance, they wondered why he had wasted his talents on such feeble, outdated fare. Tynan wrote acidly: 'Sir John never acts seriously in modern dress; it is the lounging attire in which he relaxes between classical bookings; and his present performance as a simpering valet is an act of boyish mischief, carried out with extreme elegance and the general aspect of a tight, smart, walking umbrella.'

Despite the notices Coward's play was a commercial success, running for 511 performances at the Globe. Gielgud felt he had lost his way, and was uncharacteristically depressed. 'I thought this was the end for me,' he recalled. 'I thought I would have to go to Hollywood and play ambassadors and heavy fathers.' He stayed in *Nude with Violin* for seven months, but loathed the experience. 'It was a very silly play, and I was very stupid to do it,' he said later. But his performance won the approval of one eminent theatrical figure, who told his company that, if they wanted to understand about acting, they should watch John Gielgud in *Nude with Violin*. The advice, given to the Berliner Ensemble just before his death, came from Bertolt Brecht.

27

One Man and His Show

When Gielgud speaks the verse I can hear
Shakespeare thinking.
(Lee Strasberg, founder of the
Actors' Studio, 1959)

A S with so much in his life, Gielgud owed the inspiration for
Ages of Man to Ellen Terry. His great-aunt had devised a similar
lecture-recital, *Shakespeare's Heroines*, when her career had
shown signs of fading. As a boy Gielgud had been fascinated to see her
bring Portia, Beatrice, Juliet and others vividly back to life. 'She shed
her years miraculously and seemed a young woman,' he remembered.
In 1951 Emlyn Williams had devised a one-man show as Dickens, and
when it proved a success suggested to Gielgud he do something similar
based on Shakespeare. 'Oh no,' he replied, 'that sort of thing should be
kept for one's old age.' (Williams was just fifty.) But with his career
now at a low ebb, he changed his mind. During the war his own lecture
'Shakespeare – in Peace and War' had made a considerable impact.
Now, prompted by Beaumont and John Perry, he developed it into a
full-blown Shakespeare recital. During the next ten years he was to
perform *Ages of Man* in sixteen countries, reaching new audiences and
gaining fresh recognition as the supreme Shakespearean verse-speaker.

It was George Rylands' Shakespeare anthology *Ages of Man*,
published in 1939, which gave him his title and format. Like the book,
his recital was divided into three parts: Youth, Manhood and Old Age.
The mixture of pieces was an artful one. There were speeches from his
most celebrated roles, including Richard II, Hamlet and Benedick. He
also included Romeo, admitting wistfully: 'When I was young I just
flung myself into the role, but now, when I know better how to play it,

I can't.' But he also dipped into parts he had not played and never would play: Friar Laurence, Caliban, Lorenzo, Troilus and Berowne. He added some sonnets 'to give a leavening to the dramatic passages, to rest and soothe the audience', linking the items with plot summaries and his thoughts on acting Shakespeare.

He first gave the recital in a house in St James's Square in London, with Julian Bream supplying interludes on the lute. When he gave it at the Freemasons' Hall at the 1957 Edinburgh Festival, the demand was huge: all the reservable seats were sold immediately, and hundreds queued in vain for the unreserved seats on the day. What the audience saw that August afternoon was a slim, balding man standing at a reading-desk in a sober grey suit for two hours. What they heard, by common critical consent, was a compelling rendering of some of the greatest verse in the English language, and a reminder that Shakespeare was not only a master-dramatist but a poet of genius.

Gielgud achieved variety by following Ellen Terry's example, reciting or 'indicating' the lighter pieces and the sonnets, but acting 'full out' the weightier speeches, in his case those of Lear, Leontes and Richard II. He wanted people to listen to the words and the poetry without distraction, so he kept gestures and movement to a minimum: 'The tendency in doing Shakespeare has too often been to substitute activity and restlessness for the musical and athletic power of the verse, which drives it along if you speak it correctly and are still,' he explained. 'What I have been trying to demonstrate is that the words are so wonderful that if you serve them properly they will carry you.'

Ages of Man gave him a unique opportunity to play upon what one critic called 'this magnificent violincello voice'. He did so with spellbinding effect, exciting and moving the audience with the rich musicality of his verse-speaking. Philip Hope-Wallace wrote of his Hamlet soliloquies that they were 'wonderfully called up, holding the audience in total thrall by reason of something lucid yet passionate, vibrant yet without self-conscious thespian tremolo, which sets this actor above all others as a speaker of Shakespearean verse'. But this was not just a verse recital: Gielgud was compelling also because of the passion and intelligence he brought to what was effectively a performance. Covering a great variety of parts, he moved effortlessly between Hotspur and Lear, Leontes and Romeo, Cassius and Benedick, Hamlet and Caliban.

After the Edinburgh début he could hardly contain his glee. 'The recital went wonderfully well, and they could have sold out the house several times,' he wrote to friends. 'I think it will be a useful meal ticket for my old age!' It did indeed prove a money-spinner. Within months he had performed the recital in Berlin, Milan, Antwerp, Brussels and Paris. France's two leading actors, Jean-Louis Barrault and Madeleine Renaud, had been at Edinburgh, and on their return to France paid him glowing tributes. According to Harold Hobson, in his two performances in Paris he made a greater impression as a verse-speaker than Olivier, Richardson or Redgrave had. 'At a moment when any addition to our prestige abroad is to be welcomed, Sir John has rendered us a national service,' Hobson enthused.

In the years leading up to *Ages of Man* his Shakespearean verse-speaking had also been heard on the radio. After a fine 1948 *Hamlet* he had recorded *The Tempest* twice, and *King Lear*, and also played the Duke of Buckingham in *Henry VIII*, in a broadcast to mark Sybil Thorndike's golden jubilee in the theatre. But there had been many other plays, including *Ivanov, Richard of Bordeaux*, Coward's *Present Laughter* and, finally, Eliot's *The Family Reunion*. He had also made a brief return as John Worthing in a broadcast, with Rex Harrison and Jean Cadell, of the 'lost scene' from *The Importance of Being Earnest*.

His inability to do any kind of character accent was highlighted when he and Richardson played Sherlock Holmes and Dr Watson in a series of radio dramatisations of Conan Doyle's famous tales. His brief attempt at capturing one of Holmes' disguised voices was inept – and the cause of general mirth amongst actors when it was subsequently played at parties. He was no better at it when he read E. Nesbit's *Five Children and It* for Children's Hour some years later. 'It was absolutely terrible,' his director Hallam Tennyson recalls. 'He attempted Cockney accents, and it sounded too extraordinary for words.'

The Sherlock Holmes series was one of several occasions when he worked with his brother Val. Monica Grey, Val's third wife – Gielgud once introduced her at a party as 'Val's latest wife' – says there were difficulties between them: 'They weren't close as brothers, just loyal. They were so different you could hardly believe they were from the same family. Val was very proud of John and always went to his first nights, but he hadn't got John's wit or sense of humour, and there was a kind of unspoken jealousy there. John was such a success, and he rather looked down on Val's radio work, and Val felt this.' Hallam Tennyson, who worked with Val at the BBC, takes a similar view: 'Val absolutely adored John, and thought he was the greatest actor ever. But

John gave the impression of thinking Val was an old fuddy-duddy and pretty unmemorable as a director. He was fairly snooty about him.'

Just before he started on *Ages of Man*, Gielgud became involved in radio politics. In April 1957 he joined in the protests against the BBC's controversial proposal to cut the number of hours of the Third Programme by half. With Eliot, E.M. Forster, Fry, Masefield, Vita Sackville-West, Victor Gollancz and eight other luminaries he signed a letter to *The Times*, urging the BBC to think again. It had little effect. In September, as one of the vice-presidents of the Sound Broadcasting Society, he read from Shakespeare, Webster and Dryden in a 'funeral evening' for the Third at the Royal Court.

By this time he was back in Stratford, appearing as Prospero in *The Tempest* for the third time. Once again he was tackling his favourite part and working with his favourite director, Peter Brook; Alec Clunes was playing Caliban and Brian Bedford was Ariel. Brook is now caustic about his production and what he feels were 'some very extravagant ideas', but remembers Gielgud's willingness to look at Prospero afresh.

'John and I wanted to suggest a very dynamic character. He lives a tempest, his spell on the island has brought out of this bookish man a great ferocity. It's a play of revenge, that then becomes transcended and transformed. If he's a man of reconciliation from the outset, then you have no play or story. At the time it was unusual for Prospero to be played without a beard. The tradition was a Father Christmas figure, who presided over a series of beautiful, baroque images and sweet music. That character is an operatic bore, and John and I both wanted to avoid it. Out of this came this swift, energetic, clean-shaven man.'

As with *Measure for Measure* and *The Winter's Tale*, Brook forced Gielgud to discard his mannerisms and dig deep within himself, spurring him to give a dark, angry performance. With short, grizzled grey hair, dressed in an off-the-shoulder toga and sandals to give the effect of a hermit in an El Greco painting, he subdued any gentleness in Prospero until the final reconciliation. 'I tried to play it with strength and passion,' he recalled. Although unsure about the production, most critics felt he gave a performance of supreme emotional force. Hobson thought he had never spoken verse more finely; for Darlington it was the first Prospero 'that might have satisfied Shakespeare'. Karen Blixen, whom Gielgud had invited to Stratford, was profoundly moved by the production, and returned to Denmark inspired to write her last major work, 'Tempests'.

Tynan mixed praise with characteristic venom in a celebrated comment on Gielgud's work: 'Bodily inexpressive and manually gauche, he is perhaps the finest actor, from the neck up, in the world today. His face is all rigour and pain; his voice all cello and woodwind; the rest of him is totem-pole. But he speaks the great passages perfectly, and always looks full of thinking.' Like many of his more memorable comments, Tynan's 'totem-pole' jibe was a gross exaggeration. While Gielgud was never physically agile or especially flexible in his movements, he could still convey a thought or an emotion through subtle bodily expression.

In December *The Tempest* moved to London for a seven-week run at the Theatre Royal, Drury Lane. The first Shakespeare play to be staged there for twenty years, and the first production of *The Tempest* there since Macready played Prospero in 1833, it was a sell-out. Gielgud was performing in the theatre where Kean had played many of the great Shakespearean parts, and his fan mail touched on these historical associations. 'Magnificent,' Basil Dean wrote. 'I felt I was back amongst giants.' One generous tribute must have given him special pleasure. Headed 'Fan Letter – No Reply Please', it came from Richardson: 'It is a very great achievement, simple and noble, and with tear-bringing poetry. I am sure WS would be delighted with it. It is the best Shakespearean acting I have seen.'

The following summer, at the French Embassy in London, Gielgud was invested with the insignia of a Chevalier of the Légion d'Honneur, in appreciation of his work in furthering cultural ties between France and Britain. The French singled out not just his performances of *Ages of Man* in Paris, but his recent work as director of a neglected opera by a major French composer, *The Trojans*, performed at Covent Garden. This was the first professional English stage performance of Berlioz' massive work, and the first time the two parts had been played together in one evening. The epic five-hour production, which needed three intervals, was conducted by Rafael Kubelik, and starred Amy Shuard, Jon Vickers and, as Dido, Blanche Thebrom from the New York Met.

For Gielgud's first venture into opera this was a formidable undertaking. He had always been keen on opera, and in the 1930s had been to all the Mozart productions at Glyndbourne. His love of music was profound, but technically he was no more than an enthusiastic amateur. Unable to read music, he spent six months studying *The Trojans* by listening to records. 'You can't afford to make mistakes, and you have no time for experiments,' he remarked, perhaps wistfully, during rehearsals. He was scathing about the general lack of stage technique amongst singers. 'When they act, they are inclined to act on their own, melodramatically and without any inner impulse,' he said. He had a similar problem with the 150-strong chorus, for whom he demanded an extra week's rehearsal because of the singers' inability to be expressive. One day, after several fruitless attempts to get them to show emotion at the arrival of the Trojan horse, he rushed down in frustration from the back of the stalls, shouting, 'No, no, you look as if you're seeing off some not very good friends from Waterloo.'

It was all very different from the theatre. He was amazed when the principal singers left before he could give them their notes, which traditionally they expected to get later from a secretary. He was taken aback when Jon Vickers came on in a bowler hat with an umbrella and said, 'How many calls do I take after that aria?' As for the chorus, 'I was absolutely terrified of handling them. They all brought their knitting to do in their breaks, and when they started to sing I was so excited, but then I didn't know how to get them to stop.' Eventually he had recourse to a whistle.

He also had difficulties with Blanche Thebrom, who became 'rather autocratic about her clothes', and made drastic alterations without consulting him or the designer, his friend Mariano Andreu. Olivier's problems with Marilyn Monroe during the filming of *The Prince and the Showgirl* had recently made headline news, and the press speculated on a possible Stage Knight versus Prima Donna re-run. But though Gielgud may have ruffled some feathers by admitting in an interview before the first night, 'You can't expect very much in the way of acting from singers,' his leading lady was full of compliments about his directing, at least in public: 'Sir John knows what you are trying to do even before you know it yourself,' she said. 'Being directed by him is like dancing with an expert partner: you don't realise you're being guided. He lets you get on with playing in your own way first, so *you* create the character.'

In the circumstances Gielgud did an admirable job. 'John is quite exhausted, but has found it all terribly exciting,' his sister Eleanor reported after the dress rehearsal. Most of the music critics commended him for a clear, unfussy if conventional production: Desmond Shawe-Taylor thought it 'had the great merit of theatrical good manners; he was content to allow the music to speak for itself', while Peter Heyworth called it 'extraordinarily sure-footed, discreet and decisive'. Only Ernest Newman dissented, with a pompous dismissal of the whole idea of an opera being 'produced' by anyone 'with some connection with the theatre or the films'. But *The Trojans* was greeted as a landmark operatic event, and was revived in 1961, with Georg Solti taking over from Kubelik.

In February 1958 Gielgud made a rare excursion into modern dress – only his fifth in twenty years – in Graham Greene's *The Potting Shed*. Directed by Michael MacOwan at the Globe, it also starred Gwen Ffrangcon-Davies, Irene Worth and Redmond Phillips. The critics – except Hobson, a Christian Scientist – dismissed it as creaking Catholic propaganda. Tynan felt the story of lost faith and a Lazarus-like resurrection 'shot us back overnight to the dark ages', and that Gielgud, as a seedy provincial journalist, talked to the other actors 'as if he was going to tip them'. Gielgud never really liked the play, and was relieved the run was limited: 'It would get on one's nerves after a while,' he said after the opening, with an honesty that can hardly have pleased Tennent's.

Remembering Eliot's refusal to explain *The Family Reunion* to a non-believer, Gielgud had expected his agnosticism would provoke a similar response from Greene. In fact it did quite the opposite. 'Greene and I seemed to understand each other,' he said. 'I was afraid that he shouldn't like me, that I shouldn't like him either. That he would be bleak. Well, he isn't.' Greene had no worries about an actor without a faith playing the part, and was willing to explain any aspect of his play. When Gielgud asked him if he would write another for him, he replied: 'If I do, I hope you'll like the part in it better than you did this one.'

It was eighteen years since Gielgud had acted at the Old Vic. In May he returned there as Cardinal Wolsey in *Henry VIII*, the final play in Michael Benthall's ambitious five-year plan to present the entire Shakespeare canon. A sprawling chronicle of Tudor propaganda, more like a pageant than a drama, and only doubtfully credited to Shakespeare, it appealed to Benthall's love of flamboyance. But it seemed an odd choice for Gielgud's return to his old stamping-ground. Although he retained a vivid memory of the gorgeous Casson–Thorndike production from his youth, he had no great fondness for the play, and accepted the part only on condition that Edith Evans would play Katherine.

In rehearsal he found it hard to suppress his director self: Benthall remembered seeing him often 'bursting in a corner', so he listened to his ideas, and used some of them. Though Wolsey was supposed to be fat and vulgar, 'a butcher's cur', Gielgud played him as haughty and ascetic. But after the first night Benthall, a brilliant if impatient director, told him he had made a mistake not to play him as fat. Ever willing, Gielgud added padding and devised a more florid make-up, but still played Wolsey's downfall with great pathos and dignity. The speech gave him the chance to turn on the Terry tears, which he could do with remarkable precision. But it also genuinely moved him. Daniel Thorndike, playing Suffolk, recalls him coming off with his face bathed in tears, and saying: 'I'm just a silly emotional gubbins.'

The production toured in Europe, playing in Antwerp, Brussels and, as part of the British contribution to an International Theatre Festival, at the Sarah Bernhardt Theatre in Paris. As befitted a Chevalier of the Légion d'Honneur, Gielgud made a short speech in French on his arrival. The audience for the Paris première were, according to one correspondent, 'swept away by the masterly oratory of Edith Evans and John Gielgud'.

In the summer he suffered a great personal loss. His mother had been ill for the last year, and had not seen him on stage since *The Tempest*. In August she died, aged ninety-one. She had been an intensely loving and adoring mother, and her Kensington flat was filled with hundreds of pictures recording her son's career. 'They were very, very close,' his sister Eleanor recalled. 'Her death was a terrible thing for John, it shook him to the core.' Soon afterwards he wrote to Oliver Messel: 'The death of one's mother is such a very personal and strangely final business.' Committed to tour in North America, he had to sublimate his grief in *Ages of Man*.

It was said that Beaumont and John Perry had encouraged Gielgud to do the recital because, should the scandal create any problems, no other actors would be affected. Perry in fact accompanied him on the American tour, as did a family friend Patsy Ainley, Henry Ainley's daughter, who acted as his personal assistant. It was a gruelling, badly organised tour, forcing him to zig-zag across America, from Boston to Tallahassee, from Atlanta to San Francisco, sometimes passing through the same town three times. Beginning in September, he travelled eighteen thousand miles in thirteen weeks, and gave eighty-one performances in sixty different towns. (His theme song, he said, was 'This is mein Hertz'.) At first exhilarated, he gradually became disenchanted with life on the road, as extracts from his letters to his sister Eleanor reveal.

Stratford, Ontario, 21 September The stage most impressive and beautiful, but not altogether ideal for the recital, with audience on three sides of one. However it went remarkably well, with a huge and appreciative audience. Reception after, at which I had to shake hands with about 60 people – slept till 12.30 this morning.

Montreal, 2 October The tour is going very successfully so far. Rave notices and very good attendances. Enormous house at Ottawa – 2700 people in a big cinema – but it still went splendidly ... The car drives are very easy and beautiful on superb roads, and one hires very luxurious machines which Patsy and John have driven alternately.

Philadelphia, 14 October The tour is getting very hectic, but everyone tries to make it as comfortable as possible for me. Some of the halls are movie houses and baseball courts, and are in a bad shape and beastly to speak in, but others are excellent ... Boston was really a big success, the houses are full everywhere and notices ecstatic, so I suppose it is all one could have hoped for.

Chicago, 26 October The recital has gone simply wonderfully everywhere, in houses, chapels, auditoria of all shapes and sizes. At Ann Arbor we had an audience of 3500, and it seemed not to be any more difficult to hold them, thanks to excellent PA systems. Last night only 750 and an ideal hall, rather like the Wigmore, which was a very pleasant change. But the travelling and moving is an awful grind, and one never has a minute to go about and see anything – just catching planes and driving endless miles on good but frightfully monotonous roads, and resting and doing the show, and meeting a dozen or so boring new people every day and making polite conversation.

Chicago, 9 November Endless and exhausting journeys – and ridiculously big auditoria in Milwaukee and St Louis – each holding 5000! Rather like appearing in Olympia – and of course mikes, which I hate even when they're good. Audiences of about 1100 looking like brussel sprouts huddled in the desert! Last night a college chapel and only 1000, much better, but I was too tired to enjoy it. Here again tonight, then 5000 at Minneapolis tomorrow and two colleges before Denver.

Denver, 15 November Wonderful here. Comfortable old-fashioned hotel, fine weather, crisp, mountains in the distance, and only one recital in four days. Able to unpack at last.

San Francisco, 28 November Rather a disappointing visit, except for the lovely weather and the extreme beauty of the city itself . . . Patsy and I saw a very poor Tennessee Williams programme – *Garden District* – and taxied round desperately for hours afterwards trying to get food. Tomorrow two recitals, and on to LA on Monday.

Tallahassee, Florida, 12 December Ghastly week of travelling, but it is nearly over now, thank God.

Despite this hectic schedule, Gielgud remained outwardly unruffled and apparently inexhaustible. People were amazed at the way he could transform himself, arriving crumpled and exhausted at five o'clock at a new destination, then taking the stage three hours later in his dinner-jacket, seeming fresh and buoyant. But privately he still needed reassurance, as Patsy Ainley recalls: 'He would always say afterwards, Was I good tonight? And because I'd been with him for a while I could say, No, not quite so good – and he knew it. Some nights were brilliant, some nights he just got by on that wonderful technique. But he was nearly always good, and the audiences lapped it up.'

At the start of the tour he read about half of the passages. But soon he knew them all by heart, and would only turn to the book to indicate one had ended. He continually altered the programme, adding or dropping speeches or changing the sequence to keep it fresh. At first he wore reading glasses, but gave them up, as they became misted up during the more passionate speeches. 'I am still very emotional during the readings,' he explained near the tour's end, 'but now I've done them so often I'm not quite so much at the mercy of the text as I used to be. The *hoi polloi* do like to see you shed a few tears, but the trouble is it's very hard to cry just out of your eyes. Your nose drips, and that's rather bad.'

As an instinctive actor Gielgud often used images in his mind to help him convey emotion through the words. Until his mother died he had never seen anyone dead, and he now used the memory of her in his rendering of Hamlet's 'To be or not to be' soliloquy. 'On a certain line I always thought of her, of exactly how she looked when she was dead,' he explained. 'It came into my mind, it didn't hold me up, but it gave me exactly the right feeling of the voice for the line. It came to me naturally without knowing it the first time, and it was so vivid that I thought I could never speak the speech again without thinking of it, because it would help me to make the line right, and it always did.'

He was sometimes extremely nervous before the show. Conditions were often against him, especially in the smaller towns, as Patsy Ainley recorded in her diary. In Corning 'the hall was horrid, very hard, bare and much too wide – the air conditioning was on and in the background a bowling alley – John was very unhappy and felt the audience stiff – actually they weren't'. Usually he overcame such obstacles: in Indianapolis he performed in a church, but 'was so moving in Lear, he had the audience standing, and I was weeping too'. In St Louis 'he gave a lovely performance', despite an all-in wrestling match in progress in an adjacent hall.

Towards the end the strain began to tell: in Dallas 'the hall in the university was quite awful and the man in charge extremely rude, the sound was ghastly, John became furious, cut and cut, and romped through the performance in record time, which he has never done before'. Sometimes, as in Portland, Oregon, he wanted to give up: 'For some reason he was agin everything, said he wouldn't open in New York, wouldn't do one difficult journey in the south where we have to travel all night, and was thoroughly agin the world.'

But life on the road was not all motels and poor Chinese food. While playing in Tucson, Arizona he spent the weekend on a ranch in New Mexico owned by Stewart Granger and Jean Simmons. He visited Niagara Falls, and insisted on going to Disneyland. He went frequently to the cinema, though he often walked out, and spent a lot of time in clothes stores and bookshops. There were also countless interviews for local radio and television. On one television programme in the Midwest, asked if he could name someone who had helped him get started, he replied blithely: 'Oh yes, a wonderful man called Claude Rains. I think he failed, and went to America.'

San Francisco provided a welcome diversion. 'John had a wild night on the tiles, seeing the local bars, he enjoyed and saw new people, only got in about 4am!' Patsy Ainley recorded. Two days later, 'John had a glorious time visiting all his old haunts and shopping like mad. Christopher Isherwood took him round and they had a wonderful lunch, he was bubbling with news and gaiety when I found him.' Isherwood, by now a good friend, saw the show three times. 'John

Gielgud is really a very lovable person,' he wrote in his diary. 'What is interesting is his obsession with the poetry itself; you really do feel that he has a need to proclaim it. When he recites, he actually cries.'

In Beverly Hills Patsy Ainley wrote: 'He is having a fine time with all the old chums, who flock around.' He was especially nervous before the Hollywood audience because many in it, including James Mason and Cathleen Nesbitt, were his friends. 'He hadn't done it for two days, and had been having a very good time, the combination made him dry up twice, not that many people would have noticed.' The actress Elspeth March remembered the power of his performance: 'There was this slight figure with narrow shoulders, in an ill-fitting dinner-jacket, and balding. He had no props or scenery to help him, and yet at the end I couldn't believe he wasn't dressed in finery.'

The tour brought him a host of offers of work. Gregory Peck asked him to direct or act in a theatre he planned to build in La Jolla; Jean Vilar invited him to direct at the Théâtre National Populaire in Avignon; there was an offer to go to Stratford, Ontario the following year. His attitude to such proposals was ambivalent: 'He keeps stating he wants offers, but grumbles when they come,' Patsy Ainley wrote.

Before arriving in New York he spent Christmas in Cuba with his friend Paul Anstee: 'Lie by the pool all day, and night club bars and gambling at night,' he wrote from Havana. Unconscious as ever of any political circumstances, he almost missed his opening night. 'The hotel where I stayed seemed curiously empty, and the next day the revolution broke out,' he recalled. Having forgotten to get a re-entry permit, he just caught his plane, after a frantic day at the embassy.

The tribulations of the tour were more than compensated for by his reception at the 46th Street Theater. The recital was a sell-out, broke all box-office records for a one-man show on Broadway, and had to be extended for a fortnight. 'GIELGUD CONQUERS THE GREAT WHITE WAY' ran one headline, and the show became a hot ticket on the black market. He had refused to let his title be used used in press advertisements for the show, but happily relented when it came to having it in lights on a Broadway theatre. 'After all, I went on stage with no make-up or toupee,' he pointed out proudly.

After the opening Patsy Ainley wrote:

Last night was a terrific success, and as you can imagine very emotional. The house was packed, they stood up at the end and applauded, and we were all weeping! . . . Marlene Dietrich was

the first round after the curtain fell, and took complete charge of
John and the dressing-room, it was a fascinating sight. Then came
Diana Wynyard, who made a terrible fuss over the seats she was
given . . . Gloria Swanson, Truman Capote with his squeaky
voice, Mary Martin with her hair shorn for *Peter Pan* looking
really old . . . The Gishes arrived, Lillian with a black eye! . . .
John is thrilled, but still a bit bemused by everything.

The critics marvelled at the beauty of his voice, but also at his
lightning switches between rage, reflection, passion, wit and scorn.
Brooks Atkinson called his programme a masterpiece, one that 'renews
wonder over the glory of the English language'; Richard Watts Jr felt
that 'greatness was on view'. Even Tynan, writing for the *New Yorker*,
was admiring. 'Never before have I followed Richard II's slow ride
down to despair with such eager, pitying attentiveness,' he wrote, 'and
the excerpts from Hamlet were delivered with a mastery of rubato and
a controlled energy that put one in mind of Mozart.'

It was another part of this review that prompted one of Gielgud's
more celebrated remarks. Tynan, he said, had accused him of having
only two gestures, right hand up and left hand up. 'What did he want
me to do, bring out my prick?' But Tynan's actual description of his
stage movement was nowhere near so critical: 'Now and then, when
the impulse of a speech demands it, he takes a step or two to right or
left and permits his hands, which spend much of the evening
protectively clasping each other, to fly up in gestures that claw the air,
but for the most part he is still, and better for it.' Gielgud's
embroidering of the tale was a classic example of a mischievous habit
that was to increase with age.

His Broadway triumph quite overwhelmed him. 'The success here
has been – and is – quite unbelievable,' he wrote to his sister. 'Business
and booking going up all the time – crowds in my room after every
performance, people crying and God blessing and shaking hands with
one in the street. Now *Life* magazine is doing a page with photographs,
and Roger Stevens is talking of bringing me here in *Much Ado* in
September! I also have dates with Sol Hurok, Richard Rodgers, Otto
Preminger, and Rudi Bing – lunches all this week – so the going is
definitely good! Only wish you could have been here to share some of
the reflected glory! And I feel and keep very well despite parties every
night and far too much food and drink and cigarettes!'

In public he was modest about his achievement: 'I haven't got a very big or resonant voice, but I have a useful one,' he told a journalist. Speaking about Shakespeare at a luncheon at Sardi's he observed: 'I hate to put myself up as an authority on anything.' He worried that his quick shifts in mood during the recital would make him seem insincere: 'I feel a bit like a conjuror doing a lot of tricks.' Interviewers warmed to his obvious enthusiasm, one writing: 'His eyes sparkled and his right eyebrow kept shooting up in a most lively fashion as he made his points, rattling on in his usual offstage rapid-fire delivery. "I'm absolutely dead," he said, looking absolutely alive.'

Praise was showered on him throughout the five-week run, and the recital gained him a special Tony award. John Steinbeck told him he was 'moved and uplifted in a way usually set off by great music, which of course this is, and a great musician'. Patsy Ainley reported: 'John is really the toast of the town, and much loved by all. None appears to be jealous of his success, which is a tribute. He is still jubilant and sweet about it all, and not yet swollen-headed; I don't think he could be.' Celebrities continued to crowd into his dressing-room: 'When John Neville came round he burst out weeping, Irene Selznick came in too and did the same thing, each sobbing in their corner of the dressing-room what a wonderful evening it had been. Stars float round: Lauren Bacall, Douglas Fairbanks and his wife, Katherine Cornell, and Susan Strasberg, whose father Lee Strasberg runs the Actors' Studio, and who said, "Daddy says you are the only person who can act."'

In San Francisco Isherwood thought he seemed 'obsessed by the fear of another scandal', a fear that made him have 'the keenest concern for everyone else who gets into trouble with the police'. Gielgud had certainly been anxious about his first visit to America since the scandal, but his ecstatic reception put his fears to rest. 'Not a whisper of unkindness from a single newspaper here – which is rather amazing,' he told his sister. But in the final weeks of the run a paragraph by John Gordon appeared in the *Sunday Express*. Drawing attention to the 'moral turpitude' clause in the application form for American visas, he concluded: 'All who remember a little episode in Sir John's not so distant past will wonder what influence helped him over that hurdle.' Gielgud took this snide reminder of his troubles relatively calmly: 'It *would* come from London – and when I was not even there – but I don't really think many people will take much notice – and there was bound to be *one* fly in the ointment from some quarter I suppose.'

Relishing the social buzz of New York, he kept up a hectic night life: 'He admitted to being tired last night after two performances, then went out all night!' Patsy Ainley reported. She was clear where her duties began and ended: 'He has been madly gay, people pour in, not always the most desirable ones, but then one can't keep an eye on things in a big city! I sometimes feel he must wish I would go away, but as long as he is in the theatre I cling!' She noticed, however, how hard he found it to turn down invitations: 'Between everyone J is getting more and more exhausted,' she noted; he was being 'torn asunder' by all the friends around him.

He went to parties with his close friend the writer and librettist Hugh Wheeler, and dined variously with Marlene Dietrich ('she has become my greatest fan'), Fredric March, and Lillian and Dorothy Gish. When the run finished at the end of January 1959 he made a recording of it, then took a holiday with John Perry and Binkie Beaumont in Marrakesh ('Not lucky at the Casino') and Casablanca ('very Biblical, *Chu Chin Chow* atmosphere') before returning, re-invigorated, to England.

In July he brought *Ages of Man* to the West End, where it opened the re-built Queen's, an empty shell since 1940. 'It was a wonderful night for me, the notices are spendid, and I am very happy to be back at the Queen's with all its happy memories,' he told a friend. The recital's success led to an early revival of it in April 1960 at the Haymarket. Joyce Grenfell saw it, and wrote in her diary: 'The beauty of his voice moves me so terribly that I was looking through tears. So was he. I never saw a man cry so much.' But the English critics were more cautious than the American ones. Some found the programme too sombre or over-stuffed with riches, others criticised Gielgud for presenting little more than a technical *tour de force*. Among those who approved was the young Bernard Levin, who wrote extravagantly: 'Nobody who cares for the English language, or verbal beauty, or acting, or Shakespeare, can afford to miss this gallery of performances.'

On the basis of his pre-war success there with Shakespeare, Beaumont suggested he take the recital to the provinces. Here the response was relatively poor. In Liverpool audiences were thin, while in Edinburgh – were they still recalling the scandal? – he found them 'very hard'. In Brighton attendances were so low that Alan Melville and Godfrey Winn wrote letters to the local paper, expressing outrage at the town's lack of support. This ensured full houses for the rest of the week. 'I had to write to thank them, which I found somewhat humiliating,' Gielgud recalled. Yet for some people he was now a symbol of a dying tradition. Diana Devlin, then a student, remembers his visit to Cambridge: 'Privately my friends and I were sending him up, it was so much the Voice Beautiful, we just howled with laughter. I remember thinking, he really has come to the end, he's got nothing to say in Shakespeare to the younger generation.'

Gielgud began to worry that he was simply 'doing the purple passages', that *Ages of Man* was 'a bit snobbish' because he played only patrician, kingly and heroic roles. But the recital became a global success. He performed it in Venice, Spoleto, Tel Aviv, Jerusalem, Dublin and Warsaw; in cities throughout Australia and New Zealand; in Sweden, Denmark, Norway and Finland; in Leningrad and Moscow, where he met two of Stanislavsky's children; and again in America, where the recital was networked on national television. Not all the venues were ordinary theatres. In Galilee he played in a kibbutz; in Ankara it was the State Opera House; and in Washington he performed at the White House for Lyndon Johnson. There was even a spin-off in 1966, when he and Irene Worth took a similar recital called *Men, Women and Shakespeare* to both South and North America.

The original American trip had exhilarated Gielgud. But back in London, performing alone eight times a week, sitting by himself in his dressing-room between acts, he was often lonely and depressed. 'I no longer get a great kick out of seeing my name in lights,' he said. 'One suffers from a kind of terrible malaise. There isn't the same enthusiasm.' It was, he decided, time to call a halt.

28

Othello to Albee

One doesn't want to be left behind, stuffed,
and put in a museum.

(Gielgud in 1961)

IN autumn 1959, during the Broadway run of *Much Ado About Nothing*, Gielgud declared: 'I just don't enjoy acting any more. I feel I would like to give it up completely and direct. Acting is really too responsible a job. As one goes on one has to work harder and harder – and more and more is expected of you. You've got to live up to your reputation.'

His announcement created a minor sensation. Its timing seemed contrary, for it came just as he was attracting extravagant praise from the American critics, who thought his Benedick magnificent, exhilarating, and shimmering with wit. So was this merely a temporary loss of direction or nerve, a momentary Slav mood, or something more fundamental?

His enthusiasm for acting had in fact been waning for some while: as early as 1952 he was saying he preferred directing. He had by now done all the classical parts he wanted to do; he had recently turned down an invitation from Glen Byam Shaw to head the 1959 Stratford company, and play his fifth Lear. Out of sympathy with the work of Beckett and Brecht, he found no new English plays to attract him. Meanwhile his contemporaries were plunging boldly into the work of the new dramatists. Olivier had turned in a wonderfully seedy performance as a failed music-hall artist in John Osborne's *The Entertainer*, while Richardson had re-discovered his wonderfully as the dreamy, unhappy insurance manager in Robert Bolt's Brecht-influenced *Flowering Cherry*. Ahead of them both was Peggy Ashcroft, who at the Royal Court in 1956 had played a prostitute in *The Good Woman of Setzuan*, the first Brecht production in English.

Gielgud also saw little future for himself in the cinema. Since Olivier's *Richard III* he had appeared in only three films, all shown in 1957. In *The Barretts of Wimpole Street* he struggled with an overwritten part as Elizabeth's dictatorial father. Elizabeth was Jennifer Jones, the wife of the producer David O. Selznick, who told Gielgud not to take any notice of the director, Sidney Franklin. 'I thought this a rather bad beginning,' he recalled. Fearful of being melodramatic, he tried to suggest Mr Barrett's isolation. 'Loneliness is a quality which I think I can get over,' he said. Jean Anderson recalls: 'On the studio floor his performance seemed wonderful, and yet it didn't come off.' On screen he seemed strained, conveying little of the incestuous feelings he was supposed to have for Elizabeth. 'I was awful,' he said later, claiming he only made the film in order to pay a surtax bill.

He was only marginally more successful in Otto Preminger's film version of *Saint Joan*. The screenplay, by Graham Greene, cut Shaw's play almost by half, and left him with a relatively minor role as the Earl of Warwick. He was terrified of Preminger, a notoriously bullying director. During filming he confided in Richard Todd: 'He told me he envied my apparent ease and confidence before the camera,' Todd remembers. 'He confessed that he himself felt very ill at ease.' His performance was poised and haughty, but remote.

He turned down several parts, including the title-role in *The Trials of Oscar Wilde* ('Nobody could look less like Wilde than I do, not even Peter Finch') and Pontius Pilate in *King of Kings*. There was talk of his playing the former university don running a commando school in *The Bridge on the River Kwai*, but the part went to Jack Hawkins. He did make a cameo appearance, the first of many, as a gentleman's gentleman (Olivier had rejected the part) in the ponderous and never-ending *Around the World in Eighty Days*. In his single scene he was neatly upstaged by Coward; at one moment he was caught glancing uneasily at the camera. 'I hate films!' he said soon after. It was his last one for seven years.

A frank interview he gave to the critic Robert Muller in the spring of 1960 revealed his anguished state of mind. 'What worries me is that I haven't got any grandiose ambitions left any more,' he said. 'I haven't got any strong opinions, I'm no longer sure about how I feel . . . When one is young one's mistakes are excused, but when one is middle-aged one's mistakes are not forgiven. Or you fear they're not . . . I can't find the plays, can't find the parts . . . I'm so terribly difficult to cast in modern plays. I'm not a modern-looking man . . . I feel somewhat out of my time.'

Yet his bombshell in New York proved less explosive than it appeared. Even before he finished announcing his farewell, he qualified it by adding, 'I may do the odd play occasionally.' During the following decade he was to average only one a year, but some were very odd indeed. Most were done for Tennent's, but his influence was now less with Beaumont, whose love of the theatre, according to Coward, had been replaced by 'too much concentration on money grubbing'. Lacking anyone to give him honest, sound and independent advice, Gielgud made some bad errors of judgement, and had frequent recourse to *Ages of Man* to fill the lengthening gaps between parts.

His worst mistake was *The Last Joke*, a farrago of nonsense by Enid Bagnold in which he played a Romanian count. Richardson insisted on playing the role of a millionaire art collector, but only because he wanted to act with Gielgud again. But in rehearsal the two friends became increasingly unhappy and confused. The author wanted Gielgud to play her text *à la* Noël Coward, but he was delivering it *à la* Shakespeare. On the pre-London tour, Anna Massey recalled, the cast were 'all at sea', and to Bagnold's fury Gielgud and Richardson frantically re-wrote the text. Opening in September 1960 at the Phoenix, directed by Glen Byam Shaw, the play ran for just sixty-one performances. 'We've got ourselves a stinker, haven't we?' Gielgud admitted. The critics were unanimously hostile. Robert Muller wrote: 'This great actor's search has now reached the stage of desperation. (Next week: The Telephone Directory.)'

In fact his search had already led him back to Stratford, where Peter Hall was now artistic director of the newly created Royal Shakespeare Company. So far he had resisted Hall's offer to join the RSC, writing to him: 'I feel I have done my share of pioneering work both at the Old Vic and Stratford, and my own main problem is to decide what I really want to do – am able to do – to contribute some sort of decent work, which – with luck – I have another ten or twelve years or so in which to accomplish.'

But Hall shrewdly tempted him with an offer to play Gaev in *The Cherry Orchard*, a part he had never played, and a chance to work again with Peggy Ashcroft and Saint-Denis. In reply Gielgud floated the idea of his playing the one great Shakespearean tragic role he had never attempted: Othello. The play had always fascinated him, though in his youth he had seen himself as Iago. He had once played the part to Henry Ainley's Othello on the radio in 1932, and in 1953 he had convinced Quayle that he should do the same with *his* Othello at Stratford and in America. But then came the court case. He now decided he was unable to play such a 'coarse-bred' character. 'It isn't that I think I'm grand or aristocratic, but I know that I make that effect upon an audience,' he said.

He was also unsure about playing Othello, and was always looking for his nobler side. 'Othello is a saint overcome by villainy,' he had told Richardson. For years he had felt he would fail to convince in the scenes of passion and jealousy. His success as Leontes had changed this view, and he had included the Moor's speech to the senate in *Ages of Man*. But during its American tour he decided he had 'the wrong sort of voice and quality' to play the Moor. By 1960 he had changed his mind again, writing to Hall in October: 'The only Shakespeare part I want to play is Othello – you may think this madness – and I shall not be hurt if you think so . . . I have always feared I would be too cold for the part, but, in studying it lately, I believe I could have a shot at it.'

Few people believed he would be suitable as the proud, naive and gullible Moor. 'Rude am I in my speech,' Othello declares: could anyone be less so than Gielgud, the most mellifluous verse-speaker of the age? Hall, whatever his anxieties, felt 'the extraordinary sweetness and innocence of one side of Gielgud's personality' would enable him to do it. But Gielgud continued to harbour doubts: 'Othello is generally regarded as a slow, lumbering fellow, whereas I give the impression of being swift,' he fretted, as rehearsals loomed. He was anxious to establish whether Desdemona was still a virgin when she arrived in Cyprus: if she was, he felt that made Othello less animalistic, and the part more comfortable for him. 'I think it will be all right, I don't think he sleeps with her, do you?' he asked Dilys Hamlett before rehearsals began.

His suggestions for Iago showed his judgement to be seriously off-beam. His first choice was Peter O'Toole – 'so young and wild – he would be marvellous against me', but neither he nor Burton, whom he also wanted, were available. He put forward Alan Badel and Robert Shaw as possibles, then decided Badel was 'a bit obvious'. His ideas became more fantastical: he proposed the suave and sophisticated Rex Harrison ('might be fascinating casting'), or the small and ultra-cheerful John Mills ('we *must* have an Iago of some equal status in experience and style').

The part eventually went to Ian Bannen, who also played Hamlet that year at Stratford. Unhappy with this choice – he hoped Bannen would be Roderigo – Gielgud, as he so often did, took advice. He talked to Peggy Ashcroft, Edith Evans and Gwen Ffrangcon-Davies, but gave way when he discovered all three were in favour of Bannen. But he saw problems ahead, warning Hall: 'If disaster should fall on us – either through his fault or mine – we should not bring *Othello* to London (or conceivably find a new Iago). I don't want to stress such a possibility, but I do think one should keep it as a sort of air-raid shelter in case of a desperate emergency in the back of our minds.'

His fears proved well founded, but it was his own choice of director that was to create the emergency. As Peter Brook was committed elsewhere he approached Franco Zeffirelli. The fashionable Italian director's experience was mainly in opera, but he had just made his Shakespearean début with a vibrant, realistic and very Italian *Romeo and Juliet* at the Old Vic, starring Judi Dench and John Stride. Gielgud had seen it and, after lunching with Zeffirelli, reported to Hall that 'he took my criticisms in lively but delightful part', and that they had 'exchanged some exciting and infectious ideas' about *Othello*. Before going to Stratford he stayed with Zeffirelli in Tuscany, and returned fired with enthusiasm: 'Zeffirelli is a man of such charm,' he said. 'He has a striking talent for settings and costumes because he was trained as a scene designer.'

There were difficulties during rehearsal. Dorothy Tutin, playing Desdemona, remembers the death scene: 'John was very unphysical, that kind of violence was just not up his street. I practically had to throttle myself.' He also resisted Zeffirelli's idea that Othello was a vain man. He was embarrassed by his practice of getting an actor to speak his lines from the stalls, while Zeffirelli mimed the actions on stage. 'All right for Sutherland and Callas,' he said. But the two men agreed the part should be acted naturalistically, that Gielgud must suppress any rhetorical playing, and avoid 'singing' the verse.

Dorothy Tutin watched them rehearse the reputation scene late one evening. 'Zeffirelli asked John to keep it down, and he just said he would, then did it. It was incredibly moving and beautiful. I turned to Peggy, and both of us had tears in our eyes. He had a direct line to the verse: he was swift, unmannered, there was no fluting.' For Peggy Ashcroft, playing Emilia, it was one of the most exciting rehearsal periods of her career: she believed 'John was about to give one of the great performances of his life'.

The mood changed when the actors had their first sight of the sets, which only arrived on the day of the first dress rehearsal. Basing them on Titian and Tintoretto, the opera-loving Zeffirelli had designed realistic Italianate scenery more suited to Verdi than to Shakespeare. Grandiose, elaborate, dark and badly lit, they dwarfed the actors. The company also felt constrained by their vast Renaissance costumes, and Gielgud felt weighed down with his heavy armour and cloaks. The actors began to panic, as Ian Bannen remembered:

> Some scenes weren't properly rehearsed, and John got more and more nervous. He spent time on unimportant things, like which side to come in from for the 'Put up your bright swords' speech. Franco didn't say anything: I don't know if he was rigid with fear, or just knew it was going to be a disaster. At the final dress rehearsal we worked into the early hours. I went back to my dressing-room about five in the morning, the sweat pouring off me, and as I took my costume off I heard John's voice over the tannoy saying, 'Oh Christ, we haven't done the bed scene.' The bed hadn't arrived, so he had no chance to do his 'Put out the light' speech.

The actors suggested making the first few performances public dress rehearsals, and postponing the opening night. Hall refused, assuring them he could persuade Zeffirelli to cut some of the scenery. He failed to do so: Zeffirelli insisted, as if Stratford were La Scala, that the audience wouldn't mind the wait during scene-changes if what they finally saw was beautiful. The result was one of the most disastrous first nights in an English theatre.

Dressed in prune-coloured doublet and hose, with his face blacked-up, Gielgud was almost invisible against the dark brown sets – not just to the audience, but also to the actors. The huge Corinthian pillars swayed every time he leant against them, putting him in danger of doubling the role of Samson with Othello. The unwieldy sets caused long delays between scenes, accompanied by loud thumps. Othello's line 'Chaos is come again' proved prophetic: with two intervals of thirty minutes each, the performance of what was usually a swiftly acted play lasted four and a quarter hours. At the end Peggy Ashcroft burst into tears and ran off the stage.

There had been other disasters. In a key scene with Desdemona Gielgud's beard came loose, and he had to play the rest of it in profile.

'I didn't know whether to pull it right off or try to stick it on,' Dorothy Tutin recalls. Lines were fluffed, and in the final act Bannen, exhausted and stumbling around in the dark, committed what was to become a celebrated mistake: 'We were three and a half hours in and trying to put some zip into it,' he recalled. 'Having murdered Roderigo in pitch darkness, I was turning him over, and he was whispering to me to mind the stairs, and on rushed Emilia and asked me what had happened. And I said "Cassio's slain – I mean he's almost slain." It brought the house down, I've never heard such a laugh.' Later Gielgud described the production as his unhappiest in a theatre, but on the night he somehow kept his head. 'He steadied himself, he was just determined to get through it,' Bannen remembered. 'If the blooming theatre had caught fire I think he'd have gone on. During one scene change there was a great crash: I ran off, but he bravely stayed put.'

The press was justifiably rude about the fiasco: 'STRATFORD'S BLACK NIGHT' and 'OH THE PITY OF IT, ZEFFIRELLI' ran the headlines. Yet despite the chaos, some critics were moved by Gielgud's performance, Hobson ranking him among the best Othellos he had seen. Others felt he had missed the Moor's passion. Penelope Gilliatt wrote: 'Far from suggesting he could eat Desdemona raw for breakfast, he makes one feel he would really like her served on a tray in the library.' Hall later admitted that 'the poetry was extraordinary and the naïveté was honest; but the animal wasn't there'.

For the second performance Gielgud quietly dispensed with his heavy robes, and sneaked from the Stratford wardrobe the kaftans Quayle had worn for the part. That night he required courage of a different kind, as Dorothy Tutin recalls: 'He never talked about the notices, there was no self-pity, he didn't moan or rush around saying it was Zeffirelli's fault. He just took the play by the scruff of the neck, and saved it, by doing it swiftly and rhetorically, going back to his own style of acting. It wasn't what was wanted, but I don't see what else he could have done. I remember thinking, If ever there is courage in an actor, this is it. It was very inspiring.'

Gielgud blamed himself, remarking later: 'I should never have attempted to play Othello.' Zeffirelli, on the other hand, blamed everyone *but* himself. He told Bannen that Gielgud was 'a difficult man to get to know', and pointed to the difference in temperament between an outgoing and gregarious Italian and a shy, retiring Englishman. Yet while these were certainly qualities in Gielgud offstage, in rehearsal, as Hall remarked, he was 'as quick as a thoroughbred horse', an actor who 'improvises, takes risks, lives dangerously'. Zeffirelli could hardly have been wider of the mark when he claimed: 'I'm a pragmatic director, not a theorist who has it all worked out beforehand, and that was no good with John.'

Gielgud recalled that Zeffirelli 'wasn't able to give me – or even Peggy Ashcroft – the right sort of confidence . . . We both suffered bitterly.' It says much for his resilience that by the end of the run, curtailed to eighteen performances, he was able to look positively on the experience. 'Tomorrow I pack it up with considerable relief, though I wouldn't have missed the study and execution of the part for anything,' he wrote to Christopher Fry. 'It is rather a long time to spend on a near miss, but one never expects to succeed in a masterpiece the first time, unless all the circumstances are incredibly fortunate.' Once again his optimism helped him through.

Straight after the opening Zeffirelli had left for Chicago to direct an opera, and Hall had been able to make some changes to the sets. But Gielgud refused his offer to re-direct the play so it could be brought to the Aldwych, as originally planned. He did, however, remain with the RSC when it moved in December to its London base, to appear in Saint-Denis' production of his own version of *The Cherry Orchard*.

The illustrious French director, now commuting between bases in France and America, had been working on Chekhov's last great play when the Second World War broke out. This time Peggy Ashcroft was Madame Ranevskaya, Judi Dench was Anya, Ian Holm was Trofimov, and Dorothy Tutin played Varya. Gaev, the vague, foolish and eccentric landowner, forever potting imaginary billiard balls, suited Gielgud perfectly. While the production provoked varied opinions, his wistful performance was considered richly comic. Trewin thought he topped all previous Gaevs, and devoted his entire review to what he called a 'most extraordinary piece of creative acting', while John Whiting commented: 'I defy anyone to fault it. It is impudent to write about acting such as this. It must be seen to be believed.'

Gielgud had not worked with Saint-Denis since the celebrated production of *Three Sisters* in 1938. Having the luxury of eight weeks' rehearsal time, Saint-Denis decided that for the first two they would just read the play. Roy Dotrice, playing the elderly retainer Firs, recalls Gielgud's reaction: 'At the start of the second week John said, "For God's sake, let's do some acting!" He couldn't stand it any more, and he was right: we'd read the thing out of sight, and we weren't progressing.'

There was a small difference over his costume, which Saint-Denis wanted to be faded, like Gaev's life. When the designer Abd'Elkader Farrah went to the fitting he found Gielgud dressed in much too stylish clothes. But when Saint-Denis insisted they were too stagy, he at once agreed to go for the required shabby look. He was less compliant when George Murcell, who was playing Lopahin, offered on a free afternoon to show him how to play billiards. 'Don't be so silly, I don't want to do that,' he replied, all too aware of his manual clumsiness.

During *The Cherry Orchard* he became a kind of father-figure to some of the younger actors. Judi Dench had been bullied and mocked by Saint-Denis in rehearsal, and was extremely nervous on the first night. As she prepared to go on again after the first act, Gielgud told her: 'If you had been doing that for me I'd be delighted.' From that moment she played it for him, and settled into the role. Dorothy Tutin also remembers his warmth: 'John was very sweet with Judi and me on stage, the way he put his arms around us, the way he looked at us, always in tears. Although he wasn't usually a physical actor, he *was* with us, he looked upon and treated us as children, and it was easy to nestle up to him and put your head on his shoulder.'

Perhaps it was the unusual physical closeness he had with the two young actresses that prompted him one day to make an extraordinary confession to Dorothy Tutin. 'He asked if he could come and see my boat in Chelsea, and when we were in the taxi he amazed me by suddenly saying out of the blue, "I would have loved to have had children." I was dumbfounded.' His regret seemed to be genuine, a sentiment that he would express more than once in later years.

His mischievousness was also in evidence. Once, about to go on stage, he handed Patience Collier a cucumber, said, 'Put that some-where for me, will you?', then swept on. But it was his tolerance that impressed Roy Dotrice who, according to Hobson, was the star of every scene he appeared in, and acted Gielgud and Ashcroft off the stage. Gielgud's patience with his fussy antics still astonishes Dotrice today: 'I blush to think of it, but in those days I was into the Method,' he says. 'I was busying and fiddling throughout, spilling coffee and rattling tea-trays. During John's magnificent ode to the bookcase I was picking bits of fluff off him, and generally behaving outrageously. How he put up with me I don't know.'

Gielgud followed this triumph with another in one of his most successful earlier roles, Joseph Surface in *The School for Scandal*. In his own production at the Haymarket, in a re-cast company that had

Richardson playing Sir Peter Teazle, Geraldine McEwan as Lady Teazle, Gwen Ffrangcon-Davies as Mrs Candour, and Richard Easton as Charles Surface, he took over Joseph from John Neville for a North American tour. His incisive performance showed his feeling for the period and his comic timing to be as immaculate as ever. Worsley wrote: 'While others make one conscious of the lack of substance in some of the repartee, Sir John makes every sentence seem to carry twice its weight by phrasing it so perfectly.' His acting in the famous screen scene with Richardson was particularly admired. Peter Barkworth, playing Sir Benjamin Backbite, recalls: 'He was remarkable, he got enormous laughs without apparently trying for them. He made it all seem so easy.'

Still looking for modern plays, he turned down Wynyard Browne's *A Choice of Heroes*, but agreed to play Julius Caesar in Jerome Kilty's *The Ides of March*. Based on the novel by Thornton Wilder, it dealt with events in Rome in the months before Caesar's assassination. Once more Gielgud blew hot and cold. When he first read it he was enthusiastic, if critical, writing to Kilty: 'There is a tremendous lot wrong with it, though, as Gertie Lawrence said on a famous occasion, "nothing that can't be fixed".' He made detailed suggestions for improvements, and threw in many ideas about the characters: 'Catullus, couldn't he be much more strange and disturbing – a sort of Dylan Thomas, ill, impulsive, crazy?'

Kilty followed most of his suggestions, but then fell victim to his vacillation. His letters to his wife reflect his frustration with Gielgud. In October 1962 he wrote: 'When he'd read the new version he was very enthusiastic – "vastly improved", "the play is there at last" . . . I talked to him yesterday. He was a different person. No enthusiasm – nothing . . . Will a decision be made? Who knows? I'll even try to force him to say No. But I bet he won't do that either.' Gielgud saw the play in Berlin, from where Kilty wrote: 'He loved it! We talked until two-thirty afterwards.' On Thanksgiving weekend the deadline was approaching: 'Tomorrow at eleven Sir John will give us his final word. Yesterday I talked to Philip, who said, "It's in the bag." But one never knows anymore.'

Having finally agreed to do it, Gielgud enthused to Alan Dent, 'Not since *Richard of Bordeaux* have I had such a feeling about a play,' but then added, 'It might be wishful thinking.' The company included Irene Worth, John Stride and Julian Glover, and Gielgud was enthusiastic about having the venerable Marie Löhr involved. At first all went well, as Kilty reported: 'John said it is the first time in years that he finds himself in the third week of rehearsals and *still* enthusiastic about the play.' As Gielgud's co-director he noted: 'John is still playing Joseph Surface but gradually is settling down. We seem to work well together although I often find myself having to contradict him when he wants the actors to do something I don't like. Poor actors. But they all take it with a good humour.' Told off by Kilty for crying at an inappropriate moment, Gielgud replied: 'I can't help it, I was born with my bladder too close to my eyes. I blink, and out it comes.'

More serious problems arose at the start of the pre-London tour: 'The opening was terrible as far as John and Marie Löhr went,' Kilty wrote from Oxford. 'John did the first act OK but forgot all his lines in the second part and old Marie didn't know her words anywhere.' After re-writes and cuts the play improved, as did business, and the public seemed enthusiastic. 'How else explain the stacks of fan mail Gielgud gets?' Kilty wrote. 'After several years, he says, of none at all?' But when the play opened at the Haymarket in August it was booed. The critics dismissed it as mere 'desiccated talk', a hack costume drama full of lifeless stereotypes and wooden acting. The 'experimental' mixing of new dialogue with imaginary letters from Caesar, Cleopatra, Brutus and others, and of modern and period costumes, was felt to be confusing and pretentious.

Gielgud, wearing a half-toga over a grey lounge suit, was accused of offering nothing but 'surface mannerisms'. Gerald Barry wrote: 'Here is an SOS. Will Sir John Gielgud, now believed to be wasting his great talent at the Haymarket, please return at once to the theatre of Shakespeare, where his admirers are dangerously restive.' The play closed after seven weeks. Beaumont blamed the public for failing to accept Gielgud in a new kind of play. But he himself stayed away after the first night, and when Gielgud heard about the closure it was not from Beaumont but from Marie Lohr, who wrote to Kilty: 'It's all too sad, and I still can't believe it. Poor John is right on the floor.' Kilty recalls: 'He felt personally attacked, his spirits really plunged.'

Even *Ages of Man* was no solace. 'John is as low as ever,' Marie Löhr wrote in the closing week. 'He is off to Australia with his solo play. He seems to hate the thought.' It was a further blow when he received no invitation to take part in the celebrations to mark the four-hundredth anniversary of Shakespeare's birth. He had come to a crossroads. One road led back to the past, to Shakespeare, and to the comfortable bosom of his admiring traditional public; the other into new, unexplored territory, more exciting but more dangerous. The old way no longer tempted him: fearing to become a museum piece, he decided to abandon Shakespeare. But he lacked a map and a guide for the unfamiliar new country.

During 1963 he published *Stage Directions*, a technical book about acting and directing. In the introduction he reaffirmed his belief in the theatre of colour, fun, excitement and movement, the theatre of his youth. 'I cannot bring myself to care for elaborate dialectic argument on the stage,' he wrote. 'Abstract plays have only appealed to me occasionally. I hate propaganda in the theatre ... Shapelessness, redundance, and acute class-consciousness irritate me profoundly.'

'John is in a "Wesker state",' Enid Bagnold wrote to Edith Evans. 'Dying to be new!' But much of the new repelled him; he felt it made a fetish of ugliness, that it was in bad taste. He walked out of N.F. Simpson's *One-Way Pendulum*, and booed Osborne's *The World of Paul Slickey*. During a David Mercer play, in which the actors came and talked to the audience, he told the girl who approached him to 'bugger off' ('I thought it was in the spirit of the play'). After seeing Ionesco's *Rhinoceros* he yearned for Shaw's 'clear dramatic arguments and fine English prose'. He was especially shocked by Genet's *The Blacks*, which he saw in New York. 'You can never be certain that something indecent isn't going to happen, and in a mixed audience this makes me embarrassed,' he confessed. He compared 'the honest coarseness' of the Crazy Gang to Genet's 'sophisticated pornography'.

In 1958 he had turned down Devine's invitation to play Hamm in Beckett's *Endgame* at the Royal Court, fearing he would be unable to hold an audience while being confined to an armchair and wearing dark glasses. He also disliked the play's loneliness and despair: 'It nauseates me, I hate it,' he said. 'It's depressing for me to go to the theatre and see completely gloomy and sub-human characters in despair.' He wanted to work with Joan Littlewood, but when she suggested he play the homosexual king in Marlowe's *Edward II*, he declined. Yet he longed to break into the avant-garde.

His chance came at last in 1964 – but not in England. Edward Albee had shot into prominence with his savage one-act play *The Zoo Story*, which made an impact on American theatre similar to that of *Look Back in Anger* in England. After *Who's Afraid of Virginia Woolf?* Albee was now an international figure; but his new play *Tiny Alice* was a very different work. Its story centred on Brother Julian, a lay brother who becomes involved with a rich woman, Miss Alice, but is eventually abandoned by her, and by everyone else. An obscure and portentous allegory about religious martyrdom and sexual hysteria, laced with theories of physics, it perplexed not just audiences and critics, but the actors and its director too.

Albee wanted Albert Finney to play Brother Julian, but when his producer Richard Barr secured Gielgud's acceptance, he raised no objection, even though he had hoped for 'somebody younger and more sexual'. When Gielgud read the first two acts he was torn. He failed to understand the play, and felt it was 'quite wrong and ridiculous my playing this chaste young man'. On the other hand he was intrigued: the play, he told Albee, had 'a kind of grandeur and a certain glamour which make it exciting to me'. Seeing the door marked 'avant-garde' suddenly opening he accepted, suggesting Irene Worth for Miss Alice after Vivien Leigh had turned down the part.

Foolishly, he failed to read the third act until he arrived in America to rehearse. To his dismay he found that the play ended with a mock crucifixion scene, in which Brother Julian dies after a nine-minute soliloquy. This speech became the focus of a bitter dispute with Albee. Gielgud was worried that, in seemingly identifying with Christ, his character might be considered blasphemous. 'Not being religious myself, I don't know what might offend others,' he said. But his main objection was a theatrical one: his instincts told him the speech was much too long, and that nobody would sit through it. 'They'll all be charging out getting their snow boots,' he said.

Albee, however, refused to cut the speech, at least until he had seen it done on stage. Gielgud duly rehearsed it, and played it uncut at a couple of previews, after which various versions were tried. Albee remembers: 'I was word proud in those days, and always considered I was right. When John told me he couldn't do the speech as it stood, I said in my great wisdom, "Don't be ridiculous, of course you can."'

Gielgud remained loyal publicly. But during rehearsals he continually asked Albee about the meaning of the play. Albee replied unhelpfully, 'You can't play the meaning, you have to play the reality of the characters,' and refused all pleas to consider re-writing certain scenes. The director, Alan Schneider, recalled: 'Gielgud wanted to withdraw almost daily, and was sustained mainly by post-rehearsal brandy and Irene's good-natured joshing.'

The night before the opening Gielgud predicted, 'We'll be stoned tomorrow.' He was especially worried about the climax of the second act, where Irene Worth, with her back to the audience, had to open her gown and, apparently naked, embrace him. In fact she was clothed, but this didn't prevent Gielgud from being embarrassed, and feeling the audience were too. 'It was supposed to be sort of D.H. Lawrence,' he remarked. 'It was a very phoney scene.' He confided to the actor Roddy McDowall: 'I say to myself, thank God it's just dear old Irene.'

Most of the audience were baffled by the play. Stink bombs were set off at a preview, there was booing at most performances, and it got a critical mauling. Philip Roth called it 'The Play That Dare Not Speak Its Name'; people were divided between thinking it a hoax and a masterpiece. 'I liked it because it was so empty,' said Andy Warhol. Albee called a press conference, and chided the critics for their negative reviews and for being too stupid to understand his play. Gielgud recalled the aftermath: 'Irene Worth and I both implored him to reconsider certain scenes. He promised to do so, but then he disappeared, and we never saw him again.'

Despite the fuss, or maybe because of it, the play ran for six months at the Billy Rose Theater. Gielgud gained good notices for his heroic struggle against the odds. Tennessee Williams, who found him in his dressing-room 'in fine spirits and looking remarkably young', wrote: 'Gielgud is giving a brilliant performance, I think the best I've ever seen him give.' Stanley Kauffmann described his final soliloquy: 'The audience began to murmur and rustle as he kept on and on. The buzz swelled a bit, punctuated by giggles. Towards the end he seemed isolated, separated by an invisible wall of protest. I was filled with admiration, not because of any "show must go on" hokum, but at his power of concentration, his inner ear. He had kept his own music going against a hostile chorus.' Afterwards Alan Schneider said to him: 'All I can do is thank you for your willingness, your trust and understanding.'

Three years later, in an interview due to be published in a book, Albee claimed that Gielgud had insisted the final speech be cut almost entirely, that he 'pretended' to forget sections of it and refused to learn it as written, and had behaved like a spoilt prima donna at rehearsals. Gielgud deeply resented what were clearly false accusations, and persuaded the book's publisher to delete Albee's remarks. He was bitter about Albee's behaviour, and the two of them didn't speak for five years. Albee now admits he was wrong about the speech. 'I just did a production in Connecticut, and we had to cut it even more,' he says. 'John was right: it's too fucking long, it doesn't work.' On Gielgud's performance he looks back in wonder: 'He was able to get Julian's ascetic quality very beautifully. Both he and Irene were absolutely perfect. John can handle language so expertly, without any effort. Despite the fact he goes round saying he can't understand anything, his intuitive intelligence as an actor is extraordinary.'

As with *Othello* and *The Ides of March*, Gielgud later avoided any reference to the production in his memoirs. Yet hard though the experience had been, he had made the breakthrough to the contemporary scene. But he still found no roles to tempt him in England, least of all the drag queen hostess in Osborne's *A Patriot for Me*, a part offered to him by Devine, and rejected by thirty other actors, including Coward.

Once more he turned to his beloved Chekhov, and to one of his most difficult roles. *Ivanov* is probably the least satisfying of Chekhov's plays, a work he dashed off quickly and then revised endlessly. It had never before been presented in the West End, but Gielgud had admired it ever since seeing Komisarjevsky's production at Barnes in 1925, with Robert Farquharson as Ivanov. He liked its changing moods, the mixture of farce and tragedy, the touching yet ridiculous characters. Using a literal translation by Ariadne Nicolaeff, he adapted and directed it at the Phoenix, with a top-class company that included Yvonne Mitchell as Ivanov's wife Anna Petrovna, Claire Bloom as Sasha, Roland Culver, Angela Baddeley, Richard Pasco and Nora Nicholson.

As the tortured, egotistical provincial landowner, bankrupt and out of love with his consumptive wife, Gielgud managed to avoid both monotony and melodrama in presenting a character whose anguished self-pity can very quickly pall. Many critics thought it one of his finest creations; Ronald Bryden wrote: 'Gielgud goes to the heart of his neurosis, exposing every symptom surgically, showing in every strangled gesture and protest the coil of guilty self-love-hate in which he struggles.' Claire Bloom, as the young woman who forces Ivanov to marry her, recalled how he helped her: 'When he said, "Oh my God, look at me, I'm an old man and there's grey in my hair, and I can't go through with it," I didn't have to do what is called "acting". We reached an emotional pitch together in that scene that I have never felt with anybody else.'

During this erratic period in his career a slim, handsome, dark-haired young man came into Gielgud's life. Martin Hensler, once married but now divorced, was a much-travelled Hungarian who had come to England after the 1956 revolution. Gielgud had come across him at an exhibition at the Tate Gallery, and they had become lovers. Hensler was a retiring man, something of a loner, and it took six years for Gielgud to persuade him to come and live with him in his Westminster home.

He had all the practical skills Gielgud lacked, and soon became indispensable to him. Some friends and visitors thought their relationship a curious one. The actress Pinkie Johnstone remembers a lunch at Cowley Street: 'Martin was very rude, he belittled John throughout the meal, and John just took it. He seemed quite a difficult man, hard for outsiders to like. But it was wonderful to see John with someone to love and be loved by.'

Martin Hensler pledged himself never to leave Gielgud. Few of his friends imagined then he would become his companion for life.

29

A Sense of Direction

You've controlled me so well.
(Richard Burton on Gielgud's directing,
Hamlet, 1964)

I N the decade that followed his first performance of *Ages of Man* in
1957, Gielgud spent more time directing than acting. As well as two
operas, he directed eight plays in London, four of which had runs
on Broadway. In America, in addition to staging *Much Ado About
Nothing*, he directed two new plays by American playwrights. The
quality of his work was erratic, plumbing new depths in a particularly
abysmal Tennent's production, but reaching a peak in his work with
Richard Burton in *Hamlet*. In between he gained Tony awards for his
work on two new plays, one English and one American.

In 1958 Rattigan finally persuaded him to become involved in one of
his plays, but as director rather than actor. The year before he had
played Crocker-Harris in *The Browning Version*, but only on the radio,
in a production by his brother Val. In a linked broadcast Rattigan said
he had been 'trying desperately' for twenty years to secure Gielgud for
one of his plays. But meanwhile he had been mining his life for
material: in 1954 he had used Gielgud's court case as the basis for the
second part of *Separate Tables*. Originally the fake major at the centre
of the play was arrested for 'persisently importuning male persons' on
an esplanade, but Rattigan then changed the offence to groping
women in the cinema. Representing homosexuality on stage was still
officially seen as a threat to public morals, and Rattigan feared a ban
from the Lord Chamberlain. When an attempt was made to use the
original in the New York production two years later, the American
producer Robert Whitehead warned Rattigan it would create more

'distasteful' publicity about Gielgud's case and about homosexuality in the British theatre.

Rattigan's new play also had a sexual sub-text. *Variation on a Theme* was an updated version of Alexandre Dumas fils' *La Dame aux Camélias,* based in part on the tortured relationship between Margaret Leighton and Laurence Harvey. Although it told the story of a doomed affair between a young ballet dancer and a consumptive older woman, Rattigan was also writing in code about his own homosexual relationships with younger men.

The cast included Leighton herself, Jean Anderson and Michael Goodliffe. Gielgud, embracing Guthrie's philosophy that rehearsals should be fun and exciting, gave rein once more to his helter-skelter imagination. It received a mixed response. 'I liked trying things a lot of ways, so I enjoyed his inventiveness,' Jean Anderson says. 'But some people couldn't take it, they got desperate, and rehearsals were fraught with difficulties.' One young and inexperienced actor, who thought Gielgud's directing old-fashioned, shouted at him: 'For Christ's sake, can't you make up your fucking mind?' Possibly unsuited to the part anyway, he was sacked by Beaumont during the pre-London tour.

Variation on a Theme was lambasted for being old-fashioned and novelettish; Rattigan was criticised for being out of touch, and evasive about homosexuality. The playwright Shelagh Delaney, then nineteen and unknown, thought his treatment of the subject so ridiculous she was provoked into writing her first play, *A Taste of Honey.* The message about changing audience tastes was clear: while *Variation on a Theme* closed after four months, the shortest-ever run for an original Rattigan production, Delaney's fresh and outspoken play was a vibrant success, and was soon to enjoy a good run in the West End.

Gielgud's production clearly identified him as a member of 'the old guard'. He was criticised for allowing the lavish costumes to dominate the scene: Tynan complained that the star of the show was the designer Norman Hartnell. The production was heartily disliked; Hobson thought it 'too awful to think about'. Even Rattigan criticised Gielgud privately: 'As all he does is turn his back on the players and correct their intonations, it doesn't have very much effect.' This was a caricature of Gielgud's style, prompted perhaps by the play's failure. But Gielgud had not been helped by Beaumont's insistence that its complex sexual undercurrents should be played down. 'We don't want anything unpleasant,' he had said pointedly at the first reading.

After struggling with an inferior piece by an established playwright,

Gielgud restored his reputation with a production at the Comedy of the first stage play of an exciting new writer. Peter Shaffer's *Five Finger Exercise* was a taut, bitter exploration of the hidden longings and passions within a middle-class family, whose lives are turned upside down by the arrival of a German tutor for their teenage daughter. Gielgud had recruited an interestingly mixed company, with Shaftesbury Avenue stalwarts Adrianne Allen and Roland Culver working alongside talented younger actors such as Michael Bryant and Yorkshire-born Brian Bedford, part of a new generation of actors who dressed in scruffy jeans and T-shirts for rehearsal, and were bursting with Stanislavskian ideas.

Shaffer recalled that by the end of the first week the company were rushing around 'with the galvanic urgency of a circus troupe on cocaine'. But this time young and old responded well to Gielgud's direction. Roland Culver felt his method, or lack of it, took the monotony out of rehearsals: 'Each day is an adventure and one is kept on one's toes,' he said. Brian Bedford was also enjoying himself: 'Some people find his sudden burst of ideas annoying, but I enjoy keeping up with them.' Juliet Mills, just out of boarding-school, was making her stage début: 'I was a very young sixteen, and he was absolutely sweet to me. It wasn't nerve-racking at all, he was very encouraging and lots of fun. He gave you five or six suggestions, and you chose from them. Often he would act things out, tippy-toeing round the stage on the balls of his feet.'

Michael Bryant, playing the tutor, also found Gielgud helpful, but baulked at his more bizarre suggestions. 'You felt you could do what you wanted to do, and he would help you, which is what you want from a director. He was very kind, very good to work with. He didn't object to Brian and me acting naturalistically, he was most supportive. But sometimes he seemed very vague. Once I made an exit up the stairs, and came down them on my next entrance. John said, "No no, Michael, come in through the French windows." I said, "But John, how did I get into the garden, did I shin down the bloody drainpipe?" And he said in a jokey sort of way, "Oh Michael, you're so *dreary*."'

Bryant also recalls two changes that Gielgud proposed. 'He wanted to cut a speech in which I referred to looking in the mirror in the morning. When I asked him why, he said, "They'll think you were going over there to wash your balls." Next day he asked me why I'd left the speech out; when I reminded him, he said, "Oh that was rubbish!" He also wanted to cut Walter's famous speech about my father being a

Nazi – it's in all the audition books now, but he said it was boring; that was his favourite expression. I told him that I was going to say it anyway, so it stayed in. After the first night he said, "You were right, I was wrong." He was a very generous man.'

Despite his reputation, Gielgud could be silkily tactful and empathetic when required. In 1959, while directing Ralph Richardson in *The Complaisant Lover*, Graham Greene's play about a suburban love triangle, he was on his best behaviour. Richardson was never an easy man to direct: he liked to find his own way to a character, and not necessarily let the director in on the secret. He once said there were only two things an actor needed apart from talent, a pencil to write down the director's notes, and an india-rubber to rub them out when he's not looking.

But Paul Scofield, who also starred with Phyllis Calvert, remembers that Gielgud handled Richardson skilfully. 'Ralph created a circuit of dynamic energy into which John merged with sympathy and grace, together with a smattering of misgiving. He displayed a profound understanding of Ralph, and their relationship was courteous and perfect. Deep down Ralph was his own director with his own baton beat, but John displayed unwonted tact. It was a fascinating illustration of how a director can afford release to an actor who knows precisely what he wants and needs to do.'

Phyllis Calvert remembers being prepared for the worst: 'Binkie called me in and said, "You don't know what you're letting yourself in for, you'll have a terrible time, John changes his mind all the time." But that was my idea of heaven, I don't like getting stuck with anything.' Previously, after a long and difficult dress rehearsal of *Five Finger Exercise*, Beaumont had persuaded Gielgud not to give the exhausted actors their notes the same night. This time, having little enthusiasm for the play, but for once being entirely satisfied with the company's work, Gielgud left them alone for the final week's rehearsal: 'I'm not coming in any more, I'll only ruin it,' he announced. Even when he returned during the run he resisted the temptation to make changes, though Phyllis Calvert recalls him saying, 'I'm just going down to see Ralphie, to get him to cut out a few of his dance steps.'

Gielgud helped Richardson give an inspired performance as a dreary suburban dentist in Greene's thin tragi-comedy, which ran for 402 performances at the Globe. But he could do nothing with his next Tennent's assignment at the same theatre. *Dazzling Prospect*, a trite, dull play by M.J. Farrell and John Perry, about horse-racing and the goings-on of lovable Irish country folk, was booed vociferously on its opening night, mauled by the critics, and taken off after twenty performances. Gielgud directed it out of misplaced loyalty to his friends the writers. Interviewed after the opening, forlorn and 'sad-faced' in the face of his worst notices as a director, he declined to apportion blame: 'I don't like discussing failures, it only leads to one saying bitter things one might regret afterwards,' he said. 'I did the play because I was fond of the people who wrote it. It didn't require much in the way of subtle treatment. One has to try everything once.'

Sarah Miles, whom he had spotted at a RADA public show and given her first West End part, remembers his embarrassment: 'He kept apologising for being hopeless: "Oh my God, I'm so bad at this sort of thing, I'm so sorry everybody, I'm just the most terrible director." I was amazed such an important man of the theatre should say that. Of course he knew damn well the play was a load of old twaddle. I think he was also apologising to himself for having got into it. You felt half of him was somewhere else, and he could be terribly vague. But he was caring and considerate to me. I couldn't help but love him.'

When directing himself Gielgud still tended to ignore his own performance and concentrate on the other actors. This could be disconcerting even for someone as experienced as Irene Worth. Jerome Kilty, who co-directed *The Ides of March*, recalls the problem: 'There was a line about Caesar's eyes resting on a woman, and Irene would say, "It's not Caesar's eyes that are resting on me, it's Johnny G the director's eyes."'

His mind moved so fast his mental leaps often seemed surreal. In 1967 he directed *Halfway up the Tree*, a light comedy by Peter Ustinov which had a year's run at the Queen's. He had some disagreements with Ustinov in rehearsal, though never unpleasant ones. Ustinov recalls a moment when he was given a glimpse into what he called 'the sorcerer's workshop' of Gielgud's mind: 'I said to John, "There's no conflict in that scene, the girl must be much more brutal and aggressive with her mother." He listened with great interest, and then said, "Yes, perhaps I should have allowed her to wear her hat after all." I could never work out what he meant.'

Gielgud directed two further operas during this period. His stylish production of Benjamin Britten's *A Midsummer Night's Dream* at Covent Garden, conducted by Georg Solti with stunning sets by John Piper, was a great success. His intimate knowledge of Shakespeare's play was an asset, and he enjoyed himself. Solti recalled him after one rehearsal showing Nicolas Chagrin, playing Puck, how to deliver the line, 'Lord, what fools these mortals be'. 'This great man of the theatre became a naughty little boy before our very eyes. It was breathtaking.' But he still found it difficult working simultaneously with music and drama. According to Geraint Evans, who played Bottom, 'he was somewhat disconcerted by the music and its effect on the words, so that occasionally he seemed a bit lost'.

This was vividly illustrated during rehearsals for Mozart's *Don Giovanni*, which he directed in 1968 for the Sadler's Wells Opera on the occasion of its move to the Coliseum. Unable to attract the attention of a member of the chorus, he ran down the aisle with arms waving, shouting at the conductor Mario Bernardi, 'Oh do stop that terrible music!' Derek Jarman was the set designer, but the combination of his inexperience and Gielgud's floundering proved disastrous, and on the opening night the audience hissed their efforts. The hostile reviews focused on Jarman's abstract, angular sets, but Gielgud blamed himself. 'I was so embarrassed,' he recalled. 'So many people dependent on me, and the opening of the season.'

In the years following his triumphant tour of *Ages of Man* he worked regularly in America as a director. He could still get boyishly excited about New York, his second favourite city. Juliet Mills remembers when she, Brian Bedford and Michael Bryant arrived there to start the Broadway run of *Five Finger Exercise*. 'We'd never been before, but John was as excited as we were. It was sunset, and he insisted we dump our things straightaway and see the sights. As we walked down Fifth Avenue he showed us things – here's Tiffany's, here's Cartier, here's St Patrick's – as if it were his own city. I think he got a tremendous pleasure out of other people's pleasure.'

With Jessica Tandy replacing Adrianne Allen, Gielgud tried to inject a freshness into the production after its year in the West End. He found it hard, he confessed during rehearsals, to convince some actors 'that they must be seen, heard and understood', and should not see it 'as a kind of glory in itself' to play with their backs to the audience. 'He was never happy, and we never stopped rehearsing, even during the tour in Boston and Philadelphia,' Michael Bryant remembers. 'Shaffer was there, and John kept him locked up, re-writing all the time.' Gielgud's search for perfection paid off: the play gained excellent notices and a ten-month run at the Music Box Theater, and gained him the Tony award for Best Direction.

His production of *The School for Scandal* also ended up on

Broadway. The original rehearsals for the London production had been problematic. Gielgud and the actor playing Careless had developed a mutual dislike, which affected the atmosphere. Others were irritated by his ever-changing ideas. When one actor complained he had said something totally opposite the day before, he replied, 'Ah, but I was a fool yesterday.' Pinkie Johnstone recalls his effect on the younger actors: 'Anna Massey was terrified, and he often upset me. At the end of the read-through he said, "Pinkie, you're meant to be like a little ping-pong ball dancing on top of a fountain, but you're like a slow drip of cold water." I immediately started to cry, and he said, "Oh, come and have lunch at Scott's."'

Meriel Forbes, playing Lady Sneerwell, felt the actors should not be over-obedient towards him: he was, she said, offering them pearls, but they had to supply their own string; if any of the pearls didn't fit, they should discard them. But this was not easy for less experienced actors, as Peter Barkworth recalls: 'I was greatly in awe of him, and shaking with nerves at the read-through. Suddenly he told me he thought it would be amusing if I said all my Rs as Ws. There was no explanation, it was just one of his surface goodies. I didn't like the idea, but felt I couldn't argue. But when I did what he suggested it was a real mess, and I felt humiliated.'

Richardson, a law unto himself, likened Gielgud to a catherine wheel, but claimed he was 'rather a good editor' of the shower of ideas that came from him. For his part Gielgud, like other directors, found Richardson awkward to handle: 'He has very secret ideas of what he wants to do, and is very determined to do them,' he said. This time there was conflict between them. At one point, Peter Barkworth remembers, Richardson decided he wasn't up to the part, and told the actors: 'I seem to have lost my talent, I shall have to go to the lost property office and find it.' There were arguments over his first entrance – What prop should he carry? Should he be taking snuff? – which made it impossible to start rehearsing it. Finally Richardson said: 'You know, Johnny, I prayed to God last night to tell me how to come on. And this morning God answered, "Do what it says in the text, just come on."'

Gielgud again met resistance from his friend while rehearsing for the Broadway transfer. The original production had been criticised for lacking a common style. After opening with the new cast, which included Geraldine McEwan and Gwen Ffrangcon-Davies, Gielgud told Jerome Kilty: 'I think the play is much better balanced now, though I had a good many struggles with Ralph and Laurence Naismith to persuade them to make any changes in their performances. Skilled comedians are absolute fiends when they fancy one may have interfered with some precious laugh they have spent months cooking up.' But the critics who re-visited the production, principally to catch Gielgud as Joseph Surface, found a significant improvement in the ensemble playing.

Directorial changes reached their most extreme form just before the opening at the Majestic in New York in December 1962, when Gielgud decided the actors should enter from the side rather than the back for the last scene. This change, and the adjustments to the moves that followed, had to be rehearsed during the interval of the crucial first-night performance.

The play did excellent business in Canada and America in 1963, and drew enthusiastic notices. But Gielgud's production of *Ivanov* was less well received three years later: after a short tour it lasted less than six weeks at the Shubert Theater, with the cast taking salary cuts towards the end to keep it going. Although Richard Watts Jr felt it had 'a polished and glittering expertness characteristic of Sir John', most of the critics disliked the play, and seemed strangely reluctant to accept Russian characters with English accents. But they were also clearly disappointed that Vivien Leigh, taking over from Yvonne Mitchell, should have such a relatively small part, and not appear at all in the second half.

As Ivanov, Gielgud had to say to her: 'You are dying! The doctor told me so, do you know? You are going to die. Quite soon.' Retrospectively this seems unbearably poignant since, like Anna Petrovna, Vivien Leigh herself was to die of tuberculosis within a few months. Gielgud had become devoted to her, and after her death wrote to her mother: 'You know how I loved Vivien. Her passing is unbelievable and tragic, and she will leave an irreplaceable gap amongst the very small circle of my intimate friends.' The strength of his feeling was clear when, in the presence of Olivier and the cream of the theatrical profession, he gave the address at her London memorial service in St Martin's-in-the-Fields. Emotionally open to an unusual degree, he delivered a beautifully written tribute that was heartfelt without being sentimental.

'In the first shock of losing a very dear friend one does not feel able to talk of it to other people,' he began:

Grief is a private and personal emotion, and, in some ways too, a selfish one – so many good times that will not come again, so many opportunities lost of expressing affection for the one who is gone, such bitter resentments against the suddenness, the sadness that was so unexpected and so final. To talk of Vivien Leigh in public so soon after her death is almost unbearably difficult for me . . . Her manners both in the theatre and in private life were always impeccable. She was punctual, modest and endlessly thoughtful and considerate. She was frank without being unkind, elegant, but never ostentatious. Her houses were as lovely as her beautiful and simple clothes.

He ended by saluting her 'for all she gave so generously and so gaily', and quoted as an epitaph Shakespeare's words on the death of Cleopatra: 'Now boast thee, Death, in thy possession lies / A lass unparallel'd.'

During the 1960s he created two original productions for Broadway. The first was *Big Fish, Little Fish*, a first play by his friend Hugh Wheeler, which starred Hume Cronyn, Jason Robards, Ruth White, George Grizzard and Martin Gable. It ran for over 100 performances in 1961 at the ANTA Theater, and won Gielgud his second Tony award for Best Direction. With Hugh Wheeler, who attended rehearsals and cut and re-wrote to order, he worked fast and furiously during the seventeen days of rehearsal. The strain his impetuous methods put on the actors can be glimpsed in extracts from a journal kept by Hume Cronyn.

Tuesday 7 February (First reading) No formal statements from anyone – no welcomes, introductions, explanations or psychological investigation. Just, Shall we read it? Rather a relief. We're off!

Wednesday 8 February Johnny G seems to have sixteen new ideas a minute. Write in and erase, write in and erase. Script covered with lunatic markings.

Saturday 25 February Dress-rehearsed in street clothes. John G continues to re-stage the first scene. Please God, let me remember what version we're to do on opening night.

Monday 27 February (Opening) I became increasingly peevish as the day wore on. At one point I stepped down to the footlights and said, Now John, are you changing it because it will be better – or because you're bored? John's reply was gentle and maddeningly benign: But Hume, you'll manage it beautifully.

Cronyn admired Gielgud's ability to illuminate a character with a few precise and well-chosen words. He found that, though many of his ideas seemed strange or wrong, they often proved to be inspired if you gave them a chance. He suggested Gielgud got bored in rehearsals because he expected everyone to be as good an actor as he was; when they inevitably fell short, his enthusiasm evaporated.

But Gielgud worked at full stretch on his next visit to America, to direct Richard Burton in *Hamlet*. Now an international star, Burton had always acknowledged Gielgud's influence. The year before he confessed: 'In truth from my earliest years I modelled my acting on Gielgud's though, because of our vast differences in temperament, voice and body, nobody has ever remarked on it.' For years he had been haunted by Gielgud's Hamlet, which he had seen at the Haymarket in 1944: though he had seen many since, he still thought his the best. His own at the Old Vic in 1953 he described as 'a sort of unconscious imitation of John Gielgud'. Perhaps this was why Gielgud had not been satisfied by it, as he carelessly let slip in Burton's dressing-room after seeing a performance. The two were to dine together, but Burton was delayed by a crowd of admirers. Gielgud said: 'I'll go on ahead, Richard. Come when you're better – I mean, when you're ready.' When the producer Michael Benthall returned to watch the play a few nights later, he had to tell Burton off for imitating Gielgud, mannerisms and all.

The Gielgud–Burton *Hamlet* came about by chance. It had been conceived the year before during the making of *Becket*, which Burton and Peter O'Toole were filming in the north-east while Gielgud was touring in *The Ides of March*. At the last minute Gielgud stepped in to play the small but effective part of Louis VII of France when another actor dropped out. Burton and O'Toole were drinking hard; Gielgud claimed later that you could see the red in their eyes in the finished film. There are two versions of how *Hamlet* came about, not necessarily conflicting. O'Toole's version has he and Burton deciding they would both play Hamlet soon, and tossing a coin for choice of director and location. Burton won the first, and chose Gielgud; O'Toole won the second and chose London. In Burton's version he and Elizabeth Taylor went to see *The Ides of March* in Newcastle, and afterwards Gielgud inquired what he was doing for the Shakespeare quatercentenary. Burton said he had been asked to do Hamlet in New York; then, on an impulse, told Gielgud he would only do it if he would direct him. Gielgud agreed half-jokingly, believing nothing would come of it. But Burton, who had been away from the classical theatre for eight years, was serious.

The cast was mainly American, though it included Eileen Herlie as Gertrude and George Rose as the First Gravedigger. Gielgud's work with the actors, and in particular his handling of Burton, was documented in unique detail in two books by members of the company. William Redfield's *Letters from an Actor* is an absorbing and perceptive account of rehearsals from the viewpoint of the actor playing Guildenstern. Richard Sterne's *John Gielgud Directs Richard Burton in Hamlet* is based on copious notes taken by the actor playing a Gentleman, but also on verbatim transcripts of recordings he made without Gielgud's knowledge, by means of a tape-machine hidden in a briefcase.

A striking feature of both accounts is Gielgud's scholarly and detailed knowledge and understanding of the play. He knows exactly what Barker, Dover Wilson and other academics have written about *Hamlet*. But he is wary of general theories, and contemptuous of Freudian interpretations, preferring to back his own intuition as to what is right in the theatre. His ideas about the motivation of the characters are shrewd, often brilliant, but always based on the text. He knows every line of *Hamlet* by heart, so has no need to consult the book.

From out front he acts each part with the actors, mouthing the lines, making the gestures, conveying every changing emotion through his expression. Chewing endless mints and chain-smoking his Turkish cigarettes, he sometimes has to show an actor how it's done. He leaps from his chair and rattles off a whole speech – not just Hamlet's, but those of Claudius, Gertrude and other characters. Redfield describes the electrifying effect: 'His complexion reddens, his knuckles go white; he stands on pigeon's toes; he is tense, excited, stimulated – his brow shows deep creases as though he were in pain; tears appear in his eyes. Then, like a thunderclap, the speech is over and his actors stand about him, silent and breathless.'

The actors, most of whom lack a classical background, are dazzled by these demonstrations, but also intimidated by Gielgud's mastery of the text. They are unhappy about his giving line readings and correcting inflections, both frowned on in the American theatre. Schooled in the Method, some of them feel Gielgud is too concerned with plot, pace and pictorial effectiveness, and not enough with psychological motivation. Alfred Drake, playing Claudius, says: 'When I ask John a question, I feel as though I've stuck a knife in him. All he wants to talk about is mechanics.' Others, such as Hume Cronyn, playing Polonius, believe Gielgud's brief, lightning observations about characterisation offer the actor enough to work with. 'Sometimes I know when I'm in the presence of my betters,' he remarks, adding: 'John has a near-infallible ear.'

When an actor asks Gielgud, 'What's this character *about?*' he tends to reply maddeningly, 'It's about being a good feed for Hamlet.' Invited to summarise the theme of *Hamlet,* he says: 'I don't think of it that way. I just see it as a play.' Some of the actors – though not apparently Burton – are irritated by his refusal to give them a 'concept'. But his enthusiasm and humility dissipate much of their frustration. His persistent use of the phrase 'Of course you yourself may find a better way' reassures them they can be creative, that he will not impose. They are also beguiled by his self-mockery. 'Make him terribly supercilious, like me,' he tells one actor. Once he forgets a line of the text. 'Well, there you are, you see,' he says. 'My reputation is exaggerated and fraudulent. I'm just a silly old goop who can't remember his lines.'

Although Burton and Gielgud are both intelligent, instinctive actors capable of great lyrical power, Gielgud knows that Burton will create a much more vigorous, extrovert Hamlet than his own, and that he must be allowed to do so. 'The moment I feel that I'm giving you too much what I myself would do, then I shrink from making any comment,' he says. Brilliant but uneven, Burton is a 'blood and guts' actor driven by his Celtic temperament. Gielgud's main problem is to stop him shouting and persuade him to rein in his power, to get him to match the feeling to the word, and find an appropriate rhythm in the soliloquies. Burton changes his delivery of key speeches or phrases from one day to the next, and often omits words or lines, or misquotes them. Gielgud, meticulous and all-seeing, notices the smallest error, and corrects him fastidiously.

'You've controlled me so well,' Burton says at the final run-through. Flexible and keen to learn, he agrees verbally with most of Gielgud's suggestions, but in practice takes only some of them on board – a classic actor's device that Gielgud notices, but approves of. Burton's admiration and respect for Gielgud are obvious, and their relationship in rehearsals is mutually trusting and relaxed. During the fourth week Sterne records a characteristic exchange:

> *Gielgud* Richard, you said, 'In a dreeeeam of passion.' You rather imitated my habit of dragging out a word.
> *Burton* Well, I'm working with you, aren't I? [Burton gives an affectionate imitation of Gielgud.] 'In a dreeeam of passion.'
> *Gielgud* (deliberately) 'Plucks off my beard, and blows it in my face, tweaks me by the nose, and gives me . . .'
> *Burton* Yes, love. I was doing that at half past two this morning and I buggered it up again.
> *Gielgud* Nobody will notice except me.

Remembering Barker's comment that *Hamlet* was a permanent rehearsal, Gielgud had decided on a 'rehearsal run-through' version, in which the actors would wear their own clothes, and perform on a bare stage in front of a set representing the back of a theatre. This bold idea was prompted in part by Burton's hatred of wearing period clothes, especially tights, but also by Gielgud's own experience: like most actors he had often seen or given a better performance in the last run-through than on a first night. Burton was sympathetic to the idea, and remembered a striking example. In 1953 he had attended the final rehearsal of the *Richard II* that Gielgud was about to take to Bulawayo, and rated it among the finest performances he had ever seen.

In practice the idea of using rehearsal clothes caused confusion and heartache. Unaccustomed to such freedom, the actors found it hard to choose the appropriate clothes, and kept turning up in different outfits. Gielgud changed his opinions about them from day to day. After the first preview in Toronto he rushed on to the stage after the final curtain call, and announced: 'It went well. But I'm afraid I've made a terrible mistake. It all lacks colour and majesty and it's my fault. Tomorrow night you'll all wear capes!'

Rehearsals were made more difficult because of the frenzy over the affair between Elizabeth Taylor and Burton, who were married immediately after the Toronto opening. Gielgud disliked all the publicity, and the strain it put on their relationship with each other and the company. 'It was rather sad to see them in the hotel, holed up in the suite with a man with a machine-gun in the corridor,' he recalled. 'It made it very difficult to get Richard alone.' Yet he retained his liking for Burton, 'an extraordinarily natural character in a way', who seemed to him 'a curious mixture of naïveté and sophistication'.

Elizabeth Taylor's presence during rehearsals disconcerted Gielgud, and it prompted one minor crisis. Having auditioned countless candidates for Ophelia, Gielgud suddenly decided in Toronto that the actress he had finally chosen was not right. 'It's a nightmare, and you know what a ghastly director I am,' he said on the phone to Sarah Miles, while persuading her to fly out from England as a replacement. At a party after that night's performance, fuelled by a few drinks, Burton flirted with his new Ophelia in front of Taylor. Early next morning Gielgud rang Sarah Miles in obvious distress, and asked her to pack her bags immediately. Embarrassed by the situation, he took her to the airport: 'He told me he wasn't happy with Liz Taylor being there, putting her oar in,' she says. But the new Mrs Burton continued to haunt the production. At the New York première in April huge crowds gathered outside the Lunt-Fontanne Theater, and the curtain had to be delayed for forty minutes because of her arrival.

Gielgud's production was praised as lucid, fresh, contemporary and stirring. In Toronto many drama students, fascinated by the rehearsal-style production, had been to see it four or five times. Burton was praised for a bold and virile Hamlet in notices that were mostly favourable. Helped by the extraordinary publicity engendered by the Burton–Taylor marriage, the production became the most profitable *Hamlet* in American stage history. A film was made of it after the hundredth performance, and shown in a thousand cinemas. Gielgud had left New York after the opening, and when he saw the film he was dismayed: Burton had restored much of the flamboyance and many of the tricks he had tried to discourage.

On the last night he cabled Burton: 'All congratulations. Thinking of you fondly tonight as always. Please give my love to the company. Wish I could have been with you once more.' It was his final contact with *Hamlet* in the theatre. The production ran for 138 performances, beating by six the record for the play's longest-run on Broadway – held by Gielgud himself, after his consummate performance nearly thirty years before.

PART FIVE

Indian Summer

1968–2000

30

Oedipus and *Home*

One had to risk looking idiotic.
                    (Gielgud on rehearsing *Oedipus*
                            with Peter Brook, 1968)

WHILE Burton had chosen Gielgud to direct his Hamlet, O'Toole had opted for Olivier. In October 1963 their version of *Hamlet* was chosen to mark the long-awaited opening of the National Theatre, which was housed initially at the Old Vic. Olivier, appointed its first director, guarded his territory carefully: it was to be four years before Gielgud made his début there.

Their relationship remained a difficult one, characterised by mutual wariness, and compounded by Olivier's jealous nature. Both of them were good friends of Richardson, but Gielgud was now the closer of the two, and this Olivier resented. 'I know I'm not your best friend but I believe I am the one who loves you best,' he told Richardson during a birthday tribute. He failed, however to extend that love into his friend's working life: during his ten-year regime at the National Richardson was never to appear once.

With the help of Bill Gaskill and John Dexter, Olivier had quickly established a permanent company, built around talented younger actors such as Maggie Smith, Robert Stephens and Frank Finlay. His policy of excluding established stars was eventually questioned by Tynan, now the theatre's literary manager, and it was he rather than Olivier who was instrumental in bringing Gielgud to the National. In October 1965 he sent a memo to Olivier: 'I have a marvellous idea. People keep telling me that John G. is dying to work with us. Why not ask him to play Robespierre with you as Danton, with somebody else directing. I have a further suggestion. Why don't you alternate Lear and Gloucester with him? This would have enormous historical impact because of the *Romeo and Juliet* interchange, and I needen't tell you what the box-office impact would be.'

Neither idea worked out. Nor did that of bringing the two actors together in Ibsen's *The Pretenders*, in a version by Tom Stoppard which Ingmar Bergman was invited to direct: at a late stage Olivier became ill, and the production had to be shelved. Seneca's *Oedipus* had already been agreed upon, but plans to stage *Le Misanthrope* went awry. Gielgud then suggested another Molière, *Tartuffe*, and as potential directors Roger Planchon, Jean-Louis Barrault or Jean Vilar. Planchon was hired, designed the sets, but had to withdraw, and at the last minute Guthrie was brought in.

Gielgud had not been cast in the title-role, as he had expected – it was given to Robert Stephens – but played Orgon, the rich simpleton deceived into thinking Tartuffe is a priest. He was totally miscast, not least because Stephens' playing of Tartuffe as a coarse, bucolic lout could only have fooled a complete dunderhead, a type not within Gielgud's range. Crucially, he failed to strike up any kind of rapport with Guthrie ('Tony didn't say much to me personally'), and was irritated by his direction. 'Naturally I didn't open my mouth, because one can't be destructive once one has agreed to appear in a production,' he said afterwards. Some actors might have withdrawn, but that was not his way.

Guthrie was recovering from a heart attack, and the production lacked his usual gaiety and invention. It was also hampered by a translation in rhyming couplets more suited to pantomime than Molière. Bearded and moustachioed like the Laughing Cavalier, Gielgud was clearly under-rehearsed, and gave a hesitant and disappointing performance. The critics chided the National for choosing such an unsuitable and undemanding role for his first appearance there. Invited to comment on the production, Gielgud said: 'Joan Plowright was good as the maid.'

Oedipus was a different experience altogether. Alongside Gielgud in the title-role were Irene Worth as Jocasta, Colin Blakely as Creon, and Ronald Pickup as the Messenger. Olivier had planned to direct, but was prevented again because of illness. He offered the job to Peter Brook, who accepted 'as a homage to John', but insisted on ten weeks of rehearsals. Since he and Gielgud had worked together in *Venice Preserv'd* in 1953, Brook had radically changed his approach to theatre. Heavily influenced by Artaud and Grotowski, and companies such as the Living Theatre and the Open Theatre, he put the actors through several days of physically and emotionally demanding exercises before allowing them a sight of the text.

Some of the actors thought the exercises a waste of time. On the first day everyone waited for Gielgud's reaction. Would this living symbol of an older tradition agree to take part? 'He joined in in a way I would never have believed possible,' Oliver Cotton remembers. 'He astonished us with his willingness to experiment. There were massive exercises, and Tai Chi for an hour every morning – though I don't think he did the Maori dances.' According to Benjamin Whitrow: 'He did everything he was asked to do, including the mirror exercise in pairs – although *you* had to follow *him*, he wasn't someone who would follow you.'

Brook remembers how Gielgud's cooperation closed the generation gap within the company: 'What touched everyone was that he jumped in without hesitation, forcing himself even though he was doing it clumsily. He was totally courageous and trusting. When you ask John to do something that's difficult, it just doesn't occur to him to be bloody-minded. He has this belief that if something is painful and agonising, you don't show embarrassment or have any self-pity. That's his nature, those are his values.'

Nevertheless he disapproved of the exercises, and only did them because of his respect for Brook. He found the solemn atmosphere hard to take: 'Nobody was allowed to giggle or think it funny at all,' he complained. He did his best to lighten the atmosphere. 'Morning troops,' he would say on arrival, suggesting the exercises were his punishment for not being called up in the war. Once, when they were exploring the theme of Shock, Brook asked each actor to come to the front and describe the worst thing they could imagine. After the usual offerings – nuclear war, necrophilia, my father, rats in the eyeballs – Gielgud stepped forward and said: 'We open three weeks on Tuesday.' The company collapsed in laughter.

Gielgud later called this preparatory work 'agony and misery'. But he also felt the discipline had been good for him: 'One's often had one's own way too much, and to be forced to make an effort is valuable,' he said. It had, he felt, been useful to be on the same level as the other actors. 'I made a bit of a fool of myself, which I think increased their respect for me. But it also decreased my respect for myself, and made me feel that I could afford to make a fool of myself in front of them all without lowering my prestige. One had to risk looking idiotic.'

His willingness to try out a technique so foreign to his generation of actors was impressive. When Richardson was asked to improvise during rehearsals for Pirandello's *Six Characters in Search of an Author*, he quietly rose and left the room, unwilling to risk any kind of personal exposure. Olivier was equally reluctant: according to Bill Gaskill, he tried to avoid the improvisation during rehearsals for *The Recruiting Officer*. Gielgud, though apprehensive and sceptical, accepted the challenge without hesitation. The boldness, the love of a fresh challenge, was still there.

The translation by Ted Hughes was a raw, violent and fiery version of Seneca's rarely performed play. Before rehearsals began Hughes had read it to the company. It was, Gielgud remembered, an electrifying experience: 'We huddled together spellbound by the power of the play, and especially by the poet's brilliant handling of the material.' But in rehearsal he struggled to learn Hughes's text, which was unpunctuated and more like a musical score. Brook, who liked all the company to be present throughout each rehearsal, refused to let Gielgud rehearse quietly in a corner. Anna Carteret, one of the Chorus, recalls: 'John was very uncomfortable, and finding it difficult to compete with us. One morning, when we were all writhing and humming and doing all kinds of things to colour the verse, and he was trying to speak, he shut his eyes. After a while he said, "Peter, I wonder if I could have a little spot downstage not too far from the audience?" After that we simmered down a bit.'

He often found a welcome release in humour. In rehearsal the actors sometimes had to wear false dildos on their heads. 'Just going to put on my cock hat,' he would say. Irene Worth called him 'Shakespeare's brother in his love of puns', and at the climactic moment of the dress rehearsal he proved her point. As Jocasta she had to impale herself through the womb on a spike. Finding the spike too short, she suggested to Brook it should be put on a plinth. 'Plinth Philip or Plinth Charles?' Gielgud called out from the wings. The rest of the company fell about. 'That cheered up the atmosphere a bit,' he recalled.

One of the production team, Richard Mangan, recalls his extreme nervousness before the opening, wondering what his admirers would make of such an *avant-garde* production. There were limits to his cooperation, and when Brook insisted the actors should be on stage half an hour before the start to get into their characters, he complied, but inwardly rebelled. 'I just sat there counting the audience coming in,' he recalled. 'If I thought about the part I'd have exhausted myself before I started. You've got to husband your energy.'

Brook's production – some likened it to a 'happening' – relied heavily on ritual and incantation, with the Chorus often moving around among the audience. In the centre of the frenzy and the chanting, dressed in black sweater and trousers, Gielgud played out the Oedipus story. Controversially, the play ended with what Brook intended as a form of catharsis in the manner of the ancient Greek drama. To the tune of 'Yes, We Have No Bananas' played as Dixieland jazz, a fertility dance took place round a ten-foot golden phallus, with the actors inviting the audience to join them onstage. Gielgud was embarrassed, and refused to take part; the phallus, derided by the critics, was dropped after a few performances.

Oedipus was a commercial success, but Brook's iconoclasm provoked extreme reactions. Several critics felt Gielgud was uncomfortable with the stylised acting. Irving Wardle wrote: 'Sir John Gielgud, dispensing honeyed cadences amid the carnage and registering Oedipus' blood-freezing discoveries with a testy frown, seems only marginally in contact with the show.' Others thought he displayed impressive power and control. Simon Callow, then working in the box-office at the National, saw every performance: 'Over the run he grew to a tragic stature,' he remembered. 'There was an extraordinary nobility and dignity, it was a revelation.' Olivier, who hated Brook's production, called it 'a perfect tragic performance'.

Gielgud found it very difficult to handle a part which involved sitting impassively on the side of the stage to hear the Messenger's monologue, then going on and producing the strangulated cries of the blinded Oedipus. Later he said of Brook: 'He wouldn't let me be emotional. He made me stylised and he wouldn't allow me to let go. I'd been hoping I'd have a chance to rival Larry's Oedipus with all that screaming and howling.' But Irene Worth claimed Brook forced him to dig deep into himself, pushing him to release his emotions to express the deep disgust and horror Oedipus feels. Although he found this almost impossible, the experience, she believed, 'turned him into a new kind of actor'.

In 1965 Gielgud had told Edward Albee: 'I have longed for some years, while being very doubtful of my ability to understand and interpret the new playwrights, to have a shot at one of them, because one longs to create a new part more than anything in the world, and to find a challenge for one's experience by playing something completely different.' Seemingly released by his experience in *Oedipus*, less self-conscious and concerned about his dignity, he now found what he was looking for in the work of newer playwrights such as Alan Bennett, Peter Shaffer, David Storey, Charles Wood, Edward Bond and Harold Pinter.

In accepting parts that challenged him both technically and personally, Gielgud re-created himself as an actor in startling fashion. After years of uncertainty and erratic performances, he achieved commercial success and critical acclaim, a combination that had recently eluded him. At the age of sixty-four he returned to the theatrical mainstream with a vengeance. As the theatre finally threw off the shackles of censorship – abolished in 1968 – so Gielgud threw off his mental chains, seeming to become younger with each new production, and often shocking the more conventional theatregoers in the process.

He was still playing in *Oedipus* when he was sent Alan Bennett's first play *Forty Years On*, a delicious satire, affectionate but sharp, on the absurdities of the British upper-middle classes and their institutions. It included a play within a play, performed for the parents of pupils at a seedy minor public school, and taking the form of a pageant of British history from 1900 to the Second World War. Essentially a comedy, it also had an underlying seriousness, prompted by Bennett's affection for aspects of the past. Although he had not written the part of the Headmaster for Gielgud, he could well have done so. Here was a man trying vainly to uphold vanishing traditions, feeling under pressure from a younger generation, dropping remarks of waspish but unconscious humour, yearning nostalgically for the past, yet being thoroughly aware of the need for progress. Gielgud liked it immediately.

The play included parodies of or jokes about Wilde, Sapper, the Sitwells, T.E. Lawrence, Virginia Woolf and other writers. This ignited Gielgud's quickfire wit. He asked Bennett to add a Coward parody: 'You know the sort of thing, lots of little epigrams, smart witty remarks. It wouldn't be at all difficult.' Bennett said he couldn't possibly do so. 'Why not?' Gielgud said. 'It's terribly easy. Noël does it all the time.' He knew many of the celebrities Bennett referred to, and enjoyed gossiping about them. Once he said: 'I can't think why Ottoline Morrell had an affair with Bertie Russell. Terribly bad breath, you know.' Another time, asked what he thought of Vita Sackville-West, he replied: 'Tiresome old dyke.'

Initially he had many doubts about his part and certain aspects of the play. Bennett recalled that he came up with some distinctly cockeyed ideas. Though he found the script funny, he thought having twenty-five boys on stage would be distracting, and suggested that cardboard cut-outs should be used instead. Like the Headmaster he objected to the bawdier jokes and lewd rugby songs, and even worried that the use of Churchill's favourite song 'Forty Years On' would offend Old Harrovians. He also disliked the play's opening: 'It's very doleful, the boys coming in singing that song, it's just like school,' he told Bennett. 'But it *is* school,' Bennett replied. 'Yes, I suppose it is,' Gielgud said.

In his diary Bennett pinpointed why it was difficult for those working with Gielgud to dislike him: 'He can be wayward, obstinate and maddeningly changeable, but one can forgive all these because he sets so little store by his own reputation. He is entirely without malice or amour-propre, and in a succession of gruelling rehearsals he never once loses his composure.' He also noted his positive influence: 'One realises how important Gielgud's presence is: he is always impeccably polite, and any slight flurry in his temper is followed by an instant apology. His modesty and good behaviour infect everyone else.' Bennett was struck in the days before the London opening to find Gielgud going round London with his dresser Mac, helping him to find a new flat after he had been turned out of his old one.

The company included Paul Eddington, Nora Nicholson, Dorothy Reynolds, and Bennett himself as a junior master, and the director was Patrick Garland. Eddington, who admired Gielgud above all other actors, was surprised how vulnerable and uncertain of himself he seemed. In Manchester, where the play opened, he struggled with his words and worried about his shabby gown and unkempt appearance. Above all he was nervous about addressing the audience directly. 'He was very resistant to the idea, saying it was vulgar,' Bennett remembers. Gielgud told Garland: 'You want me to do that Brecht and Peter Brook stuff, and I won't.' The small audiences in the cavernous Palace Theatre, better suited to music-hall, seemed to produce some kind of block, and the production was in deep trouble.

But Brighton, with its small theatre and appreciative audience, changed everything. 'After his first speech the audience applauded for two solid minutes, and off he went like a rocket,' Garland recalled. During the interval Gielgud said to him: 'I thought I'd try something new and address the audience, and it seems to be going rather well.' Bennett recalled: 'As soon as he stopped being nervous about it, he went much further than one imagined he could, leaning over the footlights and singling out people he knew.' Gielgud's trick was to remember a charity matinée in the 1950s, when he and Olivier and John Mills had dressed up as 'spivs' and performed Coward's 'Three Not-so-Juvenile Delinquents' song.

The trick worked. As the absurd and fastidious Headmaster he revealed a new subtlety and his abiding talent for parody. John Barber's comment on his performance crystallised the transformation: 'Gielgud dominates all with an unexpected caricature of a mincing pedant, his noble features blurred so as to mimic a fussed and fatuous egghead. From the great mandarin of the theatre, a delicious comic creation.' Gielgud later claimed that no part since Benedick had given him such a feeling of release.

Forty Years On opened at the Apollo in October 1968, and brought him his best notices for more than a decade. He stayed in it for ten months before handing over to Emlyn Williams. During his final week Bennett observed: 'I shall be sorry to see him go. He's made of the play something which I couldn't possibly have imagined it would have been.' He admired Gielgud for allowing the sillier, less austere side of his personality to come through, for being 'absolutely serious about what he does, but not taking himself seriously'. Later he suggested that when the play had come so close to disaster on tour Gielgud had time to realise 'that audiences actually loved him; that this was not respect, which he was used to, but affection'.

Gielgud's second encounter with the new generation of dramatists was much less satisfying. Peter Shaffer, now a successful commercial playwright, had written *The Battle of Shrivings* in the hope that Gielgud and Olivier would play the two leading parts at the National. The plot centred around an intellectual battle between a pacifist sage modelled on Bertrand Russell (Gielgud), and a cynical reprobate poet loosely based on Ezra Pound, who despises the self-righteousness of such idealists (Olivier). Once again Olivier's health prevented him from appearing. The play was eventually staged by Tennent's in February 1970 at the Lyric, with Peter Hall directing, and Patrick Magee playing Olivier's part.

Gielgud had doubts about the play from the start. More than three hours long, its characters were little more than mouthpieces for a bewildering, undramatic torrent of philosophical ideas. Gielgud pressed for cuts, but the management, playwright and director were at odds, and none was made. As he had shown with *Tiny Alice*, he had a fine instinct for what would hold an audience. After the play received what Shaffer called 'its public maiming', substantial cuts were made, but too late to prevent the production closing after nine weeks. Gielgud asked Shaffer: 'Will it go to New York? I do hope so, these pretentious plays usually go down rather well.'

Although his notices were complimentary, he was unhappy in a play so obviously flawed. One aspect of it might have been a disturbing factor. The sage has a liking in Italy for 'slim brown boys', and at one point decides to make 'a brief observation about homosexuality. I mean, my own.' Attitudes to homosexuality were now slowly changing, and the Sexual Offences Act of 1967 had at last removed the stigma of illegality. Yet Gielgud still chose not to discuss his homosexuality publicly, and having to do so onstage may have been an ordeal for him.

His real baptism of fire with the new writers came later that year, when he and Richardson appeared at the Royal Court in David Storey's *Home*, directed by Lindsay Anderson. Devine, who had died in 1966, had established the Court as a forum for serious, high-minded work. Essentially a writers' theatre, it encouraged polemic and argument, disliked 'camp', and opposed the values of what John Osborne called 'Binkiedom'. It was also a theatre where a new breed of actors with their roots in the regions – Peter O'Toole, Albert Finney, Colin Blakely, Joan Plowright and Frank Finlay – had been making their mark during the 1960s. While Olivier, Scofield, Guinness and Ashcroft had all appeared there during Devine's regime, Gielgud and Richardson had stayed away. In Gielgud's case it was not for lack of an invitation. Aside from his rejecting *Endgame* and *A Patriot for Me*, there had been tentative plans for him to appear with Olivier in Anouilh's *The Rehearsal.* He had also been offered the title-role in a modern-dress *Julius Caesar*, but claimed not to have received Lindsay Anderson's hand-delivered letter.

The Royal Court was now being run jointly by Gaskill and Anderson. 'It was even more contentious than it was in George's time, and John was very nervous of that,' Gaskill recalls. Fearing to be 'terribly sent up by all these left-wing boys, sitting in their blue jeans reading pamphlets on the staircase', Gielgud nevertheless arrived defiantly in a Rolls-Royce. 'I thought they would hate me,' he recalled. 'I thought they'd think me stiff and just interested in money.' David Storey remembers that first meeting about *Home*: 'John said he felt very uncomfortable because the Court was against his style of acting, which was to entertain and serve the audience. He was smiling, but full of trepidation.'

One of his worries was Lindsay Anderson, whom he felt had been hostile when they met socially. Anderson could indeed appear aggressive and behave autocratically, but in this instance had been put off by Gielgud's demeanour: 'I thought of him as a remote, distinguished planet, circling with a certain hauteur above the contemporary struggle,' he recalled. Privately Gielgud described Anderson as: 'Quite a pleasant little man, rather short, wore a funny cap, I think gay, but not quite up to it.' But *Home* dispelled the mutual wariness, and after it they became good friends.

Gielgud was intrigued by the script, which he thought very funny; but he was also fearful of it. *Home* was unlike anything he had attempted before. Only gradually does it emerge that the two elderly men at its centre live in a mental hospital. The elliptical and fragmented dialogue, the absence of background information on the characters or their situations, made him think he should refuse it. But he changed his mind when he met its author: 'Storey was so beguiling and charming and easy, I thought, I don't really understand the play, but I'd love to do it.' He then suggested Richardson as his partner.

There was uncertainty about who should play which part, until Richardson opted for the one who does card tricks. At the read-through Gielgud began to feel his part consisted of little more than non-sequiturs and single-word responses to Richardson's lengthier speeches. 'I must be mad, I'm going to be the poor old stooge,' he thought. Richardson was equally ambivalent about the play; both actors feared they were plunging into an abyss. 'We trembled like aspen leaves,' Gielgud remembered. 'We thought we were going to make such fools of ourselves.'

Storey remembers how their nerves came spilling out on the first day: 'It was like pulling the plug out, we couldn't stop them, none of us knew what the hell was going on, they just ran the lines. Lindsay's attempt to stop them every three or four lines and discuss them was totally ignored. He looked over to me and shrugged. It was like being on a stagecoach with two horses, and nothing on the reins would do anything, and we were going at full speed, and should we just jump off or hold on?'

For a while, baffled and insecure, Gielgud and Richardson were convinced they had made a mistake. 'This is a very *avant-garde* play,' Gielgud said continually. Storey was present throughout rehearsals, but refused to answer their questions about the play's meaning; he and Anderson wanted them to find that out for themselves. They therefore had to invent their own secret lives, a method quite foreign to both of them. Gaskill recalled looking in on early rehearsals. 'Lindsay was just taking them through their lines, very subtly and cleverly, easing them into it. He didn't have a concept, but he had a marvellous musical ear, which is how he related to John. He was orchestrating them.'

Anderson tried to get the two actors to remain seated during the twenty-five-minute opening scene, but Gielgud felt too exposed, and said this was impossible. After *Forty Years On* he found it relatively easy to look into the auditorium, as Anderson encouraged him to do. But neither he nor Richardson believed their silences and moments of stillness would hold the audience. Then Gielgud watched from out front a scene between Richardson and Dandy Nichols, and discovered a poetic power in the dialogue that was not apparent from the stage. 'After that I didn't feel so bare and desperate,' he recalled.

His fear of exposing his real self showed in other ways. After *Oedipus* and *Forty Years On* he had got used to working without make-up or disguise, but with *Home* there was an argument about whether he should have a moustache to play Harry. The Court's resident designer Jocelyn Herbert remembers another difficulty: 'John wanted to wear one of his smart suits, and I had a terrible job getting him into clothes that were right. It was also hard to persuade him not to wear a toupee.'

A turning-point was a run-through before an invited audience of actors, including a group from the American experimental theatre group La Mama, then playing at the Court. David Storey remembers their reaction: 'They were sitting in the dress circle, and at the end they all applauded and shouted Bravo, Bravo. John looked up absolutely astonished; he was still convinced we were going over the edge. But the cries of Bravo continued. Tears came to his eyes, and he stepped forward and said, "Oh you're so kind, but we don't deserve it." And they shouted back, "Oh yes you do!"'

Eventually Gielgud relaxed into the role. 'I just emptied my mind and tried to live my character, and Richardson did the same,' he remembered. Towards the end of rehearsals Storey noticed they had become so involved in their characters it was difficult to know where the play ended and their conversations began. When *Home* opened in June to ecstatic reviews, their magical partnership attracted huge praise. Now supremely attuned to each other's playing, they left critics wondering how one might have fared without the other. Richard Findlater wrote: 'Both performances gained immeasurably by reciprocal reflection; both actors listened magnificently.' Significantly, they were named Joint Best Actors at the *Evening Standard* awards.

Anderson was fascinated to see how Gielgud transformed himself just before going on: 'He would be chatting in his dressing-room, get his call, go to the side of the stage, and suddenly acquire great weight and authority, not as the character, but as himself.' Storey was greatly moved by his partnership with Richardson: 'They had an authority which they took for granted, but which they weren't aware of themselves,' he says. 'You were catching a glimpse of the final flowering of a tradition that was vanishing. The fellowship between them was an extraordinarily innocent one, even Edwardian; there was a genuine Babes in the Wood innocence, they came from another world. That was the magic, watching these two giants of the theatre performing what they weren't sure was performable, and doing it so superbly.'

Home soon transferred to the Apollo, where it ran for three months before moving in November to the Morosco Theater in New York. Its success demonstrated Gielgud's remarkable ability to adapt to contemporay writing and modern directing methods. It had taken courage to go to the Royal Court, and he was genuinely taken aback at how well he and the 'leftie boys' had got on. Afterwards he paid the theatre the ultimate compliment: 'Backstage was full of old cigarette packets and young men in pigtails, but they were so kind, they couldn't have worked harder at the Haymarket.'

The following summer at Chichester he met the avant-garde in a very different guise when he played Julius Caesar in Shaw's *Caesar and Cleopatra*. Although Shaw was one of his least favourite dramatists, he had often regretted turning down the part in Gabriel Pascal's wartime film. Now he decided to make amends. What he had not bargained for was that the director, Robin Phillips, would send up the play. The designer Carl Toms came up with a set that was a futuristic all-white nursery for the child-Cleopatra, played by Anna Calder-Marshall. The production was punctuated by actors bouncing beach balls, twirling hula-hoops and turning somersaults. Gielgud, in his white toga, was called on to slide down a chute and mount a rocking-horse.

While he approved of taking a fresh look at the classics, he disliked ideas that drew too much attention to the director at the expense of the text and the actors. He also felt Phillips' ideas in rehearsal were completely different from those which he had initially put forward. But he kept his doubts to himself, diplomatically praising Phillips' handling of him. Privately he was very unhappy. 'It rather broke my heart,' he confessed later.

After a lifetime under the proscenium arch he found it very hard to adjust to Chichester's open stage. On the opening night he was initially inaudible, though he quickly found the right level. But his discomfort was clear, at least to Harold Hobson, who noted: 'He sometimes stumbled over the rhythm of his lines, and got hopelessly muddled over talents and sesterces. This suggested to me he was bored by the play, as well he might be.'

While at Chichester he put together another book. *Distinguished Company* was a collection of portraits of famous players he had seen, known or worked with in his youth, from du Maurier to Gertie Lawrence, from Laughton to Mrs Patrick Campbell. Brimming with anecdotes and witty recollections, full of his relish for the foibles of the stars, it put into print the countless memories and stories with which he continued to delight his fellow-actors at the slightest opportunity.

It was also a reminder, at a moment when he was opening himself up to new experiences, of how firmly his roots and values lay in the theatre of his youth.

31

Peter Hall and Pinter

My parents would be horrified.
(Gielgud on performing in
No Man's Land, 1975)

MUCH in favour at the Royal Court after *Home*, and unabashed by a salary of £50 a week, Gielgud returned there in 1972 to appear in Charles Wood's *Veterans*. His decision to act in such a bawdy, irreverent play shocked and outraged his traditional admirers. Ironically, the main character was an affectionate portrait of himself, inspired by his work four years earlier on *The Charge of the Light Brigade*, a film which had effectively re-launched him as a screen actor.

Although he had won an Oscar nomination for Best Supporting Actor for his witty and elegant performance as Louis VII in *Becket*, it had been a brief, casual job, undertaken at the last-minute while touring in *The Ides of March*. It was Tony Richardson and Orson Welles who taught him to take filming seriously and to enjoy himself in the process.

Following his years with Devine at the Royal Court, Tony Richardson was at the centre of the British cinema's 'new wave', with seminal films such as *A Taste of Honey* and *The Loneliness of the Long-Distance Runner* to his name. He had directed Olivier on both stage and screen in *The Entertainer*, and had just scored an immense success with *Tom Jones*. In 1965 he made *The Loved One*, a crass updating of Evelyn Waugh's macabre fictional study of the American 'death industry'. Promoted as 'the motion picture with something to offend everybody', it severely damaged his reputation as a director.

One of its few delights was Gielgud's playing of Sir Francis Hinsley, an elderly English painter living in Hollywood. Basing the character loosely on Cecil Beaton – with whom he had fallen out some years before – he wafted around in a floral dressing-gown, slightly camp, terribly British, and hugely tactless – playing, in other words, himself. Regrettably he committed suicide early on, but appeared again briefly when his corpse was being prepared for its final resting-place.

Gielgud always relied heavily on his director, and the growing confidence of his playing owed a lot to a happy, warm relationship with Richardson, a difficult, volatile man who was nevertheless adept at flattering stars in a jokey, enthusiastic manner. Gielgud liked and responded to this enthusiasm, and their friendship blossomed. Richardson thought him 'the nicest, most human actor I've ever worked with, and, together with Jack Nicholson, the most intelligent'.

The following year Gielgud played Henry IV in Welles's film *Chimes at Midnight*. His relationship with the cinematic genius, whose *Citizen Kane* had influenced his wartime *Macbeth*, had not begun auspiciously. When they met in London in 1951, Welles had told him he was in town to play Othello. 'On the *stage*? In *London*?' Gielgud replied incredulously, much to Welles' displeasure. Subsequently he had turned down a role in Welles' film of Kafka's *The Trial*, believing, with some justification, he would not be paid by the often penniless director. But when Welles offered him Henry IV he accepted immediately. It was a role he had long wanted to play; when the National Theatre was about to open he had tried without success to get Ralph Richardson to play Falstaff to his Henry.

Chimes at Midnight, also titled *Falstaff*, was essentially a screen life of Shakespeare's roguish, cowardly knight, whom Welles called 'the most entirely good man of all dramatic literature'. Before the war he had created a stage version called *Five Kings*, using parts of *Henry IV* and *Henry V* as well as fragments from *Richard II* and *The Merry Wives of Windsor*, and in 1960 had revived it in Dublin. The cast of the film – apart from Jeanne Moreau, an unconvincing Doll Tearsheet – was mainly English: Keith Baxter was Prince Hal, Norman Rodway played Hotspur, and Margaret Rutherford was Mistress Quickly. Welles filmed it in Madrid, and in a variety of striking locations around the Spanish hills and plains.

He and Gielgud approached each other apprehensively. Before filming began Welles confided to Baxter: 'I'm in such awe of him. No actor can touch him in Shakespeare. I don't want him to think me just a trickster.' Gielgud, on arrival, announced: 'So kind of Orson to ask me. Will he think me old hat? He's so brilliant and I'm an old war-horse.' He did his cause no good when he remarked, in Welles' presence: 'Have you ever known an American who could play Shakespeare? Oh – sorry, Orson. Well, I always thought you were Irish, or something.'

The actors worked under extremely difficult conditions, as Welles improvised, used doubles wherever possible because he could only afford the actors for a short time, and fixed locations from day to day. Gielgud's scenes were shot in November in a deserted monastery on a hilltop in the Pyrenees, with no glass in the windows and little heating. 'I would sit in my tights and dressing-gown on my throne with a tiny electric fire to warm my feet, while Orson spent his last pesetas sending out to buy brandy to keep me going,' he remembered.

Welles created a relaxed atmosphere on the set, discouraging the idea that there was any special mystique in film acting. Put at his ease, Gielgud felt able to throw suggestions at him, some of which Welles used. Keith Baxter recalled their creative partnership: 'Nothing was more moving than seeing these two extraordinary men working in tandem so happily together, laughing unrestrainedly, so full of respect for each other.' Gielgud admired Welles' 'unfailing flair in choosing his set-ups for the camera', and his understanding of Shakespeare's text. Thus inspired, when it came to Henry's pained soliloquy 'Uneasy lies the head that wears a crown', he played it without rehearsal on the first take. 'I said all the words in the right order,' he said with a grin to an amazed crew.

Despite many flaws, including appalling synchronisation, the film was compelling and often moving, partly because of Welles' massive and poignant Falstaff, but also because of the melancholy power of Gielgud's lonely, dying King Henry. Oddly, he never acted in a scene with Welles, or saw him made up as Falstaff. Later he was disconcerted to discover that one of the scenes he thought most effective was one he had never played; Welles had simply assembled it by skilful editing of reaction shots. It disturbed him that an actor could have so little control over his performance. But he loved working with Welles. Shortly after leaving Spain he wrote to Keith Baxter: 'I do miss Orson's brilliance and all the fun.'

In 1968 he teamed up again with Tony Richardson for *The Charge of the Light Brigade*, in which he played that shining example of military incompetence Lord Raglan, the commander-in-chief of the British army. For this he roasted for ten weeks on the Crimean plains in Turkey, in the company of Trevor Howard – playing Lord Cardigan – Mark Dignam,

Harry Andrews, David Hemmings, Jill Bennett and Vanessa Redgrave, with the Turkish army masquerading as the British cavalry.

Charles Wood, who wrote the screenplay, remembers his ability to stay outwardly cool in the terrific heat: 'He was incredibly contained. He got hot with the rest of us, but nothing seemed to bother him.' Wood was also impressed with the way he handled the pseudo-Victorian language he had invented for the screenplay. 'He could sight-read it, he took to it like a duck to water. Others like David Hemmings found it very difficult, and had to ask him how to say it. When a new linking bit was needed, I always gave it to Gielgud, who would go round the corner and learn it immediately. He was inspirational.'

Richardson liked to encourage the actors to improvise within the framework of their character. Gielgud was more relaxed than before, less anxious about his looks, and more ready to exploit aspects of his own personality. Resplendent in uniform and a chestnut wig, he caught wittily and ironically the eccentric Raglan's bumbling dottiness, his inept disdain for the younger soldiers. It was a wonderfully polished comic performance, in which he made mocking use of his own idiosyncrasies. He even slipped in the old Victorian actor's habit of referring to 'me hat' rather than 'my hat'.

The experience with Gielgud inspired Wood to write *Veterans*, a comic play about two elderly actors filming in the sun in Turkey. One of them, Sir Geoffrey Kendle, is eminent, patrician, tactless, hopeless on horseback, a colleague of the Motleys ('hessian days') who has played Hamlet at Elsinore, a workaholic with homosexual tendencies. The other character, Laurence D'Orsay, nicknamed 'Dotty', was thought to be modelled on Trevor Howard, but was actually, Wood says, a mixture of several actors. There are elements of Richardson in him, and at one stage it was announced that he was to play the part.

'I got to know Gielgud superficially very well during filming, and I could hear him all the time while I was writing the play,' Wood says. 'There was a lot of sitting and waiting, so I was able to absorb his mannerisms, and listen to the way he used words, the resonances he gave them. I remember he used to open his mail: one letter asked him if he wanted to take up his old-age pension; from another he learnt that Vivien Leigh had died. The whole thing was very Chekhovian.'

Wood had earlier written his play '*H*' about the Indian Mutiny for Gielgud, who had declined it, suggesting it was simply 'monologues in front of burning cities' – a phrase Wood adopted for its sub-title. In '*H*' there had been one speech he badly wanted Gielgud to speak, so he wrote *Veterans* around it. He then sent him the script, not expecting him to do it, but in case he had any objections to his portrait. To his astonishment Gielgud wrote back giving dates when he would be free.

'The part was so well written, I couldn't resist it,' he said. But Wood was less than delighted at his reaction to the proposed casting of Geraldine McEwan. 'Oh no, she's far too grand now,' he said. 'She doesn't do anything unless it's absolutely first-class.' He had few complaints about the text: Wood adjusted a few speeches in which he felt his character was 'going on a bit'. One cut, restored in the published version, was a reference to a wife in America: 'Nobody will ever believe I'm married,' Gielgud said.

The cast included Gordon Jackson, Bob Hoskins, James Bolam and Ann Bell, with John Mills as D'Orsay. Gaskill had wanted to direct, but the job went to Ronald Eyre. Gielgud was now quite relaxed at the Royal Court. 'He worked marvellously with everyone,' Wood says. 'His theatrical intelligence was extraordinarily acute, the way he reacted to the rhythms and emotions of the other actors. All the young ones were so excited to be working with him; Bob Hoskins was like a puppy basking in his approval.'

Though it seems innocuous enough thirty years on, *Veterans* contained a good deal of sexual innuendo and swear-words: 'No fucking shop stewards watching is there?' was Hoskins' first line to Gielgud. All this shocked many of his loyal fans, who vented their feelings during the pre-London provincial tour. He and John Mills received letters saying they were a disgrace to the profession, appearing in a play with such disgusting language. One woman sent Gielgud a postal order for 40p, saying he must be hard up if he had to do this kind of filth. The reaction upset him. 'I was very unhappy to find I had to fight the audience,' he remembered. 'It is unpleasant to deliberately antagonise people who have looked forward to seeing you.'

Ronald Eyre recalled coaches arriving at Nottingham 'full of eager ladies who had seen him in *Richard of Bordeaux*, and then slowly dismay would set in'. At one matinée the audience was virtually silent, except for one man who laughed a lot. The cast thought he must be from a nearby mental institution; in fact it was Ian McKellen. In Brighton a near-riot broke out during the first act, as John Mills remembers: 'People were walking out in droves, or shouting out in protest at the language, especially that of Bob Hoskins. I could see from the wings how shocked John was. His face was a study; this kind of thing had never happened to him before.'

Wood was in the middle of the furore: 'I was four rows back, and the first three rows got up and left. Someone shouted, "If you say that word again . . ." They hated Gielgud doing it, they wouldn't have him. I don't think friends like Binkie Beaumont wanted him to continue, but he just got on and did it. People thought he was making a spectacle of himself; they didn't realise he was simply showing the genius he had for things other than the great classical parts, that he was the most brilliant comic.' Ronald Eyre recalled his courage: 'He came in for a lot of abuse, and he was fantastically brave to face it.'

The reception was quite different at the Royal Court where, as Alan Bennett put it, 'the occasional oath is part of the house style'. The first-night audience was captivated, and laughed hysterically at what Ronald Bryden called 'the most endearing portrait of an actor ever drawn', and a piece that would 'explain to the future why, since Ellen Terry, no actor has been more beloved by his peers'. Scores of actors came to see his exquisite, self-mocking performance, in which jokes about himself were timed to perfection. The four-week run was a sell-out: 'We were having a ball,' John Mills remembers. But a proposed West End run proved impossible since Gielgud, anticipating disaster, had signed up to do a film.

He was much less happy with his next Royal Court appearance, in Edward Bond's *Bingo*. He had already turned down the title-role in Bond's excessively violent *Lear*, in which the old king, among other indignities, has to examine the remains of his dead daughter. 'Oh no, I couldn't fish out the entrails,' he told Gaskill. 'Better get someone else.' *Bingo* was challenging in a different way. Bond was a fashionable author, but his plays were increasingly didactic and schematic. *Bingo* was a harsh, political play about a melancholy, dying Shakespeare caught up in a dispute about land-ownership. Gielgud, while enjoying certain poetic speeches in it, regretted the absence of humour and sympathy in Bond's portrait of his favourite playwright.

Jane Howell, co-director with John Dove, admired his courage in accepting such a difficult and exposing part: 'He had a lot to lose, he was putting his reputation on the line,' she says. 'It was all very Royal Court, very left-wing, very stark. His great fear was that I was going to go off into weird areas and do mad exercises; but I rehearsed it very simply and conventionally. I was very nervous, but after the second day I thought, This man's a poppet! He was shy, but very generous, and took any notes I gave him like a lamb. Once I said, "Frankly the way you do that is just bloody boring – oh!" But he just roared with laughter. Some of the text was hard to grasp, but he wrestled with it simply and honourably. The brilliant thing was that he would try anything – though I don't think he had much fun.'

Bond, who attended several rehearsals, was fascinated to see how he explored the language: 'I thought he didn't know his lines. Then I realised he had never made any actual mistakes. He'd been word-perfect from the beginning. But he always spoke as if he were trying to remember what to say – each thought was re-thought each time so that it never became an empty formula. It was only at the very end of rehearsals that perfect cadences came.' Twenty-five years later he remembers being very happy with Gielgud's performance: 'I'm not sure if he was much interested in the technical arguments, but he understood the human dilemmas very well.'

The critics disliked Bond's cynical, bitter Shakespeare, and the static nature of the play. Gielgud caught Shakespeare the sceptic convincingly – John Barber wrote of his 'wounded-eagle intensity' – but was generally felt to be under-used. As the run progressed he began to experiment a little. 'Sometimes he went off at tangents that weren't totally suitable,' Jane Howell recalls. 'He was very influenced by friends, and I think someone suggested there should be a few laughs in it. So he attacked certain scenes in slightly different ways.'

Gielgud always liked to keep in touch with younger actors. During *Bingo* he made friends with Oliver Cotton, and one day took him to lunch in an expensive restaurant in the King's Road. 'He talked all the time about the theatre, and the whole history of his playing Hamlet. I told him I had been in a production at Hoxton Hall. "Where's that?" he said. I told him it was in the East End. "I only know the West End," he replied. He asked me if I knew Olivier. "Rather a cold man, but he writes very good letters." He had been worried about the drunk scene he had to play with Arthur Lowe, who was Ben Jonson. "I can never play drunk because I've never been drunk," he said. Most actors would watch other people, but he didn't have any skill as a mimic. So the drunk scene was rather declaimed.'

Gielgud had not appeared at the National since Brook's controversial *Oedipus*. But once Peter Hall took over from Olivier in 1973 he appeared in five productions in three years. Reversing Olivier's policy, Hall hired star classical actors, and Gielgud, Richardson and Ashcroft were among the first to benefit. He quickly established a good relationship with Gielgud, whom he had admired since his youth. Like Gielgud, Hall had been influenced as a Shakespearean director by Poel and Barker, and shared his belief in the importance of the verse. He also admired him personally: 'It is an inspiration just to be with him – the most giving of men,' he said.

For his opening production Hall staged *The Tempest*. Worried that Gielgud might be too gentle for the harsh Prospero he had in mind, Hall had talked first to Olivier ('What on earth would *I* do with a boring old conjuror?' he said later) and then to Guinness. Gielgud had not been in a Shakespeare play in London for sixteen years, and was worried that he was out of date: 'My own speaking, which was over-praised for many years, is now something of a cliché, and of course actors don't want to talk posh,' he said. Scofield he recognised and admired as the leader of the next generation, but he was also aware of the younger, more naturalistic actors such as Nicol Williamson, whose *Hamlet* was felt to have 'removed Gielgud's shadow from the play'.

With Prospero, however, he felt on firm ground. It was a part that matched well his own remote, austere quality, and one that he loved to play. But for his fourth attempt at it he was keen not to repeat his previous performances: 'I've always found, particularly with Shakespeare, that the more often you play a part, the more often you find something new to say.' But after seeing a very avant-garde, black-leather *Julius Caesar* by the RSC, in which he felt the actors 'shouted and screamed and had no idea of character', he briefly panicked about returning to Shakespeare. Was Hall, he wondered fearfully, going to do something similar?

At first he displayed his usual neuroses. At the start of a three-hour meeting with Hall and designer John Bury he rejected his costume, refused to wear a beard, pronounced Prospero a boring man and a boring part, questioned all of Hall's suggestions, and offered a multitude of his own. Perhaps he was simply testing his director's mettle, for by the end he was telling Hall that his ideas were fascinating, agreeing to his costume and a beard, and going off happily to be measured.

He was not happy, however, about Olivier's decision to come to the first day of rehearsals, though according to Hall 'he masked it, perfectly mannered Edwardian that he is'. When Hall took him off for lunch in his office, Olivier came and joined them. 'He sat and chatted, making Gielgud feel uneasy,' Hall observed. 'It is extraordinary to watch these two giants. Gielgud is obviously disturbed by Larry, and Larry knows it.'

In rehearsals Hall found Gielgud 'volatile, mercurial, exhausting to direct, but also delightful'. Wanting a Prospero who was disillusioned with the world, who would rather stay on the island than regain his dukedom, he tried to stop Gielgud 'singing' the verse, and to get him to rein in his emotion. Gielgud readily responded, and was soon 'becoming contained and strong', impressing Hall with his desire to avoid easy solutions, and to find a humorous side of Prospero. 'He is an amazing man, and my debt to him is enormous,' Hall noted after the first preview. 'He has never complained, never been restless. He has led the company and helped me every inch of the way.'

The company included Denis Quilley as Caliban, Michael Feast as Ariel, Jenny Agutter as Miranda, and Arthur Lowe as Stephano. It seemed fitting that Gielgud, in his seventieth year and giving what was assumed to be his last Prospero, should be heading the company as a new regime began, and the first night in March 1974 had a very special atmosphere. Quite against the modern convention, Gielgud was applauded on his first entry; at the end the reception was, in Hall's words, 'absolutely wild'.

The critics, however, were less ecstatic. Having immersed himself in productions of baroque opera at Glyndebourne, Hall had not directed a Shakespeare play for seven years. He had conceived the production within the framework of a masque, with Prospero as its remote and detached stage manager, and devised many elaborate and extravagant effects which, he admitted later, sank the play's complexities. But Gielgud, in a close-fitting cap, Elizabethan ruff and grey beard, was praised for remaining aloof from what was seen as Hall's vulgarity. 'His lifelong familiarity with the text and with its infinite subtleties give his Prospero the authority of an old master,' Frank Marcus wrote. 'When he faces us bareheaded for the final epilogue, he engages our emotions most poignantly.'

His technique was a revelation to others in the company, including Denis Quilley: 'I was astonished to see how all that lightness you see out front was supported by so much physical work in the diaphragm and in the projection of his voice,' he recalls. 'It was like a swan paddling under the surface.' Michael Feast saw another aspect: 'Sometimes he actually beat out the rhythms with his feet. I noticed the shadow of it in performance, a definite physical feel in his rhythm.' For Hall, Gielgud provided the ultimate model for speaking the verse: 'He thinks Shakespeare in lines not in words, he speaks it trippingly on the tongue, it's always witty and never pompous, and he has the ability to make the antitheses and contradictions absolutely natural, as if he was thinking of them only at that moment.'

The company enjoyed Gielgud's unfailing good humour and modesty. Hall wrote in his diary: 'He keeps making self-deprecating remarks, reminding us we shouldn't listen to him, and that he is a romantic who loves the old-fashioned theatre.' Michael Feast, who stood next to him at the curtain call, remembers one particular night: 'The audience exploded into especially loud cheers and bravos. When he stepped back he took my hand and whispered, "I think the landlady must be in tonight." It was an old touring actor's comment.'

His ability to retain his humour and control his emotions was severely tested by two incidents. During a lengthy technical rehearsal the trapdoor through which Ferdinand and Miranda appear was being tested. Suddenly Gielgud fell through it. Cordelia Monsey was sitting in the stalls, and remembers the consternation: 'Peter went completely white. Nobody dared venture on the stage. Then Gielgud emerged, saying: "Oh that this too too solid flesh . . .". Not a moment of resentment or anger.' Although it was one o'clock in the morning and he was bruised and shaken, he insisted on continuing. He also remained calm on the second night when a key member of the company failed to turn up for the performance. 'It didn't seem to throw him, he remained as cool as a cucumber,' Denis Quilley recalls.

In April Gielgud turned seventy. To many he seemed years younger. Pink-cheeked, dapperly dressed, smoking endless Turkish cigarettes, he was working harder than he had been ten years before. 'I don't want to retire, I only get bored and depressed when I'm not working,' he said. Eternally youthful in spirit, he retained his blazing curiosity about the theatre, and his unquenchable love of gossip.

The gaffes continued unabated. After seeing a pen-and-ink drawing of himself by David Hockney, he remarked: 'If I really look like that I must kill myself tomorrow.' To a journalist doing a feature for his birthday he said, 'I do find these interviews a bore, don't you?' Hallam Tennyson was another victim. Gielgud used to visit him and his family at their home, where his father was also living. Some time later Tennyson said to him, 'You never come and see us now.' Gielgud replied: 'No, I used to enjoy coming when your father was alive.'

Sometimes, when roused, he could be quite waspish. Shortly after his birthday he took part in a recital of Milton's *Paradise Lost*, adapted for the stage by the newsreader Gordon Honeycombe. Martin Jarvis recalled that when Honeycombe asked him to deliver a line with a different inflection, Gielgud said: 'Well, I suppose I might say it like that if it were the nine o'clock news.'

To celebrate his birthday the BBC broadcast a selection of recordings from some of his greatest performances, presented by Ralph Richardson. 'It's a programme about a man of talent narrated by a man of genius,' Gielgud said. Friends and colleagues from all over the world wrote messages in a handsome volume specially bound for the occasion in Venice. At the end of the performance of *The Tempest* Richardson came on stage and wished him a happy birthday, a surprise gesture which provoked the inevitable tears. At a small party afterwards in the rehearsal room the actors gave him a Doulton figure of Ellen Terry.

Some years earlier Gielgud had said wistfully: 'I wish Pinter would write a play with a part I could do.' He had always liked Pinter's work, especially *The Birthday Party* and *The Caretaker*. In this he was quite different from his brother Val, who was accused of running his radio drama department 'as if it were the days of Henry Irving'. Stuck in the era of Maugham and Coward, he took a strong dislike to new writers such as Pinter and Stoppard, who began their playwriting careers in radio. 'He thought their plays were absolutely terrible, he didn't understand a word of them,' Hallam Tennyson remembers. 'His views were positively nineteenth-century, drama for him stopped with Ibsen and the well-made play. John was much more open to new ideas.'

Gielgud's prayer to Pinter was now answered: the National offered him one of the two leading parts in his new play *No Man's Land*, to be directed by Hall. Teamed again with Richardson, with Michael Feast and Terence Rigby in support, Gielgud astonished everyone with his performance as Spooner, a seedy, garrulous failed poet. With earlier roles such as Noah, Lear and Shylock he had disguised himself facially, but his own persona had shone through, vocally or otherwise. With the wickedly observed Spooner he gave an impersonation of a character for the first time. It was a radical departure and, he said later, 'the happiest theatrical experience of my life'.

The surface story concerns the efforts of the sly, disreputable Spooner ('Do you often hang about Hampstead Heath?') to worm his way into the home of Hirst, a wealthy but lonely man of letters who has brought him there after a chance meeting in a pub. Gielgud was enthusiastic about the play straightaway, but surprised Pinter and Hall by insisting on playing Spooner rather than the patrician Hirst, which was then offered to Richardson.

Quite untypically, Gielgud saw his character at once – the crumpled suit, the dishevelled sandy hair falling over one eye, the rimless spectacles, the sandals and socks, the bulging belly. His inspiration was

W.H. Auden, with whom he had recently shared a platform at a poetry recital at the Young Vic: 'When this creature came down the stairs with this extraordinarily wrinkled face, with his tie hanging out and awful sandals and a terrible soup-stained suit, I was absolutely fascinated,' he said. But he also drew on memories of the crumpled Bohemian figures he had observed in his youth in the second-hand ballet bookshops in Charing Cross Road.

A week into rehearsal he appeared in his costume looking, according to Hall, like 'a sad and dreadful creep'. Amid the general approval Gielgud observed: 'Now I must find a performance to go inside it.' This was the reverse of his usual technique, and the quest was not straightforward. 'As one gets older one gets so nervous,' he confessed during rehearsals. 'There is no obvious line of progression in this play.' As is clear from Hall's diary, one problem was his method of exploring a part: 'I am a little worried about John,' Hall wrote. 'He's over-experimenting: playing it humble, playing it conceited, playing it creepy, playing it arrogant.' He thought Gielgud was overdoing the humility, and finding it hard to capture Spooner's hardness. But soon after he saw he had found the key: 'Today John really broke through and became an arrogant and unpleasant man,' he noted.

Pinter, who got on well with Gielgud, was impressed by his openness to ideas: 'I did occasionally offer an emphasis that seemed to me to be appropriate and called for, and he would seize upon such a suggestion,' he recalled. 'He's not an egoist, that's the most extra-ordinary thing, and the truth about him.' But Pinter was charac-teristically unforthcoming about the meaning of his play. Oliver Cotton, sitting in on rehearsals as an understudy, recalls: 'John asked him many questions, but Pinter would say, "I can't answer that." It was very difficult, there was a complete block.' Gielgud told Pinter he had read a book about his work; Pinter told him he was wasting his time.

The two actors also struggled with Pinter's long sentences and his famous pauses. 'There was terror in the rehearsal room when we reached a pause, because each of them thought the other had lost his lines,' Hall remembers. 'We had to spend a great deal of time learning the pauses and understanding what they meant.' Richardson was irritated by Pinter's refusal to change any of them. Finally he said: 'In that case, sir, could you tell me how many pauses make a silence, because I need to know.' Pinter said: 'About three, sometimes four, depending on the speech.'

Gielgud found Hall a sympathetic and thorough director, liking the way he encouraged suggestions and criticisms from the actors. They shared a strong musical sense and a respect for the text, which helped Gielgud handle Pinter's taut prose. Pinter always stressed the importance in his work of rhythm and music, elements Gielgud understood. He spoke his dialogue, full of repartee, precision and menace, with immense subtlety. Many critics were baffled by the play, but Gielgud concluded pragmatically: 'Why should the play mean anything if the audience was held the whole time and was never bored?' He was now strikingly at ease with the radical spirit of the age.

Some of the audience were offended by the occasional swear-word, but the fuss was minor compared to that over *Veterans*. 'My parents would be horrified at my performing in it,' Gielgud observed, while clearly enjoying the experience. He told Pinter he had thought *No Man's Land* would be like acting Chekhov, where you ignored the audience, but that he had found it more akin to playing Wilde or Congreve, where you manipulated it.

What surprised many people was his ability to conceal his own personality. 'John's performance took me completely by surprise,' Michael Feast remembers. 'Much as I admired him, I couldn't think what he would do with this vicious old sponger. It was a miracle of transformation.' An important element in that transformation was his voice: basing his vocal delivery on the drawl affected by his brother Lewis and his Oxford friends the Huxleys and Haldanes, Gielgud made it lower and less mellifluous than usual.

This vocal adaptability was crucial to his success with the new plays he was now doing. Received pronunciation was no longer the standard, and actors were expected to find more natural rhythms in the text. 'What was wonderful about Gielgud was his ability to bridge the gap between styles while keeping the integrity of his voice,' says Cicely Berry, voice director of the RSC. 'He never sounded stilted or old-fashioned as some actors did. That was to do with an aliveness of mind, and a lack of ego. He wasn't stuck in his own sound, he was interested in the present, not just the past.'

His success was also due to his relaxed, affectionate relationship with Richardson. Michael Feast recalled their nightly conversation just moments before the play began. 'Every night I would turn up the tannoy to hear their conversation on stage. You'd hear, "Hello Johnny." – "Hello Ralph." – "Did you have a good day?" – "Yes, I met Peggy. We had lunch." – "Oh marvellous." This went on right up to the moment the curtain rose when John, pouring a drink, would go straight into the first line, "As it is?" and Ralph would reply, "As it is, yes please, absolutely as it is."' How much further, Hall wondered, could you get from Method acting?

Although Pinter had not had him in mind when writing *No Man's Land*, after the first night at the Old Vic in April 1975 Gielgud thanked him for having written 'such a marvellous vehicle for me'. In his diary Hall wrote: 'The Old Lions are pleased. John's performance was magnificent.' Spooner was hailed as Gielgud's finest role for years, and won him the London Theatre Critics' award for Best Actor. Richardson too was outstanding, giving a moving portrayal of the lonely Hirst.

Years later Olivier praised Gielgud's creation of Spooner. 'That performance created a reality I've always fought for,' he wrote. But during the run he managed to antagonise both actors. After one performance he came round and complained that he couldn't hear them and had fallen asleep. He then threatened to return the following week in the hope that they would be more audible. Hall noted the actors' reactions: 'Ralph is very upset: why is Larry so harsh? John, who is furious, is more down to earth; he says he suspects Larry is going deaf.'

No Man's Land was a huge artistic and commercial success, and also rewarding for Gielgud financially, since he and Richardson were each taking 10 per cent of the box-office income. On stage every night for two hours, they notched up 378 performances over the next two years, including a six-month spell at Wyndham's, and a transfer to the National's newly opened Lyttelton. Their partnership had an unfortunate consequence for Pinter: 'It frightened the life out of every other actor in the world, so the play wasn't done in London again for ages,' he said. 'People just wouldn't touch it, because after Richardson and Gielgud set such an extraordinary standard of performance, what could you do?'

The play was also taken to America. In Washington and Toronto audiences found it heavy going, and dozens of people walked out. Broadway was different. In November 1976 Peter Hall recorded the reaction on the opening night in the Longacre Theater: 'There was terrific excitement in the house and the actors rose wonderfully to the occasion. I have rarely seen the two Lions roar better. Fantastic reception.'

Many of Pinter's nuances and references were lost on American audiences. 'It's a great pity, it makes it difficult for us,' Gielgud said.

'But you have to take it on the chin. Googly, Jack Straw's Castle: they don't know cricket, or Hampstead, you see. They don't know the word *pouf.* They don't know the word *bent.*' His use of such words in public was another mark of his freer, more relaxed spirit. He had found a new audience, and was revelling in it. 'You need a young public to strip your work of its affectations,' he told an American journalist. 'It is a more realistic world, and I hope I have got rid of a lot of the romantic hoo-ha of my youth. The young directors – Lindsay Anderson, Peter Brook, Peter Hall – have been the making of me.'

No Man's Land marked his final stage appearance in America. New York again put him in a buoyant mood, and he lived in style: the American management supplied a Cadillac to ferry him around town, and he had a suite in the Drake Hotel. Tynan visited him there, and found him 'spruce, poker-backed, voluble, eyes wickedly gleaming'. He had lunch at the Algonquin with Richardson, during which they reminisced merrily, about previous visits to New York, American courtesy, speakeasies, and Tallulah Bankhead. Since playing together in *Home* they had given countless interviews together, been much photographed, and even been mistaken for each other in the street. Gielgud likened their partnership to 'the broker's men in *Cinderella*'.

It was one based on love and respect, tinged with mutual awe and amazement at their many differences. Gielgud loved Richardson for what he called 'a kind of level madness that was very endearing'. He admired in him qualities he himself lacked: his preference for pleasing himself rather than the audience, his ability to think carefully before he spoke, his interest in objects, machinery, animals, and all kinds of things outside the theatre. 'I'm so proud to be his friend, he's so talented, so knowledgeable, so eccentric,' he said. Not long after he was a guest on 'Desert Island Discs', and one of his choices was Richardson reading two Blake poems. 'He has such a beautiful voice and such a warmth of personality, I felt he would be a great comfort to me if I had nobody to talk to.'

Richardson was amused at Gielgud's total lack of interest in anything technological. 'I told him Concorde flies faster than sound,' he recalled. 'On cue, the bored look.' He terrified Gielgud by taking him up in a plane, and on the back of his motor-bike. 'He didn't like it, he's not a car or bike man,' he said. But when they talked Gielgud was in the driving-seat. 'You needn't say a word when you're with him,' Richardson said. 'Sometimes I will say Yes, or No, or Really? Afterwards he will tell someone, "I had a wonderful talk with Ralph."'

In 1976 the two of them returned briefly to the theatre of their youth. Gielgud had assumed *The Tempest* would mark his last Shakespearean production at the Old Vic. 'Fantastic reception,' Hall had noted after the last night. 'Gielgud obviously very moved.' But there was to be one more appearance. In February, on the National's last night at the Old Vic before the move to its new building on the South Bank, he took part – with Richardson, Scofield, Edith Evans, Sybil Thorndike and many other stars – in *Tribute to a Lady*, a celebration of the life and work of Lilian Baylis, played by Peggy Ashcroft.

Dressed in a dinner-jacket, standing on the stage where he had first played Hamlet in 1930, Gielgud gave a passionate rendering of the 'O, what a rogue and peasant slave am I!' soliloquy. He had not played the part for thirty years, and the speed, energy and precision with which he spoke the lines astonished an audience packed with the cream of the profession. It was a spell-binding farewell to the theatre where he had first shown his potential as a great Shakespearean actor.

32

The Road to Brideshead

The utter finality of a television performance
invariably depresses me.
(Gielgud after his television début, 1959)

I N 1973, under pressure from Martin Hensler, Gielgud bought a
house in the village of Wotton Underwood in Buckinghamshire,
fifty miles from London. His new home, South Pavilion, was a converted William and Mary coach-house situated at the end of a
cul-de-sac. A tall, square, red-brick building, it stood next to a larger
house belonging to the historian Arthur Bryant, from whom Gielgud
had bought South Pavilion.

The house was in a poor state of repair, and it was three years before
he was able to move in, and sell his London house. In the meantime
Martin Hensler supervised the re-decoration. A vast central room,
doubling as sitting- and dining-room, was hung with Regency wallpaper and individually lit pictures, its stained floor painted with gold
feathers. It was furnished with silk-covered sofas, Persian carpets, gilt-
edged, high-backed chairs, and lots of silver and candelabra. A grand
double staircase led up to a mezzanine where Gielgud kept his book
collection. Underneath, in a small area containing paintings and a
photograph of Craig, he would watch television.

It was all very lavish, ornate and elegant, to some tastes over-
decorated – not unlike one of his own stage sets. Outside 'Capability
Martin', as he was called, created a beautiful formal Italian garden,
with high walls, gravel paths, fine vistas, box hedges, stone figures, a
fountain, a gazebo and an aviary. 'You can hear the birds and there are
views of lakes and things,' Gielgud said. In this peaceful haven he was
to live for the rest of his life.

At first he was unhappy being away from London. He would make frequent visits, meeting friends for lunch, wandering past the theatres to see what was on. Some of his friends felt Martin Hensler had too much control over him, and had imprisoned him in the countryside against his wishes. The relationship caused problems with certain friends of Gielgud: he broke with John Perry and others, fearing the violent scenes that Hensler often created. Orson Welles noted that Gielgud was subjected to the 'constant carping of an apparently malicious Hungarian friend' during the filming of *Chimes at Midnight*. 'John, you are terrible old fashion!' Hensler would say all day long. 'Old hat, old hat! Nobody wants you!' And Gielgud would reply: 'I know, I know, it's perfectly true, perfectly true, every word of it is true!'

Hensler also took charge of his money, and after a while decided Gielgud was being exploited. He persuaded him to break with Beaumont, and appoint Laurence Evans at ICM as his agent. Gielgud was permanently anxious about money. 'Country life is costing me a fortune,' he said, pointing to the expense of maintaining his house, and 'the most awful drain' on his finances of employing a chauffeur. And then there was the taxman: he discovered when his accountant died that because of muddled book-keeping he owed £70,000 in back taxes. 'I'll never be solvent until the day I die,' he protested. At one stage he had to sell some paintings, and feared he would have to give up the house. But friends being entertained in lavish style were amused to find him pleading poverty amongst so much splendour.

'John said how wonderful it was to have a free afternoon in London,' Peter Hall noted in his diary in January 1978. 'He isn't really enjoying the country, I think: he's a town rat, as Ralph has always observed.' Now a highly accomplished television actor, Gielgud had come to record *No Man's Land* for Granada Television. Its producer Derek Granger recalls his delivery of Spooner's climatic speech: 'When he finished there was a short pause of stunned amazement, which suddenly turned into the sound of rapturous appreciation as the entire studio floor let forth a spontaneous roar of applause. John had delivered, without a single fluff, six pages of incredibly complicated monologue, not only letter-perfect but with every stress and inflection, nuance and underlining, every demi-semi-quaver miraculously intact.'

As with films, Gielgud had at first disliked acting for television, and struggled for many years to adapt to it. The first televised play, Pirandello's *The Man with a Flower in his Mouth*, had been shown in 1930. There had been a few pre-war productions, in one of which Peggy

Ashcroft played Miranda in *The Tempest*, the first Shakespeare play broadcast from the BBC studios at Alexandra Palace. But televised drama only got going seriously after the war. In the 1950s actors began to dip a toe into television, but many looked down on it. 'They tell me the TV audience is not particularly noted for taking things in,' Olivier remarked disdainfully. They also feared and mistrusted the process: plays were recorded live, so there was no scope for re-takes or editing. Coward likened the experience to being in a stage play without an audience, a radio play without a script, and doing a film in one take.

Gielgud rarely watched television, and was as mistrustful of it as most actors. In 1955 he refused requests to appear on it with Peggy Ashcroft in *Much Ado About Nothing*, arguing that failure would badly damage their reputation: 'A multitude of viewers who had never seen us might well wonder what all the fuss had been about,' he said. 'It is no good playing to millions on television if they are not ready and willing to appreciate the play.' He also saw television as 'a terrible intrusion' on social life. 'I'd rather be excited by ordinary happenings than by that nasty box. I like to be entertained in company, and I can't understand how people get together in a room and look at a set. It defeats the entire purpose of a gathering.'

His first appearance was on the opening night of commercial television in September 1955, when he performed an excerpt from *The Importance of Being Earnest* with Edith Evans and Margaret Leighton. He was glimpsed again the following year, when the cameras filmed part of *Nude with Violin* from the Globe. In 1958 Olivier made a much-publicised début in Ibsen's *John Gabriel Borkman*. 'When Sir Laurence successfully broke the ice, I thought I had better have a try,' Gielgud said soon after, politely overlooking the fact that the production provoked a massive switch-off – a reaction that put Olivier off television for many years.

Associated Television was so keen to have Gielgud appear that it offered him one of the highest fees paid for a television appearance. His choice of play was disappointingly cautious. Convinced that Shakespeare would be too 'large' for television, he opted for a modern part, deciding that if he was going to 'make a fool of myself' it would be in a play he already knew. His first choice was Graham Greene's *The Potting Shed*, but when Alec Guinness proved unavailable he thought again: 'The actor who plays the priest is bound to walk off with the play,' he said. 'I would not mind Alec's doing that, but I'll be hanged if I'll let anyone else do it.' Eventually, believing his understated part in it might adapt well to television, he chose the second-rate *A Day by the Sea*, in which he appeared with Gladys Cooper, Margaret Leighton and Roger Livesey.

The production was said to have been seen by twenty-two million viewers. The critics liked Gielgud's studied underplaying, but thought the play a poor choice. The experience alarmed Gielgud, and provoked a new set of anxieties. He missed the contact with a live audience which in the theatre settled his nerves, and felt cramped by the restricted conditions and the technical paraphernalia. Above all he hated the fact that there was no room for improvement in a performance – or scope for changes: 'There are moments when I am convinced that every viewer has switched off,' he confessed soon afterwards. 'Furthermore, the utter finality of a television performance invariably depresses me – that awful awareness of now or never. Everything is staked on one short hour and it is disturbing to know that millions are watching.'

His American television début came the following month, when he appeared with Margaret Leighton and Robert Stephens in *The Browning Version*, playing Crocker-Harris, as he had on radio. Again he felt uncomfortable: 'John Frankenheimer terrified me by sitting between my legs during the takes, and hissing directions in my ear,' he recalled. But his restrained performance was greeted with superlatives; Stephens thought he played the part 'beautifully and very movingly'. He even received a rare tribute from Olivier, with only the smallest of stings in the tail: 'Your old friend was bursting with pride and admiration – your performance was quite flawless and dreadfully moving, it haunts me still. Bravo dearest Johnnie, it's just fascinating and most inspiring the way you seem still to find room for improvement all the time.'

Gielgud announced grandly that he would only appear on the small screen if he had no stage work. In the next seven years he made only three appearances on British television, two of which were in adaptations of successful Chekhov productions: Saint-Denis' version of *The Cherry Orchard* and his own of *Ivanov*. Neither of these satisfied him: 'Chekhov is almost impossible on television,' he said. 'You want to watch seven or eight people at once and their reactions: it is their interplay and the general movement of the action which makes the play.'

His other appearance was in a shortened version of *The Rehearsal*, Anouilh's bitter-sweet comedy, in which the characters rehearse a play by Marivaux. In it Gielgud showed his unawareness of the technical difficulties of live television, as Judy Campbell remembers: 'He asked for a mirror shot in one scene in which he had to put on a hat. This was very hard to arrange, and we all had to crawl around on our hands and knees so as not to be seen. He just didn't realise the problems involved.'

He had to struggle with a more familiar problem himself. As the debauched Count he had to seduce the young nursemaid, played by Sarah Miles. As she recalls, he kept putting the scene off, and it remained unrehearsed by the day of recording. 'Eventually he came on to the set wearing silk pyjamas and dressing-gown, looking like something out of Noël Coward. He was absolutely terrified. He asked me to lead him, but I said that wasn't quite what was meant to happen. He whispered anxiously to me, "What does one do, embrace or kiss first? I never get it right." He was very sweet, but I had to nurse him through it.'

Alan Badel, with his reputation as an actor who ate directors for breakfast, was repeating the role he had played with success in the recent West End production. He disliked the adaptation, thought Gielgud wrong for his part, and was continually unpleasant and abusive. On the day of recording there was a furious row. Badel was supposed to hit Gielgud lightly in the face with his glove, but instead knocked him to the floor. Gielgud was shaken, but only later showed how much, as Sarah Miles recalls: 'The director was weak, and Alan got away with murder. John was amazingly patient. Later I watched the finished version with him in a screening-room. He was half in profile, but I could see there were tears in his eyes. At the end he stood up white with rage, and said with such hurt and fury: "God damn blast Alan Badel!" I'd never seen him so emotional.'

In 1966 Gielgud re-visited his very first stage part, that of the Mock Turtle in *Alice in Wonderland*, which he'd played at prep school. In Jonathan Miller's dreamy adaptation of the famous children's classic, he danced the lobster quadrille on the sea-shore with Malcolm Muggeridge's Gryphon, and re-told the story of his schooling in 'Drawling, Stretching and Fainting in Coils' with poetic gentleness. He was fast adjusting to the medium: in a farrago of over-acting and weird camera angles, he and Michael Redgrave (as the Caterpillar) give easily the most subtle performances.

He next appeared as Chekhov in *From Chekhov with Love*, Miller's portrait of the Russian playwright based on his letters, with Peggy Ashcroft playing Chekhov's wife Olga Knipper. Soon after he was in Dürrenmatt's two-hander about a prisoner and his executioner,

Conversation at Night, in which Alec Guinness made his British television début. Both were praised for adapting their technique to the small screen with apparent ease. Gielgud was now much more assured, but still disliked studio conditions, especially being separated from his director, and only getting instructions from the floor manager: 'You can't hear what the director is saying to him, so you become suspicious that you're being heavily criticised from upstairs and can't interfere,' he complained.

As he gained more experience he relaxed his negative attitude to Shakespeare on television. He spoke the Prologue for *Romeo and Juliet* in 1967, and played the Ghost again in Peter Wood's 1971 production of *Hamlet*, in which Richard Chamberlain was the Prince and Redgrave played Polonius. In the BBC's massive Shakespeare project, which was to cover the entire canon over six years, he spoke the first lines of the opening production, resplendently dressed as the Chorus for *Romeo and Juliet*. In the second, *Richard II*, he played John of Gaunt to Derek Jacobi's king. Jacobi remembered how intimidating Gielgud's mere presence could be for an actor: 'I was terrified, being there with one of the great Richards. I thought, he's going to wince at every wrong inflection. In fact he was marvellous to work with, very encouraging.'

Television also softened Gielgud's opinion about playing in Shaw, and enabled him to fulfil two youthful ambitions. In the title-role of *In Good King Charles' Golden Days* he worked for the only time with his friend the great German star Elisabeth Bergner. He also played Captain Shotover in that most Chekhovian of Shaw's plays, *Heartbreak House*. It was a role he had coveted for forty years, but though he was now the right age, he seemed miscast as Shaw's eccentric old sea-dog.

He fared better as the Inquisitor in *Saint Joan*, provoking high praise from George Melly, then a television critic, who wrote: 'His incredible authority as an actor made everyone else seem paper-thin. It's not that he upstages. He just has to sit there.' But during recording he still had difficulties, as the director Waris Hussein recalls: 'We shot almost continuously, with just four breaks every hour to take stock. So everything had to be very carefully choreographed. Halfway through his very long speech about mercy he forgot his lines. Not wanting to show it, he said, "What's that wretched thing coming towards me?" I said, "John, it's the camera."'

Television, in addition to offering him the predictable civil servants, diplomats, aristocrats and tycoons, enabled him to enjoy a much wider range of modern parts than he had ever had in the theatre. He now developed a neat line in men of the cloth, some less pious than others. He was a sleuth-vicar in Agatha Christie's *Why Didn't They Ask Evans?*, a fraudulent one alongside Bernard Miles in Roald Dahl's *Parson's Pleasure*, and a weird one as the eccentric recluse in Hugh Whitemore's spine-chilling *Deliver us from Evil*.

Butlers proved another rich vein. In Roald Dahl's macabre black comedy *Neck* he was the inscrutably polite but snooty butler employed by the bitchy wife of a newspaper tycoon, played by Joan Collins. Director Christopher Miles recalls: 'When I went to collect John for his opening scene he was trying to get his lines right, and I could see his nervousness. Here was a man who took it all very seriously, the work still caused the adrenalin to flow. Directing him was a pleasure – though his presence was so strong it could unbalance a scene.'

On location in Norfolk Joan Collins marvelled at his alertness: 'Every morning, throwing on jeans, shirt and headscarf, I'd totter down to the car where John awaited, dapper in tweeds, tie and waistcoat, and elegantly smoking a cigarette, his mind already as sharp as a whip.' Gielgud was politeness itself in describing their collaboration: 'People seemed to expect some kind of cataclysmic happening when Joan and I were working together,' he said. 'But Joan is a very professional actress and we got on extremely well.'

He returned now and then to costume drama, and to the turn-of-the-century period in which he was most at home. One of his most subtle performances was as Lord Henry Wotton in *The Picture of Dorian Gray*, John Osborne's adaptation of Wilde's novel. Hampered by a startling red wig, he poured forth a stream of epigrams with perfect *fin-de-siècle* nonchalance and wit. The over-elaborate production kept the homosexual nature of the characters' relationships implicit, allowing him to play 'the love that dare not speak its name' with subtle restraint, and put over the old roué's sadness with great poignancy.

He seemed startlingly youthful as Disraeli in *Edward the Seventh*: in his wavy wig and discreet goatee beard he looked younger than he had in 1940 when he played the same part in *The Prime Minister*. Yet he was very aware of the effect of time passing. Michael Feast recalls a discussion while they were filming Dostoyevsky's *The Grand Inquisitor* for the Open University: 'He said, "You'll be all right, you've got the cheekbones," and I said, "You will be too." And he said, "Yes, yes, but *this* is going" – and he pointed to his neck.'

For both *The Grand Inquisitor* and the Preacher in *Portrait of the*

Artist as a Young Man he had to learn a lengthy monologue. For an actor in his mid-seventies this was intimidating, but Gielgud relished the stimulus: 'I'm emulating Sybil Thorndike,' he remarked. 'It's frightfully important to learn new things every year, it does keep your memory flexible.' Yet this didn't prevent the usual doubts about his performance. Still striving for perfection, after having completed the twenty-five-minute Dostoyevsky solo he remarked: 'Using old tricks . . . couldn't quite get the voice . . . Shakespearean delivery . . . doesn't seem right.'

He appeared in *Special Duties*, John Mortimer's adaptation of a Graham Greene story. His continuing enthusiasm for his work is caught vividly in Mortimer's description of waiting for a private viewing to begin:

> His back is straight, his head cocked, the nose like an eager beak clearing the air, the eyes hooded as if prepared to wince in fastidious disapproval at what that inquisitive nose might discover. He has the bald head of a priest, the pink health of a retired admiral, the elegant suit of what was once known as a Man about Town, and the competent hands of an artist . . . He sits before the dead television set with the eagerness, which has never left him, of a child about to see the curtain go up on its own carefully cut-out and coloured puppet-show.

He was frequently interviewed for programmes about acting and the theatre, and was much in demand as a narrator for programmes ranging from the lives of Leonardo Da Vinci and Noël Coward, to *Peter Pan* and a documentary on the October Revolution. America was a good source of income: he was paid a handsome sum for 'hosting' the American transmission of the BBC's version of Trollope's *The Pallisers*. He was still slightly astonished at the money he was being paid: after appearing on *Stars on Sunday* he remarked with innocent glee, 'They are paying me the most enormous amount of money just for reading the Bible.'

In 1980 he presented Thames Television's historical series on *The English Garden*, which took him to famous country houses such as Petworth and Blenheim. He had always had a keen visual appreciation of the English formal garden, a feeling reflected in some of the sets in his productions. He especially loved to visit Hidcote Manor in Gloucestershire, with its beautiful vistas across the Vale of Evesham. But he treated his role of presenter with twinkling self-mockery: 'With an old ham like me they just put me in front of the camera and tell me what to say,' he said. 'It's fun to pretend one knows something about gardening, but I don't really. I just sit outside and enjoy things coming up.'

The following year he gave what was widely felt to be his finest television performance. As Edward Ryder in *Brideshead Revisited*, John Mortimer's celebrated adaptation of Evelyn Waugh's novel, he drew a memorable portrait of desiccated cruelty, of a man of supreme meanness and calculating malice. Using a range of subtle gestures and inflections to suggest his contempt for his son Charles, played by Jeremy Irons, he was simultaneously chilling and funny.

Gielgud knew the novel intimately: 'I loved the part because it was right off the page of the book,' he said. In creating it he recalled his childhood fear of his father, but in essence he was faithful to the character in the novel, which he knew Waugh had based on *his* father. Curiously, in his autobiography Waugh recalled his father reading aloud 'with precision of tone, authority and variety that I have heard excelled only by Sir John Gielgud'.

Among a distinguished cast that included Claire Bloom, Anthony Andrews and Diana Quick, Olivier was cast as Lord Marchmain. According to producer Derek Granger, he believed he should have had Gielgud's role. 'Larry was extremely cross,' Granger remembers. 'He said, "Why did you give Johnny the best and funniest part, why didn't I get it?" I told him he had to be Marchmain, as he was the one with the glamour.' But in the view of director Charles Sturridge there was never any doubt about who would play Edward Ryder: 'Gielgud was the obvious choice as someone able to conduct that particularly vicious kind of war with his son.' Olivier, he felt, was being mischievous, and given half a chance would have played all the parts.

Gielgud's presence on the set forced everyone to work at their best. Having known Oxford in the Brideshead era, he was an authoritative source on the pronunciation, manners and décor of the time. Sturridge felt he not only understood how to create a character on film, but relished doing so. 'The mark of a great film actor is that when you see a performance on film as opposed to in front of you, you suddenly see many more things than you'd actually seen when it was being shot. And I think that's certainly true of his performance as Ryder's father.' Gielgud trusted Sturridge, and liked his undeferential approach. 'He reminded me of a young Peter Brook, sitting there in his plimsolls thinking,' he said.

He decided later that *Brideshead Revisited* was the one television performance he was truly proud of. Soon afterwards he recorded an abridged version of the novel. Kitty Black remembers the moment he came to the death of Lord Marchmain. 'Everyone in the studio was in tears, including John. At lunch he said: "I'm very ashamed, I cry at everything, I cry for trumpets, I cry for queens – oh dear, I suppose I shouldn't have said that."'

Asked once about the question of retirement, he had replied: 'There's always the radio.' In the autumn of his life he continued to broadcast, tapping again into the work of contemporary playwrights such as Peter Terson, Hugh Whitemore, Peter Barnes, Rhys Adrian and John Mortimer. He also read a substantial amount of poetry, including work by Blake, Tennyson, Coleridge, Edward Lear and the war poets.

Hallam Tennyson, who directed him several times, felt he was uncomfortable with radio. 'He was worried he would fall back on his voice, and lose the character. He also didn't take easily to reading from a script. He felt inadequate, and wanted discipline; he was very keen to have good direction. I think like a lot of his generation he looked on radio as a secondary art-form.' Gielgud admitted as much. 'I was never keen on radio, except as easy money on the side,' he said. 'You've got to be very sympathetic to the medium, and treat it gently, which is not easy for me, as I'm very impatient.'

Val Gielgud had retired from the BBC in 1963, and gone to live in the country, where he married his fifth and last wife. Eventually he went into a home, and died after a long illness, aged eighty-one. Though few people came to his funeral, four of his wives attended. Gielgud had seen little of him in his last years, and wrote to Christopher Fry: 'Val had a wretched long-drawn-out decline, and one can only be thankful he is out of it at last. He was a dear, generous, talented fellow.' Later he described him as 'always just slightly the black sheep of the family', someone who 'never seemed to have quite the luck he deserved'.

Some years earlier, speaking of their relationship, Val had admitted regret that 'an intimacy has vanished which I recall as having greatly valued'. Self-contained, cool and detached, Gielgud's regal manner hardly invited intimacy, even from his friends. Clive Francis, a talented cartoonist as well as an actor, observed the contrast with Olivier: 'If you met Olivier he would give you a bear hug, punch you on the shoulder, and say, "Hello, old cock." With Gielgud there was the head held at a slight angle, the ramrod back, the eye looking warily down at you.'

Gielgud acknowledged that he was no good at drawing people out. His friends would tell him he had no interest in anyone but himself. Alec Guinness recalls his self-absorbtion: 'He would invite you to dinner, but after ten minutes you could see he was bored by the idea, and he'd put on some gramophone records. He was acutely sensitive, but I don't think he ever asked me a single thing about my life, nor did so with anyone else I know. He would go through the normal politenesses, but that was all.'

Gielgud was now settling into country life. He liked to walk his dogs, make bonfires, and sit in his garden. He continued to devour books – 'I read all the time, anything at all, thrillers, biographies' – and listen to music, especially Brahms, Mozart and Delius. But he no longer went to parties, and only very rarely to the theatre – though he still kept up to date with the latest plays, and who was appearing in what. One of his visits to London was for Arthur Bryant's eightieth birthday lunch at the Guildhall, in which he was seated between Harold Wilson and James Callaghan. 'I didn't know what to talk about,' he said. 'I can't tell the Tories from the Whigs.'

Some of his friends felt he was becoming a recluse, and complained at how rarely he went out. 'Oh,' he told Derek Granger, 'but I've been out.'

33

Late Stages

I wouldn't entirely care to go in for revelations.
(Gielgud on publishing his memoirs, 1979)

GIELGUD'S renaissance as an actor seemed to have diminished his interest in directing. Since 1932 he had been directing almost continuously, averaging more than two productions a year. But after Ustinov's *Halfway Up the Tree* in 1967 he directed no play for four years. 'Now I prefer to be directed – I'm no longer bossy,' he explained.

In the 1970s he changed his mind once more. Again it was Edward Albee who broke the pattern. He sent Gielgud his new play *All Over*, and invited him to direct it in New York with an all-star cast, including Jessica Tandy, Colleen Dewhurst, Betty Field and Madeleine Sherwood. The play was a meditation on death and dying; Gielgud liked 'that Albee quality of rowing and rudeness'. But as with *Tiny Alice* he was hard put to discover its meaning. 'Edward was not helpful,' he complained. Jessica Tandy recalled asking Albee about some contradiction in her character: 'Edward said, "I'm sure we all understand that. You understand that, don't you, John." John the fink of course said, "Well, not altogether, but . . ." I never got anything from either of them. I was lost in limbo.'

Just before the opening Gielgud told Albee he had found the play 'continually fascinating and stimulating to work on'. But it was disliked by the critics, and on the second night the Martin Beck Theater was almost empty. It staggered on with meagre audiences for four weeks, but only because the actors took cuts in salary. Albee thought the production a little cold. 'John worked intelligently and sensitively, but I don't think there was much emotional presence,' he recalls. Yet Gielgud's work won plaudits from some eminent theatrical figures, including Tennessee Williams – who praised Jessica Tandy's 'brave and beautiful performance' – and the eminent director and critic Harold Clurman, who thought his production Albee's 'most thoroughly realised interpretation'. Gielgud, meanwhile, took pleasure in the words displayed outside the theatre: 'Edward Albee All Over John Gielgud'.

'I've always longed to direct a successful musical,' he had said some years earlier. He now realised his ambition with *Irene*, a Cinderella story about a New York Irish shopgirl, updated in a new version by Joseph Stein and Gielgud's friend Hugh Wheeler. Although its star, Debbie Reynolds, scarcely knew Gielgud's work as an actor ('I saw him in Henry something, would it be the Second?'), she had met him in Hollywood while he was filming *Julius Caesar*. Hearing he was in Hollywood again, she invited him to her house.

'I wanted a director who would keep *Irene* as a dramatic story and make me work,' she remembered. 'He sat sipping a glass of wine and looking contemplative, while we played him the score and I sang him the numbers. Then he said, "I'm surprised, pleasantly surprised, in fact amazingly surprised. I'll do it." Then he added, which was very sweet, "You shouldn't really be auditioning for me, because you've got the job. I should be auditioning for *you*."'

Even before starting work he had intimations of trouble. 'I'm frightened to death,' he said. 'I'm picturing sackings, and they'll probably throw me out.' His first mistake was to admit he knew nothing about musicals, and express the hope that the company would help him learn. The actors soon lost confidence in him, and began to skip his book rehearsals so they could concentrate on their singing and dancing. There were disputes with the management about cuts and additions, and even rows about the staging of the curtain calls. 'They began to suspect I was no bloody good, and went their own way,' Gielgud recalled. 'We didn't agree about basic essentials, like what is good and bad. It was all very tricky, they thought I was too weak. It was a ghastly experience.'

Variety correctly predicted 'a big, bouncy Broadway success'. But after try-outs in Philadelphia, Toronto and Washington it became 'Goodnight *Irene*' for Gielgud: he was sacked, and replaced by the top choreographer Gower Champion, who had been responsible for *Hello Dolly!* There was, however, a silver lining. Having agreed to accept a percentage of the profits instead of a fee, Gielgud netted around £40,000 from the run at the Minskoff Theater. As the money was held in America he later gave some of it to fund a fellowship organised by the Society for Stage Directors and Choreographers, and designed to help young directors work on the classics.

Back in London Noël Coward was back in fashion. *Hay Fever* had been staged at the National, and Coward was being re-discovered as a playwright of crackling wit and supreme craftsmanship. Gielgud was invited to direct *Private Lives*, that hymn to irresponsibility and nonconformity. Arguably Coward's finest play, it was the first of his that he had directed in the West End. He got the job after Maggie Smith, starring with her husband Robert Stephens, had rejected several younger directors suggested by Beaumont, including Bill Gaskill, John Dexter, Lindsay Anderson and Peter Wood.

Gielgud's view of the director's role was more detached than usual. According to Stephens, he told the actors that Coward needed a conductor rather than a director, since the play was 'just the music of people talking' – which it clearly is not. He claimed he was no good at comic business, and suggested the two stars arrange the famous second-act fight between themselves. Was his enthusiasm for directing starting to wane?

He was aware of Maggie Smith's reputation for being difficult, for sometimes relying on mannerisms and tricks. These tended to be more evident when she was unhappy, and at this time her marriage to Robert Stephens was falling apart. The production had been partly set up by Beaumont, and agreed to by the two actors, in the hope that it would save their marriage. Gielgud said later that they kept their emotional problems out of rehearsals, but their presence below the surface can't have made his work easy. Publicly he claimed to have found Maggie Smith 'a dreamgirl to rehearse', though he admitted she was 'so full of new touches of invention that I found it difficult to decide which were the best to keep in'. For once the roles were reversed.

Coward, now declining in health, came to the first night at the Queen's in September 1972. Asked about the revival he replied enigmatically: 'I think it is right not to say anything sometimes.' But Gielgud's production was well received and, after playing to capacity audiences for nearly three months, transferred to the Globe, and then in September 1974 to Broadway. While rehearsing the American version Gielgud made one of his more wounding gaffes when he said to Maggie Smith: 'Oh, don't do it like that, Maggie, don't screw your face up. You looked like that terrible old woman you played in that dreadful film. Oh no, I didn't mean *Travels with My Aunt*.'

Gielgud continued to enjoy exchanging gossip with the actors in his productions. Pinkie Johnstone, who took over the part of Sybil in *Private Lives*, recalls his love of drama offstage as well as on. 'He was always interested in your sex-life, always saying, "I hope you slept in your own bed last night." If he thought you were having an affair he got terribly excited, and wanted to know all about it, about any kind of drama or unpleasantness, someone crying or running out into the street. He loved anything like that.'

His next assignment was Maugham's cynical and witty comment on marriage *The Constant Wife*, with a company that included John McCallum, Pauline Jameson and Barbara Ferris. It starred Ingrid Bergman, who had recently had successes in the West End with Turgenev's *A Month in the Country* and Shaw's *Captain Brassbound's Conversion*. Gielgud's main problem in directing her was her command of English. Fluent on film and in private life, on stage she was hesitant and unsure, both about pronunciation and her lines, which she never mastered during the run. An apocryphal story has Gielgud saying, 'Dear Ingrid, speaks five languages and can't act in any of them.'

Her problems failed to deter the public, who packed the Albery (formerly the New) for a year to see the famous Swedish film star in the flesh. But Gielgud's production, though admired for its meticulous re-creation of 1920s décor, costumes and lighting, was merely glittering rather than authentically stylish as his Wilde and Sheridan revivals had been.

In March 1973, while he was planning *The Constant Wife*, he suffered the loss of two men who had played crucial roles in his career. He and Ingrid Bergman had spent an evening discussing designs and touring dates with Beaumont. Afterwards Beaumont read Rattigan's new play *After Lydia*, then rang the playwright to suggest Gielgud as a possible for the male lead. During the night, aged sixty-five, he died of a heart attack. Gielgud was rehearsing Hugh Whitemore's television play *Deliver Us from Evil* and, according to Whitemore, was 'very upset and miserable'. At the memorial service in St Paul's Church in Covent Garden, the 'actors' church', he recited again the familiar 'Fear no more the heat o' the sun' from *Cymbeline*.

His professional debt to Beaumont was enormous. He had worked regularly for Tennent's for thirty-five years, acting or directing in more than seventy productions. Beaumont had allowed him a lot of freedom in his choice and casting of plays, and for much of the time dealt skilfully and patiently with his restlessness, his impetuosity, and his inability to abide by decisions. He also readily acted as axeman in situations where Gielgud shied away from the responsibility of firing an actor. But Gielgud's complete trust in his judgement, combined with his feelings of loyalty and gratitude, had often led him into productions unworthy of his talents.

Three days after Beaumont's death Noël Coward, aged seventy-three and living in Jamaica, also died of a heart attack. Gielgud's relationship with the man he had understudied in his youth was a more complex one. While admiring Coward's wit and humour and his skill as a playwright, he disliked his bossiness, and his refusal to take much notice of his friends' opinions. Having his own circle, he never really aspired to be part of Coward's, though he frequented his parties and stayed in Jamaica, where Coward thought him 'a charming house guest, amusing, talkative and most considerate'.

He felt Coward lost much of his panache once he went into tax exile. 'He didn't do a lot with his money,' he observed. 'His houses were commonplace, the food dreadful, the decoration pretty amateurish.' Though they maintained a long friendship, there was always a wariness: Gielgud never spoke as warmly about Coward as he did about other close theatrical friends. Nevertheless he was moved at his memorial service in St Martin's-in-the-Fields: when he recited Shakespeare's sonnet 'When to the sessions of sweet silent thought', his voice broke with emotion on the final lines, 'But if the while I think on thee, dear friend, / All losses are restored, and sorrows end'. At the later unveiling of a memorial stone in Westminster Abbey he read Coward's poem 'When I have fears'.

The deaths of Beaumont and Coward prompted a savage article in the *Spectator* by the critic Kenneth Hurren. Writing under a pseudonym, he attacked 'the network of homosexuality' that he claimed dominated the London theatre. There were snide references to 'the third sex' and 'twee coteries', and to Beaumont's parties, where 'there were more fag-ends walking around the room than there were in the ashtrays'. This bilious piece provoked an avalance of letters, most of them endorsing the writer's stance. Despite the change in the law, attitudes were only slowly becoming more tolerant. Although Gielgud was not mentioned by name, he cannot have relished this attack on his close friends and their circle.

Yet although he still refused to talk openly about his homosexuality in public, there were signs that he worried less about publicity. Occasional references to his living arrangements now began to appear in the press, presumably with his tacit agreement. In 1975, in a lengthy and sympathetic article on his career, John Mortimer mentioned in passing the 'friend' with whom he shared a house. Around this time he became very interested in a 'gay play' written by Hallam Tennyson. 'It was very early for such a frank piece, but he was determined to put it on,' Tennyson remembers. The director Peter Cotes, who sent him the play, recalled his response: 'He rang me the next morning, very excited and interested, saying it was a good play and he would consider it.' He got as far as casting a star actor in the lead, but was then persuaded it was not a good idea for him to be associated with such a play.

In January 1975 he revived Pinero's *The Gay Lord Quex*. 'It's a ridiculous play, terribly snobbish, entirely about money and class,' he explained with his usual tact just before rehearsals began. 'I once gave it to Gertrude Lawrence in New York but I don't think she ever read it.' The story, which concerned the efforts of a Bond Street manicurist to expose the wicked past of the aristocratic hero, involved a lot of spying behind bushes, listening through keyholes and jumping in and out of windows. It had been one of his mother's favourite plays, and this influenced his choice.

For what proved to be his last production as a director the cast included Judi Dench, Siân Phillips and Daniel Massey. His compulsion to experiment continued to the end, as Judi Dench recalls: 'Although he was always changing his mind rehearsals weren't stressful, in fact they were very funny. But he couldn't resist interrupting.' He also committed further gaffes. Siân Phillips was very conscious of her height, and after a disagreement over whether she should sit or stand after her entrance, Gielgud said: 'I know it's dreadful, but you're so terribly *tall* when you're standing up.' But some gaffes were less painful than others. When Judi Dench came on in costume at the dress rehearsal, Gielgud called out: 'Oh, no, no, no, God, Judi, you look just like Richard the Third,' leaving her weeping with laughter on the stage.

Despite such remarks, Judi Dench enjoyed being directed by him: 'He was divinely witty and had a wicked sense of humour,' she recalls. 'But he was also a very kind man. I think his dropped bricks came out of an incredible shyness.' His delight in the eccentricities of human behaviour burst out during one rehearsal, which was being held in the crypt of St James's Church in Piccadilly. In a scene more Feydeau than Pinero, two men suddenly and unaccountably ran screaming out of the lavatory, one clutching the other's trousers in his hands. Gielgud was unable to stop laughing, and rehearsals had to be suspended.

The critics were puzzled that he should bother to revive a play 'full of vapid nobodies', as John Barber described it. Although the production was praised for its elegance, its lightness of touch and care for detail, there was little more to it than that. Gielgud had allowed nostalgia to overcome his judgement, and had made no serious attempt to look at the play afresh. 'I stupidly became obsessed with the idea that I must do it exactly as it was written,' he admitted.

The play lasted a few weeks at the Albery. It was an unsatisfactory end to a distinguished directing career. Yet at the same moment he was enjoying one last taste of success as a director, for two of his revivals were running simultaneously on Broadway: *Private Lives* at the 46th Street Theater and *The Constant Wife* at the Shubert. At the time he was also acting in *No Man's Land* in London, playing Disraeli on television, and filming *Murder on the Orient Express*. 'I'm rather on show,' he said, with unconcealed glee.

After eventually finishing with *No Man's Land* he returned to the National in 1977. Prospero's epilogue 'Our revels now are ended' seemed to have brought his work in Shakespeare to a fitting end in 1974. 'I would never return to Shakespeare,' he insisted soon after. 'I'm afraid to do so, because I think I would appear to be dated, to be old-fashioned in comparison with the way it is done today.' But in March 1977, at his own suggestion, he played the title-role in John Schlesinger's production of *Julius Caesar*.

It was not his first time in the part, for he had played it in Stuart Burge's lacklustre 1970 film. Shot at Elstree with tatty sets and inappropriate costumes, it had been packed with Hollywood stars – at one point Raquel Welch had been suggested for Calpurnia. Burge was a talented theatre director, but had little experience with film, and the result was flat and uninspiring. As Antony, Charlton Heston does little more than grimace; Jason Robards is a desperately wooden Brutus; and Richard Johnson's Cassius is merely ponderous. Only Gielgud emerges with credit, catching both the proud, arrogant Caesar and the weakness of a man with 'the falling sickness'. Heston thought him superb: 'He showed us how easy it is for a great actor to be great,' he said. One critic observed that he gave such a sensitive performance 'it almost seems as if he, rather than Brutus, was the noblest Roman of them all'.

Burge recalls the impression he made on the set: 'In rehearsal he was very helpful and thorough, and the American actors all idolised him. He had a very true attitude to it all. Once he suggested doing a scene in a certain way, and then said, "Would that be effective?" I knew what he meant, it was the teaching of Saint-Denis, who would say, "Where is the comment?" None of the Americans, brought up on corrupt Stanislavsky and the Method, would have dared say that.'

Seven years later, in the stage version in the Olivier at the National, Gielgud worked with a predominantly young and inexperienced company that included Brian Cox, Ronald Pickup, Mark MacManus and Ian Charleson. 'It looked like a bunch of young thugs beating up an old man,' someone observed of the assassination. Unlike Hall, Schlesinger was not especially interested in the verse, and Gielgud, far from seeming old-fashioned, stood out as the only actor able to handle it. Schlesinger was grateful for his support during some difficult rehearsals, in which there were clashes with Brian Cox. 'The production was not a happy experience for me, I felt I had failed, and most of the actors weren't up to it,' he remembers. 'But John was wonderful, it was a privilege to have him in the middle of this very unhappy job. I never asked him for advice, and he never expressed an opinion about the other actors. He was just enormously professional and loyal.'

Behind the scenes Gielgud would occasionally express his impatience, as Oliver Cotton, one of the conspirators, recalls: 'None of us was acting well, and he obviously loathed the production. We used to come on together, and I remember him saying just before our entrance, "Oh God, they're so slow, it's not interesting."' Cotton also remembers a famous moment when Gielgud failed to appear for his second scene. 'The actors were stranded for about two and a half minutes while they tried to find him. Everyone was looking at each other, and I was nearly hysterical. Finally John ran on in a terrible panic – and dried stone dead.' He had been listening to Alan Ayckbourn's *Bedroom Farce* on the Lyttelton tannoy.

The critics disliked the production, but found much to admire in Gielgud's performance. 'He eclipses every other actor in sight,' Irving Wardle wrote. Yet while his noble, majestic qualities were noted, some critics felt he failed to capture Caesar's arrogance and harder qualities – to such an extent that the assassination seemed almost unnecessary. Schlesinger himself pinpointed this drawback: 'I liked John's grandeur, the way as a great actor he played this remarkable man seemingly without effort,' he says. 'But he wasn't really tyrannical enough: if you have Gielgud it's hard to get that quality.'

His next role was a contrast: he played Sir Politic Wouldbe, the deliciously gullible English tourist caught amongst villains, in Ben Jonson's *Volpone*. Peter Hall directed, with Paul Scofield making his

National début as the scurrilous Volpone, and Ben Kingsley playing his wily sidekick Mosca. In his diary Hall noted Gielgud's unbounding energy and enthusiasm at the first rehearsal: 'He came in like a fine-bred horse eager to career anywhere, even down the wrong road, but very creative, very brilliant, and very, very funny.'

But he was never quite at home in Jonson's grotesque comedy, which required him at one point to crawl around on his hands and knees masquerading as a giant tortoise. He found the part difficult to learn and, according to Scofield, 'didn't much enjoy it'. He experienced all the familiar last-minute doubts, deciding just before the first preview that he needed to 're-focus his performance and make it realer'. Hall rehearsed him while the stage was being prepared around them. Scolded for over-playing, Gielgud blushed and said, 'Will I never learn? Still my old tricks after years and years and years: anything for a laugh, and because of that I don't get it.'

Yet the critics warmed to his portrait of the dotty, upper-class Englishman. John Peter wrote: 'It is one of the glories of this company that this great actor remains a member of it, revealing still fresh facets of his odd, sophisticated and beguiling talent.' That talent was recognised again officially when in June he was made a Companion of Honour. He responded with his customary self-deprecation, telling Hall he had 'done nothing really except survive to seventy-three'.

His final role at the National was in Julian Mitchell's elegant but static play *Half-Life*, directed by Waris Hussein. Gielgud played Sir Noel Cunliffe, the lethally rude and witty retired archaeologist and former Master of an Oxford college. Supposedly based on Maurice Bowra, the part required him to sit centre stage for most of what passed as the action, throwing out insults, put-downs and waspish epigrams, and finally breaking down when confronted with the reality of his wasted life. The part, he felt, was longer than Hamlet.

There was considerable surprise that Hall should have chosen the 300-seat Cottesloe, supposedly the National's experimental venue, to stage what was in essence a conventional West End play, a mixture of N.C. Hunter and Noël Coward. Gielgud was again worried about seeming old-fashioned: 'I suppose some people will think a country-house play with lots of champagne and gracious gardens outside the windows is out of date,' he said. It was indeed the kind of play Beaumont might have presented at the Haymarket twenty-five years earlier. 'I've got to do it, I need a new roof for the south wing,' Gielgud told one of the actors.

Hussein, who had worked mostly in television, had problems in adjusting to the stage. 'I was very restrictive and rather limiting, but John nudged me into being more free,' he remembers. 'I was young and inexperienced, but he never took advantage. If actors are insecure they can be destructive, but he wasn't like that. In the end he had so much experience he just used his own technique.'

On the first night in November 1977 he was feeling ill and under-prepared. Although certain technical matters to do with archaeology, such as radio-carbon dating and measuring tree rings, had been regularly explained to him during rehearsals, he had found them difficult to grasp. Beset by nerves, he needed frequent prompting, and fluffed several lines, once memorably referring to someone's 'blue hair and fair eyes'.

After a sell-out run at the National, *Half-Life* transferred to the Duke of York's in March 1978, where it seemed more appropriately housed. Although again initially hesitant over his lines, Gielgud was now more in command: 'Sir John enjoys himself hugely,' Peter Lewis wrote. 'He simply sits there like a balding eagle and imposes his will on us, defying us to notice that this is a monologue.'

There were four cast changes during the run, and the usual 'alterations and improvements' were made – some of them behind the director's back. While Hussein was away filming Gielgud decided, to the bewilderment of the company, to re-direct one complete section himself. When Hussein returned he was horrified: where there had been several laughs there were now none at all. 'I went backstage and asked John what he'd done, and he said, "Well, I thought a little bit of this and that." I said, "But there isn't a single response from the audience in that section. I don't think it's a very good idea." "Oh, don't you?" he replied. "Then we better put it back to what it was." And we did. He really doesn't have a big ego.'

Like many actors, Gielgud disliked conditions at the National. Hussein recalls him arriving at the Cottesloe: 'He was shown into this tiny, windowless little cell, and this upset him. He said it wasn't what he was used to, and couldn't he have somewhere a bit better. It was a real indignity.' In general he found the National cold and impersonal, and variously likened the building to an airport, a hospital and, less predictably, a toad. 'The only decent theatre is the Cottesloe, and that's like a coffin,' he observed.

He did, however, give his support to Hall and the National during the industrial troubles that beset the opening of the new building.

Together with Olivier and Richardson he wrote a letter to *The Times*, protesting against the unofficial strikes which had recently stopped performances at the National and in the West End, arguing that if they continued 'the theatre in this country will surely and quickly sicken to extinction'. He hardly ever took part in theatre politics, but would sometimes do so when a theatre was under threat. In 1974 he had led a deputation from the 'Save London's Theatres' campaign to the Department of the Environment. There he had delivered a petition in protest against proposals to re-develop Piccadilly Circus which threatened the future of the Criterion.

After his difficulties with *Half-Life* he was frightened his memory might go. 'What would one live on?' he asked anxiously. Yet his memory for the theatrical past was as sharp as ever, as he showed the same year when he talked about his life and work on the radio. John Miller, who created the programmes, found him very difficult to interview: 'Once he got going he was unstoppable: sometimes I couldn't get a question in for twenty minutes. I got most from him by being oblique: if I asked him a direct question about his *Macbeth*, I got bugger all; but if I asked him about other interpretations, it slid in. All the time he talked he looked over my shoulder; he'd only look at me for the question, or when he'd finished. "I can't look at you," he explained to me, "I have to conjure it up in my mind's eye."'

The broadcasts formed the basis of the final version of his auto-biography, *An Actor and His Time*, published in 1979. While finalising the manuscript he made it clear what kind of book it would be: 'I do think one must be careful and kind about those of one's friends and colleagues who are still alive,' he said. 'I wouldn't entirely care to go in for revelations.' This attitude proved problematic to his publishers, Sidgwick & Jackson, since he was always toning down any passage he thought might offend. In general he omitted the more mischievous and bawdy observations that he made in real life. But he did write more honestly than before about those now dead.

Now seventy-five, he had already suffered the loss of several of his great contemporaries and friends, and was beginning to establish yet another career as a speaker or reader at memorial services. Edith Evans and Sybil Thorndike had both died in 1976. Gielgud was in Washington with *No Man's Land* when he heard of Edith Evans' death, but found time to write a tribute for the American papers, in which he called her 'a supreme mistress of high comedy and farce, a brilliant character actress rich in power and emotional conviction'. Yet like most actors he had never felt entirely at ease with her, and he wrote relatively little about her personal qualities.

Sybil Thorndike was a different matter. She had been a magnificent ally in his desperate hours after the court case. After Lewis Casson died in 1969 he had sometimes visited her in her Chelsea flat, and admired the courage with which she dealt with her acute arthritis. When her ashes were buried in Westminster Abbey he was asked to give the memorial address. It was a warm, generous but unsentimental tribute, underlining his understanding of and love for the woman he rightly called 'the best-loved English actress since Ellen Terry'.

34

'Major Movie Star'

> John Gielgud can steal a scene simply by
> wearing a hat.
>
> (Pauline Kael reviewing *Arthur*, 1981)

IN 1975 Gielgud declared proudly: 'I am not afraid of the camera any more.' Before long he gave ample evidence of his new-found confidence with a courageous, soul-baring performance in Alain Resnais' complex film *Providence*. It was his one great performance for the cinema.

Resnais had planned the film as a 'memorial to the greatest English actor of our time, and the most beautiful voice'. The story, written by David Mercer, concerns an elderly dying novelist, and his struggle, during one long night filled with drink, pills, remorse and hatred, to create a new work in his mind, using his family as the characters. Gielgud was delighted to have what he called his first truly 'butch' part, but unsure if he was 'sufficiently craggy' for it. But he seemed less anxious about certain potentially embarrassing scenes. 'I was asked to put suppositories up my bottom under the bedclothes and play a scene in the lavatory, which I confess I found somewhat intimate,' he said with obvious pride.

He was anxious about Mercer's verbose and difficult screenplay, with its complicated mixing of past and present. But Resnais showed great confidence in him, and he relaxed. He found the director 'wonderful to work with, so beautifully impassive', and called him 'the most English of French directors' – a potential gaffe which Resnais, an ardent Anglophile, treasured as a compliment.

The film also starred Dirk Bogarde, Ellen Burstyn, David Warner and Elaine Stritch. Before shooting began Bogarde organised a series of supper-parties, so that Resnais could study Gielgud the raconteur in action. Resnais sat entranced, absorbing material for possible use in the film. Gielgud soon realised he had been set up, but continued with his uninterrupted flow of reminiscence, and his views on the latest plays, books, music and films. 'He was enchanting, so witty and sharp,' Bogarde recalled. 'He loved gossip, and if he didn't have any he'd invent his own.'

Bogarde also liked Gielgud's modesty. Accustomed to being addressed as 'John' on film sets, and disliking sycophancy, he was inhibited by Resnais and the French crew's insistence on respectfully calling him 'Sirjohn', said as one word. He asked Bogarde to stop them doing this, and eventually his wish was granted. But another incident brought out a different side of him. A tape was being made as a birthday present for Resnais, and Bogarde was delegated to ask him if he would record the first message on it. 'At first he refused, and went on doing his *Times* crossword,' Bogarde recalled. 'Then I said, "But John, you have one of the most beautiful voices in the English language." He sprung to attention, outraged: "*The* most beautiful," he said. And then he recorded the message.'

Gielgud burst through the boundaries of his previous film roles, acting with huge passion and guts as well as subtlety and comic precision, and dominating the film. His performance won him the New York Film Critics' Award for Best Actor. The *Village Voice* said the film 'proves again that he is the greatest living actor in the English language'. In the *New Yorker* the eminent critic Pauline Kael vividly captured his exuberant wickedness. 'God how this old knight loves to act, loves the sound of his old sing-song,' she wrote. 'There's lip-smacking joy in his dirty-old-man rant. He's lean and wiry, turkey-faced, a tough old bird – so alive to the kinetic pleasures of play-acting that he bounces through the role savouring its pipsqueak grandeur.'

Gielgud was so pleased with his performance he called in at the Academy cinema in London, to ask when they would be showing the film. Lunching with Peter Hall at the Garrick, he feigned embarrassment, but giggled with pleasure, at the contrast between his excellent reviews and those Olivier had got for his performance in the dire Harold Robbins soap opera *The Betsy*.

In the period leading up to *Providence*, and for some time after it, he played only cameo roles in films. He became adept at suggesting a character with little more than a gesture, a sideways glance, or an inflection in his voice. 'It's rather fun to play the small parts, because you can get a good effect, and yet you haven't got the whole responsibility,' he said. Filming was now a pleasure. He no longer worried about getting up early, coping with physical discomforts, or the constant waiting. 'I find now that I am rather good at quietly doing my crossword and watching other people's scenes,' he said. 'One does, after all, have plenty of spare time to think about one's part, gossip with one's colleagues, and have fun.'

One of his best films was David Lynch's affecting and atmospheric *The Elephant Man*, in which he played the governor of a hospital with restrained sensitivity. He shone in unpleasant roles: he was convincingly nasty in Hugh Hudson's *Chariots of Fire* as the bigoted, anti-semitic Master of a Cambridge college, and effectively cold, acerbic and ruthless as the corrupt chairman of a mining company in the dreary blockbuster *Gold.* He also gave a beautifully dry, understated performance as Richard Widmark's manservant in the creaky *Murder on the Orient Express.* Denis Quilley remembers a small contribution he made to the screenplay. 'I had to ask him if the book he was reading was about sex. John said to Sidney Lumet, "Wouldn't it be funny if I looked at my watch and said, "No, it's about half past seven." Sid roared with laughter and said, "Put it in." It gets a big laugh every time.'

Some of the roles were tiny, but this never seemed to bother him. 'People might have thought it rather silly of me,' he said, 'but I think you can learn from every part you play.' He had just half a day's work on Joseph Losey's *Galileo*, in which, despite his dislike of Brecht, he played the Old Cardinal in one short scene. For television he even agreed to a non-speaking part as Lord Burleigh in Sheridan's *The Critic*: one day's work, no lines, just a cough. Other parts were shorter than they might have been. As the hell-fire preacher in Joseph Strick's version of James Joyce's *A Portrait of the Artist as a Young Man* he spent two months learning an eighteen-minute monologue, 'probably the most difficult thing I had to do in my whole life'. The final version, to his intense disappointment, was edited down to five minutes.

He could be vague about the nature of the work. 'I'm going to Budapest to do a film,' he told Anthony Hopkins. 'I don't know what the part is but they tell me it's awfully good.' Although many were unworthy of him, he took them because he hated not to be working. In the unfunny spoof comedy thriller *Sebastian* he had a thin part as Head of Intelligence, and failed to suggest any sinister quality. *The Shoes of the Fisherman*, in which he played one of his many Popes, was considered so awful it was not released in England for five years. One of his direst roles was in the disastrous musical remake in Hollywood of *Lost Horizon*. Cast as an Oriental (he replaced Toshiro Mifune) he spoke pidgin English and wore a series of unbecoming hats. The script, he admitted to Tennessee Williams, was 'sentimental crap'.

He would defend his playing of such poor roles by citing the exorbitant cost of maintaining his house, or the chance it gave him to travel. 'It's nice at my age to be able to travel all over the world at someone else's expense,' he said. 'I don't even need to take holidays any more.' He was in Libya with Anthony Quinn for *Lion of the Desert*, and in Israel for another Hercule Poirot adventure, *Appointment with Death*, with Lauren Bacall and Peter Ustinov. In December 1981 he wrote to Christopher Fry from Munich: 'This is a marvellous, clean and luxurious city. Ten weeks to do about twelve days' shooting – so there is too much time to eat and sleep a lot. But many lovely things to see – broad non-traffic streets with open markets – museums, galleries etc . . . How I do get about in me advanced years. Never thought to see this part of Europe.'

On location he remained resolutely unflustered. He spent several weeks on the coast of Yugoslavia filming *Eagle in a Cage*, the story of Napoleon's final days on St Helena, in which he played a cynical, devious Foreign Office official. Billie Whitelaw recalled him lunching with Ralph Richardson under the scorching sun, two English gentlemen unaffected by their surroundings: 'Though in full regalia, they had spread out their paper napkins to look like tablecloths, and conversed with calm and dignity. They remained courteous and dignified through all the heat and stink and mess around them.' The puns continued. The actors had to endure some tiring ascents of a craggy rock-face; Gielgud re-named the film *Climb and Punishment*. After hearing that two of the horses had thrown their riders he announced, 'I've decided to call them the Bolting Brothers.'

In 1979 he appeared in Bob Guccione's notorious *Caligula*, scripted by Gore Vidal. The story of the decadent reign of the mad Roman emperor, played by Malcolm McDowell, it was a repellent mixture of pornography, bestiality and violence. Orson Welles had rejected on moral grounds an offer of $1 million to play the title-role. Gielgud was initially offered and turned down the part of the doddering, syphilitic Emperor Tiberius. The film, he complained, was 'full of sex, smut all the way through, and I wouldn't dream of doing it'. He received a petulant letter from Vidal, whom he'd met years before with Tennessee Williams, and disliked. 'I suppose you've never read Suetonius,' Vidal wrote. 'All these things really happened. If you knew what Tennessee Williams and Edward Albee think of you you'd be more careful of the way you behave.' Gielgud laughed and tore up the letter.

Subsequently he was offered the part of the wise elderly senator Nerva, and accepted it 'rather shamefacedly'. Later he blamed his agent for persuading him that it involved 'no dirty bits, a lot of money, and only ten days' work'. For his sins he had to spend three days sitting in a bath in Rome filming Nerva's suicide. Somehow, in defiance of the trashiness of the film, he managed to make his death simple and touching. On another day he was a fascinated onlooker in a scene involving Tiberius – played without a qualm by Peter O'Toole – in which extras of both sexes cavorted naked in the imperial swimming-pool. As ever, Gielgud had an eye for the absurd: 'The moment the bell rang for lunch, they all put their hands in front of their genitals and rushed out to have pizzas with their families. It was such a funny mixture of rudery and primness.'

He was, however, severely criticised for taking part in such an appalling film, which *Variety* described as 'a moral holocaust'. Even Vidal was horrified: when he saw the finished result he sued to have his credit removed. Gielgud was invited to say he had been tricked into appearing in the film, but resolutely refused to do so. Twenty years later Malcolm McDowell said of the filming: 'John Gielgud loved it.'

After Resnais he now worked with another major European director, Andrzej Wajda. In *The Conductor* he played the title-role, that of a Polish-born musician who returns for a concert after a successful career in the West. Wajda says he was 'ravished' by Gielgud's dedica-tion and the intensity of his acting. His account of the film catches graphically Gielgud's detached attitude on the set: 'The master did not even pretend to take an interest in our efforts to make a coherent film,' Wajda wrote. 'In fact he behaved exactly as the script demanded (if we had had one): he lived his own life, immersed in his own inner world.'

Gielgud's experience with *Caligula* affected his first response to *Arthur*, the film that brought him his greatest success in America. Offered the part of Dudley Moore's supercilious manservant Hobson, he turned it down because of its supposedly risqué dialogue: 'I thought it was rather smutty and a vulgar little film, so I refused it,' he recalled. 'But each time they asked me they doubled my salary, so naturally I became reconciled to it.' But *Arthur* was not terribly vulgar, and except for a few witty one-liners its humour was exceedingly heavy-handed. Having relished Gielgud's performance in *Forty Years On*, Moore had suggested him for Hobson. His fondness for Gielgud originated in their first, chance meeting at London Airport, during the run of the hit revue *Beyond the Fringe*, which Gielgud had greatly liked. Hearing Moore was going to Italy, he suggested he call on the actress Lilli Palmer in Portofino, and wrote him a note beginning: 'Darling Lilli, This is to introduce Stanley Moon, the brilliant young pianist in *Beyond the Fringe*.' Moore dined out on the gaffe, Stanley Moon became his *alter ego*, and he used it for his character in *Bedazzled*.

Moore liked Gielgud's good humour and innocence, and also his professionalism. 'It's wonderful to work with somebody where you don't even have to discuss anything,' he said. 'You just do it.' He recalled his efforts to break down Gielgud's reserve. 'I tried to be Rabelaisian with him as much as possible, to gee him up and get him going.' Gielgud lapped it up: 'I loved Dudley Moore's humour and his sense of invention,' he said. After appearing with him in 1988 in the sequel *Arthur on the Rocks*, he confessed: 'I got to know Stanley Moon rather well by the end of the two films.'

The director of *Arthur*, Steve Gordon, was an anxious and insecure man, and Gielgud, according to Liza Minnelli, caught his insecurity. 'John had a huge sense of humour, but he was never quite sure he was being funny,' she remembered. 'He kept turning to Dudley and me and asking, "Was that funny?"' Moore thought Gielgud's performance wonderfully witty, because 'he really didn't change his approach that much from the way he would play a dramatic scene, he played it with the same seriousness, the same gravity'.

In a variety of dashing hats and suits, Gielgud gave an exquisitely deadpan and witty performance. But there was pathos mixed in with the acerbic humour, culminating in a touching death-bed scene that Gielgud timed to perfection. But what especially amused American audiences was Gielgud's coarse language, his delivery of remarks such as 'You little shit' and 'Go screw yourself' in the haughty, bejewelled tones of South Kensington.

Yet he himself had always enjoyed 'talking dirty', making sexual or scatalogical jokes, or reciting risqué limericks. Once, asked by Vivien Leigh to record on tape something for her parrot to imitate, he came up not with a Shakespeare sonnet but with, 'Shit and sugar, shit and sugar.' Another time he announced during a Chekhov rehearsal, 'Just been to see *Splendid up the Arse*.' Watching the naked marathon athletes that Charlton Heston insisted should be used in *Julius Caesar*, he declared, 'Buttocks wouldn't melt in their mouth.'

Arthur was the surprise hit of 1981, a huge success that would eventually gross £80 million worldwide. America went overboard for Gielgud. Pauline Kael suggested he 'may be the most poised and confident funny man you'll ever see'. He won an Academy Award for Best Supporting Actor, and the New York and Los Angeles Critics' Awards. He was now, according to *Time* magazine, 'the hottest young talent around' and 'a major movie star'; his face was seen 'on more screens than the MGM lion'. Other countries also discovered him: in Germany five fan clubs were started; some time later, while filming in Berlin, Gielgud was pursued around the city by his fans.

Although he thought *Arthur* a silly film, he was delighted to reach a wider, different audience: 'I got a new public all over the world who had never seen me play *anything*,' he said. 'They didn't know what to expect. They were just amused by my performance. That was why it was so gratifying.' Like many actors he disliked the Oscar awards: 'I think they're so invidious, all that comparing of people, and the people who are disappointed,' he said. 'I dislike the assumption that some people are better than others.' He refused to attend the awards ceremony, so Dudley Moore collected the statuette on his behalf. Gielgud put it in his bathroom.

Early in 1982 he went to Vienna to work on Tony Palmer's *Wagner*. This epic, overblown television film, with Richard Burton playing Wagner, became celebrated for its length – eight hours, cut to five for the cinema – but also for bringing Gielgud, Olivier and Richardson together onscreen for the first time since *Richard III*. Uniquely, as wily ministers at the court of Ludwig II, they shared a scene together. During it, according to Palmer, each tried in a gentlemanly manner to upstage the other two. Richardson, he said, proved the most adept at it.

Gielgud's friendship with Burton had remained a warm one, despite a notorious gaffe about Elizabeth Taylor he had committed some time before. Over dinner with Burton and Taylor he said, 'I had lunch the other day with that charming fellow Michael Wilding. What a pity he got mixed up with all those dreadful tarts.' To which Taylor replied, 'I was one of them, John.' Burton never lost a chance to tell the story, with huge delight.

In Vienna his first words to Gielgud were: 'Are you all right for money?' Over bacon and eggs in Burton's caravan they reminisced about Stratford and *The Lady's Not for Burning*. But Gielgud was upset by Burton's physical condition, caused in part by his excessive drinking. 'Richard seemed dreadfully sad and ravaged, lonely and unhappy,' he told Emlyn Williams. When Burton threw a dinner-party for the three theatrical knights he became viciously drunk, and verbally abused them in turn: Olivier for being all technique and no emotion, Richardson for having lost his memory, and Gielgud for being homosexual. According to Tony Palmer, Gielgud looked disdainful and sad at this behaviour by one of his greatest admirers. When he finished filming, Burton gave him an expensive present. 'I suppose he is so lavish as a kind of guilt complex,' Gielgud wrote. 'All very sad.'

His fifty-year friendship and professional partnership with Richardson was coming to an end. After *Wagner*, they appeared together in the film *Invitation to the Wedding*, in which Gielgud played a stetson-wearing Southern evangelist with an unconvincing Deep South accent. There was a happier collaboration on *Six Centuries of Verse*, a sixteen-week television series on poetry in English: Gielgud presented it, and he and Richardson, together with Peggy Ashcroft, featured as speakers. And in the summer of 1982, when the Queen Mother came to tea at Wotton Underwood – profiteroles, strawberries and fifteen kinds of sandwiches – the 'Old Lions' delighted her with an unending stream of theatrical anecdotes.

Richardson died in October 1983, after a series of strokes. His death cut Gielgud to the quick, and he was too upset to comment publicly. In a tribute to 'a most dear friend' published a few days later he wrote: 'How sadly I shall miss his cheerful voice on the telephone . . . and his patience with my chattering tongue.' He knew how essential Richardson had been to their success in the Pinter and Storey plays. 'Now he's gone I'll never find such a partner again.' At the memorial service in Westminster Abbey, reading from Bunyan's *Pilgrim's Progress*, his voice broke when he came to the final lines: 'So he passed over, and all the trumpets sounded for him on the other side.' A few months later Burton too died, aged just fifty-eight, and Gielgud read a Hamlet speech at his memorial service. He performed a similar function at those held for Michael Redgrave, James Mason and several other actors. After reading a sonnet at Marie Rambert's service he remarked: 'Sometimes I feel as if I may as well stay on for my own.'

In April 1984 he celebrated his eightieth birthday. There was a dinner at the Garrick, where his health was proposed by Peggy Ashcroft. The critic Michael Billington compiled a celebratory radio portrait, and plays by Rhys Adrian (*Passing Time*) and Peter Barnes (*Glory*) were broadcast. There were also two books: a heavily illustrated 'celebration' by Gyles Brandreth, and *The Ages of Gielgud*, an affectionate and revealing collection of essays by actors, playwrights and critics, edited by the playwright Ronald Harwood.

The second book had two notable omissions amongst the contributors: Richardson, who had died before finishing his piece, and Olivier who, despite frequent prompting, had failed to produce one. One essay that *was* included seemed out of place. Brooding on Gielgud's fascination with the Terrys, Harold Hobson called him 'a family man without a family except among the dead', and perversely suggested he would have been happier and more successful, and not 'fallen to some sickening depths', if he had had a wife and family. This thinly veiled reference to the 1953 scandal provoked a row, as Hobson explained to Christopher Fry: 'John's friends are distressed by it and have asked me to withdraw it.' He refused to do so.

Gielgud claimed to have stopped enjoying his birthdays. At a party held on the Old Vic stage he suggested again that such celebrations were 'only because I've survived, because I haven't much else to offer at the moment'. His fellow-actors marvelled at his stamina and energy. Michael Pennington, playing the title-role in the television *Oedipus the King* two years later, recalls the force of his performance as the blind Teiresias: 'What struck me was the full-bloodedness of his acting, the power that he generated physically. At that age the sheer passion was astonishing.'

After *Arthur* Gielgud accepted some dreadful film parts. Asked how he coped with a poor script he replied: 'I say the lines very quickly, with a slight smile.' During the 1980s he had plenty to smile about. He reached an all-time low with the disastrous *Scandalous*, widely deemed a waste of celluloid. Playing an aristocratic con-man he turned up, among other disguises, in chains and black leather as a Hell's Angel. 'The role wasn't very demanding, in fact I thought it rather fun,' he commented blithely. There might have been worse: he only escaped appearing in *Space Vampires* when his huge original fee was suddenly reduced by half.

He turned down a part in Derek Jarman's *Caravaggio*, telling Jarman bluntly that, after *Caligula*, he was 'very wary of indulging in my advanced years in semi-pornographic films'. At one point he was doing so many cameos he had little time to get to know the director. Ronald Harwood recalled a dinner some years later with Albert Finney and Gielgud. Finney enthused about *Arthur on the Rocks*, and asked Gielgud who directed it. 'I don't know, I never took him in,' he replied.

There were still a few worthwhile parts in better films. He played the eccentric anti-bloodsports campaigner Cornelius Cardew in *The Shooting Party*, a role which won him the Los Angeles Film Critics' Award. As Lord Irwin, sternly upholding the empire in Richard Attenborough's impressive epic *Gandhi*, he was suitably granite-like, registering his contempt for Gandhi's activities with fine imperial disdain. He played Cardinal Wolsey in a version of *A Man for All Seasons* filmed for American television, and directed by Charlton Heston. And he was perfectly cast as the priggish hypocrite Herbert Muskett, the solicitor who caused D.H. Lawrence's paintings to be banned, in Christopher Miles's under-rated film about Lawrence's life with Frieda, *Priest of Love*.

He was always worried that directors would be overawed by his reputation. 'People may not have the courage to tell me when I'm not good, when I'm boring, or using a lot of old tricks,' he suggested. David Lynch was certainly awestruck on their first day together on *The Elephant Man*: 'I was putting on my underwear and thinking, "Today I am going to direct Sir John Gielgud", and it was a horrible, horrible feeling.' Yet once the ice was broken he found Gielgud extremely receptive and technically adept. 'If you want to change just one little word, just a slight bit, you can introduce the psychological reasons, and the next time he does it that change is incorporated effortlessly and perfectly. The timing, the phrasing of every line is just beautiful.'

In the film of David Hare's *Plenty*, alongside Meryl Streep and Charles Dance, he gained another Los Angeles Critics' Award for his performance as an imperious civil servant who resigns over Suez. Director Fred Schepisi, whom he thought excellent, recalled: 'He's not large, you don't have to bring him down or get him to adapt his stage performance to film; he's got a natural instinct for that. And he's a very good observer, I noticed he was watching Meryl and the others. You can see his mind ticking over all the time, seeing if there is anything else he can learn.'

Meryl Streep's acting certainly impressed him, but so did the way in which she and other actresses he worked with managed to combine film careers with having children. 'How they do it, even with nannies and cots and things, I can't imagine,' he said. Motherhood was a mysterious concept to him and also, according to Pinkie Johnstone, a worrying one. 'He tried to ignore the fact that you had childen, he was frightened you might talk about childbirth,' she says. 'Anything to do with ladies below the waist absolutely terrified him.'

Star actors meeting him for the first time were struck by his good humour and lack of pretension. 'He exudes such a sense of ease,' Faye Dunaway remarked; Joan Collins thought him 'deliciously self-deprecating'. Others were struck by his good manners, especially in the face of provocation. Peter Ustinov worked with him on *Appointment with Death*, directed by the arch-vulgarian Michael Winner. 'John thought Winner was awful, and was acutely embarrassed by his behaviour,' he recalled. 'But he was always very polite.'

Others remember the generous help he gave them on the set. Jane Birkin was playing Katherine Mansfield in *Leave All Fair*, in which Gielgud was cast as Middleton Murry: 'He had finished for the day, but I was having problems with one scene,' she recalls. 'Most actors would have gone home, but he stayed behind for an hour and a half, refusing to sit, just standing behind the camera and producing tears. He really wanted to help me.'

The actress Mavis Walker, for many years his travelling companion on film assignments, saw contrasting sides of his personality. 'He was enchanting to be with, so funny and sensitive and courteous,' she recalled. 'But you had to move with his moods. If he talked, you talked; if he didn't, you didn't. I never brought in my own life, and he never wanted to know anything about it. If there was absolute silence you knew there was something wrong, but he wouldn't get angry – although once, during the shooting of *War and Remembrance*, when I said, knowing he was tired, that he should only do one more take, he was furious.'

War and Remembrance, made for American television, was a mini-series about the Holocaust, in which Gielgud played a Jewish-American writer who dies in Auschwitz. Part of the filming was done in the camp building itself, where some of his Polish relatives from Cracow had been. He found the experience harrowing, likening its emotional impact to rehearsing *King Lear* four times a day. Yet even here his humour broke through. In the climactic scene he had to march naked into the gas chambers with a hundred other men, some of whom were then thrown on top of him. After one take the director Dan Curtis asked him if he minded doing another. 'Oh bliss!' he replied.

Other roles he played for American television were notably harsh. As the Torturer he supported Anthony Hopkins' tormented Quasimodo in *The Hunchback of Notre Dame*; he was Albert Speer's haughty father in *Inside the Third Reich*; and in *The Scarlet and the Black* he played a severe, unrelenting Pope Pius XII, refusing to speak out against the extermination of the Jews. But for British television he played more eccentric roles, such as the tense, tight-lipped and partially blind Jasper Swift in Molly Keane's sharp and witty *Time After Time*, which was filmed in Ireland.

It was a part he was very keen to do because of his friendship with Molly Keane, who lived nearby and watched some of the filming. But there were practical problems, as director Bill Hays remembers: 'He was supposed to cook, but he couldn't do it: I had to show him how to use an egg-whisk. We had to change the script to allow for things he couldn't do. He also disliked cats, which he was supposed to feed and fondle. "Oh can't we do the fucking cats tomorrow and get them out of the way?" he asked me.'

Like other directors, Hays found Gielgud a joy to work with. He was always willing and cooperative, and often declined to have a stand-in for technically difficult scenes. Nor did he play the grand star: he refused to have a trailer, or to take his meals separately, preferring to mix with others in the canteen. His wit was as sharp as ever, as Hays recalls: 'We all had a meal in this wonderful restaurant, during which we were introduced to the Bishop of Kerry. Afterwards John and I went to the gents, where the bishop was in the middle stall. I'd had a glass or two, and I said, "Ah, that must be a bishopric." John said quick as a flash: "They call it a diocese now."'

Hays directed him again in Simon Gray's brilliant and touching play *Quartermaine's Terms*. As the joint head of a language school with his male companion, Gielgud caught beautifully the waspish cruelty behind the man's amiable mask. He had turned down the part in the original stage production, partly because of the homosexuality of the character. But according to Hays he had no problems playing it on television. 'He was quite relaxed about it, and talked quite openly about the cottaging incident. In the final speech he had to break down while speaking of his companion's death. We rehearsed that in private, but only because it was so long and difficult.' Gielgud played that last, emotional scene with moving restraint.

His most surprising screen role was in a commercial for Paul Masson's Californian white wine, in which he was asked yet again to play a butler. Unable to resist the $1m fee, he accepted on condition the ad would not be shown in Britain. Three years later he was still making new ones for the company, and boasting of how an entire baseball team had been flown to London to film with him. Like Orson Welles, who had appeared in earlier Masson ads, he seemed to have no qualms about doing the work, no fears that he might be thought to be prostituting his talent. Besides, there was a precedent: Richardson had told him that classical actors should never undertake commercials, but Gielgud then discovered that he had done one on the sly for Concorde.

His real ambition, he said, was to do an underwear commercial. For this the opening line would be: 'At my time of life, all's quiet on the Y-front.'

35

Swan Songs

Very strange isn't it, getting old – somehow one
never thought it quite possible.
                              (Letter to Emlyn Williams, 1971)

FOR some time now Gielgud had been missing the theatre: the camaraderie of rehearsals, the contact with a live audience. 'I'd love to go back if I could find a good part,' he admitted. He had rejected many roles, both from the subsidised theatres and from commercial managements in Britain and America. He turned down Aubrey's *Brief Lives,* feeling unable to match Roy Dotrice's original performance. He declined Angela Huth's play *The Understanding,* which gave Richardson his last part. He refused to go back to a recent success, resisting an offer to revive *Forty Years On.* Soon after turning eighty he did make a brief return – but only to play the Goose King for a single night in *Mother Goose,* staged to raise funds for the Theatre Museum. 'I do hope to goodness no one thinks of it as a comeback,' he said, 'because I don't feel I've actually gone completely away.'

There was talk of a final Lear at the National, a 'chamber' production at the Cottesloe, with Peter Hall, Peter Gill and John Dexter variously mentioned as director. 'I still remember most of it, I rehearse it in the car going down to the country,' Gielgud said. But in the end he was 'frightened of not being up to it', and, according to Peter Hall, backed out in 'a welter of sorrow, mortification and disappointment'. He was anxious about a proposed European tour, and about promoting the play in the media, of having to 'go along with all that Parkinson–Harty stuff and meet hundreds of people'. But there was another factor: 'We couldn't decide on the cast or the director,' Gielgud recalled. 'Then Olivier looked me rather boldly in the eye and said, "Johnny, you don't want to play Lear again, do you?" I saw that he wanted to do it very much, so naturally I didn't.' Olivier played the part on television, his final Shakespearean role.

In October 1987 he made a rare trip to London, to attend a private view of a major exhibition celebrating his life's work in the theatre. On display at the Theatre Museum in Covent Garden, where a gallery was named after him for the occasion, it focused on his work not just as an actor but also as a director, using photographs, paintings, costumes, stage designs, posters, programmes and copies of reviews. It revealed that his career had spanned 130 roles in over 200 productions. That weekend, with perfect timing, Gielgud announced plans to play number 131.

His return to the West End after ten years away was marked by a familiar mixture of impetuousness, nerves and indecision. Hugh Whitemore's play *The Best of Friends* was based on letters between the scholarly museum curator Sydney Cockerell, the abbess Dame Laurentia McLachlan, and Shaw. The latter parts were taken by Rosemary Harris and Ray McAnally, and Gielgud accepted Cockerell almost immediately. But when Whitemore and director James Roose-Evans arrived at his house to discuss the play he was already back-tracking. The play was too static, he said, it would be better done on the radio. Hugh Whitemore recalls the delicate negotiations:

'Martin brought in the tea, took me to one side, and said, "He's nervous, just bear with him. I think he should do it, it's a marvellous part." That encouraged me, so I said to Gielgud, "Is there anything I can do to the text to help you?" He suggested a walk – he was very proud of the garden. We walked around, and he said: "The trouble is, the part is nowhere as good in Act Two as it is in Act One. I think Shaw has got all the laughs." I suggested I could build up the part in Act Two, and give *him* some laughs, and he said, "Then of course I'd love to read it again." So I re-wrote the part.'

Before rehearsals Gielgud declared: 'The great thing is to keep the memory going, and that's really why I'm coming back.' But he also admitted that 'study and memory are more of an effort than they used to be'. Privately he confessed that he was 'very apprehensive at the responsibility of acting in the theatre again after so many years'. Rehearsals, Roose-Evans remembered, were a daily torture for him: he experienced several small black-outs that made him stamp his foot in frustration. He felt he was making a fool of himself, and contemplated giving up. He was anxious about being left alone after the death of the two other characters, and suggested the actors remain onstage, 'dead' in their chairs. As soon as the idea was tried he realised it wouldn't work: 'It's like sitting in a Pharoah's tomb!' he said. Yet his instinct for what would work was mostly sound, as Whitemore recalls: 'Sometimes he would query the timing of a move, or suggest pauses to the other actors. They didn't mind; he was always right.'

His salary for the part was less than £100. He had agreed to play it on certain conditions: no tour, a maximum of twelve weeks at the Apollo, and a fortnight of previews to ease him in. Once again he was galvanised by having an audience, as Roose-Evans recalled: 'At the first preview he seized hold of the opening speech as he had never been able to do before, and delivered it with enormous energy and pace.' There were minor mistakes at subsequent previews. At one he forgot his last line, and the curtain was brought down; at another he spoke of 'a man with a lot of children and no money', paused, then said, 'I mean, a man with no children and a lot of money'. Both he and the audience roared with laughter.

On the opening night in January 1988 there were occasional fluffs, but he skilfully wove these into Cockerell's character. Afterwards he wrote to Roose-Evans: 'I hope you will continue to correct my faults and to be on the look-out for any small improvements I may hope to make.' In general he was in control: because *he* was not embarrassed if he forgot his lines, neither was the audience. 'Sir John himself has acquired the rich patina of a valued friend,' the critic Jack Tinker wrote. 'To him the audience responds instinctively with genuine affection, admiration and warmth.' Yet before each subsequent performance he was apprehensive: 'He would sit on stage, quietly waiting for the play to begin, looking drawn and anxious,' Roose-Evans remembered. 'And each night, at the curtain call, he would look years younger, like a boy in love.'

Whitemore watched several performances from the wings. 'I got that sense of a great actor commanding an audience,' he says. 'I was astonished by the way he phrased the part. I've never known anyone control long sentences so well, and he used his hands quite wonderfully.' On the final night he watched from the front, then slipped backstage for the curtain call: 'Suddenly there was this extraordinary noise. I thought it was an IRA bomb, but it was all the seats banging as everyone stood up. The applause went on and on, and when the curtain finally came down, John turned to Rosemary Harris and said, "Well my dear, I hope the next time we meet it will be under happier circumstances."'

Audiences often found it difficult to separate Gielgud from his character. Cockerell's last line – 'I might pop off tomorrow. Who knows?' – had all the obvious resonances. Many had come to witness what they guessed would be his farewell to the stage. Richard Briers remembers the atmosphere: 'He wasn't being funny, but everyone around us was smiling, because he was just enjoying himself so much. People were pleased to see him, and his great love of the theatre and the public just soared across. The feeling wasn't just, What a wonderful actor, it was also, What a wonderful man.'

It had in fact been an immensely difficult experience. Even though he was staying at the Ritz he disliked being in London, and told more than one friend that he was miserable. He had regretted agreeing to a two-week extension of the run: the effort, he said, had nearly killed him. He had now finished with the theatre for good.

However, he continued to work without a pause in films and television. In John Mortimer's *A Summer's Lease* the following year he played a reprobate, down-at-heel, elderly writer on holiday with his family in Italy. 'I find it amusing not to play for sympathy, to show the worst side of a character,' he said. In straw hat, silk cravat and white jacket, a cigarette permanently in his mouth, he turned a subsidiary character in the novel into the dominant one on screen, with a performance of sparkling wit and consummate rudery. Mortimer caught him in action on location in Tuscany: 'He seems as elegant and entertaining as ever, his head cocked to catch a whisper of gossip, ready to end his musical sentences in a little burble of laughter at many things, including himself.'

Early in the filming he had to return to England for a prostate operation. Michael Pennington, playing his son-in-law, noticed how work acted as a tonic when he returned: 'I thought he looked terribly frail, and he had difficulty with his first scene. But once he was working again it was like an iguana on a rock, the air begins to puff it up. He was doing what he loved doing, and all was well. It was a wonderful process to watch.' His performance won him an Emmy award in America – which he managed to avoid collecting by taking a holiday in Scotland.

It was in Tuscany that he heard the news of Olivier's death. Pennington walked round the location with him that evening: 'He was just so extraordinarily warm and generous,' he remembers. 'Without any sort of affectation or envy he said, "Of course there are things Larry could do that I couldn't even begin to do, performances he gave that I couldn't begin to approach." In a completely unforced way he drew attention to what Larry had that he didn't – but not the other way round.' He was unable to attend the funeral, but sent a wreath of flowers, and the message, 'With loving memories, John'. At the memorial service in Westminster Abbey he spoke John Donne's holy sonnet 'Death be not proud' and Hamlet's 'Not a whit, we defy augury'. It was an extravagantly theatrical occasion, with leading actors processing down the aisle carrying significant objects from Olivier's career. Gielgud's gift of Kean's sword brought up the rear. Asked to whom he would be handing it on, Olivier had replied: 'No one. It's mine.'

In a tribute published just before the service Gielgud acknowledged Olivier's greatness, praising his daring, his technical expertise and his 'magnificent panache'. He also tactfully denied the existence of any rivalry between them. Yet jealousy undoubtedly existed, though more in Olivier's mind than in Gielgud's. That jealousy had led Olivier, despite professions of complete and lifelong devotion to Gielgud, to criticise him cruelly and unfairly on many occasions, both privately and in print. Gielgud, publicly loyal at the time of Olivier's death, later acknowledged their 'curious love–hate relationship', and admitted that when they worked together 'we were never happily in harness'.

The constant references made to their rivalry sometimes proved too much for him. Mention of it during the celebrations of his eightieth birthday prompted an uncharacteristic outburst. 'I hate being put up against my contemporaries,' he said. 'All those terrible arguments! All those questions! "What do you think of Olivier and what does he think of you?" It's all such rubbish.' Yet he could be sensitive to any suggestion that Olivier's status within the profession might be greater than his. The actor Richard Bebb had commissioned bronzes of Olivier as Oedipus and Mr Puff in Sheridan's *The Critic*, and of Gielgud as Hamlet. When he presented Gielgud's to him at the Garrick, he suggested a further one of him as Richard II might be created. Gielgud said he felt one was enough, but when he was told that two had been done of Olivier, he decided that Richard might be a good idea after all.

In recent years their mutually polite but distant friendship had been damaged by Olivier's autobiographical *Confessions of an Actor*, an indiscreet and ungenerous book which embarrassed many people in the theatre. Gielgud had been deeply upset by the newspaper extracts detailing Olivier's over-candid revelations about his marriage to Vivien Leigh, and refused to read the book itself. He publicly defended her in interviews, arguing that this was not the Vivien Leigh he knew. 'I was really Vivien's friend,' he said. 'I've rarely seen Larry since she died.'

Olivier's death provoked him to reflect on the reasons for their poor relationship. 'I cannot help feeling sad, and somewhat ashamed too, that I did not strive to know him better,' he said. He wrote to Olivier's widow Joan Plowright, regretting their lack of contact in his final years: 'I hadn't wanted to burden him with my wellness when he was so ill,' he explained. 'The truth was that I was always a little afraid of him.' In her reply she wrote that Olivier had been rather afraid of *him*.

In 1991 he fulfilled a long-held ambition, and in doing so gave one of his most remarkable screen performances. Ever since his youth, when he had seen Beerbohm Tree in a silent film of *The Tempest*, he had wanted to play Prospero on screen. In 1951 Michael Powell announced plans for him to do so with the dancer Moira Shearer as his Ariel, but she turned it down. For the last fifteen years Gielgud had been trying to set up the film, hoping to leave a record of one of his Shakespearean roles, as Olivier had done. 'Larry left his Lear which he made towards the end,' he said. 'I thought it would be nice if I left another old man who might be a bit of a contrast.'

After Benjamin Britten agreed to compose the music Gielgud put together a short treatment, then searched with remarkable persistence for a suitable director. He talked to Giorgio Strehler of the Piccolo Theatre in Milan, and the controversial American director Peter Sellars. After *Providence* he asked Resnais, who felt his English was not up to Shakespeare. He told Welles he could raise the money if he would play Caliban, but Welles felt he was too old. He approached Bergman, who refused to discuss the idea. He wrote to Kurosawa, whose *Rashomon*, a version of *King Lear*, had greatly impressed him. There was no answer. But when Derek Jarman invited him to play the older Prospero in *his* film, he rejected the offer, pleading his committment to playing the part in the BBC Shakespeare series – from which he then withdrew.

He had reluctantly given up on the idea when in 1990 Peter Greenaway asked him to appear as Virgil in his television film *Dante's Inferno*. Gielgud, who had greatly admired Greenaway's *The Draughtsman's Contract*, told him of his *Tempest* project, and showed him his treatment. Before long he received a complete shooting script for what was to become *Prospero's Books*. He was amazed when Greenaway suggested he speak all the parts, but excited when the director explained his idea: to have Prospero not just as the manipulator of people and events, but as the creator of the drama called *The Tempest*, who devises the characters and speaks their dialogue in order to act out his fantasies. 'The whole concept was modelled on Gielgud's voice,' Greenaway explained.

He was intrigued by Greenaway's ideas, and stimulated by his remarkable imagination and feeling for colour. As he did with only a handful of other directors – Resnais, Brook, Barker, Peter Hall, Lindsay Anderson – he trusted Greenaway's judgement, believing he would give him honest criticism. 'The best directors don't say much, you have to just trust them,' he said. He admired Greenaway for being 'so challenging, such a painterly director, enormously cinematic'.

Filming took place in Amsterdam, from where Gielgud wrote: 'Having most fascinating time here . . . Superbly original script but only WS dialogue – very considerate crew and staff, most efficiently organised.' The work required a lot of physical courage. The first scene required him, at the age of eighty-six, in February, to go naked in a pool in a disused shipyard building in the docks. 'The nudity soon ceased to be surprising,' he said afterwards. 'Greenaway ignored it completely, so one didn't feel self-conscious.' He was surrounded by scores of cavorting extras, naked except for their body-paint. 'He was amused by his entourage and made a lot of unrepeatable jokes,' Greenaway remembered.

The result was a film of startling originality and visual extravagance, unlike anything previously made by a British director. Though some critics felt Shakespeare's work had been damaged in the process, Gielgud's severe, often brutal performance was widely praised, not least by Greenaway himself: 'He was the still, calm figure in the midst of this pyrotechnical extravagance,' he said. 'Whatever else is going on, it is him you watch.' *Prospero's Books* was an appropriate testament not just to Gielgud's voice and poetic skills, but also to his openness to experiment and fresh ideas. He himself thought the film an apt summation of all his Prosperos: 'I think you will find it most original and fascinating, if a bit over-elaborate,' he told a fellow-actor.

To coincide with its release, he was persuaded by John Miller to put together what he called 'rather a frivolous little book' on Shakespeare. Essentially it was a further volume of personal reminiscence, laced with anecdotes old and new, but with some fresh thoughts on many of his Shakespearean roles. 'I am neither a scholar nor an intellectual, and I have naturally hesitated to trespass on so many well-trodden and controversial paths,' he wrote in the foreword. He thought the original

title *Acting Shakespeare* too grand, and suggested instead *Shakespeare –*
Hit or Miss? But when this was later discovered to be the name of a
secondhand-clothes store in America, he agreed that the US edition,
and later the UK paperback, should carry the original title.

As he moved through his eighties his fellow-actors began to die off
at an alarming rate. 'Most of my friends seem to be dead, deaf, or
living in the wrong part of Kent,' he said with a Wildean flourish. But
in more sombre moments he admitted that 'the loss of so many friends
and people dying and incapacitated depresses me a great deal'. Peggy
Ashcroft's death in 1991 hit him especially hard: the mere mention of
her name brought tears to his eyes and an abrupt change of subject.
Their warm and abiding professional friendship was reflected in the
tribute he paid to her not long before her death. 'Consummate actress,
darling friend, impeccable partner and colleague, a beneficent
member of every enterprise and company,' he wrote. He loved her
defiance and fighting spirit, and likened her 'shimmering radiance and
iridescence and a kind of forthright, trusting quality' to that of Ellen
Terry. When she won an Oscar for Best Supporting Actress in *A*
Passage to India he was delighted: 'So wonderful for her to receive
world appreciation after so many years of wonderful modest triumphs
in the theatre,' he said.

Although they had not acted together since *The Cherry Orchard*
thirty years earlier, they had taken part in many special events,
including several poetry recitals. In the Old Vic tribute to Lilian Baylis
they had waged one more merry war of words as Beatrice and
Benedick. In 1987 Gielgud had read three Shakespeare sonnets as part
of her tribute evening at the Old Vic, and in 1988 they had jointly led
a Celebration of Literature held in Westminster Abbey. Now,
returning to the Abbey, Gielgud joined in a service of thanksgiving for
her life, paying an affectionate tribute, reading the speech from *Antony*
and Cleopatra about 'a lass unparallel'd', and closing the service with
Prospero's 'Our revels now are ended'.

The following year it was the turn of Gwen Ffrangcon-Davies, who
died two days after reaching the age of 101. She had been one of
Gielgud's staunchest leading ladies, notably in *Richard of Bordeaux* and
his wartime *Macbeth*, and he had looked upon her as a great actress of
extraordinary range, as well as a cherished friend. He always
remembered how as Juliet she had come to his rescue during his first,
near-disastrous attempt at Romeo, winning his undying admiration for
'her remarkable professional skill and tolerance of my inexperience'.

After *Prospero's Books* Gielgud played his final Chekhov role. His one-act play *Swan Song* was the story of a drunken, failed old actor left behind in a theatre after a performance. With only his memories and the prompter for company he re-lives some of his Shakespearean parts. Gielgud had performed it for the troops during the war, as part of his ENSA programme. Now he was invited to play the part on film by Kenneth Branagh. In his youth Branagh had seen Gielgud as a godlike figure: at RADA he had been overwhelmed when, on a casual visit, Gielgud had given him helpful advice after he had, in his view, wrecked Hamlet's 'O, what a rogue and peasant slave am I!' soliloquy. 'I was hypnotised by the humility of the man,' he remembered. 'He spoke to me not as a teacher but as one professional to another. He was completely beguiling.'

Swan Song was twenty-two minutes of unalloyed joy. Gielgud brilliantly catches the humour and the melancholy of the old actor, and even manages to be a moderately convincing drunk, at least in the opening minutes. Re-creating some of his old parts and finding a new vigour in doing so, he and the character seem to merge into one. As he speaks Romeo's farewell, skips through a Hamlet soliloquy, and defies the storm as Lear, there are sudden glimpses of the young Gielgud who once set the West End on fire. It's a performance that's touching in itself, but poignant too for its references to his past triumphs.

Branagh recalled that Gielgud was 'never too grand to take a note'. Richard Briers, who played the old prompter Nikita, remembers how well he worked with a director nearly sixty years younger than himself. 'He was totally obedient to Branagh, totally cooperative. He was always learning, a lesson to us all not to get big-headed. But rehearsals had their sad side. They took place on the stage of the Criterion, where he had done *Musical Chairs* in the old days, and he talked a lot about the ghosts of the past.'

The film was not Gielgud's own swan song on screen, for he continued to work at a level that would have exhausted a man thirty years younger. During the 1990s he added fourteen film roles and nine television appearances to his extensive list of credits, astonishing his friends and fellow-actors with his unflagging zest. 'I get restless if I have nothing to do,' he explained. 'I enjoy meeting new young actors and actresses, being in the thick of it, as it were.' Some of his conversational gambits surprised even those who knew him. Judi Dench remembers meeting him at the BBC while he was filming J.B. Priestley's *Summer's Day Dream*: 'He invited several of us to join him for lunch, all devotees.

We sat down and waited for him to say something. There was a pause, and then he said: "Have any of you had any obscene phone calls?"'

As he approached his ninetieth birthday he finally began to acknowledge his frailty, though in characteristically flippant style. 'I try not to take on more than one or two days' filming, in case I drop dead in the middle of it,' he joked. 'If I die on the job they'll give it to Michael Denison, and that I couldn't bear.' Though he could no longer work on location, Pinewood and Shepperton studios were only a short, chauffeur-driven journey away. Allowed to work a shortened day, he was spared the early morning starts.

'GIELGUD IS GOD' ran the predictable headline in 1991, when the BBC announced plans to broadcast the entire Bible in dramatised form. He opened the series of daily ten-minute readings with *Genesis*, and brought it to an end with *Revelation*. John Theocharis, the producer, recalls his empathy with one of the characters in *Genesis*: 'He was in the middle of reading a chapter – "and Abraham was ninety years old and nine when he was circumcised in the flesh of his foreskin" – and he suddenly stopped, took off his glasses, looked at me with real concern, and without changing his pitch said, "Can you imagine the sheer horror of it?" Then he went on, "Ishmael, his son . . .". He identified, as all good actors do.'

Gielgud very rarely lost his temper, but Theocharis was witness to a rare moment of anger during the Bible readings. 'I had wanted his voice to be at its best, and had dropped an indirect hint on the phone about refraining from smoking. Next day he emerged from the car, a cigarette hanging Maigret-like from his lips, one eye closed because of the smoke. That day I thought his voice a bit gravelly, so I said: "Sorry John, it's not working at the moment. Maybe you should rest for three or four days, and refrain from smoking during that time?" He went red, and said with controlled anger: "I have never been asked to do anything like that. Except for one day in 1926 when I had a bad cold, I've been smoking for seventy-four years without interruption." I then made the mistake of saying, "I'm afraid it's beginning to show, John." At this he said: "Please ask the girl to call my cab. I'll see myself out. Good day to you."

'I was very upset, and wrote to him saying I was sure it would be all right, the tape had shown that it was better than I thought, and I looked forward to our next session. He rang me the next morning and said: "I was most touched by your letter. You know, since I left the studio last night I haven't had one cigarette." He said it in such a way that I felt like saying, "Light up, have one on me!" When he came a few days later to record *Revelation* he said: "I haven't smoked for a week." Then he added, "But don't spread it around." '

In 1992 he was persuaded by Branagh to play the Ghost in his radio *Hamlet*. 'The Ghost is very difficult,' he explained. 'You have to be very strong and commanding and at the same time ghostly and insubstantial.' He proved to be both. His very substantial presence in the cast made the event something of a media circus, especially when he and Branagh appeared sharing a skull on the cover of *Radio Times*. 'A great deal of nonsense was talked about pretenders to the throne and heirs apparent, which Sir John treated with his customary Olympian loftiness,' Jack Tinker wrote.

The following year he took part in Branagh's radio version of *Romeo and Juliet*, and then played his fourth and last radio *King Lear* in April 1994, in another Branagh production broadcast to celebrate his ninetieth birthday. The all-star cast included Judi Dench (Goneril), Eileen Atkins (Regan), Michael Williams (Fool), Richard Briers (Gloucester), and Emma Thompson (Cordelia), with actors such as Bob Hoskins, Simon Russell Beale and Derek Jacobi happy to take on minor roles. There were fears Gielgud would not be up it: to some he seemed tired and frail, and he played the part sitting down. But Branagh found him alert and inventive as ever, and virtually directing himself: 'He's already thought of all the suggestions you offer,' he said. 'All you do is provide a reminder service.'

Gielgud himself was not satisfied, feeling he lacked power: 'I can't act any more!' he told Judi Dench during one rehearsal. Once more he had under-rated his performance: his intense and strongly articulated Lear was universally enjoyed and marvelled at. The role an ailing, emaciated Olivier had courageously tackled at seventy-five on television, Gielgud – spry, resilient, striving to improve – had now matched at ninety. Michael Billington wrote: 'This is not something wistful, embalmed and elegaic, but a compelling and urgent study of an imperious tyrant splintering into madness. And that is nothing less than you would expect from Gielgud.'

He spent his birthday quietly at home with Martin Hensler. At his insistence there were no celebrations. 'Such talent as I have, I've only developed without knowing,' he remarked. 'I haven't sat and studied for hours like an astronomer or a statistician.' He wrote to the Garrick Club cancelling a planned dinner, and to the impresario Duncan Wheldon forbidding any gala event. 'It would sound like my obituary,' he said. 'I'd much rather work and show I can still do a bit than just get congratulations on the past.'

He did agree to take part in a tribute put together for the BBC's *Omnibus* programme. Presented by Branagh, with Gielgud reading linking passages from his memoirs, it provided a faithful if over-reverential record of his career. There were two more celebratory books. One was an affectionate anthology of reminiscences from friends and colleagues, *Sir John: The Many Faces of Gielgud*, compiled by Clive Francis, who illustrated it with wittily accurate cartoons. The other was *Notes from the Gods: Playgoing in the Twenties*, an illustrated collection of Gielgud's youthful play reviews, edited by Richard Mangan. 'I find it rather hard to believe the present generation will be much interested in these juvenile reminiscences,' Gielgud wrote to him. But when Mangan sent him the typescript for approval he was unable to resist filling in the background with further stories and opinions, many of which were included in the book.

One planned celebration went temporarily awry. At the recent Olivier Awards ceremony it had been announced that a West End theatre would be re-named the Gielgud. It was a gesture many thought long overdue, and some four hundred members of the profession – including Peter Hall, Judi Dench, Harold Pinter and Richard Eyre – mounted a campaign to have the Apollo or the Queen's named after him. The owners, Stoll Moss, rejected the idea, arguing that the name 'Gielgud' was too austere for contemporary West End audiences, and for the kind of shows they might want to present in those theatres. Alongside this argument another producer offered the hardly more frivolous one that, if the Queen's were to be chosen, there would be a danger of the new 'Gielgud' being referred to as 'the old Queen's'.

Eventually Stoll Moss agreed to re-name the Globe, where Gielgud had acted in fifteen productions over four decades, including *The Importance of Being Earnest* and *The Lady's Not for Burning*. At the ceremony in November, looking healthy and trim in a white goatee beard and moustache, he gave a witty, barbed speech spiced with anecdotes and memories, provoking tears and laughter in an audience that included Guinness, Scofield and Wendy Hiller. 'This is a kind of crown for me,' he said with obvious pride. He had never announced the end of his stage career, but now he did so. 'I don't think I will ever act in the theatre again,' he said. 'The discipline of eight times a week and the labour of making up on stage is too much for me.' Though he missed the applause and rehearsals, he would not be acting in 'his' theatre. But at least he would recognise one name now as he walked down Shaftesbury Avenue: his own.

'What appeals is a good part with a couple of good lines, a good entrance and a good exit,' he said that day of his film work. 'A bit of limelight on me and that's all I ask for.' Although his appearances were becoming ever more fleeting, he still lent a genuine distinction to many a king, nobleman, pope, judge and aristocrat. He hugged Julia Ormond as a village elder in the absurd Arthurian tale *First Knight*, and smoked a cigarette and died in Jane Campion's pretentious version of *Portrait of a Lady*. One of his more substantial parts was as David Helfgott's piano teacher in *Shine*, which he played with startling dash and energy. There were two final Shakespeare appearances, in *Richard III* and as Priam in Branagh's *Hamlet*. In his last feature film, *The Tichborne Claimant*, in which he played a judge, he was clearly more delicate, but still produced a credible cameo performance.

In his last years he was the recipient of many honours. He was made the first honorary fellow of RADA, and awarded honorary doctorates by London University and the Open University. In 1993 he gained the first annual Shakespeare Globe Trust Award for his contribution to the enjoyment of Shakespeare. There was recognition too from abroad. In 1994 the Gielgud Award for Excellence in the Dramatic Arts was established in America by the Shakespeare Guild. The Japan Arts Association gave him its Imperial Prize, declaring that in the theatre 'there is no one else who occupies such an international role in everyone's conscience'. But the award that pleased him most, according to his sister Eleanor, was the Order of Merit, given personally by the Queen to 'individuals of exceptional distinction'. Kipling, Eisenhower, Elgar, Churchill, Florence Nightingale and Mother Teresa were among previous recipients. Gielgud was only the second actor to receive it; the first had been Olivier.

As a friend of the Queen Mother he was driven occasionally to Windsor to read poetry to her. He also took part in a recital at Buckingham Palace, as Simon Russell Beale recalls: 'Rather than Prospero, he'd chosen to do Lorenzo's speech to Jessica from *The Merchant of Venice*, which was amazing. He did it without the book, but then he dried. Samatha Bond nudged the script towards him, but he put out his hand and stopped her. He just took his time, and then went back to it.' Otherwise he rarely went to London: 'All those despatch riders and plastic bags everywhere, you can't stroll around the West End any more,' he shuddered. 'I hear people are sleeping in the

Strand.' He did, however, brave these horrors in January 1995, to unveil a plaque at the Haymarket commemorating the theatre's links with the work of one of his favourite playwrights, 'that brilliant, witty man' Oscar Wilde.

He unveiled another two years later, on the house in Chelsea where Edith Evans had been living and working as a milliner when she was discovered by William Poel. From a first-floor window he gave a lively speech to a crowd gathered below. John Mills recalls the occasion: 'It was one of the hottest days on record, but he spoke at length, and all off the cuff. It was wonderful stuff.' The event enabled him to correct the persisting story that Edith Evans had once said he had a face like a camel. 'She said I *walked* like a camel,' he explained. 'It didn't rankle at all. She may well have been right.'

Aside from his radio broadcasts he was also in demand in his last years to make recordings for audio-books and cassettes: he read works by Dickens, Wilde, Evelyn Waugh, Alan Bennett and many others. In 1998 he played Gower in *Pericles* for a new series of Shakespeare recordings. 'I hope it made sense,' he said at the end to the director. 'I'd be very glad to do any of it again.' There was still the occasional cameo 'to pay the butcher and baker': television appearances in *Lovejoy* and *Inspector Morse*, and in *Gulliver's Travels, Dance to the Music of Time* and *Merlin*.

Old age finally began to catch up with him, though he hated to be seen as old offscreen; a photograph showing him being wheeled on to a film set upset him a lot. He took to wearing an expensive hearing-aid, and had to use a stick when he took his Tibetan terriers for walks. He spent an increasing amount of time at home, and modified his lifestyle slightly, giving up spirits and drinking wine only in the evenings. But he refused to follow any diet, or give up smoking Turkish cigarettes. 'It's so boring saying one mustn't smoke, one mustn't eat eggs, one must wear a seat belt,' he complained. 'There's almost nothing left except sex, and I'm too old for that, unfortunately.'

He pottered around the garden, read trashy novels by Judith Krantz and Harold Robbins, and watched too much television. For some years he had been devouring soap operas, first *Dynasty* and *Dallas*, then *EastEnders*, and finally '*Cheers* and other rubbish'. Sometimes he would phone home while filming on location to catch up with the latest twist in the plot of the latest soap. He loved them for their silliness, but he also still loved to watch actors act.

It was television that belatedly opened his eyes to what was going on in the world. Brooding on his obsession with the theatre, he began to feel ashamed he had not taken more interest in other areas of life. 'The theatre's been an escape for me, which I'm not particularly proud of,' he confessed. 'The miseries of the world are so great these days. In the past I was always too busy to notice, I suppose. But now I find it very hard to rise above it all.'

There was one unexpected gesture of political engagement. In 1993 he became involved in a campaign by the American animal rights group People for the Ethical Treatment of Animals. Its aim was to draw attention to the cruel force-feeding of ducks involved in the production of *pâté de foie gras*. On a hard-hitting video Gielgud appealed to people to stop buying the delicacy or ordering it in restaurants. 'I had no idea that the animals suffer so dreadfully,' he said. 'Now I know the truth.'

He occasionally sent money privately to the gay rights group Stonewall, but resisted this being made public, as Ian McKellen recalls: 'When I wrote to him on his ninetieth birthday asking him if I could let this be known, I got the quickest reply of my life – No, no, no! He just wouldn't talk about it. Many years before he had said to me, "When I die I'm just going to be known as the first queer to be knighted." Yet in today's world that would be something to be proud rather than ashamed of.'

At the end of his life he also became active in efforts to preserve the character of his local village. He helped pay for planning appeals when some fields in Wotton Underwood were threatened by developers, and after buying two fields he had trees planted on them to try to keep the development at bay. He also paid for oaks and chestnuts to be planted at the entrance to the village, to help preserve its rural atmosphere.

He brooded again on the question of children. What he had said to Dorothy Tutin he had hinted at later to others, as Hallam Tennyson recalls: 'He sensed that I was bisexual, and was fascinated that I was also a married man. He kept asking me, in what I thought was a meaningful way, how I liked being a father. I felt he would have liked to have been one himself.' At ninety, in one of his last radio interviews, he said: 'Never having had children, I've never experienced that very interesting thing of seeing people growing up around me. There I do feel I've missed something very important.'

Though he tried hard not to dwell on it, his thoughts inevitably turned to the question of death. While often speaking vaguely of 'Somebody up there who knows what's going on', he had no real faith or a belief in an after-life, and experienced moments of great depression. But he could also joke about the subject: 'I think people see it as an indecent race between myself, the Pope and Boris Yeltsin.' No doubt he enjoyed the exaggerated reports of his death that circulated in the week of his ninety-fifth birthday, prompting one newspaper to start ringing his fellow-actors for their reactions.

He had remained close to his sister Eleanor, ringing her three or four times a week at her Gloucestershire home, and becoming very anxious if she was unwell. 'I think he looks on me as the next best thing after Mother, but I never feel I can live up to that,' she said in 1998. When she died aged ninety-one at the end of that year he was very distressed. He was also upset after breaking an ankle in a fall, which left him unable to walk more than a few steps without help. But his greatest blow was the death of Martin Hensler. Though Hensler had cancer – he was a heavy smoker – he kept his illness from Gielgud for as long as possible. In hospital he refused to eat or drink, and was allowed home to die. Devastated by this loss, unable to work, Gielgud was low for months, refusing to see all but one or two close friends. Aside from his deep emotional attachment to his companion of nearly forty years, he had relied on him totally for everything practical.

As the century ended he gave what turned out to be his last interview, for the BBC's *Newsnight* programme. Sitting on the stage of the Old Vic, dapper as ever in a well-cut, charcoal-grey suit and floppy patterned tie, he was noticeably frail, the famous voice now diminished in strength. At ninety-five his mind had slowed, and he took a moment to absorb the questions put by Jeremy Paxman. He spoke sadly of all the friends who had died, and of his guilt at not taking more interest in the world outside the theatre. But he ended positively: 'If I had it all over again, I wouldn't do any of it differently.'

His chauffeur, who had been with him for thirty years, and his young gardener were now effectively his carers. At his own wish he spent New Year's Eve alone, as he and Martin Hensler had always done in recent years. As the new millennium began he seemed to revive a little. The contest for London Mayor prompted a characteristic piece of political insight: 'Glenda Jackson was a wonderful Cleopatra, and she would have made a wonderful Lady Mayoress,' he said. On his ninety-sixth birthday he was back at work, filming for two days in London in Samuel Beckett's play *Catastrophe*, directed by David Mamet for Irish television. It was a key role, but a non-speaking one: 'I don't understand a word of it,' he said. Asked if he minded working on his birthday, he said it was a great surprise to be still acting at this age.

Pinter was also taking part. 'He was extremely frail, and his features very gaunt,' he recalls. 'He was brought on to the set in a wheelchair, but he stood without a stick, very upright and wonderfully focussed. It was impressive, and affecting.'

A month later Margaret Harris of Motley died. Gielgud was upset by the loss of yet another cherished theatrical figure from his past, but agreed to come to her funeral in London. But on Sunday 21 May, the day before it was due to take place, he collapsed in his drawing-room, and died in the arms of his chauffeur. The next day the West End theatre lights were briefly extinguished in his memory, and in the theatre that now bore his name actors and audience joined in a one-minute silence.

The funeral service, held in his local church, was a simple, private affair, attended by some fifty close friends and colleagues, including Alec Guinness, Maggie Smith, Richard Attenborough and Irene Worth. At his request there were no flowers or hymns. John Mills recited John Pudney's poem 'Johnny Head in Air', and Paul Scofield movingly delivered the Shakespeare sonnet, 'No longer mourn for me when I am dead'. Later that day Gielgud's body was cremated in Oxford.

Greatly offended by what he saw as the tastelessness of Olivier's memorial service, he had left strict instructions that none should be held for him, and these were honoured. 'Public celebrations are awfully embarrassing, they've become society functions,' he had said. Modest to the end, he believed he had no right to be commemorated in Westminster Abbey, that he was not important enough.

'My work stands for what it is,' he said. 'That's all.'

Conclusion

IN his heyday Gielgud was a radical and an innovator. As such he had a profound influence on the theatre of the twentieth century.

In his youth, at a time when Chekhov's plays were generally unappreciated and misunderstood in England, he helped to establish his reputation as a serious dramatist. His fresh, bold approach to Shakespeare rescued his plays from the fustian traditions of the previous generation, and made them both popular and commercially successful in the West End. His outstanding achievement as an actor-manager between the wars, when he seemed at times almost to be a one-man National Theatre, helped to set new standards of production in the West End.

At the root of his achievement lay his unceasing search for quality and perfection. This was evident in his desire, so unusual then for a star, to surround himself with the best actors he could find. In establishing his 'Cabinets of all the Talents' at the New and then the Queen's, and insisting on the importance of a permanent ensemble, he provided a crucial blueprint for the subsequent setting up of the Royal Shakespeare Company and the National Theatre.

In the theatre an actor's life is writ in water. Gielgud's later work in films and television give a very limited idea of his power and range as a stage performer. Widely acknowledged as the supreme romantic actor, he moved and thrilled audiences with his lyrical intensity and incomparably melodious voice. But Alec Guinness's memorable likening of it to 'a silver trumpet muffled in silk' was only half the story: as was seen most strikingly with his Hamlet, Gielgud's vocal beauty was allied to a formidable intelligence.

It was the combination of his innate musicality and his understanding of the verse that established him as the age's greatest interpreter of Shakespeare. Yet he also made an indelible mark in high comedy: his comic creations, full of wit, vigour and mockery, brought a freshness and a new naturalism to the playing of Wilde, Sheridan and Congreve, while his witty Benedick was one of his greatest glories.

As a director he had considerable influence. Though he lacked the flamboyant boldness of Guthrie or the startling vision of Peter Brook, his fertile imagination and passion for design resulted in many distinctive productions, notable for their beauty and elegance, and their high-quality ensemble work. He was also one of the first to use a permanent set, and to stage Shakespeare's plays in swift, continuous action, as he felt Shakespeare intended them to be played, and as is now commonplace.

But his impetuosity and butterfly-mind prevented him from becoming a great director. Actors in the end need security, and Gielgud was not a good provider of it. 'Once one makes a decision life becomes unbearably dull,' he once said. While many actors were stimulated by the quick, intuitive, surface ideas that he threw at them, others were deeply frustrated by his fatal inability to keep to a decision. Nor was detailed analysis of character and motivation his way, as several American actors discovered to their cost when looking to him for guidance. 'Get yourself a small Cordelia,' he once said to an actor hoping for some advice on playing Lear. What interested him was what was 'effective' on stage, the mechanics rather than the psychology.

Great actors never really grow up, and Gielgud did so less than most. Throughout his life he retained a child-like innocence, which left him hopelessly adrift in the real world. 'I am a very timid, shy, cowardly man,' he once said, with characteristic honesty. He was also aloof in manner, remarkably detached, and self-contained to a degree. Never drunk, scarcely ever angry, he always kept his emotions rigidly in check in his everyday life.

In the theatre it was a different matter. Here he could allow himself to be guided by his instincts and emotions. 'Acting is half shame, half glory,' he once said. 'Shame at exhibiting yourself, glory when you can forget yourself.' Acting allowed him to forget his shyness and timidity, and in doing so he found release. He was, as he himself admitted, somewhat repressed in everyday life. His innate shyness and reserve were part of this, as was an Edwardian upbringing which emphasised politeness and good manners. But so too was the need during most of his life to conceal his homosexuality. In the theatre he was able to use and exploit his repression, and in the process get rid of some of his frustrations.

Throughout his career he was driven by an insatiable appetite for the new, and an unflagging desire to improve and learn. It was this that made him as interested in his failures as his successes. His ego was never very large: actors were struck by his unselfishness on stage, the way he consistently refused to play the star actor. They were also surprised by his modesty and humility, the way he constantly sought reassurance about his performance, even from the most inexperienced member of a company.

Tactlessness, that fatal offshoot of his impetuosity, seems to have been part of his make-up from the beginning. In later years it achieved legendary status, helped in no little part by Gielgud himself. Genuinely embarrassed by his gaffes, most of which seemed to be free of malice, he nevertheless enjoyed re-telling some of the more notorious examples. His sense of mischief was well-developed: noticeably free of the self-importance so often found in leading actors, he never took himself too seriously.

His essentially happy and optimistic disposition was one of the causes of his longevity: he was rarely bitter or resentful, and nothing got him down for long. Yet while he loved to gossip and tell his theatrical stories, he was in many respects a solitary person, someone who could be quite satisfied with his own company. 'I'd be rather happy there, I don't think I'd make a raft,' he said, when asked how he would cope on a desert island.

In his long life he had his share of setbacks and disappointments, and one moment of trauma and desperation. He made some rash decisions and poor judgements during his career, and for a time seemed to have lost his way as an actor. But in the end he achieved most of his ambitions. In the theatre he played almost all the parts he wanted to play. He worked with the century's finest actors and directors, and played a major role in modernising the English theatre. He was acclaimed as a great actor in his youth, and once again in old age.

Above all, he never stopped working. The toy theatre was not just for Christmas, but for a lifetime.

Chronology

This chronology excludes amateur productions, charity matinees, excerpts from plays, and touring performances outside London and New York.

THEATRE: ACTOR

1921   Old Vic: Soldier/English Herald in *Henry V*. Walk-on in *Wat Tyler*.

1922   Old Vic: Walk-on in *Peer Gynt, King Lear, The Comedy of Errors, As You Like It*.
New, Oxford: Lieutenant Manners in *The Wheel*.

1923   Regent: Felix in *The Insect Play*. Aide in *Robert E. Lee*.
Comedy: Charles Wykeham in *Charley's Aunt*.

1924   Oxford Playhouse: Johnson in *Captain Brassbound's Conversion*, Valentine in *Love for Love*, Brian Strange in *Mr Pim Passes By*, Young Marlow in *She Stoops to Conquer*, Prinzivalle in *Monna Vanna*.
RADA Theatre: Paris in *Romeo and Juliet*.
Regent: Romeo in *Romeo and Juliet*.
RADA Theatre: John Sherry in *The Return Half*.
Oxford Playhouse: Eugene Marchbanks in *Candida*, Naisi in *Deirdre of the Sorrows*, Paul Roget in *A Collection Will be Made*, A Domino in *Everybody's Husband*, Antonio in *The Cradle Song*, Erhart Borkman in *John Gabriel Borkman*, Zurita in *His Widow's Husband*, Augusto in *Madame Pepita*.
Charterhouse: Lieutenant George Graham in *French Leave*.

1925   Oxford Playhouse: Algernon Peppercorn in *Smith*, Trofimov in *The Cherry Orchard*.
RADA Theatre: Ted Hewitt in *The Nature of the Evidence*.
Aldwych: Castalio in *The Orphan*.
Comedy/Little: Nicky Lancaster in *The Vortex*.

Lyric, Hammersmith: Trofimov in *The Cherry Orchard.*
Garden: Julien de Boys-Bourredon in *The High Constable's Wife.*
Oxford Playhouse: A Stranger in *The Lady from the Sea,* The Man in *The Man with a Flower in His Mouth.*
Apollo: Valentine in *The Two Gentlemen of Verona.*
Little: Konstantin in *The Seagull.*
New, Oxford: Good Angel in *Doctor Faustus.*
Little: Sir John Harrington in *Gloriana.*
Prince's: Robert in *L'École des Cocottes.*

1926   Savoy: Ferdinand in *The Tempest.*
RADA Theatre: Richard Southern in *Sons and Fathers.*
Barnes: Baron Tusenbach in *Three Sisters,* Georg Stibelev in *Katerina.*
Royal Court: Rosencrantz in *Hamlet.*
Garrick: Armand Duval in *The Lady of the Camelias.*
Royal Court: Wilfred Marlay in *Confession.*
New: Lewis Dodd in *The Constant Nymph.*

1927   Apollo: Cassio in *Othello.*
Strand: Dion Anthony in *The Great God Brown.*

1928   Majestic, New York: Grand Duke Alexander in *The Patriot.*
Wyndham's/Arts: Oswald Alving in *Ghosts.*
Globe: Gerald Marloe in *Holding Out the Apple.*
Arts: Jacob Slovak in *Prejudice.*
Shaftesbury: Vernon Allenby in *The Skull.*
Royal Court: Alberto in *Fortunato*; Felipe Rivas in *The Lady from Alfaqueque.*
Strand: John Marstin in *Out of the Sea.*

1929   Arts: Konstantin in *The Seagull.*
Little: Fedor in *Red Rust.*
Prince of Wales: Paul de Tressailles in *Hunter's Moon.*
Garrick: Henry Tremayne in *The Lady with the Lamp.*
Arts: Bronstein (Trotsky) in *Red Sunday.*
Old Vic: Romeo in *Romeo and Juliet,* Antonio in *The Merchant of Venice,* Cléante in *Le Malade Imaginaire,* Richard in *Richard II,* Oberon in *A Midsummer Night's Dream.*
Prince of Wales: The Prologue in *Douaumont.*

1930   Old Vic: Mark Antony in *Julius Caesar,* Orlando in *As You Like It,* The Emperor in *Androcles and the Lion,* Macbeth in

Macbeth, The Man in *The Man with a Flower in his Mouth,*
Mr Hughes in *The Rehearsal,* Hamlet in *Hamlet.*
Queen's: Hamlet in *Hamlet.*
Lyric, Hammersmith: John Worthing in *The Importance of Being Earnest.*
Old Vic: Hotspur in *Henry IV Part I,* Prospero in *The Tempest,* Lord Trinket in *The Jealous Wife,* Antony in *Antony and Cleopatra.*

1931   Old Vic: Malvolio in *Twelfth Night,* Sergius Seranov in *Arms and the Man,* Benedick in *Much Ado about Nothing,* Lear in *King Lear.*
His Majesty's: Inigo Jollifant in *The Good Companions.*
Arts: Joseph Schindler in *Musical Chairs.*

1932   Criterion: Joseph Schindler in *Musical Chairs.*
Arts: Richard in *Richard of Bordeaux.*

1933   New: Richard in *Richard of Bordeaux.*

1934   Wyndham's: Roger Maitland in *The Maitlands.*
New: Hamlet in *Hamlet.*

1935   New: Noah in *Noah.*
New: Mercutio, then Romeo, in *Romeo and Juliet.*

1936   New: Trigorin in *The Seagull.*
Empire, New York: Hamlet in *Hamlet.*

1937   St James's, New York: Hamlet in *Hamlet.*
Queen's: Mason in *He Was Born Gay,* Richard in *Richard II,* Joseph Surface in *The School for Scandal.*

1938   Queen's: Vershinin in *Three Sisters,* Shylock in *The Merchant of Venice,* Nicholas in *Dear Octopus.*

1939   Globe: John Worthing in *The Importance of Being Earnest.*
Lyceum: Hamlet in *Hamlet.*
Kronborg Castle, Elsinore: Hamlet in *Hamlet.*

1940   Haymarket: Macheath in *The Beggar's Opera.*
Old Vic: Lear in *King Lear,* Prospero in *The Tempest.*
ENSA tour, UK: Henry Gow in *Fumed Oak,* Peter Gilpin in *Hands Across the Sea,* Old Actor in *Hard Luck Story,* William Shakespeare in *The Dark Lady of the Sonnets.*

1941   Globe: William Dearth in *Dear Brutus.*

1942   Piccadilly: Macbeth in *Macbeth.*
Phoenix: John Worthing in *The Importance of Being Earnest.*
ENSA tour, Gibraltar: *Christmas Party.*

1943   Haymarket: Louis Dubedat in *The Doctor's Dilemma.*

Phoenix: Valentine in *Love for Love.*

1944　Haymarket: Arnold Champion-Chesney in *The Circle,* Valentine in *Love for Love,* Hamlet in *Hamlet.*

1945　Haymarket: Oberon in *A Midsummer Night's Dream,* Ferdinand in *The Duchess of Malfi.*
ENSA tour, India and Far East: Hamlet in *Hamlet,* Charles Condomine in *Blithe Spirit.*

1946　New/Globe: Raskolnikov in *Crime and Punishment.*

1947　Royale, New York: John Worthing in *The Importance of Being Earnest,* Valentine in *Love for Love.*
National, New York: Jason in *Medea,* Raskolnikov in *Crime and Punishment.*

1948　Globe: Eustace Jackson in *The Return of the Prodigal.*

1949　Globe: Thomas Mendip in *The Lady's Not for Burning.*

1950　Memorial, Stratford: Angelo in *Measure for Measure,* Cassius in Julius Caesar, Benedick in *Much Ado about Nothing,* Lear in *King Lear.*

1951　Royale, New York: Thomas Mendip in *The Lady's Not for Burning.*
Phoenix: Leontes in *The Winter's Tale.*

1952　Phoenix: Benedick in *Much Ado about Nothing.*

1953　Lyric, Hammersmith: Mirabell in *The Way of the World,* Jaffeir in *Venice Preserv'd.*
Royal, Bulawayo: Richard in *Richard II.*
Haymarket: Julian Anson in *A Day by the Sea.*

1955　Palace: Lear in *King Lear,* Benedick in *Much Ado about Nothing.*

1956　Globe: Sebastien in *Nude with Violin.*

1957　Memorial, Stratford: Prospero in *The Tempest.*
Freemason's Hall, Edinburgh: *Ages of Man* recital.
Drury Lane: Prospero in *The Tempest.*

1958　Globe: James Callifer in *The Potting Shed.*
Old Vic: Cardinal Wolsey in *Henry VIII.*
46th Street, New York: *Ages of Man.*

1959　Queen's: *Ages of Man.*
Lunt-Fontanne, New York: Benedick in *Much Ado about Nothing.*

1960　Haymarket: *Ages of Man.*
Phoenix: Prince Ferdinand Cavanati in *The Last Joke.*

1961　Royal Shakespeare, Stratford: Othello in *Othello.*

Aldwych: Gaev in *The Cherry Orchard.*

1962   Haymarket: Joseph Surface in *The School for Scandal.*

1963   Majestic, New York: Joseph Surface in *The School for Scandal.*

Haymarket: Julius Caesar in *The Ides of March.*

1964   Billy Rose, New York: *Tiny Alice.*

1965   Phoenix: Ivanov in *Ivanov.*

1966   Shubert, New York: Ivanov in *Ivanov.*

1967   National (Old Vic): Orgon in *Tartuffe.*

1968   National (Old Vic): Oedipus in *Oedipus.*

Apollo: Headmaster in *Forty Years On.*

1970   Lyric: Sir Gideon Petrie in *The Battle of Shrivings.*

Royal Court/Apollo: Harry in *Home.*

Morosco, New York: Harry in *Home.*

1971   Festival, Chichester: Caesar in *Caesar and Cleopatra.*

1972   Royal Court: Sir Geoffrey Kendle in *Veterans.*

1974   National (Old Vic): Prospero in *The Tempest.*

Royal Court: William Shakespeare in *Bingo.*

1975   National (Old Vic)/Wyndham's: Spooner in *No Man's Land.*

1976   National (Lyttelton): Spooner in *No Man's Land.*

Longacre, New York: Spooner in *No Man's Land.*

1977   National (Olivier): Caesar in *Julius Caesar,* Sir Politic Wouldbe in *Volpone.*

National (Cottesloe): Sir Noel Cunliffe in *Half-Life.*

1978   Duke of York's: Sir Noel Cunliffe in *Half-Life.*

1988   Apollo: Sir Sydney Cockerell in *The Best of Friends.*

THEATRE: DIRECTOR

1932   New, Oxford: *Romeo and Juliet* (OUDS).

Arts: *Richard of Bordeaux.*

St Martin's: *Strange Orchestra.*

Old Vic: *The Merchant of Venice.*

1933   New: *Richard of Bordeaux.*

Wyndham's: *Sheppey.*

1934   Shaftesbury: *Spring 1600.*

New: *Queen of Scots, Hamlet.*

1935   New: *The Old Ladies, Romeo and Juliet.*

1936   New, Oxford: *Richard II* (OUDS).

1937   Queen's: *He Was Born Gay, Richard II.*

1938   Queen's: *The Merchant of Venice*.
       Ambassador's: *Spring Meeting*.

1939   Globe: *The Importance of Being Earnest, Scandal in Assyria, Rhondda Roundabout*.
       Lyceum: *Hamlet*.
       Kronborg Castle, Elsinore: *Hamlet*.

1940   Haymarket: *The Beggar's Opera*.
       ENSA tour, UK: *Fumed Oak, Hands Across the Sea, Hard Luck Story, The Dark Lady of the Sonnets*.

1941   Globe: *Dear Brutus*.
       Apollo: *Ducks and Drakes*.

1942   Piccadilly: *Macbeth*.
       Phoenix: *The Importance of Being Earnest*.

1943   Phoenix: *Love for Love*.
       Westminster: *Landslide*.

1944   Apollo: *The Cradle Song*.
       Lyric: *Crisis in Heaven*.
       Phoenix: *The Last of Summer*.
       Haymarket: *Love for Love*.

1945   Haymarket: *Lady Windermere's Fan*.
       ENSA tour, India and Far East: *Hamlet, Blithe Spirit*.

1947   Royale, New York: *The Importance of Being Earnest, Love for Love*.
       National, New York: *Medea*.

1948   Haymarket: *The Glass Menagerie*.
       Globe: *Medea*.

1949   Haymarket: *The Heiress*.
       Memorial, Stratford: *Much Ado about Nothing*.
       Globe: *The Lady's Not for Burning*.
       Apollo: *Treasure Hunt*.

1950   Lyric, Hammersmith: *Shall We Join the Ladies?* and *The Boy with a Cart*.
       Memorial, Stratford: *Much Ado about Nothing, King Lear*.

1951   Royale, New York: *The Lady's Not for Burning*.
       Criterion: *Indian Summer*.

1952   Phoenix: *Much Ado about Nothing*.
       Memorial, Stratford: *Macbeth*.
       Lyric, Hammersmith: *Richard II*.

1953   Lyric, Hammersmith: *The Way of the World*.
       Royal, Bulawayo: *Richard II*.

Haymarket: *A Day by the Sea.*
1954   New: *Charley's Aunt.*
        Lyric, Hammersmith: *The Cherry Orchard.*
1955   Memorial, Stratford: *Twelfth Night.*
        Palace: *King Lear* and *Much Ado about Nothing.*
1956   Haymarket: *The Chalk Garden.*
        Globe: *Nude with Violin.*
1957   Royal Opera House: *The Trojans.*
1958   Globe: *Variation on a Theme.*
        Comedy: *Five Finger Exercise.*
1959   Globe: *The Complaisant Lover.*
        Lunt-Fontanne: *Much Ado about Nothing.*
        Music Box, New York: *Five Finger Exercise.*
1961   Royal Opera House: *A Midsummer Night's Dream.*
        ANTA, New York: *Big Fish, Little Fish.*
        Globe: *Dazzling Prospect.*
1962   Haymarket: *The School for Scandal.*
        Majestic, New York: *The School for Scandal.*
1963   Haymarket: *The Ides of March.*
1964   Lunt-Fontanne, New York: *Hamlet.*
1965   Phoenix: *Ivanov.*
1966   Shubert, New York: *Ivanov.*
1967   Queen's: *Halfway up the Tree.*
1968   Coliseum: *Don Giovanni.*
1971   Martin Beck, New York: *All Over.*
1972   Queen's: *Private Lives.*
        US tour: *Irene.*
1973   Albery: *The Constant Wife.*
1974   46th Street, New York: *Private Lives.*
        Shubert, New York: *The Constant Wife.*
1975   Albery: *The Gay Lord Quex.*

FILMS
1924   Daniel Arnault in *Who is the Man?*
1929   Rex Trasmere in *The Clue of the New Pin.*
1932   Henri Dubois in *Insult.*
1933   Inigo Jollifant in *The Good Companions.*
1936   Ashenden in *Secret Agent.*
1941   Benjamin Disraeli in *The Prime Minister.*
1953   Cassius in *Julius Caesar.*

1955 Duke of Clarence in *Richard III*.
1957 Edward Moulton-Barrett in *The Barretts of Wimpole Street*.
   Earl of Warwick in *Saint Joan*.
   Foster in *Around the World in Eighty Days*.
1964 Louis VII in *Becket*.
1965 Sir Francis Hinsley in *The Loved One*.
1966 Henry IV in *Chimes at Midnight*.
1967 Curt Valayan in *Assignment to Kill*.
1968 Head of Intelligence in *Sebastian*.
   Lord Raglan in *The Charge of the Light Brigade*.
   The Pope in *The Shoes of the Fisherman*.
1969 Count Berchtold in *Oh What a Lovely War*.
1970 Caesar in *Julius Caesar*.
   Lord Sissal in *Eagle in a Cage*.
1972 Chang in *The Lost Horizon*.
1974 Meecham in *11 Harrowhouse*.
   Farrell in *Gold*.
   Chief Constable in *Frankenstein: The True Story*.
   Beddoes in *Murder on the Orient Express*.
   Old Cardinal in *Galileo*.
1976 Headmaster in *Aces High*.
1977 Clive Langham in *Providence*.
   Preacher in *Portrait of the Artist as a Young Man*.
   Doctor in *Joseph Andrews*.
1978 Lord Salisbury in *Murder by Decree*.
1979 Nerva in *Caligula*.
   Brigadier Tomlinson in *The Human Factor*.
   Jan Lasocki in *The Conductor*.
1980 Carr Gomm in *The Elephant Man*.
   Abdu Hamdi in *Sphinx*.
1981 Sharif El Gariani in *Lion of the Desert*.
   Master of Trinity in *Chariots of Fire*.
   Abraham Esau in *The Formula*.
   Hobson in *Arthur*.
   Herbert G. Muskett in *Priest of Love*.
1982 Lord Irwin in *Gandhi*.
1983 Pfistermeister in *Wagner*.
   Hogarth in *The Wicked Lady*.
   Uncle Willy in *Scandalous*.
1984 Cornelius Cardew in *The Shooting Party*.

1985   Clyde Ormiston in *Invitation to the Wedding*.
        Sir Leonard Darwin in *Plenty*.
        Middleton Murry in *Leave All Fair*.
1986   Sir Adrian Chapple in *The Whistle Blower*.
1988   Bluebeard in *Bluebeard, Bluebeard*.
        Colonel Carbury in *Appointment with Death*.
        Hobson in *Arthur on the Rocks*.
1989   Sir Gordon Munday in *Getting it Right*.
1990   Prospero in *Prospero's Books*.
1991   Headmaster in *The Power of One*.
1992   Konrad Friedrichs in *Shining Through*.
1993–1999 Cameo appearances in:
        First Knight, Richard III, Haunted, Portrait of a Lady,
        Looking for Richard, Shine, Hamlet, Dragon Heart, Elizabeth,
        The Tichborne Claimant.

TELEVISION
1959   Julian Anson in *A Day by the Sea*.
        Crocker-Harris in *The Browning Version*.
1962   Gaev in *The Cherry Orchard*.
1963   The Count in *The Rehearsal*.
1964   Ghost in *Hamlet*.
1966   Ivanov in *Ivanov*.
        Stockbroker in *The Love Song of Barney Kempinski*.
        Ages of Man.
        Gabriel Kontara in *The Mayfly and the Frog*.
        Mock Turtle in *Alice in Wonderland*.
1967   Chorus in *Romeo and Juliet*.
1968   Chekhov in *From Chekhov in Love*.
        Inquisitor in *Saint Joan*.
1969   The Writer in *Conversation at Night*.
1970   Charles II in *In Good King Charles's Golden Days*.
1971   Caliph in *Hassan*.
        Ghost in *Hamlet*.
1972   Streeter in *Probe*.
        Harry in *Home*.
1973   Frederick William Densham in *Deliver us from Evil*.
        Clinton-Meek in *QB VII*.

1975   Mr Ferraro in *Special Duties.*
        Benjamin Disraeli in *Edward the Seventh.*
1976   Lord Henry Wotton in *The Picture of Dorian Gray.*
1977   The Grand Inquisitor in *The Grand Inquisitor.*
        Captain Shotover in *Heartbreak House.*
1978   Jelks in *Neck.*
        Spooner in *No Man's Land.*
        John of Gaunt in *Richard II.*
        Chorus in *Romeo and Juliet.*
        Gillenormand in *Les Misérables.*
1980   Reverend Thomas Jones in *Why Didn't They Ask Evans?*
        Cyril Boggis in *Parson's Pleasure.*
1981   Marquis of Caterham in *The Seven Dials Mystery.*
        Edward Ryder in *Brideshead Revisited.*
1982   Torturer in *The Hunchback of Notre Dame.*
        Lord Burleigh in *The Critic.*
1983   Pope Pius XII in *The Scarlet and the Black.*
        Albert Speer Senior in *Inside the Third Reich.*
1984   Major Sir Louis Cavagnari in *The Far Pavilions.*
        Lord Durrisdeer in *The Master of Ballantrae.*
        De Lacy in *Frankenstein.*
        Duc de Charles in *Camille.*
        Charles Woodward in *Romance on the Orient Express.*
1986   Jasper Swift in *Time After Time.*
        Doge of Venice in *Marco Polo.*
        Teiresias in *Oedipus the King.*
        Teiresias in *Antigone.*
        Sir Simon de Canterville in *The Canterville Ghost.*
1987   Eddie Loomis in *Quartermaine's Terms.*
        Aaron Jastrow in *War and Remembrance.*
1988   Cardinal Wolsey in *A Man for All Seasons.*
1989   Haverford Downs in *Summer's Lease.*
1990   Virgil in *A TV Dante.*
1991   Sir Sydney Cockerell in *The Best of Friends.*
1993   Svetlovidov in *Swan Song.*
1993–1999 Cameo performances in:
        Inspector Morse, Summer's Day Dream, Under the Hammer,
        Scarlett, Lovejoy, Inspector Alleyn, Gulliver's Travels, Dance to
        the Music of Time, Merlin.

RADIO PLAYS

1929	*The Man with a Flower in his Mouth.*
1931	*The Tempest, Will Shakespeare.*
1932	*Othello, Hamlet.*
1933	*The Tempest.*
1937	*He Was Born Gay, The School for Scandal, Present Laughter.*
1939	*The Importance of Being Earnest, Hamlet.*
1940	*Hamlet, The Laughing Woman, The Importance of Being Earnest.*
1941	*Prince of Bohemia, King Lear, The Return of Mr Oakroyd, Richard of Bordeaux.*
1943	*The Great Ship, Suicide Club.*
1948	*The Family Reunion, Hamlet, The Tempest.*
1950	*Measure for Measure.*
1951	*The Importance of Being Earnest, The Cross and the Arrow, King Lear, Helena.*
1952	*Richard of Bordeaux.*
1953	*The Tempest.*
1954	*Ivanov, The Adventures of Sherlock Holmes, Henry VIII.*
1955	*Sheherazade.*
1956	*Present Laughter.*
1957	*The Browning Version.*
1959	*Oedipus at Colonus.*
1960	*The Way of the World.*
1961	*Richard II, Arms and the Man.*
1967	*King Lear.*
1973	*Forty Years On.*
1975	*Mr Luby's Fear of Heaven.*
1976	*Henry V, Much Ado about Nothing.*
1977	*Henry VIII.*
1981	*The Winter's Tale.*
1983	*Passing Time.*
1989	*The Tempest.*
1990	*Between Ourselves, Tales my Father Taught Me.*
1991	*The Best of Friends.*
1992	*Hamlet.*
1993	*Romeo and Juliet.*
1994	*Laughter in the Shadow of the Trees, King Lear.*

Gielgud also gave many talks and poetry readings on the radio, and took part in several programmes about the theatre or tributes to actors. He also made recordings of numerous plays, including ten of Shakespeare's.

Source Notes

REFERENCES are to the main published sources for each chapter. Publishing details are given here for books not included in the bibliography.

1 A Terry Childhood
Marguerite Steen, *A Pride of Terrys*. Memoirs: Kate Gielgud, Val Gielgud.

2 Gielgud Minor
The Letters of Aldous Huxley (Chatto & Windus, 1969). Aldous Huxley, *Eyeless in Gaza* (Chatto & Windus, 1936). For Gielgud's early theatre reviews, *Notes from the Gods*. Memoirs: Kate Gielgud, Val Gielgud, Arnold Haskell, *In His True Centre* (London, 1951), Naomi Mitchison, *All Change Here: Girlhood and Marriage* (Bodley Head, 1975).

3 Atkins, RADA and Playfair
Notes from the Gods. Biography: Barker/Eric Salmon.

4 Oxford Apprenticeship
Humphrey Carpenter, OUDS (OUP, 1985). Norman Marshall, *The Other Theatre*. Don Chapman, *Agamemnon and After*, a history of the Oxford Playhouse (forthcoming). George Rowell and Anthony Jackson, *The Repertory Movement*. Memoirs: Guthrie, Emlyn Williams (*George*). Biography: Janet Dunbar, *Flora Robson* (Harrap, 1960), Kenneth Barrow, *Flora* (Heinemann, 1981), Elizabeth Talbot Rice, *Tamara* (John Murray, 1996).

5 Coward, Chekhov and Komisarjevsky
Notes from the Gods. Anthony Curtis (ed.), *The Rise and Fall of the*

Matinee Idol (Weidenfeld & Nicolson, 1974). Biography:
Coward/Philip Hoare, Agate/James Harding.

6 Man about Town
Norman Marshall, *The Other Theatre*. Memoirs: Fabia Drake.
Biography: Peter Parker, *Ackerley* (Constable, 1989).

7 The Search for Stardom
Norman Marshall, *The Other Theatre*. Memoirs: Basil Dean.
Biography: Coward/Philip Hoare.

8 Mrs Pat and Lilian Baylis
Biography: Mrs Patrick Campbell/Margot Peters, Edith Evans/Bryan
Forbes, Lilian Baylis/Richard Findlater.

9 The Old Vic
Memoirs: Harcourt Williams, *Four Years at the Old Vic* and *Old Vic
Saga*. Biography: Lilian Baylis/Richard Findlater, Wolfit/Ronald
Harwood.

10 Matinée Idol
Memoirs: Harcourt Williams, *Four Years at the Old Vic* and *Old Vic
Saga*. Biography: Richardson/John Miller, Richardson/Garry
O'Connor.

11 Young Producer
Peggy Ashcroft in *The Ages of Gielgud*. Memoirs: Anthony Quayle.

12 *Richard of Bordeaux*
Memoirs: Jessie Matthews, *Over My Shoulder* (W.H. Allen, 1974).
Biography: Marion Cole, *Fogie* (Peter Davies, 1967),
Rattigan/Michael Darlow, Rattigan/Geoffrey Wansell.

13 *Hamlet*
Val Gielgud, *British Radio Drama*. Memoirs: Emlyn Williams
(*Emlyn*), Alec Guinness (*Blessings in Disguise*). Biography: Ted
Morgan, *Somerset Maugham* (Jonathan Cape, 1980).

14 Saint-Denis and *The Seagull*
John Elsom and Nicholas Tomalin, *The History of the National*

Theatre. Biography: Devine/Irving Wardle, Edith Evans/Bryan Forbes.

15 Enter Larry
Memoirs: Laurence Olivier, *Confessions of an Actor* and *On Acting*.
Biography: Olivier/Anthony Holden, Olivier/Thomas Kiernan,
Peggy Ashcroft/Michael Billington, Rattigan/Geoffrey Wansell,
Rattigan/Michael Darlow, Vivien Leigh/Hugo Vickers.

16 A Prince on Broadway
Rosamond Gilder, *John Gielgud's Hamlet*. Brooks Atkinson,
Broadway. Biography: Ronald Howard, *Leslie Howard: Trivial Fond
Records* (Kimber, 1982), Mrs Patrick Campbell/Margot Peters.

17 Actor-Manager
Emlyn Williams in *The Ages of Gielgud*. Memoirs: Alec Guinness
(*Blessings in Disguise*), Michael Redgrave. Biography: Peggy Ashcroft/
Michael Billington, Guthrie/James Forsyth, Devine/Irving Wardle.

18 Binkie, *Earnest* and Elsinore
Biography: Dodie Smith/Valerie Grove, Beaumont/Richard Huggett,
Rattigan/Michael Darlow, Rattigan/Geoffrey Wansell,
Edith Evans/Bryan Forbes, Olivier/Thomas Kiernan.

19 Barker and *King Lear*
Biography: Barker/Eric Salmon, Devine/Irving Wardle.

20 ENSA and *Macbeth*
Agate, *Ego 6*. Memoirs: Val Gielgud (*Years of the Locust*), Kitty Black,
Michael Wilding, *Apple Sauce* (Allen & Unwin, 1982). Biography:
Beaumont/Richard Huggett.

21 The Haymarket Season
Agate, *Ego 7* and *Ego 8*. Memoirs: Peter Brook. Biography:
Tynan/Kathleen Tynan, Peggy Ashcroft/Michael Billington,
Beaumont/Richard Huggett, Olivier/Anthony Holden,
Richardson/John Miller.

22 Travelling Player
Agate, *Ego 9*. Cecil Beaton, *Selected Diaries*. Memoirs: Peter Ustinov,
Denys Blakelock, *Round the Next Corner* (Gollancz, 1967).

Biography: Olivier/Anthony Holden.

23 Rattigan, Fry and Burton
Christopher Fry in *The Ages of Gielgud*. Memoirs: Tennessee .
Williams, Peter Bull, *I Know the Face But...* (Peter Davies, 1959).
Biography: Rattigan/Michael Darlow, Rattigan/Geoffrey Wansell,
Richardson/John Miller, Peggy Ashcroft/Michael Billington,
Burton/Paul Ferris, Burton/Melvyn Bragg.

24 Stratford and Peter Brook
Sally Beauman, *The RSC*. Peter Brook in *The Ages of Gielgud*.
Memoirs: Anthony Quayle. Biography: Peggy Ashcroft/Michael
Billington, Richardson/John Miller.

25 From Hollywood to Hammersmith
Tynan, *Persona Grata*. Biography: Peter Manso, *Brando* (Weidenfeld
& Nicolson, 1994).

26 Dark Days
Memoirs: Michael Denison (*Double Act*). Biography: John Casson,
Lewis and Sybil (Collins, 1972), Beaumont/Richard Huggett,
Vivien Leigh/Hugo Vickers, Peggy Ashcroft/Michael Billington,
Devine/Irving Wardle, Edith Evans/Bryan Forbes,
Coward/Philip Hoare.

27 One Man and His Show
Humphrey Carpenter, *The Envy of the World*. Christopher
Isherwood, *Diaries 1939–1960* (Methuen, 1996).

28 *Othello* to Albee
Memoirs: Franco Zeffirelli, *Autobiography* (Weidenfeld & Nicolson,
1986), Claire Bloom. Biography: Peter Hall/Stephen Fay,
Peggy Ashcroft/Michael Billington, Judi Dench/John Miller,
Albee/Mel Gussow.

29 A Sense of Direction
Richard L. Sterne, *John Gielgud Directs Richard Burton in Hamlet*
(Random House, 1967). William Redfield, *Letters from an Actor*
(Viking Press, 1967). Memoirs: Hume Cronyn, *A Terrible Liar*
(William Morrow, NY, 1991). Biography: Rattigan/Michael Darlow,

Rattigan/Geoffrey Wansell, Richardson/John Miller, Vivien
Leigh/Hugo Vickers, Burton/Paul Ferris, Burton/Melvyn Bragg.

30 *Oedipus* and *Home*
Peter Brook, Irene Worth in *The Ages of Gielgud*. Kenneth Tynan,
Letters (Weidenfeld & Nicolson, 1994). Memoirs: Alan Bennett,
Writing Home (Faber & Faber, 1994), Gaskill. Biography:
Richardson/Garry O'Connor, Richardson/John Miller.

31 Peter Hall and Pinter
Hall, *Diaries*. Edward Bond in *Sir John*. Memoirs: Keith Baxter, *My
Sentiments Exactly* (Oberon, 1998), Tony Richardson, *Long-Distance
Runner* (Faber & Faber, 1993). Biography: Barbara Leaming, *Orson
Welles* (Weidenfeld & Nicolson 1985), Michael Billington, *The Life
and Work of Harold Pinter* (Faber & Faber, 1996),
Richardson/John Miller, Richardson/Garry O'Connor.

32 The Road to Brideshead
Derek Granger in *The Ages of Gielgud*. Charles Sturridge in *Gielgud
Stories*. Memoirs: Joan Collins, *Second Act* (Boxtree, 1996).

33 Late Stages
Hall, *Diaries*. Biography: Albee/Mel Gussow, Beaumont/Huggett,
Coward/Philip Hoare, Judi Dench/John Miller, Michael Coveney,
Maggie Smith (Gollancz, 1992).

34 'Major Movie Star'
Memoirs: Dirk Bogarde, *An Orderly Man* (Chatto & Windus, 1983),
David Lynch, *Lynch on Lynch* (Faber & Faber, 1997). Peter Greenaway,
Prospero's Books: A Film of Shakespeare's 'The Tempest' (Chatto &
Windus, 1991). Biography: Barbra Paskin, *Dudley Moore* (Sidgwick &
Jackson, 1997), Burton/Melvyn Bragg, Richardson/John Miller.

35 Swan Songs
James Roose-Evans in *Sir John*. Memoirs: Kenneth Branagh,
Beginning (Chatto & Windus, 1989).

Quotations from John Gielgud's books are mainly from *Early Stages*
and successive volumes of his autobiography. I have also drawn on a
large number of articles by and interviews with him, from 1929 to 1999.

Bibliography

JOHN GIELGUD
Books by:
Early Stages, Macmillan, 1939; revised edition, Hodder & Stoughton, 1987.
Stage Directions, Heinemann, 1963.
Distinguished Company, Heinemann, 1972.
An Actor and His Time, Sidgwick and Jackson, 1979; revised edition Pan, 1996.
Backward Glances, Hodder & Stoughton, 1989.
Shakespeare: Hit or Miss?, Sidgwick & Jackson, 1991; revised edition, *Acting Shakespeare*, Pan, 1997.
Notes from the Gods: Playgoing in the Twenties, Nick Hern Books, 1994.

Books about:
Gordon Anthony, *John Gielgud: Camera Studies*, Geoffrey Bles, 1938.
Gyles Brandreth, *John Gielgud: A Celebration*, Pavilion Books, 1984; revised edition, 1994.
Clive Fisher (ed.), *Gielgud Stories*, Futura, 1988.
Hallam Fordham, *An Actor's Biography in Pictures*, John Lehmann, 1952.
Clive Francis (ed.), *Sir John: The Many Faces of Gielgud*, Robson Books, 1994.
Rosamond Gilder, *John Gielgud's Hamlet*, Methuen, 1937.
Ronald Harwood, *The Ages of Gielgud: An Actor at Eighty*, Hodder & Stoughton, 1984.
Ronald Hayman, *John Gielgud*, Heinemann, 1971.
Robert Tanitch, *Gielgud*, Harrap, 1988.

Books containing essays by or interviews with:
Hal Burton (ed.), *Great Acting*, BBC, 1967.

Bibliography

Richard Findlater (ed.), *At the Royal Court: Twenty-Five Years of the English Stage Company*, Amber Lane Press, 1981.

Lewis Funke and John E. Booth, *Actors Talk about Acting*, Thames & Hudson, 1961.

Ronald Harwood, *A Night at the Theatre*, Methuen, 1982.

Ronald Harwood (ed.), *Dear Alec: Guinness at 75*, Hodder & Stoughton, 1989.

Ronald Hayman, *Playback*, Davis-Poynter, 1973.

Alfred Rossi, *Astonish Us in the Morning: Tyrone Guthrie Remembered*, Hutchinson, 1977.

GENERAL

Brooks Atkinson, *Broadway*, Cassell, 1971.

Sally Beauman, *The RSC: A History of Ten Decades*, Oxford University Press, 1982.

Michael Billington, *One-Night Stands*, Nick Hern Books, 1993.

Humphrey Carpenter, *The Envy of the World: 50 Years of the BBC Third Programme and Radio 3*, Weidenfeld & Nicolson, 1996.

Edward Gordon Craig, *On the Art of the Theatre*, Heinemann, 1911.

Nicholas de Jongh, *Not in Front of the Audience: Homosexuality on Stage*, Routledge, 1992.

Charles Duff, *The Lost Summer: The Heyday of the West End Theatre*, Nick Hern Books, 1995.

John Elsom, *Postwar British Theatre*, Routledge, 1976.

John Elsom and Nicholas Tomalin, *The History of the National Theatre*, Jonathan Cape, 1978.

Richard Findlater, *These Our Actors*, Elm Tree Books, 1983.

Bryan Forbes, *That Despicable Race*, Elm Tree Books, 1980.

Val Gielgud, *British Radio Drama 1922–1956*, Harrap, 1957.

Norman Marshall, *The Other Theatre*, John Lehmann, 1947; *The Producer and the Play*, Macdonald, 1957.

George Rowell and Anthony Jackson, *The Repertory Movement: A History of Regional Theatre in Britain*, Cambridge University Press, 1984.

Michael Sanderson, *From Irving to Olivier: A Social History of the Acting Profession 1890–1983*, Athlone Press, 1984.

Kenneth Tynan, *Persona Grata*, Allan Wingate, 1953; *Curtains*, Longmans, 1961; *A View of the English Stage 1944–1965*, Methuen, 1984.

Audrey Williamson, *Theatre of Two Decades*, Rockliff, 1951.

Bibliography

MEMOIRS/BIOGRAPHY

Felix Barker, *The Oliviers*, Hamish Hamilton, 1953.

Jean Benedetti, *Stanislavsky: His Life and Art*, Methuen, 1999.

Michael Billington, *Peggy Ashcroft*, John Murray, 1988.

Kitty Black, *Upper Circle: A Theatrical Chronicle*, Methuen, 1984.

Claire Bloom, *Leaving a Doll's House*, Virago, 1996.

Melvyn Bragg, *Laurence Olivier*, Hutchinson, 1984.

Melvyn Bragg, *Rich: The Life of Richard Burton*, Hodder & Stoughton, 1988.

Peter Brook, *Threads of Time: A Memoir*, Methuen, 1999.

Simon Callow, *Charles Laughton*, Methuen, 1987.

Michael Darlow, *Terence Rattigan*, Quartet, 1999.

Basil Dean, *Seven Ages: An Autobiography 1888–1927*, Hutchinson, 1970.

Michael Denison, *Overture and Beginners*, Gollancz, 1973; *Double Act*, Michael Joseph, 1985.

Diana Devlin, *A Speaking Part: Lewis Casson and the Theatre of his Time*, Hodder & Stoughton, 1982.

Fabia Drake, *Blind Fortune*, William Kimber, 1978.

Stephen Fay, *Power Play: The Life and Times of Peter Hall*, Hodder & Stoughton, 1995.

Paul Ferris, *Richard Burton*, Weidenfeld & Nicolson, 1981.

Richard Findlater, *Lilian Baylis*, Allen Lane, 1975.

Richard Findlater, *Michael Redgrave*, Heinemann, 1956.

Kate Fleming, *Celia Johnson*, Weidenfeld & Nicolson, 1991.

Bryan Forbes, *Ned's Girl: The Life of Edith Evans*, Elm Tree Books, 1977.

James Forsyth, *Tyrone Guthrie*, Hamish Hamilton, 1976.

William Gaskill, *A Sense of Direction: Life at the Royal Court*, Faber & Faber, 1988.

Mark Gatiss, *James Whale*, Cassell, 1995.

Kate Terry Gielgud, *An Autobiography*, Max Reinhardt, 1953.

Val Gielgud, *Years of the Locust*, Nicholson & Watson, 1947; *Years in a Mirror*, Bodley Head, 1965.

Valerie Grove, *Dear Dodie: The Life of Dodie Smith*, Chatto & Windus, 1996.

Alec Guinness, *Blessings in Disguise, My Name Escapes Me, A Positively Final Appearance*, Hamish Hamilton, 1995, 1996, 1999.

Mel Gussow, *Edward Albee*, Oberon Books, 1999.

Tyrone Guthrie, *A Life in the Theatre*, Hamish Hamilton, 1960.

James Harding, *Agate*, Methuen, 1986.

James Harding, *Gerald du Maurier: The Last Actor-Manager*, Hodder & Stoughton, 1989.

James Harding, *Emlyn Williams*, Weidenfeld & Nicolson, 1993.

Ronald Harwood, *Sir Donald Wolfit*, Secker & Warburg, 1971.

Philip Hoare, *Noel Coward*, Sinclair-Stevenson, 1995.

Anthony Holden, *Olivier*, Weidenfeld & Nicolson, 1988.

Richard Huggett, *Binkie Beaumont*, Hodder & Stoughton, 1989.

Martin Jarvis, *Acting Strangely*, Methuen 1999.

Thomas Kiernan, *Olivier*, Sidgwick & Jackson, 1981.

John Miller, *Ralph Richardson*, Sidgwick & Jackson, 1995.

John Miller, *Judi Dench*, Weidenfeld & Nicolson, 1998.

John Mills, *Up in the Clouds, Gentlemen Please*, Weidenfeld & Nicolson, 1980.

Garry O'Connor, *A Life of Peggy Ashcroft*, Weidenfeld & Nicolson, 1997.

Garry O'Connor, *Alec Guinness: Master of Disguise*, Hodder & Stoughton, 1994.

Garry O'Connor, *Ralph Richardson*, Hodder & Stoughton, 1982.

Laurence Olivier, *Confessions of an Actor*, Weidenfeld & Nicolson, 1982.

Laurence Olivier, *On Acting*, Weidenfeld & Nicolson, 1986.

Tony Peake, *Derek Jarman*, Little, Brown, 1999.

Margot Peters, *Mrs Pat: The Life of Mrs Patrick Campbell*, Bodley Head, 1984.

C.B. Purdom, *Harley Granville Barker*, Rockliff, 1955.

Anthony Quayle, *A Time to Speak*, Barrie & Jenkins, 1990.

Michael Redgrave, *The Actor's Ways and Means*, Heinemann, 1953.

Michael Redgrave, *In My Mind's Eye*, Weidenfeld & Nicolson, 1983.

Eric Salmon, *Granville Barker: A Secret Life*, Heinemann, 1983.

Donald Sinden, *A Touch of the Memoirs, Laughter in the Second Act*, Hodder & Stoughton, 1982, 1985.

Robert Speaight, *The Property Basket*, Collins/Harvill Press, 1970.

Marguerite Steen, *A Pride of Terrys*, Longmans, 1962.

John Russell Taylor, *Alec Guinness: A Celebration*, Pavilion Books, 1984.

Kathleen Tynan, *The Life of Kenneth Tynan*, Weidenfeld & Nicolson, 1987.

Peter Ustinov, *Dear Me*, Heinemann, 1977.

Hugo Vickers, *Vivien Leigh*, Hamish Hamilton, 1988.

Geoffrey Wansell, *Terence Rattigan*, Fourth Estate, 1995.

Irving Wardle, *The Theatres of George Devine*, Jonathan Cape, 1978.

Emlyn Williams, *George*, Hamish Hamilton, 1961; *Emlyn*, Bodley Head, 1973.

Harcourt Williams, *Four Years at the Old Vic 1929–1933*, Putnam, 1935; *Old Vic Saga*, Winchester Publications, 1944.

Tennessee Williams, *Memoirs*, W.H. Allen, 1976.

B.A. Young, *The Rattigan Version: Sir Terence Rattigan and the Theatre of Character*, Hamish Hamilton, 1986.

LETTERS AND DIARIES

James Agate, *Ego*, Hamish Hamilton, 1935.

James Agate, *Ego 2–9*, Harrap, 1938–1948.

Richard Buckle (ed.), *Self-Portrait with Friends: The Selected Diaries of Cecil Beaton 1926–1974*, Weidenfeld & Nicolson, 1979.

Peter Hall, *Diaries*, Hamish Hamilton, 1983.

Kerrison Preston (ed.), *Letters from W. Graham Robertson*, Hamish Hamilton, 1953.

Tennessee Williams, *Five O'Clock Angel: Letters from Tennessee Williams to Maria St Just 1948–1982*, André Deutsch, 1991.

Acknowledgements

MY greatest debt is to John Gielgud, who generously gave his blessing to my book, and kindly granted me permission to draw on his letters, books and other material. He also gave me the green light to approach those who had worked with him during his long and distinguished career. As a result I was able to talk to more than a hundred fellow-actors, directors, playwrights and friends, and correspond with many others. I would like to thank them all warmly for the time they gave me, for their willing co-operation, and for their kind hospitality.

I interviewed the following people: Patsy Ainley, Edward Albee, Jean Anderson, Frith Banbury, Ian Bannen, Alastair Bannerman, Peter Barkworth, Geoffrey Bayldon, Sam Beazley, Cicely Berry, Jane Birkin, Kitty Black, Dirk Bogarde, Richard Briers, Peter Brook, Michael Bryant, Stuart Burge, Helen Burns, Phyllis Calvert, Judy Campbell, Anna Carteret, Mary Casson, Helen Cherry, Alma Cohen, Peter Copley, Peter Cotes, Oliver Cotton, Michael Denison, Diana Devlin, Ninette de Valois, Roy Dotrice, Olga Edwardes, Beryl Evans, Gemma Fagan, Trader Faulkner, Michael Feast, Clive Francis, Leslie French, Christopher Fry, Bill Gaskill, Eleanor Gielgud, Cooks Gordon, Marius Goring, Prudence Goring, Derek Granger, Dulcie Gray, Monica Grey, Kate Griffin, Alec Guinness, Ian Haines, Dilys Hamlett, Margaret Harris, Bill Hays, Jocelyn Herbert, Wendy Hiller, Jane Howell, Waris Hussein, Barbara Jefford, Pinkie Johnstone, Rachel Kempson, Jerome Kilty, Michael Langham, Moira Lister, Terence Longdon, Alan MacNaughtan, Virginia McKenna, Richard Mangan, Elspeth March, Olive Markham, Ian McKellen, Sarah Miles, Christopher Miles, John Mills, Juliet Mills, Keith Michell, John Miller, Tanya Moiseiwitch, Cordelia Monsey, Penelope Munday, John Nettleton, Nancy Nevinson, Valerie Newman, Muriel Pavlow, Michael Pennington, Denis Quilley, Simon Russell Beale, Patsy Rodenburg, Paul Rogers,

Acknowledgements

Sheila Ronald, Chattie Salaman, Peter Sallis, John Schlesinger, Margaretta Scott, David Storey, Judith Stott, Nora Swinburne, Hallam Tennyson, John Theocharis, Edward Thompson, Daniel Thorndike, Frank Thornton, Geoffrey Toone, Dorothy Tutin, Peter Ustinov, Mavis Walker, Hugh Whitemore, Benjamin Whitrow, Nora Williamson, Margaret Wolfit, Charles Wood and Jack Wood.

For answering my questions by letterr I am most grateful to John Allen, Judi Dench, Piers Haggard, Pauline Jameson, Deborah Kerr, John McCallum, Paul Scofield and Richard Todd.

I am also indebted to the following people for answering my requests for information: Tony Ainley, Pekoe Ainley, Edward Bond, John Bowen, John Bury, Nicholas Butler, Daphny Clunes, Maurice Denham, Anna Ford, James Forsyth, Howard Goorney, Kate Grimond, Valerie Grove, Nigel Hawthorne, Gillian Howell, Stanley Kauffmann, Angela Lansbury, Corin Redgrave, Pauline Rumbold, David Spenser, Robert Tanitch, Wendy Toye and Andrej Wajda.

Particular thanks go to Michael Darlow, for allowing me to see the transcript of his interview with Gielgud about Terence Rattigan; to Don Chapman, for making available sections of his forthcoming history of the Oxford Playhouse; to Patsy Ainley, for allowing me access to her diary and letters covering the American tour of *Ages of Man*; to John Miller, for lending me tapes and transcripts of his interview with Gielgud; to Nancy Nevinson, for allowing me to use extracts from her diary of Gielgud's trip to India and the Far East; to Gervase Farjeon, for granting me access to his father Herbert Farjeon's archive; to Ann Playfair, for showing me her husband Giles Playfair's essay on the Lyric, Hammersmith; and to Colin Ward, for his generous help in tracking down several rare theatre books.

For help with contacts, letters and other information I would like to thank Alastair Bannerman, Nicholas Blyth, Ted Braun, Alice Douglas, Anne Harvey, Tony Lacey, John Miller, Jinx Nolan, Ann Queensberry, Tamara Ustinov and Julia Wood.

Thanks also to the staff in the following libraries, museums, archives and theatres: the Theatre Museum in Covent Garden, the British Newspaper Library in Colindale, the Oxford Playhouse, the Northamptonshire Record Office, and the Shubert Archive in New York. I am grateful to Margaret Weare, the curator at the Ellen Terry museum at Smallhythe Place, Kent, for allowing me to spend a morning looking through the records of the Ellen Terry Memorial Fellowship, and to her husband Tony Weare for showing me round the

Barn Theatre; and to Sarah Morris, keeper of the theatre collection at the University of Bristol, for her valuable help. I want to record my special gratitude to Richard Mangan at the Mander and Mitchenson Theatre Collection, for his untiring help and patience during my many visits to that magnificent collection; and also to his assistant Donna Percival.

Finally, I am especially grateful to Nicki Household for reading an earlier draft of the book with her usual critical and discerning eye, and to Jenny Overton for many helpful editorial suggestions. My thanks are also due to Michael Earley, Max Eilenberg, David Salmo and others at Methuen, for their help in producing the book, and to my agent Derek Johns at A.P. Watt for his constant encouragement and support.

I am grateful to the authors and publishers of the many books which I have consulted in writing this biography. Full publishing details appear in the source notes and bibliography.

For permission to quote from letters and diaries I am grateful to the following: for the letters of Sybil Thorndike and Lewis Casson to John Casson; for the letters of Peggy Ashcroft to Lord Hutchinson of Lullington; for the letters of Jerome Kilty to their author; for the letters of W. Graham Robertson to Hamish Hamilton; for the letter of Aldous Huxley to Chatto & Windus; for the extracts from the diaries of Christopher Isherwood to Methuen; and for the letters of Shaw and Barker to The Society of Authors, on behalf of the Bernard Shaw and Harley Granville Barker estates.

For permission to use photographs acknowledgements to: Gordon Anthony 14, 15, 16, 17; Jane Bown 28; Granada Television 27, 29; Ronald Grant 20, 21, 30, 31; Angus McBean 23; Mander and Mitchenson Theatre Collection, frontispiece, 1, 6, 7, 9, 10, 11, 12, 13, 18, 19, 22, 24, 25; News International 32; John Timbers 26.

Every effort has been made to trace copyright owners. Full acknowledgement will be given in future editions to any details omitted.

Index

Index

Index

Index